THE SPECULATION ECONOMY

ALSO BY LAWRENCE E. MITCHELL

Progressive Corporate Law, editor (1995)

Stacked Deck: A Story of Selfishness in America (1998)

Corporate Irresponsibility: America's Newest Export (2001)

THE SPECULATION ECONOMY

HOW FINANCE TRIUMPHED
OVER INDUSTRY

❖

LAWRENCE E. MITCHELL

BK

BERRETT-KOEHLER PUBLISHERS, INC.
San Francisco
a BK Currents book

Berrett-Koehler Publishers, Inc.
235 Montgomery Street, Suite 650
San Francisco, CA 94104-2916
Tel: (415) 288-0260   Fax: (415) 362-2512   www.bkconnection.com

ORDERING INFORMATION
QUANTITY SALES. Special discounts are available on quantity purchases by corporations, associations, and others. For details, contact the "Special Sales Department" at the Berrett-Koehler address above.
INDIVIDUAL SALES. Berrett-Koehler publications are available through most bookstores. They can also be ordered directly from Berrett-Koehler: Tel: (800) 929-2929; Fax: (802) 864-7626; www.bkconnection.com
ORDERS FOR COLLEGE TEXTBOOK/COURSE ADOPTION USE. Please contact Berrett-Koehler: Tel: (800) 929-2929; Fax: (802) 864-7626
ORDERS BY U.S. TRADE BOOKSTORES AND WHOLESALERS. Please contact Ingram Publisher Services, Tel: (800) 509-4887; Fax: (800) 838-1149; E-mail: customer.service@ ingrampublisherservices.com; or visit www.ingrampublisherservices.com/Ordering for details about electronic ordering.

Berrett-Koehler and the BK logo are registered trademarks of Berrett-Koehler Publishers, Inc.

Printed in the United States of America

Berrett-Koehler books are printed on long-lasting acid-free paper. When it is available, we choose paper that has been manufactured by environmentally responsible processes. These may include using trees grown in sustainable forests, incorporating recycled paper, minimizing chlorine in bleaching, or recycling the energy produced at the paper mill.

Library of Congress Cataloging-in-Publication Data
Mitchell, Lawrence E.
   The speculation economy : how finance triumphed over industry / by Lawrence E. Mitchell.
      p. cm.
   Includes bibliographical references and index.
   ISBN 978-1-57675-400-9 (hardcover : alk. paper)
   1. United States—Economic policy.   2. Industries—United States.   3. Corporations—United States.   4. Finance—United States.   5. Speculation—United States.   I. Title.

HC103.M684 2007
330.973'08—dc22

First Edition
12 11 10 09 08 07   10 9 8 7 6 5 4 3 2 1

Produced by Wilsted & Taylor Publishing Services
   Production management by Christine Taylor ▪ Production assistance by Drew Patty
   Copyediting by Nancy Evans ▪ Design and composition by Yvonne Tsang

For Dalia

אני לדודי ודודי לי

CONTENTS

PREFACE

The formative era of American corporate capitalism took place between 1897 and 1919. The American industrial landscape of the late nineteenth century had been characterized by independent factories. No matter what their size, they typically were owned by entrepreneur industrialists, their families and often a few business associates. Almost overnight American business transformed into a vista of giant combinations of industrial plants owned directly and indirectly by widely dispersed shareholders. Business reasons sometimes justified these combinations. But they might never have come into being if financiers and promoters had not discovered that they could be used to create and sell massive amounts of stock for their own gain. The result was a form of capitalism in which a speculative stock market dominated the policies of American business. The result was the speculation economy.

Historians have studied virtually every aspect of the Progressive Era, including the social and philosophical changes that took place in Americans' ways of living and thinking about their world, the dramatic technological and economic developments that occurred, the rise of big business, the growth in importance of the federal government, the fitful creation of American industrial policy, the establishment of the bargain between labor and capital, the changes in political relations between government and big business, the development of new styles of regulation and America's assumption of its turn as the world's dominant economic power. Vincent P. Carosso, Alfred D. Chandler, Jr., Louis Galambos, Eric F. Goldman, Samuel Hays, Richard Hofstadter, Morton J. Horwitz, Morton Keller, Gabriel Kolko, Naomi R. Lamoreaux, R. Jeffrey Lustig, Ralph L. Nelson, Mark J. Roe, William G. Roy, Martin Sklar, Hans B. Thorelli, James Weinstein and Robert H. Wiebe, among many others, have provided rich pictures of different aspects of the dramatic and related economic, social, political, legal, business and financial transformations that occurred during that period. The story that remains to be told is of the creation of American corporate capitalism through the birth of the giant modern corporation, the stock market it produced and federal efforts to tame both.

The story I tell is the economic equivalent of the political creation of the Republic. It is a story that needs to be told for many reasons. There is of course the simple virtue of understanding why the American corporate economy has taken its distinctive form, a good and sufficient reason in its own right. But that corporate economy recently has been beset with problems ranging from short-term management horizons that can damage the long-term health of business to the increasing willingness of corporate managers to externalize the costs of production for the benefit of their stockholders. The speculation economy is one in which business management focused on production is replaced with business management focused on stock price. Such a management goal might be consistent with healthy, sustainable and responsible business practices, but it also might not. Understanding the complex development of American corporate capitalism can help us better improve and sustain the strength of the American economy.

One lesson of the formative period is that meaningful reform can be achieved only by reforming the market, by reforming finance itself to create the incentives for stockholders and managers to relearn the lesson that profits come from industrial production, not from the breeze that blows toward tomorrow. It is a lesson that was often forgotten during these formative years and many times since.

And the story of the creation of American corporate capitalism illustrates the possibilities of capitalism and the variety of forms it can take. Some of these were present in the American corporate economy of the late nineteenth century. Closely held industrial capitalism, bank finance capitalism, capitalism in which publicly held permanent investments like bonds characterized the principal source of corporate finance, even a heavily regulated state-guided capitalism, all were possibilities before the election of Warren Harding. Many of these different forms of capitalism have appeared successfully in different regions, cultures and countries during the twentieth century. American corporate capitalism—stock market capitalism—was neither the necessary nor inevitable form of the American economy.

The story of the formative period is a story of problems misperceived, transformations not yet understood and misguided regulation. One lesson of this story is that modern American corporate capitalism is the result of human choices. It is a system we maintain out of choice. It is a system that has ramifications beyond the economic that have helped to embed social norms of individualism that interfere with the cooperation necessary for a successful economy and a thriving society. It is within our power either to change it, to modify its rough edges or to accept it as it is. But these choices can only be made with understanding. The story of the formative period provides critical insights into the making of modern America.

⧼⧽

I have written this book for a number of reasons. First was my deep curiosity about how it came to be that the American economy today is so deeply grounded in the stock market. Several years into my research, I began to realize that this story had yet to be told and that it had greater significance than simply the intellectual engagement that sustained me. I began to see in the formation of American corporate capitalism the reasons for a number of contemporary business, economic and social problems, problems which so many are trying to solve today without understanding some of the important causes that this history helps to identify. Perhaps as important, I started to see the way our speculation economy affects the norms of American society, how it has pushed American social norms from a vision of collective life that achieved some currency during the Progressive Era to a more atomistic form of individualism that has both recalled an earlier American ideal and driven the future. Nowhere in American society is violent, competitive individualism more rampant than in the modern stock market.

Historians of the era, and those interested in history, are likely to be engaged by this critical phase of the development of modern America, and it is for them that I have tried to take such care in telling the story as accurately as my research has led me to understand it. But I hope that people engaged in business, public policy and law, and Americans who are concerned about the shape and direction of our society find this book equally helpful for the way it highlights the important ramifications of this transformation for American economic and business welfare and the character of American society.

Finally, the story I tell holds important lessons for citizens of other nations, even as the American form of corporate capitalism has affected the different ways many other countries do business. For almost two decades now, many countries have been at a decision point as to whether they will adopt the American way or pursue their own, or even whether they have much choice in the matter. This book teaches them that they do.

⧼⧽

I have many people to thank for helping me through this project. First and foremost, my brilliant wife and colleague, the historian and legal scholar

Dalia Tsuk Mitchell, deserves my gratitude for suggesting I explore history in the first place, for answering my endless questions about historiography, for sharing her knowledge of, and insight into, the Progressive Era, for listening to my endless lectures on the subject, for critically reading the manuscript over and over, for reminding me of the sources I had not yet read, for never letting me accept what I had shown her as good enough and for providing love and encouragement when I needed it the most. Theresa Gabaldon, Ira C. Lupu, Andrew Mitchell, Mary A. O'Sullivan, Daniel Raff, Christopher Ruane, Philip Scranton and Michael Selmi gave helpful feedback on various portions of the manuscript and a number of other colleagues throughout the country took the time to discuss aspects of the project with me. Arthur Wilmarth was more than generous in sharing his encyclopedic knowledge of the financial and regulatory history of the era and by commenting on a number of chapters. Donald Braman, Charlie Cray and Renée Lettow Lerner were enormously kind to read and comment on portions of the manuscript at a relatively late stage. The comments by Berrett-Koehler's readers—Charles Derber, Steven Johnson, Marjorie Kelly, Jeffrey Kulick and Steven Lydenberg—were sometimes mercilessly helpful and forced me to sharpen my argument. Early workshops at the University of California, Los Angeles, Rutgers University and The George Washington University helped me begin to organize what at the time was nothing more than muddled thinking about some interesting research, and participants in workshops and conferences at the University of Pennsylvania, the University of Illinois, McMaster University, Columbia University, Washington & Lee University and Georgetown University, among others, helped me to sharpen and refine my ideas. Matthew Mantel of the Jacob Burns Law Library at The George Washington University Law School, aided at times by Leonard Klein and Germaine Leahy, was an indispensable help, as was the hardworking staff of the interlibrary loan department. My assistant, Toinetta Foncette, undertook the rather large task of keeping everything reasonably organized. I am also grateful for the assistance of librarians and archivists at the Baker Library of Harvard University, the Library of Congress, the New York Public Library, the Newark, New Jersey, Public Library, The National Archives Research Administration at College Park, the New York Historical Society and the American Jewish Archives.

My deep appreciation goes to my agent, Susan Schulman, for her constant faith in me. My debt to my publisher is perhaps unusually large, because working with Berrett-Koehler gave me the chance to work with the kind of corporation I have idealized throughout my career. My editor, Steve Piersanti, challenged me to write and think with a new level of clarity. Ian Bach, Peter Cavagnaro, Mike Crowley, Tiffany Lee, Dianne Platner and Rick Wilson were remarkably open to my comments, ideas and suggestions and made the process of producing and marketing a book both interesting and a pleasure, as did the production team at Wilsted & Taylor Publishing Services, especially my enormously patient copy editor, Nancy Evans. Jeevan Sivasubramaniam's warmth, patience, humor, understanding and respect made him the managing editor every anxious author dreams of and, I hope, a real friend.

Finally, I am indebted to several excellent research assistants at The George Washington University Law School, including Matthew Benz, Martinique Busino, Zal Kumar, Adam Marlowe, Jacques Pelham and Misha Yanovsky. My very special thanks go to two extraordinary research assistants whose efforts during the last year of work made it possible to complete the book in a timely fashion, Alexis Rose Brown and Emily Vincent.

It was a pleasure to work with all of you.

Washington, D.C.
April 2007

⊰ PROLOGUE ⊱

A recent survey of more than four hundred chief financial officers of major American corporations revealed that almost 80 percent of them would have at least moderately mutilated their businesses in order to meet analysts' quarterly profit estimates. Cutting the budgets for research and development, advertising and maintenance and delaying hiring and new projects are some of the long-term harms they would readily inflict on their corporations. Why? Because in modern American corporate capitalism the failure to meet quarterly numbers almost always guarantees a punishing hit to the corporation's stock price. The stock price drop might cut executive compensation based on stock options, attract lawsuits, bring out angry institutional investors waving antimanagement shareholder proposals and threaten executive job security if it happened often enough. Indeed, the 2006 turnover rate of 118 percent on the New York Stock Exchange alone justifies their fears.[1]

The problem has been noticed. In 2006 two of the nation's most prominent business organizations, The Conference Board and the Business Roundtable, published reports decrying the short-term focus of the stock market and its dominance over American business behavior. They each suggested a variety of solutions to allow executives to manage their businesses for the long term in a manner they saw fit without constantly having to answer to the market's insistent demands for continuous price appreciation. The problem of business short-termism caused by the link between executive incentives and the stock market has become a popular subject of discussion in business, academic and policy circles. It was the central problem that I addressed in a book of my own in 2001.[2]

There is little question that short-term market behavior has created an increasingly troublesome business problem over the last twenty-five years.

But the stock market's pressure on business and business's response is nothing new. The short-termism of the late 1990s and early twenty-first century simply is an exaggeration of a quality that was embedded in the American economy a hundred years ago. The typical public corporation we know today, what I will call the giant modern corporation, was created during the merger wave of 1897 to 1903. It gave birth to the modern stock market. As it did, it transformed speculation from a disruptive game, played by a few professionals and thrill-seeking amateurs that from time to time erupted into a major frenzy, into the very genetic material of the American stock market, American business and American capitalism.

❧

The roots of the modern American stock market lie in the creation of the giant modern corporation. Born of the seeds of destructive competition that seemed to threaten the future of industrialization in late-nineteenth-century America, the giant modern corporation provided a solution that at first promised to stabilize new businesses and maintain the upward trajectory of industrial growth. But the stock market that it brought into being quickly came to be the main thrust behind business, the power behind the boardroom. The stock market started as a tool that helped to create new businesses. It ended by subjugating business to its power.

The modern stock market became an exacting taskmaster for American managers. It came to drive their investment, operating and planning decisions, and the path of American economic development itself. The market transformed from an institution that served businessmen by providing the means of making things and selling things. It became instead a thing apart, an institution without face or form whose insatiable desire for profit demanded satisfaction from even the most powerful corporations it created. In the end, the modern stock market left behind its business origins and became the very reason for the creation of business itself.

The significance of the market's development was not fully appreciated by regulators of the time. Controlling the perceived monopoly power of giant trusts was the issue of the day. Thus it was through the lens of monopoly that most contemporary observers and almost all lawmakers understood every aspect of the merger wave that created the giant modern corporation, including its causes, the legal forms it assumed, questions of operating efficiency and management and, perhaps most important of all, how the new corporate combinations were financed. While commentators were close to unanimous in locating the underlying cause of the merger wave in businessmen's attempts to control the often destructive competition that came to plague many of the new industries of the industrial century, they were equally unanimous in their agreement on its immediate and proximate cause—the opportunities it created for financiers to create wealth for themselves.

Destructive competition had been a problem for years. But it was only during the last few years of the nineteenth century that business distress combined with surplus capital searching for investment opportunities, changes in state corporation laws, and the creative greed of private bankers, trust promoters and the newly evolving investment banks created the perfect storm that shifted the production goals of American industry from goods and services to manufacturing and selling stock. Within twenty years the strong ripples of the merger wave had transformed the nineteenth-century industrial corporation into the giant modern corporation, and the stock market into the focus of American business life. While regulators were embroiled in questions of monopoly, the speculation economy subtly took form.

The history of the creation of the giant modern corporation and the modern stock market is complex. It is a story of industrial development, intellectual transformations, innovations in law and finance, rapidly changing social trends and the federal government's attempts at regulation. By the end of the period all of the ingredients for the modern stock market were in place and the major regulatory outlines of the securities laws that would be passed a decade hence had been laid out in Congress. Those laws took the speculation economy as a given.

The legal and regulatory changes of this period were driven by transformations in finance and the stock market. Waves of watered stock created by the giant modern corporation brought average Americans into the market for the first time. The instability of these new securities and the corporations that issued them provided enormous opportunity, both intended and not, for ordinary people and professionals alike to speculate, leading sometimes to mere bull runs and sometimes to widespread panic. This type of speculation had long existed in American markets. Whether or not the merger wave had taken place, whether or not the financial and business transformations had occurred, this type of speculation would almost certainly have continued.

New conditions brought with them a new kind of speculation. Modern historians understand speculation in terms of the type I have just described, the type of speculation that characterized market bubbles in 1899 and 1901, 1928 and 1929, the mid-1960s, and 1998 through 2000, among others. But the lasting kind of speculation as it was understood by some perceptive observers at the beginning of the last century was speculation intrinsic in the capital structure of American corporations. This second type of speculation permanently changed American business and the way it was regulated. It created an economy inseparable from speculation. That economy was embedded in a market characterized by increasing numbers of small common stockholders.

※

The modern stock market developed in three distinct stages. The first was the direct product of the merger wave, which drew substantial numbers of middle-class investors into the market for the first time. Starting with railroad bonds, which were considered the only truly safe corporate investment, they began to buy the somewhat riskier preferred stock of the new industrials, and sometimes even the highly speculative common stock, as investment opportunities multiplied through the beginning of the twentieth century. They came and they stayed, some of them, through the Rich Man's Panic of 1903. They were joined by others, sobered by the financial carnage but faithful to the new finance. Together they built a bull market that lasted until early 1907.

Writers and thinkers from many walks of life began to come to terms with the changes the new economy had brought to America. This they did by reaching back to what they had known from an earlier time, by reinventing the stock market as a new form of property, a property that could fill the evaporating role of the land and small business in classical American life and thought. Leaders, progressive and conservative alike, joined to encourage their countrymen to own this new property, hoping to restore greater equality of wealth and build a strong defense against creeping socialism. I exaggerate only a little to say that this idea of corporate securities as the new family farm helped to legitimate the stock market as an American institution, even as the plutocracy continued to dominate it.

The modern market continued to develop in the wreckage of the Panic of 1907. Nineteen-eight marked a year of strong market recovery, although recovery masked the beginning of a broad economic depression. The market first rose and then dropped by a quarter in 1910 to a plateau where it held tenaciously until 1914. Like mammals in the age of disappearing dinosaurs, small investors increased their numbers, held their securities and began to pick among the bargains that were the leavings of the plutocrats. Common stock began to be considered safe for investment, and its higher promised returns made it an attractive alternative to preferred stock and a favorite with small investors.

The third and final stage of the modern market's development began with the reopening of the New York Stock Exchange in December 1914 after months of darkness that fell as the guns of August roared. Not until April did the party really get going but, when it did, it erupted in a roaring bull market that continued straight up until the "return to normalcy" in 1920. It was sobered by only one bad year when the United States entered the war and had to figure out how to finance its own participation.

This was a different market than those that had come before. Brokers were honing their sales tactics and, by 1919, the securities arms of national banks, like "Sunshine Charley" Mitchell's National City Company, were driving the development of retail brokering into branch offices from Manhattan to Middletown. Individual investors found themselves more comfortable with common stocks as war prosperity brought high returns from companies churning out war materiel. And the Liberty Bond drives of 1917 and 1918 created 25 million new American investors. The brokerage industry watched, salivating, anticipating the day when the Iowa farmer no less than the New York lawyer realized he could do better than to take the bargain-basement interest on his Liberty Bonds and turned them in for a share of the new corporate boom economy. A long year of depression followed Harding's election and, in 1922, the great bull market of the 1920s began to take flight.

-≡⊫-

Like the modern stock market, securities regulation, as one of several federal responses to the dislocations caused by the merger wave, also grew in three steps. While each phase looked to disclosure as its central regulatory device, each had a distinctly different goal and used the tool of disclosure for a distinctly different purpose. Naturally there was overlap. But what we recognize as modern securities regulation, consumer-type investor protection, did not become its purpose until after the First World War.

The first phase of securities regulation grew out of federal attempts to regulate monopoly by controlling the watered stock created by the combinations of the merger wave. This was the antitrust phase of securities regulation and ran from the beginning of the century until 1914. Antitrust reform proposals and the related federal incorporation movement tried to compel corporate disclosure of financial information in order to reveal the true values of corporate capitalizations to help the federal government identify and prosecute monopolies under the Sherman Antitrust Act. The United States Bureau of Corporations, created as an investigatory body in 1903, embodied this antitrust policy. The securities market was of no particular concern in its own right.

The second step in the development of securities regulation, antispeculation regulation, overlapped the antitrust phase. It began almost immediately following the Panic of 1907 and continued in full force until its failure in 1914. From that point on it reemerged in fits and starts until it reached fruition in the Securities Exchange Act of 1934. Like the antitrust phase, the antispeculation stage was driven by the effects of the watered securities that flooded the market following the merger wave. But this time the goal was not to regulate monopolies. Rather it was to protect American financial stability, and particularly the banking system, which was episodically threatened by financial institutions' taste for stock speculation of the traditional type, either directly or by making large and highly profitable margin loans to brokers and speculators. Disclosure again was emphasized, but again as a regulatory tool. The purpose of disclosure during this second stage was to enable regulators and banks to control overcapitalization in order to maintain the safety of bank portfolios, not so much for the security of any individual bank but for the safety of the system as a whole.

The final development of securities regulation aimed at consumer protection. It began with a model of Wilsonian progressive legislation, proposed after the war by the Capital Issues Committee in a form that would serve as the matrix for the Securities Act of 1933. This was the modern type of mandatory disclosure, grounded in a philosophy that providing information to individual investors would allow them to make self-reliant, informed investment decisions and keep the market efficient, safe and stable. While the first stages of securities regulation were grounded in the new collectivism of the early Progressive Era, this final phase philosophically was born of the unique combination of individualism within collectivism that characterized Wilson's brand of progressivism. It was also the stage of securities regulation that institutionalized and legitimated the speculation economy.

⚉

The story proceeds as follows: The first three chapters describe the creation of the giant modern corporation, the legal changes that made it possible and the financing techniques that created the modern stock market. Chapter Four examines the first stage of the development of the modern stock market, paying particular attention to the way that social and cultural changes helped to legitimate the stock market as part of American society. Chapters Five through Seven trace the federal government's attempts to make sense of the economic transformations created by the giant modern corporation, showing an evolution from antitrust to the beginnings of securities regulation, all thematically unified by the dominant focus on corporate securities at each stage. In Chapter Eight I show the shift in the quality of the market during its second stage of development from the end of the first decade until the First World War as ordinary Americans turned from investing primarily in bonds and preferred stock to embracing speculative common stock as a favored investment vehicle. Chapter Nine examines the first failed attempt at federal securities regulation during the early Wilson administration and the way that it began to establish the conceptual bases and, in a crude way, the regulatory mechanisms for the successful regulation that would be passed by the New Deal Congress following the Great Crash of 1929. Chapter Ten concludes the history with a look at how the federal government's need for massive financing during the war and the Liberty Bond drives that satisfied it created new ways of marketing securities and a giant new class of investors and potential investors, even as federal moves toward securities regulation completed their conceptual development toward consumer protection. I conclude by reflecting briefly upon the development of this story over the succeeding eighty years and its consequences for the future of American business and the American economy.

⊰ ONE ⊱

THE PRINCIPLE OF COOPERATION

The creation of the giant modern American corporation was not a slowly evolving process. Individual proprietorships, partnerships and corporations gradually grew in size and number throughout the Industrial Revolution of the nineteenth century. But what we have come to know as the modern American corporation, the giant, publicly held corporation, appeared in a flash. America collectively turned around one day and was staring at the balance sheet of U.S. Steel.[1]

THE GIANT MODERN CORPORATION

The large corporation was already in late adolescence by the time of the great Chicago World's Columbian Exposition of 1893, that wonderfully quirky celebration of technological achievement and cultural progress that raised the curtain on a devastating four-year depression. The fruits of industrialization on display there had grown from saplings planted many decades before, produced by the large businesses dotting the landscape from Boston to Baltimore, from Pittsburgh to St. Louis and beyond. They had arrived by means of one of the greatest engines of the American economy, the railroads, whose tracks sprawled across the continent, north and south, east and west. The industrialization that had begun at the turn of the nineteenth century had been kicked into high gear by the insatiable material demands of the Civil War and gave birth to factories from which flowed steel, farm machinery, packaged meat, beer, wheat flour and sewing machines; mines that brought forth copper enough to wire the country for newly generated electricity; oil refineries that lighted homes from California to Europe; great dry goods empires and the Sears Roebuck catalogue. Left to themselves, these remarkable businesses might well have grown, financed with debt and their own retained earnings, created new products and services and supplied America's wants and needs for evermore. But the large corporations of the nineteenth century were soon to become the raw materials of a new kind of business, a business created for finance rather than for production.[2]

The businesses of the industrializing nineteenth century were, more often than not, organized as partnerships or closely held corporations. The stock of these enterprises was owned by the founders and their families or a small group of friends and business associates. Standard Oil was owned by Rockefeller and the refiners and suppliers he bought out. Carnegie Steel was a series of partnerships. Only the railroads and a very small handful of industrials issued stock that traded on the markets in any volume. The machinery of finance was in its infancy. When industrial corporations needed money, they dipped into their earnings, went to the bank, or sold bonds.[3]

The giant modern corporation was a phenomenon distinct from the forms and processes of industrialization. Its reasons for being were different from those of the nineteenth-century corporation. Earlier enterprises in the age of industrialization were built to take advantage of improvements in shipping, or new production technologies, or new ways of marketing or packaging. The giant modern corporation was created for a new purpose, to sell stock, stock that would make its promoters and financiers rich.[4]

It took only seven years. In the space of that explosive period, from 1897 to 1903, the giant modern American corporation was created by the fusion of tens, and sometimes hundreds, of existing businesses. The new corporations that emerged from this merger wave transformed the very nature of American business.

The inspirations that first drove businessmen to abandon competition to combine the plants that became the great corporations were business problems. Destructive competition threatened the success, and often the existence, of some of the new industries. Efficiencies of size and efficiencies of management prompted the combination of others. Cooperation was the solution. The great nineteenth-century trusts were the result. Before very long, these business motivations were combined with a different goal. That goal was to manufacture stock.[5]

Corporations created for this purpose transformed the structure of American corporate capitalism. They dumped huge amounts of new stock on the market, dispersing ownership from small numbers of men who managed their businesses to hundreds, and then thousands, and then hundreds of thousands of men and women who invested their savings in small blocks of bonds and stock. Although it would take a while to realize their promise, they forever changed the nature of the American economy by distributing the ownership of corporate wealth across the growing middle class. They also transformed American law and politics, leading the federal government to blossom from a small and undistinguished institution of limited domestic powers to a sovereign state that found, in the regulation of business, a central reason for being.[6]

The creation of the giant modern corporation gave birth to a new class in American society, the capitalists. There existed men who were called capitalists well before the 1890s, men who provided the funds to finance new enterprise. Their wealth came from the profits of land or from trade, and sometimes from the industrial plants they created. The businesses they financed were run, for the most part, by industrialists for industrialists. There were of course the rogue plungers and speculators in corporate stocks and bonds who found their wealth by gambling with the business lives of railroads. But men like these were a sideshow. The business of business was business.[7]

Matters had changed by 1903. Still there remained industrialists of the classic mold, but John D. Rockefeller was growing wealthier in retirement as an investor and Andrew Carnegie had sold his empire into the combination created by the very embodiment of the new breed, J. Pierpont Morgan. The nineteenth-century industrialist was *passé*. As Carnegie put it, "he and his partners knew little about the manufacture of stocks and bonds. They were only conversant with the manufacture of steel." J. P. Morgan and his men knew little about steel, but they were masters of the manufacture of stocks and bonds.[8]

The world of American business belonged to this new breed of capitalist. J. P. Morgan, John R. Dos Passos, the Moore brothers and Charles Flint became the symbols of modern American capitalism. These were the men who released billions in securities by rearranging the companies created by the captains of industry. When John "Bet a Million" Gates decided to create American Steel & Wire, he did not do it by building blast furnaces and rolling mills. He did it by buying almost thirty different plants, from Everett, Washington to Worcester, Massachusetts, using stock as his currency and taking stock as his profit. The giant modern corporation was created for the sake of finance.

The giant modern corporation did more than transform business into finance. It also displaced classical ideas about American individualism. Collective in its very nature, it complicated American social thought born in notions of fervent independence, of rugged individualism. It spread across the landscape cooperative enterprises that organized a new kind of social spirit even as it threatened to subjugate the individual. While it roiled the social order, it nevertheless seemed to pave a road back to older ways of thinking. In its creation of a new kind of property, corporate stock, it put forth a substitute for the traditional ownership of land and small enterprise, the iconic yeoman farmer, the traditional opportunity of the frontier. The stock market was the new frontier and Americans were eager to explore it. The giant modern corporation made Wall Street our wilderness and corporate stock our grubstake.

THE RISE OF FINANCE

The Industrial Revolution was a different phenomenon from the consolidations that created the giant modern corporation. American industrialism started from a base of relatively small owner-operators before the Civil War. A few important American business corporations can be traced as far back as the beginning of the nineteenth century. These were mostly local companies, locally owned and locally managed, even if their raw materials came from the cotton plantations of Mississippi, even if their products were widely sold and even if their stock was sometimes traded on the Boston Stock Exchange. Business use of the corporate form really blossomed in the 1840s and 1850s with the expansion of railroads, with their special needs for large amounts of permanent capital and the protection of limited liability. The stock of many railroads traded on exchanges, but more often than not it was controlled by a small group of insiders. As the railroads grew, they came to be financed largely with debt. When railroad stock traded in any great volume, it almost always meant that different factions were clawing for control or speculators were toying with the stock.[9]

The factory system itself appears to have been firmly established by the 1840s and 1850s. Significant growth took place between the end of the Civil War and 1890, with perhaps the greatest increase in the number of factories from 1879 to 1889. The class of wage earners grew from just over 2 million in 1869 to 4.25 million in 1889.[10]

While industrialization created new jobs, especially from around 1880 on, the creation of the giant modern corporation did relatively little for workers. Almost 53 percent of the gainfully employed population worked in agriculture in 1870, and only 19 percent in manufacturing, 39.5 percent when transportation, mining, construction and trade are included. The number of employees engaged in manufacturing, mining, construction transportation and trade had grown to exceed those employed in agriculture by 1890. But this increasing dominance of manufacturing and related industries was already in place by the time of the merger wave. Manufacturing jobs increased at a fairly steady rate during the last two decades of the century, by 33.4 percent between 1880 and 1890 and 34.2 percent between 1890 and 1900. During the decade following the merger wave, manufacturing jobs continued to increase, but at a rate of 30 percent, a slower rate of increase than occurred during the preceding two decades. The merger wave's role in job creation was insignificant.[11]

The merger wave did not create many new manufacturing jobs. It did not even create new factories. The jobs and the factories were already there. The giant modern corporation was an aggregation of existing factories, already fully staffed. The financial imperative that created the giant modern corporation created stock, not jobs. Only in finance and real estate, insignificant employers before 1900, were substantial numbers of jobs created by the merger wave.

The giant modern corporation combined existing jobs and factories under a single corporate umbrella. But it had an enormous financial impact. Although difficult to determine with precision, its magnitude seems to be beyond dispute. According to one contemporaneous study by Luther Conant, Jr., the total capitalization of American industrial combinations of plants with capital greater than $1 million was $216 million in 1887. It had grown over twenty times to more than $4.4 billion by 1900. Slightly over $1 billion of this had been added before the crash of 1893. Relatively little occurred during the following depression, but from 1896 to 1900 almost $4 billion of capitalization by combination was added to American industry. Hans Thorelli's later study, based on slightly different criteria, showed $262 million in combination capitalization in 1893 rising to an aggregate of almost $3.9 billion in 1900, with another $2.3 billion added by 1903. Neither study included railroads, the dominant industry, or public utilities. Thorelli excluded the portion of corporate capitalization represented by bonds, but Conant showed that bonds were a relatively small percentage of combination capitalization.[12]

John Moody, in his 1904 book, *The Truth About the Trusts*, calculated that "the aggregate capitalization outstanding in the hands of the public of the 318 important and active Industrial Trusts in this country is at the present time no less than $7,246,342,533," representing the consolidation of almost 5,300 individual plants. Two hundred thirty-six of these trusts had been incorporated after January 1, 1898, and represented more than $6 billion of his estimated capitalization. Adding public utility and railroad combinations, Moody calculated a total capitalization of almost $20.4 billion, comprising 8,664 "original companies." Ralph Nelson, whose numbers set the modern standard of analysis and are based upon a more restricted definition of merger, calculated 2,653 "firm disappearances by merger" with a total capitalization of $6.3 billion between 1898 and 1902. Turn-of-the-century economist Edward Meade pointed out that between 1898 and 1900 alone, 149 large business combinations comprising plants in every industry were formed with an aggregate capitalization of $3.6 billion, including Standard Oil of New Jersey, "the United Fruit Company, the National Biscuit Company, the Diamond Match Company, the American Woolen Company, the International Thread Company, the American Writing-Paper Company, the International Silver Company, The American Bicycle Company, and the American Chicle Company," as well as combinations in whiskey, tobacco, beer, coal, iron, steel and chemicals, among others. And all this was before the creation of the first billion-dollar corporation, U.S. Steel, in 1901. No matter how you look at it, the financial economy created by the merger wave was like a tidal wave crashing over American society.[13]

With all of this new capitalization, the value of stock in the hands of Americans rocketed. Individual (nonagricultural) and nonprofit net acquisitions of corporate stock increased from $105 million in 1897 to a peak of $715 million in 1902, declining to $475 million in 1903, the year of the Rich Man's Panic that effectively called an end to the merger wave. Net acquisitions of corporate and foreign bonds were $58 million in 1897 and $82 million in 1903, with major concentrations ranging from $287 million to $465 million in 1899 and 1902, respectively.

The effect was more than dollars. The merger wave created dramatic increases in the number of shares of stock traded throughout the nation. Seventy-seven million shares were traded on the New York Stock Exchange (NYSE) in 1897, almost all of them issued by railroads. Trading volume reached 176.4 million shares in 1899 and, after a brief decline to 138.3 million in 1900, charged up to 265.6 million in 1901, fluctuating between a low of 161 million and a high of 284.3 million shares during the succeeding decade. At the end of that decade, the number of industrial stocks listed on the New York Stock Exchange passed the railroads for the first time and stock ownership had begun to be widely dispersed among Americans.[14]

"INDUSTRY IS CARRIED ON FOR THE SAKE OF BUSINESS"

The dominance of the stock market over business in American economic life was foreseen by Thorstein Veblen even as the events that would cause it were unfolding. Veblen understood concepts like value and profit in terms of human behavior; what people did, instead of what people made, was the real key to understanding profit. This led him to develop a critical distinction between "industry" and "business." Industry was the physical process of making things. It involved factories, raw materials, workers and end products. The industrial process developed to increase productive efficiency and coordinate among the various intricately related aspects of manufacture. In order best to serve the community, the various industrial processes had to be kept in balance. It was the businessman interacting through business transactions who was to maintain this balance. The business transaction was something different from the process of industry.

Veblen observed that "industry is carried on for the sake of business, and not conversely." Businessmen were driven by the chance for future profits. And the businessman, in contrast to the industrialist, found those profits in disturbing the balance of the system, the industrial equilibrium, which his transactions ideally were supposed to maintain. By creating these disturbances among the corporations of industry, he could make much more money for himself than he could earn from the mere profits of production. Just as a grain speculator could make money whether the market was good or bad, so the businessman could profit whether industrial profits were high or low. The community's well-being, its need for industrial stability and its dependence upon the products of industry were of no concern to the businessman. Indeed, maintaining that community in balance would deprive him of these opportunities for gain.

In order to achieve his ends, the businessman had to "block the industrial process at some one or more points." For example, businessmen seeking to form combinations would first have to make it difficult for the industrial components to remain independent. The goal was to freeze out competitors or drive them toward bankruptcy.

Who were these businessmen? After all, Veblen's distinction between industry and business as well as his attention to combinations were based on the realization that many independent industrial plants owned by individuals or small groups existed throughout the country. And there were industrialists who were content to stick to their knitting. But the description of the true businessman, the businessman whose goal was to arbitrage industrial imbalances that he himself created, "seems to apply in a peculiar degree, if not chiefly, to those classes of business men whose operations have to do with railways and the class of securities called 'industrials.'"

Veblen saw corporate securities as the principal tool for industrial disruption. Dealings in railroad securities were for manipulation, consolidation and control. This was no less true in the late 1890s for industrial combinations than for railroads, as industrial combinations came together through the medium of stock. Thanks to an increasingly developed market, these securities could be far more easily manipulated by overcapitalization, speculation and the like, than entire factories could be.

Veblen understood the developing domination of finance over industry. "From being a sporadic trait, of doubtful legitimacy, in the old days of the 'natural' and 'money' economy, the rate of profits or earnings on investment has in the nineteenth century come to take the central and dominant place in the economic system. Capitalizations, credit extensions, and even the productiveness and legitimacy of any given employment of labor, were referred to the rate of earnings as their final test and substantial ground." As he further wrote: "[T]he interest of the managers of a modern corporation need not coincide with the permanent interest of the corporation as a going concern; neither does it coincide with the interest which the community at large has in the efficient management of the concern as an industrial enterprise." The interest of managers, including corporate directors and large stockholders, was "that there should be a discrepancy, favorable for purchase or for sale as the case may be, between the actual and the putative earning-capacity of the corporation's capital." Business in the giant modern corporation was not about industry. It was about arbitraging the stock.[15]

LAISSEZ-FAIRE

Before the giant modern corporation could be created, the social, intellectual and legal environments that would make it acceptable had to develop. The story of the end of the nineteenth century is thus a story of the shift from *laissez-faire* in economic and social thought to an appreciation of, and desire for, more collective and cooperative forms of endeavor. It is a story of deteriorating business conditions that imperiled the new industrialization as railroad and then industrial overbuilding and competition appeared to threaten to create a few giant monopolies and put every small operator out of business. And it is the story of how businessmen tried to cooperate in the face of laws that made cooperation all but impossible until New Jersey, for reasons of its own, came to fix it. It is a story of the transformation from competition to cooperation that fertilized the ground in which the giant modern corporation took root.[16]

The social and intellectual environment in which the giant modern corporation flourished helped to rationalize changes in public thinking about the respective virtues of competition and cooperation. The transformations in American life that came along with accelerating industrialization caused social and economic dislocations as the old doctrine of *laissez-faire* impeded effective regulatory redress. Well-known social and political upheavals, characterized by the Grange movement, Populism, labor agitation, Socialism and religious movements like the Social Gospel, were one result. Another was a fervent defense of the old order in new terms, from the Social Darwinism of William Graham Sumner to its reconceptualization and humanization in Andrew Carnegie's Gospel of Wealth. The ferment led to larger popular concern, and also to iconoclastic scholarly debate within academic circles by young scholars educated in, or under the influence of, the collective spirit of Germany. These young economists provided much of the intellectual apparatus necessary to legitimate the new order and for that reason alone they are important. But they are important for another reason, too. Among their number was the young Professor Woodrow Wilson who, as president of the United States, would help transform some of this thinking into economic regulatory policy.[17]

The doctrine of *laissez-faire* dominated the America of the middle century. Following the Civil War, economists, businessmen and public intellectuals adopted the idea in a version more extreme and inhumane than that of Adam Smith or John Stuart Mill. Business was, for the most part, unregulated. Social services that could deal with economic dislocation existed, if at all, only by virtue of charity. The war economy had hastened industrialization and the pursuit of wealth became a widespread goal. Andrew Carnegie's "Gospel of Wealth," William Graham Sumner's *What Social Classes Owe to Each Other* and Supreme Court jurisprudence all provided variations on an idealized theme of an unregulated society of business in which competition created benefits for society and riches to the victorious. It did not hurt that *laissez-faire* had religious foundations deep in American and British Protestantism for, as John Maynard Keynes noted in *The End of Laissez-Faire*: "Individualism and *laissez-faire*. This was the Church of England and those her apostles."[18]

But in real-life America, and especially in the America of railroad men and new industrialists, *laissez-faire* was a dangerous idea. Riches were fleeting and ruin quite frequent. The promised benefits hardly showed. Wall Street financiers and modest Midwest farmers decried *laissez-faire* as a practical ideology as they saw how disastrous competition could be when applied to the conditions of modern American business. Grangers in the West howled as railroad rates threatened to absorb their profits even as they watched large millers and meatpackers ship their goods at much lower rates. Oil producers in Pennsylvania were forced to succumb to Standard Oil's domination of the railroads. The damaging effects of increasing urban poverty and unsafe working conditions stimulated reformers motivated by humane concerns. Even as the Sumners and Carnegies preached their gospels, churchmen, philosophers and economists were writing a new one. *Laissez-faire* as a way of life was in its death throes.[19]

Laissez-faire was a philosophy. It was a way of economic thought that, like the American ideal of individualism itself, derived from Enlightenment ideas upon which the republic was based. The Lockean idyll of individual freedom and individual property went hand-in-hand with the classical economic ideas of Adam Smith. If the appropriate actor in American political and social life was the individual, pursuing his interests as he saw fit, the appropriate actor in economic life was likewise the individual, pursuing his economic goals as he saw fit, all in competition with other individuals doing precisely the same thing.

This individualism had a sacred provenance, for it expressed the foundational American principle of equality as much as it did its partner ideal of freedom. If the goal was to liberate all men to pursue their interests, the practical corollary in a nation of justice was that individuals were roughly equal in their opportunities. In the absence of rough equality, freedom for all would rapidly lead to dominion by some and increasingly less equality for others.

Tied to the ideal of individualism was the sanctity of private property. Property's almost mystical power in American social thought derived from the notion that it was the extension of the individual, the product of the individual's motivations, interests, talents and efforts. Private property was also the basis for wealth, wealth produced by the nominally free economic activity that domesticated property, increased its value and indirectly boosted the welfare of all. It was the medium through which individuals exercised their freedom, a freedom expressed through unhindered competitive transactions with other individuals. Individualism, in its idealized form, meant much more than the pursuit of wealth—it also held the freedom to express one's own ideas, practice one's own religion, set one's own life goals. But it was the relationship between freedom and equality, and the individual's pursuit of happiness through economic activity, that laid the foundation for mainstream mid-nineteenth-century thought.

THE RISE OF INDUSTRIAL COMPETITION

Americans experienced conflict between these ideals and the reality of an industrializing America in which some people had more than others, whether as a result of birth or talent, effort or luck. The problem was less pronounced before the Civil War, at least to the extent that one ignores the hard-to-ignore issue of slavery. That was a time when the overwhelming majority of white, male Americans lived mostly as small farmers, merchants or tradesmen, although there were regional disparities in wealth concentration, with middle Atlantic and north central states dominating other regions.[20]

Americans' opportunities to acquire great wealth began to increase following the Civil War, at first slowly and then with increasing speed. Among the first were the railroads, often monopolies, which also created larger markets for those who owned land or did business in the favored locations where depots were located. Farmers had new outlets for their crops; merchants had new outlets for their wares; manufacturers had new outlets for their products. And investing in the railroads themselves made men rich.

The railroads did not go everywhere at first. From 1830 to 1840, aggregate track mileage increased from 23 miles to almost 123 times that amount. These lines were, for the most part, local or regional, and mainly served to supplement existing canals. Most of them were fairly short lines, sometimes connecting with other short lines to span longer distances radiating out from Boston, New York, Philadelphia and Baltimore. Funds were raised by local subscription and by debt, which was mostly sold in New York and Europe.[21]

Railroad construction exploded following the Civil War. Seventy thousand miles of track were in operation by 1873, which grew to almost 200,000 miles by 1900. At the same time, new technologies increased the productivity of farmers. Factories began to churn out combines and threshers and harvesters to help them increase their crops. Modern refrigerator cars, developed in 1881, permitted the safe and efficient shipment of beef from the Midwest to the East Coast. The explosion of railroad construction created an insatiable demand for steel. The growth of cities led to the need for massive amounts of lumber and, later, steel for building and kerosene and natural gas for energy. Inventions like the telegraph, the ticker tape and the telephone provided businessmen with almost instantaneous means of communication. Electric power led to the invention of new conveniences and comforts for modern life, providing new entrepreneurial and manufacturing opportunities. The railroads' development of national markets also gave birth to new kinds of merchants, sellers of branded commodities such as oats, soap and tobacco, and catalogue houses that could capitalize on new economies of scale because of quick shipping and communication technologies. Big business started to grow.[22]

These new opportunities attracted interest from people in all walks of American life. And so first with the railroads, and then with other businesses that could now expand their markets thanks to the new transportation facilities, competition erupted, competition wholly in the grain of the American ideal. Even as this competition led to the burgeoning industrialization that disturbed the earlier relative income equality, and even as relative equality in the ownership of property was transformed into the increasing concentration of wealth in the hands first of individuals and then of corporations, the courts, especially the Supreme Court, continued to hold competition as sacred. The problem was that competition was destroying business.

The American ethic was individualism. Its economic expression was *laissez-faire* competition. But in the age of the railroads, as in the age of growing industry, the American ethic of individualism created a tension with American prosperity that required combination to sustain itself. The incomes and comfort of increasingly large numbers of Americans were coming to depend upon the railroads and new industry. Americans' real *per capita* income grew almost 45 percent between 1879 and 1899. In order to allow people to realize the benefits of new businesses, and in order for businesses to be able to take advantage of this new wealth, they had to survive. Survival increasingly required cooperation. But the law demanded that they compete or, more precisely, made it very difficult for them to cooperate. Unless a way to facilitate cooperation could be found, the American economy confronted a severe threat, a threat that existed because of a legal culture that still embraced an outdated ideology.[23]

THE PRINCIPLE OF COOPERATION

The assault on traditional ideology began to develop at around the same time that railroads were experimenting with various forms of cooperation, all of which turned out to be ineffective and legally unenforceable. *Laissez-faire* philosophy had come under attack on a number of fronts by the late 1870s. The Social Gospel movement confronted the Gospel of Wealth. Economically sophisticated clergymen, led by Washington Gladden, preached that the restoration of Christian ethics could remedy the damage done by the unbridled and unregulated pursuit of wealth. And a group of young economists, coalescing in the mid-1880s, were deeply affected by this religiously based social movement and the turmoil they saw around them. Many of them had studied in Germany and were heavily influenced by the historicist school of economic thought. The ideas of that school arose from the history of social development and accompanying ideas of collective solidarity, deeply grounded in time and place. As one of their number, Edwin Seligman, succinctly wrote in 1886: "The modern school, the historical and critical school, holds that the economic theories of any generation must be regarded primarily as an outgrowth of the peculiar conditions of time, place, and nationality under which the doctrines were evolved, and that no set of tenets can arrogate to itself the claim of immutable truth, or the assumption of universal applicability to all countries or epochs."[24]

Troubled by the inhumane implications and universalistic claims of *laissez-faire*, these young economists developed a belief in both regulation and cooperation. Most of them acknowledged the importance of competition, but the competition of their imagination was a civilized competition, a sort of competition that was grounded in a society more organic than traditional American individualism acknowledged, a society that ameliorated the horrible casualties of unrestrained battle. Some saw the evolution of industrial society itself as leading to a new kind of competition, a competition of groups against groups, of corporations against corporations, rather than of individuals against individuals or even individuals against corporations. All acknowledged the urgent need for some kind of cooperation in both business and society. And all saw the need for a degree of state intervention that would regulate competition in a manner consistent with the more humanistic values they were introducing into American economic thought. Many were frustrated as they faced rejection by an older school of American economists, a school steeped in David Ricardo and John Stuart Mill and hewing to the orthodoxy of *laissez-faire*. But, at least in the beginning, they fought back.[25]

In the spring of 1885, members of this group discussed the need for a new association that would counter the old orthodoxy by committing itself to the independent scientific study of economics. Liberated from political ideology and preconceived prejudice, they would encourage "perfect freedom in all economic discussion." Among them were Henry Carter Adams, E. J. James, John Bates Clark, Edwin Seligman and Richard T. Ely. They were joined by Ely's former Johns Hopkins student, Woodrow Wilson, a young political scientist just about to embark upon his new academic career.

Ely, perhaps the most radical of the group, drafted a prospectus that he, along with Adams and James, sent out, inviting a larger group of economists and fellow travelers like Gladden and Cornell President Andrew White to a meeting. It was scheduled for early September in Saratoga Springs to coincide with the annual meeting of the American Historical Association. At four o'clock on the afternoon of September 8, 1885, the session was called to order in the Bethesda Parish Building for a discussion of the objects and platform of the new American Economic Association (AEA). Among the members of its original council were Woodrow Wilson and Lyman Abbott, the latter of whom succeeded Henry Ward Beecher as pastor of the famous abolitionist Plymouth Congregational Church in Brooklyn and would become a close friend, editor and informal advisor to Theodore Roosevelt.

The platform as presented began: "We regard the state as an educational and ethical agency whose positive aid is an indispensable condition of human progress. While we recognize the necessity of individual initiative in industrial life, we hold that the doctrine of *laissez-faire* is unsafe in politics and unsound in morals; and that it suggests an inadequate explanation of the relations between the state and the citizens." The statement captured the group's spirit, but its language was hotly debated. Some of the members agreed with it precisely as written. Some rejected strict *laissez-faire* but did not like the implication that they were opposed to unregulated competition in all circumstances. Indeed, all members of the group thought that some degree of competition was important. Some thought *laissez-faire* was generally acceptable in times past but that modern economic circumstances had made the doctrine impractical. A very few asserted a continuing belief in *laissez-faire* although, as in the case of Benjamin Andrews, it was tempered by a humanism found in the moral theories of Adam Smith that seemed to have been abandoned in the new industrial world. In the end, the final "Statement of Principles" retained its first sentence dealing with the indispensability of the state to aid "human progress," but dropped the following sentences decrying *laissez-faire*. The complete denunciation of *laissez-faire* was defeated. But the doctrine was on its deathbed.[26]

The new economists often disagreed on details but unanimously held the principle that the age of economic cooperation was arriving and that the government was, at a minimum, a necessary midwife. A few examples of the individual thinking of the AEA's charter members will help to fill in the contours of the new economic thought in America. The writings of Clark, Adams, Ely and Seligman stand out, especially for their emphases on the positive benefits and normative desirability of the shift from competition to cooperation.

Clark, who taught Thorstein Veblen at Carleton College, would return more closely to free market ideas as the century closed. Indeed, he achieved his lasting fame with his writings on marginal utility theory and a return to the centrality of competition. But in the late 1870s and 1880s, Clark's thinking embraced what he referred to as "true socialism." His was not the political socialism that was popular in Europe, a centralizing socialism at odds with the structure of American government. It was instead a socialism based on the rather modest notion that property rights were grounded in social organizations rather than individuals. The object of property rights was to distribute wealth on the basis of justice, not to the survivor of harsh competition. Clark called this a "practical," not an ideological, socialism, a statement of fact about the ultimate direction in which the American economy was moving. The corporation, itself a social organization capable of being endowed with property rights, was its leading actor.

So Clark claimed to describe the world as he saw it. But he also approved of this new direction. Cooperative ownership and production were the markings of a much more advanced state of society than free market competition. Competition would not, and should not, be abolished. But in the new world of cooperation, competition would take place between collective institutions such as corporations rather than between individuals, even if this meant that competition would wind up as something "latent or residual" instead of an actual state of economic affairs. The possibility of competition would be enough to preserve the benefits of competition without its dangerous flaws. Traditional views of competition might have been appropriate for the age of liberation in which the work of Adam Smith emerged, but realities had changed. The evolution of society into a higher order meant that a new economic principle had to be found. Clark called it "the principle of cooperation."[27]

Adams, while acknowledging that *laissez-faire* contained "some truths," harshly criticized it as "illogical" and unscientific. Society was the proper object of economic study, and society included both the individual engaged in business and the state itself. Competition was neither malevolent nor beneficent but had to be evaluated "according to the conditions under which it is permitted to act." Adams approved both of appropriately measured competition and of Clark's worldview, and set out the general principle by which governmental regulation of industry should be evaluated: "It should be the purpose of all laws, touching matters of business, to maintain the beneficent results of competitive action while guarding society from the evil consequences of unrestrained competition." This included permitting monopolies to exist, because monopolies could be highly beneficial to society while regulation could prevent their excesses. Adams's work would echo twenty-five years later in Woodrow Wilson's regulatory program.[28]

Wilson's teacher was the most controversial of the group. As one historian described him, "Wherever he turned, Ely seemed to step on somebody's toes." It was Ely who had drafted the original AEA platform, and he took perhaps the strongest position among his colleagues against *laissez-faire*. He was also one of the greatest proponents of the humanization of economics and emphasized historicism and induction over the more formal approach of classical economics. Ely at times expressed his views (including his appreciation of Marx) so forcefully that he was accused of being a socialist. It was a label he correctly rejected.

In his 1889 *An Introduction to Political Economy*, Ely identified sociology as the master social science, with political economy as a subdivision within the broader study of society. Christianity itself "offers us our highest conception of a society which embraces all men, and in that conception sets us a goal toward which we must move." Society was an organism, and the ideas of political economy could not be considered separate and apart from that organism. To his credit, Ely did not claim to be writing a comprehensive treatise, and the list of readers he thanks—Franklin Giddings, John Bates Clark, Woodrow Wilson and Amos Warner, as well as his research assistant, John R. Commons—suggests from the beginning a work perhaps more ideological than positive.

Ely drew a sharp distinction between monopolies and trusts, accepting and even praising the latter as big businesses seeking the gains of economies of scale and therefore greater efficiency. Indeed, while Ely understood competition as "the foundation of our present social order" and believed that it functioned best among large enterprises, he argued that the "moral and ethical level" of competition needed to be raised. But, despite his approval of competition, Ely, like Clark, saw the evolution of society as heading in the opposite direction. As he put it, "cooperation is the great law of social growth." Yet the interdependence among men and their differential status required even cooperation to be regulated. Only regulation could lead to the realization of "freedom and individuality" that were at the heart of the American ideal.[29]

Edwin Seligman, noting the "serious defects" in free competition, made his colleagues' arguments for cooperation appear to be more consistent with traditional thought by dressing the new collective theories in classical economic form. Classical economists argued that the individual, working in his own self-interest, incidentally produced benefits for society. Seligman observed that corporate combinations also worked for their own benefit. But while "[t]hey better their own condition, in so doing they often better the public condition." *Homo economicus* became, in Seligman's thinking, the economic group. Besides, combinations existed and monopolies were facts. They had already so shifted the price system that prices were set by the "artificial manipulation" of the combinations and not by free competition. This was often to the public good, but there were evils to be prevented. While bemoaning the relative inefficacy of the Interstate Commerce Commission, Seligman argued that it provided a good regulatory model for trusts that ought to be improved upon and followed.

Clark, Adams, Ely and Seligman, like others of their young colleagues, each had different visions of the principle of cooperation. But the new economists almost unanimously agreed that cooperation had become a necessary principle of economic organization and that competition had to be controlled if it were to be preserved at all. Even the conservative Arthur Hadley, who would soon join the AEA, wrote that "[a]ll our education and habit of mind make us believe in competition." But industrial cooperation was inevitable and necessary.[30]

THE NEED FOR COOPERATION

The new economic thinkers, attuned as they were to social problems, were keen observers of business. The greatest business reality in America during the mid-1880s was the self-destruction of the railroads. And the most significant barrier to their self-preservation was the absence of legal devices that could allow them to cooperate effectively.

The railroads had grown up in an era of free competition, although ironically many were granted monopoly power within some range of their roads. The trouble was that free competition proved too much in the face of rapid industrialization and concentrating wealth. In their eagerness to take advantage of increasing market opportunities, and as new operators entered the market, the railroads became heavily overbuilt, with parallel lines criss-crossing the countryside and converging on the major cities in the East and Midwest. This overbuilding produced competition with a vengeance, competition that many of the roads could not handle. One of their significant business characteristics was that they had high fixed costs for track maintenance, rolling stock and personnel, as well as substantial debt service obligations on the large volume of bonds they issued to finance their construction and expansion. In order to pay these costs, let alone make a profit, they needed to generate revenue from passengers and freight. With too many lines serving the same routes and thus competing for the same customers, this was a difficult goal to accomplish. It was not long before railroad lines were so numerous and covered so much parallel territory that their operators had to engage in self-mutilating rate wars simply to stay alive.[31]

Shippers between St. Louis and Atlanta had their choice of twenty different routes as early as the 1870s. In the budding days of Standard Oil, when many of the nation's refineries were centered in Cleveland, Rockefeller had a warm-weather choice between shipping over the Great Lakes and using the Lake Shore Railroad. The Lake Shore was happy to accept Standard's guaranty of sixty full cars every day in exchange for deeply discounted rates. The Erie, the Great Atlantic, the New York Central and the mighty Pennsylvania all fell before Rockefeller's ability to fill their cars. He even managed to demand kickbacks from the Pennsylvania's shipment of other people's oil.

Too many lines, rebates to customers who filled cars, differential rates for long- and short-haul shipping and out-and-out price gouging by lines on some routes in order to generate the cash to support others became the pricing practices of the entire industry. Railroads dropped their freight rates to such low levels that they often could not cover fixed costs. Bankruptcy and reorganization became a rite of passage in a typical railroad's life.[32]

While the railroads were struggling to survive they were helping to destroy competition in a different way. Businesses that were big enough shippers could command bargain rates, adding significant cost savings to the tools that let them dominate their industries. The rails were a road to monopoly.[33]

In 1901, surveying the enormous popular and scholarly literature about trusts that had appeared from 1897 to 1901, economist Charles J. Bullock described a class of trust literature dealing specifically with the relationship between the trusts and the railroads. He quoted one author as noting that "the trusts have the railroads by the throat," and another as classifying discriminatory railroad rates as "most prominent among ... [the trusts' evils]." The United States Industrial Commission in its Final Report in 1902 noted: "There can be no doubt that in earlier times special favors from railroads were a prominent factor, probably the most important factor, in building up some of the largest combinations.... The evil effect of such discriminations upon the rivals of the combination is self-evident." And among the recommendations of the Bureau of Corporations in its Report of 1904 was "prohibition of discriminations by public service companies."[34]

The railroads were the first of America's large corporations, and thus the first to face the problems of excessive competition. Manufacturing and the extractive industries followed as technology increased production (and fixed costs) and railroads expanded product markets from localities and regions to large sections of the nation. Within a short period of time industries throughout the country were fighting one another to keep their shares of the market. Competition might have produced efficiency. But it often produced destruction. Cooperation was the solution.[35]

A significant portion of American industry was in hypercompetitive pain. A way to cooperate had to be found. One method that might appear obvious in modern times would have been to combine the corporations that owned the railroads or competing factories, or perhaps to form a single corporation to buy up competing properties. But those solutions were not available. The constraints of nineteenth-century law were, for the most part, preclusive.

THE LIMITS OF COOPERATION

The railroads had brought with them the first widespread use of the corporate form of conducting business. The corporate form provided advantages that were unavailable to sole proprietorships and partnerships. Corporations provided the best means of bringing together the large amounts of capital necessary to build the railroads, and later other large businesses, by allowing them to issue massive debt under the protection of the limited liability of their shareholders while at the same time permitting the shareholders to retain control through their ownership of common stock. The corporate form also made it easy to transfer stock ownership and change personnel without disturbing the capital structure. And it allowed the centralization of management that was an essential key to the growth of giant corporations. All of this created a means of consolidation. But the restrictions on consolidation imposed by state corporation laws made any sort of widespread cooperation using the corporate device difficult if not impossible.

Corporations were the creations of the individual states. What the state created the state could restrict and, as a general matter, the states restricted the powers of corporations to join forces or freely grow for a number of reasons. Not the least of these was to keep within the states the businesses upon which they increasingly came to rely for jobs for their citizens and tax revenues for their services. Even as railroads crossed state lines, the corporations that owned them could not freely cross state lines to join with other corporations. The common result was that lines in one state were owned by a corporation in that state and connected at the state border with a line owned by a different corporation in the adjacent state. This not only prevented consolidation, but also for a time created problems for management and the technical standardization of railroads. Different lines owned by different corporations often used different gauge track. At least until the mid-1880s, a train arriving in Virginia from New York or Pennsylvania might have to empty its passengers and freight into the Virginia cars in order for the passengers and freight to continue.[36]

A lingering mistrust of corporate privilege and a growing fear of monopoly led states to restrict corporations' abilities to combine even within individual states and to operate interstate businesses. Capitalization, and thus the ability to grow by means of outside financing, was limited. Nineteenth-century ideas about corporate personhood constrained judicial interpretations of the purpose clauses of corporate charters so severely that corporations usually were not allowed to own stock in another corporation. Notions about the nature of incorporation itself led to requirements almost impossible to meet before corporations could combine by merger or consolidation. By the 1880s, state corporate law restrictions were supplemented by state antitrust laws, with at least fourteen in effect by the time Congress passed the Sherman Act. The obstacles to cooperation were substantial.

Businesses attempted to use other devices, again led by the railroads. Railroads tried to form pools. The pools consisted of railroad managers coming together and appointing a central coordinator to determine rates or allocate traffic. Starting as early as the middle 1850s, but concentrated in the 1870s, some of the pools actually held together for a time. The pool formed by William Vanderbilt under the so-called 1873 "Saratoga Agreement" lasted for six months. The far more successful Southern Railway & Steamship Association was created in 1875 with a formally appointed director to allocate traffic and lasted for a decade. Other pools came and went but never were enduring, and rate competition always returned as pool members, drawn by their own greed, defected. There was little the other pool members could do to prevent this. Under the common law dealing with restraints on competition, the pools were unenforceable.

As the pools continued to fail, businessmen tried to devise ways to create what were generally referred to as "communities of interest." These were often enforced by intercorporate investments—cross-holdings of stock—to satisfy the members' self-interest. There might be enough business for everyone if business simply could be rationalized in a way that distributed the opportunities more evenly. But, as with the pools, the problem of maintaining these communities of interest was real. The competitive impulse always remained; cooperation might persist for a while but, even with intercorporate stockholdings, the incentives to cheat and defect could be irresistible.[37]

STANDARD OIL AND THE TRUST

There had to be a way to make cooperation legally effective. Corporations were generally prohibited from owning the stock of other corporations, a rule which, together with restrictions on size, purpose and fundamental changes like mergers, made the corporate device unavailable to solve the problem. The pooling agreement was unstable. Communities of interest were difficult to assemble. Both were hard to maintain and unenforceable in court.

The first significant solution was discovered by oil. The American petroleum industry had experienced dramatic competitive problems during the late 1860s and early 1870s, with overproduction in the fields and refining overcapacity in Cleveland, Pittsburgh, the Allegheny Valley, Philadelphia and New York. The Pennsylvania Railroad's Tom Scott tried to resolve the problem by engaging with a small group of refiners, including John D. Rockefeller, and the major trunk lines in the region to create the South Improvement Company, a device to monopolize and control the industry. The South Improvement Company became a political and industrial nightmare that collapsed before it ever engaged in business. But Rockefeller, who understood the benefits of combination, was beginning his plan to rationalize the oil industry by acquiring it.

Standard Oil spent the 1870s expanding its business and, significantly, buying new companies and properties in the major oil refining and producing states. By 1879, the Standard group was a hodgepodge of corporations, wells, refineries, pipelines and other assorted assets, loosely organized and difficult to manage. Ohio corporate law made it almost impossible for Rockefeller and his associates to assemble these properties in an economically and managerially rational form. The law prohibited Standard from owning the stock of corporations in other states, and its charter limited its business only to refining, shipping and selling petroleum. The business had grown more complex than that, and Standard Oil of Ohio itself, the flagship corporation, owned substantial properties in Pennsylvania, Maryland and New York, in addition to Ohio.[38]

Rockefeller and his associates already controlled the oil industry. But their control was dispersed. As he acquired the companies that built his monopoly, Rockefeller achieved a modest degree of centralization by placing their stock in trust, usually with Henry Flagler as trustee. But this kept the businesses separated and without a centralized management.[39]

In 1879, Samuel C. T. Dodd, then a relatively obscure Cleveland lawyer described by one contemporary as being "so fat that . . . he was the same size in every direction," and said to possess questionable legal ethics, had come into the Standard Oil orbit. He was "a wizard at contriving forms that obeyed the letter but circumvented the spirit of the law." In 1882 Dodd, together with Rockefeller and Flagler, came up with a solution. Separate Standard Oil companies were incorporated in Ohio, New Jersey, Pennsylvania and New York to own Standard's properties in each of those respective states. This would centralize all of Standard's property in those states and keep the property separate by state. The owners of each corporation's common stock put that stock in a trust, a perfectly lawful device designed for people who wanted to put the legal control of their property in faithful hands while retaining its economic benefits. The stockholders received trust certificates in exchange for their shares. The formal consequence of this arrangement was to unify the stockholders while the corporations were kept technically separate. The trust was born and with it a name that was used to refer to large corporate combinations of every legal stripe for decades, whether or not they actually had the legal form of the trust (and most did not).[40]

While the trust was a recognized legal device and therefore safer than the pool, it was not without risk. It complied with the letter of the law but, used as a device for accomplishing the otherwise illegal goal of uniting different corporations under the same control, it was an obvious subterfuge. Courts came up with reasoning to destroy it. In 1890, New York's highest court declared H. O. Havemeyer's Sugar Trust illegal by looking through the technical unification of the shareholders to the combined corporations and holding that corporate combination was beyond the constituent corporations' powers. This was followed by the Ohio Supreme Court's more direct breakup of the Standard Oil Trust in 1892. Although only a handful of technical trusts were formed, they seemed to be the last best hope for cooperative business. Now, again, business combination became difficult if not impossible. A new way to combine corporations, to promote cooperation, had to be found.

The pools and communities of interest were illegal or at least unenforceable. The trust was in jeopardy. The corporation was a form subject to significant limitations, especially for interstate businesses. The legal devices that made combination possible had yet to be invented. But the need for a legally effective cooperative business device was clear, and the social acceptance of business cooperation was growing. Beyond pockets of populist demagoguery, the death of *laissez-faire* had been proclaimed by economists and the reality of the American business landscape. The influence on a wide cross-section of the population—progressive reformers, businessmen and even some labor leaders—was decisive. Americans from all walks of life now began to see the new attempts at combination as the inevitable evolution of American capitalism and sometimes as beneficial to consumers and workers, even as they worried about the power of the trusts. The public increasingly was concerned with ensuring economic order so business could grow, not without competition, but with orderly competition that took account of the need for cooperation and prevented ruin.[41]

And New Jersey was poised for discovery.[42]

⊰ TWO ⊱

SANCTUARY

As you drive the interstate highways of the United States and pass from one state to another, you typically are welcomed by a sign announcing the fact that you are crossing the border into new territory. The sign usually radiates local pride, proclaiming the state's nickname or its motto, depicting its emblematic animal or flower. Entering New York you are welcomed to "The Empire State." Heading south, New Jersey announces that you are in "The Garden State." Maryland warmly implores you to "Enjoy Your Visit." Drive along Interstate 95, and whether you cross the Delaware Memorial Bridge or come from the south, tiny Delaware, "The First State," "Little Wonder," greets you with another sign, a smallish blue sign with white lettering that is nevertheless hard to miss: "Home of Tax Free Shopping." How does such a small state, with little industry to speak of, obtain the revenues to eliminate sales tax?[1]

The answer is that Delaware gets rich from the revenue it rakes in from chartering and taxing corporations. Along with this money comes the taxable wealth of the substantial industry of lawyers and corporation service companies that has grown up to assist them, together with the rest of the professional infrastructure necessary to maintain the corporate law business. And corporate law is big business in Delaware. In 2005, Delaware's total tax revenues were $2.7 billion. Nine percent of this came from corporate income taxes, that is, from taxes paid by corporations earning money in the state. But $700 million—almost 26 percent—came from corporate licensing fees paid by corporations that buy into Delaware law and operate throughout the rest of the world. Take away the business of DuPont, the chicken farms, tourism in the Brandywine Valley and the lovely beaches, and Delaware's main industrial product is corporations. Corporations that have their legal *pied-à-terre* in Delaware pay the bills that keep the population free from taxes.[2]

It was not always so. Delaware was an also-ran at the end of the nineteenth century. The state was not even among the top five states of incorporation. At the end of that century, the empire of corporate law was New Jersey. Known by muckrakers as "the traitor state," "the mother of trusts" and a variety of other less printable epithets, New Jersey presided over the degradation of corporate integrity from 1889 until 1913. Only then did Woodrow Wilson, on his way to the White House, persuade New Jersey's legislature to toughen up its corporate laws. The legislature took it back after Wilson was safely in Washington. But it was too late.[3]

Wilson's legacy to New Jersey was a corporate exodus to the promised land. As if crossing a corporate Red Sea, guided by a pillar of cloud by day and fire by night, New Jersey's companies made a beeline across the Delaware River to a land where they were welcomed with open arms and have lived happily ever after. Perhaps this is New Jersey's most important legacy to the nation, or at least to its corporations. But the important story for now is not the present; it is how New Jersey changed the face of American corporate capitalism.

New Jersey did not create the giant modern corporation. But, saddled with debt and politically controlled by its own railroads that refused to pay it taxes, its politicians sensed an entrepreneurial opportunity in marketing corporate charters. The state provided laws that made it easy to cooperate by combination, and the charters it sold allowed corporations to solve the problem of destructive competition. Competitors that previously had to work at the margins of the law through trusts, pooling arrangements, or communities of interest now could legally combine operations under a single corporation that owned all their stock. The structure that resulted looked almost exactly like the outlawed trusts. But New Jersey inscribed that structure into its corporate law. The trust structure was no longer a subterfuge. The holding company transformed it into a perfectly legal device.

New Jersey made it easy for corporations to take advantage of these holding companies. The law provided a financing technique that allowed promoters and bankers to put the combinations together without having to use cash. It gave them a financial printing press that let them create vast amounts of new stock to pay the owners of the corporations coming into the combinations. Promoters could also take that stock as their pay and then dump it on the market, to be scooped up by an emerging middle class eager to participate in the new business world. When J. P. Morgan's syndicate had finished creating the New Jersey holding company that was U.S. Steel, it paid itself 1.3 million shares of Steel stock. It promptly sold that stock to the public for $62.5 million (almost $1.5 billion in 2006 dollars) in order to cash in on its enormous fee. New Jersey provided the magic words that allowed financial wizards to conjure up the giant modern corporation.

New Jersey solved the problem of corporate cooperation even as it created problems for American finance, law and society, problems that would persist long after Delaware had taken the lead. New Jersey is not solely to blame for the dilemmas that confronted all Americans, whether Granger, Populist, Progressive, Socialist or Conservative, as they struggled to deal with the giant corporation. But the Garden State's role in the development of American corporate law and the troubles it created for the entire nation were pivotal. And so my story of the giant modern corporation continues in New Jersey.

THE POWER OF THE STATES

Corporation law—the law that governs the creation, financing and management of corporations—has always been left to the states. The members of the Constitutional Convention refused to delegate the power to create that law to the federal government. James Madison saw the future better than most. He wanted the Constitution to give the federal government the power "to grant charters of incorporation in cases where the Public good may require them, and the authority of a single State may be incompetent." When might the "authority of a single State" be incompetent? When corporations were engaged in interstate commerce. And it was the federal government that had the power to regulate interstate commerce. Madison had some supporters. He pushed the issue several times. But the Framers' fear of monopoly privileges that had long been associated with corporations and their even greater fear of concentrating economic power in the federal government won the day. The creation and regulation of corporations stayed in state hands.[4]

The states granted corporate charters the way they had been granted in Britain. Corporate charters were granted by special act of the legislature, as in Britain they had been granted by the Crown. Because each was granted separately, it was tailor-made to suit the needs of the particular corporation. This meant that these charters contained whatever rights and powers the incorporators could negotiate with the state. That might include more freedom or less, depending on the project and the promoter's relationships with legislators.[5]

The point is important because it laid the foundation for an eventual revolution in the way that American state charters were granted. Special legislative favors, like corporate charters, were undemocratic. And many state legislatures granted monopoly privileges in corporate charters just as the Crown had done in England, and just as undemocratically. Even when a monopoly was not explicit, the idea of the corporate charter was frequently thought to convey it. The issue was joined in the 1837 *Charles River Bridge* case, where the United States Supreme Court held that a corporate charter did not imply a monopoly in the business for which it was granted. The Court would revisit this issue under various constitutional provisions through almost the end of the century. The fear of corporate monopoly power and other "undemocratic" privileges stirred up general anticorporate sentiment that reached its peak in the democratic maelstrom of Jacksonian America. But corporations were useful, even though their real utility was not to be realized until the development of the railroads and the age of industrialization. So state legislatures granted charters and created corporations.[6]

This practice of legislative chartering could not survive in the land of equality. In order to make the corporate form fit with the equality promised by democracy, states—starting with New York in 1811—slowly began to develop general incorporation laws. These laws allowed anybody to form a corporation simply by following the proper procedures. Most states had adopted some form of general incorporation law by the middle of the nineteenth century.

General incorporation laws were democratic. But the advantages of tailoring a charter to a corporation's needs sustained the practice of special chartering, even after general incorporation laws were commonplace. For example, a special legislative charter could loosen tight statutory restrictions on the amount of capital a corporation could have and the nature of its business. Special charters, like any other statute passed by a legislature, could more or less contain whatever terms the legislature chose to include. So a charter could include privileges beyond those included in general incorporation laws.

There was another, somewhat darker, advantage to special charters. They could have a certain attraction for the poorly paid lawmakers themselves. Legislators could get by with a little help from their friends as those friends showed appreciation for the special privileges put in their corporate charters. So most states continued to allow special legislative incorporation along with these general incorporation laws until the 1870s, when they began to outlaw the practice. It was special incorporation in the age of Jackson that got New Jersey into the financial mess that its late-century corporate law was designed to fix.[7]

WHY NEW JERSEY?

New Jersey identified itself with corporate interests early in its statehood. The state's first significant attempt to attract corporate business was realized in Alexander Hamilton's Society for the Establishment of Useful Manufactures, which planned to develop an industrial city alongside the Passaic Falls. The state was so eager to establish its importance in business that it gave the corporation some of its own sovereign powers, including the power to take private property for the corporation's use. It also made the corporation's profits exempt from taxes. These privileges, modified a bit, became common in many state railroad charters, but New Jersey mastered the practice of delegating its power to corporations.

After the failure of the Society for the Establishment of Useful Manufactures, New Jersey tried again. It gave these powers, and more, to two corporations that would join together to dominate its business and government until the Panic of 1873. These were the Delaware and Raritan Canal Company and the Camden and Amboy Railroad Company.[8]

The State of Camden and Amboy

New Jersey's story really began as the legislature created the Delaware and Raritan and the Camden and Amboy. The War of 1812 had painfully showed up the inadequacies of existing transportation and communication facilities between New York and Philadelphia. New transportation routes were needed. Canal promoters started clamoring for a charter to build a cross-state canal as they came to see New Jersey's transportation potential. They soon found themselves competing with railroad promoters who also wanted to grab the New York–to–Philadelphia connection. Each group wanted the kind of monopoly charter that had characterized Robert Fulton and Robert Livingston's steamship monopoly of New York Harbor. Both were granted their wishes in a legislative compromise. On February 4, 1830, the corporate twins, the Delaware and Raritan Canal Company and the Camden and Amboy Railroad Company, were born.[9]

Their charters were similar but, because the Camden and Amboy is the name by which the monopoly was best known, I will focus on that charter. According to one account, "the monopoly of the Delaware and Raritan canal and Camden and Amboy railroad companies was unique in American history." The Camden and Amboy's corporate charter protected it from competing lines built within three miles of its track for nine years. But far more significant was the fact that it also made the corporation completely exempt from taxes. Tax exemption, usually for a limited period of time, was characteristic of many of the early railroad charters. The Amboy's was permanent. It did have to charge a modest transit tax of ten cents for each passenger and fifteen cents for each ton of shipped materials. But this applied only to passengers and freight traveling across the entire state. The Amboy was exempt from the transit tax for New Jersey residents who traveled and shipped within the state. And the transit tax would disappear completely if the New Jersey legislature chartered another railroad that ran within three miles of the Amboy's terminal points. This was unlikely to happen because, only a year later, the legislature amended the Amboy's charter to give it a truly extraordinary privilege — veto power over the grant of additional railroad charters. The Amboy held these powers until 1868, when the two companies surrendered their charters, and 1869, when the legislature eliminated both the transit tax and the railroad's unique privileges.[10]

The Camden and Amboy, under the control of the extraordinary Stevens family of Hoboken, was almost immediately successful. The canal company failed. But success was at hand. Captain Robert Field Stockton, a young man not yet thirty who had earned his stripes in the War of 1812, returned home to New Jersey after military exploits in Europe and Africa. He quickly involved himself in New Jersey politics. He also persuaded his wealthy father-in-law to invest heavily in the canal company. At this point, just to cover his bases, he asked the Trenton legislature to amend its charter to allow it to run a railroad line right alongside the canal.

This was not as daft an idea as it seems. Railroads in that time before dawn were pokey, unreliable things. They were mostly used to supplement other forms of transportation, and the idea of running a railroad along a canal would be helpful to its business. Stockton got his railroad amendment despite the Camden and Amboy's resistance. This threatened the Amboy enterprise. Stockton was hardly guaranteed success either, although the canal had grown profitable. Competition between the canal and the Amboy would hurt them both. So Stockton accepted Stevens's offer to combine the Delaware and Raritan Canal Company with the Camden and Amboy. Thus it was that their capital, their assets, their routes, their management and their boards of directors were joined together under the "Marriage Act" of February 15, 1831. The new "Joint Companies" controlled the fledgling Jersey transportation industry, with the canal eventually running from New Brunswick to Trenton and the railroad from South Amboy to Camden. Just to secure its position with the Trenton government, the Joint Companies gave the state one thousand shares of stock (the Amboy had already given it one thousand), to be paid for out of their joint revenues.

The legislature gave the Camden and Amboy complete veto power over grants of all railroad charters for about $30,000 in anticipated dividends and transit taxes. The corporation had begun its control of state policy. New Jersey rapidly became known as the State of Camden and Amboy. So important was the railroad to New Jersey history that at the 1893 Columbian Exposition in Chicago, the fabled "White City," New Jersey's contribution was the original Camden and Amboy train that had begun its run in 1834.[11]

Eighteen thirty-two saw the birth of another railroad company, the New Jersey Railroad and Transportation Company. The Camden and Amboy exercised its veto power. Evidently the incorporators of the New Jersey Railroad had good friends in the legislature, because the legislature ignored the Amboy and granted the charter. The New Jersey Railroad successfully began to operate a line between Jersey City and New Brunswick. This gave it quicker access to New York by way of the ferry from Jersey City than from the Amboy's own terminal farther to the south. Legal fights followed. The rulings looked bad for the Amboy. In order to stop the litigation and save the Joint Companies, Stockton bought control of the New Jersey Railroad. He pulled the plug on the litigation and gave his control to the Amboy. But there was one final battle before the Amboy's empire was secure. The Pennsylvania-incorporated Philadelphia and Trenton Railroad threatened to run a line along the Straight Turnpike between the Philadelphia ferry landing at Trenton and the New York ferry at New Brunswick. The Amboy bought control of this line, too.[12]

The Camden and Amboy, now operating under the corporate name the United Railroads and Canal Companies, controlled New Jersey's rail lines, its shore line and its access to New York. Passage from Philadelphia to New York—at least rapid passage—required paying tribute to the Amboy. And the Amboy was not shy about exacting its tribute. It charged extortionate rates to through-passengers and consistently cheated the state out of its transit tax, the only revenue (besides returns on its stock) that the state could expect from it. It was easy to cheat. Accounting was still on the far side of primitive and the Amboy could keep its books any way it chose—and it chose to keep them dishonestly. By 1871 the Amboy controlled 456 miles of track, including the principal New York–to–Philadelphia lines, and 65 miles of canal.[13]

The crumbs from the Amboy's table were enough to keep the state going for a time. As New Jersey's nineteenth-century historian John Raum described it:

> It was the duties paid by these companies [the Camden & Amboy and later the United Companies] that built our State Prison and

Lunatic Asylums, of which structures our State may well feel proud; also, our beautiful State House, which a late writer in Massachusetts observes, "is not surpassed by any in the United States;" and in fact the means for all our internal improvements, as well as a large amount towards the support of our magnificent system of public schools, is derived from this source, thereby saving our citizens from an enormous yearly tax, which must have accrued through our extensive internal improvements, did we not have some other means of meeting these expenditures.

The Amboy was in control. The Amboy more or less picked New Jersey's legislators and its governor. It was able to produce a complete whitewash of two investigations authorized by the state in 1848 and 1849, brought to investigate charges by the famous economist Henry C. Carey, writing anonymously as "A Citizen of Burlington," that the Amboy was cheating the state and its own stockholders. The Amboy continued to buy up tax-free land at the same time that it continued to refuse to pay the state what it was due. The tax burden fell squarely on the cities and towns.

What little the Amboy provided was enough for New Jersey through the Civil War. But while the state had been beyond the range of physical destruction during that conflict, financial destruction was another matter. It had accumulated crushing Civil War debt, crushing, at least, if it lacked the revenue to pay it back. At the same time, it continued to provide the substantial public services demanded by its citizens, including upkeep on that "beautiful State House" and the "State Prison and Lunatic Asylums." The New Jersey legislature did not want to suffer the political heat of imposing property taxes, and much of the taxable property was owned by the Amboy anyway. Local officials complained bitterly about the amount of property taxes they had to assess in order to provide public services that they believed the state should provide. And while some state tax revenue came in from other corporations, it was not much.[14]

Finally, desperate for funds and pressured by would-be competitors, New Jersey broke the Amboy's monopoly by passing a general railroad incorporation act. But the Amboy had already, in June 1871, leased its lines to the Pennsylvania Railroad for 999 years. Following an unsuccessful shareholder suit to enjoin the lease, the Amboy transferred its property to the Pennsylvania at the stroke of midnight between November 30 and December 1, 1871. Somewhat desperate, the state finally taxed the United Companies itself. So the Amboy paid New Jersey approximately $298,000 in 1876 on combined earnings of $5 million, a rather modest 5.9 percent. New Jersey's awakening was too little and too late. The state was desperate for cash. The solution lay in corporate law.[15]

Despite the Amboy's control, New Jersey's general corporation law was frequently amended between 1846 and 1886 to resemble a responsible corporation law, similar to that of most states. But responsibility was expensive, especially if you were a New Jersey legislator. Special chartering continued to be a highly popular form of incorporation until the 1870s, at least for those with money and influence.[16]

Other states were tightening their corporation laws. This became particularly true in the 1880s as businesses grew following the depression of the previous decade. The first of the large trusts appeared in order to combine in a manner that evaded corporate law restrictions. Standard Oil made everybody nervous, and the growth of several other large trusts during the 1880s, including the American Cotton Oil Trust, the National Lead Trust and the Sugar Trust provoked a general awakening to the coming changes in the American industrial and financial landscape. In response several states, including Kansas, Michigan, Missouri, Nebraska, North Carolina, Tennessee and Texas, passed relatively strong antitrust measures by 1891. The Sherman Act of 1890 became federal law. Public policy, not yet adjusted to the new realities, continued to oppose corporate cooperation. But business was desperate for a new legal form that would control competition for survival and profit. It was New Jersey—poor and accustomed to submitting to the demands of corporations—that in 1889 was poised to give birth to the giant modern corporation.[17]

New Jersey Finds Its Fortune

It is fair to say that in 1889 pretty much every sentient being in America was watching what was happening in the business world. A few states, sensing an opportunity to help facilitate business cooperation, had liberalized their corporate laws. They hoped that the congenial homes they created would lead to revenue from franchise fees and taxes. Delaware and West Virginia decked out their laws to attract needy businesses. And in order to make the most of it, they sometimes took to the road. In 1888, the secretary of state of West Virginia set up a table at New York's Fifth Avenue Hotel, "the social center of the financial world," where he displayed the seal of the state proudly beside him and explained the advantages of West Virginia law, selling charters to all who cared to buy one.[18]

Recall that it was about this time that the New Jersey legislature was facing huge deficits because of the state's unpaid Civil War debt and its unwillingness to tax its corporations seriously. While the incorporation business had been profitable for politicians, the pressure to solve the state's financial problems had become irresistible. The stage was set for an uphill battle waged by New Jersey to tax the previously untaxed or undertaxed railroads. So in 1882 the state swept away all tax exemptions from corporate charters. Tax legislation was passed. The railroads became taxpayers. The Amboy continued to cheat. Taxes went largely unpaid and the state's treasury remained unfilled. In order to try to make some money, the New Jersey legislature imposed a franchise tax on corporations in 1884.[19]

And then James B. Dill rode into town. Dill was a New York lawyer who lived in the Garden State. John Wayne with a briefcase, Dill went to Trenton to rescue New Jersey from its financial woes. In so doing, he helped to change the face of American corporate capitalism.

Dill was, as his friend and critic Lincoln Steffens put it, "a masterpiece." Although a young man at the time, he eventually became, according to Upton Sinclair, the highest-paid lawyer in New York. Born in 1854, by the time he was forty-six he had reportedly been paid $1 million, "the largest fee ever paid to an attorney in the United States," for mediating negotiations between Andrew Carnegie and Pierpont Morgan that led to the creation of U.S. Steel. A year later, he was described in *Frank Leslie's Popular Monthly* as "the greatest trust lawyer in the United States." By 1898 he had written the first of his several treatises on New Jersey corporate law. By 1899 he had testified as an authority on New Jersey corporation law before the United States Industrial Commission and regularly attended meetings of the American Economic Association. By 1902 he had given a speech to the Seminary in Economics at Harvard, in which he advocated the creation of a national incorporation law that would deal with the problem of the irresponsible state corporate laws he had helped to create. And in 1905 he became a member of New Jersey's highest court, the Court of Errors and Appeals. There was no commission of the government, no conference of academics, no gathering of experts, no major newspaper, which failed to call upon him for testimony, speeches or comments. Everybody knew James B. Dill. And this is how he was referred to. One could speak of (although not to) Morgan as "J.P.," but Dill was universally referred to as "James B. Dill" or, at the very least, "Mr. Dill." By the time of his death in 1910, Mr. Dill's opinion on virtually every aspect of the modern corporation was given the greatest deference.[20]

Dill was hugely successful. But he was a bit of a misfit among his powerful and famous contemporaries. One account described him as follows:

In appearance he suggests none of the traditions of the ideals of the lawyer who has been successful beyond the most rosy dream. He has none of the suave dignity that distinguished Evarts; none of that genial and yet, after all, reserved quality that made Choate both admired and feared. There is not an expression or a mannerism that suggests a profound student.... To see Dill hurrying through Wall Street one would surmise that he was the Clearing House or Stock Exchange representative of some one of the greater financial institutions ... muttering to ... [himself] in a manner which in a more secluded environment would cause ... [his] mental balance to be suspected.

This, then, was one of the most respected and best paid lawyers of his day. But in the late 1880s, Dill was a relatively young man on the make. He observed West Virginia's and Delaware's attempts to attract corporate business and, so watching, came up with a plan. He presented this plan in New York, whose corporate laws were of the generally more respectable type. But New York was not interested. According to Lincoln Steffens's entertaining account of the matter, Dill naively failed to explain to the New York political bosses how they could personally benefit from the plan. So he crossed the Hudson to his home state.[21]

Dill explained his plan to Governor Leon Abbett, a reformer who twice became governor despite crossing New Jersey's political machine. Abbett was trying his best to obtain control over New Jersey's chaotic finances. So he listened. As Dill explained it, the plan came in two parts. First, the legislature would build on its holding company act and corporate finance laws to pass the most liberal corporation law in the country. But the mere passage of new laws would not bring New Jersey the business it sought. After all, other states had lax laws, too.[22]

The second part of the plan revealed Dill's real genius. This was to create a corporation to advertise New Jersey's paper bounty. The Corporation Trust Company of New Jersey was born. Its job was to sing the praises of the New Jersey corporation to businessmen throughout the land. It would do all of the necessary work to incorporate, service and maintain these companies which, under New Jersey law, would not have to do a penny of business in their new legal home. But the Corporation Trust Company of New Jersey was hardly a public service company. Its founding stockholders included not only James B. Dill himself, but also Secretary of State Henry Kelsey, Allan L. McDermott, clerk of the Chancery Court, United States District Attorney Henry S. White, Charles B. Thurston, secretary of the successor corporation to Hamilton's Society for the Establishment of Useful Manufactures (which had been acquired by the Amboy and now was controlled by the Pennsylvania Railroad), and Governor Leon Abbett himself.[23]

Here is how the company worked. Anybody who was interested in incorporating in New Jersey had only to write to the Secretary of State. That functionary would send in return a treatise on New Jersey law which carefully explained the latitude it gave corporate managers and directors in structuring and financing their corporations. The Secretary of State would then refer the inquiry to the Corporation Trust Company or one of its later competitors, which would service the client, sending the necessary legal forms and offering to complete the entire incorporation process for the promoter, all at a modest fee.

The New Jersey approach was later widely imitated, sometimes even more blatantly. The Secretary of State of South Dakota, for example, referred interested parties both to that state's corporation trust companies and also to the librarian of the State Supreme Court. This devoted public servant offered promoters his own personal incorporation services for $10 by letters written on the court's official letterhead. No matter how brazen the efforts of the also-rans, New Jersey had such a head start that, by 1904, 170 of 318 industrial trusts studied by John Moody, including all of the largest trusts, had incorporated in New Jersey.[24]

The eight years that it took New Jersey to refine its laws did not damage the plan. Eighteen ninety-three was a year of major panic, followed by a serious four-year depression. By the time recovery slowly began in 1896 and the merger wave broke with a fantastic return to prosperity in 1897, New Jersey was poised to jump out in front, and jump out in front it did. The revenue from New Jersey's new business in corporate franchises paid off the state's debt within a decade. The number of New Jersey incorporations grew from 567 in 1888 to 1,155 in 1891 and 1,212 in 1892, dropping into the 800s and 900s during each of the depression years of 1893 to 1896, and exploding from 1,118 and 1,104 in 1897 and 1898, respectively, to 2,186 in 1899, 1,995 in 1900, and 2,353, 2,255 and 2,035 in each of 1901, 1902 and 1903. By contrast, New York did not show anything close to a comparable number of incorporations until 1901 and Delaware did not even get out of the hundreds until 1909.[25]

Dill's marketing plan spoke more or less for itself—the proof was in the dramatic increase in the number of New Jersey corporations and Trenton's rapidly filling treasury. But what exactly made New Jersey law so attractive?

In order to understand what was meant by the liberalization of corporate law, it helps to have some idea of what corporate statutes that were considered to be responsible looked like. Take, as an example, the law of Massachusetts.

Its citizens were proud of the fact that their corporation law probably was the most demanding in the nation. The powers of directors and officers were limited. Stockholders had to approve all conveyances, mortgages, long-term real estate leases and business expansion. Directors could only issue stock after business had started by offering it at par to existing shareholders, regardless of the actual value of the stock. Stock could be issued for cash or property but a majority of the directors as well as the officers had to make a sworn statement that described and valued the property and the Commissioner of Corporations had to certify that, in his opinion, the valuation was reasonable. Directors and officers were personally liable for certain actions that damaged creditors, like paying dividends when such payment would make the corporation insolvent, issuing debt in excess of capital and watering stock. Massachusetts corporate law would not look like that of other states until 1903, when the legislature amended it in a futile attempt to catch up with New Jersey. Here is how New Jersey's law was different.[26]

THE LEGAL FOUNDATION OF THE GIANT CORPORATION

The transformation of New Jersey law came in stages. Historians generally mark the passage of the 1889 holding company act as the most important reform. That law reversed the old common-law rule by allowing New Jersey corporations to buy and hold stock in other corporations. But, as I will show, the holding company act was not the essential development, although it was useful. Rather, the critically important change was the law that allowed corporations to buy shares in other corporations with their own stock, leaving the matter of price entirely within the discretion of corporate directors. This development was perfected in 1896, the year before the merger wave began.[27]

The Holding Company

The traditional rule in the various states, including New Jersey, was that corporations were generally not allowed to own stock in other corporations. The law was particularly stringent with respect to stock purchases made by one corporation for the purpose of controlling another. Rare exceptions were made when a corporation had express legal permission or the purchase was incidentally necessary to its business. While a small handful of states took the opposite approach, this rule had long been entrenched in American and British law and continued as the law in most states even after New Jersey had authorized the holding company.

Courts provided several justifications for this rule. First, a corporation was only allowed to engage in the specific activities described in its charter.

There was good reason for this. Nineteenth-century Americans were not entirely comfortable with corporations. Their acceptance—or tolerance—of corporations depended upon the states' willingness to keep them under control. One of the best methods of preventing corporations from running amok was to limit their activities.

A second, relatively ancient, reason for the rule was that courts presumed that stockholders of a particular corporation were investing their money in that particular corporation conducting those particular activities allowed by its charter with its particular management. In the language of modern economics, stockholders chose only the risk of a given business, not any other business the corporation might buy into.

A final reason, which started to appear frequently in the early 1880s as the antitrust debate heated up, was that a corporation buying the stock of other corporations, especially in the same business, was the mark of monopoly. Courts enforced the rule, and the treatise writers through the late 1880s expressed it as black letter law.[28]

New Jersey's holding company act was important. It paved the yellow brick road from competition to cooperation. But it took a few tries for the lawmakers to get it right. The 1889 holding company act allowed corporations "of this state, or any other state, doing business in this state *and authorized by law to own and hold shares of stock and bonds of corporations of other states* [emphasis added]" to do so, and to do so "with all the rights, powers and privileges of individual owners of shares." The statute served its purpose as an opening salvo. But it was not enough. The 1889 law applied only to corporations otherwise legally entitled to hold stock in other corporations. Only a handful of states allowed this under almost any circumstances, and even the New Jersey law itself was not an outright license for New Jersey companies to own stock in other companies—they had to have express permission in their charters. Courts differed in their interpretations of what corporations owning stock with the rights of "individuals" meant and, in particular, whether a corporation owning stock in another corporation had the right to vote that stock unless that right was expressly stated in the charter.[29]

So on March 14, 1893, the law was improved in a way that would induce promoters to incorporate in New Jersey. It now provided that "any corporation" created under the New Jersey corporation act could own stock in corporations of any state and specifically provided that the rights of individual owners included "*the right to vote thereon, which natural persons, being the owners of such stock, might, could, or would exercise* [emphasis added]." The legislature could not have been much clearer in permitting corporations to vote the shares they owned to control their subsidiaries.[30]

But there was more. Evidently the meaning of the rights of "natural persons" exercising rights they "might, could, or would" exercise was not clear enough. So, in 1896, the statute was amended one more time to eliminate the phrase "natural persons" and "might, could, and would." Now it simply allowed a corporation, "while owner of such stock" to "exercise all the rights, powers, and privileges of ownership, including the right to vote thereon." Finally, in 1899, the law achieved its final form. A holding company was allowed to exist as a finance company alone, to exist solely for the purpose of owning another corporation's stock. In a complete perversion of the nineteenth-century view of the corporation, the twentieth century dawned with corporations that had no specific businesses of their own.[31]

The promoters of New Jersey corporations could buy all the stock of competing corporations in any state, adding them to the corporate structure in the same way that an individual stockholder added stock to his portfolio. Since most states, including New Jersey until 1918, prohibited mergers of corporations across state lines, the holding company could have been the Holy Grail of cooperative business.[32]

But most combinations were not holding companies until the last few years of the merger wave. The dominant form of transaction appears to have been what was sometimes known as "fusion," in which the assets and liabilities of the constituent corporations were directly absorbed by the new combination in exchange for stock or, occasionally, cash. This left the constituent corporations in place with no other assets than the new company's stock or cash. The old corporations then dissolved and distributed the consideration to the shareholders of the selling corporations. If a constituent corporation had taken stock for its assets, its shareholders then became shareholders of the combination.[33]

Why was the simpler holding company form not more widely used? One reason is fear of the unknown. Lawyers then, as now, were conservative in counseling clients. The holding company act, and the holding company itself, were untested both as a corporate law matter and as an antitrust matter. Holding companies looked almost exactly like trusts except that a corporation held the stock instead of trustees. Lawyers and their clients were afraid that holding companies would be treated like trusts, exposing them to prosecution under the Sherman Act as the Supreme Court then applied it. Many were emboldened by Standard Oil's reorganization as a New Jersey holding company in 1899, which significantly increased the use of the holding company during the final years of the merger wave. But their fears were confirmed by the Supreme Court's ruling in the 1904 *Northern Securities* case that holding companies were subject to the Sherman Act. Only with the 1911 decisions in the *Standard Oil* and *American Tobacco* cases did the Supreme Court make it clear that the Sherman Act applied to single consolidated corporations too, thus making the choice of form less consequential than its behavior from an antitrust perspective. The holding company only reached its full potential, and that as a control device, in the 1920s.[34]

The holding company was important as the first apparently unassailably legal form of combination. It was a symbol of New Jersey's willingness to accommodate corporate combinations when most other states were clearly hostile. It was also an invitation, quite express if you consider the role of the Corporation Trust Company, for promoters to come to New Jersey with the implicit assurance that nobody would bother them as they put together their combined corporations. Seen this way, the holding company served a transitional purpose, as a bridge between the trust form of organization and combinations of assets within a single giant corporation.

Selling Stock for Property

New Jersey's more critically important contribution both to the growth of the giant modern corporation and the American stock market was made in 1896. It was then that the state amended its corporation law to allow corporations to buy stock for property in a manner that gave the directors the exclusive right to value the property, and thus its price in stock. This development was determinative for the success of the merger wave because it allowed promoters to pay as much as they wanted for corporations with the stock of the new combination. They did not need cash.

In one sense, there was not as much new about this law as there had been about the holding company act. New Jersey law, like the laws of other states, had long allowed corporations to buy stock for property. The key difference was that the earlier rules did not give the directors' valuation the finality of the 1896 New Jersey act. Under the old law, directors could be liable to creditors and sometimes shareholders if their valuation was wrong, and shareholders could be liable to creditors, too. Under the new statute, the directors had no liability to creditors or shareholders (or anyone else) if they turned out to be wrong unless their valuation of the property was clearly fraudulent. And fraud was a technical legal concept that was very hard to prove.

The old law also said that property had to be bought for the full value of the stock. It is unclear from the statute what "full value" meant, although New Jersey courts would provide the surprising answer. The 1896 amendment left no statutory question—it was up to the directors alone to decide whether or not full value had been paid.

This standard was the real key to creating the giant combinations. And

New Jersey's lawmakers knew it. In their introduction to the 1896 revision of New Jersey's corporation laws, the commissioners noted that "a few substantial changes have been made, but they are generally only the insertion of the well settled decisions of the court. For instance, in Section 49 ... we have provided that in paying for property purchased by the issue of stock, the judgment of the directors as to the value of the property, shall, in the absence of actual fraud, be conclusive." The assertion that this provision merely reflected well-settled law was misleading, as I will discuss below, but the important point to note is that this was the only provision of the entire act that the commissioners separately discussed. They did not mention the holding company act except as part of a broad overview of the revised statute.[35]

The Corporation Trust Company gave the same prominence to the stock-for-property act in its brochure describing the advantages of New Jersey law, and repeated the same misrepresentation. After describing the process of incorporation, the brochure laid out the benefits of New Jersey law. As one of seventeen briefly mentioned points, it noted the power of corporations to own stock. But after setting out these seventeen points, it went on to discuss one special feature:

> A most important example calls for special mention. In that section which authorizes the issuance of stock for property, the statement that the judgment of the directors as to the value of property is absolutely final in the absence of fraud was first flatly stated in the law in 1896, but the Courts for many years previous to this laid down the same principle and had repeatedly affirmed it. Since the Courts and Legislature thus supplement each other's efforts, every provision of the law is the rational result of long experience.

Thus, among all of the statutory provisions that the Corporation Trust Company identified as important, the most prominence was given to the stock-for-property provision. Together with the Report of the Commissioners and the observation by the Industrial Commission that stock of a combination was the most frequent form of payment to the sellers, this almost certainly clinches the argument that at least New Jersey's lawmakers and lawyers believed the stock-for-property provision was the most important of New Jersey's "reforms."[36]

A proper understanding of the development of the giant modern corporation also supports this conclusion. It is extremely difficult to appraise the value of property. In one sense, value is whatever a willing buyer will pay a willing seller. But what if there are only a few buyers or only one buyer? And what if the property is unique? Take an easy case like real estate. In most populated markets today, valuing a piece of real estate is relatively simple. A house in a suburban housing development, where most houses are fairly similar, will sell for a price that is somewhere in the range of what the last house in the development sold for (holding constant for variables like the condition of the house, interest rates, the frequency of sales and the like). A two-bedroom coop apartment on West End Avenue in Manhattan will sell within some range of the last one sold in the same building, assuming roughly the same condition and the same layout. Bic pens will sell within pennies of one another from one city to the next. Shares of Microsoft stock trading on the New York Stock Exchange move by tiny fractions based on immediate supply and demand. Value is relatively predictable.

But what about an oil refinery in Philadelphia in 1870? What about a Pittsburgh steel mill in 1890? What about a Chicago slaughterhouse, a trunk line between Cleveland and New York, a flour mill in Minnesota? Each of these, for a variety of reasons, was unique—its location, the quality and cost of railroad service or other shipping, the reliability of its customer base, the goodwill of its name and the quality and stability of its suppliers. Properties like these were swept up into the new giant corporations in the corporate combinations of the 1890s. While some of their owners insisted on cash, most were happy to take all or part of the purchase price in stock of the new combination as long as the price was high enough.

When these new corporations were formed by combining existing corporations into a new corporation or under a holding company, their promoters and financiers had to decide upon a capitalization, a financial structure consisting of some combination of bonds, preferred stock and common stock. They had to determine how much to issue and to assign a value to each of these different types of securities. Together these values would make up the capitalization of the corporation. And the value had to be based upon something. But what?

Promoters had almost irresistible incentives to put high values on the assets they were buying. The more they valued the assets, the higher the amount of capital they could justify and the more stock they could issue. The more stock they could issue, the more stock they could take for themselves. And the more stock they could take for themselves, the more they could sell in the market for cash. Promoters were not the only greedy ones. Sellers had to be given attractive prices to persuade them to sell their properties, all the more so if the promoters expected them to take untested stock. So promoters had every incentive to make the initial volume of shares—the capitalization —as big as possible.

The New Jersey amendment pretty much allowed the directors to assign the properties any value they chose. As a result, it allowed them to capitalize the new corporations at whatever values they chose and to issue as much stock as they wanted. The New Jersey courts, vainly attempting to uphold their state's honor, did the best they could to eviscerate the statute. Nobody cared.[37]

THE NEW JERSEY COURTS — A FUTILE ATTEMPT TO MAINTAIN INTEGRITY

The New Jersey law revision commission did not completely lie. The stock-for-property provision did develop out of common law, and New Jersey even had various statutory forms of the rule that well predated the 1896 revision. The lie was in the implication that directors had long had virtually absolute discretion in valuation. The truth was otherwise. This rule had been judicially adopted only in 1890 and, without much additional litigation, remained somewhat ambiguous.

The original rule was grounded in democracy even as its later statutory revision enabled the creation of plutocracy. Courts reasoned that it allowed people with little cash, but valuable assets, to have the chance to participate in corporations. But this rationale limited the discretion directors had to determine the value of the property. While courts wanted to provide opportunity, they also had to protect corporate creditors who could rely only upon the corporation's assets for repayment in the event of failure. And stock that was issued for property worth less than the face amount of the stock would mislead creditors as to the value of the corporation's assets.

Corporate laws that protected creditors were a tradeoff for the relatively new general privilege of limited shareholder liability, as New Jersey's highest court explained in 1882 in *Wetherbee v. Baker*. Limited liability meant that stockholders had to pay the corporation only the par value of their stock. Creditors could not come after their individual assets. The rule for partners was different. All of the partners were liable for the business's debts, even if payment had to come from their personal assets. The law that stock had to be fully paid was a way of compensating creditors for protecting shareholders with limited liability.

Besides, as the *Wetherbee* court saw it, the statute did not really change anything about this creditor-protective rule. All it did was create a different way for shareholders to pay for their stock. It certainly did not provide a different method of valuing that payment. Property given for stock was expected to have a cash value something close to the par value of the stock in order to be considered "fully paid." Only then would limited liability attach. While creditors of a bankrupt corporation could not go after shareholders' personal assets when the shares were fully paid, at least they had the comfort of knowing that the shareholders had paid what they promised.[38]

There were limits to how much stock you could sell for property under the common law and early statutes. These limits largely grew out of what was known as the "trust fund doctrine." This doctrine treated the amount stockholders paid to the corporation in par value as a trust fund to be held for the benefit of creditors. The trust fund included money that shareholders owed for the stock but had not yet paid. Now note the problem. If "fully paid" stock was issued for property that was worth less than the stock, the creditors' protection was largely meaningless—the trust fund would be empty, or relatively so. So in *Wetherbee*, the New Jersey court held that it was not enough for the directors of a corporation to make a good-faith attempt to value the property being purchased. That value had to be a "fair bona fide valuation" in "what may fairly be considered as money's worth." This was known as the "true-value" rule. Unless the property met this standard, the stock was considered to be a fraud upon the corporation's creditors. Shareholders (who in these cases were usually the promoters and directors) would have to pay the difference between the true value of the property and the unpaid portion of their stock until the creditors were paid off. The rule of *Wetherbee* gave the directors no real discretion. It held them almost to a form of strict liability.[39]

The true value rule began to bend. The United States Supreme Court, relying both on common law and New York's 1880 move from the true-value rule to a "good-faith" rule, held in 1886 that shareholders would be liable to the corporation's creditors for unpaid subscriptions (which included the difference between the true value and the overvalued property) only if the directors or shareholders had engaged in "actual fraud." If "the shareholders honestly and in good faith put in property instead of money in payment of their subscriptions, third parties have no ground of complaint."[40]

In 1890, New Jersey's equity court again addressed the issue. In *Bickley v. Schlag*, the corporation's authority to issue stock for property came not from a statute but from a provision in the corporation's charter that was almost identical to the statutory language. The distinction between charter provision and statute did not matter to the court, which adopted the good-faith rule articulated by the United States Supreme Court. New Jersey law had just been judicially amended and, before the dust settled, would be amended again.[41]

The problem with the New Jersey statute up to this point was that it authorized the issuance of stock for property "to the value thereof." *Whose* valuation mattered—directors or courts? While courts ordinarily would defer to the judgment of the corporation's directors under the good-faith rule, their judgment still was subject to the chance that a court would hold that the property was not worth what the directors said it was.

The moment of truth came in *Donald v. American Smelting and Refining*, the first case to be decided under the 1896 revision. This revision had added the language "and in the absence of actual fraud in the transaction the judgment of the directors as to the value of the property purchased shall be conclusive." This language was vitally important. It was the language the Corporation Trust Company touted and said the courts supported. Unlike the good-faith rule, and certainly unlike the true-value rule, it did not leave room for judicial valuation. But that did not stop the court. It used the *Donald* case to read this new language out of the statute.

Donald is interesting for several reasons. It was the first case under the new statute, and the first that involved a corporate combination of the type that characterized the merger wave. It is also interesting because counsel for the defendants, Samuel Untermyer, was one of the best-known and highest paid corporate lawyers in the country. Like his contemporary, Louis Brandeis, he would forsake his origin as corporate lawyer and trust promoter (again, like Brandeis, after he had become very wealthy), to redeem himself by making the national case against the abuses of trusts, corporate law and the stock market. Untermyer's most prominent and public role would be as counsel for the Pujo Committee in 1912 and 1913, and as an advocate for stock market regulation. We will meet him again in this role in Chapter Nine.

American Smelting bought various Guggenheim properties, including smelting and refining plants. (The Guggenheims, who made their money in mining, were among New York's Jewish aristocracy. But although they were among the richest of "our crowd" they were of a slightly lower social standing than Schiffs and Kuhns and Warburgs and Lehmans. Not only were they considered *nouveau riche* in that crowd, but mining was also considered socially inferior to banking as a way of making money.) American Smelting would pay for the Guggenheim properties with $6 million in cash and $45 million in its own stock, and increase its capitalization from $65 million to $100 million to finance the deal. Shareholders of American Smelting sued to prevent it, and the court agreed.[42]

The court found the language of section 49 "explicit." "To the value of the property" meant that the property's value "must at least equal the face value of the stock," specifically citing the old true-value rule of *Wetherbee*, which the statute was designed to overrule. The court noted that the judgment of the directors was entitled to "considerable weight," although the court claimed the right to determine the value for itself in complete disregard of the new statute. And it loosened the meaning of the statute's language, "actual fraud." Actual fraud was a precise legal concept with clearly established meaning. But the court said that if the directors had not engaged in "due examination" of the property's value, or if they included other "assets" that were not really property (apparently goodwill and capitalized future earnings), or if their judgment was "plainly warped by self-interest," that would be fraud enough. None of these behaviors even approached the legal test for actual fraud.

What about the new language that made the directors' decision final, the new language that was designed to attract the promoters? The court effectively rewrote the statute. When a deal involved valuation *before* the stock was issued, as the American Smelting deal did, the court held that its version of the true-value rule applied. The statute only applied as written if a stockholder or creditor brought a case *after* the stock had been issued. The court's policy goal was clear. Promoters who capitalized the new combinations for their own benefit were not to be trusted. Only shareholders who later bought the stock were to be protected. While the court's reading had logical force, it was not what the statute said.[43]

The press followed the case closely and applauded the court's decision. The *New York Times* reported that "[t]he decision is looked upon here as one of great significance with respect to the incorporation of companies under New Jersey laws in the future." Fear was expressed that corporations would flee from the state, although others thought that fear was overstated. There was no flight from New Jersey.[44]

Nobody left New Jersey because everybody ignored the court. Its ruling in *Donald* did not even matter to the parties themselves. The plaintiffs did not care about protecting creditors or shareholders at all. Leonard Lewisohn and H. H. Rogers, who both resigned from the American Smelting board in protest of the deal, were worried that the Guggenheim deal would wind up cutting their own United Metals Selling Company out of its role as selling agent for American Smelting. On March 30, 1901, the day after the court's decision, the parties negotiated a settlement. The Guggenheim deal would proceed as planned and United Metals would continue as the Smelting Company's selling agent. Who cared if New Jersey's highest court said the directors' valuation of the deal was a lie?[45]

New Jersey's courts did their best to stymie the legislature in its attempt to sell New Jersey's dignity. While *Donald* represents the judicial interpretation of the 1896 act, there is one more case worth discussing which, although decided five years after *Donald*, relied upon the 1889 act. Although the acts had somewhat different language, the differences appear to have been entirely irrelevant to contemporaneous commentators and almost entirely irrelevant to the New Jersey courts. *See v. Heppenheimer* is a classic of the era and provides the most thoughtful and carefully reasoned discussion of the entire issue.[46]

The case again involved Untermyer. This time he was serving as a principal in the deal, a promoter as well as lawyer for the allegedly fraudulently valued Columbia Straw Paper Company. The business was formed in 1892 explicitly to monopolize the straw paper industry. It was bankrupt by 1895. The court relied on *Donald*, disregarding the fact that a different statute applied. Again it ignored the words "actual fraud" and adopted the constructive fraud rule.

The deal in *See* was in some respects even worse than that in *Donald*. The whole purpose of the Untermyer scheme was to promote and organize the corporation, capitalize it with overvalued property, get it running, and dump the stock on the public. The deal was meant to be accomplished by means of a misleading public prospectus drafted by Untermyer, whom the court called "the managing genius of the whole transaction," and a privately circulated "confidential" prospectus. Without mincing words, the court called this whole operation an "intrinsic" fraud.

Untermyer had a defense. The promoters had, in fact, carefully valued the property. But they did so, wrote the court, on the basis of anticipated monopoly power. That meant that the value the directors assigned the property included future profits which the court in *Donald* had said was not "property" at all. The question of corporate valuation was squarely raised, but for now the important question was what the courts would accept as value, regardless of what businessmen and economists might think. Could the board value the corporation's property on the basis of "prospective profits"? The answer was no. Only tangible assets could be used.

The court was more financially sophisticated than might appear from this conclusion. Prospective profits could not be used as value, but the court did say that the directors could use goodwill in valuing the property bought with stock. The court was, with good reason, rather unclear in describing the difference between prospective profits and goodwill. But it did not matter in this case, because the new corporation had not done any business. It had no goodwill, however one defined it, and as far as the court was concerned the goodwill of the constituent corporations was already included in their purchase prices.[47]

See v. Heppenheimer was embraced by commentators. Where *Donald* had damaged one of the principal attractions of New Jersey corporate law, the valuation methodology approved by the *See* court completely destroyed it. Yet corporations continued to flock to New Jersey after *Donald* and *See*, and the previously formed giant New Jersey corporations did not run away. Why?[48]

The *See* court's own language provides an answer worth quoting at length:

> But the defendants say the practice of so valuing property under our statute has been indulged in frequently before, and numerous corporations have been organized and have existed upon such a basis, so that, they argue, the practice has become well nigh crystallized and sanctioned by long usage.
>
> I am sorry to feel constrained to admit that this practice has been frequently indulged in, and, further, that it has brought obloquy upon our state and its legislation. But I am happy to be able to assert, with confidence, that such practice is entirely unwarranted by anything either in our statute or in the decisions of our courts, and whenever it has been indulged in it has involved a clear infringement of, if not fraud upon, the plain letter and spirit of our legislation.

"Frequently indulged in" indeed. By hundreds of corporations, including almost all of the largest corporations in the United States. But in order for a corporation to be held liable under the court's revision of the statute, it had to be sued by creditors after the corporation had run out of money to pay them or by stockholders diluted by the promoters' stock. These suits almost never materialized. The court rose to protect the maiden's honor. But the maiden had willingly gone astray and the court's efforts were far too little and far too late.[49]

New Jersey's courts could try to cover the state's shame. But Dill's legislation was ultimately what mattered, and what continued to pay the tax bills. Writing in 1909, Taft's attorney general, George Wickersham, complained about the confusion created by the New Jersey courts and proposed instead a mandatory corporate disclosure law to allow shareholders to figure out corporate value on their own. At the same time, he noted that if the rule of *See v. Heppenheimer* "should be applied to all the corporations organized under the laws of New Jersey during the past ten or fifteen years, a very considerable number would no doubt be found to have their capital stock not fully paid, and the stockholders, to their great surprise, liable in the event of insolvency for the debts of the corporation." While Wickersham was right, there really was little to worry about. New Jersey remained safe for corporate plutocracy.[50]

This entire discussion raises the vitally important question of how the stock of a giant corporation was to be valued. While I have just touched upon the topic here, I will discuss the matter at greater length in the next chapter. Meanwhile, there were a few other advantages to incorporating in New Jersey.

YOU NEVER HAVE TO LIVE IN JERSEY AND OTHER FEATURES

New Jersey law acquired some other attractive features in the 1896 Act. Included among these were the corporation's right to incorporate "for any lawful purpose." This was a dramatic liberalization of the restrictions placed on the scope of corporate business by legislative charters and other general incorporation laws. New Jersey corporations also were given the power to amend the corporate charter at will (in order, among other things, to alter its capital stock and to create different classes of stock), and to pay minimal taxes for the privilege.[51]

With these reforms in place came perhaps the crowning glory. Companies could incorporate in New Jersey and never have to conduct any business there at all. It was enough that they maintained a registered office in the state. And the corporation service companies were ready to do all the work for a modest fee. Testifying before the United States Industrial Commission in October 1899, Howard K. Wood, assistant secretary of the Corporation Trust Company, told the commission that his corporation served as the registered New Jersey office of, and represented, six to seven hundred companies. How could the Corporation Trust Company accommodate so many different corporate offices in one building? It did not. Complying with the letter of New Jersey law, it covered the outer walls of the building with plaques, each stating the name of a corporation and noting that the building contained the corporation's registered office. Thus all six to seven hundred corporations whose plaques were on the wall were present and had a registered office in the state.[52]

And there was more. New Jersey actively defended its corporate citizens against the resentments and retaliations of other states. In 1894, New Jersey passed a law that taxed every corporation of other states operating in New Jersey at the same rate that those states taxed New Jersey corporations operating in their states. This precluded other more responsible or ambitious states from retaliating against New Jersey through taxation.

In 1897 the legislature passed a law that protected stockholders, directors and officers of New Jersey corporations from any criminal or civil action brought in New Jersey courts under the laws of any other state. The law was not the result of a random thought. It was passed eighteen hours after being introduced for the purpose of protecting the officers of the Sugar Trust who were about to find themselves in big trouble in New York. As Lincoln Steffens described it:

> The Albany legislature appointed a committee to investigate all Jersey trusts that were operating in New York, and that committee came down to New York City after the Sugar Trust. But the Sugar Trust put its books on a boat and rushed them over to Jersey, and Jersey, under the guidance of her New York corporation lawyers, drew up and rushed through the Trenton legislature a bill to protect her own.

With the passage of the new legislation, New Jersey's "conquest" was complete.[53]

WHERE WERE THE OTHER STATES?

New Jersey prospered. Other states howled with indignation, and perhaps some envy, at New Jersey's crass and selfish takeover of corporate America. But the other states were not powerless, and one might well ask why they did not use their own corporation laws to combat New Jersey's profligacy. Why, for example, did Nebraska not prohibit the stock of a Nebraska corporation from being owned by another corporation, or at least a corporation from another state? If all of the states had enacted such laws, New Jersey's holding companies would have been of little use. And states could have prohibited New Jersey corporations from raising money by selling watered stock in their states. (That was not to happen for more than a decade.) New Jersey corporations would only have been able to grow in New Jersey.

There are several answers to the question of why the other states did not retaliate. In the first place, attacking New Jersey would be counterproductive. Restrictions against New Jersey corporations would simply induce all corporations that wanted to combine to reincorporate in New Jersey, thus taking away any control over them by their home states, and relying either on local finance or help from residents of states that failed to retaliate. Moreover, these other states imposed franchise taxes on foreign corporations, revenues they were unwilling to lose by antagonizing New Jersey. Besides, New Jersey corporations could simply use their stock to buy the assets of corporations in other states rather than the corporations themselves, so it would have been ineffective for states to retaliate by restricting what their corporations could do.

If this were not enough to discourage state self-protection, there was the collective action problem of one state retaliating against New Jersey, uncertain of what other states would do. If all states had retaliated, they could have contained New Jersey's apostasy. But one or a few states, challenging New Jersey by themselves, would suffer. It was not long before more than half of the nation's largest corporations were incorporated in New Jersey. U.S. Steel was a vital employer in Pennsylvania and much of the Midwest, as was Standard Oil from Cleveland to Baltimore. It was the same as if all states today prohibited Delaware corporations from having subsidiaries or doing business in their states—economic devastation for most. So there was little to be gained and much to be lost for a state at the turn of the century to retaliate against New Jersey. Although officials from nine states in the Mississippi Valley met in St. Louis in 1899 to develop a set of uniform laws, they ultimately failed with a "ludicrous fizzle" because the delegates could not agree on a policy toward trusts and, I suspect, states were unwilling to suffer the economic consequences of bucking the trend New Jersey had begun.[54]

The attitude that resulted was, if you can't beat 'em, join 'em. New York passed its own holding company act in 1892. And, before long, other states followed and even outdid New Jersey's liberality. The entire complexion of American corporate law changed. Even Massachusetts, the bastion of corporate integrity, rather resentfully joined along in 1903. But despite (or perhaps because of) the domino effect created by New Jersey, the new situation did not go unchallenged.[55]

The federal government did not rise to its modern prominence in domestic matters until the New Deal. But it was during the Progressive Era that it began to lay the theories and create the models upon which federal regulation was based. The corporations question more than any other issue helped it set that groundwork. Even as the federal government tried to regulate trusts, the multiple problems created by corporate combination in New Jersey confused regulatory attempts. This was especially true of corporate overcapitalization, which resulted in promoters dumping huge numbers of questionable shares on the market. The issue of overcapitalization became the regulatory centerpiece of everything from antitrust reform to railroad rate regulation and eventually led to the first federal efforts to enact securities legislation. But before examining this regulatory history, it is important to see how New Jersey law combined with economic circumstances to create the merger wave, to make the business of America into the business of finance, and, in the process, to transform the American stock market.

⊰ THREE ⊱
TRANSCENDENTAL VALUE

Overbuilt industries engaged in ruinous competition created the circumstances that made business cooperation the rational strategy to ensure industrial survival at the end of the nineteenth century. New Jersey met business needs by providing the mechanisms of cooperation. Together they almost certainly would have increased the pace of business combination along the lines that companies like Standard Oil had achieved.

The process of continuing combination to rationalize industry using the New Jersey holding company would probably not have led to a merger wave of the intensity and proportions that occurred between 1897 and 1903. It almost certainly would not have transformed the stock market as it did by dramatically increasing corporate capitalization and the dispersion of massive amounts of stock into the American market. That consequence of the merger wave, the transformation of the stock market, depended upon yet other factors and introduced into the mainstream of business a new leading actor whose goal was profit from stock and not from industry.

The factors that set the timing of the merger wave and led to its transformation of the market were a dramatic late-nineteenth-century run-up in surplus cash looking for investments and the opportunity it created for promoters to use the New Jersey stock-for-assets law to put together the giant modern corporation and enrich themselves in the process.[1]

The new leading actor was the trust promoter. The trust promoter was sometimes a conservative banker like J. P. Morgan and sometimes a freewheeling speculator like John Gates. The difference between the way Gates and industrialists like Rockefeller and Carnegie did business can be summed up, at the extreme, by noting that Gates "was said to have spent a rainy afternoon on a way train betting with a companion on which of the raindrops coursing down the windowpane would reach the bottom first—at a thousand dollars a race." Gates's travel activities and his work as a promoter were similar except that in the latter capacity he bet on stock instead of raindrops. Morgan was not a gambler but, like Gates, his inventory was composed of stocks and bonds. Working sometimes together, and sometimes in competition with one another, Gates, Morgan, Charles Flint, the Moore brothers and others created the giant modern corporation and, with it, the modern stock market.[2]

The state of the American economy at the end of the nineteenth century and the rise of the modern stock market are the subject of the next chapter. The story for now is how promoters used New Jersey law to reap enormous profits while putting together the business combinations that became the giant modern corporation. It explains how promoters' abilities to overcapitalize corporations provided the incentives they needed in order to create them. And it shows how this overcapitalization created a perennial and unsolvable regulatory problem that was grounded in a legal regime that had yet to embrace the reality of big corporations and in economic thinking that did not fully grasp the mechanisms of finance.[3]

OVERCAPITALIZATION

While New Jersey provided the machinery for cooperation, it also created the potential for mischief. Perhaps the single greatest issue wafting up from its statutory reforms was the problem of overcapitalizing corporations or watering stock. Overcapitalization allowed promoters to issue enough shares to induce the industrialists to sell their plants into the giant combinations and to pay themselves huge fees. It was also how they created the modern stock market.[4]

The term capitalization, as used at the time, meant the nominal (or stated) value of the stocks and bonds that a corporation was authorized by its charter to issue. A corporation's capitalization might not, and typically did not, reflect either the amount of the securities that it actually issued, nor their value as they traded on the market. Yet a corporation's capitalization commonly was used as a proxy for its size.

Overcapitalization and watering stock were the terms used to describe the situations we saw in the *Donald* and *See* cases. Overcapitalization meant that the corporation was capitalized in an amount that was greater than the cash value of the assets that appeared on its balance sheet. Stock was watered when a corporation issued stock backed by tangible assets worth less than its nominal value. Although the concepts can be separately understood, in practice during the merger wave they largely amounted to the same thing. I will use the terms interchangeably.

The problem of watered stock was nothing new in the nineteenth century. The phrase, if not the practice, is credited to mid-century stock speculator and Erie confederate Daniel Drew. Drew began his career as a young man early in the century as a cattle drover in his native Putnam County, New York. He perfected a trick in this first business venture that would make him rich when he later applied it to stock instead of livestock. Drew would drive his herd almost the entire distance to the drovers' market in Harlem without letting them drink along the way, but providing them with liberal amounts of salt. Naturally they arrived hot and thirsty. Just before he delivered them to market, he brought them to drink. Needless to say, they drank a lot. By the time the cattle arrived at market they were bloated, registered higher weights and sold for substantially more than they were worth. Drew's stock was, quite literally, watered. It was not long before he was rather quickly driven to Ohio to escape his angry victims. But when he returned to New York he indulged in the same practice with a different sort of animal. Corporate stock was not literally watered but the principle was the same. Drew and his imitators issued stock at a par value higher than a corporation's tangible economic value. The difference was called "water." Like Drew's cattle, the stock appeared to have more value than it was worth.[5]

Stock watering made its first serious public appearance with the railroads. One of the games Drew played in his battle for control of the Erie with that old "yokel from Staten Island," Cornelius Vanderbilt, was simply to print stock whenever he wanted more, most strikingly to dilute Vanderbilt's holdings to below the level of control. Share capital of the "Scarlet Lady of Wall Street" increased from $17 million to $78 million in a four-year period without any appreciable increase in earnings or assets. That was an extreme version of watered stock. There was no economic value so all of the new stock was water. Other roads used only slightly more subtle techniques. Corporations declared stock dividends of 100 percent, doubling their capitalizations with the stroke of a pen. More commonly, corporations paid stock dividends ranging from 14 percent to 80 percent of the company's capital, increasing the number of shares without increasing the corporation's wealth.[6]

Stock watering may not have been new, but it raised the appearance of a crisis during the merger wave. Contemporaries believed that the practice created serious antitrust and economic problems. As a result, debates about overcapitalization dominated reform discussions for over a decade, befuddling congresses, presidents, economists and reformers. Lawmakers chased after an issue that proved, in the end, to be a red herring that diverted them from their main task in the long struggle to regulate competition and protect consumers from monopolies. At the same time, investors were only too happy to encourage overcapitalization by buying the water. While reformers' attention was diverted, overcapitalization during the merger wave created the modern stock market.

Before going any further, I need to take a moment to be clear about the claims I make in this chapter, for the concept of overcapitalization will sound foreign to modern ears. Economic theory has more or less dismissed the possibility that a corporation, especially a publicly traded corporation, can be overcapitalized. However much stock and bonds a corporation has issued, whatever their par values and whatever the prices at which the corporation issued them, the capital markets will determine their value, and thus the corporation's capitalization, in light of fundamental economic characteristics like risk, earnings and cash flow. If overcapitalization is an illusion, why spend a chapter talking about it?

Overcapitalization may be an illusion, but that is not the way it was understood at the turn of the twentieth century. Overcapitalization was widely believed to cause or to conceal monopolies, to create massive amounts of speculative securities that led to corporate mismanagement and economic instability, and to serve as the means by which Eastern plutocrats robbed ordinary Americans of their financial well-being. Overcapitalization became one of the main entry points of legislative efforts to control monopoly and became a rallying cry for antitrust efforts. Overcapitalization was one of the most talked about issues in the corporate debate from the turn of the century until well into the next decade. Illusion or not, overcapitalization was the apparent way that massive amounts of new securities were created and sold on the market. The problem of overcapitalization is a key to the triumph of finance over industry and to the shape that regulatory efforts to control giant corporations took.[7]

Overcapitalization was a real issue because it affected real behavior. Whether or not overcapitalization was a real economic problem, whether it affected corporate profits or the way stock performed, does not matter for my narrative. Historians have debated the issue, some concluding that it had negative effects on corporate success and some concluding that it did not, but it does not matter whether combinations formed during the merger wave ultimately justified their capitalizations by regular dividend payments, increased investments and retained earnings, whether they responded to overcapitalization by behaving like monopolists, or whether their businesses succeeded or failed. These are important historical questions, but they are beside the point in an explanation of how the modern stock market was created by the giant modern corporation and how federal securities regulation grew out of numerous and sustained efforts to deal with the apparently unrelated problems of trusts and monopolies. Whether overcapitalization was economically possible is not the issue. It is enough that the principal actors believed that it was or at least behaved as if it were.[8]

A QUESTION OF VALUE

Contemporary observers thought that overcapitalization created three major problems. First, a corporation that issued more stock than the value of its tangible assets would have to charge unfairly high prices in order to make enough money to pay dividends. The assets simply were not productive enough to generate the necessary income on the basis of fair prices alone. The second problem was that overcapitalization made it hard to identify and regulate monopolies. The "water" hid monopolistic rates of return by spreading the extra monopoly profits over far more nominal capital than actually worked to generate the profits. This lowered the corporation's apparent rate of return and destroyed one of the few ways lawmakers had of figuring out whether a particular company was a monopoly. A third problem that attracted greater attention later in the decade was that the speculative stock created by overcapitalization increased the volatility of the nation's capital markets and threatened the stability of its banking system.

How were contemporaries able to determine when a corporation was overcapitalized and how much of a problem it presented? The question ultimately came down to one of value. How were you supposed to decide what a new combination was worth? How much in bonds, preferred stock and common stock should a new corporation issue? Once you get beneath the law reform proposals, the accusations and counteraccusations of fraud and bad faith and the fiery political rhetoric, the overcapitalization debate was as much a fight about financial theory as it was about rapacious monopolies and fleeced investors. The lack of consensus or even clear thinking on the valuation question made the overcapitalization problem impossible to solve for both economists and politicians. As late as 1935, Shaw Livermore wrote that "an objective standard to measure the 'truth' of overcapitalization has always been lacking." The question remained alive for years to follow.[9]

Most courts, like New Jersey's, accepted some form of the argument that the value of a corporation's stock should be based on the determinate, measurable cash value of its tangible assets. Plant owners relied upon the corporation's earning power and goodwill, although their abilities to measure these were often too tentative for lawmakers' comfort. Economists tended to agree with businessmen but were more equivocal about the appropriate measure of value at the time the corporation was formed. The corporate valuation problem was a relatively new one in economics and finance because the giant modern corporation was a relatively new phenomenon. There was no consensus solution. All economists seemed to understand that the value of a going concern was the value of its expected profits, at least in theory. But for a variety of reasons I will discuss below, many drew back from theory and, following the courts, concentrated their attention on tangible assets, too.[10]

Corporate promoters and financiers—Veblen's true businessmen—determined the value of their companies on the basis of their projected earnings and anticipated goodwill, but at least as often created capitalizations based on what they had to pay in order to induce plant owners to sell into combinations. The lack of technical sophistication they seemed to bring to the task made the whole methodology suspect. Consider the case of the Sugar Trust. Its creator and head, Henry O. Havemeyer, described the way he capitalized that trust to the Industrial Commission in Washington on June 14, 1899. What he had to say is typical of the financiers and promoters of the age.

The questioning was done, as it frequently was, by Cornell economist Jeremiah Whipple Jenks. Jenks served as a consultant to the Commission and would serve in a similar role with the Commission's successor, the Bureau of Corporations. He was a noted scholar and public speaker on trust issues and his 1900 book, *The Trust Problem*, is a classic in the field. He was a close adviser to McKinley and Roosevelt. Of all the economists writing during this period, Jenks was perhaps the most prominent and the most equivocal. Reading his work is sometimes maddening because of his hesitancy to take a strong position on almost anything. He generally favored large corporations but, financial conservative that he was, he was especially mindful of the various problems that could be caused by a corporation capitalized beyond the value of its physical assets.

Havemeyer was the force behind the Sugar Trust. He was born into a family that already dominated much of the American sugar business. His grandfather and great-uncle started their refinery in Greenwich Village in 1802 and rapidly became the largest refiners in America, bringing the wealthy family into the ranks of New York's social elite. The various Havemeyer refineries, run by different branches of the family, spanned the waterfront in Williamsburg, Brooklyn and Jersey City. By 1886, the year before Havemeyer created the Sugar Trust, his firm, Havemeyer & Elder, controlled 55 percent of the nation's refining capacity, and the various branches of the Havemeyer family together held 70 percent.[11]

Havemeyer was a highly public figure, celebrated by some and reviled by others. He was widely considered to be the most significant trust organizer in America after John D. Rockefeller. He was aggressive, outspoken, blunt and often admirably honest about his monopolistic intentions and blatant self-interest. Under questioning by Jenks, he was characteristically forthright and direct:

Q. There has been a great deal said at different times with reference to the capitalization of the American Sugar Refining Company, with reference to the amount of [stock] certificates they issued for the different plants, and so on. What was the general principle that you adopted in fixing the valuation of the different plants that came into the organization?

A. Well, we bought the stock at what we could buy it for, which was considered the value, according to what we termed value. I would rather have the brand of a refinery as value than to have a building worth millions of dollars, and that feature which is called good will in the brand was undoubtedly well estimated.

Q. That is exactly the question. I wanted to get at the meaning that you yourself attach to the term "value" in capitalizing the industry.

A. Well, I do not think we thought much of it then — of defining the value of each particular plant. Some plants we bought probably more on account of the real estate value; others we took because they were going concerns; others we took for their standing; others had very valuable trade-marks; all of these things figured in; but how we can separate or divide them I can never tell.

Q. The question was: Would they contribute to the profit of the new organization?

A. Yes.

Q. Then your general basis of valuation was the paying capacity of the plant?

A. You know I know nothing about it except so far as my own plant is concerned. We figured up that our plant was worth so much money and they accepted it, and we have always felt we sold it at an inconsiderable price compared with its real value.

Q. The real value there again being what one could make out of it?

A. Yes; being the value of the trade-mark, the name of Havemeyer as identified with sugar.

—❧❧—

Q. So as regards the capitalization of the American Sugar Refining Company at the present time, then, in round numbers, $30,000,000 to
$35,000,000 is about what it would cost to build the refineries?

A. As mere buildings?

Q. As mere buildings.

A. I think the brand of Havemeyer & Elder would bring thirty-five millions
alone.

Q. That is the question I have in mind, as to how far this building value
should be considered, and how far good will and other matters of that
kind?

A. I never separated them. This is the first time that question has ever been
put to me, and I have never given it any thought.

To be fair to Havemeyer and other industrialists who participated in the
creation of trusts, his holistic approach to valuation almost certainly came
from a thorough knowledge of the sugar industry, his own business and keen
intuition. Nonetheless, one could not expect the public, creditors and shareholders to rely on the intuitions of people who were in business to take their
money, and trust promoters and underwriters did not have the same deep
knowledge of the businesses as the men who ran them. As Edward Meade
wrote of trust promoters: "The promoter, in his endeavor to estimate the
economies of combination, was reduced to elastic approximations. . . . [The
trust promoter's] calculations were at best inaccurate guesswork." There were
more scientific methods of determining value, and to them we will turn
shortly. But before we do, it is important to understand the concept of overcapitalization and the problems that the practice was thought to create.[12]

THE LEGAL BACKGROUND OF WATERED STOCK:
THE CONCEPT OF PAR VALUE

In order to see how and why overcapitalization became such a dominant issue it is important to understand some basics of corporate finance law. The
starting point is the concept of par value.

Corporate charters, and later general incorporation laws, had long required stock to have a stated par value. This was an amount that represented
the minimum amount of capital per share that each shareholder committed
to the corporation. Par value is now a museum piece of corporate law, first
fatally weakened when New York, after years of debate, authorized the issuance of no-par stock in 1912. Its demise was very slow and it now survives

more as a corporate formality than for any serious policy reason. But well into the first part of the century, par value was intended both to protect creditors and to ensure that stockholders actually paid in full for their stock. In the absence of par value, the overcapitalization problem would almost certainly never have existed.[13]

Say that a corporation's common stock had a par value of $100, a fairly common amount. Multiply $100 by the number of authorized shares and you have the capitalization with which the corporation began business. Par value allowed shareholders to be confident that they paid neither more nor less for their stock than other shareholders and gave creditors some assurance that the corporation really did have the value its stock represented.[14]

The corporation was not required to keep cash in the amount of par value. Paid-in capital was an accounting entry representing an equity cushion, but the money was invested in productive business assets. Even so, if the corporation kept its books honestly (and in an age of primitive accounting, what "honestly" meant was a complicated question) creditors could take some comfort in believing that the paid-in capital represented corporate investments in valuable assets equivalent to the stated amount.

A brief illustration of the early way par value worked will help to clarify the issue. Traditionally, stock was sold by subscription. A promoter, perhaps a mill owner, would decide to incorporate his mill to raise money for expansion. To find this money, he would go to his friends and business acquaintances, to local merchants and bankers, and ask them to subscribe for the stock. If they were interested, they would sign a subscription agreement, a contract to buy a given number of shares at a set price. In the early days, the price was set at par value. The promoter would then go the legislature and get a corporate charter, allowing him to incorporate with a specified amount of capital.

Subscribers did not actually have to pay for the stock until the promoter had sold subscriptions for a minimum number of shares and the corporation was formed. But even when these conditions were fulfilled, shareholders did not always have to pay the entire price at once. It might be the case that the promoter did not need all the money right away. If not, he would "call" from the shareholders the amount of cash he needed, maybe 25 percent of the purchase price. Each of the subscribers (now shareholders) was still obligated to pay the remaining 75 percent whenever the promoter (now board of directors) made additional capital calls. Until a stockholder had paid in the full amount of par, the stock was considered to be watered by an amount equal to the difference between the par value and the amount the shareholder actually had paid.

The essential legal matter was that a stockholder remained on the hook to creditors in an amount up to the total par value of the shares for as long as his subscription was not fully paid. If the corporation went bankrupt before this happened, creditors could go after the shareholders directly. This arrangement gave the corporation and its shareholders financial flexibility while it provided some protection for creditors. In the eyes of more than a few courts, this entire par value arrangement was the trade-off for allowing shareholders to enjoy the privilege of limited liability, which protected their assets from creditors' claims.[15]

Although courts took par value seriously, no sensible creditor relied upon it. Instead they put their faith in the banker who underwrote the bonds. If you bought your bonds from Morgan, you knew that somebody responsible was protecting you. If not, you took your chances. Watered stock came to matter as an issue of corporate privilege and monopoly, not as a fraud on investors.[16]

WATERING STOCK

There are three main recipes for making watered stock. Here is the first: Set par value and take one part cash and one part nothing. If the corporation needed more cash than its shareholders paid, it could borrow the money. The corporation would pay dividends on the full par value of the stock, but with only half of the stockholder's money invested. So the stockholder's rate of return would double. Now, as I noted above, this could be risky, because the stockholders would have to pay up if the corporation went bankrupt. But they might never have to pay more if the corporation succeeded and, in the meantime, they would enjoy an extra-high rate of return.

The second recipe for making watered stock was the recipe used by the giant modern corporation. Using this method, the corporation identified property it wanted to buy to use in its business. Assume the market price was $5,000. The seller wanted cash for his property. But maybe the corporation did not have enough cash, or did not want to use its cash to buy the property. The promoters, or board of directors, set the par value of the corporation's stock at $100. Naturally this would suggest that the property was worth 50 shares.

But here's the trick. As we saw in the last chapter, New Jersey law gave the board the right to decide how much the property was worth because property was often unique and hard to value and, presumably, because the directors knew their corporation's needs better than other people. Maybe the property was a parcel of land especially well-placed for the corporation, or perhaps the patent for a new machine. The directors, using their discretion, decided that it was worth $10,000 to their corporation. They offered the seller 100 shares. Now the seller could be interested. He might be willing to forgo cash for a chance to acquire stock at what amounted to half price. If the corporation succeeded he would enjoy a rate of return that was double what it otherwise would have been on the $5,000 of property he actually invested. But the corporation would be overcapitalized; it had issued twice as much stock as the $5,000 property was worth. The seller got a bargain and the directors bought the asset without spending any cash.

A third recipe for watering stock was typically used by the railroads. As we have seen, the railroads were funded mostly with debt. Debt service was a heavy fixed cost the roads had to meet and could be a serious burden when competition became fierce and revenues declined. So they looked for a way to keep interest rates down. If bond buyers agreed to a lower interest rate, the railroads would give them "bonus stock" as part of the deal. The bondholders did not pay for this bonus stock. All of it was water. If the railroad turned out to be successful enough to pay dividends on the stock, bondholders had that much additional gain on the upside while the security of their bonds protected them on the downside. The railroads became the first industry that thrived on watered stock.

Industrial stock before the merger wave was owned mostly by the founders and managers of the corporation, and the financial interests of the creators, like Rockefeller, provided little incentive for overcapitalization. Stock watering would only have diluted their wealth. Besides, no significant public market for industrial securities existed and so there was nobody to buy the watered stock. Matters changed when the market was ready. As we will see in Chapter Four, it was ready by 1897 when surplus capital created a hungry demand for new investments.[17]

As the promotion of combinations flourished and taking stock in untested combinations with high capitalizations became increasingly risky, entrepreneurs who sold their businesses into combinations became more reticent about accepting stock instead of cash. Plant owners were not foolish. The new combinations, now saddled with heavy debt service and dividend obligations, could fail. But they could get all or most of their money back if the combination failed and the assets were liquidated as long as they held stock worth at least the value of the corporation's tangible assets. So to make stock more attractive as currency, the combinations organized by promoters began to issue preferred stock in the amount of these assets, protecting the sellers on the downside by giving them a more certain return on their investments and priority over common stockholders in the event of liquidation.

At the same time, it did not make much business sense for plant owners to part with their businesses for only the cash value of their assets, especially taken together as a going concern. They knew their own profit histories and understood perfectly well that the goodwill value they had created was worth more than tangible asset value. So they demanded a premium, reflecting the future profits to be generated by that goodwill. The promoter would already have offered enough preferred stock to cover the value of each seller's tangible assets. The combination had to create more stock in order to pay this premium. It issued common stock, which increased its capitalization well above the value of its tangible assets but gave sellers a chance to share in the potential gains of the combination. And promoters could do this because New Jersey's stock-for-property law gave the combination's directors almost complete discretion in determining the value of the plants they were buying.[18]

The promoters had to be paid as well, and expected to be paid very handsomely. The cheapest way for the combination to pay them was also in stock, which promoters would commonly dump on the market during the initial excitement surrounding its creation. This way they could cash out before the business faltered. A problem was that the promoters had nothing to sell but their services. The merger wave occurred at a time well before most states, including New Jersey, allowed corporations to exchange stock for services performed. In order to reap their rewards, promoters typically would buy options on each of the plants to be sold into the combination and either exercise those options themselves, selling the overvalued plants to the combination, or sell the options directly to the combination at high valuations that supported their payment in stock.[19]

The more stock promoters could issue, the more stock they could sell to the public. That meant more money—in real cash—in their pockets. The fact that no authority except the NYSE and some states mandated corporate disclosure helped promoters sell the stock of untested corporations, at least during periods of high demand for investments. Most corporations ignored the NYSE rules because they were not enforced much anyway, and the disclosure required by states and the NYSE went only to them, not to the shareholders or the public. Voluntary public disclosure, when it occurred, was almost meaningless. By protecting their secrets, promoters and plant owners could cash out by selling their stock to the public before the new combination had to endure the test of the capital markets.[20]

WATERED STOCK IN ACTION: THE CASE OF U.S. STEEL

Perhaps the best, or at least the biggest, example of an overcapitalized company is the combination that resulted in U.S. Steel. The project was organized by Pierpont Morgan and was, with a capitalization of approximately $1.4 billion, bigger than any corporation previously created. Compared to Steel's $1.1 billion of stock and $300 million of debt, its tangible assets were worth $676 million. This meant that excess capitalization, or water, was $727 million.* The Bureau of Corporations explored the various ways one could justify this extensive watering. Perhaps it could be attributed to good-will. But the total market price of the stock of the companies absorbed into Steel was only $793 million. And these market prices should already have reflected goodwill. Even on a market value basis, Steel contained $610 million of water.

Other estimates also found water. The "departments of the businesses" themselves estimated tangible property at $682 million, which left water of $721 million. More modest estimates of Steel's overcapitalization were made by the Industrial Commission in 1901 at ranges of $302 million to $390 million.

Part of the explanation for this overcapitalization lies in the promoters' needs to pay premiums to the owners of the component corporations, some of whom, like Henry Frick and Andrew Carnegie, were negotiators the equal of J. P. Morgan. (Carnegie was confident that he had outfoxed Morgan. Morgan told Carnegie he would have paid the latter more if he had only asked.) But part of the water also represented Morgan's profit as promoter. The Morgan syndicate took 1.3 million shares as its fee, which it dumped on the market for the rather tidy sum of $62.5 million. Economists of the time, like Edward Meade and Charles Conant, left no doubt that promoters' and bankers' profits were to come from the sale of stock, not from holding the stock and receiving dividends. No matter how you look at it, watering stock was a profitable business for everyone except, perhaps, the public stockholder.[21]

DEFENDING OVERCAPITALIZATION

Promoters insisted that overcapitalization was necessary to encourage business growth. Their attitude was perhaps most forcefully expressed by corporate lawyer and trust promoter John Dos Passos in his testimony before the U.S. Industrial Commission in December 1899. Dos Passos's defense may have been a bit overheated, but it reflected the common opinions of promoters and financiers. The Commissioners sat politely for what must have been hours, listening to Dos Passos hector them for passing the Interstate Com-

---

*The careful reader will notice that $676 million and $727 million exceed $1.4 billion. For ease of reading here and throughout, I have rounded aggregate numbers but retained the component numbers as they appear in the different reports.

merce Act of 1887. He extolled the virtues of the free market like a revivalist preacher. Dos Passos evidently was so pleased with his own rhetoric that he published his testimony as a book.[22]

Dos Passos was a fiercely antiregulatory Social Darwinist. After leaving his tempestuous family in Philadelphia, he became an office boy in a law firm and began to read law, interrupted only by his service as a drummer in the Civil War. Upon his return from Antietam, where he had been put out of commission by dysentery, he apprenticed himself to a lawyer and attended night classes at the University of Pennsylvania's law school, entering the bar in 1865. Two years later he moved to New York, where he quickly established an important reputation by his successful defenses of two accused murderers. He earned particular notoriety for his victory in the case of socialite Edward S. Stokes, who killed Jim Fisk in a fight over Fisk's mistress. Forming a partnership with his brother in the Wall Street area, Dos Passos started to represent brokerage firms. He earned the bulk of his wealth as a trust lawyer, putting together Havemeyer's Sugar Trust as well as several others. Among his projects was the first tunnel connecting New York and New Jersey beneath the Hudson River. It was a project he abandoned to the young William Gibbs McAdoo, who later became Wilson's treasury secretary and son-in-law.

Dos Passos was a passionate man, and one of his passions was free-market capitalism. He had a "flamboyant personality, flair for the grand gesture, and inordinate powers of persuasion," such that he could have "talked the blindfold off the goddess of justice herself with only half a tongue." It was this last quality that must have led the Industrial Commissioners to tolerate hours of his bullying testimony.[23]

Dos Passos admitted that overcapitalization was an "undoubted" although curable "evil," but claimed that it was necessary, at least in the formation of the railroads and, by implication, the big industrial combinations. Recall that one of the ways railroads overcapitalized was by issuing bonus stock, the speculative stock that gave creditors a chance to share in the future profits of a corporate combination. Dos Passos explained that this potential for profit was the key to persuading skittish Europeans to invest in railroad bonds: "Now, before you dissolve [the Commission], call before your commission those men who talk about overcapitalization and examine them; get at the facts; ... I am not defending inflation. I am speaking of the facts. I am giving you the facts, and showing you that there was no possibility of money being raised except through the instrumentality of these large bonuses...."[24]

Sam Untermyer, who gave up watering stock to become a crusader against Wall Street, agreed with Dos Passos as late as 1914 when the issue was still hot in some quarters. Minnesota's Senator Knute Nelson, questioning Untermyer in a hearing on stock exchange regulation, suggested that the New York Stock Exchange should be banned from listing companies with watered stock. Untermyer's response reflected the standard business defense of overcapitalization: "That would be a pretty drastic proposition, and I hope we are not going so far as that. I, for one, am not prepared to urge such a drastic program as that, because you never would have had a railroad built if that had been the program. It would not allow anything for the goodwill of any project, and goodwill is quite an essential element of value, as much so as physical assets, and frequently more essential." Necessity was the mother of invention. Whatever the benefits or detriments of watered stock, there would be no railroads, there would be no industrial America, without it.[25]

Looking back from 1929 to the merger wave, Seager and Gulick noted that competitors could rarely be persuaded to combine their businesses without financial incentives. "The sensational progress of the ... trust movement was possible only because a group of shrewd, plausible, and aggressive promoters was at hand." No matter how the promoters persuaded each plant owner that the valuation they put on the business was fair, corporate promoters and financiers always needed stock above the tangible value of the assets to get the deal done.[26]

THE WATER WAS DEEP

How common was the practice of watering stock? There are several different ways to get at the answer. We know that a characteristic watering pattern was for a corporation to issue preferred stock in an amount equal to the tangible assets (and some intangibles, like patents) and simultaneously to issue the same amount of common stock. So we can look at a number of combinations to see how prevalent this practice was.

Available data show that in the five-year period from 1887 through 1891, only twenty-four of sixty industrial corporations, or 40 percent, issued preferred stock. That proportion leaped to 90 percent in 1892. From that point until the end of the century, virtually every industrial combination issued preferred as well as common stock. The representation of tangible assets by preferred stock provided cover for corporations to issue completely watered common stock.[27]

Capitalizations using preferred and common stock easily reveal the water. From 1887 until 1896, sixteen of ninety-five industrial corporations, or almost 17 percent, issued an amount of common equal to the amount of preferred. Many observers took this as sufficient evidence of overcapitalization. The practice boomed during the merger wave. In 1898 alone, 55 percent of the combinations issuing both classes of stock issued equal amounts of common and preferred.[28]

Some promoters did use more finely tuned methods of valuation to determine the appropriate capitalization of their combinations. One was for the plant owners to determine the amount of their past earnings and demand common stock based upon a multiple of those earnings. So, for example, if earnings had been $1 million in the past year they might choose a multiple of three and demand $3 million in common stock for their company. Often these multiples were not randomly chosen. Plant owners knew their businesses and their industries and chose multiples based on their estimates of their companies' relative competitive positions and performances. This was better than simple guesswork but it still required a great deal of judgment and opinion, colored by the seller's interest in making as much money on the sale as he could. Sometimes the promoters made a crude estimate of the combination's goodwill. The promoters of the American Chicle Company put such a high value on the brand that they issued preferred stock in an amount three times the combination's tangible value, along with an amount of common stock double that of the preferred. They declared this valuation to be conservative in light of the fact that the company earned six times the dividends on the preferred. But while it may have been conservative as to the preferred, that explanation still stretched credulity as to the value of the common. Contemporary and later studies of combinations described how overcapitalized combinations later tried to bring their capital structures more in line with business realities, "squeezing out" the water by retaining earnings, among other methods.[29]

On the other hand, capitalization could be determined in a reasonably precise and conservative way that reflected the present value of the corporation. Sears, Roebuck & Company, for example, capitalized its business in 1906 when it publicly issued stock underwritten by a partnership between Goldman, Sachs and Lehman Brothers. Preferred stock was authorized in an amount equal to the company's $10 million in "material assets" and common stock was authorized to capture the promise of future profits. The company's profits, net of preferred dividends, were $2.1 million that year. The company capitalized its earnings at a rate of 7 percent, which led it to authorize $30 million of common stock in addition to the preferred. Seven percent was a high capitalization rate for the era. The prevailing yields on corporate bonds were 3.55 percent on thirty-year bonds and 4.75 percent on one-year bonds. This was a time in which most people believed that common stock yields should not be significantly higher than bond yields, but Sears' business was considered to be particularly risky. This example demonstrates that sensible and modern capitalization could be undertaken. But it is worth noting the fact that this particular capitalization was structured by a company that was not a combination and that, unlike the combinations, already had some performance record at the time it was recapitalized to go public.[30] As to combinations, the report of the Industrial Commission confirms the conclusion that valuation was very much in the eye of the promoter. In the words of Seager and Gulick, "[t]his meant inevitably overcapitalization."[31]

We can also look at the profits to be made from overcapitalization, surmising that the more lucrative the practice, the more common it would be. We have already seen the fee paid to Morgan for creating U.S. Steel. Alexander D. Noyes, speaking at Harvard in 1904, described the magnitude of the potential profits in the water. He noted that: "during the full year 1899 the total [capitalization of new corporations] rose to $3,593,000,000, of which respectable sum $2,354,000,000 was the common stock, which by frank confession of promoters, then and afterward, simply was water." In other words, the promoters and sellers of those corporations had created for public consumption stock whose only value was hope in an amount almost twice that of the value of the tangible assets of the issuing corporations. The U.S. Industrial Commission studied 183 industrial corporations and found that corporations with tangible assets worth $1.5 billion issued stock and bonds in the amount of more than $3 billion, overcapitalizing corporate America by more than 100 percent. And economist Arthur Dewing found that substantial amounts of stock were issued in excess of the value of the assets in all but one of the mergers he studied, ranging from a low of 35 percent to six that were overcapitalized by between 70 percent and 80 percent. While there are dissenters from the view that overcapitalization was either a problem or a meaningful historical fact, the consensus among observers of the era and some later writers seems to be that it certainly was commonplace.[32]

We hardly need more than "the frank confession of promoters" to understand the widespread belief that overcapitalization was common, and its enormous profit potential supports the conclusion. But we have more. Economist Luther Conant, Jr., writing at the beginning of the twentieth century, concluded that the evidence was clear that industrial combinations were motivated not only by the desire to avoid competition but also, perhaps equally, by the opportunity for promoters to dump stock on the market. As the investment-conservative *Wall Street Journal* noted in 1902: "Investors should bear in mind the fact—unfortunate fact though it is—that many schemes are promoted for the sole purpose of getting their money, that the promoters do not expect the enterprise to be a business success, but propose to unload stock on the public, and then let the public stockholders manage the business the best they can." They were joined in this conclusion by James B. Dill, among many others. Theodore Burton, writing in 1911, observed of the merger wave that it was "sometimes called the promoters' period," and that "the formation of a combination often partakes of the nature of a stock-jobbing operation, the aim being ... to afford profits to promoters and underwriters." And economists Seager and Gulick, looking at the merger wave thirty years later, concluded that "to explain the veritable furore for combination that developed we must give due credit to the professional promoter," agreeing that it was promoters' profits that were a driving force of the merger wave. It was widely recognized at the time that the profits to be made from overcapitalization gave promoters and plant owners alike the incentives they needed to combine.[33]

CAPITALIZATION VERSUS REAL CAPITAL

One has to be careful in discussing overcapitalization even from the perspective of the era to understand the relationship between the amount of a corporation's capitalization and the amount of bonds and stock it actually issued, as well as the prices at which they were issued. For example, International Paper Co. was organized in 1898 with $25 million in preferred stock and $20 million in common, yet the issued and outstanding amounts of each were, respectively, $20.5 million and $13 million. During the year the preferred traded at a low of 85 and a high of 95 while the common traded at a range of 48 to 67, suggesting that the market considerably discounted the stocks' par values of $100.[34]

Similarly, the Rubber Goods Manufacturing Co., a combination put together in 1899 by leading trust promoter Charles Flint, began with an aggressive capitalization of $50 million, half of which was common and half of which was preferred, based on tangible assets of $6.2 million and an 1898 net income of $1.1 million. Preferred stock in the amount of $6.2 million, representing total tangible assets, was issued at $84 per share. Only $11.8 million of the $25 million in common was issued, at a price of $33 per share. Again the market appears to have significantly discounted the combination's nominal capitalization to adjust for the risk of the investment. One suspects that some of the unsold stock was reserved for new acquisitions, since later that year Rubber Goods acquired both Empire Rubber and Dunlop Tire Company, and the stock does not appear to have been traded during the year.[35]

The United States Flour Milling Co. consolidated nineteen flour mills in 1899 with total assets of $6 million (including real estate, other tangible property, brands, trademarks, goodwill and $1.25 million in cash). It capitalized at $25 million in stock, half preferred and half common, and $15 million in bonds. Half of the bonds, $5 million of the preferred and $3.5 million of the common were issued to acquire the property, and $4.5 million in bonds were offered at 102½ upon the company's creation. The bonds remained inactive on the market. The preferred and common dropped from highs of 58¼ and 78½, respectively, on September 15, four days after they began un-listed trading on the NYSE, to 12 each by the end of the year, suggesting that the company's capitalization was optimistic and the market corrected for it. It also did not help matters that Charles A. Pillsbury died almost immediately following the beginning of trading, thereby unloading a significant block of stock on the market and depressing the price.[36]

These three examples, drawn from the height of the merger wave, demonstrate the way that the market, even in the absence of significant amounts of corporate information, could and did correct almost immediately for potential overcapitalization. These stories could be repeated for other combinations and, indeed, they are, in the pages of the *Commercial & Financial Chronicle*, which also published simple balance sheets for many of them. If the market was working against overcapitalization, it should not have been an issue. But it was one of the biggest issues in the corporate debates throughout the entire decade.

WHAT WAS THE PROBLEM?

Why was corporate overcapitalization considered to be one of the biggest public problems created by the merger wave? The nineteenth-century concerns with creditor protection and stockholder equity were no longer significant. The traditional legal remedies had become largely irrelevant. The combinations issuing stock during the merger wave were dumping buckets of it on the market and taking on thousands of shareholders. Even if a corporation went under, it would be completely impractical for its creditors to try to collect from shareholders. Creditors were well aware of the watering and could not seriously be said to have relied on a corporation's nominal capital. Nor, as I have shown, could sophisticated shareholders, since frequently only part of the authorized stock of combinations was issued and often traded well below par. And, as we will see, some courts were willing, at least in theory, to consider goodwill as part of corporate valuation, and this latitude allowed corporations to justify issuing more stock. Accepting goodwill as a valid corporate asset meant that stock that was thought to be water could have real value based on the corporation's expected earnings.[37]

The traditional concerns that led to laws against watered stock did not make sense in the new context, although many people still would not let them go. And overcapitalization was not yet considered to be the investor problem it would later become. Some people did see it as a problem for investors, despite the fact that at some level the market appeared to be working. Economist Irving Fisher, whose understanding of finance was second to none, wrote: "It is sometimes said that stock-watering is not wrong as long as all the terms and conditions are known. This is much like saying that lying is not wrong, provided everybody knows that it is lying." While lawmakers sometimes expressed similar concerns as well as a belief that overcapitalization could mislead bondholders and stockholders and cause destabilizing speculation, these are problems that were not seriously addressed until after the Panic of 1907. There were some lawmakers and policymakers, especially from the Midwest and South, who despised the very idea of the giant modern corporation, and overcapitalization was an easy point of attack for them. But these arguments were more or less peripheral. Even in the nonindustrial regions, most people understood that the giant modern corporation was here to stay.[38]

What, then, was the problem? Overcapitalization in the last years of the nineteenth century and at least the first decade of the twentieth was primarily an antitrust problem. It was thought to create a financial imperative for promoters to monopolize an industry and hide the supernormal profits that could prove that a corporation was indeed a monopoly. The debate on overcapitalization was a debate about monopoly regulation.

The best way to understand the antitrust problem is by simple example. Assume that a combination was worth the cash value of its assets, for that was the mainstream view. Also assume that a promoter brought together a combination of corporations with total assets of $25 million, and capitalized the new corporation at $50 million. He did this by issuing 25 million shares of preferred stock and 25 million shares of common stock, which he used to pay the plant owners a bonus price for the stock or assets of the constituent corporations, as well as his own fee.

Now assume, for simplicity's sake, that the total average dividend that the corporation committed to pay on all of the common and preferred stock was 7 percent. It is important to stress here that dividends at the time were paid as a percentage of par value, not as a percentage of profits as is the case today. Seven percent on par value would require total dividends of $3.5 million, assuming all of the stock had been issued. But $25 million of the capitalization represented no tangible assets at all and therefore was thought to have had no earning power. So the dividends were really only earned on the corporation's $25 million of productive assets. Seven percent of $25 million is $1.75 million. But the corporation had announced that it would pay a 7 percent dividend on all $50 million of stock. This meant that it still had to pay out $3.5 million to its shareholders, or a real dividend rate of 14 percent on the $25 million of productive assets.

In other words, a corporation capitalized at twice its value had to produce the full amount of dividends using only the half of its capital that represented its productive assets. The money had to come from somewhere, and it was not coming from the water. Many of the combinations were, for a time, able to sustain these high dividend payments either through monopoly rents or on the simple strength of their businesses. But it was difficult to earn this income consistently over the long term. For example, the enormously successful Sugar Trust increased its capital by four and a half times over fifteen years. During that same period, sugar consumption increased only about two and half times, and the trust's market share dropped from almost 90 percent of the nation's refining capacity to approximately 57 percent. With capitalization steady or increased and profitability dropping, there were very few ways a combination could meet its dividend promises. The obvious solution was to raise consumer prices.[39]

This presented one kind of antitrust problem. Consumers would have to pay exorbitant prices to allow shareholders to receive their dividends. Lawmakers treated this as a very important issue at the height of the merger wave. But, by the end of the first decade, this concern was increasingly limited to natural monopolies like common carriers and utilities. Consumer demand for those services was inelastic. People had no choice but to buy from the monopolists. Greater competition among industrial producers forced them to reduce their prices along with price reductions that came from efficiency gains. Worries about industrial combinations shifted from monopoly to speculation and economic stability in the years following 1907.[40]

The other kind of antitrust problem presented by overcapitalization was that water could wash over supernormal rates of return. A higher-than-average rate of return could be pretty good evidence that the corporation was a monopoly because it signaled the corporation's ability to charge monopoly prices. But concealing this power under watered stock made it harder for the government to identify and prosecute monopolies. Take the corporation I described above. It was overcapitalized by $25 million at its nominal capital of $50 million. Assume that it actually earned net profits of 10 percent on its entire $50 million of capital. That would be $5 million. The corporation still had absorbed $25 million of water so, as in our previous example, all $5 million was being produced by only $25 million of assets. That $5 million dollars now represented a whopping 20 percent rate of return on tangible assets. The extra 10 percent, which could suggest monopoly, was hidden beneath the water.

This second kind of problem—concealing monopoly profits—and the problem of protecting investors that developed during the next decade, could have been solved by mandating disclosure. But, as I will discuss more thoroughly in Chapter Four, meaningful disclosure was rare in corporate America. Corporate secrecy combined with primitive accounting and valuation methods to almost guarantee that public investors would remain ignorant of how much they paid, and consumers how much they were charged, for water. As the Industrial Commission (which was generally in favor of corporate combination) put it: "It is striking that not one of these statutes [regarding trusts and industrial combinations] aims especially at securing publicity regarding the business of the large industrial combinations, through detailed reports, in order that the publicity itself may prove to be a remedial measure."

Both problems could also have been solved by eliminating par value, which would have created transparency in rates of return as a function of real assets and earnings rather than as a function of an arbitrary number like par value. It also would have discouraged investors from making even the rough equations they did between nominal value and economic value. But even though New York authorized corporations to issue no-par stock as early as 1912, par value retained significance until the Depression. Meanwhile, promoters and financiers dumped their stock on the public while their corporations were still able to make dividend payments and the stock price was high. Mandatory disclosure was a solution for the future.[41]

TRANSCENDENTAL VALUE
The Legal Origins of Valuation

The entire question of overcapitalization turned on how one determined the value of the corporation. In order to figure out whether a corporation was overcapitalized, one had to assume that there was a reasonably determinate way of valuing it. If not, valuation would be subjective and leave no basis for judging the legitimacy of a corporation's capitalization.

The valuation concept that underlies my discussion so far is the legal model that had existed for decades. This was the implicit starting point for most public debates about overcapitalization and it was the model that continued to dominate in the courts. The legal model defined the value of the corporation as being the cost of its assets, although one can sometimes see statements in judicial opinions suggesting that intangible future profits and goodwill might have some bearing on value. But economic concepts like future profits and goodwill played little role in regulatory discussions of overcapitalization for the first decade of the century.[42]

There are several reasons why the legal model dominated. The first, and simplest, was the novelty of the problem. While railroad stocks had been trading for a long time, industrial stocks were rarely publicly traded before the merger wave. The merger wave brought large numbers of industrial stocks to market for the first time, creating a new need for sophisticated methods of valuing the stock of public companies. Going-concern value, the value of future profits and goodwill, was hard to determine, especially in a context where accounting was relatively undeveloped and promoters had strong financial incentives to cheat. Few economists had thought much about the matter. Virtually none had a ready way of figuring out going-concern value with any precision, especially when corporations did not disclose much financial information. Businessmen seemed to have less of a problem determining value, which might suggest a disparity in the comfort levels of those trying to create a science and those engaged in actual practice.[43]

Legal methods of determining the value of corporate capital had been around for decades, designed for the purpose of assessing whether corporations had received cash or property equal to the par values of their stock. Thus, at a time when even economists treated nominal value as having some meaning, the law's emphasis on the cash value of assets provided at least the parameters of a ready test. Law was the touchstone because it provided some developed method of valuation. The problem was that the legal solutions had been developed to address different problems in different contexts. They simply did not address the problem of heavily capitalized combinations at all. And even the legal solutions were full of ambiguities. As late as 1930, David Dodd wrote that when it came to valuing stock, judicial definitions were not helpful because "the concepts of value which the court itself entertains are too vague to permit of a nice definition."

> In defining the word "value" for the purposes of deciding whether stock has been watered, courts frequently do nothing but repeat the qualifying adjectives that are used in the statutes and constitutions of the various states. These statutory definitions include such phrases as "reasonable value," "full value," "cash value," "fair valuation," "fair value," "actual value," "real value," "true money value," "real present cash value," and other similar expressions. Terms such as these are merely question-begging phrases and really add nothing to the mere word "value."

Statutes provided no helpful definitions of value. And courts repeated "the meaningless phrases which have become current in all types of judicial valuation." But economists had yet to develop a consensus of their own and legal tests were readily available.[44]

The problem of valuing future profits and goodwill became even more complex when the corporation to be capitalized was a new combination that had not yet engaged in any business. Of course the individual plants had a track record, so one could try to determine the going-concern value for each, add them together and come up with a value for the new combination. One still had the problem of how to calculate going-concern value for the individual plants. And this method did not take account of any additional value, like monopoly rents or increased productive efficiency, that might be created by the combination itself.

Capitalizing future profits was a theoretically sound method. Courts and lawmakers understood the value of intangibles like goodwill and future profits, but were skeptical of their susceptibility to precise valuation and their relevance to capitalization at the time of formation. Their doubts were exacerbated by conflicts of interest between the combination's future shareholders and the directors and promoters hoping to profit by selling the stock to them. Promoters had every incentive to overcapitalize and everybody knew it. So the more indeterminate the valuation method, the more dubious it was in the eyes of the courts. The crude ways promoters typically determined value did not help their credibility, either. Simply issuing common stock in amounts equal to, double, triple, or sometimes greater multiples of the value of a new company's physical assets could hardly have provided the reassurance of integrity that courts and lawmakers needed. As a result, while many courts, including those of New Jersey, California, Illinois and New York, allowed capitalized earnings to be introduced into litigation concerning overcapitalization, the general standard was the reasonableness of the estimate. The burden of proof fell on promoters and directors. It appears clear that, no matter what factors courts ultimately looked to, their rhetoric, while vague and imprecise, supported conservative approaches to valuation.[45]

Finally, some of the blame for the general mistrust of valuing intangibles can be placed on the first big corporations and consumers of water, the railroads. The railroads presented two special problems that colored discussions of overcapitalization. First, successful railroads could charge monopoly prices. Using the pricing practices of known monopolies as the basis for valuation would defeat the purpose of capitalizing earnings to identify monopolies. Second, railroad rate behavior in the competitive environment of the late nineteenth century provided unreliable data for economists trying to determine an average return on capital from which they could then discover monopoly pricing.

Valuation was the central problem underlying the capitalization debate, but determining value required one to look through a kaleidoscope. Even as economists developed more refined theories and methods of valuation, the problem persisted well into the twentieth century. For now, let us look at the law and economics of *fin de siècle* corporate valuation.

The Economists

Economists of the era were divided in their approaches to valuation. While many studied trusts and finance, few discussed the matter of valuation, and certainly not in any systematic manner. This is surprising, since all of them expressed opinions about overcapitalization. It is hard to understand how they could have concluded that overcapitalization was a problem without some idea of value. Only Meade and Fisher clearly identified their preferred valuation methods.[46]

There were several reasons economists did not spend much time on the technical problems of corporate valuation. First, overcapitalization had historically been a legal issue. The law created the subject, and the law was where it received the most attention. The law's conservative approach had a significant impact on economic thought. As Henry Steele Commager explained the economics of the late nineteenth century, "postwar economists united with jurists to insist that the laws applicable in the past to real property were no less valid for intangible property" instead of taking account of the "widespread use of the corporate device." Second, academic economists were deeply interested in the trust problem, competition and the growth of big business. But many simply assumed overcapitalization because of promoters' incentives. Perhaps too, the lack of enough publicly available information to permit economists to evaluate whether corporations were overcapitalized frustrated their efforts, but this would have been no block to theory and enough data could probably have been drawn from the *Commercial & Financial Chronicle*. It appears that most economists accepted traditional concepts of valuation, especially legal concepts, as a default, because they were there.[47]

Another possible reason for the absence of an economic consensus on financial valuation is that it was a relatively new issue. As John R. Commons explained, valuation had a long history in the law. But academic economists were still struggling with the theoretical concept of value. Besides, the demand for practical application of valuation principles to corporations and corporate stock was very recent. Ralph Badger, a fan of capitalized earnings, noted in the introduction to his book, *Valuation of Industrial Securities*: "The writer realizes that he is entering a somewhat new field. . . . [T]he infinite variety of conditions which surrounds security valuation makes it difficult to lay down rules susceptible of universal application." And this was in 1925. The issue of valuation was that much newer and more complex at the turn of the century. There had not been enough time for any consensus to develop.[48]

The strong influence of legal concepts of valuation on economic thinking is particularly notable in an age in which economists were writing furiously to establish the groundwork of the new science of economics and finance. Paul-Joseph Esquerre, in his remarkable 1914 book on accounting, stated that accounting theory evolved from, among other things, "the application of the principles expressed by judicial decisions in litigation brought about through business relations, from the doctrines of the law merchant, of the common law, and of modern statutes." Economists generally assumed the legal methodology, even as they worked to develop their own theories of value.[49]

One might, therefore, dismiss the ideas of economists in favor of the practices of businessmen, lawyers and financiers who were putting the combinations together. But this would distort history. For it was the academics like Meade, Ripley, Jenks, Hadley, Ely and Fisher who advised the commissions, counseled presidents and senators, and testified before Congress. Their influence drove the shape and pace of public policy and legislation. The practitioners went on creating modern finance, but they did so against a background of regulatory debates that were shaped by academics.

To obtain a more nuanced understanding of the problem of valuation in the arena of public policy, we need to look at the ideas of some of the more prominent economists who wrote on the trust issue. It is clear that they generally favored the more conservative legal approaches to valuation. Most merger era economists did not seem to appreciate the way the trust debate was complicated by a notion of overcapitalization grounded in legal precedent that had developed for other purposes. A very few, like Meade, advocated economically sound methods of valuation apart from any legal provenance. If courts and lawmakers had followed these approaches, there would have been no overcapitalization problem because overcapitalization would have become a meaningless concept. The legal issues addressed by antitrust and securities regulation in the early twentieth century would have likely been very different.

Meade was a pragmatist. He unambiguously supported the capitalized earnings approach. In fact he explicitly rejected valuation based on physical assets. Like many of the other new economists he began with the proposition that "value is a social fact." As a result, "to identify it with cost is impossible." Oddly, he continued to place significance on par value despite his otherwise economic understanding of corporate finance, suggesting that even his ultimate touchstone was legal. Overcapitalization, according to Meade, was the difference between the face value of a corporation's securities and its capitalized earnings. "Proper capitalization" was achieved when the market value of a corporation's securities was equal to its par value. As he put it, "[t]he object of every corporate management should be to make its shares worth at all times their face value." There were two obvious difficulties in applying this definition to the trust problem. First, it was the role of economics to determine whether economic value was equal to par value, and economics did not have an answer. Second, corporations had no market value at the time their capitalizations had to be determined. Meade's solution was for the corporation to maintain proper capitalization by issuing more stock if market value rose above par and repurchasing it if the opposite were true.[50]

Other economists ranged from equivocal to conservative when it came to the subject of capitalization based on future earnings. William Z. Ripley, whose omnipresence in the trust debates rivaled that of Jeremiah Jenks, was unimpressed by arguments that capitalizing earnings was necessary to adjust reward to risk. Most of the trusts' permanent capital, claimed Ripley, came from debt. Stockholders did not provide the real risk capital and therefore were not entitled to the returns of risk takers.

Most of Ripley's valuation work was devoted to the specific problems of railroads and public service companies, but even when he wrote about industrials he remained skeptical of capitalizing earnings. He accepted its economic logic, but was highly sensitive to its potential for abuse. He also worried that the "extreme complexity" of the problem did not provide easy solutions. In the end, he punted: "For all classes of corporations," he wrote, the "ultimate remedy . . . must come from courts and legislatures."[51]

If Ripley equivocated in 1905, his opposition to capitalized earnings grew more pointed during the next decade. And even if one could interpret his writings in 1915 to potentially include capitalized earnings, he was quite explicit in his opposition by the mid-1920s. In his 1926 classic, *Main Street and Wall Street*, he warned his readers: "Ware of a company with a huge item of goodwill on its balance sheet!" While goodwill "theoretically" represented capitalized earnings, in truth it was "the outward expression of inward unsubstantiality." Hearkening back to "the good old days of trusts," he recalled the water flooding balance sheets of the time that equaled or exceeded a corporation's "real possessions." Affected by the memory of the "bitter experience" created by that watered stock, "the trend among the better sort of corporations has been in the direction of elimination of this water." Ripley understood the economic logic behind capitalized earnings, but he never trusted it in practice.[52]

Jeremiah Jenks understood the distinction between legal and business valuation, between the cash value of assets and capitalized earnings. Jenks understood that capitalizing earnings under normal economic conditions would, at least in theory, approximate the cash value of assets taken as a whole. But he warned that supernormal earnings could distort this equation. High valuation might be justified if high returns were the result of unusual economic prosperity or superior management. But monopoly power could also generate supernormal returns and thus lead to high capitalization. Periods of prosperity were fleeting. A sustained normal rate of return on high capitalization usually indicated monopoly power. In Jenks's view, businesses preferred to capitalize earnings in order to hide their monopoly power in the water. He had "no doubt" that high capitalization put pressure on managers to raise prices in order to make dividend payments.

Jenks characteristically favored a solution that did not commit him to choose a valuation methodology. He simply called for promoters to disclose their valuations of assets brought into their combinations, together with enough information to permit investors to make their own estimates. Yet he worked with Congress in drafting laws for Puerto Rico that mandated actual cash valuation in its corporation law.[53]

As one can readily see, economists were caught between the pragmatic problems of overcapitalization and the theoretical issues that had to be resolved in order to determine whether it really was a problem. The best one can say is that leading economists of the period generally accepted the legal method of physical valuation and the legal definition of overcapitalization as the bases for their analyses of the antitrust issue. Traditional legal concepts validated the belief that overcapitalization was indeed a problem. It was not until the 1930s that economists converged on earnings and cash flow valuations and the problem began to go away.[54]

A few words from a contemporary professional appraiser reinforces the conclusion that the problem of valuation was far more practical than theoretical and that pragmatism was rooted in legal ideas of value. Herbert G. Stockwell, president of the Audit and Appraisement Company of America, described the object of an appraisement as nothing more than ascertaining "the true position of a business by estimating the amount of cash which would be realized if the business were closed out and the assets converted into cash." Stockwell realized that valuing a going concern led to other considerations, like determining the value of a plant to the ongoing business. By this he meant cost less depreciation, again a conservative, cost-based approach.

But Stockwell recognized the possibility of efficiency gains, and thus at least implicitly the need for capitalizing earnings. In an efficient combination, the consolidated corporation's earnings should be more than the earnings of the individual components, provided that the latter were not overpriced. The problem was with the promoters. Honest promoters would hire appraisers, who would value each plant using cash-based valuation methods together with an audit of the books. Appraisers probably had little influence in the merger wave because, as Stockwell observed, the average promoter was unlikely to retain an appraiser.[55]

The Courts and Value Revisited

I have spent a fair amount of time searching for a consensus understanding of value among economists because value was, after all, an economic issue. But we have seen little agreement except for a pronounced tendency toward legal conservatism. That conservatism was, as we saw in the case of New Jersey as well as other states, the governing principle of state courts that were called upon to make legal determinations of overcapitalization.

We have also seen that judicial pronouncements mattered little to promoters. While they might be made more frequently in other contexts, such as taxation and eminent domain, judicial involvement in corporate matters of overcapitalization generally was confined to cases of corporate bankruptcy. But troubled combinations usually wound up in reorganization or were consolidated into another combination, from which creditors would have emerged with securities, instead of undergoing liquidation, where creditors' recovery might depend upon proceeding against promoters' personal assets. It was also quite rare for stockholders who purchased their stock from promoters to sue, for, as one authority noted, their position was "hopeless." Based on an exhaustive review of judicial methods of valuation in the case law, David Dodd concluded that it "has not been possible to subject the truth or falsity of the ... charges against stock watering to quantitative demonstration."[56]

In contrast to the goals of theoretical economists, the purpose of valuation in the courts was the very practical one of deciding whether a corporation's paid-in capital was worth the amount it represented itself to be. While the "average businessman" believed that capitalizing earnings was the most appropriate method of valuing corporate stock, courts were more hesitant to adopt that method. In fact, New Jersey's famous "Seven Sisters Act" of 1913 expressly prohibited valuation using capitalized earnings.

The problem was that the property corporations bought with their stock typically was unique and hard to value, and this was even more true for entire corporations than for a patent or a copper mine. Often courts paid lip service to capitalizing prospective earnings, leaving going-concern value as the theoretical standard, but they did not explain how to determine it. Perhaps one of the most important factors, according to Dodd, was the cost of the asset to the promoters, which served as a proxy for value. But if the question was overcapitalization, that is, the overvaluation of assets, the cost to promoters had limited utility.

Ultimately it did not matter much because courts rarely engaged in appraisal. A more common legal technique they used when confronted with overcapitalization was to put the burden of proof on the promoters to establish value. If the promoters failed to prove their firm's value, they lost the case. This approach allowed the court to react to evidence rather than to engage in the valuation process itself.

The New Jersey cases of *See* and *Donald* show that the courts allowed for the theoretical possibility of valuing goodwill or prospective earnings (sometimes, as in *See*, using the terms interchangeably). At the same time, they were reluctant to attribute goodwill value to new combinations. The predominant judicial approach to valuation was precisely that found by Commons over the course of the history of Anglo-American jurisprudence. Courts would accept the directors' valuations of corporate assets as long as they were reasonable.[57]

Legislative Approaches to Value

We are back to precisely the concept of valuation with which we began. The work of legislative bodies did not contribute much to an understanding of valuation, but it is worth spending a few moments on the views of two public bodies that mattered, the United States Industrial Commission and the United States Congress, because it is from them that policy emanated. The Industrial Commission was appointed by an unambiguously pro-business administration. Congress, while also dominated by Republicans, had to answer to broader constituencies and was more progressive in its outlook. But the Commission and Congress arrived at the same basic conclusions.

The Industrial Commission produced nineteen volumes of testimony and reports covering a wide range of issues over a period of five years. Many of those testifying were forthright and, indeed, proud of what they had accomplished, so their words have the ring of credibility. Moreover, the Commission's staff performed thorough surveys of the relevant literature, including cases. So the Commission's understanding of actual practice gives us another perspective on the issue. Although its most extensive commentary on capitalization was focused on railroads, the Commission observed that the problem of overcapitalization was also widespread in industrial combinations, and that the same issues existed in both.

The Commission recognized that "the popular theory" of valuation was the cash value of assets approach, which included capitalized earnings. It noted that this approach seemed to be fair at first blush. But sometimes this method would either overstate or understate capitalization. Capitalization would be too high when a corporation was characterized by inefficiency and waste, and too low in cases of unusually efficient management. The Commission thought inadequate capitalization would typically result from using the original cost of assets and that particularly skillful and efficient management should be rewarded by higher capitalization.

The Commission noted the railroads' preference for capitalizing earnings. The "two legitimate arguments" the railroads gave to support this practice were that it was the best way to reward risk and that the greater quantity of salable shares helped raise relatively cheap working capital. The Commission dismissed the first argument as nonsense, echoing Ripley's belief that most recent railroad construction involved very little shareholder risk. It was more persuaded by the idea that using capitalized earnings to produce higher valuations gave the railroads a way to obtain working capital by selling more securities. But it also recognized that railroad franchises were considered to be perfectly good collateral that could be used for commercial borrowing to obtain the necessary working capital.

The biggest and, to the Commission, the most important objection to capitalizing earnings was that it "obscures the relation between rates, wages, and profits," allowing corporations to reap "exorbitant profits." The Commission insisted upon drawing limits to capitalizing earnings in order to avoid this problem. It also showed some interest in the reproduction cost method of valuation. But at least one Supreme Court case held that reproduction cost by itself was inadequate because it failed to account for goodwill.

The Commission's conclusion is confused and confusing. Following the Supreme Court, it wrote that the only fair way to determine capitalization was to use a combination of methods that included original cost, the cost of improvements, the market value of the corporation's securities, reproduction cost and earning capacity. To this it added a technique used by economist Henry C. Adams to determine the "franchise value" of railroads. Adams took net earnings, subtracted the cost of capital and capitalized the balance at an appropriate discount rate. Having rejected economically sound methods of going-concern valuation in favor of the Supreme Court's more conservative approach, the Commission wrote of Adams's technique: "This method of valuation would seem to give the true basis of capitalization." It appears that after doing everything it possibly could to shy away from capitalizing earnings, the Commission seemed to endorse exactly that approach, using a formula that could even approximate goodwill. One can only conclude that the Commission was as uncertain about the appropriate basis for capitalization as everyone else.[58]

For its part, Congress was quite certain that capitalizing earnings was inappropriate. The Committee Report on the Littlefield bill of 1903, which was aimed largely at preventing overcapitalization, noted that while "it is undeniable that the dividend paid upon a stock or the interest paid upon a bond largely determines its market value, it by no means follows that capitalization can be based upon earning capacity." The committee's logic reflected Jenks's thinking as well as that of Attorney General Philander Knox. Capitalizing earnings exaggerated the importance of timing. Corporate profits were higher in good times, consumers paid higher prices, and a corporation capitalized under such circumstances would be overcapitalized when the economic situation normalized and overall prices fell. But corporations that had been capitalized during those good times would have to keep charging higher prices in order to meet their interest and dividend payments. "By capitalizing the profits you deliver the public bound hand and foot to the capitalist, whom they must continue to serve that he may receive the stipulated reward." The records of the House debates reveal a similar attitude.[59]

⋙⋘

After a long and inconclusive search for the principles of valuation that would provide a common basis both for resolving the overcapitalization debate and for assessing the extent of the problem, all we can conclude is that promoters had significant incentives to overcapitalize corporations and sophisticated economists, as well as courts and lawmakers, were highly sensitive to this fact. Modern business and financial conditions made it unlikely that promoters would ever be called to account except by the market, and more often than not they would have already unloaded all or most of their stock by the time the market could force them to a reckoning. Legal valuation methods that were developed to deal with different economic problems remained the touchstone. We are left with no choice but to take the overcapitalization debate on its own inconclusive terms.

Born of business's desire to cooperate, New Jersey's license to promoters for overcapitalizing and manufacturing stock gave them the tools they needed to create the giant modern corporation. Their ability to realize these profits depended upon enough surplus capital and a sufficient population of potential investors. This is where corporate promoters introduced the new middle class to the stock market, and it is here that both investor and market were transformed.

FOUR

THE NEW PROPERTY

FROM DEPRESSION TO PROSPERITY

Eighteen ninety-three was the year of the great Columbian Exposition in Chicago, a corporeal celebration of more than sixty years of industrial success. It was also a year of financial panic, a year followed by a long and dismal depression that was then perhaps the worst in the nation's history. Crop prices were low, hundreds of banks and thousands of businesses failed, railroads continued their slide into bankruptcy and almost four million Americans were out of work. Business retrenched and farmers had to pay off their mortgages or sell their farms. The American gold supply hovered frighteningly close to depletion and a currency crisis ensued, leading the federal government, with significant controversy, to rely upon J. P. Morgan to bail out the nation and restore its gold reserves.

Even if money had been available for investment, there were other reasons for investors to be cautious. The great monetary debate that followed the Civil War was reaching fever pitch with the 1896 presidential contest between William Jennings Bryan and William McKinley. Eastern "gold bugs" had reason to fear that the champions of free coinage and inflation would prevail as Bryan, the Boy Orator of the Platte, gained support across the nation. The market remained lackluster for much of the middle of the decade, except for recurrent destabilizations due to periodic bear raids and Wall Street's fear of Bryan. Matters were not helped by the approaching war with Spain, and anxious investors remained on the sidelines.[1]

But all was not bleak for finance. Eighteen ninety-six brought McKinley's election and, with it, the likelihood of a continued gold standard. (Sound money was assured with McKinley's reelection in 1900.) An immediate drop in interest rates followed, freeing up cash. Matters were stirring on the broader economic front as well. As Alexander D. Noyes, perhaps the most prolific financial observer of the time, wrote, the nation was poised "to enter upon a very remarkable chapter in American finance." This chapter entailed "such reversal of its position by the United States that, instead of the crippled industrial and financial state of 1894, with the country's principal industries declining, its great corporations drifting into bankruptcy, and its Government forced to borrow on usurious terms from Europe ... there was presented, in the short space of half a dozen years, a community whose prosperity had become the wonder of the outside world." Europeans had reason to fear a flood of American goods that would threaten their own industries and economic well-being. In short, the American economy exploded at the end of the nineteenth century, igniting the chain reaction of corporate combination.[2]

The light on the horizon was reflected by gold and grain. World gold production registered modest increases during the 1890s with output 28 percent higher in 1896 than in 1893 and 51 percent higher in 1899 than three years earlier. One result of this dramatic rise was increasing bank gold reserves that expanded their loan capacities. This increased production of gold would not alone have helped the American economy. But America, more than any other nation, received the lion's share of the new gold. The reason was that America increasingly supplied the world's grain and other commodities.

World commodity prices generally hit their nadir by around 1896. The American wheat crop that year, while small, had begun to show increased prices, but not enough to affect the overall level of economic well-being. Then came the crops of 1897 and 1898, among the largest ever. Wheat crops in India failed, transforming that nation from a world exporter to a wheat importer. The Russian, French, Austrian and Balkan crops failed too in 1897, dropping European production by at least 30 percent. Europe's demand for food led to large increases in American exports at very high prices, aided by "wild speculation on the Chicago Board of Trade." Wheat prices rose about 40 percent between 1897 and 1900. Corn, oats and cotton also boomed, with 1900 cotton prices increasing 32 percent over 1897. Other commodities, like iron, also soared, as the demand for buildings, railroads and industrial equipment that had been suppressed during the depression was released with the new return to prosperity. Iron prices in 1900 were a full 65 percent higher than had prevailed only two and a half years before. The result was a dramatic increase in the nation's gold reserves.[3]

The agricultural and commodity boom stimulated business. Newly prosperous farmers bought supplies they had held back on during the years of depression, and businesses began investing not only to build up the necessary inventory but to expand their productive capacities as well. Wages increased toward the end of the century and bank clearings more than doubled between 1894 and 1899, signaling the return to prosperity. War with Spain, when it came in April 1898, lifted employment as the unemployed went to work replacing those who had gone to fight in Cuba. American industrial exports to Europe doubled between 1893 and 1899. Money in circulation reached a peak by early 1900. Capital surplus was high.

Money was looking for places to go. Ray Stannard Baker noted that, while a boom was brewing on Wall Street, "still there were not stocks enough to supply the demand, and idle capital still sought investment." Prices of the so-called Granger railroads began to climb, with other railroad stocks increasing along with them, despite the fact that approximately 40 percent of American roads were in receivership. The increase in railroad stocks produced a good year for the market in 1897 and was followed by a boost in the new industrial stocks in 1898 as the economic recovery got seriously under way and the quick victory against Spain inspired American optimism.

Edward Meade, writing at the time, noted that "the people believed that good times and high prices had come to stay, and the national feeling found instant expression in the quotations of securities." The boom in the market was sporadic at first, with a downturn as the war approached and a short-lived crash in 1899 when the Transvaal declared war on Great Britain. The speculative bubble that had built up, and continued to build as the century turned, burst with the Northern Pacific corner in 1901. But money was still sitting around, waiting to be invested.[4]

THE MODERN MARKET

The modern stock market developed in fits and starts. Most investors generally looked upon buying common stock simply as gambling until well into the second decade of the twentieth century. Andrew Carnegie was no exception. Almost all of the owners who sold their companies into the U.S. Steel trust in 1901 took the risk of being paid with a combination of preferred stock, based mostly on tangible asset value, and watered common stock, based solely on the combination's anticipated earnings. Not Carnegie. He insisted on his payment of $217.8 million in the form of U.S. Steel first mortgage bonds.

The average investor at the turn of the century avoided common and even preferred stock except during periods of fevered speculation like the spring of 1901, which abruptly ended with the stock market–roiling battle between James Hill and E. H. Harriman for control of the Northern Pacific Railroad. Financial advice columns continually cautioned him (and often her) to stay away from stock. Although the get-rich-quick bug of the merger wave led many to ignore their advice, investment columns typically warned would-be stockholders that the lack of reliable corporate financial information was reason enough to stay away from stock, except for the stock of railroads, for which some form of information was regularly provided. And there was the intrinsically unstable nature of a market in which professionals regularly launched bear raids and other manipulative tactics to move prices to their profit. Finally, the investment columns warned the public of the dangers of watered stock and advised them to keep away from investments that seemed to promise unusually large returns.

Women investors in particular were advised to look after the conservation of their principal as the best investment strategy and only to invest where they were likely to receive average returns. And if you must buy stock, the papers warned, invest only in stocks with good dividend records, focus on railroads and keep away from industrials. *The Wall Street Journal* warned investors in 1899 to worry about the safety of their principal rather than their rate of return. "We occasionally receive inquiries as to whether there is any way of telling whether a stock or bond can be regarded as a safe investment. ... As a general rule stocks should not be regarded as an investment, because it is optional with the management of a company whether it pays a dividend or not.... Therefore the outside investor should always take bonds instead of stock."[5]

Investment advice came from all corners of society. Preaching from the pulpit on the Sunday following the Northern Pacific corner, the Reverend Daniel H. Overton of Brooklyn's Greene Avenue Presbyterian Church cautioned his flock: "The real value of stock in any concern is in its security and in its dividend paying power, the latter, perhaps, being the greater standard." In any event, buying securities was an activity primarily engaged in by citizens of the Northeast because Southerners and Westerners tended to put their surplus capital into land. But this was changing by 1904.[6]

The wealthy were just like the rest of Americans. *The Wall Street Journal* reported that even the richest citizens, who had made their fortunes by taking great risks, protected those fortunes by investing in railroad bonds and banks. Those who could not afford to take risks should follow the example of the wealthy and invest safely. Conservative investors were sufficiently skeptical of corporate securities of all types that the New York State Savings Bank Association actively opposed proposed legislation to permit savings banks to invest in "first class" railroad bonds, the most conservative corporate investments the nation had to offer.[7]

Throughout this first stage of the market's development, the bull market of the merger wave, it remained clear to most knowledgeable people that the stock market was not for everyone. The basic theme of investment advice to ordinary people continued to be to keep their money in savings banks or, if they had to invest, to invest in solid first mortgage bonds. In responding to a letter written in 1900 from "A Poor Man," a young man who had inquired whether the *Times* would recommend that he invest his savings in the stock market, the *Times*'s unequivocal answer was "no." Stock market speculation was no better than "the races or the faro table." Concern for principal was the *Times*'s counsel, as it was the mantra of most investment advice columns. Preserving principal meant, as the *Times* told the "Poor Man," putting his money in savings banks, at least until he had money enough that he could afford to lose.

Caution was thrown to the wind in speculative periods, especially between 1900 and 1901 and again between 1905 and 1907. Among the big losers in the Northern Pacific corner were "people of limited means" who had been drawn into the market by the prospect of quick riches, but they soon returned. Investment advice also blew with the winds of Wall Street. On March 30, 1901, as the speculative bubble was just over a month away from bursting, even the conservative *Wall Street Journal* tentatively approved of speculation. For years before (and years after) the *Journal* preached the sermon of caution quoted above. But now it encouraged speculation, albeit cautiously, at least for those who knew enough about an industry or a company. "Blind speculation is folly, but there is such a thing as intelligent speculation in industrial stocks."

The advice did not hold. After the market collapsed in May, the *Journal* turned back to bond investments as the appropriate posture, and did its best to take advantage of its conservatism. In August 1901 its editors wrote rather smugly that "the people at large are giving more thought than ever before to the question of investing their money wisely.... This is shown in the swelling volume of subscriptions to the Wall Street Journal." By December 1901 the *Journal* clearly was back to its old advice; protect principal and accept lower returns.

Very gradually, as one reads the investment advice columns, one sees a slow but increasing chorus touting industrial stocks as appropriate investments. The *Journal* anticipated this shift as early as 1901, when during the bull market it editorialized that "It is as certain as anything in the future that industrial securities will form the principal medium for speculation in this country." With the convergence of investment and speculation in common stock ownership at the beginning of the second decade, the entire character of American corporate capitalism began to change.[8]

The end of the merger wave provided a rough lesson for both the new investors and the combinations in which they invested. The giant overcapitalized combinations had assumed that when they needed working capital they could always turn to the short-term credit markets. This proved not to be the case, at least not at reasonable interest rates. New England Cotton Yarn, which had paid a 7 percent dividend, suddenly in need of affordable cash, had to issue a capital call to its stockholders. U.S. Steel stopped dividend payments altogether. More of the new combinations faltered. The highly respected Pennsylvania Railroad had to raise cash in 1903 by publicly issuing stock for a bargain price that was $37 below the market price of its outstanding stock. U.S. Steel tried to float $50 million in bonds. There were no takers. The stock prices of the great combinations tanked.[9]

John Moody reprinted a 1903 chart from *The Wall Street Journal* showing that the hundred largest industrials lost a total market value of almost $1.8 billion from "the high prices of the boom" (which presumably meant 1901) with none of the hundred losing less than $1 million. U.S. Steel common dropped from an aggregate market value of $508.5 million to $216.1 million and its preferred fell from $430 million to $192 million. Stock prices depended on dividends. That was the return investors expected.[10]

The market made a quick recovery that would plateau at the beginning of 1906. Small investors may have been hurt, but they had also learned. As early as the months following the Panic of 1907, it appeared that the big bargain hunters on Wall Street were not the rich professionals but the small investors. The *New York Times* noted that many women were among the bargain hunters, since women "never enter the market until it is at its lowest ebb." By 1908, turnover on the New York Stock Exchange had dropped to a still very high 100 percent from over 200 percent during several of the preceding years. This suggests, as I will explore in detail in Chapter Eight, that professional speculators were moving aside as smaller investors, who were beginning to buy speculative securities, were becoming more prominent actors in the market.[11]

What had happened to turn the focus of American business from its production of goods and services to the stock market? Although it will take the rest of this book to answer the question, this chapter describes the foundation of the transformation.

SOCIALIZING THE MARKET
Preserving American Ideals

One of the most important consequences of the rise in American investing during the first decade of the twentieth century was the way that owning stock was treated as creating a new opportunity for the average person to express his or her individualism in American economic life. Sometimes this was expressed by Progressive thinkers trying to make sense of the new society in terms of older ideas. Sometimes it came in the exhortations of conservative businessmen and politicians who were fighting to stave off the challenges of the newly displaced, which showed most clearly in episodic and occasionally bloody labor unrest. Whatever its source or the motivations of the speakers, Americans of all political viewpoints worried that the giant trusts were squeezing out the individual entrepreneur, transforming worker-owners into wage laborers and destroying the very nature of private property upon which American individualism and, with it, American democracy were built. Many saw the threat of creeping socialism and its challenge to private property as quite real. But even as early as the end of the nineteenth century, those who were most concerned with the disappearance of individualism could foresee ways in which the growth of giant corporate combinations created a chance for every American to own a piece of the new America.

Most Americans, and especially the members of the new middle class, simply were trying to figure out what was happening around them and how to find their places in the new society. Historian Robert Wiebe describes the Progressive Era as a time when "the ambition of the new middle class [was] to fulfill its destiny through bureaucratic means," noting that the Progressive mind attributed "omnipotence to abstractions." Richard Hofstadter describes "the central theme" of Progressivism as "the complaint of the unorganized against the consequences of organization." Either way, the bureaucracy of the corporate world provided a path to professional success, increased wealth and middle-class comfort. And the abstractions of Wall Street, made tangible in the form of stock, provided the individual with a path not only to achieving wealth but also to finding a place in this new America.[12]

What was true of the middle class may have become increasingly true, if on a smaller scale, of wage earners. Despite their uncertain legal status, labor unions began to grow after the Civil War, accelerating through the 1880s before declining and then gaining real strength after the depression of the middle 1890s. The average American worker found his job as a part of the new industrial machinery, and much of his autonomy as a worker absorbed by a labor organization. Whatever individuality the worker previously had in his efforts to make a living was melded into collectivity at both ends.

The United States Industrial Commission expressed concern with the worker's loss of control over his working life in 1902, observing that democracy and self-governance were only learned by practice, and the man who was accustomed to "absolute submission in industry" carried the consequences of that submissive posture into civic life. There was some reason to seek a solution in the stock market. "The philanthropic hope has not quite disappeared that workingmen will attain a share in their industrial government by becoming stockholders." But the Industrial Commission had little faith in this possibility, suggesting that organized labor was the only real potential counterbalance for the working man against corporate power and concluding that, "in view of the enormous and increasing size of the units of industrial control, any expectation of an effective participation of wage-earners in the government of the great industries by any method based on their individual ownership of shares of the capital is chimerical." The Commission undoubtedly was right in its gloomy forecast from a governance perspective. But there was no reason to think that even the wage earner was precluded from individual financial participation in the new collective economic life by means of share ownership.[13]

Attentive Americans demonstrated a growing understanding that the stock market was the future of America, and with this perception came the belief that the stock market had to be made safe for democracy. Market reforms were needed that demanded the kind of honesty and disclosure necessary to bring small investors like "A Poor Man" into the market. One writer questioned: "Is there not something radically wrong with our system which allows the millionaire to increase his millions by hundreds per cent, while the small capitalist is confined to a trifle of interest from savings banks or investments which are of questionable value?" The writer expressed his hope that honest markets could open up investment in corporate stock to "the workingmen and the general public, furnishing the means for their development." It was clear that the time had come for the stock market to fulfill the role in urban, corporate America that land had played in the early years of the republic.[14]

Many contemporary thinkers, and especially those supportive of the new corporate economy, encouraged stockholding as a reimagining of the Jeffersonian ideal. Writing in *The American Law Review* in 1905, conservative federal judge and trust activist Peter S. Grosscup said that the principal problem with trusts was that they had taken property away from working Americans. While Grosscup spoke and wrote mostly in favor of industrial consolidation, he noted that the American people, raised in a culture of proprietorship, had come to realize that they did not own their businesses any more. This was the real trust problem, he argued. The giant combinations, the new society of organizations, robbed Americans of the kind of entrepreneurial spirit and individualistic impulse they had enjoyed as farmers and small proprietors. The solution for Grosscup was clear. Ordinary Americans should buy stock in the great trusts, restoring ownership to the people. But this could only happen if corporations were honestly capitalized under a federal incorporation law.

Grosscup extended his argument a year later, addressing not only the problem of the relationship between the individual and corporate property but also the link between stock ownership and civic responsibility. As individuals came to own corporate stock and slowly recaptured the traditional sense of relationship to their property, "corporate ownership more and more will become transactions with people, man with man; and into such relations is breathed always a sense of responsibility, the pride of doing the right thing, a respect for others, and a yearning for that respect that distance cannot command."[15]

Some commentators put the issue in different, but equally traditional, terms. *McClure's Magazine*, editorializing in 1908, reimagined Frederick Jackson Turner's famous thesis of American history, arguing that the old closed physical frontier had been replaced with a new financial one. The *McClure's* editors wrote that the new corporate culture presented "a frontier of civilization," and that it was essential to make investing in securities as safe for the "man of moderate means ... as producing farm-land." Safe investment could only be assured by government regulation, in order "to establish an orderly and safe civilization, where property and enterprise of the individual will be properly protected by the state." These observers linked the new financial economy to the old frontier, and stock to the land, and they also directly tied stock to the same kind of "property and enterprise" that had been valued and protected in the ideal of Jeffersonian America. Some people even took the connection literally. In 1907, a promoter in Nebraska came up with the idea of incorporating and consolidating farms, using exactly the same techniques used by Morgan in creating U.S. Steel.[16]

Replacing Jeffersonian agrarian individualism with stock market individualism came to be a leitmotif of business leaders and can even be seen to have begun to become internalized in the culture. Former comptroller of the currency and later Coolidge vice president, Charles G. Dawes, advising small investors, wrote: "Be self-reliant. Make your own investigation in investments." While the latter phrase simply was good investment advice, the former echoes the great American philosopher of individualism, Ralph Waldo Emerson.

As early as 1899, *The New York Times* implied that investing in securities more or less fulfilled the demands of Locke's labor theory of value. "As soon as a capitalist is willing to be troubled further, as soon as he begins to take a personal interest in his investment, and to give his personal attention to look-

ing after it, he ceases to be a mere capitalist, and his return from his investment becomes, not merely the interest on his money, but also something in
the nature of wages for his own services in the way of superintendence."[17]

The idea that American individualism and the virtue of private property were best served by turning Americans into stockholders had a number
of goals behind it. There was the more or less abstract goal of maintaining
traditional American values, a Jeffersonian ideal of individualism and self-
reliance within the constraints of collective industrial society. Combined
with this was the hope that if Americans owned corporate stock they would
maintain the kind of stake in society that would help to cure the ills of industrialization, urbanization and labor unrest.

Investment as Civic Obligation

Broad-based stock ownership was seen as a way of building the strength of the
American economy and preventing class warfare between labor and capital.
Leading businessmen encouraged American investors to take greater financial risks in order to maintain national greatness. Ownership was not just a
matter of individualism; it was an obligation of citizenship. Frank Vanderlip,
vice president of the National City Bank, gave a speech in October 1904
describing France as "a nation grown rich by thrift, a nation whose economy
has become a disease, and in the growth of it all initiative for new accomplishment has been lost." Millions of Frenchmen held investments, but they
invested almost wholly in railroads and state enterprises, the safest sort of
investments and not the type to stimulate the growth of a great capitalist
economy. *The Wall Street Journal*, while withholding judgment on France,
agreed there was no doubt "that economy in a nation of individuals, as in a
single individual, may be carried to such a point that it becomes a disease,
turning the careful person by degrees into a miser, and the economical nation into a country incapable of great initiative."

Although the *Journal* saw in Americans the "more attractive" trait of
prodigality, a trait it nevertheless insisted had to be curbed, it agreed with
Vanderlip that American money should be put to work by Americans taking
ownership of our great public enterprises. Not only ought we to become a
nation of small investors, advised the *Journal*, but also, as stockholders, we
should take an active interest in the companies in which we invest and assert
control over the corporation's management and policies. "Let the people
own the stocks and bonds of the corporations, and they become true owners
of the country's wealth." At that point, traditional values would return and
there would be no reason to fear socialism.[18]

Widespread stock ownership was the answer. As the *Times* observed in

1908, "it is clear that the theory and practice of Socialism, as it is ordinarily understood, are not likely to make much headway among the two millions of shareholders or among those indirectly interested who understand their own interests."[19]

U.S. Steel put a blend of these ideas into practice in 1903 when it approved a "profit-sharing plan" to permit its workers to buy Steel preferred at a price set slightly below the market. (Three years later, steelworkers were complaining that the stock price was too high and declined to invest.) Carnegie criticized the company for encouraging workers to take risks with their wages, but understood the purpose of the plan. Ownership would keep workers happy, productive and away from strikes.[20]

The more telling social significance of the plan came from the workers themselves. Some union members were concerned that they were compromising their status by buying Steel stock. How could labor betray its class by becoming part of capital? The Amalgamated Association of Iron, Steel, and Tin Workers, perhaps more subtly understanding the opportunity offered by U.S. Steel in the manner characterized by Grosscup and the *Times*, gave them full permission to participate in the plan. Despite the strong ties of union membership and identification with workers, stock ownership was an individual decision to be made individually. By 1908, 35,000 of Steel's 165,000 workers had purchased Steel preferred. By the 1920s, the corporate practice of offering employees stock ownership had become reasonably widespread.[21]

Industrialist and former New York mayor Abram Hewitt, in a farsighted speech in 1890 that *The New York Times* quoted in 1903, argued that "The harmony of capital and labor will be brought about by joint ownership in the instruments of production, and what are called 'trusts' merely afford the machinery by which such ownership can be distributed among the workmen." The *Times* approved: "Self-reliance, the sturdy striving of every man to do what he could to make himself better off in the world, and a disposition to shun a weak reliance upon co-operative devices and nostrums—these were the qualities which MR. HEWITT admired in a man." They were to be realized, among other ways, by increasing opportunities for workers directly to invest in American industry.[22]

The new stock market could even be seen as a permanent solution to the labor problem by eliminating the troubling wage system. United States Labor Commissioner Carroll D. Wright said in 1903 that the essential problem of the wage system was that it treated labor as a commodity to be disposed of at market prices. But workers had begun to demand an opportunity to attain a "higher standard of life." The answer, Wright predicted, was that the wage system would disappear. In its place would arise "profit sharing and cooperative plans. The work [*sic*] people will then acquire the interest of investors, the more capable will rise to their opportunities, and the less worthy will find their level." The *Times* disapprovingly described Wright's vision as "state socialism."[23]

Stock Ownership—The Antidote to Socialism

Class warfare was one thing. The fear of socialism developing through the ownership of concentrated wealth was another, and the new financial economy was tainted with its touch. Although private rather than public, the increasing concentration of corporate control was worrisome. As the American Bar Association opined in 1903, "If the time ever comes when there is only one or a dozen or a hundred corporations controlling the industries of this great land, and having their directors and managers elected by the stockholders, it will be but a very easy step to legislate that those directors and managers shall be elected by the people."[24]

Substantial institutional ownership of securities created its own kind of socialist anxiety. National banks, disregarding the spirit and sometimes the letter of the law, were big investors, and so were insurance companies. But savings banks had also started to acquire large stakes in corporate America. In 1898, New York passed a law permitting savings banks to invest in first-class mortgage bonds issued by railroads that had paid dividends on their common stock consistently for at least ten years. By February 1904, the same class of securities could be used as collateral for government deposits in national banks. By the spring of that year, savings banks owned over $2 billion of securities as investments and held another $350 million as collateral for loans. Insurance companies owned around $2.25 billion in securities as the laws restricting their investments were liberalized in the early years of the new century to permit investment in corporate securities. And these figures do not account for increasing securities ownership by national banks and trust companies as well. Concentrated wealth was becoming a problem in the capital markets as it was in American industry. Business managers were hardly irrational in their concern over the kind of concentrated ownership that could lead to government privatization and socialism.[25]

One report noted in 1905 that "It would be possible to show that practically the entire trust power of the United States, which has been estimated at $20,000,000,000, or one-fifth of the total wealth of the country, is under the direct control of about fifty or sixty men, controlling the policies of the railroads, the leading industries and the leading banks, with influential connections in the chief money markets in Europe." This particular study argued that, despite this concentration of industrial control, these men could not control American capital markets because of the overwhelming power of international markets. But the concern with concentration to which it was responding is hard to miss. It would come to fruition in the Money Trust hearings of 1912 and 1913.[26]

Business leaders, in turn, were worried about the more immediate possibility of direct state ownership of corporate America through the currency system. The fact that the federal government now allowed banks to use railroad bonds as collateral for government deposits created the specter that it would come to own industry. The way this could happen in the ordinary course of banking was simple. Government guaranteed the bank notes secured by these bonds. If the notes defaulted and the government foreclosed on the bonds, corporate, or at least railroad, ownership gradually would transfer to the federal government. The Treasury Department had opened the door to this possibility and the conservative voice of *The Wall Street Journal* called upon it to stop.[27]

The shifting nature of institutional investing also posed the threat of intrusive federal business regulation. The types of securities banks and trust companies invested in changed, as it did for other Americans, through the first three decades of the century from bonds to preferred stock to common stock. The transition was incremental. The earlier forms of investment did not disappear. Instead, the new form of investments became increasingly popular, and this was especially the case with common stock. The move from bonds to stocks linked the performance of the banking sector, and thus the money supply and the nation's entire economy, to the performance of the stock markets. National banks slipped around the restrictions imposed by the National Banking Act and set up their own investment affiliates, typically as separate corporations, which they then might spin off to their shareholders. The separation theoretically shielded bank deposits, but underwritings and margin loans funded by bank affiliates from their parents like National City Bank and First National Bank did not, exposing the banks' cash reserves and depositors to the threat of loss.

Trust companies were not authorized to act as banks, but, taking advantage of a legal loophole, nonetheless found a way to become heavily involved in the banking business, accepting deposits and making loans without being subjected to the cash reserve requirements of national and state banks. They had much wider investment discretion than banks and used that discretion to trade heavily in securities.

The threat these investment practices posed to the integrity of the national banking system was first realized in the October Panic of 1907, with several major trust companies failing and the rest draining down reserves to keep themselves afloat. Many sound institutions found themselves faced with runs by anxious depositors. It took all of the power of Morgan and the cooperation of a compliant federal government to hold the system back from collapse. Among the results were a major investigation into speculation and the first significant public calls for securities regulation.[28]

The Ownership Society

Americans were investors, or at least were well along the way in the decades-long process of becoming so. Although I will refine the numbers in Chapter Eight, a preliminary perspective is helpful. Estimates of American shareholdings are wide-ranging. One study concluded that at least 10 percent of Americans in 1904 were investors, almost all through savings banks and insurance companies. Another estimated that only half a million Americans directly owned stock in 1900, approximately 0.625 percent of the population of 80 million. *The New York Times* estimated ownership by two million people in 1908, although by its own admission it almost certainly overstated the number because the *Times* included the shareholders of each corporation without factoring in the likelihood that most stockholders owned stock in multiple corporations. (The *Times* also failed to distinguish between individual owners and institutional owners.) One of the more widely accepted estimates was provided in 1924 by H. T. Warshow. Although also a flawed study, which he was quick to admit, he estimated 4.4 million shareholders in 1900 growing to 14.4 million in 1922. The 1922 number seems plausible, and in considering the 1900 number one must take into account that, despite a fall in the market, 1900 was in the middle of the merger wave bull market. Leaving absolute numbers aside, Warshow's study is particularly noteworthy for his evidence demonstrating that the distribution of stock among the middle class dramatically increased between 1917 and 1920. More than 53 percent of all dividends paid in 1923 went to people with incomes below $20,000. The largest proportional increase came in the $1,000 to $5,000 annual income category ($11,800 to $59,000 in 2006 dollars).

While all of these estimates suggest that only a relatively small percentage of the population directly owned securities, the market was increasingly important in politics, economics and society. Widespread stock ownership could serve as an antidote both to class warfare and to the increasingly bureaucratic corporate economy's effect on individual initiative, independence and enterprise — the traditional American values that would become the leitmotif of Woodrow Wilson's first presidential campaign in 1912. Americans increasingly found that the most meaningful opportunities to exercise their economic individualism lay in the stock market. By the century's second decade, stock manipulators, bear raiders and plungers had become the nation's heroes.[29]

America had changed. People tried to hold on to the founding values in the face of the new economic realities, but the gradual acceptance of common stock as the new property slowly transformed the grounded ideology of the land into the more ephemeral promise of future profits. These new values found expression in the stock market. Conservative voices tried to root the new property in the old, but the stock market had a force of its own.

SPECULATION — A MATTER OF KNOWLEDGE

Ballade of the Sure Thing

Why should you capital invest
  And draw a paltry 5 per cent?
We here and now invite a test—
  You try us and you won't repent.
Directors all are prominent,
  With probity they fairly ooze.
It isn't an experiment,
  We guarantee you cannot lose.

Our methods are the very best—
  Conservative, intelligent—
We'll feather anybody's nest,
  Tho some concerns are pestilent,
More privateers with pirate crews.
  Our own is vastly different.
We guarantee you cannot lose.

Your capital—we do not jest—
  We'll double. Nothing can prevent
Its doubling. It is manifest,
  To this our energies are bent,
Your money will be wisely spent,
  For to success we hold the clews.
There cannot be an accident,
  We guarantee you cannot lose.[30]

As Americans moved from bonds to common stock over the first decade of the twentieth century, the conservative investment advice of the early years gave way to an increasing popular interest in speculation. Speculation for the average investor did not mean investing for price appreciation as it would after the war. Before the war almost everyone but professional speculators invested for dividends. But securities considered to qualify as investments were those with reliable and regular returns and thus a steady value, like the stock of the Pennsylvania Railroad. Speculative securities were those in which the probability of constant dividends was more tentative and their value more volatile, with higher promised dividend rates to compensate for the increased risk. Even so, while dividends were the expected fruits of stock ownership, investors were also keenly aware of the possibility of price appreciation, as the often jagged ups and downs of the early market clearly showed.

Edward Meade identified two different kinds of securities buyer and two kinds of securities. As to buyers Meade wrote, "the investor buys after making a judgment of value based on the demonstrated earning power of the property. The speculator buys a prospect; he seeks to control a property the value of which is destined to fluctuate wildly." He distinguished the types of securities by contrasting the Pennsylvania Railroad with "the Lucky Chance Oil Company of West Virginia." The former had existed for enough time to allow the investor to make a considered judgment of its earning power. The latter had not. Putting it differently, he classified as investment securities those "whose value is certain because based on known conditions, and those whose value is uncertain, and therefore speculative."[31]

Meade was somewhat unusual for financial writers at the turn of the century, not only, as we have seen, for his embrace of capitalizing earnings, but also, and relatedly, because he was willing to classify at least some stocks as investment grade. (Meade used the term "stock" without qualification, but his valuation theory would suggest that he probably considered the common stock as well as the preferred stock of well-established companies to be investment grade as, for example, when he wrote about the Pennsylvania.) Nonetheless, even Meade keyed his understanding of investment to safety of principal. "The investor will not buy a security whose value is in any way doubtful. He demands in a stock or bond, before anything else, the virtue of stable value. He must be reasonably sure that his principal is safe." The only way that an investor could have this assurance would be to put his money in reputable bonds or, if he were willing to tolerate some risk, high-grade preferred stock.[32]

Meade maintained this somewhat schizophrenic advice as the second decade began. Writing a five-part series of articles in *Lippincott's Monthly Magazine* in late 1911 and early 1912 at a time when the market had stagnated, he maintained that ordinary investors had no chance to win by speculating on Wall Street, especially on margin. He held to his argument that ordinary investors should buy bonds instead of stock.

At the same time, Meade did repeat his earlier position that stock could be an acceptable investment, but he favored railroad stocks rather than industrials. Finally, he noted two instances where an ordinary investor could profit by speculating in stock on margin—either by purchasing convertible bonds or by buying stock on the increasingly popular installment plan. Neither of these devices were conventional margin buying, but they operated on a similar financial principle and the investor's downside was more limited.[33]

Investing itself was not especially easy. You had to know something about the company in which you were investing to be as certain about the security of your principal as Meade and the other investment columnists of the early years suggested you should be. And that was a significant challenge.

Our Business Is Our Business

Looking at financial statements might have been a good idea if you could have found them in the first place and if they would have told you something useful. The absence of disclosure was, to say the least, a problem, one recognized by the Industrial Commission, the Bureau of Corporations and almost every leading economist and policymaker. The absence of disclosure was the result of two problems: the unwillingness of corporate owners and managers to disclose financial information at all, and the primitive state of financial accounting.[34]

The average American's lack of access to corporate financial information was one of the biggest barriers to stock investments, although basic balance sheets and earnings reports of some corporations regularly appeared in the pages of the *Commercial & Financial Chronicle*.[35]

Those who controlled public corporations saw little benefit in disclosure. Businessmen prized secrecy for a variety of reasons, not the least of which was to hide information from competitors and regulators. In his letter to the stockholders of Westinghouse Electric and Manufacturing Company, in its 1901 Report of the Board of Directors, George Westinghouse explained the absence of reports since 1897, noting that "if some should be surprised that more complete statements have not been previously submitted to them, it can only be said that the Directors, as well as the stockholders who own the largest amounts of stock, have believed that in view of the existing keen competition and the general attitude toward industrial enterprises, the interests of all would be served by avoiding, to as great an extent possible, giving undue publicity to the affairs of the Company." Westinghouse's next annual report was distributed in 1906.[36]

A deeply held belief in the sanctity of private property also led some businessmen to a fundamental conviction that nobody but management was entitled to information. One of the principal spokesmen for this view was John Dos Passos.

Testifying before the U.S. Industrial Commission in 1899, Dos Passos argued, with justification, that the purpose of the trust form of combination itself was to maintain secrecy. His client Henry O. Havemeyer was perhaps the leading proponent of the policy of corporate secrecy, as the Sugar King revealed in his famous 1899 testimony before the Industrial Commission: "Let the buyer beware; that covers the whole business [of selling stock]. You cannot wet-nurse people from the time they are born until the day they die. They have got to wade in and get stuck and that is the way men are educated and cultivated." While Havemeyer was perhaps more frank than most, his attitude was commonly shared. Even some serious scholars agreed. In 1903, *The Wall Street Journal* took issue with Yale professor J. Pease Norton, who argued that the "private information of the entrepreneur ... [is] in the nature of patent rights and not so useful to the public that does not understand it."[37]

The need for disclosure in various forms seemed the only point of consensus among many of the experts testifying before the Commission. Although Dos Passos opposed mandatory disclosure as staunchly as he opposed all federal regulation, he gave testimony that squarely illustrated its necessity:

> A trust was not a novel proposition when it was introduced into dealings in corporations shares. It was the application of an old principle of law to new conditions. The object of it was this: To keep people who had no business to know from knowing the secrets of that trust. That is the object of a trust (a perfectly innocent and a perfectly laudable object, in my estimation). If they had formed one corporation and put the six constituent companies into one corporate body, it would have been heralded to the world, and the world would have had the right to go into the county clerk's office, or the office of some other officer entitled and authorized to receive those papers, and to look at them.... The object of the creation of the trust was to avoid that publicity.

In questioning later in his testimony, Dos Passos did concede that one circumstance justified publicity. He agreed that publicizing the cost of a corporation's assets to its existing stockholders would let them assess the future value of the stock. But he stopped short of supporting disclosure to potential stockholders, or anyone else for that matter. Existing stockholders were already part of the corporation—they were entitled to financial information because the corporation was their business. But it was nobody else's business, even if they wanted to buy stock in the company, for, "no man need buy a stock if he doesn't want to."[38]

The Commissioners saw publicity as an important key to dealing with the corporations problem. But publicity in this early stage was not principally about investor protection. While Dos Passos and Havemeyer spoke of publicity to stockholders the Commission was, as I will later explain, far more focused on publicity to regulators and the way that publicity would reveal monopoly power.

Disclosure was rarely required, even in the face of businessmen's intransigence. Railroads were relatively early practitioners of regular financial disclosure, partly because of their traditional reliance on debt and foreign money and partly because they had to report to the Interstate Commerce Commission. Other regulated corporations like banks, insurance companies and public utilities tended to disclose as well. But, as Alfred Chandler noted, the railroads had largely developed their accounting for internal needs, not financing needs, so the information was of limited use to investors. And even these reports could be sporadic and incomprehensible.[39]

State laws generally did not require significant corporate financial reporting, either to the state itself (which treated even the small amount of disclosed information as confidential between the state and the corporation) or to stockholders. Twenty-seven states required some kind of the former by 1900; almost half the states required some form of the latter. But the form and content of financial reporting were rarely specified. Some ambiguous form of balance sheet was the most common requirement. Profit and loss statements were not required and were rarely voluntarily disclosed. The primitive state of the accounting profession and the lack of agreement on standards and principles also meant that the form and content of reports that were made varied widely across corporations and even year to year within the same corporation. Corporation laws typically did not require management to mail reports to shareholders. The only way a shareholder could be sure of getting a copy was by attending the corporation's annual meeting.[40]

The New York Stock Exchange was the principal authority that actually demanded financial disclosure, at least in theory, during this period of stock market development that lasted until the New Deal. Its listing requirements had required companies to file an annual report of some kind in addition to financial disclosure as part of the listing application since 1866. But most companies ignored the annual reporting requirement and the Exchange rarely enforced it. It was only with the Kansas City Gas Company's 1897 announcement that it intended to report profits at least semiannually that a listed company fully complied. The willful noncompliance of listed companies, together with the NYSE's lack of enthusiasm in enforcing the rule, had led the Exchange to create an unlisted securities department in 1885. That is where Havemeyer's company and many other industrials traded, marked only by an asterisk next to their quotations to indicate their unlisted status. (The unlisted department was eliminated in 1910 in the face of regulatory threats following the Panic of 1907.)[41]

But a market for financial information was beginning to develop along with Americans' broadening participation in the stock market. Alexander Noyes noted that, by 1899, newspapers had regularly begun to publish weekend financial articles reviewing the week's activities and, indeed, a review of the evidence suggests that these columns were starting to appear as early as 1890. These reviews "concerned themselves all but exclusively with the Stock Exchange. They rarely discussed agricultural events or incidents of politics or problems of manufacture." They rarely discussed business itself, although there were exceptions like Barron's *The Boston News Bureau*, which proclaimed itself as published for the benefit of public shareholders. The perennial topic of discussion was not business but the performance of the markets. Gradually the markets became the centerpiece of American corporate capitalism.[42]

Misleading Disclosure

Despite small advances in disclosure, the Kansas City Gas Company was unusual. Profit and loss disclosure was virtually absent, even for companies listed on the NYSE, and alternative sources of financial information—the *Commercial & Financial Chronicle*, investment columns and market reports in newspapers, *The Wall Street Journal* starting in 1889, John Moody's manuals beginning in 1900, and the like—were hardly a substitute for corporate financial reporting. The creation of the first professional school for financial accountants at New York University in 1900 was a good sign, but its fruits were still in the future.[43]

While there was a paucity of formal corporate disclosure, misleading disclosure was abundant. It was common for corporate promoters to manipulate financial reporters, and many reporters were only too happy to supplement their incomes by obliging. The appearance of "tipster reports" and corporate advertisements of their securities hardly constituted the kind of financial reporting that would help legislators, regulators, or investors. *The Wall Street Journal* itself, although a bit self-serving, blamed much of the misinformation on "the general newspaper" (in contrast to the financial newspaper), "and especially that deplorable kind which endeavors to give its readers an exaggerated idea of their own intelligence by offering them pseudo-scientifics in a popular form, which sins against the light." Pseudo-scientifics were not even necessary. Some newspapers obliged by sprinkling brokers' ads written to appear as articles throughout the news, with no differentiation in type. To a 1900 reader of *The Portsmouth (N.H.) Herald,* it would have seemed that the paper itself was reporting that "Seldom, if ever, in the history of our country was there ever seen such an opportunity for securing bargains and making money," and noting that the "remarkably correct Reports" of Wm. Committ Cone & Co. of Broad Street had made that firm "most popular."

The real news could be enticing, too. Papers frequently described the successes of those who had gotten rich quick. Alexander Noyes reported that during the speculative bubble of 1901 and the brief bull market leading to the Rich Man's Panic of 1903, newspapers were "full of stories of hotel waiters, clerks in business offices, even doorkeepers and dressmakers, who had won considerable fortunes in their speculations." Advertisements for securities with outlandishly high returns were commonplace, as were ads for books like one that appeared in 1902 in the Des Moines *Daily Reader, How to Speculate in Wall Street.* Information, such as it was in the popular press, was highly questionable. Some of it was paid for by investment banks and brokerage houses to educate investors as to the different kinds of investment instruments, but the amount of paid advertising to hawk specific securities generally exploded from the beginning of the century on.[44]

Meade, claiming to draw upon "a large number of prospectuses" but without disclosing names "out of respect for the feelings of those directly interested," gave a wicked account of the typical stock promotion. This included a depiction by the promoter of "enormous wealth" when in reality all that existed was "a flat plain, a precipitous mountain, or a prospect of monopoly profits." Then came "a mass of expert testimony of this or that 'professor' whose wealth of technical detail is most convincing" with respect to a new feature of the business—technology, resources, or organization. Maps and charts, "strongly worded testimonials" of well-known businessmen or politicians advising investors to "'provide for the children' by investing a few dollars" in the project, and the like, rounded out the promotional materials, along with the complete and certain assurance of large dividends. The widespread circulation and success of this kind of promotion led one writer to note that more information would not make a difference, at least to Chicago's "incorrigible investors," who were happy to be suckered into any scheme to "get rich quick," regardless of the quality of information.[45]

The Morganization of Disclosure

There were significant exceptions to the policies of nondisclosure and false disclosure. General Electric's annual reports from 1893 on are remarkable for their detail and thoroughness as well as their narrative reports and precise auditor's opinions. Historians of accounting also mark U.S. Steel's first annual report for 1902 as a watershed event, as much for the fact that it was voluntary as for its completeness, although it was not nearly as elaborate as General Electric's. The American Telephone and Telegraph report, after Morgan became involved with the company in 1906, is also noteworthy. These reports do present carefully detailed and comprehensible information that would be useful to anybody interested in the companies' financial positions. But it is significant to note that these were Morgan corporations, and the House of Morgan was well known for its integrity in protecting the investors to whom it sold mostly bonds by appointing directors and keeping a close watch over its companies. Morgan's entire success was based on reputation, which was only enhanced by his companies' financial reporting.

There were other exceptions. The United Fruit Company Reports of the early century are unaudited but a model of corporate reporting of the time, including financial statements and detailed narrative descriptions of the assets and conduct of the business. But statements of this depth, even with differences in reporting detail and styles, were rare. For example, International Paper's annual reports consisted of a terse one-page balance sheet and one-page income statement, although the reports were audited. Not every corporation was even this committed to disclosure. And most companies that did seem more open to informing investors rarely disclosed anything meaningful.[46]

The best any historian of accounting can say about corporate disclosure in general is that some corporations did disclose, although very few provided anything like the Morgan companies, and what they provided they provided sporadically. Ripley, looking back in 1932 at a time when, he vehemently argued, disclosure still remained inadequate, recounted a history of this early period in which disclosure was rare, a position consistent with that he had taken in 1905.[47]

The Infancy of Accountancy

The state of American accounting was highly underdeveloped, especially when compared with that of Britain, where the institute of chartered accountants had been royally chartered in 1880 and the British Companies Act of 1900 demanded extensive and detailed disclosure. Internal accounting was important to the management of increasingly large and far-flung businesses as well as to investors and government. But this did not lead to the kind of accounting that the British profession had created.

What is clear is that balance sheet disclosure long preceded income statement disclosure as a regular practice. It is also clear that even though a number of nineteenth-century accounting books were published, the accounting profession was beginning to organize and accounting education was developing, there was nothing resembling agreement on accounting techniques or generally accepted accounting principles. A comparison of the two Morgan-backed Steel and Harvester reports, both of which are accompanied by early forms of auditors' certificates, shows very different accounting and presentation practices. Even as late as the passage of the New Deal securities acts, observers reported significant deficiencies in accounting practice. So while scholarly debate about the level and sophistication of disclosure during this period does exist, it seems beyond question that very little that would help the ordinary shareholder or regulator was readily available.[48]

The absence of reliable information turned almost all investment into speculation as ordinary Americans were beginning to enter the market in significant numbers. Perhaps the best an investor could have done would have been to look at a corporation's interest payment record and its dividend history as a proxy for investment safety. There was no guarantee, of course, that the past would predict the future, but at least in nonspeculative periods this information would give the investor something to work with. Business remained recalcitrant. Regulation was needed. But the federal government was, at the time, consumed by a different regulatory agenda.[49]

⊰ FIVE ⊱

THE COMPLEX WHOLE

B y 1900, the creation of the giant modern corporation and its outpouring of watered stock brought the problems of antitrust into alignment
with the first stage of federal securities regulation in the form of the
federal incorporation movement. The bond that united them was overcapitalization. While some Americans, especially in the West and South, were
anxious about the sheer size of the new enterprises, most were agitated by
their perceptions of monopolistic price gouging to satisfy the demands of
capital and that individual opportunity was rapidly being wiped out by the
giant combinations. Some, especially in the South, tempered their qualms
with envy. They looked longingly toward the wealth of the North and hoped
for a piece of the action. They did not get it.[1]

Businessmen had their own problems. The Supreme Court's somewhat
schizophrenic interpretations of the Sherman Act created troubling uncertainty as to the lawful methods of cooperation. Congress was struggling too,
fitfully feeling its way to the limits of its authority. The Court had clearly
severed federal jurisdiction at the state line, restricting the range of the
government's power. Manufacturing was beyond the federal government's
regulatory reach, even if the entirety of a factory's output ultimately found its
way outside the state of production. States, courts and Congress made their
own attempts to regulate the new monopolies. The difficult issues sprang
from questions of federal jurisdiction, states' rights and, most important, the
two tablets of private property and contractual freedom. The Senate business
leadership impeded reform and McKinley's indifference in the face of the
merger wave made regulatory progress increasingly unlikely.[2]

The novelty and complexity of the issues often confused the regulatory
agenda throughout the first decade of the twentieth century. Like nesting
snakes, issues of monopoly, overcapitalization, speculation, railroad regula-

tion, currency reform, minority shareholder protection, tariffs and the like, swarmed together in the hands of lawmakers. For a moment or two one might peel off from the others, only to be drawn back into the tangle. It was not until each issue grew and matured with the developing economy, not until each began to present a clear identity of its own, that reformers could get their hands around them and tame them on their own terms.

Antitrust concerns dominated the public agenda. Monopoly was a relatively easy concept to grasp and the issue had been receiving attention for years. But the merger wave also spawned a second set of problems that centered on the new securities. The merger wave delivered into the American economy a new kind of corporation, the finance corporation, created by promoters to reap their profits by producing and selling stock. Contemporary observers failed at first to understand that many of the issues raised by the financing techniques used by the giant combinations were qualitatively different from those created by the earlier industrial monopolies. The combination of competitors with the currency of securities produced waves of water that cascaded through the stock market, swamping investors and destabilizing the economy. But reformers saw the problems of antitrust and overcapitalization as sufficiently intertwined that they typically took them up as one. The issue centered on monopoly. The integrity of the new securities for the investment market was, for the time being, a distant concern.[3]

Reform was the topic of the day, but for the federal government it remained little more than a topic of discussion, debate and legislative failure for more than a decade. What successful legislation there was aimed at the more focused problems of the railroads, with which lawmakers had developed experience over forty years. The problems of industry were of only recent vintage, and industry was inseparable from increasing American prosperity. All but the most radically populist Republicans and Democrats took care to avoid damaging the economy. This was especially true in the Senate, which was run by the business quartet of Nelson Aldrich, Orville Platt, John C. Spooner and William B. Allison. This senate leadership group was completed by two powerful outliers. Matthew Quay, Pennsylvania's ruthless boss, was a free agent but chose to use his power for the security of capital. Ohio's Marcus Hanna, a self-made businessman, generated his independent power as the architect of McKinley's rise to the presidency. Despite occasional tensions and conflicts among the "Big Four" and Quay and Hanna, business was politically secure. By 1888 the Republicans had undeniably become the party of big business.[4]

Political pressure for some kind of reform became intense. Almost the entire assortment of business and financial issues drew together after 1900 in the form of the first major federal incorporation movement. Calls for federal corporation laws were heard from time to time during the century that followed. None were as hotly pursued or so protracted as the efforts that took place during the long decade from 1900 to 1914.

There were two distinct models of federal incorporation. The most sweeping would have required state corporations engaged in interstate business to reorganize themselves under a federal incorporation law. The law that governed the financing, management and managerial responsibilities of these corporations would have been significantly more stringent than, say, the laws of New Jersey or Delaware or West Virginia. More typical and less organic were proposals that would have required state corporations to obtain federal licenses before they could engage in interstate business. These licenses would carry with them a set of governance, financing and disclosure regulations that would overlie the fundamental laws of state incorporation.

The federal incorporation movement joined two related but distinct problems into a single legislative chorus and kept them there for most of the first decade of the twentieth century. Antitrust was the tune, but overcapitalization was the counterpoint that harmonized them into one. By the end of the decade these themes began to unravel, with antitrust reform leading to the creation of the Federal Trade Commission (FTC) and the Clayton Antitrust Act of 1914 and overcapitalization growing into the new issue of securities regulation, designed to curb speculation and stabilize the economy.

The federal incorporation movement failed, but it provided the foundation for the Department of Commerce, the Bureau of Corporations, the Federal Trade Commission and the Clayton Antitrust Act and enhanced railroad regulation through various amendments to the Interstate Commerce Act. It also created the fundamental conceptual underpinnings of the New Deal securities laws.

THE FAILURE OF FEDERAL INCORPORATION

Federal incorporation failed for five major reasons. It failed because almost all of the proposals were either too limited in the problems they confronted or too ambitious in their sweep; because it aggravated deep-seated fears of centralized federal power, enhanced by Roosevelt's aggressive pursuit of the imperial presidency; because disempowered Southern Democrats remained committed to notions of states' rights; because a growing fear of socialist influences made aggressive federal regulation difficult to achieve; and because the problems presented by the giant modern corporation changed during the long first decade of the twentieth century even as Congress grappled with the issues of the nineteenth century.

Federal incorporation proposals often encompassed regulation aimed at antitrust concerns, corporate finance, the obligations of directors and officers, stock speculation and railroad rate regulation in the same bill. Congress, like the rest of the nation, was trying to sort through its bewilderment with the dramatic transformations in American economics and business. Political pressures on each party (and within parties) pulled in different directions. The issues created by the giant modern corporation were new and difficult to keep conceptually distinct. Congress could hardly be blamed for its failure to achieve legislative coherence when the relationships among the problems were often ambiguous.

The next three reasons for the failure of federal incorporation are distinct but at the same time deeply related. First was the pronounced and often stridently articulated public concern with centralizing power in the federal government—the very same concern that had led the Constitutional Convention to reject Madison's bid for federal incorporation, leaving the matter to the states. Some longed for the Jeffersonian romance of a limited central government and would fight any attempt to expand its power past that necessary for defense and the protection of interstate commerce. Romantic or not, the fear of centralized federal power at times united Southern Democrats and big business Republicans, although for different reasons.

Teddy Roosevelt's personality and revolutionary ideas about presidential power made these fears tangible. While Roosevelt remained relatively cautious following the public shock of his inauguration, he did little to conceal his belief in a strong executive branch led by a particularly strong president. Roosevelt the reformer became an obstacle to reform because the imperial Roosevelt scared even the reformers into passing pale legislation. The far more modest and politically conservative Taft, less skilled in dealing with the legislature, pursued statutory reform half-heartedly. The successful regulatory compromises blended federal oversight with a largely self-regulatory approach that characterized the progressive politics of Woodrow Wilson.[5]

The third stumbling block for federal incorporation lay in a more painful history. Reconstruction was a deep scar, and Southerners ceded states' rights reluctantly. Nonetheless, Democrats, the party of the South, had long fought for trust reform. They held extensive hearings on trusts in the late 1880s under Grover Cleveland and, although they produced no legislation, their campaign platforms of 1900 and 1908 included a federal incorporation plank, and their platforms of 1896, 1904 and 1912 all demanded trust regulation. Bryan, the party's presidential candidate from 1896 to 1908 (relieved by Alton Parker in 1904) was a persistent fan of federal incorporation. But the issue of federal corporate control unavoidably irritated the sore spot of states' rights. The Democrats wanted regulation. Yet the idea of federal incorpora-tion overriding the prerogatives of the states fueled strong emotions.[6]

Also related to the fear of centralized power was the widespread concern with creeping socialism that raised its head during the federal incorporation debates. America was becoming far more of a collectivist society than its self-image and founding myths allowed its leaders to acknowledge. Corporations, labor unions, trade associations, civic associations and a variety of other col-lective centers of identity and interest formed quickly. Intellectuals of the era were keenly aware of, and wrote widely about, the phenomenon, while the public sensed it and the leadership warned of it. Cries of imminent socialism were echoed by Democrats and Republicans throughout the country.[7]

The final reason that federal incorporation failed was that the problems changed during the fourteen years of reform efforts. The monopoly powers of the giant industrial combinations proved less than enduring. The Supreme Court's interpretation of the Sherman Act evolved into workable and often effective regulation. The securities markets underwent dramatic transforma-tion. Banking practices changed. Yet the regulatory approach remained con-stant, even as the nature of the problems was quickly shifting.[8]

Federal incorporation sometimes came close, but it never really had a chance.

A PRELUDE TO FEDERAL INCORPORATION—
THE CHICAGO CONFERENCE ON TRUSTS

The trust problem had become a subject of serious study even before the federal debate got rolling. The meteoric rise of Standard Oil, which in less than a decade had captured virtually the entire domestic petroleum mar-ket, was perhaps stimulus enough. Economists and popular writers had been studying the problem since the 1880s, but the merger wave brought with it a literary explosion. Economist Charles Bullock, in his 1901 review of the popular and scholarly literature on trusts, wrote that in a three-year period "the production of trust literature has kept pace with the process of industrial consolidation."[9]

Widespread public interest in the trust issue led to action as concerned citizens grouped together to find their own solutions. The congressionally created Industrial Commission provided the beginnings of a federal response in 1898, but that organization was designed as much to placate the public, and especially labor, as it was to pave the path to meaningful reform. McKin-ley, who was indebted to business for his presidency, paid no attention to the trust issue until the election of 1900 drew near. Only then did he reluctantly conclude that political wisdom required the administration to affect concern about the trusts. Safe again after the election, McKinley completely ignored the trust problem in his second inaugural address and even hinted that public agitation over the issue was counterproductive. By the summer of 1901, he recognized that he had little choice but to engage the problem directly or leave it exclusively to his voluble, energetic and ambitious vice president. Yet even in his fateful final speech in Buffalo on September 5, McKinley did not mention trust regulation. He took the occasion to praise the accomplishments of American industry.[10]

Public activism on the trust question had begun to coalesce during the last year of the century. Its first organized manifestation was the Chicago Conference on Trusts, which convened in the Central Music Hall on September 13, 1899, and ran for almost four days. The Conference, sponsored by the Civic Federation of Chicago, was the first major public trust event following the formation of the Industrial Commission. Naturally it drew wide attention from a national press serving a people hungry for information and for action.

The Civic Federation of Chicago (CFC) had been created in 1894 by a reform leader named Ralph Easley as a group of "business men, professional people, social workers, labor leaders, and rank and file citizens" coming together to address the problems visited especially heavily on Chicago by the depression of 1893–97. Political corruption and industrial crisis were its main focal points, sharpened by rising unemployment and poverty, increasing labor agitation, evaporating philanthropy and general social turmoil as the order of the day. Jacob Coxey's Army went on the march in 1894 to protest the federal government's passivity, frightening thousands with the specter of mass revolt. The CFC had much to occupy itself.

By 1900 Easley had transformed the CFC into the National Civic Federation (NCF). The NCF was probably the era's most visible civic force behind legislative and social reform. Both the CFC and its successor gained legitimacy and influence from the range and variety of its members, including labor leader Samuel Gompers, social reformer Jane Addams and an assortment of businessmen and their lawyers, among them steel leader Elbert Gary, Morgan partner George Perkins, Andrew Carnegie, August Belmont, Jr., Cyrus McCormick and prominent lawyer Charles Bonaparte. But they were, for all the diversity of their membership and their progressive agenda, more or less resolutely in favor of big business and it was largely from business and finance that they drew their leadership. The NCF reform proposals followed suit.[11]

The Chicago Conference on Trusts was capacious both in its attendance and its scope of inquiry. The organizers asked the state governors to appoint delegates to the conference. Among them were "represented every interest in the respective states, including congressmen, ex-congressmen, ex-governors, ex-supreme court judges, attorneys-general, presidents of banks, presidents of railroads, manufacturing and commercial organizations, and representatives of labor, agricultural, and educational interests." Despite the impressive list of delegates, *The New York Times* reported that "less than half the delegates appointed by the various States" were present on opening day but that tardiness and absences had been expected. Ultimately there appears to have been broad participation and substantial attendance. The official roll reported 744 attendees.[12]

CFC President Franklin H. Head of the conservative National Business Men's League called the conference to order, identifying education as its goal. The CFC claimed to be responding to what it perceived as the great public interest in the trust question and a paucity of public education and information about the matter. Men of "every shade of opinion" had been invited to pursue this great inquiry into the nature and problems of trusts. With this in mind, Head claimed: "It is not a trust or an anti-trust conference, but a conference in search of truth and light. With this end in view the attendance has been solicited of men of every shade of opinion upon the general subject."

And men (and a barely perceptible handful of women) of every shade of opinion they were, as the lengthy published proceedings attest. In addition to the gubernatorially appointed delegates, representatives of almost every type of relevant organization imaginable filled the hall. There were members of Granges; industrial associations like the Millers National Association, the Association of Western Manufacturers and the Farmers' National Congress; labor unions; civic organizations ranging from the New Orleans Board of Trade to the Commercial Club of Terre Haute; regulatory bodies like the Interstate Commerce Commission, the U.S. Industrial Commission and a variety of state railroad commissions; and representatives of issue-oriented groups like the Single Tax League of the United States, the American Anti-Trust League and the Tariff Reform Committee of the Reform Club of New York. There were presidents and faculty of universities, representatives of the American Academy of Political and Social Science and a variety of at-large representatives from thirty-three states and territories, all forming, as appears from the proceedings, not only a formidable program but a rather active and vocal gallery as well.[13]

As to it being "neither a trust nor an anti-trust conference," one could be forgiven for some doubt. Head and a number of other speakers took note of the "crying need for education" to distinguish beneficial trusts from harmful monopolies, suggesting at least some attempt to clear big business of the general charges of evil being levied against it in the heartland.

The proceedings were lively, often detailed and sophisticated in their discussion of the issues, and sometimes hotly debated. There were speakers who worked to be analytical and balanced. Jeremiah Jenks, a trust supporter, opened the substance of the conference with characteristically noncommittal remarks: "It is certainly true that a long step has been taken toward the solution of any problem when the problem itself has been clearly stated." He then proceeded, in good scholarly and painfully dull fashion, to analyze each aspect of the problem, finishing each section with a series of unanswered questions that required resolution before trusts could be thoroughly understood.

The tedium of speakers like Jenks was relieved by the performances of the real crowd pleasers—partisans whose flourishing rhetoric maintained the entertainment value of the proceedings. Dudley G. Wooten of the Texas legislature opened his remarks by reflecting on the decline in American values that was causing concern among progressives and conservatives alike. "We [Texans] believe that there are some things more valuable, more to be desired and more worthy to be contended for by a free people than mere industrial activity, commercial progress or the accumulation of worldly wealth." The proceedings show that Wooten's remarks—the first of the conference taking an *anti*trust standpoint—were well received. "The gallery audience was sympathetic with [Wooten's] views, and carried away by the eloquence of the gifted orator, punctuated his address with salvo after salvo of applause," especially labor delegates and those from the South and West; "the Easterners generally smiled critically and kept their arms folded."[14]

Charles Bonaparte was a Baltimore attorney who would, in 1908, become Teddy Roosevelt's attorney general and thus the man charged with enforcing the antitrust laws. He foreshadowed in his remarks a strain of what, within a decade, would become mainstream Progressive thought. "I regard the tendency of combination as an inevitable feature of modern civilization from which no free and enlightened country can escape, and which has force in proportion to each country's freedom and enlightenment."

All eyes were upon the Great Commoner as William Jennings Bryan indulged in his customary flamboyant rhetoric. He was received with "warm and vigorous" applause. "I want to start with the declaration that a monopoly in private hands is indefensible from any standpoint, and intolerable." But even Bryan showed some caution in defining the enemy. The target was monopoly, not big business *per se*, and Bryan was careful to state that he used the term "trust" interchangeably with "monopoly." "I venture the opinion that few people will defend monopoly as a principle, or a trust organization as a good thing, but I imagine our great difference will be as to remedy." He proceeded to discuss the need for a federal remedy, saving especially harsh words for New Jersey and Delaware. Federal incorporation was Bryan's answer, and it is fair to say that his enthusiasm for it raised suspicion among those Republicans who were otherwise inclined to see its virtues. It was naturally hard to separate economics from politics, even as some broad consensus was developing on the appropriate contours of the economic landscape.[15]

While the proceedings were sometimes analytical, sometimes raucous and sometimes plain dull, the conference produced more show than substance. Conference President William Howe, speaking unofficially, summarized what he saw to be the common themes of the speeches and papers. States should pass laws to outlaw those trusts and restraints of trade that judicial opinion had condemned. Such legislation should be as uniform as possible. States should pass corporation laws that were as uniform as possible. Watered stock should be prohibited. Corporations should be required to make reports and subject themselves to government inspection to the extent that it preserved their legitimate need for secrecy. The lowest common denominator of the conference clearly was very modest.[16]

The formal conclusion of the conference was even more of a disappointment for those who demanded reform. Introduced as a resolution by Cyrus G. Luce, former governor of Michigan and chair of the committee on resolutions, it was probably the only aspect of the conference about which there was no debate. Luce disarmed the reformers by emphasizing the educational, nonpolitical purpose of the conference, concluding: "Therefore, be it resolved, That in the opinion of the committee on resolutions, this conference is without authority, and it would be inexpedient for it to adopt resolutions purporting to declare the sense of the conference upon any aspect of the subject of discussion." It would have been hard to get excited about a resolution resolving nothing. But the public debate had begun to coalesce.[17]

FROM ANTITRUST TO FEDERAL INCORPORATION

The CFC, as a voluntary civic organization, could afford to follow through on its stated educational mission without any resolution of the debate. McKinley, whose constituency was grounded in the business community, was not in any rush to do much, either. It might be an understatement to say that the administration was hardly vigorous in enforcing the antitrust laws. In fact, McKinley initiated only three of all lawsuits ever brought under the Sherman Act. Harrison and Cleveland, whose presidencies took place before the trust issue became nearly as pressing, together brought twelve.

Congress and Trust Reform Before the Turn of the Century

McKinley could afford to ignore the trust issue. Attention to his political fortunes certainly encouraged his disinterest. Congress did not have the same luxury. Trust agitation was widespread and elected representatives could not afford to ignore the groundswell of public opinion that led to the Chicago Conference. Congress responded. Between 1881 and Roosevelt's rise to the presidency in 1901, congressmen introduced forty-five separate pieces of antitrust legislation. Three constitutional amendments were also proposed during this period, designed to resolve the debate over the federal government's power to regulate trusts.[18]

In order to see what Congress was worried about before the turn of the century, it is worth taking a moment to examine what these bills were designed to do. Most proposals directly outlawed trusts. A handful of them proposed to deal with the problem by defining and taxing trusts. Taxation as a remedy for corporate ills was consistently suggested from the beginning of the antitrust debate through the New Deal era. It became especially important during the first years of the new century for several reasons. The federal power to tax, unlike its commerce power, was relatively unambiguous as a constitutional matter. It could also be used, as Taft wanted, as a form of regulatory disclosure designed to squeeze information from corporations.[19]

Two bills were unique in focusing on the causes of trusts rather than attempting to regulate them directly. A bill introduced in 1894 proposed eliminating tariffs on any trust-produced articles. This followed the widespread, if contested, belief that tariffs encouraged trust formation (although there was little doubt that the Sugar Trust had blossomed thanks to the protection of high tariffs). The idea was that tariffs protected American industry from foreign competition and created artificial price discrimination between foreign and domestic goods. Trusts were spawned in the shelter of these pricing privileges. Eliminating the tariff with respect to trust-produced categories of goods became an important part of the Democrats' position during the next decade.[20]

Another bill introduced later that same year aimed at a different perceived cause of trusts—patents. The whole purpose of patents was to create temporary monopolies by giving their holders the exclusive use of the subject inventions. The idea that patents substantially aided in the creation and protection of trusts had substantial support. Innovative means of production were vitally important both to the growth and the products of industry. Patents, even if limited in duration, even if other inventors could get around them, provided significant starting advantages to those who held them. The proposed bill would have nullified patents used by trusts.[21]

The U.S. Industrial Commission and its successor Bureau of Corporations, both conservative in conception and orientation, downplayed the role of tariffs and patents in trust formation. In the end, neither bill received any consideration. Tariff reform created a rift between conservative and progressive Republicans, and Democrats watched this internecine battle with amusement until the issue helped to provide an opportunity for them in 1913, when Wilson and his Democratic Congress succeeded in reducing tariffs.[22]

A shift in the approaches of proposed legislation began to occur around 1897. Republican Phillip Low of New York introduced a bill in the House to provide national supervision of corporations. The bill was interesting for two reasons. It was the first federal incorporation bill introduced in Congress. It was also the first proposed trust measure of any kind to use the word "corporation" instead of "trust." I do not want to overstate the significance of this shift, but by moving from the word "trust" to the word "corporation" the bill reflected the increasing threat of monopoly posed by businesses that were taking advantage of New Jersey's legal reforms. It also conceptually expanded the nature of the thing that was being regulated. No longer was it the trust alone that was the subject of regulation, but also the giant modern corporation in and of itself. Part of the explanation for the shift is a change in the form of business cooperation from trusts, pools and communities of interest to large corporations that contained within them the assets of former competitors. It was not clear that the Sherman Act's prohibition of agreements in restraint of trade applied to the corporation, because a corporation, as a single entity, could not contract or conspire with itself. So the regulatory focus shifted to the Sherman Act's proscription of monopoly and thus a concern with how even the unitary corporate entity behaved, rather than on combination *per se*. Beyond this, though, the new legislative efforts also focused on problems caused by aspects of corporate governance and finance that had been made possible by states like New Jersey. The conflation of trusts—that is, monopolies—with corporations, could and sometimes did exacerbate the confusion of issues in the federal incorporation debate.[23]

Only three bills proposing any form of federal corporate supervision were introduced during this period, along with three bills that would have prevented overcapitalization. These latter bills were introduced during the merger wave. This makes perfect sense, because it was during the merger wave that overcapitalization as a serious and widespread public problem first came to characterize corporate combinations in the minds of many. Antitrust reform remained an important legislative concern until its resolution by the creation of the Federal Trade Commission in 1914, but, starting around 1903, it began to share the stage with other important corporate issues. The overall record suggests that the early 1880s up to 1900 should be classified legislatively as the golden age of antitrust. Despite widespread public concern, little federal attention was paid to other aspects of liberalized state corporate law until the end of this period.[24]

The United States Industrial Commission

The real beginning of legislative attempts to regulate corporations in a more sweeping way than simply controlling monopolies came in 1898. That was the year when Congress created the U.S. Industrial Commission, charging it, among other things, to "investigate questions pertaining to . . . manufacturing, and to business, and to report to Congress and to suggest such legislation as it may deem best upon the subjects." The Commission was important— it was the first concerted federal effort to investigate what was going on inside the new giant corporations. Remember that corporations were highly secretive. The only information most people, including lawmakers, had to go on in evaluating their behavior was rumor, capitalization, dividends and securities prices. The Commission was organized to investigate all aspects of the new economic conditions of the United States.

But the Commission was also created as a parry, an attempt by the Republican Congress to satisfy public opinion at the same time that it delayed any serious regulation. Writing in *The North American Review*, one of the Commission's own members, S.N.D. North, admitted as much: "It recognizes in itself a sort of safety valve for the country." A "large part" of Congress' motivation in creating the Commission was to provide a forum for anybody who felt wronged in the new economic order to come and complain, understanding that "people who suffer wrongs, either real or imaginary, always feel better when they are allowed an opportunity to ventilate them before some recognized governmental authority." The Commission was created to placate more than to reform.[25]

The Commission was instructed to hold hearings should it deem them necessary, and in this respect it did its work quite well. It took extensive testimony over the course of its existence, with several sessions focused largely on the problems created by the liberalization of New Jersey law. Those testifying were a who's who of American business and finance, including John D. Rockefeller, Charles Schwab, John Dos Passos, James B. Dill, H. O. Havemeyer, Elbert Gary, "Morgan's Attorney General" Francis Lynde Stetson, a number

of officers of New Jersey corporation trust companies and a wide range of
industrialists, financiers, labor representatives, lawyers and economists.[26]

The Commission's broad mandate led it to study a variety of topics, ranging from the trust problem generally to issues of transportation, labor and
agriculture, among others. In just a few short years it produced thousands
of pages of transcripts and reports, published in nineteen volumes. The first
direct federal salvo against state corporate regulation was fired in one of the
closing sentences of the Commission's seven-hundred-page Final Report:

> It is important to observe that whenever any State has put conserva-
> tive restrictions upon corporations, either as to their formation or
> their management, other States have taken advantage of the situa-
> tion and enacted such liberal laws that corporations have removed
> to them from other States. Two or three States have apparently, for
> the sake of securing a certain revenue easily collected, bid against
> each other by offering more liberal inducements to corporations.
> This demoralizing tendency in corporation legislation, and the
> great variety of corporation laws in our forty-five States and four
> Territories, makes the task of controlling large corporations exceed-
> ingly difficult.

New Jersey! Delaware! West Virginia! The states were unreliable. The states
were irresponsible. The states were greedy. So the Commission discussed
federal incorporation and federal franchising as solutions to the problem of
state corporate control. The specific issue creating perhaps the most controversy was whether it was constitutional for the federal government to regulate
corporations doing interstate business and supplant various aspects of state
corporate law. Special attention was reserved for New Jersey law, especially
the provisions that eased the way for corporate combinations and overcapitalization.[27]

Disclosure was also an issue, although disclosure at this point meant regulatory disclosure, a tool to facilitate legislation and prosecution rather than
a remedy to protect investors. The supplementary opinion filed by Commissioner Thomas W. Phillips with the Final Report put it squarely on the table.
Whatever the method of regulation, the government needed information.
And most state law, as we have seen, did little or nothing to compel corporations to provide it. Anticipating the securities laws by thirty-one years, Phillips wrote: "[For federal control of corporations] to be efficient, a system of
public accounting must adopt two separate methods. First, each corporation

should be required to make periodical reports of its business, supplemented by other reports upon official demand, all verified by the oaths of certain of its officers." Some variation on this suggestion would be present in virtually all of the proposed federal incorporation measures.[28]

As early as 1866 the New York Stock Exchange required listed companies to file annual reports. In 1900 it demanded balance sheets and income statements as part of a corporation's listing application. As we have seen, these requirements were more often than not ignored. Such financials as were provided were relatively meaningless, and were not available to the public or stockholders. So it was during the Industrial Commission hearings that publicity as an essential tool in law enforcement received its first thorough airing.

One centrally important issue for the Commission was corporate valuation and proper corporate capitalization. The Commission was confused by the issues of valuation that underlay the problem of overcapitalization, as we saw in Chapter Three. But everyone questioned seemed to agree on one point: the absolute size of a corporation did not matter. This is an especially important observation, because progressive corporate reform in this era has often been identified with attacks on corporate size. It is true that some reformers, most prominently Louis Brandeis, held to a populist notion of small business and condemned large business as an evil in and of itself. But it is clear from the historical record that progressive reformers—from Eugene Debs to Woodrow Wilson—were not troubled by bigness alone. Indeed many saw large corporate size as the product of the inevitable evolution of business.

The Industrial Commission was commendably thorough in its work. But it was not without bias. For the most part the Commission, appointed by the Republican-controlled Congress, was in favor of big business. At a minimum it accepted the natural inevitability of big business. Much more important than sheer size was whether bigness necessarily led to monopoly, whether it allowed a particular trust or corporation to drive out competition, squelch entrepreneurial opportunity, dictate prices and harm consumers. This was a heavily debated issue.[29]

The eventual result—encouraged by big businessmen themselves—was the creation of the FTC, which was intended in part to work through regulatory disclosure by engaging in investigations and eventually providing regulatory determinations of the antitrust implications of their intended combinations and contracts, giving businessmen some of the certainty they were seeking. But that was a solution for the future.[30]

The Final Report of the U.S. Industrial Commission

The Commission's Final Report was published in 1902. By this time Roosevelt was feeling his oats as president. Despite his initial assurance to the American people, and especially the business representatives of his own party, that he would continue McKinley's policies, he enthusiastically took up the issue of trusts. While his actions were more tentative than his words, and even his words were often measured, he saw the need for action more clearly than his predecessor. Less than three weeks after the Commission submitted its Final Report, Attorney General Knox (a former trust lawyer who had been appointed by McKinley) sued the Northern Securities Holding Company under the Sherman Act. A furious J. P. Morgan met with Knox and Roosevelt. Morgan, referring respectively to Knox and Stetson, told Roosevelt that "if we have done anything wrong ... send your man to my man and they can fix it up." When Roosevelt demurred and Morgan anxiously inquired as to whether he planned to attack "my other interests," the new president responded: "Not ... unless we find out ... they have done something that we regard as wrong." The McKinley days were over.[31]

The Commission's Final Report was especially important in this new environment. It contained massive amounts of information about the way big business was put together and run, and also made recommendations that would provide the legislative themes for the next decade.

The Commission rejected federal incorporation as a solution, mostly because it would centralize business regulation in the federal government "to a degree to most people unthought of, in connection with our form of government." Instead, it recommended a federal licensing law that would require all corporations engaged in interstate commerce to be licensed and registered with a bureau of corporations. The law aimed at two major issues: controlling monopolies and, vitally tied to this goal, mandatory corporate publicity (which anticipated greater accountability of corporate officials). The Commission also recommended a federal law prohibiting stock watering (and thus overcapitalization) modeled on the Massachusetts anti–stock watering law. Much more than the monopoly issue itself, this attack on over-capitalization aimed at the heart of business—finance—that had been controlled entirely by the states.[32]

There was broad public sentiment in favor of some form of federal corporate law. Leading businessmen and lawyers who were frustrated by having to comply with a variety of conflicting state laws were among its supporters. John D. Rockefeller favored the idea. James B. Dill himself, speaking at Harvard in 1902, dismissed the modest proposal of federal licensing and wanted to go all the way with federal incorporation: "I view with favor the enactment of a National Incorporation Act as distinguished from a national control of state-created corporations." Continuing, and with an apparent complete lack of self-consciousness as the Mephistopheles of New Jersey's Faustian bargain, he said:

> A national corporation act should be based upon the public de-
> mand for cleaner legislation and for purer politics premised upon
> the assumption that it is more feasible to obtain from the national
> body proper regulation and control than in and from various state
> legislatures, some of which are to-day engaged in a competitive war-
> fare for revenue from corporations.

Like other business leaders, he bemoaned the fragmented nature of corporate regulation: "We have the members of the great financial combinations practically located in New York, with their millions of capital, relegated to the courts of New Jersey for a determination of their rights as stockholders."[33]

Dill's sincerity is difficult to judge. He remained on the record as stridently in favor of federal incorporation, yet his business was based largely on his status as the leading expert in New Jersey corporate law. Lincoln Steffens, who was fascinated not only by the trust issue but also by Dill himself, expressed his chagrin after he listened to Dill recount what Steffens regarded as horror stories of the behavior of New Jersey corporations. Late in his life, Dill explained to Steffens why he had fed the muckraker such detailed inside stories of legalized corporate misbehavior: "'Why, Dr. Innocent,' he said, 'I was advertising my wares and the business of my State. When you and the other reporters and critics wrote as charges against us what financiers could and did actually do in Jersey, when you listed, with examples, what the trust-makers were doing under our laws, you were advertising our business—free.'"[34]

Alton Adams, writing in 1903 in the *Political Science Quarterly*, also noted the benefits to business of federal incorporation: "Trust advocates ... see in national incorporation laws a means of escape from state regulation." While state law had become lax, the states still had the power to "tax, regulate, and exclude." The prospect of tightened regulation in each state in which they did business worried businessmen. Scholarly examination of the possibilities of federal incorporation was rapidly becoming a popular pastime.[35]

The Democrats' Dilemma: Regulating Trusts and Federal Power

On May 15, 1900, the House Judiciary Committee reported on a joint resolution of Congress calling for the Sixteenth Amendment to the Constitution to be passed by Congress and submitted to the states for approval. The amendment was designed to put to rest all doubts about the federal government's constitutional power to regulate trusts. Had it passed, it would also have ensured the constitutionality of federal incorporation. While there were several proposals, the amendment as reported was simple and direct. First: "All powers conferred by this article shall extend to the several States ... and all territory under the sovereignty and subject to the jurisdiction of the United States." In its operative language, it would have given Congress the power to "define, regulate, prohibit, or dissolve trusts, monopolies, or corporations." Finally, it acknowledged "the rights of the states to exercise any of their own powers not inconsistent with the amendment."[36]

It is unnecessary here to discuss the details of the committee report. It spoke of the need to regulate trusts and the desire to ensure the regulation's constitutionality. I will review many of these arguments in the next chapter when I discuss the debate over the Littlefield bill. The minority report is much more important for now.

The Democrats, more than the Republicans, had long favored trust regulation. While a number of progressive Republicans sincerely wanted to regulate trusts to protect the public, the party of McKinley was a latecomer to the cause. The Senate in particular, under the firm control of the Big Four, was not especially eager to see meaningful trust regulation enacted. The Democrats were wholly in favor of trust regulation, but the Supreme Court's interpretation of the commerce clause following the *E. C. Knight* case (which drew a sharp distinction between manufacturing, which Congress lacked the power to regulate, and interstate commerce, as to which it did have power) left real questions about the constitutional scope of federal trust regulation. The proposed Sixteenth Amendment would have resolved all doubts in favor of federal regulation. But the Democrats opposed it. Indeed, the Republicans used this opposition to accuse them of forsaking their regulatory opportunity.

Why did the Democrats oppose a real solution to a problem they had been trying to address for years? The answer is revealed in a minority report filed by De Armond of Missouri, Lanham of Texas, Fleming of Georgia, Terry of Arkansas, Elliott of South Carolina, Clayton of Alabama and Smith of Kentucky. The Democrats' legal argument was that the amendment was unnecessary. Trusts could be controlled by amending or eliminating the high tariff, using the undisputed federal taxing power to tax trusts, amending the federal patent laws to prevent monopoly and using the federal postal laws to prevent interstate fraud through the mails. The federal government had unquestionable jurisdiction over these matters, and any of these remedies, separately or together, would have gone a long way toward regulating trusts. But the majority had proposed a constitutional amendment.

The Democrats made clear their general disdain for constitutional amendments. Noting that only three had been adopted since the nation's founding era (which, it is worth noting, were the Civil War amendments), the minority expressed some horror at constitutional amendment as a general proposition. States' rights was the reason.

The minority report devoted only a few paragraphs to states' rights and they were among the most moderate of the minority's arguments against the amendment, except in their conclusion: "But State [*sic*] rights need not be involved in the discussion, and we leave them for consideration at a more convenient season. The proposed amendment would take power from the States and lodge it in Congress, with the proviso that if the States could find something left when all had been taken away they might make use of what they might find where there remains nothing to be found."[37]

Corporate regulation traditionally had been left to the states. Federal power was limited and adequate. The issue of states' rights had a powerful grip on the South and thus on the Democratic Party. This particular amendment, broadly drafted as it was, would have invited Congress to take over almost the entire field of corporate regulation. The Supreme Court's holding that the commerce clause did not apply to manufacturing would have disappeared. The federal government would have the power not only to regulate but also to define what "trusts, monopolies, or combinations" meant, "whether existing in the form of a corporation or otherwise." Such limitations as were read into the commerce clause would have evaporated. Congress could effectively have defined its own power. While the Democrats would eventually vote unanimously in favor of the one piece of federal corporate regulation to reach a vote during the decade, they preferred to take their chances with judicial interpretations of the commerce clause rather than with a new amendment that would have indisputably increased federal power.

ROOSEVELT DISCOVERS THE TRUSTS

The executive branch and its attitudes toward big business had changed by the time the Industrial Commission had published its final report. With McKinley's assassination in September 1901 and the feisty Teddy Roosevelt's descent from the Adirondack Mountains to ascend to the presidency, public scrutiny of business shifted from congressional commissions and civic associations to the White House. The myth of Roosevelt as "trust buster" was largely false; he was far more sympathetic to the concerns of big business than legend suggests. But while he saw its inevitability and benefits as clearly as anyone, Roosevelt wanted the federal government to take a more active role in business regulation. By federal government, Roosevelt meant himself, and this is one of the reasons that the regulation that Congress actually passed was far less reaching than it might have been.[38]

It is difficult to tell how strongly Roosevelt really opposed the trusts. His initial interest in the issue seems to have been largely to ensure his own political safety. In fact, he thought public antitrust agitation was overblown. In a letter to editor and sometime power-broker Hermann Kohlsaat in August 1899, while governor of New York, he wrote: "How about trusts? I know this is a very large question, but more and more it seems to me that there will be a good deal of importance to the trust matter in the next campaign, and I want to consult with men whom I most trust as to what line of policy should be pursued." He went on to note his concern with "popular unrest and popular distrust on the question," as to which he wrote: "It is largely aimless and baseless," but without some plan "multitudes will follow the crank who advocates an absurd policy." Two days later, writing to his close friend Henry Cabot Lodge, he described "the agitation against trusts ... [as] largely unreasonable and ... [as] fanned into activity by the Bryan type of demagogue," again articulating his fear that some "quack" would make bad policy unless cooler heads began to develop more reasonable measures. In other correspondence of the time he described the agitation against trusts as "largely irrational." But toward the end of August with an election year approaching, he had started to develop his own trust policy based on his belief in the benefits of disclosure.[39]

Despite his apparent uncertainty as to how serious the trust problem might be, if indeed there was a problem beyond the political, it is possible that Roosevelt's increasing desire to address the issue was partially motivated by his reaction to significant business opposition to his governorship. As early as January 1898 he saw that "the great corporations" were working hard to raise money for his opponents. He did not much endear himself to corporate interests by signing the Ford Franchise Tax Act in May 1899 after a hotly contested fight. The "interests" represented by "Easy Boss" Thomas Platt set out to push him from office. In fact it was Roosevelt's firm (and correct) belief that New York corporate interests put enormous pressure on Senator Platt and other party leaders to make sure Roosevelt was nominated for the vice presidency, an office that rarely led to the presidency and from which he could cause no trouble for New York corporations. This was a fate Roosevelt wanted to avoid. He revealed his fears to Lodge in a letter penned on April 9, 1900: "The big corporation men ... are especially anxious to have me gotten out of New York somehow. In default of any other way, they would like to kick me upstairs."[40]

Roosevelt was also frustrated by business opposition because businessmen failed to understand, or so he claimed, that his policies ultimately would protect business. He wrote that his balanced approach to trusts was the only way to maintain Republican control in New York and protect corporations from regulation by fanatics. He could not understand why business leaders did not appreciate that he was really their friend.

Roosevelt's unhappiness with being misunderstood was coupled with the need to be liked, both by Platt and by people in general. He was almost fawningly courteous in an extraordinary letter to Platt on May 8, 1899, during the fight over the Ford Franchise Tax Act. At the same time, he tried to persuade the senator that his position was really favorable to corporations, if for no other reason than that it would help to keep the party in office and prevent more damaging legislation. He also tried to absolve himself for taking the position he did: "... I only did take action when it was forced upon me, after an immense amount of thought and worry." To a correspondent in April 1900 he protested that because he supported corporations "when they are right," they ought to know that this gave him a corresponding right to demand their responsible behavior. And writing to Joseph Bishop that same month he insisted that Platt personally liked him, despite the growing corporate pressure on Platt to oppose him, repeating this assertion to John Proctor Clark that same week: "Platt and Odell really like me." To Samuel Hill he wrote: "I cannot help thinking that in the end the big corporation men whose support is really worth having, will understand that I am their friend." The same pattern would repeat itself with the formerly antagonistic "Uncle Mark" Hanna when Roosevelt became president and with whom he developed a warm if complex personal relationship. Roosevelt wanted to be liked and wanted to be understood. He also very much wanted to be elected.[41]

Reading the correspondence leads to the conclusion that part of the reason Roosevelt's trust rhetoric heated up and he became increasingly interested in the problem was that he came to take business's antagonism toward him quite personally. The letters range from defiant to hurt, and some of his antagonism also seems to have developed from his firsthand view of corporate political attitudes and tactics. Both of these reactions are illustrated once he became president, by his authorizing Knox to start the Northern Securities litigation in 1902 and his interactions with the coal operators during the anthracite coal strike later that year. But emotional or not, Roosevelt knew politics. As we will see in Chapter Six, his overwhelming ambition to be elected president in his own right led him to make a dramatic shift from promoting a fairly strong antitrust measure to one that was largely toothless.[42]

Both Roosevelt's emotional attitude and his political astuteness can be seen in the way he developed his annual governor's message for 1900. In early December he sent a draft to Secretary of War Elihu Root, asking him to pass it on to the attorney general. He made a point of noting that he had asked for assistance from Jenks, Hadley and Dill, all of whom were trust supporters and could hardly be described as anything other than conservative.[43]

Roosevelt, like many progressives as well as conservatives, believed the large corporations that were then being assembled "are an inevitable development of modern industrialism." As governor of New York, he gradually began to speak out against trust abuses in a moderate and measured way and concluded his last annual message to the New York State Legislature by listing a catalogue of trust evils and calling for corporate publicity. Corporate misrepresentation of material facts, overcapitalization, unfair competition, monopoly pricing and unfair treatment of workers had to be stopped. In his letter accepting the nomination for the vice presidency he took a stronger position on trusts balanced with respect for the accomplishments of business, noting "real abuses" at the same time that he repeated his caution against unwise legislation. He clearly saw the need to mollify the antitrust agitators for the sake of American prosperity. Publicity, taxation and "regulation, by close supervision, and the unsparing excision of all unhealthy, destructive and anti-social elements" were Roosevelt's remedies.[44]

As president a year later he delivered a message to a joint session of Congress in which he argued for federal supervision of trusts to be coordinated with regulation by the states. (In the same speech he proposed the creation of the Department of Commerce and, within it, the Bureau of Corporations.) Caution and moderation were again the watchwords: "Many of those who have made it their vocation to denounce the great industrial combinations which are popularly, although with technical inaccuracy, known as 'trust,' appeal especially to hatred and fear. These are precisely the two emotions, particularly when combined with ignorance, which unfit men for the exercise of cool and steady judgment."

Speaking on April 9, 1902, at the Charleston Exposition, Roosevelt packaged his ideas about business regulation as compactly as possible while he also made clear the need for federal intervention:

This is an era of great combinations both of labor and of capital. In many ways these combinations have worked for good; but they must work under the law, and the laws concerning them must be just and wise, or they will inevitably do evil; and this applies as much to the richest corporation as to the most powerful labor union. Our laws must be wise, sane, healthy, conceived in the spirit of those who scorn the mere agitator, the mere inciter of class or sectional hatred; who wish justice for all men; who recognize the need of adhering so far as possible to the old American doctrine of giving the widest possible scope for the free exercise of individual initiative, and yet who recognize also that after combinations have reached a certain stage it is indispensable to the general welfare that the Nation should exercise over them, cautiously and with self-restraint, but firmly, the power of supervision and regulation.

Roosevelt tried to preserve the good of big business while carefully regulating its excesses despite the occasional bold public gesture like the Northern Securities suit. Of all the remedies he favored, the one he called for most frequently and before all others was publicity, one of the most conservative of the various approaches to trust regulation then on the table. In the end he neither attacked the trusts aggressively through litigation nor presided over the passage of meaningful trust law reform.[45]

Roosevelt's speeches regarding trust regulation were typically reasonably balanced and respectful of honest big business, despite the occasional war whoop. As the 1902 midterm elections drew closer and his attempt to settle the anthracite coal strike that fall antagonized many business leaders, he became cautious again as the administration embarked on the project of drafting trust legislation. But he was keenly aware of the loud public demand for some kind of reform. The trick was to keep both sides happy and, at least until the elections had passed, Roosevelt did a masterful job.

A speech he gave in Cincinnati on September 20 following a late-summer speaking tour through New England illustrates his caution. A hand-edited copy of a typed draft of the speech is included in the Roosevelt papers. The speech was much like others on the subject, praising the contributions of great businessmen and big business even as he called for regulation of unscrupulous businessmen and monopolies. The edits are especially revealing of Roosevelt's efforts to temper himself in his comments about business and to increase the intensity of praise he heaped upon businessmen.

For example, the phrase "Wherever monopolistic tendency exists" became "Wherever a substantial monopolistic tendency can be shown to exist." Instead of arguing that monopolies should be "curbed," he wrote they should be "controlled." "The evils in big corporations" became "any evils in the conduct of big corporations." "The trusts" became "the so called trusts." "Moreover, in but very few cases" do trusts monopolize became "in very few, if any, cases," do trusts monopolize. Similar changes appear in the markup of a speech given at Providence in August. If nothing else, this illustrates Roosevelt's considerable political skill as he tried to walk the tightrope between the progressives and plutocrats of his own party.[46]

The trust problem was a fast-moving target. Early in the summer of 1902, Roosevelt publicly designated Maine Representative Charles Edgar Littlefield as the administration's congressional point man to develop trust legislation. Knox worked with Littlefield to prepare what became the Littlefield bill, H.R. 17, taken up by Congress in a slightly different form in February 1903. The Littlefield bill inaugurated the federal incorporation era. It would also serve as its high point.[47]

⇥ SIX ⇤

MUCH ADO ABOUT NOTHING

THE FEDERAL INCORPORATION ERA

The long decade from 1900 to 1914 unleashed a flood of corporate reform activity in Congress. No fewer than sixty-two unsuccessful bills embraced federal incorporation or federal licensing. An additional eight attacked overcapitalization and seven more tried to create some form of securities regulation. Six would have protected minority shareholders from abuses by controlling interests, signaling that this new class of public investor was becoming an increasingly influential force in American economic life. A slowly dawning comprehension of the complexity of the corporations problem is reflected by the fact that only five purely antitrust measures were introduced.

Antitrust concerns remained central. But the growing congressional understanding that the corporations problem was bigger than monopoly alone led federal incorporation or licensing proposals to become the most frequently introduced type of antitrust legislation. Antitrust reform came to share the stage with other matters.

Thirty-two federal incorporation bills were introduced between the Industrial Commission's final report in 1902 and the Panic of 1907, with an average of about five a year during the next three years and only three in each of 1912, 1913 and 1914. The relatively steady march of the bills reflects the strong desire of the elected branches to constrain the Supreme Court's freedom to interpret the Sherman Act, a desire that began to relax only when the Court adopted the flexible and economically sensitive rule of reason in the 1911 *Standard Oil* case. The trajectory of the bills tracks Congress' expanding appreciation of the distinct issues of trust regulation, corporate regulation and financial regulation.

Internal corporate governance matters, which traditionally were regulated by the states, sometimes figured in the federal incorporation debate. A number of bills proposed during this period would have imposed strict federal standards of managerial and directorial conduct. A few were so bold as to demand prison for malfeasant managers.[1]

Bills introduced in 1905 and 1906 focused largely on monopoly and required federal incorporation or licensing for interstate businesses. A frequent target was businesses supplying food or fuel products for which consumer demand was relatively inelastic. Bills of this sort were introduced as late as 1909 as were federal incorporation bills in 1910. Proof that a corporation was neither overcapitalized nor a monopoly was a universal requirement.[2]

The shift in issues addressed by federal incorporation bills over time shows the influence of the developing stock market. All of the bills that dealt only with overcapitalization, and thus securities, were proposed between 1907 and 1910. This was a natural response to the Panic of 1907, which exposed the speculative risks some banks and trust companies had taken and the serious damage they inflicted upon the nation's economy. Regulating overcapitalization now was treated as much as a banking and economic problem as it was as an antitrust problem. Securities bills, starting in 1907, focused on the same concerns.[3]

A few measures demonstrated a growing understanding of the way the giant modern corporation had shifted American business from industry to finance and had transformed the stock market from a forum for allocating capital to an institution that facilitated the accumulation of wealth from speculation. Perhaps the most extraordinary illustration of this increasing awareness is S. 232, introduced in the Senate late in the game in 1911. Its focus on overcapitalization aimed at the heart of the antitrust attack. It would have replaced traditional state corporate finance law by preventing companies from issuing "new stock" for more than the cash value of their assets, addressing both traditional antitrust concerns and newer worries about the stability of the stock market by preventing overcapitalization. But it would have done much more.

S. 232 was designed to restore industry to its primary role in American business, subjugating finance to its service. It would have directed the proceeds of securities issues to industrial progress by preventing corporations from issuing stock except "for the purpose of enlarging or extending the business of such corporation or for improvements or betterments," and only with the permission of the Secretary of Commerce and Labor. Corporations would only be permitted to issue stock to finance revenue-generating industrial activities rather than to finance the ambitions of sellers and promoters.

S. 232 would have restored the industrial business model to American corporate capitalism and prevented the spread of the finance combination from continuing its domination of American industry. Following as it did the Panic of 1907 and the resulting depression, it also was designed to preserve the market as a tool for allocating capital rather than as a speculative playground.

Just as S. 232 tied together antitrust, business and securities issues, traces of the new interest in securities regulation appeared throughout the federal incorporation period. Securities regulation as an independent force would slowly begin to emerge from a legislative chrysalis after 1907. Conceived in the wake of the panic and the investigations that followed, it pursued its own legislative path to maturity in the aftermath of the Great Crash. On its way, it passed through three stages, each with a different focus: the antitrust stage, the antispeculation stage and the final and successful consumer protection stage. Securities regulation for trust control was a perennial aspiration and with it came a more subtle but nonetheless palpable hope that new laws could control the economically destabilizing speculation that distorted the market's allocative functions. Speculative binges brought on by the instability of watered stock increased margin trading and short selling and threatened the stability of a banking system suspended within a decentralized and loosely regulated currency system. Banks held barrels of stock as collateral for margin loans, collateral that could turn back into water after a bad week or two on Wall Street. Sheltered by the dark corners of the National Banking Act, banks sometimes conjured up other ways to profit from speculation. Securities regulation scored for banking and economic stability became the theme following the Panic of 1907. The first two stages, the antitrust stage and the antispeculation stage, united, with no success, in 1914.

The federal incorporation period mostly involved regrafting antitrust reform onto a matrix woven of publicity, corporate finance and, to a lesser but nonetheless distinct extent, corporate governance. Overcapitalization was the central antitrust issue that held the framework together; while it started to lose its grip by the end of the decade, it remained important for several decades more, particularly with respect to products with inelastic demand like agricultural commodities. Railroads, as natural monopolies, received perennial attention and attempts to control utility overcapitalization followed later in the decade. The disclosure remedy envisioned by the proposed legislation was a regulatory tool aimed principally at exposing overcapitalization to reveal monopoly and speculation, yet hints of investor protection began to emerge.[4]

This was the landscape of the federal incorporation era. It was gradually laid out over the economic and financial topography of the United States. Congress and the executive tried to shape these developments at the start of the century, to take hold of the new corporate economy and mold it in ways that would subjugate corporate behavior to some notion of responsible public conduct. But resistance by conservative Republicans and Roosevelt's own erratic behavior disrupted any regulation that might seriously have interfered with business. Rather than control the developing corporate economy, they chased it, so that business regulation became a cooperative project between business and government rather than one of federal control. In the end, business was allowed to organize, capitalize and manage as it saw fit. By the time of the major federal antitrust reforms in 1914, the Clayton Act and FTC Act, the moment for federal regulation of business had passed. All eyes were turning to the stock market.

The federal incorporation movement was a failure, but some modest reform did emerge. The only significant corporate legislation, except for some railroad rate regulation that gradually increased the powers of the ICC, was the Nelson amendment to the Department of Commerce bill. The resulting Bureau of Corporations, an investigative body, essentially served as a continuation of the Industrial Commission. One political effect of its creation was perhaps at least as important as its work. Its introduction into the debate over federal incorporation threw sand in the gears of progress of far more extensive regulation. It succeeded admirably. It also placed such minimal regulatory power as was created directly into the hands of Theodore Roosevelt.

THE LITTLEFIELD BILL OF 1903

The most important bill in the history of the federal incorporation movement was the Littlefield bill. First introduced in the House in 1901, the Littlefield bill was reintroduced as a substantially changed draft in 1903, debated by the House in February 1903 and passed unanimously before it was amended and killed in the Senate. The Littlefield bill was important because it was the only federal incorporation measure during the fourteen-year period from the turn of the century to the start of World War I to be seriously debated in either house and passed by at least one. Only the tepid Nelson amendment, which created the Bureau of Corporations within the Department of Commerce and Labor, succeeded as an indirect corporate control measure.[5]

The Littlefield Bill as Federal Incorporation

The Littlefield bill was called an antitrust measure. Its principal focus was overcapitalization. But it was also among the very first federal incorporation proposals. As the Committee Report both stated and illustrates, the premise of the bill was that overcapitalization was the principal "evil" created by the

trusts and the cause of all others. These included monopoly, corporate financial irresponsibility, managerial misbehavior and, almost as an afterthought,
investor fraud. While nominally an antitrust measure, the Littlefield bill
would have operated precisely like most federal incorporation bills. The only
meaningful difference was the absence of a federal incorporation or licensing requirement. But the bill's reporting requirements and its proposed ICC
rulemaking and investigatory powers served the primary purposes of federal
licensing. Coming as it did directly on the cusp of the transition from direct
antitrust regulation to federal incorporation, and in light of its broad substantive overlap, the Littlefield bill should be considered to be among the latter.
The story of its failure reveals a lot about why the federal incorporation movement failed. It is also a personal drama of political rise, betrayal and fall.[6]

Littlefield

Charles Edgar Littlefield was Teddy Roosevelt's choice to lead the charge for
trust reform in Congress. He was first elected to the House as a Republican
from Maine in 1899 and almost instantly asserted leadership, making several
impressive and bold speeches on important issues. He was "admired almost
without exception throughout the party in the House." McKinley consulted
him on matters of policy, which both reflected and increased Littlefield's
early influence. And Littlefield was known as a leader in the antitrust crusade, as one account put it, a "household name."

Littlefield's prominence and reformist bent made him an understandable choice to represent trust reform. But he was, perhaps, a poor political
choice to manage the antitrust fight for a controversial president only recently described by Mark Hanna as "that damned cowboy." He had many of
the more fearsome qualities the plutocracy attributed to Roosevelt without
the underlying political wiliness. He was idealistic, persistent and, perhaps
fatal for any politician but Roosevelt, arrogant and obstinate to a fault.

Littlefield's capacity to make enemies almost equaled his president's.
In November 1902 he led an unsuccessful insurgency to topple Joe Cannon and make himself speaker of the House. Cannon emerged with little
more than a scratch. The *Chicago Daily Tribune* reported the president's
neutrality during the battle and described Littlefield's "pretensions" as meeting "with laughter," at least in part because he had "bolted his party on practically every important question which has arisen since he became a member
of the house." Littlefield found himself increasingly isolated. The powerful
conservative Republicans on the Senate side fretted over his increasing radicalism. But he had been named as Roosevelt's lieutenant and worked with

Attorney General Knox throughout the fall of 1902. In light of public attitudes toward Littlefield it is hard to imagine that the politically savvy Roosevelt would have taken him very seriously. In the end Littlefield's president and party would desert him.[7]

The Bill

The issues raised by the Littlefield bill and during the course of its debate encompassed most of the problems that plagued all later efforts to pass a federal incorporation law. Littlefield introduced H.R. 17 on December 2, 1901, and it was immediately referred to the House Judiciary Committee. That relatively modest piece of legislation required every corporation engaged in interstate commerce to file financial and capitalization reports with the secretary of the treasury, who would publish annually "for free public distribution" a list of all filing corporations together with information on their financial conditions. False filings were to be prosecuted as perjury. More aggressively, all corporations with watered stock had to pay an annual tax equal to 1 percent of their issued and outstanding capital stock.[8]

When the Committee brought the substitute H.R. 17 before the House on January 26, 1903, it was a bill transformed. In some measures it had been diluted, in others strengthened. Filing was no longer to be with the executive-branch secretary of the treasury but with the independent Interstate Commerce Commission. The filing requirement no longer applied to "every corporation engaged in interstate commerce" but instead to "every corporation *which may be hereafter organized*" and which engages in interstate commerce. This protected the combinations formed during the great merger wave from the bill's reach. Instead of annual reports, corporations only had to file reports "at the time of engaging in interstate or foreign commerce," which may or may not have made a practical difference depending upon how the ICC interpreted it. The Committee bill no longer required the report to include a balance sheet and income statement, but it did give the Commission rulemaking power to enforce the law.

The bill's finance provisions had changed, too. The overcapitalization tax was gone. On the stronger side, while corporations still had to report their capital, the bill now required them to disclose the method they used to determine the cash market value of property received for stock, "especially" whether they had done so by capitalizing earnings.

The substitute bill did cover corporate governance matters not addressed in the original. Each corporation had to file its charter and also "a full, true, and correct copy of any and all rules, regulations, and bylaws adopted for the management and control of its business and the direction of its officers, managing agents, and directors." In contrast to the earlier bill, which asked only the corporation's treasurer to certify its information, the Committee bill required that the "president, treasurer, and a majority of the directors of such corporation shall make oath in writing on said return that said return is true."

While the overcapitalization tax had been dropped, the committee bill approached the underlying issue of monopoly in a more traditional way. The three new substantive sections it added would be its downfall in the Senate, said Alabama Representative Henry Clayton, reflecting the Democrats' skepticism that the Republicans had drafted a bill that was intended to pass. A new section 5 prohibited common carriers from granting rebates and other similar advantages to shippers in interstate commerce. Section 6 denied the use of the means of interstate commerce to any "corporation engaged in the production, manufacture, or sale of any article of commerce" that accepted rebates granted in violation of section 5, tried to monopolize its industry, or otherwise attempted to destroy competition in "any particular locality." And section 7 penalized interstate common carriers for knowingly transporting products that were produced, manufactured, or sold in violation either of the Littlefield bill or the Sherman Act. Finally, the committee bill added a provision for a private right of action and treble damages for any person or corporation injured by any behavior made illegal by the act.[9]

The minority report issued on January 29 foreshadowed the terms of the debate. The Democrats wanted the bill to make overcapitalization a ground for declaring bankruptcy, ensure that corporations operating in interstate commerce remained subject to state jurisdiction, impose a capitalization tax on all corporations with capital of more than $200,000 and remove the tariff from a list of domestically trust-produced items.[10]

The Debate

The Littlefield bill failed because of politics. But the debate itself remains important because a number of policy arguments aired during its course were repeatedly used to block federal incorporation throughout the decade. Both sides understood that the American public demanded some kind of trust legislation and that Congress had to provide it. Almost any congressman voting against the bill would have put himself in political jeopardy. Hence the bill passed the House without amendment on February 7, 1903. The vote was 246 to 0, with 6 members answering "present" and 99 members not voting. Nobody could vote against it. But not everybody would vote for it. Many Democrats did not think the bill had gone far enough in regulating trusts or corporations. Many Republicans were beholden to their big business constituents.[11]

The Democrats' Support

Democratic support for the measure was clear and conflicted. Contrary to some accounts of their position during this period, one issue that was not on the table was corporate size. Democrats were not opposed to big business and they did not ground their opposition to trusts in the notion that big was bad. In fact, leading members of the Party repeatedly acknowledged the efficiencies and other benefits created by large corporations.

The real issue was the way the large enterprise was used. Combinations created for monopoly should be restrained. So should combinations created for the sake of finance. Even the largest industrial corporations were legitimate as long as they stuck to their business.

The first aspect was distilled by the brilliant Mississippi congressman John Sharp Williams: "The Democratic party is not afraid of the right sort of combinations of capital. Nobody is afraid of combinations of capital.... It is not a question of the amount, but it is a question of the method in which the combination of capital uses, and is permitted by law to use, its energies after the combination is formed." Corporations formed to monopolize industries were improper uses of capital combination.[12]

Democrats also meant to maintain the business of business as business. Corporations formed for the purpose of industry, to make and sell things, were legitimate. Corporations formed for the purpose of serving the financial goals of their promoters were not. North Carolina Representative Claude Kitchin captured his party's appreciation of the distinction between finance and industry: "We are not against men or riches, or corporations, or big corporations. We admit that large *capital* or large *manufacturing plants* can produce more cheaply than small ones. No man denies their right to this advantage. We deny the necessity of enormous *combinations* for economical production." Industrial corporations, even the very biggest, were assets to the nation. Combinations that were formed for financial purposes were not.[13]

The Democrats were also chagrined that regulation they believed they had nurtured as their birthright might be stolen by a Republican congress. Federal incorporation had been a plank in the Democrat's platform in 1900, and the Democrats had, for years, been clamoring for strong trust legislation. But Congress and the executive branch had been controlled by Republicans since 1895 and Republican Benjamin Harrison had presided over the brief interlude between 1889 and 1891 during which the Republicans again controlled both houses. It was on this Republican watch that the Sherman Act was passed. The Sherman Act had proven to be difficult to use in the hands of the Supreme Court and new legislation was needed. Palpable in the debates was the Democrats' resentment that Republicans, having come late to the cause of effective trust regulation, would be credited with its enactment.[14]

Henry Clayton made the point: "Hereafter, when you discuss the Darwinian theory, which is applicable in the case of mollusks and monkeys, make some application of it to the Republican party.... That party has at last reached the monkey stage, where it has vertebrae and a tail, and monkey-like imitates some of the good actions of the Democratic party."[15]

The Democrats were also convinced that the Republicans were hypocrites. The Littlefield bill was weak regulation to begin with and had been further watered down by the committee. Stronger measures were needed. It also rapidly became clear to all involved that the Senate, under the firm control of the pro-business Republican leaders, would never allow it to pass. Thus the House Democrats were especially bitter that their Republican rivals would reap the political rewards of trust reform without bearing the burden of alienating the plutocrats.

Support it as they did, the Democrats were unhappy about having to rally behind such inadequate reform legislation. One particular complaint was that the Littlefield bill failed to address the high tariffs that many Democrats and a number of economists and businessmen credited with substantially stimulating the growth of trusts by creating a protectionist environment in which they could flourish. Besides, the bill was mostly a publicity measure and the Democrats thought that publicity alone simply was not enough to address the trust problem.

The Issues

The overwhelming concern with overcapitalization and overcharged consumers as the primary problems created by trusts resounded throughout the reports and debates. The Committee Report was quite explicit. It began by surveying the statements of a number of policymakers and authorities. It quoted Roosevelt as well as the attorney general on overcapitalization: "Overcapitalization is the chief of these [trust evils] and the source from which the minor ones flow." It also quoted at length from James B. Dill's testimony before the Industrial Commission on this issue and the Chicago Conference on Trusts transcript as well as from other sources on the value of publicity in preventing trust overcapitalization. Overcapitalization was believed to hurt investors too, but few people yet treated this as an important concern.

Publicity was the principal remedy proposed by the bill. Its main purpose was to expose overcapitalization to the public, especially consumers, in a way that would discourage the practice or lead to government action against the trusts. While the concerns with large corporations were broad and general, it nevertheless becomes clear upon a careful reading of the literature of the period that the major problem was monopoly above all else, and certainly above investor welfare. Only some Americans were investors, but all Americans were consumers. At a time when trusts dominated the supplies of necessities like beef, sugar, kerosene and the like, the problem of overcapitalization leading to overpricing was serious.

The Committee Report made this clear. "It is through the medium of consumers, the purchasers of its products, that the overcapitalized combination finds its most extensive and oppressive contact with the public." While there was some concern expressed for investors, it was far from central.

> The real purposes of overcapitalization are believed to be of an entirely different character, and they all have an injurious effect upon the public. The purpose to create for the stock a fictitious value and thus arbitrarily increase the wealth of the persons interested is undoubtedly the main purpose in overcapitalization. In order to accomplish this, in nearly every instance the price to the consumer must either be increased or maintained above its natural normal level.... As capital is entitled to a fair return, the public is vitally interested in the amount of capital necessary to carry on a given enterprise.

Finance caused monopoly. "The attempt to monopolize the market is not the principal purpose, but an incident thereto, and follows as a necessary corollary of the condition.... Unwarranted dividends and not monopoly are the moving cause. Monopoly is invoked to produce that result."[16]

This was a striking statement, coming as it did from a Republican-controlled Congress and Committee. The principal beneficiaries of stock with "fictitious" values were the very financiers the Republicans were accused of helping. The benefit was not so much in holding the overcapitalized stock but in the ability to unload it on the public that expected the large dividends promised by promoters. To sustain these dividends on the stock of an overcapitalized company, and thus to retain the credibility to create and unload more watered stock, meant promoters had to ensure that their corporations charged high consumer prices.

Overcapitalization was not the only issue. The Democrats repeatedly described the high tariff as creating an incubator for trusts. Railroad rebates had been an issue in trust formation since the 1860s and were a particular hot button for congressmen from the South and West, whose constituents had to pay published shipping rates as they watched the trusts ship for a relative pittance. Issues of states' rights and federal jurisdiction were sometimes raised during the debate and it appears clear that the Democrats as a whole were uncomfortable with the federal government's power to regulate trusts using the potentially elastic commerce clause. As we have seen, the Democrats preferred to use the more limited federal taxing power in their proposed legislation as, for example, to tax watered stock. The Democrats could accept federal power within clearly defined constitutional limits but did not want to create the opportunity to allow it to expand.

Later in the decade, when public investment in common stock became more widespread, public attention returned to more general issues of corporate regulation. When it did, its focus was no longer on governance and overcapitalization. It was on the securities markets.

THE FAILURE OF THE LITTLEFIELD BILL

The Sovereign President

The Littlefield bill presented Roosevelt with a prime political opportunity. The president wanted trust legislation, and indeed needed trust legislation, in order to demonstrate the Republican commitment to reform as the critical midterm elections approached in November 1902. As the issue evolved over time, he also came to see how the right kind of trust legislation could satisfy his personal need for power.

Roosevelt and Knox signed on with Littlefield in July 1902. The campaign for trust reform began in Pittsburgh on Independence Day. The president and his attorney general were in that leading industrial city to attend a dinner in honor of Knox, its native son. Roosevelt's speech kicked off the administration's drive to pass trust legislation during the 57th Congress, well in time for him to begin his presidential campaign. It also marked the subtle beginning of what would become a blatant reach for power.

The Pittsburgh address was similar in tone to Roosevelt's other early speeches calling for intelligent and moderate federal regulation. But now he slipped in another theme, the theme of the administration of wealth. Among the problems caused by modern industrialization, he said, were the rise of great individual and corporate fortunes that skewed the national distribution of wealth and power. But wealth was good. Its image stimulated, and its achievement sustained, the creation of great and beneficent enterprise. The thing that really mattered was how the wealth was used. "It is immensely in the interests of the country" that great wealth existed, as long as it was used for good. The polestar was to be justice. And the administration of justice required a powerful authority. New legislation was required, but, whatever its form, "it is infinitely more important that [the new laws] be administered in accordance with the principles that have marked honest administration from the beginning of recorded history."[17]

The speech is intriguing. It contains some hints about why, by February 17 of the following year, Roosevelt would describe the Littlefield bill as "perfectly idiotic." It also begins to reveal his vision of the presidency. Roosevelt gave no details of the proposed bill in the Pittsburgh speech. But he did stress several times the overwhelming importance that any legislation be fairly and justly administered. Administration, more than the law itself, was the key to justice and efficiency. It is not surprising that administration of the law would be a natural theme in a speech that ended by honoring Roosevelt's chief legal administrator. It is also quite evident that administration of the laws was the constitutional function of the president, not Congress or the courts. The powerful authority that would administer justice was none other than Roosevelt himself.

Roosevelt's desire for personal control of trust regulation had been developing over the course of his young presidency. A good example is his speech at Providence in August in which he characteristically called for judicious, careful and intelligent control of trusts rather than radical measures and noted:

> I believe that the nation must assume this power of control by legislation; and where or if it becomes evident that the constitution will not permit needed legislation, then by constitutional amendment. The immediate need in dealing with trusts is to place them under the real, not nominal, control of some sovereign to which, as its creature, the trust shall owe allegiance, and in whose courts the sovereign's orders may with certainty be enforced.... In my judgment, this sovereign must be the National Government.

He was even more direct in Cincinnati in September: "The necessary supervision and control in which I firmly believe as the only method of eliminating the real evils of the trusts must come through wisely and cautiously framed legislation which shall aim in the first place to give definite control to some sovereign over the great corporations." This would be followed by a system of disclosure. While these speeches do not directly identify executive power, in contrast to general federal power, as the repository for trust regulation, the Nelson amendment creating the investigative Bureau of Corporations, which Roosevelt would turn to instead of the Littlefield bill as his most important trust reform, put the power squarely in the hands of the president.[18]

There is more underlying Roosevelt's reach for presidential control than a simple desire for power, although that there surely was. Implicit in these addresses, as in many of Roosevelt's trust speeches of the period, was a strongly held belief in the supremacy of a leader of a certain type, a supremacy necessary for the public good. It was a belief born of his intellectual and class heritage, a heritage that had passed through Henry Adams to the difficult and imperious John Hay and was the birthright, too, of Roosevelt's close friend Henry Cabot Lodge. It was a peculiarly mandarin philosophy that understood a certain class of best men to be the appropriate repository of American leadership. Roosevelt saw himself as the embodiment of the qualities of his class. The Littlefield bill would have dispersed what Roosevelt came to believe was his rightful power into the new model of the relatively uncontrollable and dangerously democratic independent regulatory agency. In the end, as Roosevelt recognized, the federal government got less power than it might have, but at least it was power in his own hands.[19]

By the time the Littlefield bill was taken up in the House, Roosevelt was already more confident of his own command following the party's success in the midterm elections. Yet he remained cautious in light of his powerful ambition to be elected president in his own right. His confidence in his political ability and policy judgment had also been reinforced by positive public reaction to the way he helped settle the disruptive and very public Pennsylvania anthracite coal strike that took place during the summer and fall. Perhaps a bit immodestly and with a touch of exaggeration, in letters to Lodge and his Harvard classmate (and Morgan partner) Robert Bacon, he compared both his travails and his instincts to Lincoln's, the last president to have accumulated and exercised the strong centralized power that Roosevelt sought. He identified the modern struggle for justice between labor and capital as comparable to Lincoln's own struggle to save the Union and saw his duty as achieving that goal: "[I]f I had failed to attempt [to settle the strike] I should have held myself worthy of comparison with Franklin Pierce and James Buchanan," Lincoln's two predecessors whose inactivity and appeasement helped to bring about the Civil War.[20]

Roosevelt was personally disgusted by the behavior of the coal mine operators during the strike and their expressed attitudes toward the miners themselves. In contrast he was, at least at first, deeply impressed by the quiet dignity and common sense of United Mine Workers' President John Mitchell. The plutocrats needed to be controlled by someone with the strength to control them and the working man—elevated in Roosevelt's estimation by Mitchell's demeanor—deserved protection.[21]

Roosevelt walked a fine line during that autumn of 1902. His sympathy for the miners, especially after he had supported Knox's filing of the *Northern Securities* suit, brought the wrath of Wall Street crashing down on his head. Its already intransigent friends in the Senate were resistant to reform. The Littlefield bill was perceived to be highly regulatory and the Senate leaders made their opposition clear. Although the debate over the Department of Commerce bill had been strenuous enough, its Nelson amendment provided for emasculated regulatory power and, as a consequence, had a fighting chance of passing. The combination of political feasibility and Roosevelt's desire to expand his own powers, his power to administer the laws with justice, were important factors in the way the successful legislation was drafted and Littlefield defeated. His antitrust rhetoric and the fact that power under the bill was lodged in the hands of the "trust buster" assured reasonable public support.[22]

Roosevelt Betrays Littlefield

The combination of political realities and Roosevelt's growing desire for the personal power to regulate business led to his betrayal of his chosen lieutenant. While Littlefield's fall from presidential grace appeared to be swift, it had begun almost from the moment Roosevelt asked him to join forces. On July 5, *The New York Times* reported from Oyster Bay that Roosevelt and Knox had asked Littlefield to work with Knox to prepare the administration's trust bill. Although correspondence with powerful senators during this period is sparse, it must have been the case that swift reaction from the Senate leadership, and presumably others, quickly diminished Roosevelt's enthusiasm for the command of the scrappy congressman from Maine.

Roosevelt embarrassed Littlefield in an incident widely reported by the press that foreshadowed what was to come. He began his speaking tour through New England and the Middle West in August. Among the stops he was scheduled to make was, at Littlefield's personal request, the latter's hometown of Rockland, Maine. Roosevelt simply cancelled the appearance without any explanation. The press had a bit of a field day at the expense of the controversial congressman, with the *Times* noting that the "fact that Rockland had been dropped from the itinerary excited widespread speculation and many smiles." Commenting on the event the paper interjected, perhaps disingenuously, that "[o]f course there is not the slightest reason to believe that Mr. Littlefield has been 'turned down' by the President after the latter had encouraged him to go ahead with his anti-trust plans." The *Times* more generously attributed the cancellation to Roosevelt's wish to avoid further talk of the trust "triumvirate of Roosevelt, Knox and Littlefield," perhaps motivated by Roosevelt's desire to avoid the appearance of a power grab.[23]

It is a curious fact that Roosevelt's papers include no correspondence between Roosevelt and Littlefield during the entire period from July 4 through the adjournment of Congress the following March. One might have expected to see some written communication between the two of them on a matter of such great importance to the president. Correspondence might be all the more expected because Roosevelt spent most of the summer in relative official seclusion at Sagamore Hill and would not likely have had much personal contact with Littlefield. It is at least plausible to infer that, between July and late August, Roosevelt had been lobbied heavily by Republican senators, although there is little written evidence to back this up. Indeed, the manuscripts show very little correspondence to or from Roosevelt with anybody on the trust issue between July 1902 and March 1903. Nonetheless, in several letters written from Oyster Bay in August 1902, he reported that the Republican National Congressional Committee was expressing deep concern about the midterm elections, especially about the lack of campaign contributions, acknowledging that perhaps he had alienated business Republicans by overstating his case against the trusts. Roosevelt's fall correspondence was focused mainly on the coal strike and the midterm congressional elections, while foreign affairs began to dominate somewhat later in the winter of 1903.[24]

Knox gave an important speech in October in Pittsburgh, where he had been sent by Roosevelt as a personal substitute. In it he confirmed the administration's determination to pass the kind of comprehensive legislation Littlefield was drafting. Knox outlined trust measures more aggressive even than Littlefield's approach and certainly more intrusive than the measures ultimately passed. The speech was considered so important that it became the public touchstone for discussions of the administration's antitrust policy. As we have seen, the House Committee Report treated it as authoritative. The *New York Times* referred to it as "being accepted on all sides as a classic on the subject of trust legislation."[25]

Meanwhile, and apparently unknown to Littlefield, Roosevelt had been meeting with Senate Republican leaders and came to realize that a bill as "radical" as the Littlefield measure could not pass. As early as November 1, it was reported that the president was supporting " 'the Attorney General's anti-trust bill,' " an apparent reference to Knox's outline in the Pittsburgh speech. Knox drafted three bills representing the administration's position for the House Judiciary Committee in the late fall. At the same time, "the administration" signaled that the Nelson amendment and the Elkins anti-rebate bill were acceptable substitutes. Massachusetts Senator George Hoar introduced his own bill in early January and his close friendship with Roosevelt's confidante, Henry Cabot Lodge, led to some public speculation that his was the bill that the administration would support. While Littlefield continued to work on the basis of Roosevelt's earlier support and his association with Knox, the ground was shifting beneath him.[26]

Perhaps he should have sensed this shift in all of the confusion of reports. It is hard to believe that he did not read the newspapers. Perhaps he did, and did not care. Littlefield, in the heat of his crusade and perhaps intoxicated by the public attention after his defeat for the speakership, worked either oblivious to or in disregard of the president's changing attitudes. As early as the fight with Cannon, the *Times* reported that there had in fact been no solid basis to conclude that Littlefield was leading the administration's charge on trust matters, and indeed that Roosevelt had largely cut him out. Subsequent events suggest that this was true. On January 23 it was reported that the president was not happy with the Littlefield bill: "It is made clear that it is not an administration measure and does not represent entirely the views of the administration on what anti-trust legislation should be enacted by this congress." But it was only when the bill was languishing in the Senate several weeks later that Littlefield visited Roosevelt to affirm his backing. It was then, and evidently for the first time, that the president told him, with characteristic bluntness, that his bill was worthless. Without telling Littlefield, and even as the debate over his bill proceeded in the House, Roosevelt had shifted his support to three separate, and ultimately successful, measures: the Elkins Anti-Rebate Act outlawing price discrimination by railroads; a bill to allow the courts to expedite antitrust prosecutions; and the Department of Commerce Act which, with the Nelson amendment creating the Bureau of Corporations, became known as the administration's antitrust measure.[27]

It is hard to feel terribly sorry for Littlefield. It appears that few of his contemporaries did. He must have read the newspapers and felt the lack of communication from Roosevelt. Perhaps he was reassured of the president's support because of Knox's cooperation, but by early November it was clear to everyone else that the president himself had cut Littlefield out of the anti-trust campaign and that Knox was drafting his own bill. Perhaps his own "tenacity of opinion when he once makes up his mind" contributed to a certain blindness that extended to his party's fairly strong opposition to trust legislation in the Senate. The Department of Commerce bill had been making its way through the Senate since its introduction on December 4, 1901, and the Nelson amendment finally had been introduced on February 9, 1903. He had to have seen that the politically vital Senate, where real control of the Republican Party rested, would be pushing its own measures.[28]

Roosevelt's own account of the matter suggests a later date for his abandonment of Littlefield at the same time that he provided evidence of an earlier switch. In a single letter where he specified the timing of his change, he described his own embrace of the new approach to have been as early as Knox's Pittsburgh speech. Writing on February 3 to Lawrence Abbott, the son of Roosevelt's friend and frequent editor, Lyman Abbott of *The Outlook*, he explained: "In the trust matters I am having one astounding development here. A month ago I had the fight definitely as to whether we should have legislation or not.... I then asked for the three measures which Knox had been devoting himself to preparing along the lines of his Pittsburgh speech." Those measures were the three successful measures introduced in and pushed by the Senate, of which only the rebate measure was at all similar to anything in the Littlefield bill. Of these he wrote, "[p]ersonally I regard the Nelson amendment on account of the supervision and publicity clauses as the most important." Roosevelt reported "very much secret opposition" to the Elkins and Littlefield bills, with "the extremists" plotting to have the House reject the Nelson amendment and the Senate reject Littlefield, leaving no trust legislation at all.[29]

Political Realities

It made good political sense for Roosevelt to shift to the Nelson amendment, which focused on investigation and publicity as the remedy, rather than the Littlefield bill, which even in its diluted form provided more intrusive and substantive regulation. The Nelson bill allowed him to claim victory in the trust battle and thus to have fulfilled his promise to the public without unduly alienating the conservatives of his own party. At the same time, the location of the Bureau of Corporations in the cabinet-level Department of Commerce gave him the centralized control he so badly wanted.

Despite his own professed success, Roosevelt remained sensitive to possible public accusations of betraying the cause of trust reform. On December 27 he complained bitterly to a correspondent who was pushing him to insist on stricter trust measures than the simple and attenuated publicity contained in the Nelson amendment, claiming with some justification that he had always stood for publicity as the appropriate regulatory approach: "But are you aware that to make publicity an issue is mere nonsense unless I frame legislation which will give us a chance to get it? Are you also aware of the extreme unwisdom of my irritating Congress by fixing the details of a bill, concerning which they are very sensitive, instead of laying down the general policy?" Knox and he had started to work more cooperatively with Congress, Roosevelt having come to understand that dictating legislation was sure to cause him trouble.[30]

Roosevelt had not exactly ingratiated himself with Wall Street, either. The *Northern Securities* suit that Knox filed the previous spring had "stunned" Morgan. Roosevelt's sympathy for the workers and undisguised distaste for the operators during the anthracite coal strike made things worse. The *New York Sun*, edited by Morgan's friend and client, William Laffan, had attacked Roosevelt so bitterly that he impugned Laffan's editorial integrity by accusing him of speaking the voice of Morgan. In response, Laffan denied that Morgan had applied any pressure on the paper to attack Roosevelt and took full responsibility for the article. Roosevelt's friend, "the professional journalist, sycophant, and anti-Semite, Joseph Bucklin Bishop," on the other hand, wrote that Morgan indeed was behind the *Sun*'s attack, describing "his bitter personal feeling toward you." But Roosevelt's troubles ran deeper: "There is in his circle in Wall Street an undercurrent of hatred toward you of which this is a surface indication." While it is likely that this is overstatement, it must have hurt Roosevelt who, as we have seen, cared deeply that the powerful liked and respected him.[31]

Roosevelt did keep a pipeline open to Morgan through Bacon and Bacon's partner in the Morgan firm, George Perkins. Roosevelt had also developed a real friendship with Hanna, who seems to have become both fond and respectful of Roosevelt following his initial dismay, grounded only partly in his genuine affection for McKinley, at Roosevelt's ascension to the White House. Hanna was a particularly important asset to Roosevelt because he was independent of Aldrich, Spooner, Platt and Allison at the same time that his business *bona fides* were unquestionable. His childhood friendship with John D. Rockefeller gave Hanna even greater business credibility. Roosevelt had to have realized through these allies that he would have significant trouble achieving any sort of trust legislation and that it was critical that anything he supported would at least be acceptable to Wall Street.

The End of the Littlefield Bill and the Creation of the Bureau of Corporations

The shift from proposals to statutes happened fast. Politics was the driving force. And Roosevelt was at least as much a follower as a leader. Pressure came both from Republicans and Democrats. On January 17, J. C. Shaffer, president of the *Chicago Evening Post*, warned him, "I discovered in the past three days that there was a great change in the sentiment of some of the leading senators, and the progressive men in the house, in regard to needed legislation on trusts [and] finances." The scheming was not over. On February 3, Jeremiah Jenks wrote a somewhat agitated letter to Roosevelt describing "an ingenious plan" by the Democrats that he learned of while in New York several days earlier. Jenks reported that they were plotting to introduce a bill permitting corporations to incorporate voluntarily under a federal law that would mimic the New York Business Companies Act of 1900. Roosevelt had approved that very law while governor. "They think that it will rather seriously embarrass the Republicans to reject it, and that it is too rigid a bill for them to approve." Jenks characteristically waffled, noting to the president at this late date and with rumors of the Democratic plot, that federal incorporation "is probably constitutional." He had earlier objected to federal incorporation while he served the Industrial Commission because "it was altogether too centralizing." Now Jenks changed his mind and informed the increasingly imperial Roosevelt that he would support such a bill if proposed. But the path of legislation had been plotted out and was in the process of following its course. House debate on the Littlefield bill would begin the next day.[32]

The Littlefield bill's progress was closely followed by the national press, which reported every step along the way. But it progressed through a legislative obstacle course. The Department of Commerce bill had been debated, passed by both houses and was in conference committee at the time the Littlefield bill was taken up. On February 9, the Senate conferees approved the Nelson amendment. That amendment added a new Bureau of Corporations to the Department of Commerce and was considered, in its investigatory and publicity capacities, to be the Senate's antitrust measure. The House strenuously objected to this last-minute Senate interjection into its own antitrust debate, correctly fearing that it was designed to displace the Littlefield bill. The Elkins Anti-Rebate bill, covering railroad rebates and thus overlapping Section 5 of the Littlefield bill, had been introduced in the Senate on January 21, 1903: Senate leaders were pressuring Littlefield to drop the anti-rebate section of his own bill on the same day that debate on that measure had begun in the House. A legislative race to set the terms of trust legislation had begun between the House and Senate.[33]

During the three-day House debate on the Littlefield bill, the Senate passed with almost no comment the Elkins bill, the expediting bill and the Nelson amendment. It referred these measures to the House before that latter body's debate on the Littlefield bill had even ended. The day after the Littlefield bill passed, the conference committee on the Department of Commerce bill agreed to include the Nelson amendment which, according to *The New York Times*, was "the anti-trust measure favored by the administration." It was clear by then that nobody thought the Littlefield bill had a prayer.[34]

The Littlefield bill was killed off in the Senate on February 27 after that body voted to strengthen it by amendment. Littlefield, almost completely isolated now and refusing to accept reality, fought to the end, voting as the lone House Republican against the Department of Commerce bill and refusing to vote at all on the Elkins bill. That latter measure passed the House with lukewarm Democratic support on February 13. The expediting bill and the Department of Commerce Act along with the Nelson amendment passed on February 5 and 14, respectively. These results were celebrated in some quarters as the best that could be achieved, while most accounts recognized the acts as relatively ineffectual. Business interests were generally pleased. What had happened?[35]

Teddy Roosevelt's political survival instincts had gotten the better of him. The Republican Senate, despite the presence of some reformers, was run by Aldrich and his cronies, and as discussions continued throughout January it became obvious to Roosevelt that he would never win the more aggressive measures he favored. But his political survival might have been in jeopardy if it looked as though he were running from the strong trust program he had announced and that he and Knox had been publicly pursuing. Even as his agenda changed, he could not withdraw his support for the Littlefield bill without a credible alternative that would pass with the conservatives but at the same time could be displayed as a public victory against the trusts. Thus, until he was secure that trust legislation of some form would pass, he had to remain publicly committed to the Littlefield bill.[36]

The Department of Commerce and Bureau of Corporations promised to give Roosevelt considerable control. The Department itself, as a cabinet-level agency, concentrated a great deal of plenary authority for American business regulation in the nation's chief executive. As Nelson's biographer put it: "President Roosevelt was quite enthusiastic over the establishment of the department of commerce and labor and the reorganization and rearrangement of boards and bureaus which it affected."[37]

Even when the new legislation was at hand, Roosevelt was hardly home free. Although House Democrats were skeptical of the Littlefield bill's chances from the beginning, Roosevelt had to deal with a united House in the face of the Senate's last-minute, and considerably weaker, measures. There was hardly consensus in the Senate, with the pro-business Republican wing still balking at the idea of any trust legislation at all. Roosevelt was also keenly aware that the public had been expecting strong antitrust action.

Roosevelt threatened to call a special session of Congress as a House-

Senate standoff became a real possibility. It was at that point that he pulled off a political stunt that assured that the Nelson amendment would pass.[38]

On February 7, the day the Littlefield bill passed the unanimous House, Roosevelt announced that it had come to his attention that telegrams had been sent by Standard Oil to six key senators stating Standard's opposition to any antitrust legislation and bearing the signature of the retired John D. Rockefeller. The telegrams notified the senators that they would be called upon to discuss the matter by Standard's counsel. With this, it was also revealed that Standard had been pressuring the administration to kill the Littlefield bill and was especially dismayed by the Nelson amendment. The opposition certainly was plausible. It would have been consistent with the interests of the notoriously secretive Rockefeller in light of the investigative and publicity powers the bill would have given the Bureau of Corporations. As Roosevelt intended, the news set off a tempest in Congress and among the public and gave the president the kind of political leverage he needed to kick through the Nelson amendment over conservative opposition. In fact, one story reported him as "very well satisfied with the effect produced" by reports of the telegrams. It was apparent that the Littlefield bill would die in the Senate. It all worked as he had planned. But there was a catch.

Roosevelt's story was not true—or at least not entirely. One of the senators identified as receiving a telegram said the telegrams were fake. Four of the identified senators denied receiving telegrams at all. One senator close to the administration confirmed the story, but when asked to show his telegram it obviously had not been signed by John D. Rockefeller. Matt Quay published the telegram he had received but its text made clear that it was sent as a response to Quay's own letter. While some reports credited Roosevelt's account as true, at least in part, far more suspected that any telegrams that had been sent were instigated by Roosevelt in order to ensure passage of the Nelson amendment. One historical account, although not identifying source materials, claimed that the telegrams never had existed, were Roosevelt's pure invention, and that he later admitted this, claiming the important thing was that he had gotten his legislation.

Rockefeller's biographer, Allan Nevins, told a different story. He reported that Rockefeller did not send the telegram, "but it can now be revealed that his son had done so." John D. Rockefeller, Jr., wrote to Senators Allison, Lodge, Hale and Teller articulating Standard's objection to all legislation except the Elkins Act. Other Standard employees wrote telegrams opposing the Nelson amendment. John Archbold, Standard's counsel, did intend to meet with senators, although in the end he thought it necessary to meet only with Aldrich who had, after all, become part of the Standard Oil family after his daughter's marriage to John D. Rockefeller, Jr., in 1901. Nevins, sympathetic biographer that he was, did not let Roosevelt off the hook. He noted that Lodge had all the facts and could have told them to the president and, implying that Roosevelt either knew or ignored what Lodge knew, concluded that "it is evident that he had deliberately used the Rockefeller bogey to promote his special purposes."[39]

What happened to Littlefield? By early February, Roosevelt was calling the Littlefield bill "idiotic." Even as debate on the bill had begun, members of the House became aware of the fact that the president had withdrawn his support, which, along with the activity in the Senate, accounts for repeated Democratic comments during the debate accusing the Republicans of cynicism in their support for it. This evidently was the first time that Littlefield showed that he was aware of the fact that his president had abandoned him. He went to the White House and was told rather pointedly that the administration's support was for Elkins, Nelson and the expediting bill. Littlefield continued anyway, railing like King Lear in the face of an increasingly dwindling audience. By the end of the debate he was being openly mocked.[40]

Things went downhill for Littlefield from that point on. He had been so ostracized by his own party that he was not permitted to speak during the brief House debate on the Elkins bill. His downfall pleased the House leaders whose positions he had so recently challenged. Although he lost the fight for the speakership, he had earlier led the insurgents against the House leadership and won significant internal reforms. He had risen to power quickly, exhibited hubris and fell just as fast. The battle over the Littlefield bill left him politically weakened and publicly ridiculed. But Littlefield was resilient and, evidently, forgiving. Before he retired in 1908 to practice law in New York, he and Roosevelt had one last chance at federal incorporation, in the Hepburn bill of 1908.[41]

Federal incorporation as a regulatory approach failed for a number of reasons. But the Littlefield bill failed largely because of Roosevelt's ambition.[42]

SOUND AND FURY—THE FIRST REPORT
OF THE BUREAU OF CORPORATIONS

Congress was not going to get explicit constitutional power to regulate trusts. Neither was Roosevelt going to be granted the power he wanted for himself. He was not shy about his goals. In his *Autobiography* he wrote: "My view was that every executive officer in high position, was a steward of the people bound actively and affirmatively to do all he could for the people, and not to content himself with the negative merit of keeping his talents undamaged in a napkin." The president did not need specified powers to fulfill this stewardship, wrote Roosevelt. He was to do his duty implicit in the office, unless his action was specifically prohibited by the Constitution or under law. Sensitive to charges about his desire for power, he continued: "I did not usurp power, but I did greatly broaden the use of executive power."[43]

The early phase of the federal incorporation debate ended with the creation of the Bureau of Corporations. Its charge was to gather information about trusts and industry and report that information to the president, who would decide whether to publicly disclose it, initiate litigation, or propose legislation. Thus the Bureau of Corporations, headed by the highly respected and politically connected lawyer (and son of a former president) James R. Garfield, served almost the same mission as the Industrial Commission had, except for its position in the federal government. And so the Bureau picked up where the Industrial Commission left off, engaging in elaborate and detailed industrial studies and recommending legislation and litigation. For all its good work, though, the Bureau reinvented the wheel. The Bureau's recommendations returned precisely to those of the Industrial Commission.[44]

The Bureau set upon its task quickly and aggressively with a distinguished staff of economists and lawyers under Garfield's able direction. During its existence from 1903 until its merger into the FTC in 1914 it produced a substantial number of thorough industry studies, ranging from meatpacking to oil (both of which resulted in successful antitrust litigation against the Beef Trust and Standard Oil, respectively). But the Bureau's function that is relevant here—its first official act—was to recommend a federal franchise law to address a variety of corporate problems. On December 21, 1904, President Roosevelt delivered the first Report of the Commissioner of Corporations to Congress.[45]

The Report had been eagerly awaited. According to the *New York Times*, even the Report's release date was significant, coming as it did immediately before a congressional recess "so as to give the fullest opportunity for consideration and discussion while Congress is not in session, so that when Congress returns it will be able to deal with the subject more fairly and with better information." The *Times* also noted the Report's direct attack on the products of the merger wave: "The report does not mince words in denouncing the present State system. It contrasts the corporation law of Massachusetts with the 'piratical possibilities' of other States, and it declares that 'a majority of the corporations organized of late years have been organized for the stock market.'" The *Times* article picked up the "leading evils" identified in the Report as being secret and dishonest promotion, overcapitalization, rate discrimination in transportation, unfair competition and dishonest financial disclosures.[46]

The rest of the national and local press also jumped on the news. As the *Philadelphia Public Ledger* reported on December 25, 1904: "Mr. Garfield is keeping in close touch with the newspapers on his annual report, recently made public. 'These criticisms are welcome,' said Mr. Garfield. 'We want the views of every man on the subject, because the question is an important one and deserving of the most careful consideration of the more thoughtful of the American people.'"[47]

Garfield had a great deal of criticism (and praise) with which to contend and the *Public Ledger*'s account of his attention to the newspapers is borne out by a file consisting of hundreds of pages of newspaper clippings, arranged by state, in the Bureau's records. This mass of articles, often on the front pages of their respective papers, appeared mainly between December 22, 1904 and early January 1905. Surely this is testimony to the intense degree of public attention paid to the matter—and Garfield's concern with it.[48]

One reading these articles could be forgiven for reaching the conclusion that the Report argued for a sweeping change in America's founding ideals and its very way of life. One could be forgiven for reaching the conclusion that the Report recommended a massive overhaul of corporate law and even of the structure of the nation's republican form of government. One could certainly be forgiven for concluding that the Report advocated changes that would radically alter the complexion of corporate America and, with it, the nation itself. But a careful reading of the Report would rapidly disabuse one of these conclusions. For what that reading reveals is that the alarmism of so many newspapers picks up on what might be referred to as the Report's "sound and fury." In the end, while not exactly signifying nothing, the Bureau's reform suggestions were very modest indeed.

Nonetheless public debate, at least as reflected in the newspapers, was intense. The political aspect of the debate that perhaps is hardest to sort out is that favorable and critical reactions were not clearly drawn along party lines or regional lines. (There were more than a few newspapers that suggested that Roosevelt both anticipated and manipulated this nonpartisan reaction, a perfectly plausible suggestion.) The Report's reception among big business leaders was, at worst, tolerant and, more commonly, wholly supportive. After all, many of them—including John D. Rockefeller—had testified in support of such a plan before the Industrial Commission. There was a substantial midday decline on the New York Stock Exchange the day the Report was released, but the market's recovery by day's end suggests that Wall Street took the plan in stride. Traders seemed to discount the likelihood that serious regulation would result.[49]

In contrast to the support of business leaders, more than a few newspaper accounts reported that leading corporation lawyers were opposed to it. This was misleading. Certainly one, the ubiquitous James B. Dill, was opposed, but on the ground that the Report did not go far enough toward recommending federal control of trusts. A similar "oppositional" attitude was expressed by Sam Untermyer.[50]

Indeed, the fact that big business supported the plan was one of the critical refrains in the press. Even worse, one Ohio newspaper reported that the Report's recommendation was virtually identical to a plan suggested by both John Archbold of Standard Oil during his testimony before the Industrial Commission and by John D. Rockefeller himself. The *Cincinnati Commercial Tribune* referred to this revelation as an "interesting and somewhat humorous development," noting that it had "attracted much attention" in Ohio, although the newspapers of that state, where the reviled Standard had been spawned and had left its indelible mark, were virtually unanimous in support of the plan. Some failed to see the humor. The *Mansfield (Ohio) Shield*, misstating the nature of the plan, wrote: "The fact that the Rockefeller interests approve the proposition of Commissioner Garfield for the federal incorporation of the trusts throws a strong shade over the plan."[51]

Reports critical of the plan repeated the idea that business support proved that the federal government would make it easier for the trusts than did the states. In one critique, the *New York World* stated its opposition to any such federal reform until "a corrupt-practices law is enacted" forbidding corporate contributions to federal elections.[52]

Virtually none of the opposition was directed to the general idea of regulating big business. The *Wheeling (West Virginia) Register*, while opposing the plan, gave a remarkably frank assessment of the situation, noting that the leading states in charter mongering, specifically West Virginia, New Jersey and Delaware, were "wholly to blame" for the federal proposal. The newspapers more or less universally recognized that the uncontrolled growth of big business regulated by lax state laws allowed for the evils of overcapitalization, overcharging, fraud and managerial self-dealing.[53]

The central objection was the way the plan diminished state power in favor of the federal government. There is some weak evidence that the opposition on these grounds broke down over state lines, with more opposition in the South and in chartermongering states like New Jersey and West Virginia, and somewhat more mixed views among the New England states and those of the far West.[54]

New York City is where the newspaper battleground was the most bloodsoaked. The Democratic *New York Times* printed dozens of articles on the subject in this short period, sometimes writing on what appears to be the verge of hysteria. (Although the *Times* was Democratic, it does bear noting in light of its strong opposition to the plan that Morgan had helped finance Adolph Ochs's purchase of the paper in 1896 and briefly remained as an investor.) In one article the *Times* suggested that the plan was designed to "abolish the states." In another, it howled that Garfield was attempting to erect "a trust Gibraltar" in Washington and in yet another it claimed that Roosevelt had duplicated Bryan's plan and that "The Socialists are highly satisfied with both of these rivals in radicalism." The progressive *New York World* equally opposed the plan, seeing in it the "nullification of constitutional government" and suggesting that "Emperor" would be a title inadequate to describe Roosevelt's aspirations. The *New York Daily News* predicted that Roosevelt would soon be running American business and the *New York Commercial Bulletin* called the plan "a complete subversion of the policy established by the Constitution of the United States." What appears to the modern eye to be a suggestion for the most modest of business regulations was at the time treated as rising to the level of a constitutional crisis.[55]

The Wall Street Journal was a relatively strong supporter of the plan. It described the states' rights arguments as a tactic used by regulation's opponents to give legally (and politically) legitimate cover to their general opposition to regulating business, a claim that correctly represented the views of many Republican states' righters but was unfair to the understandable concerns of the proregulation Democrats. While the *Journal* was no fan of centralized federal power, it nonetheless concluded: "However much we may deplore and fear the increased centralization of power in the Federal government, which is involved in this direct control of interstate commerce, it cannot be doubted that it is the only solution of the corporation problem that now appears feasible." And what was that problem? The failure of the states "to protect those dealing with corporations as employes [*sic*], creditors or consumers, and to protect the public from the abuse of economic power coupled with little personal responsibility [among directors and officers]."[56]

That the debate over the Roosevelt-Garfield Plan should have so confused interests, regions and parties, both in support and in opposition, may be attributed at least in part to what several papers referred to as the "Rooseveltian" nature of the plan. This was its capacity to steer between (or, less charitably, pander to) both sides in the trust debate, without fully satisfying either. Continuing states' rights concerns, exacerbated by Roosevelt's aggressive talk of centralization, also hindered rational evaluation of the proposal. The intense negative reaction to the Report was more a function of Roosevelt's increasingly strong rhetoric in favor of executive power, coupled with his actions in the coal strike, than the specific details of the plan itself. Controversial or not, Congress would ultimately not let go of the idea of federal incorporation or licensing until 1914.[57]

The Bureau's Recommendations—A Modest Proposal

The fact that the Garfield plan aroused such strong emotions is surprising in light of how conservative it was, measured even by Roosevelt's ambitions as expressed by Knox in his Pittsburgh speech two years earlier:

> The conspicuous noxious feature of trusts existent and possible are these: Overcapitalization, lack of publicity of operation, discrimination in prices to destroy competition, insufficient personal responsibility of officers and directors for corporate management, tendency to monopoly and lack of appreciation in their management of their relations to the people, for whose benefit they are permitted to exist.

Knox had articulated the administration's policy as attacking a set of concerns that, when taken together, amounted to much of the regulation traditionally expected under state corporate law. But Roosevelt wound up backing something far different and aimed almost exclusively at only one feature of that platform—monopoly.[58]

Consistent with the Industrial Commission's concerns, the Report concluded: "Under present industrial conditions, secrecy and dishonesty in promotion, overcapitalization, unfair discrimination by means of transportation and other rebates, unfair and predatory competition, secrecy of corporate administration, and misleading or dishonest financial statements are generally recognized as the principal evils." It is no surprise that at the conclusion of a merger wave in which overcapitalization appeared as one of the most prominent issues, dishonest promotion and capitalization ranked high among the Bureau's concerns. It is also clear that the railroads remained an active problem, as did the fear of monopoly expressed by the Bureau in its talk of "unfair and predatory competition." Finally, corporate secrecy and dishonesty in financial reporting remained paramount as a consistent refrain throughout these reform efforts, leading mostly to calls for regulatory disclosure.[59]

The Bureau invoked its congressional charge to find remedies for these ills through legislation, noting its desire to reserve criminal sanctions for only the gravest abuses. Its preferred solution was to create better processes. Its approach, by its own admission, was to be "conservative" in keeping with the Roosevelt administration's practical approach to regulating big business. Suing a financial holding company like Northern Securities was one thing (and it did not hurt that the suit allowed Roosevelt to make a symbolic statement that he was beholden to nobody). But killing the goose that had laid the golden egg, the engine of American prosperity, was entirely another. Reform, if it were to proceed, would proceed cautiously.[60]

The Report acknowledged the degree to which industry had become overtaken by finance. It noted that the speed of corporate growth and combination had allowed corporate America to be captured by the financiers, the segment of corporate America that the Report most strongly criticized. The Report acknowledged that "the forces that have shaped" corporation law fail to distinguish the "purely financial interests" from "production," showing sophisticated economic sensitivity to the difference between industry and finance. Elaborating on this concern, the Report noted that the divisibility of corporate interests into shares "permits the creation of stock and its use as a sort of currency; taken in connection also with the transferability of stock interests, it allows speculative manipulation." Finally, this divisibility of interests allowed the controlling interests of a corporation to take advantage of the minority shareholders, an observation consistent with the recent history of promoters dumping buckets of watered stock on the market. The Bureau of Corporations understood that finance dominated industry. It did precious little about the matter.

The focus on the way the merger wave privileged finance over industry and the Bureau's concern with it was clear. But the Bureau, and thus the Roosevelt administration, squandered the chance for the federal government to take control of regulating business away from the states.

The Bureau's solution makes this apparent. After examining the crazy quilt of state laws and the cupidity of state legislatures (for chartermongering at this point had spread well beyond the borders of New Jersey), the Report concluded: "The present situation of corporation law may be summed up roughly by saying that its diversity is such that in operation it amounts to anarchy." And, rather more pointedly, "The net result of this State system is thoroughly vicious." The Bureau's solution to this anarchy was clear; the federal government had to seize some control over corporate regulation, bring order to the process of interstate and foreign trade and stop the abuses of the preceding decade.

The Report presented and discussed two possible solutions: federal chartering for corporations engaged in interstate commerce and federal licensing or franchising of such corporations. The Bureau rejected federal chartering. One reason was the lingering uncertainty as to whether Congress constitutionally could create corporations engaged in interstate trade with the power to "produce or manufacture" within the states. The Supreme Court had clearly distinguished between trade and manufacture. If Congress had no power to regulate manufactures, it could not create useful corporations to operate within state lines.

The second reason the Bureau rejected federal incorporation is more puzzling. The Bureau expressed significant concern over the constitutionality of state power to tax federally chartered corporations. Interstate corporations were producing substantial amounts of taxable income, and if the states could not tax them they would lose a significant source of revenue. While one can easily see the federal government's practical desire to preserve state revenue, the Bureau's position was a bit of a paradox. The successful modernization of state corporation law had its genesis in New Jersey's financial problems. It was precisely the states' attempts to make money by abusing their powers to regulate corporations that created the demand for federal regulation in the first place. While one can imagine that the federal government did not want to pick up the bill, the Bureau's reasoning left the corporations problem right back where it was created.

Finally, the Report expressed concern that federal incorporation might accelerate "the centralization of power in the Federal government," an odd concern in light of Roosevelt's express desires. Given the political battles of February 1903, it is obvious that federal incorporation was the least feasible option. Yet it probably would have been the most effective regulatory approach as the giant modern corporations were growing sufficiently powerful potentially to dominate the federal government itself.

The Bureau's recommended approach was federal licensing or franchising. Federal franchising would maintain the status quo of state chartering under state law and preserve the states' abilities to tax their corporations. At the same time it would allow the federal government to impose standards of conduct, mandate regulatory disclosure and prohibit corporations that violated those requirements from engaging in interstate commerce. It was regulation of a sort. But it was not business regulation.

The Garfield plan was a peculiar compromise. Peculiar because, in its conservatism, it failed to allow for enough federal regulation to address the problems of disparate state laws; peculiar because the Report, short on details, did not specify whether and how federal licensing would address the main problems the Bureau identified (overcapitalization, financial misbehavior and the abuse of minority shareholders); peculiar because it seems as though the plan was designed as much to avoid legal and political challenge as it was to solve the problems identified by the Bureau and the Industrial Commission.

While the federal licensing plan was never passed, it would find its ultimate realization, albeit in a purely antitrust form, in the FTC, a body that used regulatory disclosure to aid its enforcement. It was only an administrative body with particular expertise that could make judgments based on the particulars of each case. So while the antitrust problem was eventually resolved, the federal government would never adequately address the internal problems of corporate finance and minority shareholder abuse that were the subjects of so much public concern.

The Garfield Plan came to nothing. Its legacy was to set the subject of federal incorporation squarely on the legislative table as the administration's project. Roosevelt was hardly a quitter, and while he turned his attention to railroad regulation for the next several years, he would bring back a comprehensive and far-reaching federal incorporation measure as his second term drew to a close. That term was also marked by the Panic of 1907, an event that brought the economic dangers of speculation in the securities of the giant modern corporation to the forefront of public concern and gave Roosevelt a last chance at achieving federal incorporation. As federal incorporation proceeded, so did the first federal steps toward securities regulation.

◄ SEVEN ►

PANIC AND PROGRESS

T he Panic of 1907 was a watershed event for currency regulation, banking regulation and securities regulation. It was the first serious economic panic to occur after the creation of the giant modern corporation had brought significant numbers of ordinary Americans into the stock market and demonstrated the impact that the new market could have on American business and the overall economy. It led Roosevelt, who was blamed by conservatives for causing the panic by attempted overregulation, to make a final unsuccessful push for federal incorporation. The seeds of federal securities regulation that had been planted in the antitrust debate began to grow out of both that effort and the various investigations that followed. Federal securities regulation started to receive distinct attention in its own right as the antitrust phase of securities regulation gave way to the antispeculation phase. These earliest attempts at securities regulation were notable for their halting efforts to address the consequences of the dominance of finance over industry created by the merger wave and the rapidly developing speculation economy. All of them failed.[1]

The new generation of individual investors that had recently entered the market created its own set of problems. Uneducated and uninformed individuals put too much money into speculative securities. While a few might get rich, the best they could do for the most part was to see their wealth diminish in a bursting bubble. Or they could lose their investments in worthless stock. While this troubled some lawmakers and the president, its importance as a public concern remained minimal during an age in which *caveat emptor* still had some currency. And while the number of individual investors was increasing, the absolute numbers were not large enough to create a constituency for change. This was especially true when the executive and both houses of Congress were Republican and remained there in substantial part by the grace of business.

Concern over the tie between bank stability and speculation was also an outgrowth of the Panic, branching off from the antitrust debate's focus on overcapitalization. As early as the turn of the century, elastic state laws and federal convenience in an age of decentralized currency liberated banks, insurance companies and, especially, trust companies to increase their profits by becoming big investors in speculative securities. But until the Panic, the problem of banking stability, like the issue of investor protection, remained subjugated to antitrust concerns.[2]

The unstable banking system created by banks' and trust companies' increasing direct and indirect investments in corporate securities presented a new federal problem as the first decade wore on. Some looked to the stock exchanges to help stabilize the financial markets. The stock exchanges, including the single most important one—the NYSE—were private associations, answerable only to themselves. The NYSE sometimes adopted new rules to stave off federal regulation, as it would in 1913 following the Hughes Committee report on speculation and in the middle of the Pujo investigations of the Money Trust. But enforcement of these often ambiguous rules was entirely discretionary with the Exchange, which persisted in doing little to regulate itself. In fact the only violation that could get a member permanently expelled from the NYSE was sharing or cutting commissions. Fraud, stock manipulation and other forms of cheating customers could only be punished with brief suspensions. As with its members, so with the corporations it listed. The Exchange did little to enforce its disclosure laws. The New York state government also showed little appetite for exchange regulation.

THE PANIC OF 1907

The Dow doubled between 1904 and 1906. Old-style speculation was pervasive. Mining stocks were the driving force, as they would be the catalyst of the panic. But the winter of 1907 brought a rude if brief awakening. The money market tightened and credit increasingly was hard to come by, not least for brokerage houses. Railroads had been put under severe monetary pressure the previous year. Some brokerages closed up shop. Now a March stock panic crushed prices on the NYSE, wiping out $2 billion in market value.[3]

U.S. Steel's resumption of dividends and an increase in Union Pacific dividends brought temporary relief. But the Egyptian and Tokyo exchanges collapsed in April. The summer brought more bad news. New York failed to attract buyers for two bond issues, and San Francisco repeated New York's failure. The New York street railway combination went into receivership, as did Westinghouse Electric Company in October, just as the panic was getting under way. U.S. Steel announced lower earnings. J. P. Morgan's ambitious and poorly conceived shipping trust failed. Judge Kenesaw Mountain Landis ruled that Standard Oil had violated the Elkins Act and stuck it with a $29 million fine in the fall. Standard's stock price dropped 10 percent.

Crises on the Hamburg and Amsterdam exchanges in early October created an outflow of U.S. gold to Europe. Problems on the Montreal Exchange soon followed. An attempted corner of United Copper stock by F. Augustus Heinze and Charles W. Morse collapsed. Several important banks and trust companies were involved in financing their effort, and the result was the looming insolvency of some of them. A bank panic was at hand.

The trust companies had caught the speculative fever without keeping sufficient reserves to protect their obligations to depositors. Among these were the banks involved in the United Copper play. One clearinghouse, the National Bank of Commerce, announced that it no longer would perform clearing operations for New York's third-largest trust company, the Knickerbocker, which had been involved in the copper scheme. Trust companies like the Knickerbocker were not clearinghouse members and had to rely on member banks like the National to complete their banking transactions. The National Bank of Commerce's action meant certain death for the Knickerbocker. It failed in mid-October after shutting its doors because it could not meet the run on its deposits. The real Panic of 1907—a bank panic—had begun.

The panic was a bank panic, but the banks' losses that led to runs on their deposits were caused at least in part by bank speculation in securities. The Aldrich-Vreeland Act of 1908, the Federal Reserve Act of 1913 and finally the Glass-Steagall Act of 1933 were designed to respond to this irresponsible banking environment. At the time, though, no effective federal mechanism existed to control the banks.

The intervention was led by the nation's *de facto* central banker, J. P. Morgan, asked by the administration to save the American money supply as he had during the gold crisis of 1895. Treasury Secretary George Cortelyou went to New York, where he deposited $25 million from the Treasury to be loaned for the most part as Morgan saw fit—mostly to bail out failing brokerage firms. The story is well known: Morgan's hasty return from an Episcopal retreat in Richmond, Virginia, and the all-night meetings at the Morgan mansion on Madison Avenue, attended by George Baker of the First National Bank, James Stillman of the National City Bank, E. H. Harriman and other financial luminaries. Morgan demanded the infusion of additional funds by each of the attendees in order to shore up the failing trusts. (Morgan refused to support the Knickerbocker because of its particularly bad behavior and heavy demands. Its president, Charles T. Barney, committed suicide, but almost every account of the story suggests that perhaps Mr. Barney had not been his own executioner.)[4]

The panic continued and Morgan's circle of financial deputies widened. He invited more than fifty New York bank and trust company presidents to his library. He locked the door. He opened it again only when each had agreed to kick in their respective shares of the $25 million needed to prevent the bankruptcies of more than sixty brokerage houses and the ruin of their customers as well. John D. Rockefeller put in a share, and deposited $10 million with Stillman's bank. Morgan bailed out New York City from its impending bankruptcy by uniting with Baker and Stillman to issue bonds to keep it afloat. He bought up bills of exchange to force the flow of gold from Europe to the United States.

In a tarnished last-minute deal, he saved a large brokerage firm, Moore & Schley, which was on the verge of ruin. The arrangement was for Morgan-controlled U.S. Steel to buy Moore & Schley's principal collateral. This was the stock of the Tennessee Coal, Iron & Railroad Company, one of U.S. Steel's major competitors. The deal was made only after Morgan received personal, if perfunctory, approval from Teddy Roosevelt. Morgan's bailout was probably overkill in terms of what Moore & Schley needed to keep it afloat. U.S. Steel's acquisition of Tennessee Coal almost certainly violated the Sherman Act, which let Roosevelt in for a lot of public criticism and ultimately resulted in his testifying as a witness in the investigations that led up to the Taft administration's antitrust suit against U.S. Steel. The panic drew to a close in November and a thirteen-month industrial depression followed.[5]

One result of the Panic of 1907 was seven more or less lean years in America. But as Chapter Eight will show, it was a time when individual investors rapidly expanded their presence in the market.

ROOSEVELT'S LAST CHANCE — FEDERAL INCORPORATION,
THE HEPBURN BILL AND THE FAINT BEGINNINGS
OF INVESTOR PROTECTION

The federal incorporation debate continued despite the failure of the Littlefield bill and the Bureau of Corporations' federal licensing proposal. Congressmen regularly introduced new bills and Roosevelt renewed his attempts to secure federal incorporation under his control after he took a postelection break to focus on railroad regulation with the Hepburn Act of 1906. The

Hepburn bill, which was different from the Hepburn Act, was introduced in the House on March 23, 1908. It was Roosevelt's last chance to achieve federal incorporation. It was also the last chance for Littlefield, who chaired the subcommittee that conducted hearings on the bill in his final year in Congress.

The bill was drafted by the National Civic Federation. As presented to Roosevelt by its president, Seth Low, the bill was an antitrust reform measure, far more limited in scope than a federal incorporation or licensing proposal. By the time it was ready to present to Congress, it had been transformed by the administration into its most potent federal incorporation effort.

The bill came into being rather modestly as an amendment to the Sherman Act. But Roosevelt diverted it from the initial goals of the National Civic Federation and reshaped it in his own regulatory image. Perhaps frustrated with the modesty of his achievements in trust regulation and stung by the blame he had taken for the Panic, Roosevelt increasingly came to see trust regulation as a crusade. He concluded a letter on the subject to Charles Bonaparte by quoting the last paragraph of Lincoln's Second Inaugural Address and closed a January 1908 *Special Message to Congress* with the same words. Although Roosevelt blamed business for his failures, he retained his appreciation of the value of the giant modern corporation and wanted to bring it under sensible regulation. But Roosevelt was not Lincoln and the trust battle was not the Civil War. Despite his use of the latter's immortal words of healing, Roosevelt continued to prosecute his case in increasingly hot rhetorical terms in a vain effort to attain the control over business that had eluded him. The Hepburn bill was condemned to failure for the same reasons that Roosevelt's earlier power grabs had failed. Its importance was that, coming as it did upon the background of the Panic of 1907, the bill and the congressional debates over it introduced the issue of federal securities regulation in its own right, independent of antitrust concerns, as well as the first serious calls for investor protection.[6]

The Need for Certainty

The Hepburn bill was a different kind of federal incorporation measure despite its continued focus on trust reform. It would have permitted interstate corporations to register with the Commissioner of Corporations to give them the privilege of advance review of their contracts or combinations in restraint of trade. The Commissioner then would have had the power to determine whether they were reasonable and, if so, to exempt the registrant from federal prosecution unless the government decided that conditions had changed.

Corporations that did not register continued their business practices at their legal peril.

Business had been clamoring for certainty. The Bureau of Corporations' files contain a raft of letters from businessmen around the country inquiring as to whether they could federally incorporate or, more frequently, whether the Bureau would give them advance guidance or approval of their plans, a matter which Garfield and his successor, Herbert Knox Smith, regularly had to reply was beyond their authority. Ralph Hill of Mount Vernon, Iowa, wrote to Smith asking flat out whether the Bureau had jurisdiction to advise a corporation "how it may change its policies or organization so as to conform to the Sherman Anti-trust Act." More plaintively, the Bain Wagon Company of Kenosha, Wisconsin, sent Smith a letter claiming that only the merger of a number of wagon makers could save many of them from bankruptcy and asking for the Bureau's sanction of their combination. In 1907, an agent of the Traveler's Insurance Company wrote to Smith enclosing a newspaper article attacking the Bureau for creating such great uncertainty that entrepreneurs found it difficult or impossible to raise capital:

> I fear you do not begin to realize the great amount of trouble and financial distress you are helping to bring about by the methods you are pursuing in the management of your Department. It is affecting many lines of business and causing anxiety in many homes. If you want Harriman or Rockefeller, why not go out and lasso them instead of disturbing all the smaller business interests, and thus disturbing the whole country.

A number of trade associations like the Building Material Men's Exchange of Jefferson County, Alabama, the National Petroleum Association, the Wisconsin Retail Lumber Dealers' Association and the Bituminous Coal Trade Association wanted advice or assurance from the Commissioner that they were in compliance with the antitrust laws. In one unusual letter, Charles W. Chase of Chicago wrote on behalf of his client, the Chicago–New York Electric Air Line Railroad Company, asking if it could provide all of its relevant corporate and financial information to the Bureau so that the Bureau could publicly release it and reassure potential investors as to the soundness of the enterprise. This Garfield refused to do and Smith, then his deputy, suggested that the company simply wanted to use the Bureau both as a shill and a stamp of approval.

These inquiries reflected a growing mood of uncertainty and anxiety about antitrust concerns among businessmen of all types and in all regions of the country. Many businessmen were generally in favor of the Hepburn bill. Others opposed it because they wanted clear rules as to the legality of specific types of combinations and restraints of trade instead of regulatory guidance on a case-by-case basis. Some small businessmen worried that the bill's regulatory process would end up legalizing trusts to their competitive disadvantage. Most small businessmen opposed the way the bill effectively made labor boycotts lawful under the Sherman Act. There was much for some people to like in the Hepburn bill, but reading the hearings suggests that there was something for everyone to loathe.[7]

The Provenance of the Hepburn Bill

The Hepburn bill itself was the product of the NCF's Chicago Conference on Trusts and Combinations, held from October 22 to 25, 1907, as the panic in New York was raging. Among its final recommendations was that Congress create a nonpartisan commission to study ways of easing the effects of the Sherman Act on big business, specifically to create a system of federal incorporation or licensing that would distinguish between those trusts that served the public and those that damaged it, and also to ease the crunch of the Sherman Act on organized labor. It also recommended that Congress expand the role of the Department of Commerce and Labor to require the disclosure of corporate information.

A final amendment to the recommendations asked outgoing NCF President Nicholas Murray Butler to appoint a delegation to present its ideas to Congress and the president. The delegates met with congressional leaders in late January 1908. Aldrich evidently told NCF executive director Ralph Easley that trust legislation was unlikely to be considered during that congressional session but that the NCF ought to create a commission to investigate changes along the lines of the conference resolution.[8]

The story of the bill's origin, development and hijacking by Roosevelt, comprehensively detailed by Martin Sklar, is long and complex. What started as an outgrowth of the trust conference was taken over by the NCF in the wake of the recent Danbury Hatters' case. There the Supreme Court unanimously ruled that the Sherman Act applied to combinations of labor, a ruling that galvanized labor leaders and supporters from Gompers to Bryan to seek outright amendment of the Sherman Act to protect the unions instead of the indeterminate process of committee investigation that had been resolved upon by the conference.

NCF President Seth Low was a former president of Columbia University and mayor of New York. Conservative and open-minded, he supported organized labor. Low testified that the legislators had asked him to draft a proposed bill while he was in the process of contacting representatives Jenkins and Hepburn to arrange the presentation of the conference's thoughts to Congress. The conference had not authorized such action, so the NCF took over, although Low assured the committee that nothing in the bill was inconsistent with the Chicago resolutions.[9]

Low set up the committee. Despite the rich variety in its membership, by this time the NCF was largely dominated by the business and financial members who "carefully controlled" participation in the 1907 Conference. Its principal participants included August Belmont, Elbert Gary, Henry Lee Higginson and Isaac Seligman, together with a few labor leaders like Samuel Gompers and John Mitchell. Rounding out the committee were two eminent corporation lawyers, Victor Morawetz, counsel to the Atchison, Topeka and Santa Fe Railroad, formerly a partner in the prominent Cravath firm and the author of perhaps the first modern American treatise on corporate law, and Francis Lynde Stetson, who drafted the bill.[10]

The Hepburn Bill

While the individual eminence of its members gave the NCF access to all levels of government, the organization historically had little legislative influence or broad public support. It had begun this new project hoping to cooperate with the administration on its development. It worked closely with Roosevelt, who repaid the NCF by seizing the chance to transform the measure from Sherman Act amendments to an elaborate registration and regulatory scheme that would have put the power over American industry that he wanted in the president's hands.[11]

The bill that was ultimately introduced in the House, from which it never emerged, was an extreme expression of Roosevelt's vision of the presidency. While it followed his policy of publicity, allowing corporations to register with the Commissioner of Corporations, the real power of publicity would lie with the president. The president, not the commissioner, would be given direct rulemaking power over the initial application requirements. And this power was broad:

> [T]he President shall have power to make, alter, and revoke, and
> from time to time, in his discretion, he shall make, alter, and revoke,
> regulations prescribing what facts shall be set forth in the statements

to be filed with the Commissioner of Corporations ... and what information thereafter shall be furnished by such corporations and associations so registered, and he may prescribe the manner of registration and of cancellation of registration.

The importance of the Hepburn bill to my story is that it served as a bridge between the antitrust-based federal incorporation debate and the rising public concern with securities speculation and stock market regulation brought on by the panic. This is partly reflected in the different requirements the bill would have imposed on business corporations and not-for-profit corporations and partly in direct testimony during the hearings. The not-for-profits that the bill contemplated primarily were labor unions. The influence of the growing stock market was evident in the provisions that would have applied to business corporations.

Business corporations would have had to file their organizational materials and all of their contracts, statements of financial condition and corporate proceedings under regulations "made by the President." Not-for-profits would only have to file their charters and bylaws, the addresses of their principal offices and the names and addresses of officers, directors and members of standing committees.

The periodic filing requirements were different, too. The president would be given authority to create regulations for periodic filings by business corporations that presumably would include significant financial information, while not-for-profits were not required to file anything beyond the registration materials, except for updated registrations as required by the Commissioner of Corporations. As a trade-off, not-for-profits were unable to take advantage of the Commissioner's rulings on the reasonableness of their contracts. But the bill's attempt to exempt labor boycotts from the Sherman Act would hardly have made this a problem.[12]

Why the difference? Low, testifying in favor of the bill, explained. "Corporations for profit appeal to investors for their money; corporations not for profit do not." Corporations that sought money from investors were obliged to provide the kind of financial information that would allow investors to make reasoned decisions.

Low's view of "the large measure of publicity" of corporate information that would be released if the bill passed was sophisticated and anticipated the New Deal acts in policy as well as philosophy. He identified the "advantages of publicity [as] two sided. Men whose corporate activities, within proper limits, are to be matter of public record are likely to be careful not to do anything they are not willing the public should know." By the same token, appeasing business interests, he noted that much of the public criticism of corporations came from ignorance, and disclosure would bring understanding that would portray corporate dealings in a better light. While not so obviously shareholder-related, the first reason was aimed at controlling corporate misbehavior and the second at assuring investors that American corporations were safe places to invest their money. Under the Hepburn bill they would presumably limit the formation of illegal trusts.[13]

The strongest hint of investor protection came relatively early in the extensive hearings, during an interchange between Littlefield, Low and Jeremiah Jenks. Littlefield had been questioning Jenks on the federal government's power to require interstate corporations to disclose information of the type contemplated by the bill, including capitalization and financial information. Jenks, despite his regular protestations that he was not a lawyer, did not hesitate much in giving his legal opinions. The use of publicity for investor protection emerged from the use of publicity to control trusts.

Low focused the discussion on trust concerns. Referring to interstate corporations that sought financing from the public, he asked: "Is it not a perfectly legitimate thing to ask that corporation, it if wants to do interstate commerce on the basis of all sorts of stocks and bonds, for the benefit of the investor whose money is to be engaged in interstate commerce, to state the conditions upon which that money is to be used in interstate commerce?" Low clearly meant to suggest that publicity would alert potential investors to the possibly illegal use of their money and thus allow them to decide whether to invest. But Littlefield redirected the question. "That comes right down to the question as to whether, under our power to regulate commerce, we have any power to protect the investing public as a part of the regulation of commerce." Jenks demurred and Littlefield became even more specific. "Do we have any power, under the power to regulate commerce, to so regulate it as to protect the security or value of the investing public's investments?" To this Jenks answered in the affirmative.[14]

While such a brief and seemingly off-the-point exchange in over seven hundred pages of hearings hardly proves a major development in federal thinking, it does provide an important illustration of the beginning of legislative attention to the securities market. The Panic of 1907 was the elephant in the antitrust hearing room. Jenks testified again, this time on the relationship between trusts, securities and overcapitalization, and approvingly introduced into evidence the British Companies Act of 1900 with its detailed prospectus requirement for the protection of investors. Under Littlefield's questioning, he also gave particular attention to the relationship between overcapitalization and speculation.[15]

The Hepburn bill was not securities regulation. But the connections between the creation of the giant trusts, monopoly, speculation and investor fraud were becoming clearer. Clarification allowed lawmakers to begin to understand and address each problem on its own distinct terms while keeping the whole of the corporations problem in view. One can see the way a growing stock market and concern with speculation began to manifest itself in legislative proposals to protect investors in the last federal incorporation gasp of the Roosevelt administration.

Roosevelt himself had begun to speak out more widely on the subject of investor protection, although he was firm in his insistence that the shareholders of illegal trusts, rather than the officers, should bear the brunt of the penalties. "Nothing is sillier than this outcry on behalf of the 'innocent shareholders' in the corporations," he wrote Bonaparte. The shareholders controlled the corporations, after all. Shareholders hurt by overcapitalization were different, and Roosevelt believed that it was necessary to protect them in their purchases by disclosure, although his legislative efforts had at best an indirect influence on investor protection. But once the stockholder owned shares, the corporation's misbehavior was his responsibility, even if the corporation was dominated by a controlling interest. "That stockholder is not innocent who voluntarily purchases stock in a corporation whose methods and management he knows to be corrupt; and stockholders are bound to try to secure honest management, or else are estopped from complaining about" the government's enforcement of the laws against the corporation. Roosevelt saw a clear difference between defrauding investors by selling them watered stock and the responsibilities that came with stockholding. It was at almost precisely this time that securities regulation took off as a legislative project in its own right.[16]

THE ROOTS OF SECURITIES REGULATION

Overcapitalization, federal incorporation and the trust question largely remained consumer pricing issues through the Panic of 1907. Those who made law and policy did not entirely ignore investors, and calls for securities regulation were common. But securities regulation was not the subject of legislative activity except to the extent lawmakers thought it was necessary to remedy trust abuses. The investing class was not yet a major constituency for anybody except perhaps politicians from New York, and their most influential constituents were getting rich from securities just the way they were. The antitrust stage of securities regulation was important to the development of securities law mostly because it focused lawmakers on the various consequences of widely held corporate stock. Yet while the middle class was entering the market in larger numbers, the idea of securities regulation *as* consumer protection (treating securities as consumer goods) in contrast to securities regulation *for* consumer protection (to reduce monopoly prices caused by corporate finance) had only limited acceptance and was not yet embraced as a federal responsibility.

Arising as they did in the aftermath of the Panic of 1907, proposals for securities regulation through the beginning of the war were designed to control speculation and thus stabilize the economy. But while economic stability was the focus, the interests of investors were also starting to matter more as the middle class increasingly turned not only to securities in general but also to common stock more specifically. The antispeculation and consumer protection stages of securities regulation began together, although the former dominated. The antispeculation stage would end in failure, but some of its concerns would be addressed with the creation of the Federal Reserve System in 1913, whose evolution largely paralleled this second stage. It was the consumer protection stage that would result in effective regulation and help to legitimate the speculation economy.

Four important governmental efforts at the end of the long decade show the progress of these developments. The investigation by the Hughes Committee in 1908, the debate over the Mann-Elkins Act in 1910, the Report of the Railroad Securities Commission in 1911 and the Pujo Committee investigations of 1912 and 1913 spanned the antispeculation stage of securities regulation. It began in New York, the site of the Panic, before migrating to the federal government.[17]

The Hughes Committee

Governor Charles Evans Hughes of New York, the scene of the debacle, appointed the Governor's Committee on Speculation in Securities and Commodities in 1908. It was charged with determining "what changes, if any, are advisable in the laws of the State bearing upon speculation in securities and commodities, or relating to the protection of investors, or with regard to the instrumentalities and organizations used in dealings in securities and commodities which are the subject of speculation." While the Committee focused on the broad economic effects of speculation, investor protection was present as a reform theme. Despite its asserted aims, the Committee is widely understood to have been created largely for the purpose of forestalling more serious federal regulation.[18]

The Committee delivered its report on June 7, 1909, after slightly more than six months of work. Its efforts have received scholarly attention, with some historians noting the extent to which it lashed out at the New York

Stock Exchange. In fact it did nothing of the sort. Its Report is probably best characterized as gentlemen calling the attention of other gentlemen to the disagreeable fact that there were a few scoundrels in their midst who needed a good thrashing.

The Committee's composition made its conclusions predictable. Horace White, who chaired the Committee, had impeccable Republican credentials. Born in 1834, White worked as a reporter for the *Chicago Daily Tribune.* He covered the Lincoln-Douglas debates, befriending Lincoln and eventually serving as his paper's Washington correspondent during the Civil War. An ardent abolitionist, he spent time in the 1850s funneling money, arms and supplies as assistant secretary of the National Kansas Commission to the Free State pioneers. After brief service with his friend Henry Villard on the Kansas-Pacific Railroad and the Oregon Railway & Navigation Company, he moved to the *New York Evening Post* and the *Nation*, along with Carl Schurz and E. L. Godkin and, later, Villard's son Oswald, taking over financial and economic reporting for the two journals. Eventually White became editor-in-chief of the *Post*, from which he retired in 1903. His young associate and fellow mugwump, Oswald Garrison Villard, described him as ranking "as a great economic conservative," "blind to much that was going on about him in our economic life" and particularly the depredations of Wall Street. This attitude is illustrated by his refusal to believe that the Panic of 1907 had anything to do with stock speculation.[19]

Charles Sprague Smith, an educator, romantic and idealist, founded the People's Institute at Cooper Union and revitalized Cooper Union itself. Also a member of the Committee was David Leventritt, a New York lawyer whose nomination to the New York State Supreme Court was unsuccessfully opposed by the elite—and anti-Semitic—Association of the Bar of the City of New York, in an attack led by Elihu Root, which catalyzed the creation of the founding of the more pluralistic New York County Lawyers' Association. Despite the progressive ideals of some of its members, the Committee's conclusions toed the Republican Party line. Dissent was voiced only outside the context of the Committee report. Committee member John Bates Clark wrote a separate letter to the governor, cosigned by only one colleague, urging stringent regulation, and David Leventritt, believing state regulation to be impractical, suggested that the governor should ask Congress to pass federal legislation.[20]

It is worth noting, in light of the Committee's conclusions, that White expressed an understanding of the purpose of the market that gave pride of place to its function as a forum where investors could gain liquidity rather than as a mechanism for allocating capital to industry: "The very *raison d'être* of the stock exchange is to supply a market where invested capital can be quickly turned into cash, and vice versa." Thus it is unsurprising that the Committee found that speculation which, in contrast to gambling, was legal in New York, was not all bad. In fact, it helped to stabilize prices. But speculation had started to get out of control and threatened to destroy the economic service performed by the NYSE. "It is unquestionable that only a small part of the transactions upon the Exchange is of an investment character; a substantial part may be characterized as virtually gambling." Gambling should be stopped.[21]

The trouble for the Committee was that distinguishing good speculation from bad speculation, or gambling, was really impossible. The Committee's principal speculative concern was futures trading, and the forms and methods of futures trading that were legitimate and gambling were indistinguishable. The Committee also studied the speculative effects of short selling, which had been outlawed by New York in 1812 and restored in 1858. Again the Committee demurred, largely because of the serious financial problems Germany had experienced after trying to regulate the practice. The Committee did urge brokers to require higher margins to dampen the speculative effects of margin trading. It also criticized other speculative practices. Price manipulation, wash sales and matched orders were not mere speculation but more like fraud. These, it was "convinced," could be controlled by the Exchange.[22]

Exchange self-regulation was the Committee's principal solution, although the Exchange had been notoriously unwilling to regulate its members. The Exchange pretty much ignored the Committee until, under attack by the Pujo Committee in 1913, it adopted several vague and perfunctory rules against the most obviously fraudulent kinds of manipulation.

The Committee also expressed some concern for investor protection in addition to its primary focus on speculation. It considered and rejected the idea of a mandatory registration and disclosure system like that embodied in the British Companies Act of 1900. Two problems precluded this logical step. The Committee was afraid that New York might lose business to states that did not adopt such regulations. It also expressed its concern that state registration might lead investors to think the state had actually evaluated the quality of the securities. The former concern was implausible in light of New York's towering dominance in financial matters. The latter concern often came up in debates over securities regulation and became more credible in the next few years as state blue-sky laws did precisely that.

The Committee suggested some pallid legislation, in particular a sort of antifraud law for advertising. It would have required that any person placing an ad for securities had to sign a statement accepting responsibility for it with the newspaper's publisher. But this was the extent of its willingness to impose legal requirements.

So much for a consumer-oriented disclosure law. Perhaps, the Committee suggested, the Exchange ought to verify corporations' listing information. But this, too, it rejected, arguing again that the public would rely too heavily upon the required audit as state verification of the quality of the security. The Committee instead recommended that the Exchange should require more detailed information in its listing requirements and that "means should be adopted for holding those making the statements responsible for the truth thereof."

The Committee was especially critical of fraudulent and misleading securities advertising. But here, too, it was reluctant to suggest that anybody bear any obligation for anything. Again it displayed perhaps an unjustifiable (and ultimately unjustified) faith in human nature by choosing to forgo law and recommend that investors trust in the fact that bankers and brokers of good reputation naturally would protect that reputation by refusing to advertise in papers that accepted such "swindling advertisements." Directors, too, should have the character to pay attention to the accuracy of their companies' publicity. In the end, the Committee, putting its faith in the NYSE, did little more than to ask the Exchange itself to pay a little more attention to the miscreants.[23]

That organization, still characterized by all of the trappings of a private club, more or less ignored the Committee. The market largely remained as it was.

Brief Interlude—Taft and Investor Protection

Roosevelt's hand-picked successor, William Howard Taft, continued the advance of securities regulation as an antitrust issue, especially with respect to the railroads, but also began to articulate it as an issue of investor protection and the health of American industry. Taft unsuccessfully pursued securities regulation both in the Taft-Wickersham federal incorporation bill of 1910 and in his attempt to regulate the issuance of railroad securities with the Mann-Elkins Act. He did not care much about the fates of individual investors. But he was keenly sensitive to the fact that the continued success of the American economy required individuals to remain willing to invest their money in industrial development. He believed that in order to attract investors, industrial development required capital to be used for the growth of business, not for the enrichment of promoters.

The Panic of 1907 had its influence on Taft as on everybody else, but his interest in the relationship between investor and industrial well-being had been formulated well before Americans became buyers of common stock. Early-formed opinions were important for Taft. As the editor of Taft's speeches put it, "it is hard to avoid the sense that Taft's political character, political opinions, political prejudices even, were formed early and thoughtfully and thereafter changed little." One of his most deeply held convictions was the sanctity of private property and its relationship to liberty. It was this belief in property rights that underlay his concern, however limited, for investors.[24]

As early as 1895 Taft, who was then a federal circuit judge, saw overcapitalization both as a fraud on bondholders, whom he viewed as the true owners, and a hindrance to the advance of industry. In a speech before the American Bar Association in Detroit on August 28, 1895, he criticized state corporate law for allowing promoters and managers to water corporate stock that they then issued to themselves, giving themselves control over the corporation, which, by virtue of the watered stock, could only be mismanaged and was mismanaged for their benefit.

> The real owners, the bondholders, are at the mercy of this irresponsible management until insolvency comes. The reckless business methods which such an irresponsibility and lack of supervision invite create an unhealthy and feverish competition in every market, wholly unrestrained by the natural caution which the real owner of a business must feel. The concern is kept going with no hope of legitimate profit, but simply to pay large salaries or to favor unduly some other enterprise in which the managers have a real interest.

Only after making this observation did he proceed to assert a "distrust of corporate methods" in their use of large amounts of capital "to monopolize and control particular industries."[25]

Taft's deep belief in the sanctity of private property as necessary for liberty drove his interest in investor protection, less for the sake of the investors themselves than for the safety of the American industrial system. Campaigning during the midterm elections of 1906, he argued that the use of capital to reproduce itself was "a virtue." It was the corporation that made this possible "and the incident of the transfer of shares of stock is what enables so many millions of people to have an interest in these immense corporations which they have helped to build up by contributing their modest savings." The prosperity of all of the people depended upon the institution of stock to permit the distribution of corporate wealth.[26]

Taft was primarily interested in securities regulation for the sake of industrial health and growth. In Columbus, Ohio, in August 1907, he made his concerns plain, noting "recent revelations" of railroad overcapitalization that bilked "innocent investors." This was not a federal problem, according to Taft. What was a federal problem and had to be dealt with was the manner in which overcapitalization "has a tendency to divert the money paid by the public for the stock and bonds which ought to be expended in [railroad improvements and maintenance] into the pockets of the dishonest manipulators and thus to pile such an unprofitable debt upon a railway as to make bankruptcy" likely. He extended this view to industrial corporations generally following the Panic of 1907, demanding federal supervision of securities issues as a means of improving corporate management and with it public confidence in corporate America. Finance had to be made to serve industry rather than the other way around.[27]

Taft was happy to leave antitrust regulation of industrial corporations primarily to the courts at the beginning of his term, subject to a Sherman Act amendment clarifying when combinations were illegal, but overcapitalization, and especially railroad overcapitalization, was a problem that required legislative and administrative action. His first concern was the way promoters used watered stock to obtain control of railroads with other people's money, but it gradually shifted until he was fighting against watered stock both as a fraud on investors and as destroying the railroads by encouraging the financial mismanagement of a vitally important commercial facility. By 1910 he had returned to the idea of federal incorporation, proposing the extensive Taft-Wickersham bill. This measure would have, among other things, imposed strict federal administrative control over corporate securities issues, including federal determination of the fair value of stock issued for property. Taft's clear purpose continued to be to ensure that money raised by corporations was invested in those corporations for business health and stability. He continued to push for federal incorporation until almost the end of his term.[28]

Investors were not irrelevant. His early concern for bondholders now included stockholders as well. The only purpose of watering stock, he said, was to deceive investors into paying too much for it. These investor concerns were manageable with disclosure. Indeed, one of the principal benefits he saw in corporate taxation was the fact that reporting corporations would be disclosing far more information than ever they had before, aiding investors in evaluating a corporation's stock as well as the government in collecting taxes. His concern both with the sanctity of private property and with maintaining a healthy investor base had grown and he warned that proposed amendments to the Interstate Commerce Act should avoid damaging the interests of railroad shareholders and maintain a healthy market for their stock.[29]

Taft was not particularly focused on the investor as investor. In fact, one biographer suggested that Teddy Roosevelt had to coach him to show concern for the small investor during the 1908 campaign. But he helped to highlight and publicize the need for securities regulation in the context of his broader concerns for the protection of the American industrial economy from irresponsible finance.[30]

CAPITAL VERSUS THE CONSUMER: SECURITIES REGULATION THROUGH THE RAILROADS

Congress devoted a significant amount of attention to the securities of common carriers for antitrust purposes. Overcapitalization made it difficult for the issuers to earn enough money to meet the stated dividends on their watered stock. To ameliorate the problem, they overcharged consumers.

By the end of the first decade of the twentieth century, many economists and public actors had come to accept as a matter of economic reality that competitive markets would eliminate the possibility of overcharging consumers. Manufacturers and retailers had to set their prices to meet the competition that increased when prices rose and made industries attractive to new entrants. Only in a few industries that could sustain monopolies did overcapitalization remain an intractable problem, both for the consumer and for the uninformed stock buyer. Railroads, especially the new urban rail and streetcar lines, and public utilities often were natural monopolies. They could charge monopoly prices, and overcapitalization added the necessity of meeting dividend payments to their other incentives to overcharge consumers for a service which had no real alternatives. Thus securities regulation remained a central focus in railroad and utility regulation as the broader antitrust debate that had begun in the 1880s moved toward its conclusion during the second decade. Again the focus was the relationship between watered stock and monopoly. But consumer legislation for securities investors became an increasingly frequent issue in the debate as the general public continued to enter the market. In this context, too, it played second fiddle to the issue of banking and economic stability.

The Hepburn Act of 1906

Investors were not the object of concern when Congress passed the Hepburn Act of 1906. The Hepburn Act, which enlarged and strengthened the Interstate Commerce Commission and gave it real power to prohibit excessive rates, was introduced as an antitrust measure, ensuring that rates charged by common carriers would be "just and reasonable" and giving the Commission the express authority to set maximum rates. The Act did require substantial and detailed financial reporting by all common carriers to the Commission, but this requirement was designed to keep the Commission itself informed, not investors.

Shareholders' interests were not completely missing from the debate. Democratic Senator Benjamin Tillman of South Carolina, who supported the bill, submitted a lengthy statement. Overcapitalization, while occupying only a small portion of his analysis, was a problem he stressed, and he stressed it on behalf of shareholders:

> [I]t is impossible not to reach the conclusion that there has been an immense amount of overcapitalization deliberately planned and carried out for a specific purpose; and that purpose can be no other than the foisting on the people of railroad securities which have no actual value and the only motive for whose creation and sale was to add to the gains of a coterie of multimillionaires, whose energies are now directed toward compelling the business interests of the country to "make good" by increasing the earnings of the roads with a view to paying dividends upon this fictitious valuation of the properties.

Tillman remarked that the proceeds of the inflated securities, while allegedly needed for improvements to the roads, were mostly pocketed by the controlling interests. His concerns were threefold—railroad performance, consumer overcharging in order to make dividend payments and shareholder protection. But shareholders were the least of it. By far the greater problem was excessive rates. The senator was particularly concerned with the section of the statute that allowed the Commission to determine the "just and reasonable and fairly remunerative rate." "Fairly remunerative" on what? The watered capitalization or the value of the tangible property?

> There can be no justice in compelling the people as a whole to pay dividends on watered stock primarily for the purpose of increasing the fortunes of men already too rich. The poor dupes who have been led to invest their savings in such stocks can better afford to lose them than to have the labor of the country saddled with the burden of paying perpetual tribute in the shape of dividends on dishonest valuations....

⫷⫸

All issues of railroad securities in the future ... should be under the control of the Interstate Commerce Commission and there should be a speedy readjustment of capitalized values ... while protecting, as far as possible, the innocent holders of watered stock. It may be that these can not be protected under the law and that the holders of first-mortgage bonds and of preferred stock, who will be found in the end to be the multimillionaires who have perpetrated the scheme of injustice, will retain their advantage, while the poor dupes who have been led to buy the products of railway printing presses will lose what they have invested.

Tillman might have been concerned about shareholders, but not nearly so much as he was with the consumers and railroad patrons who were his constituents. As with the legislative proposals on federal incorporation, the seeds of stockholder concern were present in the Hepburn Act debate, but it decidedly remained a side issue.[31]

The Mann-Elkins Act of 1910

The Hepburn Act was not effective enough, so Congress passed the Mann-Elkins Act in 1910 at Taft's request. Originating in the Roosevelt administration, and indeed outlined in detail in Roosevelt's March 1907 letter to the ICC, it was drafted, in Rooseveltian style and to congressional consternation, by Attorney General George Wickersham. The Republican platform of 1908 promised new legislation to restrain railroad rate abuses. Although the Republicans still controlled both houses, the Act's passage was ensured only by a combination of progressive Republicans and progressive Democrats.[32]

Most of the Mann-Elkins Act is unimportant in explaining the evolution of securities regulation. The part that matters is the one that was amended out of the bill, which addressed the domination of finance over the railroad industry through the medium of securities. All new securities to be issued by railroads had to be paid at par value, in cash and, if in services or property, at fair value to be determined by the Interstate Commerce Commission. Like some federal incorporation measures of these years, the draft prohibited railroads from issuing securities until they had received Commission approval after the Commission had determined that all of the proceeds were to go to finance the railroad and not into the pockets of shareholders or promoters. All railroad combinations had to receive Commission approval. The Commission also had the authority to approve the capital structures of reorganizing railroads.

Investor protection was not the purpose of this capital regulation, as it might appear at first blush. Rather, it was to prevent the kind of overcapitalization that diverted wealth from industry and led railroads to overcharge customers in order to make high dividend payments. Like virtually all other business regulation during this period, the debates leave no room for doubt that the regulation was largely about monopoly. Yet it clearly addressed what its supporters saw as the distortion of industry to serve finance through the use of watered stock.

The corporate finance provisions of the bill were fiercely debated before they were defeated. The debate reveals one reason why securities regulation for investor protection had not previously received much attention. As Tillman demonstrated during the Hepburn Act debate, congressmen from regions other than the Northeast were not particularly sympathetic to the suppliers of capital, no matter how modest their means, when returns on that capital were reaped from the fields of their constituents. The House minority report clarified these concerns: "The apparent purpose of this proposed drastic and unprecedented legislation is to protect and guarantee the owners of capital stock of a railroad that has engaged in overcapitalization." This was a theme repeated throughout the debate. As William Adamson of Georgia put it, the only reason for the corporate finance provisions was to protect already existing railroad monopolies and the value of the securities held by their owners: "Their evident purpose is to anticipate and set up by indirection, for the advantage of present security holders, the impossible federal incorporation act ... to take control of the subject of investments and look after securities in speculation. If that is a good purpose, it should find manifestation in an honest effort to enforce the antitrust law instead of trying to invent means to nullify it."

Were these provisions to pass, he continued, Southern and Western railroads would be unable to raise capital and transportation throughout the country would be controlled by existing monopolies. If overcapitalization and corporate mismanagement were problems, he said, the states and not the federal government ought to assert responsibility over them.[33]

In response, James Mann of Illinois, House sponsor of the bill, argued that it would help to create economic opportunity for railroad entrepreneurs and work to the industry's benefit. After noting that the purpose of the provisions was to ensure only reasonable returns on railroad securities in order to keep rates down, he said: "[The corporate finance provisions] will protect the public; it will give to an unknown corporation which has no market value for its stock or its bonds, in a new part of the country . . . an opportunity to obtain money from the issuance of its stocks and bonds on such reasonable terms as may be allowed." The securities regulation provisions would help railroads raise capital by ensuring the integrity of their securities. They would create opportunities and foster competition, not limit them.[34]

The Senate debate was largely along the same lines as that in the House. After Albert Cummins of Iowa noted that he favored legislation regulating the corporate finance of all businesses, not just railroads, he too attacked the proposed bill on the ground that it perpetuated the status quo and left wealthy promoters and monopolists in charge.[35]

The dominant concern remained monopoly, the target high rates and the battle between capital and the consumer. The centrality of this point is brought home by Cummins's objection to a section in the corporate finance provisions that sustained the validity of securities of overcapitalized corporations as long as they were in the hands of "innocent purchasers." All purchasers would fit this category, he said, and the wealth they held was illegitimate because it was born of fraud and monopoly. More important, the purpose of the statute was to prevent overcharging consumers, and this purpose would be defeated if corporations were permitted to continue paying dividends on watered securities, no matter how innocent the purchaser.

The corporate finance provisions were eliminated and the bill passed with substantial majorities in both houses. All that was left of them was a provision authorizing the president to appoint a commission to investigate railroad securities.

The debate over the corporate finance provisions of the Mann-Elkins Act illustrates an important turning point in the development of federal securities regulation, despite its otherwise conventional concern with monopoly. For what this debate, along with the Hepburn hearings and the Hughes Committee, shows is the growth of a new branch of the trust debate, a branch with two prongs. The new branch grew out of regulatory concern with securities from a business standpoint, an antitrust concern over competition, opportunity and consumer pricing. It grew into public concern about regulating securities as securities, about regulating securities from an investor's standpoint, with a particular goal of reining in finance to serve the purposes of industry that had been perverted by the creation of the giant combinations. This branch of the debate would have worked to ensure that finance served the needs of business and not the financiers.

The faster-growing prong of this new branch focused on a particular category of investor, banks and financial institutions, whose stability and support of the economy were affected by their investments in corporate securities. The other prong focused on securities regulation for the protection of investors. Significant evidence of this appears in the report of the Railroad Securities Commission, whose creation had been authorized by the Mann-Elkins Act.[36]

The Hadley Commission—Protecting Investors

The Railroad Securities Commission was chaired by Arthur Hadley. Hadley's eminence as an economist put his appointment beyond question. But he was a perfect choice to chair the commission if the goal were to preserve the status quo. Hadley had been an economist for over thirty years at the time of his appointment, most famous for his 1896 book, *Economics*. He was also expert on the subject of railroads. One reviewer approvingly noted of *Economics* that "The work is a long argument for the general rightness of what is." Another observer wrote of the book that it was "as intelligent an apologia and as judicious a defense of the economic institutions of the day as the American literature contains." His son and biographer, Morris Hadley, agreed with this, noting that "Hadley did believe that the economic institutions of the day, with all their faults, were a better basis for future development than any of the rival schemes proposed by socialists or others." It is notable that his appointment came at a time when Taft was in the process of abandoning Roosevelt's interventionist approach to regulation in favor of a more conservative attack on the trusts through the courts.[37]

Hadley was not a great believer in regulation. In an 1890 speech in Denver he argued that misbehaving corporate executives should be socially shunned rather than punished by law, because this was clearly an "all-powerful remedy." As early as 1885, while serving as Connecticut's Commissioner of Labor Statistics he had, on more practical grounds, suggested only mild legislative reform, "believing that it would be quite hard enough to enforce [the reforms he suggested] and out of the question to enforce more sweeping ones."[38]

Hadley had a long history of opposing securities regulation in particular. In his 1885 book, *Railroad Transportation*, he dismissed the idea of regulation while acknowledging the distorting effects of speculation on business: "Legislation against commercial crises is about as effective as legislation against chills and fever." Legislation against speculation, even if it were a good idea, would be impossible, Hadley wrote, because there was no way to distinguish between "good speculation" and "bad speculation." These words would echo throughout the Commission's Report. If Taft wanted to prevent regulation, he had chosen the right man.[39]

Hadley exercised tight control not only over the Commission but also over its purpose. He responded to Taft's invitation to chair the Commission with a letter exploring the different forms a special commission could take. A commission that took testimony "and on the basis of this testimony ... draft a statute which shall represent intelligent public opinion and have the force of intelligent opinion behind it" held no interest for him. He was, however, quite willing to chair a commission of "experts, selected for their knowledge of the specific matters involved," to advise the government on the basis of their expertise as to what reforms might be "practicable."

While a commission of experts was appointed, their deliberations were not always easy. Hadley wrote to his wife after one meeting that "'Sessions of the Commission were squally, but interesting. How we are ever going to agree on a report is more than I can see.'" But the final report was unanimous, a point in which Hadley took special pride. While he noted that he had to make concessions to achieve this result, the Report reads more or less exactly as one would have predicted based on his earlier work.[40]

Despite Hadley's distaste for hearings, the Commission did hold public hearings in New York, Chicago and Washington, where it took testimony from thirty-four witnesses. It received hundreds of letters commenting on railroad securities regulation and studied the literature on the subject as well as the congressional debates over the Mann-Elkins Act. The Commission submitted its Report to the President on November 1, 1911.[41]

The Mann-Elkins Act had been designed as progressive legislation to assert more aggressive federal control over the railroads. The Report and its recommendations with respect to securities regulation were a model of conservatism. Most telling was the Commission's reliance upon disclosure as the device best calculated to control overcapitalization and financial manipulation in the railroad industry. We have seen that disclosure up until this time was almost entirely regulatory in function, designed to give the government information to enable it to enforce the law. Disclosure as a remedy, to ensure investor protection, was mentioned from time to time, as it was by scholars and other prominent thinkers and activists, but it had never been a central part of the regulatory agenda.

Disclosure for the protection of investors took center stage in the Report. The Commission identified two ways that overcapitalization could damage the public. The first, now familiar, way was to induce common carriers (and other businesses) to pay dividends that were, in effect, "an unnecessary tax on interstate commerce." But, and quite outside the scope of its charge, the Commission identified a second evil, one that hearkened all the way back to a reason for par value itself. This was the deception of bondholders by over-capitalization, leading them to believe that their bonds had a meaningful equity cushion when in truth they were floating on water. The Commission showed little sympathy for the individual bond holder, suggesting that state law and his own intelligence could protect him. But it did see that systemic overcapitalization could shake the confidence of creditors generally and thus result in higher borrowing costs for railroads that legitimately needed the funds.

Perhaps the most interesting thing about the Report is the extraordinary skill with which the Commission transformed this last concern, which was a matter of broad economic regulation, a matter of ensuring the financial viability of common carriers, into an investor concern and, at the same time, introduced modern financial thought into the regulatory debate.

The Commission recommended that common carriers report the actual funds they received in relation to nominal capital to the Interstate Commerce Commission. And this was not just for the purpose of discovering monopolistic practices. Managers should do what they wanted in terms of financing, "but they must make it plain to the investor today and to the public tomorrow" how much cash lay behind stated capital.

This conservative form of regulation would eventually serve as the federal model that developed through the Wilson administration. Management's discretion to finance the corporation as it saw fit should not be circumscribed by the federal government; state corporate law should not be superseded. It was regulation enough to ensure that every stockholder was informed of the facts. Publicity was the answer. Publicity alone should be the federal remedy. All of a corporation's financial information should be disclosed to the ICC, the ICC should have authority to investigate the corporation in order to determine the accuracy of the information, the ICC itself should have the power to set accounting rules and corporate directors should disclose all of their personal interests in the corporation.

At the same time, the Report reflected the Commission's more modern economic sophistication. Some degree of stock watering could be tolerated as long as it had a business purpose. The Commission specifically noted that it was financially legitimate for a corporation to offer its existing shareholders stock at a par value below the market value as long as management disclosed that fact. Such an issuance would dilute the market value of the stock, but the Commission acknowledged the demands of financial reality in recognizing its occasional necessity.

This was the second transformative aspect of the Report, its introduction of modern financial thinking into the debate over federal corporate regulation. I described in the preceding paragraph the Commission's acceptance of the necessity of market value dilution for a distressed railroad in need of cash. The public's failure to understand the difference between stock and bonds was another issue the Commission identified as a serious impediment to appropriate finance. This misunderstanding was natural in light of the fact that stock, especially common stock, had only recently come into popular use as an investment vehicle. But it was compounded by the standard practice of identifying common stock at its par value, typically $100. A bond with a stated par value of $1,000 represented a promise to repay that money to the bondholder, but common stock with a stated par of $100 represented no such thing. "It has at best only a historical importance, as showing property was or purported to be worth at time of incorporation." It was par value that created the problem with overcapitalization, not necessarily the overcapitalization itself. If investors knew the actual value of the corporation's assets and income, they would be able to assess for themselves the worth of the stock. "[T]he investor must depend upon his own intelligence to protect him from loss. The function of the government is to see that correct information is available."

Throughout its report, the Commission sounded the theme of share value based on capitalized earnings, recognizing that common stockholders could not rely upon the promised dividend for their return but rather on the profits actually realized by the roads. This was not the same thing as accepting capitalized earnings as a valuation method for the roads' initial capitalizations, but instead an understanding of the financial reality of the limited use of stated capital as an assurance of returns. In thirty brief pages, the Report focused governmental attention on the factors that determined the value of common stock. Future profit, not historical cost, was the true determinant. It was a lesson that the public would absorb only too well during the 1920s.

The Report was presented to President Taft. Nothing was done. Yet even as investigations continued, the middle class entered the market in ever-larger numbers, for the first time becoming a phenomenon to be reckoned with.

⊰ EIGHT ⊱

THE SPECULATION ECONOMY

While Congress and two presidents were battling over antitrust reform, federal incorporation and railroad regulation, the flood of securities spread out by the merger wave continued to transform the American stock market. As I discussed in Chapter Four, the first phase of the modern market's development began with the merger wave and then quickly picked up steam. Many small investors could not resist blind speculation in manic markets like the one that swelled during the early spring of 1901. But their investment behavior in general was characterized by relative conservatism, with railroad bonds, a handful of high-grade industrial bonds and sometimes preferred stock serving as the most prominent investments. The socialization of the market was under way, too, as business, political, social and labor leaders encouraged Americans to invest in the new property not only for the sake of their own futures but also for the preservation of American ideals.

As we have seen, stock ownership among ordinary investors had been increasing over the previous decade and with increasing speed. While the years from the turn of the century to the Panic of 1907 marked one stage of growth, driven by the masses of new securities created by the merger wave and its aftermath and taken up by Americans experiencing a new prosperity, the period from the panic to the war formed a second stage. The financial press and retail brokerages were proliferating, industrial stocks became normalized as investment vehicles, and preferred and even common stock no longer frightened the average investor. In fact, some reports characterized the market following the panic as middle-class bargain hunting. Speculation was no longer an evil word; advisors and policymakers only cautioned the public to speculate intelligently rather than gamble. For a still small but growing class of Americans, the stock market had become part of the ordinary course of American life.

Lawmakers had begun to pay attention to the increasing importance of the market. Portions of the debates over the Hepburn bill and the Mann-Elkins Act explicitly addressed issues of investor protection, while the Hughes Committee and the Hadley Commission studied the effects of speculation on the market and problems of investor protection. With memories of the Panic still strong and the growing number of middle-class investors a perceptible reality, Congress would turn its attention more explicitly to market regulation during the Pujo hearings of 1912. Meanwhile, the market continued to expand and investment styles started to change. Investing for a modest return on safe principal gave way to speculation as preferred stock and then common stock became increasingly attractive to average investors and more widespread across the population. As it did, speculation took on a whole new character. No longer just the manipulations of a handful of professionals nor the blind buying of a frenzied public, speculation had now become simply a matter of buying common stock. The speculation economy was a common stock economy.

THE NEW SPECULATION

The nature of speculation changed during the course of the market's growth from its first stage during the merger wave to its second stage in the early years of the next decade. The speculation that brought average Americans into the market during that first stage was of a sort familiar to American markets, the kind of gambling that had taken place in bull markets like the one that had collapsed in 1873, ruining the father of American investment banking, Jay Cooke, and plunging the nation into depression. The sudden outpouring of securities during the merger wave at a time of large economic surplus, which allowed ordinary Americans to take their first shot at profiting from developing American industries, created its own bubble and, like all such bubbles, it burst. But unlike the aftermaths of panics like 1873 and 1893, there was no depression this time. The market quickly came roaring back.

Writing in 1965, historian Robert Sobel observed that "never before or since did the turnover rate of listed shares reach the levels of the 1900–1907 period. During four of these years the rate was over 200 per cent," rising to 319 percent in 1901, the year in which Hill and Harriman rocked the market with their battle for control of the Northern Pacific Railroad. This was speculation of the traditional kind, speculation for profits from increasing stock prices in a market characterized by new conditions like substantial surplus capital, the abundant flow of securities issued by new kinds of corporations and frenzied buying and selling. It rode up and down in several waves and collapsed with the Panic of 1907.[1]

Noyes characterized the early period as the birth of the "New Era." What made the era new was the attitude of the speculators, an attitude that he wrote was seen again in 1905 and 1908. As Noyes later put it:

> In one of its particular phenomena, the public excitement of 1901 foreshadowed 1929 more closely than most people of later date remembered. Probably 1901 was the first speculative episode in American history that based its ideas and conduct on the assumption that Americans were living in a New Era; that old rules and principles of finance were obsolete; that things could safely be done to-day which had been dangerous or impossible in the past.

Noyes was right about the changes in attitude, but there was not all that much new about the speculation he described. It was very much the same kind of speculative mania that Americans had seen in the nineteenth century, though now it had broader public participation. The importance of the new attitude is not found in the behavior of traders during this early period, but rather in the underlying changes in the nature of investing. It is found in the evolution over the long first decade of a new and more permanent concept of speculation.[2]

Speculation as it developed during the first fourteen years of the twentieth century was conceptually different than before. It was not the speculation of a manic market, although the new kind of speculation certainly did not eradicate the episodic occurrences of manipulated markets or overwrought trading. While these roaring bull markets and market bubbles could be extraordinarily disruptive both to the market and sometimes the larger economy when they collapsed, they have never signified a permanent change in the basic structure of the American economy.

The new kind of speculation that developed during the early part of the century did represent such a permanent change, a change that transformed ordinary Americans, acting as a market, into Veblen's businessman writ large, into an institution that dominated industry. This new and permanent form of speculation took hold as American investors became comfortable buying common stock—the watered stock of the merger wave issued not on the basis of productive assets or past profits but on the possibility of profits to come at some unspecified point in the future. They demonstrated their willingness to invest on faith, all for a possible share in the wealth that had come to other investors about whom they read in their newspapers and popular magazines. In making this shift, they clearly signaled their increasing comfort with common stock that until that point had been treated not as the stuff of investment but as mere promise.

These stock buyers were speculators simply because they were willing to buy the future in the hope of higher profits. This new kind of speculation was intrinsic to the investment rather than the behavior of the investor. During the course of the first decade, even as the more traditional kind of speculation led to manic markets from 1899 to 1901 and again from the end of 1903 through 1906, investors began to shift to a more permanent kind of speculation based on the nature of the securities in which they invested. This is the kind of speculation financial writers were describing when they were not referring to the traditional speculative devices of margin buying, short-selling, futures trading and quick turnover during periods of peak market activity. Railroad preferred stock and even high-grade industrial preferred stock became more acceptable as investments. By the beginning of the next decade, average investors started to demonstrate their comfort with common stock as an appropriate investment, too. The characteristics of the different securities had not changed. What had changed was their perceived suitability as repositories for the savings of ordinary people.

The significance of this transformation for business was profound. The securities that had been considered as fitting investments for ordinary Americans were bonds and preferred stock. The principal characteristic of these securities was that they provided a steady promised return. Bonds paid interest at a set rate. Preferred stock, while somewhat more risky because directors had discretion in paying dividends, also promised a fixed return as a percentage of the stock's par value.

The difference in risk between bonds and preferred stock was more of a difference of degree than of kind. Dividend payment may have been discretionary in law, but directors skipped preferred stock dividends at their peril. Failure to pay dividends on preferred stock was the sign of a failing corporation. It also meant that directors could not pay dividends on the common stock. This was especially important because preferred stock dividends were often cumulative, which meant that all dividend payments skipped on the preferred stock had to be fully paid before directors could pay even a quarterly dividend on the common stock. Moreover, consistently missed dividends affected a corporation's credit and thus its ability to borrow money either from banks or on the bond market. The critical point is that investors in both kinds of securities expected no greater profits than they had been promised when they bought them, nor were they contractually permitted to demand any more. They also knew that behind their investments stood tangible, productive assets that could be sold or distributed should the company fail.[3]

Common stock was different. Few if any salable assets underlay the common. More important, the potential returns from common stock were boundless. The entire residual of the corporation's profit was theoretically available for dividends on the common stock once the interest and principal on the bonds and the dividends and par value on the preferred had been paid. This made common stock the most risky of investments, but potentially the most profitable as well. It was entitled to whatever the corporation earned. The more money the corporation made, the more money the common shareholders made. While stockholder voting was largely ineffective—either because of the presence of a controlling group or because directors controlled the machinery of voting—dissatisfied shareholders could sell their stock, causing significant drops in prices that could threaten both the managers' positions and the ability of the corporation to raise capital from other sources. U.S. Steel, among other combinations of the merger wave, suffered both of these consequences during its first few years of existence. Its stock price plummeted, Charles Schwab lost his job to Elbert Gary and the company could not sell its bonds. As common stock with its unlimited profit potential became the dominant form of investment security, the stockholders who owned it and the market in which it traded created profit pressures that were unknown in the days when bonds and preferred stock were the securities issued to the public while controlling interests retained the common stock. As corporations needed to retain cash to grow and dividends became a smaller share of corporate profits, price appreciation followed as a substitute for dividends. And prices could appreciate as quickly as the corporation's profits grew.[4]

The new speculation put new pressures on business. The nineteenth-century industrialist produced profits to his own satisfaction and at his own pace. But the managers of the giant new combinations had to satisfy the demands of a hungry market increasingly populated by common stockholders who expected their dividends. Veblen's businessman was the stock market and the dominance of finance over industry had begun to move to a new and more powerful level.

Lawmakers and reformers witnessed these changes. Some, as we have seen in the various legislative debates, worried about the stranglehold finance was coming to have over industry, although most were more limited in their vision. But the growth of the American stock market focused regulatory efforts on controlling speculation. And the speculation they sought to control was of the traditional type: the bear raids, short-selling, highly margined trading and quick turnover that characterized bubbles and panics. Even as they observed Americans adopting common stock as significant portions of their investment portfolios, it was perhaps too early for them to see that it was the stock, not the behavior, that created permanent change. Their efforts were not entirely misdirected because the new order of a common stock market required honesty, transparency and a measure of stability that could only be achieved by controlling abuses, and their labors were vindicated in portions of the Securities Exchange Act of 1934. But the new common stock market demanded more. In order for it to serve the American economy as well as the American investor, it required conditions that would help the new speculators understand the businesses in which they invested and understand the sources, nature and potential limits of the profits available from industry. The New Deal securities acts went some way toward serving these ends at the same time they accepted and legally sanctified the speculation economy that had by then developed.[5]

THE NEW SPECULATION TAKES ROOT

Speculation as a function of the nature of the investment rather than the behavior of the investor began to develop in a way that forever changed the American stock market by the middle of the first decade. In 1906 *The Wall Street Journal*, in its regular (and regularly conservative) column *Investment and Speculation*, marked a significant turn by identifying seven classifications of securities ranging from "investment" to "speculation," including a class it called "semi-speculative investments." These semi-speculative investments generally consisted of high-yield bonds and preferred stock that were appropriate purchases for "businessmen" hoping to receive income as well as price appreciation. The article capped a long conservative streak in which the *Journal* discouraged all but the securities professional from engaging in speculation. It now treated speculation almost as a form of investment.

Cautious advice was still prevalent. John Moody, writing in 1906, claimed that "we may put it down as axiomatic that only those are legitimate investments where the primary motive is the safe securing of one's principal and the rate of return thereon is looked upon as secondary." Conservatism still counseled the middle class to invest in the kinds of securities that were traditionally classified as investments. But a speculative wind was blowing and the public smelled money in the air.[6]

Protecting principal remained the dominant theme of investment advisors. But the old speculation of the years following the merger wave continued. *The National Banker* opined in 1907 that it was not the small investor who was losing money but rather the rich plunger, admittedly because the small investor was "as a class ... as careful and cautious and conservative as the man who invests his thousands." But the small investor proved to be impatient with small returns, although interest rates had risen to 5 or 6 percent by 1907. It was the small investor who appeared to be bargain hunting in the immediate wake of the Panic of 1907. With New York threatening to regulate or prohibit the traditional forms of speculation, professionals told investors that their speculation helped to move market prices in the right direction. The *Times* predicted that small investors had become so well educated in the ways of the market that they would reap the profits of the next boom, and in fact small investors appeared to be among the profit-takers in the brief market recovery following Taft's election in November 1908. Even Western farmers were using some of their surplus funds to engage in speculation.[7]

Alexander Noyes warned investors of the distorting effect that professional speculators' margin money could have on their own investments. Writing in *The Atlantic Monthly*, he noted that times of high interest rates combined with rising stock prices signaled a coming drop in the market. High interest rates meant that the borrowing capacity of speculators was strained, and that many soon would have to liquidate their market positions. The result would be a collapse in prices as professionals, scrambling to close out of their margin positions, unloaded their high-priced securities on the unsuspecting investor. Conservative advisors still favored high-grade railroad bonds. If an investor really insisted on a higher rate of return, their advice was at least to be sure of the security of his principal.[8]

The old-style speculative frenzy that lasted from 1905 to 1907 was caused by record wheat, corn and cotton crops and a worldwide increase in the money supply. But the speculation continued despite increasing worldwide demands for money and increasing interest rates. The gold-bound inelastic money supply was strained by funding demands for the Russo-Japanese War, the rapidly increasing cost of living and industrial expansion. European demands for money also increased as traditional speculation infested European stock markets. Bank reserves were dropping and margin loan rates in New York ranged from 25 percent to 125 percent. According to Noyes, the early part of this stock market boom did not involve the small investor but the wealthy, the captains of industry, newly rich from the merger wave and trading heavily on margin. They simply borrowed from Europe when U.S. margin rates became too high. On January 4, 1906, Jacob Schiff predicted a spectacular panic if "currency conditions" did not change materially. Ultimately it appears that the Panic of 1907 was caused in part by America's demand for more capital than the industrialized world possessed. It was as if the New York markets were trying to corner the world's cash.[9]

The Panic of 1907 and its aftermath had an unexpected effect on the investment decisions of average investors. While conservative advice still prevailed, newspapers, magazines and investment advisors encouraged speculative investing. But the speculation they envisioned was of the new type. In the summer of 1909 *The Wall Street Journal*, comparing American and European investing habits, described the English and the French as looking for safety and the Americans and Germans as looking for large returns and capital appreciation, which could only be realized by investing in common stock. At about the same time, Adolph Lewisohn, who made his fortune in copper at the end of the nineteenth century, wrote in *The New York Times* that "[i]t is very difficult to draw the line between where investment ceases and speculation commences." It was a statement that almost nobody would have made just a few years earlier.[10]

Even more surprising, *The Wall Street Journal* both redefined and encouraged speculation by reprinting an article, with evident approval, from the *Economist* penned by "A Stockbroker." Speculation, which the author saw as endemic in, and beneficial to, society, "may be defined as the realization of a will to run more or less calculable, and consequently reasonable, risks, which should be rewarded by a special gain." People of means should speculate because it helped to stimulate new industry. The *Journal* also remarked upon widespread speculation by Americans of all classes and noted the "growing popularity of substantial stocks and bonds." In the summer of 1910, as the lifeless market that had begun that year drifted on, the *Journal* chided Americans for their extravagant spending habits, also characteristic of this period, and encouraged them to invest in American industry to keep it out of foreign hands. Somewhat conservatively, it noted that while stock speculation would not soon return, "there will undoubtedly be a considerable amount of buying of the best dividend paying issues." Other newspapers continued to warn investors to stay out of common stock unless they had full information about the corporation, which, as we have seen, they were unlikely to have had.[11]

By 1914, individual investors were well along the way toward shifting their objectives to higher returns rather than safety of principal as they moved from bonds and preferred stock to common stock. Although it remained true until the middle 1920s that small investors buying stock still deeply cared about their dividends, their desire for higher returns—whether through dividends or, increasingly, price appreciation—led them to move from more conservative "investments" to engage in "speculation" in stock. The shift was significant enough to lead Theodore Roosevelt and others to call for action to curb speculation as early as 1908 and the appointment of the Hughes Committee in New York to study the problem that same year. But this early concern with speculation was not so much for the safety and well-being of the investor as it was for the way that old-style stock speculation destabilized banking and the American economy.

The American economy had fallen into a state of mild depression by the time of Woodrow Wilson's election. As Noyes put it: "Exploits of Captains of Industry no longer occupied front pages of the newspapers. 'New Era' propaganda had entirely disappeared; so had Wall Street's dream of a New York which was about to become the financial centre of the world; even New York City had found it necessary to place its bonds in Europe." The stock market reacted in an entirely unexpected way.[12]

THE NEW COMMON STOCKHOLDER

Fundamental economic changes were taking place beneath the decline in irrational exuberance from 1908 to 1914 that not only raised serious concerns about speculation in the market but also, and more important, set the groundwork for the great shift in market structure and investment mentality that flowered after the war.

The market remained flat in 1911 and 1912, producing general economic *ennui* in 1913. Not even savings banks were buying, perhaps not a surprise after the Panic of 1907, although the *Journal* encouraged them to invest in the bond market. But there was life in the market again by 1912. Significantly, it appeared that average investors were turning from the dominant railroads to industrials, which until that time had largely been considered too speculative. This shift revealed a greater appetite for risk on the part of the public. Not only were they buying industrials; they were also buying common stock. The American Sugar Refining Company Statement of 1910 noted its total number of shareholders as 19,359, with average holdings of less than fifty shares. Forty-nine percent of shareholders owned ten or fewer shares. Almost 90 percent of U.S. Steel's common shareholders and 92 percent of its preferred shareholders owned fewer than one hundred shares in 1911, with the overwhelming majority of each class owning fewer than fifty shares. Chauncey Depew, president of the New York Central Railroad, noted his surprise that "people of relatively small means are becoming gradually but surely the majority owners of the stock of the New York Central," as the average investor increasingly put his money into stock.[13]

The average investor's turn to common stock was becoming unmistakable. Numbers from the period are not entirely reliable, but the trends are clear. As I noted in Chapter Four, it is likely that the absolute number of new stockholders remained relatively small as a percentage of the population. But the speed with which their participation in the market was increasing, and its direction toward common stock, signaled the growing centrality of the stock market to American business, culture and individual wealth at the same time that it foreshadowed a transformation in the structure and character of American corporate capitalism.[14]

There is at least some reliable and specific data to support this conclusion in finer detail. The National Civic Federation's Distribution of Ownership in Investments Subcommittee, chaired by economist E.R.A. Seligman, began a study in 1914 to figure out how widely distributed capital ownership had become. The NCF was simultaneously studying the division of American wealth between labor and capital and the degree to which socialism had spread in the United States. Its stock study was prompted by its pronounced fear of creeping socialism. Widespread stock ownership would provide some evidence that the socialist threat was weak.[15]

The NCF study used several different databases. The first were publicly available. In February 1914, *The Wall Street Journal* had published articles detailing the distribution of stock ownership in a number of railroads and industrial corporations. In contrast to the NCF's concern with socialism, the *Journal*'s purpose was to demonstrate to the federal government, during a period of intense legislative activity, that regulation would hurt Americans of modest means rather than plutocrats. The *Journal* found that seventy-two railroads had 461,445 shareholders. From June 1912 to June 1913, the number had increased by 11 percent even as capitalization had increased by only 2 percent. Average shares per holder decreased from 141 to 133. The *Journal* sampled a few industrial corporations for which December 1913 data were available and observed the trend continuing. The clear conclusion was that the number of shareholders, and especially the number of small shareholders, was increasing even in a bad market environment. Important, too, the average par value of these individual holdings was approximately $14,000 in 1912 and $13,320 in 1913. While this last number is $273,800 in 2006 dollars, it is important to remember that the market typically imposed heavy discounts on the par values of common stock, so the average market value of these holdings was likely to have been considerably less than the numbers suggest. In any event, these average holdings hardly represent the kind of plutocratic ownership suggested by popular accounts of the market during this era. Regrettably, data is unavailable to derive the distribution of this ownership, but it does seem indisputable that at least the middle-class investor was a dramatically increasing presence in the market. As the *Journal* put it, the odd-lot investor was the "backbone of the investing world."[16]

The evidence presented by industrial corporations was even more striking. Three hundred twenty-seven companies had 790,023 shareholders with average holdings of 85 shares at an average par value of $8,500 ($174,722.60 in 2006). There was, as the *Journal* noted, duplication of shareholders in industrials and in industrials and railroads, but its conclusions were "not materially affected." Corporate capital ownership was clearly becoming more widespread.[17]

In addition to the information published by the *Journal*, the NCF developed its own database. The subcommittee wrote to more than one hundred corporations requesting stock ownership information. The records of the study in the NCF archives suggest that it was never completed. But the available data is highly suggestive.

Many corporations responded to the survey with more or less detail, which makes it difficult to classify the information, but one can identify three broad categories. Some companies provided very specific information, for varying years, on the distribution of shares (one to five shares, six to ten, etc.), sometimes by type (common and preferred) and sometimes in the aggregate. A larger number simply provided the average number of shares owned by each shareholder. A significant number of companies also provided information on the extent of their shares owned by women and foreigners. In addition to this raw data, there is a compilation in the NCF files of seventy-five of the responding corporations' average holdings in 1901, 1906 and 1913. Presumably those included were the only corporations in the survey that had remained in continual existence during that period.

Taken together, the information in the NCF archives permits modest but telling claims about the distribution of shareholdings in terms of the size of blocks owned, the growth of small investors and the increasing trend toward speculation by means of common stock ownership. Several respondents themselves expressly noted increases in small shareholdings, greater distribution of their shares, the extent of duplication and the extent of institutional ownership.

The data show a significant spread in share ownership across the population from the turn of the century on, both directly, in holdings of less than one hundred shares, and indirectly in the form of increased stock ownership by insurance companies and savings banks. Large holdings (over one thousand shares) were very small proportions of almost every company's stockholdings. The compiled data show an increase in the number of shareholders from 140,072 in 1901 to 197,264 in 1906 to 414,945 in 1913, or 41 percent between 1901 and 1906 and 110 percent between 1906 and 1913, with an overall increase of almost 200 percent during the period. Some of the more pronounced leaps included U.S. Steel, whose shareholders increased from 32,000 to 125,000; General Electric, from 2,900 to 10,450; and American Telephone & Telegraph, from 8,143 to 53,737. It is particularly striking to see the extent of growth from 1906 on, both because the period encompassed the highly disruptive Panic of 1907 and its aftermath and because most of the period from 1910 to 1914 was one long flat market underscored by broad economic stagnation.

The raw data demonstrate the increased popularity of common stock as an investment vehicle, with significant amounts of small holdings as well as increased amounts of outstanding common stock for almost every corporation. Consolidated Gas of Baltimore went from 6.3 million shares of preferred in 1906 to 4.1 million in 1914, a period during which its common shares went from 6.3 million to 11.4 million with only a modest increase in par value. (The company did not provide a breakdown of its capitalization between the common and preferred.) Holding capitalization almost constant, the Chicago & Alton Railroad saw the number of its preferred shareholders rise from 314 in 1906 to 408 in 1914, while the number of common shareholders went from 219 to 671. Companies like Borden's Condensed Milk, Eastman Kodak, Federal Light & Traction, General Motors, Proctor & Gamble, Seaboard Air Line Railroad and Southern California Edison all had more common than preferred shares and, typically, shareholders. Some companies, like The Texas Company and The Silversmiths Company, had only common stock outstanding. Even in the flat years of 1910 to 1914, common stock was becoming the game.

Interestingly, the data also show the very strong presence of women investors, both in common stocks of speculative companies and as investors more generally. Women's ownership ranged from 25 percent to over 40 percent in virtually every company reporting such statistics including General Motors, B. F. Goodrich, Borden's Condensed Milk Co. and National Carbon Company, except in cases like American Locomotive Company, where they owned a majority of the preferred stock, and American Express Company and the Delaware, Lackawanna & Western Coal Co., where they owned an outright majority of all stock. One can tentatively conclude that speculation of the new type had begun to become part of the culture of small investors.[18]

As I noted, indirect ownership had increased as well. Fourteen insurance companies identified in the NCF files had 3.5 million life insurance policies in force in 1913, and the NCF noted that 40 million life insurance policies were then effective in the United States. The handful of insurance companies identified in the NCF archives together owned 20 million shares of railroad stock.[19]

Despite largely adverse economic conditions, buying common stock, which had been looked upon only a few years earlier as intrinsically speculative and therefore out-of-bounds for the small investor, became an increasingly normal activity. From 1898 to 1915, the predominance of the "secure" railroad securities traded on the NYSE fell and the number of "speculative" industrials increased from 20 to 173. The language of Wall Street had even developed to include a phrase that marked the transition of a stock from speculative to investment quality; the stock was " 'put on an investment basis.' "

A broader overview of market trends supports the conclusion that average Americans were buying common stock. Capital seeking investment began to grow dramatically in the first decade of the twentieth century, bank assets more than doubled and life insurance assets did even better. As I noted in Chapter Four, the number of individual stockholders increased dramatically. This was the critical transformation for the speculation economy.[20]

Increased popular press coverage of the market, increased advertising, the rise of retail brokers, the growth of industrials as investment opportunities, the stabilization of the early century combinations by 1914 and the rise of new industries all contributed to bring the individual investor into the market.

Buying stock had never been easier. Investors with little to invest now could have a piece of the action, and new investors entered the market. The rapidly growing practice of selling stocks and bonds on the installment plan provides strong evidence of the small investor's increasing activity. A typical plan for stock purchases in 1912 would have been for $30 down on stocks priced between $100 and $150 and $5 per month thereafter. (The downpayment was $50 on higher-priced stocks and $20 per hundred in principal on top-grade bonds, with $5 per month thereafter.)

For those who still preferred bonds, corporations began to break the venerable tradition of offering their bonds at $1,000 par value by issuing "Baby Bonds" at $100 par. Investment banking firms like Kidder, Peabody and Lee, Higginson, among others on the retail brokerage side, and Goldman Sachs and Lehman Brothers, underwriting the new light industries, huge retailing houses like Sears Roebuck and consumer products companies like General Cigar, began to bring securities to the masses much in the way the new businesses were bringing their new products to all corners of the country.[21]

Finally, even the law began to encourage small investors to enter the stock market. New York passed the first no-par statute in 1912 in part to help investors understand the difference between nominal and financial value, and other states, beginning in 1916, allowed corporations to set par value as low as they cared to.

Attitudes toward speculation had changed. The dramatic increase in small holdings of common stock reflected this, as did financial discussion in general. More specifically, almost all of the companies providing detailed information on their capitalizations showed that outstanding common stock exceeded outstanding preferred stock and, while the sample is small, the fact is significant. Little had changed to increase the amount of reliable information available to shareholders, and a flat market and poor economy was hardly like the bubble of the merger wave or the period leading up to 1907, in which speculation increased at least in part as a function of the frenzied environment. It remained for Wilson's Liberty Bond drives to cement in the public mind the idea that investing in securities was the sort of thing that regular people did, in order to fully transform the character of the stock market into a central part of American culture.

OLD-FASHIONED SPECULATION
AND THE SECOND NEW ERA

The establishment of common stock as a legitimate investment vehicle was critically important in determining the course of American corporate capitalism. So was the change in investor expectations, a change that showed itself from time to time throughout the century's first two decades and reached full flower during the 1920s. That was the shift from investing for income to investing for capital appreciation. The result was a combination of the traditional form of speculation with the new. The increasingly widespread ownership of common stock made speculation in terms of the nature of the security a permanent feature of the American economy. It also amplified the traditional forms of speculation.[22]

While preferred and then common stock gradually overtook bonds as popular investment vehicles, effectively obliterating the difference between speculation and investment, most investors during the first two decades did focus their attention on dividends. For the average investor speculation during that period was more a matter of holding stocks, the dividends of which were more uncertain and higher, than profiting from trading. As Benjamin Graham and David Dodd noted in their classic 1934 treatise *Security Analysis*, before World War I "[i]nvestment in common stock was confined to those [stocks] showing stable dividends and fairly stable earnings; and such issues in turn were expected to maintain a fairly stable market level."

But things changed fast. "During the postwar period, and particularly during the latter stage of the bull market culminating in 1929, the public acquired a completely different attitude toward the investment merits of common stocks.... The new theory or principle may be summed up in the sentence: 'The value of a common stock depends upon what it will earn in the future.'" In this mode, dividend rates and asset values were completely irrelevant. All that mattered was the potential future stock prices, what once had been called the "water." Meade's insistence on capitalizing earnings, the promoters' practice of selling watered common stock, Veblen's and Commons's theories of value, all had come to be realized in the new market in a way that would not have been possible had bonds and preferred stock continued to be the individual investor's way of participating in the market. Water there may have been, but to the new investors it had lost all meaning. The problem of overcapitalization was a thing of the past.[23]

The widespread shift from buying for income to buying for price growth had profound consequences for American corporate capitalism that would not have existed without the trend to common stock. When you bought for income, you had to pay attention to whatever you might learn about the company in which you were investing. You were buying to hold, after all, not to trade. Again in the words of Graham and Dodd:

> Another useful approach to the attitude of the prewar common-stock investor is from the standpoint of taking an interest in a private business. The typical common-stock investor was a business man, and it seemed sensible to him to value any corporate enterprise in much the same manner as he would value his own business. This meant that he gave at least as much attention to the asset value behind the shares as he did to their earnings records.... Broadly speaking, the same attitude was formerly taken in an investment purchase of a marketable common stock.

The shift from investment to speculation, from a time when most Americans saw corporate securities as a way to get a steady return while protecting their principal to a time when Americans saw the stock market as a place to trade on the fluctuations of an increasingly volatile market, took place over the second and third decades of the twentieth century. Certainly speculation had been part of American capital and commodities markets for as long as they had existed. But while anybody could speculate in the market and often did, the capital markets were, as we have seen, for most people a place of investment.[24]

In order for a common stock investor to properly evaluate the wisdom

of an investment, he had to understand the business. You might think that a speculator would also have to understand the business to evaluate the potential earnings growth of a corporation. Not so, according to Graham and Dodd. They noted that in earlier speculative times the classic method (still in use) of evaluating future earnings growth was to capitalize earnings. This did not technically require much knowledge of the business, but it did at least force a speculator to look at financial statements. In the postwar period, the speculator did not bother with past earnings—he simply assumed a level of goodwill for Radio Corporation of America or Wright Aeronautical Corporation, or simply watched their price movements.

Lawrence Chamberlain, general counsel to the Investment Bankers Association and another major financial writer of the period, agreed with Graham and Dodd. He observed the postwar shift from investment to speculation with dismay:

> Not only was the utmost possible heresy rampant in our own profession, but this heresy was routing conservative practice in business life with amazing rapidity and on a colossal scale. We were being told in high places and low that long-term investment did not pay, that intelligent speculation was investment, and that Americans lived in a chosen country to which had been vouchsafed a "new era" in which all one had to do was to buy "well-selected" stocks at any time, at any price, and hold with sufficient patience in order to sell for more than one paid and thereby realize on the "investment."

This was the principal difference between the prewar and postwar stock buyer. The prewar buyer was, for the most part, interested in industry, even if he invested in speculative stocks. He knew the corporation. He paid attention to the business. The postwar buyer did not care about the corporation. He cared about price trends, reputations and rumors. While Noyes described the turn-of-the-century trader as believing in a "New Era," the postwar market demonstrated the birth of a "Second New Era."[25]

Dividend-paying common stock sometimes was considered investment grade despite its capitalization as goodwill (or water) and the absence of corporate financial disclosure. Non–dividend-paying stock—what today is called growth stock—was considered nothing but speculative, and the speculator needed no knowledge of the business in which he was investing. As Chamberlain put it: "If learned financial counsel are right in calling non–dividend paying common stocks investments by virtue of a capital gain that may or

does come to them, then the essence of investment is not inherent in income at all." He was right. It was inherent in the nature of the security. Bonds with secure principal and steady interest were investments; common stock with its potentially unlimited returns was speculative. As the public's taste for common stock developed, the distinction made earlier in the century between investment and speculation was lost. "Second New Era" investing had profound consequences for the development of American corporate capitalism with its focus on finance.[26]

Traditional speculation itself had sometimes come to be treated as acceptable. The Pujo Report, picking up on a distinction made by its predecessor investigatory committees, itself distinguished between "wholesome speculation," which even its reformist counsel Untermyer admitted was vital to the economy, and "unwholesome speculation." While noting that speculation was best left to the man who had the appropriate amount of time to spend on it, one popular financial writer opined that speculators did more for society than investors, because they were the people who provided entrepreneurial capital. He believed "that the moral standards of the average speculator before the latter half of the nineteenth century . . . were below par." At one point "the Hebrews, the leaders of the world's business, practically monopolized speculation. . . ." But "with the changing times, speculation has been placed upon a higher moral level than formerly." Now speculators could be described as "gentlemen." The market had proven itself to be important, and all but the most radical politicians were concerned that it not be destroyed. Evidence of the adverse effect of antispeculation laws, most prominently those of Germany, cautioned against heavy-handed regulation.[27]

The market was becoming an important repository of wealth, and common stock a normal part of American life, but this was not the time for radical reform. The year and a half leading up to the European war was a time of industrial depression and a flat stock market. The largest bankruptcy at that point in U.S. history, the collapse of the famous Claflin dry goods empire in June 1914, produced panic in a White House that had come to power on a blended platform of classical conservative and progressive business reform but that had never known economic good times and was beginning to fear the consequences. That would change with a remarkable and, perhaps, improbable reversal of fortune as war broke out in Europe. America's entry into the war would provide economic rejuvenation and the training ground for massive new numbers of stockholders. When securities regulation finally came into its own, it would embrace the new reality of the speculation economy. But, until then, the shadow of the merger wave continued to loom over legislative efforts.

NINE

THE END OF REFORM

T he beginning of the end of the Progressive Era in business took place
on June 25, 1914. That was the day the Claflin dry goods empire declared the largest bankruptcy in American history and the day that
President Wilson chose to pronounce himself as unambiguously for business. The preceding fifteen months had been among the most active business and financial reform periods in American history. By the end of his first
year in office Wilson had played a major role in pushing through Congress
two controversial bills, a major tariff revision and the Federal Reserve Act,
which he signed into law on December 23, 1913. Wilson also worked hard for
the 1914 passage of the Clayton and FTC Acts, which ended twenty-five years
of political agitation for antitrust regulation. The FTC Act reflected Wilson's
reform blend of progressivism and conservatism, representing a compromise
between executive, judicial and market control of the antitrust issue. It
lodged regulatory supervision in an independent federal agency, giving the
new FTC authority "to investigate, publicize, and prohibit all 'unfair methods of competition.'" But it left the Sherman Act in place with the courts, following the 1911 Supreme Court embrace of the rule of reason, as the source
of final judgment, and with it the power to review FTC decisions.[1]

When Wilson abandoned the Progressive business agenda he left two
pieces of legislation on the cutting-room floor of the Congress he had thus
far so effectively led. The Rayburn bill, a version of which would ultimately
pass in 1920, was a railroad regulation bill that was a direct descendant of
S. 232 and the corporate finance measures cut out of the Mann-Elkins Act.
Cast in terms of securities regulation, it was an antitrust measure that, following the dominant pattern of antitrust thinking, addressed overcapitalization
as the principal problem. Its method was to give the ICC power to determine

whether or not individual railroads could issue new securities. True to its heritage, shareholder protection was no direct part of its concern.

The less intrusive yet more controversial Owen bill was the first true securities regulation measure. But it was not yet modern securities regulation. It grew out of the same concerns as the investigations of the Hughes Committee and Hadley Commission, the effect of securities speculation on economic stability. At the same time it demonstrated an interest in protecting stockholders, picking up on strands of the earlier investigative and legislative efforts. The Owen bill would never pass. But it was a great leap forward. Securities regulation was now federal business.

Woodrow Wilson made almost no direct contribution to securities regulation. But his indirect contribution, his philosophy of regulation, emerged in the legislation that finally passed under his Assistant Secretary of the Navy, Franklin Roosevelt. Neither a radical progressive, a Jeffersonian conservative, nor a classic Southern Democrat, Wilson was far more economically and business savvy than most historians acknowledge. His peculiar blend of ideas included progressive realism forged by his teachers at Johns Hopkins and refined by his observations of the world around him, Southern conservatism that included at least an intellectual appreciation of, and sometimes political commitment to, states' rights, a belief in a strong and active presidency and an understanding that big business had become the centerpiece of American life and politics. Together this created a style of regulation that drew from, even as it moderated, Teddy Roosevelt's, and that helped to transform political ideas about business regulation. As I will show in the next chapter, by the time Wilson was engaged in his futile battle for Versailles and the League of Nations, the modern stock market had emerged and modern regulatory ideas with it.[2]

THE DEMOCRATS RETURN

The 1912 election provided a Democratic sweep of Congress and the White House. The party had been out of power since 1895, which meant that inexperienced leaders were continuing the job of establishing and managing a ruling party that had begun with their gaining control of the House in 1911. It also meant that a significant number of important congressional and executive positions were filled by Southerners, including almost all of the relevant committee chairmanships. Historians dispute the extent to which Southern Democrats shared a consistent, common ideology, but while it seems clear that there were significant Progressive and even radical voices from the South, those voices were a counterpoint to a fundamentally conservative chorus.

Southern conservatism, unlike the business conservatism of the Republican Senate leaders, unlike the conservatism of Taft, was an older sort of American conservatism, a conservatism of individualism, states' rights and limited federal power. Thus it is all the more striking that almost every leader of the Wilson reforms that established the federal government's dominance in business and financial regulation was Southern born. The president, his treasury secretary William Gibbs McAdoo, advisors Samuel Untermyer and Louis Brandeis and congressmen Carter Glass, Robert Latham Owen, Robert Lee Henry, Henry Clayton and Arsène Pujo, among others, all were raised in the South. While their views were hardly monolithic, they came together to create the modern financial regulatory state.

The Republican Party had effectively protected business from meaningful regulation for twenty-five years, even as it preached progressive regulation from the bully pulpit. Progressive and pledged to business at the same time, it failed to achieve sufficient regulatory reforms that would have maintained that protection while at the same time responding to the almost universal demand for some measure of federal control. To be fair, it was the Republicans who were in charge during the most rapid, and thus perplexing, period of American economic transition. Nevertheless the natives of Jeffersonian soil, the anticorporate heirs of Jackson, the states' rights Democrats, achieved exactly the kind of balanced regulation the progressive Republicans had sought. It was this group of Southern Democrats that made America safe for business.[3]

WILSON AND BUSINESS

Wilson, a minister's son, grew up in comfortable middle-class circumstances. He spent most of his youth in the South both before and, for a time, after his college years at Princeton, studying first at Davidson and later at Virginia, where he spent a year working toward a law degree. The traditionalism that characterized the instruction at these institutions was exploded at Johns Hopkins, where Wilson earned his doctorate under some of the most innovative economic and political thinkers of the day. As a son of the South, his birthright was both Democratic and conservative. It was a birthright he used well in delivering the Democratic Party from the radical ineffectuality of William Jennings Bryan. Yet this conservative Southern Democrat who spent his formative years in a South dominated by the Civil War and Reconstruction was no real conservative. Wilson's presidency defined the Progressive Era. It also ended it.

Wilson was hardly the type of candidate that newspaperman William Allen White, a staunch Republican, expected to find himself hailing as the great hope for American progressivism. But as governor of New Jersey he fought the party regulars to win battles ranging from civil service reform to remaking that state's infamous corporation law into one of the strictest in the country. He campaigned for president first and foremost on a platform of completing the antitrust program that had been almost twenty years in the making. But he was also the president who insisted upon segregating the United States Civil Service. A Southern gentleman with that character's notion of chivalry toward women, he opposed women's suffrage until the war forced him to it, asserting states' rights grounds even as he promised suffragettes his support in 1918. He politically opposed a variety of progressive social reforms he had specifically advocated in his early writings, including child labor laws, minimum wage laws and federal aid to health care and education, in part on the same states' rights grounds. Wilson's neo-Jeffersonian New Freedom, according to Herbert Croly, one of the leading intellectual spirits of the progressive movement, was in direct opposition to the collective, communitarian and regulatory aims of progressivism.[4]

Croly was right. Wilson talked far more of the importance of the individual than the orthodoxy of progressivism allowed. But Croly was also wrong. The New Freedom was a political campaign, not a complete social vision. And the man who was the candidate was still Tommy Wilson, the young professor who was a founding member of the iconoclastic American Economic Association. Wilson's graduate education at Johns Hopkins under Herbert Baxter Adams and Richard Ely and Wilson's own intellectual development helped him try to weave together a philosophy that combined a Jeffersonian vision of individual responsibility with acceptance of the evolutionary and consequently natural collective reality of modern life. The New Freedom, properly understood, was the translation into presidential politics of the young century's attempt to find the place of the individual in collective urban industrial society.[5]

The Centrality of Business Regulation

As early as 1889 in his book *The State*, Wilson had attempted to navigate between the goals of socialism, which he described as having "the right end in view" even if its methods were "mistaken enough to provoke the laughter of children," and *laissez-faire* competition, which was harsh and destructive. His conclusion at that time, a conclusion he maintained throughout his economic legislative program, was that competition was desirable, but it was only just when it occurred between equals. Given modern circumstances, equality of competition could only be achieved through regulation. Socialist regulation was extreme. "The regulation I mean is not interference: it is the

equalization of conditions so far as possible, in all its branches of endeavor; and the equalization of conditions is the very opposite of interference." That regulation, equalizing information, access and power, was the type of regulation embodied in the FTC Act. Even more, it was the very essence of the New Deal securities acts.[6]

Business regulation was part of the very nature of the state, as Wilson saw it, and as his views evolved he came to understand it as central to the state's function. Business and the state were deeply tied together. The state must not only regulate but also learn from business. In his famous 1887 article, *The Study of Administration*, Wilson wrote that administration of the government itself was but a branch of business. But while the state was to regulate, it was to do so with a light hand. As he noted in 1912, "You cannot establish competition by law, but you can take away the obstacles by law that stand in the way of competition." At that time this meant preventing monopolies from blocking access to capital and opportunities for individual entrepreneurs and smaller businesses. But regulation should be approached with caution. It should be carefully tailored so that business would not become "partners or creatures of the government itself."

Roosevelt's approach had been far too interventionist. "Recent proposals of regulation have looked too much like a wholesale invasion by government itself of the field of business management." It would be characteristic of the Wilson style of regulation that it left business largely to business. And indeed candidate Wilson, accepting the 1912 presidential nomination of the Democratic Party, proclaimed "I am not one of those who think that competition can be established by law against the drift of world-wide economic tendency." The very trend toward cooperation he and his teachers observed in the 1880s had become reality. But there was no mistaking Wilson's demand for regulation. Although, as Martin Sklar points out, Wilson scholars have attempted to classify his thought into periods moving from various types of conservatism to "militant progressivism," Wilson's economic progressivism was a leitmotif of his writings and speeches throughout his adult life, even when superimposed upon a Southern conservative foundation. The early influences of Ely, Hopkins and the American Economic Association never really left him.[7]

Jeffersonian Business

To the extent Wilson can properly be classified as conservative, his conservatism was a function of the manner in which he believed that progressive change should take place rather than the question of whether change should take place at all. As such, his conservatism was pragmatic, not principled. Indeed he understood that modern circumstances left the state and society no choice but to change. The world had become what it was, and it was for the state to adapt rather than to combat. The historicist views of his German-trained teachers remained important components of his thinking. As he noted in his first inaugural address, in words consistent with those he had been speaking for twenty-five years: "We shall deal with our economic system as it is and as it may be modified, not as it might be if we had a clean sheet of paper to write upon." At the same time, "practical wisdom," not the "long process of historical experience," was what allowed states to change their practices with changing circumstances. New theories followed new experience, not the other way around. This very pragmatism was consistent with "the rule of historical continuity," rejecting clean breaks with the past and instead adopting past ideas to new circumstances.[8]

Nowhere was this evolutionary, historically sensitive, yet eminently practical approach more evident than in Wilson's rhetorical attempts as a politician to connect Jeffersonian thought to the new world of big business. Wilson clearly was not a Jeffersonian. As early as the late 1880s, he favored cooperation over the real-world state of individual competition as long as it did not lead to monopoly. And very much like progressives of both parties, he was untroubled by big business, a position he continued to articulate with increasing frequency as he came closer to assuming progressive leadership. "I regard the corporation as indispensable to modern business enterprise," he told the American Bar Association. "I am not jealous of its size or might." In fact, "modern business is no doubt best conducted upon a great scale." The problem was not the existence of huge combinations, but monopolies that deprived others of business opportunities. And as he moved toward the presidency, Wilson argued that it was combinations of combinations, including the Money Trust, that posed the threat to individual initiative, not the great combinations taken individually. Indeed in the winter of 1912 he reiterated the evolutionary understanding he had developed at Hopkins, telling the General Assembly of Virginia that "I am not here to enter an indictment against business. No man indicts natural history."[9]

He drew on Jeffersonian metaphors even as he rejected Jeffersonian thinking. Federal regulation was not inconsistent with Jeffersonian ideals. Wilson transformed the maxim often attributed to Jefferson, "that government is best which governs least," into an understanding that the best government should regulate as far as it had to in order to eliminate arbitrary interference with individuals and to eliminate "undesirable transactions." He might depart from Jefferson on the need for federal regulation, on the one hand, but on the other hand find common ground in the fact that it was for the sake of the individual that regulation was to be had.[10]

Wilson reconceptualized the corporation as a Jeffersonian form of property much in the same way that business leaders and other thinkers had been encouraging the American middle class to discover stock as a substitute for the land: "The corporation ... is an arrangement by which hundreds of thousands of men who would in days gone by have set up in business for themselves put their money into a single huge accumulation and place the entire direction of its employment in the hands of men they have never seen, with whom they never confer." The yeoman farmer had become the yeoman stockholder, but the separation of stock ownership from corporate control limited the manner in which the individual could assert his individual autonomy through his ownership of property. Jeffersonian terms were insufficient for modern conditions, no matter how evocative of American tradition. "We have changed our economic conditions from top to bottom, and with our economic conditions has changed also the organization of life. The old party formulas do not fit the present problems." This required changes in the laws, which were still based upon the idea of business done by individuals. They needed to be adapted for business done by giant corporations in order to liberate the individual within the organization.[11]

Sklar describes a fairly sharp break between Wilson and Jeffersonian thought. But there was some continuity that is consistent enough with Wilson's writings that Wilson's talk of Jefferson seems to have transcended mere political rhetoric. In his address at the 1912 New York Jefferson Day banquet, in a remarkable speech entitled *What Jefferson Would Do*, Wilson not only built on the Jeffersonian theme of individual opportunity but also transformed the Jeffersonian ideal of competition among individuals to competition among corporations. Completely dismissive of Jeffersonian fears of bigness, he said: "[I]n the general field of business [Jefferson's thought] would ... see that, whether big or little, business was not dominated by anything but the law itself, and that that law was made in the interest of plain, unprivileged men everywhere." Squared with Wilson's acceptance of the reality of the giant modern corporation, he seems to have meant that the individual would be free to enjoy the Jeffersonian ideal as long as economic opportunity, in its new form, was not denied him.[12]

Wilson tried his best to maintain a healthy respect for states' rights, but ultimately his view of the presidency overcame his native instincts. In *The State*, as well as in his later work, he argued that most business regulation should be left to the states and, indeed, if the variety and inconsistency of state regulations were causing business problems it was up to the states to get together and correct them. At the same time he described commercial regulation, which was necessary to ensure the survival of the states, as "the chief object of the Union."

Gradually the states more or less disappeared from his business legislative program. This was an inevitable result as Wilson refined and to a degree achieved the imperial presidency developed by Roosevelt. He lamented the fact that the presidency had faded into irrelevancy as early as 1897. The contrast between the strong leadership of the nation's first three decades with the pallid presidential leadership (excepting Lincoln) that followed had given rise to scattered congressional government. He acknowledged that Congress was rightly jealous of its legislative prerogatives. But as president he did not hesitate to wade into the legislative chamber, participating actively and consistently in the legislative process, trumping even Roosevelt's heavy involvement. It was Wilson who broke the century-long tradition that barred the president physically from the Capitol as he began the practice of addressing Congress in person.[13]

One final place where the classic American individualistic thought commonly associated with Jefferson appears consistently in Wilson's thinking is his demand for individual accountability, even in the context of the corporate form of business. Corporations themselves were unpunishable. "Corporate responsibility lacks vitality, corrects nobody." The individual was the actor, whether within a corporation or otherwise, and only the individual could be punished and corrected, just as the individual was the only bearer of natural rights, the only appropriate political actor. Collective responsibility simply would not do.[14]

Woodrow Wilson, son of the South but grafted onto the North, adapted traditional notions of individualism to the permanence of the new collective society that he fully accepted, from the collectivity of life in cities, in tenement houses and apartment buildings, to the collectivity that was the corporation. He knew that this collective society could not flourish under the minimalist state that preceded the transformative presidency of Roosevelt, no matter how ideally attractive. Organizational life demanded a government that did more than simply prevent harm. It required a government that regulated organizations.

THE COLLECTIVE SOCIETY

The society of private individuals conducting their lives through private ordering had been transmogrified in large part into a society where safety in housing and employment, for example, could no longer be left to private arrangements but had become matters of public concern. The society of individuals had become a society of groups, with the consequence that the concerns of individuals had become the concerns of groups, including the giant corporations. Only the federal government was in a position to lay down the rules for group behavior in American life.

Wilson's regulatory approach therefore centered upon the ideas of publicity necessary to ensure competition among equals, whether those equals were individuals or corporations, by ensuring access to capital, information and opportunity for those with initiative. The idea of the regulated free market was Wilson's attempt to square classical American philosophical liberalism with the economic reality of the new collectivism. The regulated free market was Wilson's lasting legacy to American economic life.

As part of this vision of a regulated free market, Wilson was interested in securities regulation as a means of providing opportunity. "When you offer the securities of a great corporation to anybody who wishes to purchase them, you must open that corporation to the inspection of everybody who wants to purchase." Disclosure would permit the individual to make free economic choices. But by the time securities disclosure was on the legislative table, other matters had become more pressing. An industrial depression had persisted for almost two years along with a flat and lifeless stock market. Even new demands created by the war in Europe that would bolster American industry would take time to show. Meanwhile Wilson, facing the midterm elections of 1914, had grown increasingly impatient with economic stagnation and was under significant political pressure from Wall Street to slow the pace of reform. As a result, he shifted rather quickly from his philosophy of conservative progressivism to firm support for big business. Business had been regulated enough. He withdrew his support for securities regulation and, indeed, any other economic reform. Another twenty years would pass before securities regulation was provided by the federal government. When that regulation came, it embraced the regulated free market, progressive conservatism of the Wilson philosophy.[15]

THE FEDERAL RESERVE

When Wilson took office, the House Banking and Currency Committee had been hard at work. It had created two subcommittees in delayed response to the flaws in the American monetary system revealed by the Panic of 1907 and continuing populist agitation over the perceived concentration of the American economy on Wall Street. One subcommittee was chaired by Virginia Representative Carter Glass and had been directed to draft remedial banking legislation that would make the necessary currency reforms. The other, chaired by Louisiana Congressman Arsène Pujo, was charged with investigating Wall Street's control over American finance.

The work of the Glass committee would culminate in 1913 with passage of the Federal Reserve Act creating the central banking system of the United States. Controversial currency legislation was already in place. Nelson Aldrich had introduced an emergency measure after the Panic of 1907 that took form as the Aldrich-Vreeland Act of 1908. That act lay completely dormant until its one moment of glory, when it served to stabilize the American economy following the collapse of the European currency markets at the start of World War I.

Almost everybody agreed that some form of currency reform was needed. But, as we have already seen, a long-running political dispute centered on the twin questions of the appropriate powers of the federal government and the desirability of centralizing power in Washington. Even more frightening to some than centralizing power in Washington was centralizing power on Wall Street. The very real possibility of the latter was reflected in the predominant reform proposal, the Aldrich plan, which had been developed by Aldrich as head of the Monetary Commission and banker Paul Warburg. Aldrich wanted a central bank controlled by the bankers. This deeply worried progressives of both parties who were concerned with Wall Street's already concentrated financial power.

The legislation that emerged, with its balance of centralization and decentralization, government and business control, was very much in the Wilsonian style of regulation. The Bryanite wing of the Democratic Party favored complete federal control of the money supply. This idea troubled those who disliked too much government power and naturally bothered the bankers themselves. When the Southerner Glass became chair of the subcommittee in 1912, he was opposed to a central bank at all. But, working with his friend Warburg, he developed a more decentralized version of the Aldrich plan. The progressives opposed this, as did Treasury Secretary William McAdoo who, with the support of Untermyer and Owen, wanted to establish the central bank within the Treasury Department. Wilson, on the advice of Louis Brandeis, backed the plan for government control. Enormous controversy raged from all sides as Wilson, McAdoo and Glass carefully fought one battle after another until the Federal Reserve Act, linking the federal government with the existing private banking system, became law on December 23, 1913. The fast-moving legislation and its enormous impact on the banking and currency system held much of the country's attention as the Pujo Committee was preparing its report.

THE PUJO COMMITTEE

The Pujo Committee had been appointed by the House after years of clamoring for an investigation of the financiers of Wall Street, dubbed the "Money Trust." To some, the Money Trust, of which J. P. Morgan was reputedly the head, was just like any other trust, a conspiracy in restraint of trade. In this view, the trust was a loosely bound small group of banks and investment banks that controlled the money supply and the New York Stock Exchange. Thus it controlled the ordinary person's access to credit and to fair terms on the stock market itself. Others, including Pujo Committee counsel Samuel Untermyer, saw the Money Trust simply as an excessive concentration of financial power in several New York (and some Boston) banks and investment houses. Whatever the Money Trust was or might have been, populist agitation demanded an investigation. The House had little choice but to authorize it.[16]

Looking back from the prosperity of 1926 on the economic history of these early Wilson days, Alexander Noyes gave credit only to the work of the Glass Committee. The Pujo Committee, the subcommittee focused on the Money Trust and the stock market, was "long forgotten." Long forgotten it may have been in the sunny days of 1926. But not in 1933, when Untermyer was one of the first experts to be asked by his old colleague from the Wilson administration, Franklin Roosevelt, to draft a securities bill. More, the Pujo Committee's hearings and recommendations produced the Owen bill of 1914 and thus put securities regulation squarely on the federal agenda.[17]

The Owen bill failed for a lot of reasons, including the president's political needs, Wall Street opposition, widespread fear of centralized government power and, perhaps, some congressional exhaustion after frustrating decades of debating economic regulation. Also among the reasons for its failure was, I suspect, the controversial character of the bill's principal proponent, Samuel Untermyer.

The Crusader

[T]he [Pujo] subcommittee might more properly bear the counsel's name than the name of its chairman.[18]

There is no doubt that the Pujo Committee was Untermyer's committee. One of the most colorful members of the Wilson circle, Samuel Untermyer was born in 1858 in Lynchburg, Virginia, two years after Wilson and only sixty miles as the crow flies across the Shenandoah Mountains. The two men were dramatically different in background, style and upbringing, but they shared both idealism and ideals. Their uncompromising idealism led each to his own separate downfall, Untermyer in the Pujo-Owen fight, and Wilson in the settlement of the war.[19]

Untermyer was an early Wilson supporter and a major, if largely unofficial, influence on Wilson's economic policies. Despite an early hint of personal distaste for Untermyer that crops up periodically if subtly in Wilson's papers, Republican Simeon Fess could say of him, if perhaps hyperbolically, that his "utterances are the final word for this administration." As time wore on, Wilson appears to have developed a real fondness and deep respect for Untermyer.[20]

Untermyer began life as a Southerner but his was not a Southern life. The garrulous and passionate Untermyer recalled, as one of his first childhood memories, running out of his house in Lynchburg and crying "Hurrah for Jeff Davis" as Union troops marched through the city's streets. His father, a Confederate lieutenant who lost a fortune in Confederate bonds, died shortly after Appomattox, and Untermyer's mother moved the family to New York, where she opened a boardinghouse. While Wilson was formed by Princeton, Virginia and Hopkins, Untermyer's work as an office boy in a New York law firm served as his undergraduate education. He started at fifteen, and a few years later enrolled in Columbia Law School, graduating in 1878. With his half brother, Randolph Guggenheimer, he formed the firm of Guggenheimer & Untermyer. The firm remained a prominent institution in New York business law until its dissolution in 1986.

Untermyer was smart and ambitious. By the age of twenty-five he was earning $50,000 annually as a lawyer and trust promoter, and was a millionaire by age thirty. According to his obituary, which rated a page-one placement in *The New York Times*, "he was one of the first lawyers to see the advantage of combination of capital in great industrial enterprises." And, employing the business ethics of the era, he sometimes got into trouble, as we saw in the *American Smelting* and *Columbia Straw Paper* cases.[21]

Untermyer was an idealist. The kind of passion that led to the young Untermyer's protest against Union occupation led him to turn, like his older contemporary Brandeis, from trust promotion to economic reform. He cut his reformist teeth working with Charles Evans Hughes on the insurance industry investigation of 1905; he challenged controlling shareholders of giant corporations who he thought were trampling on the rights of minority shareholders; and he fought his most famous battle against the irresponsibility of the New York Stock Exchange. His life was a life of causes, undertaken typically without pay. He was involved in drafting the Federal Trade Commission Act, the Clayton Act, the Federal Reserve Act and numerous other measures. Like Brandeis, Untermyer turned a successful business law career into a career as a lawyer for the people.[22]

He was an early supporter of Wilson's presidential candidacy as well as a member of the Tammany-controlled New York delegation to the 1912 Democratic National Convention in Baltimore, which he left before the final balloting for his annual trip to Baden-Baden. He wrote to candidate Wilson from the R.M.S. *Caronia* and from the spa in order to fill him in on the Pujo Committee's preliminary findings and to offer him whatever help he might need.[23]

Despite his influence, Untermyer was frustrated in his attempt to obtain an official appointment in the Wilson administration. He wanted the ambassadorship to Germany and, failing that, France. But Wilson was conflicted in his early feelings about Untermyer, in part because of his earlier notoriety as a trust promoter. When Colonel House reported in April 1913 that he had received word that "Samuel Untermyer would like to become Ambassador to Germany ... the President smiled and said it was interesting and he was glad to know that Mr. Untermyer would be pleased if he should be sent." House further reported in his diary a conversation with the president on November 29, 1913, concerning Untermyer's possible appointment to the French mission. Wilson noted that Democratic Party Chairman William McCombs had suggested Untermyer and House pressed the case, but Wilson was "quite emphatic in his decision not to appoint him. ... I related a discussion I had heard concerning Untermyer, one man taking the stand that his success had a bad influence upon the youth of the country, the other contended that his failure to obtain public recognition was in itself a good lesson to the youth of the country. The President thought both gentlemen were correct."[24]

Untermyer was both charming and abrasive. He was arrogant, controlling and unrelenting in the pursuit of what he perceived as justice. His partner in reform and Lynchburg neighbor, Carter Glass, despised him, characterizing him most kindly with sarcasm as "that shy and painfully reserved gentleman, Mr. Samuel Untermyer, of New York City, well known and greatly admired for his fine aversion to notoriety of every description." While Glass had a personal ax to grind, it is true that Untermyer had no trouble grabbing the spotlight when he wanted it.[25]

The Pujo Committee's creation, no less than its ultimate success, appeared to depend upon Untermyer's participation. In January 1912, while resolutions forming the Committee were being drafted and debated, Robert Henry, chair of the powerful House Rules Committee, penned this postscript to a letter pleading for Untermyer's help: "You must not fail me — Action will soon be taken — delay and postponement are dangerous — So to carry forward plans you must obey the request and summons — Henry."[26]

The Committee

House Resolution 405 authorized the creation of a special committee to investigate whether a money trust really existed on Wall Street and the extent of its power over American business and banking. The committee would have been charged with discovering the relationship between the bankers and the New York Stock Exchange and investigating the methods by which interstate corporations were financed and their securities marketed. H.R. 405 was rejected by the Democratic leadership. But progressive House Democrats continued to push the issue.[27]

As a result, a second significantly diluted resolution did pass and simply empowered the committee "to obtain full and complete information of the banking and currency conditions of the United States for the purpose of determining what legislation is needed." In the end, at Untermyer's insistence, Arsène Pujo of Louisiana successfully introduced an amending resolution on April 22, House Resolution 504, which largely reinstated the failed H.R. 405. That final resolution gave broad investigative powers to the committee for the purpose of gathering information and suggesting "remedial and other legislative purposes."[28]

The successful H.R. 504 followed directly from the legislative activity we have seen developing in previous chapters. The opening clauses refer to bills "pending or under consideration to regulate industrial corporations engaged in interstate commerce through Federal incorporation, supervision, and otherwise," and legislation "believed to be necessary to further control the incorporation, management, and financial operations of railroad corporations." The committee also was empowered "to investigate the methods of financing the cash requirement [sic] of interstate corporations and of marketing their securities." Securities regulation of industrial corporations was finally going to receive thorough congressional investigation.[29]

The Counsel

Untermyer's application for the job of counsel to the Pujo Committee was characteristically unsubtle. In late 1911, when agitation for the investigation was growing, he gave what *The New York Times* characterized as an "unusual address" before The New York County Lawyer's Association, calling for substantial corporate reform, mostly in state law. In late December 1911, he made a widely reported speech before the Finance Forum of New York City, in which he argued that a Money Trust did indeed exist in the concentration of finance on Wall Street.[30]

There was never any question that Untermyer would be retained as counsel. The infamous stock speculator turned muckraker, Thomas Lawson, described him as having "either prosecuted, defended, or had an inquisitorial finger in every sword-swallowing, dissolving-view, frenzied finance game that has been born or naturalized in Wall Street within the decade." It was Untermyer who, at Henry's request, drafted the original H.R. 405. After its defeat and the passage of the watered-down substitute resolution, he claimed to have lost interest in the investigation because of the Committee's limited power. Writing to Henry in April 1912, he complained of the "very narrow scope of the Investigation" and concluded that "[u]nder the present restricted form of Resolution the Inquiry is bound to prove worse than fruitless." Henry invited him to draft a new resolution, incorporating the powers that originally had been included in the defeated H.R. 405. Meanwhile Pujo invited Untermyer to become counsel to the Committee. Untermyer declined. But he artfully described in his response the powers the Committee would need to be granted in order for him to change his mind. These were the broad investigatory powers that had been contained in Untermyer's failed H.R. 405. The next day, after some back and forth, he conditionally accepted the position. On April 25, 1912, H.R. 504, introduced by Pujo in the form demanded by Untermyer, passed by a vote of 237 to 15.[31]

Pujo appointed James Farrar of New Orleans to serve as co-counsel to the Committee. But there would be no doubt as to who was in charge. Writing, at first somewhat diffidently, to Henry on April 15, 1912, Untermyer noted the honor it would be to serve with Farrar as associate counsel. "At the same time I am unwilling to make the sacrifices that would be involved in my undertaking this work unless I am to direct—with the aid of the Committee—the lines of policy on which it is to be conducted and am to have the leading part in its conduct." He was even more direct with Pujo. He would not represent the Committee unless he could "have charge of the preparation and presentation of the evidence and the examination of witnesses incident thereto."

Untermyer was not entirely comfortable with his imperious demands. He lied about drafting the initial resolution that created the Committee, even to Pujo himself. Later, while presenting the Owen bill to the Committee in January 1914, he denied that he was the sole draftsman of the resolution and even more strenuously denied that he had demanded or been given the exclusive power of questioning witnesses.[32]

Yet, on May 6, Untermyer asserted his authority to the Pujo Committee in a letter, cosigned by Farrar, so breathtakingly demanding that it amounted to a bloodless coup. Untermyer laid out exactly how and when things would be done and concluded: "We cannot undertake any such task unless it is clearly understood that we are to have the widest possible latitude and authority from the Committee as to the scope of the Inquiry and the witnesses who are to be examined." Not only did Untermyer effectively usurp the Committee's power, he did so while holding it hostage: "We desire also at this time to expressly, and separately as to each of us, reserve the right to resign our employment and to publicly state the reasons for so doing if an irreconcilable difference should hereafter arise between the Committee and Counsel as to the scope or manner of conducting the Investigation." The investigation was followed closely by the public. The Committee members would have faced political disaster if Untermyer had resigned.

These hearings would be Untermyer's hearings and both the investigation and the bill that came out of them bore the stamp of his personality and ideology. He was warned by Wall Street critic and NCF member Alfred Owen Crozier that, if the Democratic Party failed to pursue the financial reform plank in their platform and the investigation failed to produce concrete results, Untermyer would be blamed: "But you have long been known as a great corporation lawyer with offices on Wall Street. When the people find, if they do, that they have been tricked and betrayed . . . and that the barn door was deliberately left open by the Committee until the horse was stolen, you will be made the one 'scapegoat' of the whole proceeding and the country will believe that you were put in charge by Wall Street 'interests' for the express purpose of accomplishing that very result." Untermyer's reputation as crusader was at stake.[33]

Untermyer raised a significant problem almost immediately after his appointment, one that would ultimately cripple the investigation. On April 30 he wrote to Henry noting that the National Banking Act contained a provision that would have prevented the Committee and its staff from investigating the records—particularly the client records—of the banks that would be the subject of investigation. A judicial order or an amendment to the Banking Act was needed or Untermyer and the Committee would be unable to follow the money. On May 18 the House unanimously passed an amendment to the Banking Act giving the Committee the powers it needed. It would never find its way out of the Senate.[34]

With no progress on the Senate side, Untermyer turned in the fall to the administration for help. He could not demand the banks' records, but the comptroller of the currency had at least some of the information the Committee wanted. Taft had never been in favor of the investigation, but on

September 24 Untermyer wrote to him to ask that he release the comptroller's information. Taft turned the matter over to Wickersham and Untermyer started to push harder. He got nowhere until, late in December, a lame-duck Taft instructed the comptroller to release some information. It was, wrote Untermyer, only "the least important of this data." As a result, he felt that the Committee had never properly completed its investigation. In January 1913, Pujo retired from Congress after an unsuccessful campaign for the Senate, leaving Glass in charge of the Committee. It was left to the unelected Untermyer to wrap up the work.[35]

As persistent as he was, Untermyer was also sensitive, and took criticism personally. Before the Pujo Committee had even been created he was complaining to Henry about his treatment in the press. His complaints would continue throughout the process in letters to friends like Henry and Bryan, associates like Pujo and the press itself, ranging from field reporters and Washington correspondents to William Randolph Hearst. He became particularly angry when his character was challenged, as it was at times because of his aggressive behavior and at times because of anti-Semitism.

One event in particular was a tremendous source of personal agitation: his insistence on obtaining the testimony of the allegedly dying William Rockefeller. Although Untermyer traveled to Rockefeller's home on Jekyll Island and worked with his doctors to obtain that testimony as painlessly as possible (he allowed Rockefeller's own lawyers to put the questions to him and waited on Jekyll Island for days until doctors were willing to let Rockefeller speak), he was roundly lambasted for his inhumanity. The fact that Rockefeller was healthy enough to return to New York shortly after the hearings ended and lived until 1922 went more or less unremarked upon.[36]

Untermyer professed his customary confidence in the ultimate results of the investigation from the very beginning. His later statements that he had begun without bias simply are not credible, especially in light of his early speeches and letters. On January 16, 1912, a week before his first appearance before Congress and months before passage of the Committee's authorizing resolution, he wrote to Henry: "Further reflection confirms me in the opinion that a thorough, painstaking, well-directed investigation will uncover a vicious financial system which must be corrected by remedial legislation before we can hope for any fundamental relief in the existing Trust and Monetary conditions." By June 12, when the investigation had barely begun, he was writing Henry that "[w]e have already shown more than enough basis for remedial legislation affecting Clearing House and Stock Exchange to justify Investigation." On June 28: "We have however already proved enough to satisfy reasoning men of the despotism of the financial concentration of money in New York." And, as I noted earlier, he wrote to candidate Wilson from Baden-Baden, laying out the "facts"—a full indictment of Wall Street—as the Committee had already found them, even while its investigation was still very much in progress.

Untermyer did try to maintain the appearance of fairness during the hearings, despite his predetermined conclusion and aggressive questioning of witnesses. His correspondence shows him reaching out to his former friends on Wall Street. Among other conciliatory gestures, he arranged a conference at New York's Lotos Club in October 1912 to discuss possible legislative solutions with some of the leading villains of the Money Trust: Albert Wiggin of Chase National Bank, Frank Vanderlip of National City Bank, A. Barton Hepburn of Chase National Bank, Walter Frew of the Corn Exchange Bank and Morgan partner William H. Porter, among others. He negotiated appearance dates with witnesses, perhaps most elaborately with Francis Lynde Stetson. He may well have believed that he was being fair. On the first day of hearings on the Owen bill on February 4, 1914, he said: "I resent the suggestion that there was anything unfair or partisan about the conduct of that investigation." Unfair? Probably not. Partisan? Without question.[37]

The Report

Pujo submitted the Committee's interim report to the House on February 28, 1913. It was the only report the Committee ever delivered. The Report itself reveals why the Committee never finished its work. As I noted earlier, the Committee had suspended its hearings in the early summer of 1912. Part of the reason was to give the Senate time to pass the necessary Banking Act amendment. Perhaps equally important was the Committee's expressed concern that the hearings not appear to be partisan and influence the upcoming presidential election. (It is likely that the Democratic House was far more concerned with the possibility that widespread Republican opposition to the hearings might energize Taft's campaign than that populist and progressive approval of the investigation would help Wilson.)

The Committee felt pressured to deliver something to show its progress. Time was short, with a new Congress to take office in 1913 and, with it, no assurance that the investigation would continue. Important witnesses would be left unexamined. The Senate's failure to amend the Banking Act and the Comptroller's refusal to disclose information to the Committee "seriously embarrassed your committee" in its efforts to explore the ties between banking houses. Thus the Committee presented its report as interim and suggested that its work be continued in the new Congress. It never was.[38]

Interim or not, it was hardly a surprise that the Report concluded that

American finance and industry were controlled by a small group of men principally associated with Morgan, including the First National Bank; National City Bank; Lee, Higginson; and Kidder, Peabody. The Committee made a number of recommendations designed to break up this concentrated control and restore stability and opportunity to the financial system. Among these was a draft of the bill that would be introduced the next year as the Owen bill.

THE OWEN BILL

The ground had been laid for the Owen bill during the first two stages of stock market growth. The Hughes Committee, the Hadley Commission and a spate of bills in Congress reflected growing concern with the stock market as a matter of national financial stability. They struggled with ways to curb speculation, especially futures trading, margin buying, short selling and wash sales that by general consensus had turned the nation's securities markets into gambling dens. Recall that this concern grew from the Panic of 1907, which was blamed at least in part on the banks' irresponsibility in financing the securities industry and in securing their own collateral. A common tool that runs throughout these bills is disclosure. The goal of disclosure was, as it had been in the overcapitalization debates, to provide otherwise unavailable information necessary to permit the executive branch to enforce the law.[39]

The Owen bill was in this tradition but it was also something different. Its structure of self-regulation, supervised loosely by state governments through the medium of exchange incorporation and the federal government through its power to regulate the mails, was very much in keeping with the Wilsonian progressive approach to federal regulation. While aimed at economic stability, it also would have worked to improve the safety of investors. As such, it tried to correct for some of the problems in corporate governance and finance created by state law. The bill would have required exchanges, most of which were unincorporated associations, to incorporate under state law, with their charters and bylaws to include regulations to protect the integrity of transactions and quotations. These regulations were to prohibit members from using their customers' securities as collateral for their own loans, from lending securities left by customers with them as collateral, from engaging in certain types of fraudulent speculation, and to require them to keep full and complete records of all transactions, which would have been open for inspection by the Postmaster General.[40]

Incorporation was the prerequisite necessary to permit the exchanges and their members to use the mails to transmit offering information, advertisements, quotations and purchase and sale information with respect to securities. The incorporation requirement was the basis for allowing the government to insist upon effective exchange self-regulation to ensure investor protection and economic stability.

Other provisions of the bill aimed directly at investor protection. The rules of all exchanges engaged in interstate commerce had to require listed corporations to provide financial information, approved by resolution of the corporation's board, "verified by the oath of an officer thereof," and "certified by an independent accountant or firm of accountants," including balance sheets describing "the nature, amount, and value of the tangible and other property, assets, and effects of the corporation" along with its liabilities, an income statement covering the preceding three years and similar statements as to corporate subsidiaries. The corporation's filing package also had to include every contract, written or not, relating to the corporation's sale of its securities.

Other provisions for investor protection focused on the treatment of investors by management. Listed corporations were required at least annually to file with the Postmaster General, "for public inspection and use," updated profit and loss statements, agreements with officers and directors or entities with which they were affiliated, and of the "profits, emoluments, salaries, commissions, or other compensation or benefits" received by the officers and directors. Charters of all listed companies had to have provisions preventing officers and directors from engaging in short selling unless reported to the corporation's board of directors and entered into its minutes.[41]

The bill received some, but not extensive, attention in the press, possibly because the president's indifference to its passage made it unlikely that it would become law. The absence of a committee report for the Owen bill makes it difficult to say more. A report was prepared by the Committee and submitted to the Senate on the day of the Claflin bankruptcy. Owen himself had just sailed for Europe, and Gilbert Hitchcock of Nebraska rose almost immediately to challenge the Report on the ground that it had never been approved by a quorum of the Senate Banking and Currency Committee. A lengthy parliamentary debate took place the next day and Hitchcock's motion to recommit the bill was approved. Hitchcock then requested that the report be "withdrawn from the files."[42]

Unlike previous proposals, the Owen bill was directed at least in part at investor protection, although the bill primarily was, like its predecessors, aimed at ensuring the integrity of the market for the sake of the health of the economy and the banking system. This conclusion is reinforced by a jurisdictional fight between the Banking Committee and the Post Office Committee following reintroduction of the bill in 1915. Owen argued that his committee had jurisdiction over the measure precisely because it was designed to protect the banking and currency systems. Securities were used as collateral for bank loans, so "the stability of the banking system of the United States is vitally concerned in the proper conduct of the stock exchanges." The Post Office Committee's argument for jurisdiction was that the bill regulated the use of the mail. This aspect of the bill was the one most clearly directed at investor protection, and investor protection served as a leitmotif throughout the hearings. Although the Owen bill retained the traditional concern with broad economic factors that had been the focus of the Pujo hearings, it did for the first time bring investor protection to center stage. And it did so in a particularly Wilsonian way, by leveling the playing field for all investors. When the president finally came out in support of securities regulation in 1919 it was for a bill that marked the third stage of securities development, a bill that was almost entirely a consumer disclosure measure for the benefit of investors.[43]

INCORPORATING THE EXCHANGES — THE PATH TO ENFORCEMENT

The incorporation requirement was central to the hearings and the bill. A substantial portion of the debate revolved around this provision. The issue of exchange incorporation had a fairly developed recent history. In England, a committee of Parliament had examined the question in 1875 and concluded that it would be unwise to force the incorporation of the London Stock Exchange. A German committee also recommended against incorporation for the Berliner Börse in 1892. The idea seems to have made its first public appearance in the United States with the Report of the Hughes Committee, which also rejected it. Governor Sulzer (who, as a congressman, had battled the Littlefield bill) proposed it to the New York legislature in 1913. Untermyer argued in opposition to this particular measure. It was, he said, "nothing but a blind," because it would have put the books of NYSE members beyond public inspection. The New York measure was overwhelmingly defeated, although Untermyer continued to argue in favor of meaningful exchange incorporation. During the Owen hearings, the NYSE's central argument was that traditional exchange self-regulation would produce better broker conduct than would law.[44]

Incorporating the exchanges might seem like a curious thing to fight about. Yet exchange officials fought this proposal more fiercely than any other. Untermyer insisted that it was necessary to the entire regulatory program in order to ensure adequate publicity of brokers' transactions, the integrity of price quotations, the proper enforcement of exchange regulations and the facilitation of federal regulation. The exchanges' principal objection was that incorporation would subject their charters to constant legislative amendment and would deprive them of the right to discipline their members.[45]

On the face of it, neither side's reaction makes much sense. New York did not have a particularly stringent general incorporation law. By the time of the Pujo Report, the state had passed rules against stock manipulation, the "bucket shop" laws proposed by the Hughes Committee. It also had enacted the country's first statute permitting no-par stock that made overcapitalization either undetectable or impossible, depending on one's point of view. There was no reason to believe that the state would make its corporations law tighter. The Committee and the NYSE officials knew this, as they also knew that New York had already rejected exchange incorporation. With lax corporation laws that by this time resembled New Jersey's, what did the Exchange have to fear from the New York legislature?[46]

One reason for the Committee's approach might be found in Wilsonian progressive thought and political realities. The Federal Reserve Act, the FTC Act and the Owen bill all avoided centralized federal regulation as much as possible in a manner consistent with giving the legislative and executive branches and, in the case of the FTC Act, the courts, an opportunity to provide needed controls. Regulation should, as much as possible, remain with the states and private entities such as corporations under broad federal guidance. Incorporation was perhaps the surest way to achieve this kind of regulation through state and federal charter requirements built into the corporation's very structure, allowing the corporation to otherwise act freely in the market. As the Pujo Report stated:

> Whilst, of course, [the exchanges] can not now do anything contrary to law, nevertheless the State can not exercise in their case that comprehensive control and close and summary supervision which it may exact of corporate bodies as a condition of permitting them to exist at all. If such exchanges were required to incorporate, the State could write into and enforce in their charters provisions calculated to restrict them to legitimate purposes and suppress the abuses described.[47]

To Wall Street, the Owen bill appeared to centralize in the federal government the power to interfere with the operations of what had become the very heart of American capitalism and to make a matter of public control an institution that nearly the whole financial community considered to be private business. Concerns over the effective transformation of wholly private property into quasi-public property had been pervasive in the railroad regulation and antitrust debates. Untermyer must have realized that too much centralized power in the federal government, especially in the executive branch, would surely have killed any chance that the bill had for passage. As it was, the bill's opponents correctly noted that, incorporation or not, the exchanges could be subjected to the authority of the Postmaster General, who was given supervision over the act in order to avoid jurisdictional questions of federal regulation under the commerce clause. Decentralization, self-regulation and continued private ownership were essential if any form of the bill was to pass.

These arguments seem sensible enough. They fit the market-oriented progressive ideology of the president and the central concerns of his party. But these were not the terms of the debate, nor do they cast stock exchange incorporation in a light that suited the Committee's attitude and its ultimate agenda. For the Pujo Report also noted the Committee's desire to correct the inconsistency and laxity of state law by using the exchange to create uniform and responsible regulation. Witnesses at the Owen bill hearings as well as opponents in the press argued that this sort of regulation, including regulation over corporations' securities issuances, should be directly done by the federal government rather than indirectly through the stock exchanges.

It does seem odd that legislation designed to fix irresponsible state law would rely upon incorporating the exchanges under those lax state laws that were supposed to ensure that the exchanges imposed meaningful corporate regulation. And no Wilsonian progressive, no matter how committed to localism, could possibly have wanted to embrace the State of New York as a laboratory for regulatory experimentation through incorporation of the NYSE. That state traditionally had been reluctant to regulate the Exchange and the lobbying pressures the Exchange and its friends in Wall Street would have brought to bear on the legislature would most likely have resulted in very weak corporate regulation. It was easy enough for the state legislature to prohibit outright fraud, especially since the NYSE had recently adopted some of the recommendations of the Hughes Committee. It seems highly unlikely that the Committee assumed that New York would have adequately regulated the Exchange.[48]

Even if these arguments support the Committee's proposal, they do not suggest any good reason for strong opposition by the Exchange. It is not enough to think that the members of the Exchange simply reactively objected to any regulation. Indeed, one of the Exchange's persistent objections to the duties that Washington sought to impose on it was its position that securities regulation should be a federal responsibility, not an Exchange responsibility. And this was not just talk. The Exchange was, for example, in favor of the Rayburn bill precisely because it placed regulatory responsibility for railroad securities on the federal government and not on the Exchange. The underlying issue of private property, reflected in the club-like structure of the exchanges, was an understandable fighting point. But the kind of regulation proposed by the Owen bill hardly rose to the level of interference entailed by stringent railroad rate regulation or federal control of corporate capitalization.

The Exchange's formal response, summarized in a brief submitted to the Committee by its counsel, John Milburn, argued that incorporation would interfere with its ability to discipline its members by involving the courts, that legislation would result in "constant appeals to the legislature" for modifications and amendments, and that incorporation was unnecessary in order for Congress to impose regulation. These were the arguments the Exchange had used to defeat incorporation legislation in New York, and they seem just as irrelevant as Untermyer's.

The biggest problem the Exchange had with judicial intervention was the difference between disciplinary decisions made "from a strictly legal point of view and with the legal habit of mind" and those made by the Exchange's governors "looking at it from the point of view of practical men of great experience in the actual transactions of the exchange." No doubt the Exchange believed it was a better regulator, but Milburn gave neither evidence nor a principled defense of this position. Moreover, New York had earlier adopted a statute permitting unincorporated associations like the NYSE to be sued in their own names, much like corporations, and judicial review of internal decisions by associations was a common, if not completely settled, practice.[49]

The idea that lobbying would create uncertainty and weaken the power of the Exchange was at once overstated and beside the point. Lobbying occurs with respect to all legislation and there is no reason to have expected the State of New York, which had already shown deference to the Exchange, to become more aggressive. Finally, the Exchange was right—incorporation was not necessary to regulation.

The incorporation debate does not seem to make a lot of sense as it was presented by the parties. Handing over the job of regulating to New York was not likely to tighten or ensure the enforcement of the rules by which the Exchange operated. There was no significant public benefit and no serious potential for harm to the Exchange. And Untermyer's continued insistence on incorporation threatened the likelihood of the entire bill's passage. While it appears from the record and the parties' correspondence that their arguments were sincere and should thus be taken at face value, another driving force, discernible from both legal analysis and indirect historical support, may have been at stake.

The explanation lies in the way compelled exchange incorporation would have affected the members' property, exposing it to legal liability in a manner that was not possible with unincorporated exchanges. Milburn correctly noted that an unincorporated association like the NYSE could be sued in its own name just as it could have been were it incorporated, but this evaded the underlying property issue. In order to give regulation real teeth by exposing the exchanges' wealth to legal liability, the federal government or any private plaintiff would have had to satisfy itself with the meager assets of the NYSE or prosecute each member individually in order to collect damages. Incorporating the exchange would most likely have collectivized its members' wealth, at least to the extent of their exchange memberships, and made that wealth available to satisfy judgments.

Although the Owen bill's penalties were modest fines for crimes that would have been classified as misdemeanors, and the exchanges' own central economic risk (in contrast to that of their members) was prohibition of the use of the mails, this specter of increased financial exposure that would have resulted from incorporation clearly troubled several witnesses. The hearings provide some evidence that collective liability was an important, if unspoken, issue. Hjalmar Boyesen, counsel for the Consolidated Stock Exchange, noted in passing that the members of an unincorporated association could not be held liable for one another's debts. Milburn's testimony revealed that the NYSE had no tangible assets. The purchase and sale of seats were private matters between members for which the Exchange received no compensation. Its building was worth $5 million, placed in a corporation owned by the Exchange for the benefit of its members. But the collective value of members' seats (individually worth $55,000) was $50 million. Incorporating the NYSE would presumably have required members to exchange their seats for shares in the newly incorporated Exchange, thereby giving it a net worth of at least $50 million and exposing that newly collective wealth to federal (and perhaps private) judgments in litigation against the Exchange, a result not possible under its status as an association. Seen in the context of the weak arguments articulated on both sides, this issue appears to justify the intensity of the battle over exchange incorporation.[50]

The controversy early in the century over the incorporation of labor unions supports the conclusion that while collective exposure was largely unarticulated, it was nevertheless a deep background concern. As one illustration, a debate of sorts had taken place in 1902 between Louis Brandeis and Samuel Gompers over this issue. Underlying that debate was a recent British decision holding an unincorporated union liable in damages for the actions of its members during a strike. Brandeis supported incorporation, arguing that it would enhance the responsibility of union leaders and members and make the unions more acceptable to the public. Broadly stating the laws applicable to unions, he made a comment that could not have been especially persuasive to union members and makes precisely the point I believe underlay the battle over exchange incorporation: "[W]hile the rules of legal liability apply fully to the unions, though unincorporated, it is, as a practical matter, more difficult for the plaintiff to conduct the litigation, and it is particularly difficult to reach the funds of the union with which to satisfy any judgment that may be recovered." It should be obvious that Gompers opposed the measure. Every participant in the stock exchange debate had to have been aware of this issue. It is striking that it never explicitly came up.[51]

In order for the federal government to regulate through the exchanges, it was best if they were incorporated.[52]

The Owen bill and the FTC bill were two logical outgrowths of the federal incorporation debate. In its disclosure provisions aimed at responsible corporate governance and finance, the Owen bill bridged the gap between federal incorporation and economic stabilization through securities regulation. The FTC Act took up the dimension of federal incorporation proposals that demanded meaningful federal antitrust legislation. Both the Owen bill and the FTC Act completed the separation of the two major problems that had confounded the federal incorporation movement. And both measures, like most of the federal incorporation proposals that preceded them, relied upon disclosure and relatively light federal control to encourage the self-regulation of business. Both provided remedies when self-regulation failed.

The New Deal securities acts imposed a slightly heavier federal hand but still maintained the spirit of the Owen bill and the Wilsonian approach to regulation in general. They had important similarities, particularly in the areas of corporate disclosure and the regulation of brokers and dealers. Like the 1934 Securities Exchange Act, the Owen bill relied largely on the exchanges themselves for self-regulation rather than detailed federal control, directly addressing itself only to those practices—manipulation, short selling and margin trading—that the NYSE had shown itself unwilling to correct effectively for itself. Finally, like the FTC and Federal Reserve Acts, it relied more heavily on voluntary cooperative conduct with the private sector than it did on heavy-handed federal regulation.

THE END OF BUSINESS PROGRESSIVISM

The economic context in which the Pujo hearings concluded, the Owen bill was debated and business progressivism ended was complex. Nineteen thirteen, the year of Wilson's inauguration, was a depression year, a continuation of the lackluster economy that had prevailed since the panic. Alexander Noyes described it as an odd time, with indications of potentially improving trade owing to expected bumper crops, an influx of gold and some industries, like iron, working almost at full capacity. But there was no recovery despite the optimistic atmosphere in which the year began. Some blamed the tariff reduction bill, others the ICC's failure to raise railroad freight rates. Some blamed the uncertainty in European markets that were evaluating the possibility of war.[53]

Despite occasional bursts of activity from 1911 to August 1914, the depression continued, affecting Wilson's taste for business regulation. Hope dawned with 1914. Surveys of businessmen as well as the general economic environment promised improvement. The Federal Reserve Act had been passed and the tariff revised downward. Wilson expressed the hopes of many that the economy would improve as this legislation took effect, even as he signaled that it was time for the government to leave business alone. The settlement of the government's antitrust suit against the New York, New Haven & Hartford also suggested the possibility of better government-business relations. Railroad executives in Chicago were looking forward to passage of the pending Rayburn bill, which would provide uniformity in an area complicated by divergent state regulations.

But hope was not uniform across the nation. Boston had been particularly bowed by the depression and the collapse of the New Haven, precipitated by that city's own Louis Brandeis, had hit New England investors especially hard. Businessmen in Boston remained gloomy. *The Wall Street Journal* reported with less optimism than others, too, focusing on the tightness of the money supply and the undeniable problems in the railroad industry caused by low freight rates, problems that in turn dragged down related industries like steel. Finally, despite his reassurances to business, Wilson clearly intended to push his trust legislation, and its ultimate form was uncertain. The fate of the Owen bill was still unclear. While many businessmen expected the trust legislation to be rather mild, the uncertainty produced anxiety.[54]

The year also began with another hopeful sign. After two years of badgering by the Pujo Committee, five major Morgan partners announced their resignations from a total of thirty directorships on January 2. Thomas Lamont, speaking for the firm, noted that these resignations had been long-planned because the directorships simply were too time consuming, and that it had only been the partners' senses of obligation toward their clients that had kept them on. The move met with broad approval. Untermyer, characteristically, complained that the resignations did not go far enough. They were in fact relatively insignificant because, busy or not, these Morgan partners remained on the boards of most banks and financial companies and of their most important industrial companies as well.[55]

Interest rates dropped throughout the month and the stock market began to rally. Wilson gave a real boost to the market in his personal address to a joint session of Congress on January 20. Most striking in this speech was his announced conciliation with business. Calling his business legislative agenda and its approaching end a "constitution of peace" with business, he declared that "the antagonism between business and government is over." He acknowledged the damage that continued legislative uncertainty caused business and pledged to complete his program quickly. The market rallied, but it was a rally that would barely survive the month. The president may have declared a truce but business was far from certain.[56]

Wilson was clear about what he would and would not support. His basic guideline was the Democratic platform of 1912. This meant that he would push trust legislation and also support the Rayburn bill. He would not, however, support federal incorporation, nor the Owen bill, on which hearings were to begin in February. Neither measure was part of the platform.

The strength of Wilson's opposition to the Owen bill was unclear. *The New York Times* described him as firmly opposing it, but the *Wisconsin State Journal*, among other papers, more tentatively described him as not opposing but not supporting the bill either. It appears that Wilson was of a mind to do the minimum amount of business regulation that he had promised and no more. As he would make clear by June, he was ready to let business be business.[57]

The hopeful air of January rapidly faded. Congress got to work on the legislative program, which the administration began to push hard to complete despite some recalcitrance in Congress. The beginning of February found the capital markets—stocks, bonds and money—substantially improved. The president was given credit for boosting investor confidence and for distancing himself from the Owen bill, which one commentator called "the most advanced proposal toward the Federal espionage over and regulation of private affairs and personal ethics that the radical tendencies of the age have yet evolved." Strong European buying also helped. But the first week of February was to prove the financial high point of the year.[58]

Legislation that had begun in an atmosphere of promise hit major snags by March. The Investment Bankers' Association opposed even the relatively mild trust legislation that would become the FTC and Clayton Acts, as did former President Taft. Securities markets had been flat and trade had slowed considerably. The odd thing about this situation that puzzled almost everyone was that the money supply was easing and business inventories were low, both of which ought to have produced a boost in commercial activity. But no such boost was forthcoming. Legislative uncertainty continued to be identified as a cause of the malaise, as did a lack of confidence created by a number of fraud-induced railroad failures.[59]

Mid-April saw a significant price break on the stock market. The downward trend this started was to continue until the New York Stock Exchange and, with it, all other American stock exchanges, closed for war on July 31. Wilson's increasing insistence on passing trust legislation before Congress adjourned gave business some reason to be afraid that perhaps the resulting statute would not be quite so benign as it had hoped. The proposed anti–stock-watering provisions, which would have given the federal government supervisory powers over all corporate securities issues and prohibited corporations with watered stock from engaging in interstate trade, became a major sticking point in the trust bill. The Rayburn bill had been on track but railroad presidents were now trying to derail it, pushing for federal incorporation instead as a measure that would provide much greater efficiency. Opposition to the program was beginning to infest the president's own party. The market dropped again and the new possibility of war with Mexico did not help.[60]

Not all was lost. The Rayburn bill was reported to the House in May with the approval of the New York Stock Exchange. This bill provided the kind of federal securities regulation, instead of exchange regulation, that the NYSE had called for in the Owen hearings. The measure was designed, as I have noted, to prevent common carriers from issuing watered stock, and it principally served as an antitrust measure. Indeed all of the antitrust reasons that had made stock watering a major public issue for years formed the rationale underlying the bill. While Rayburn himself made it clear that its goal was not to protect investors, Chairman William Adamson of the Interstate Commerce Committee proclaimed that, in addition to its antitrust effect, it also targeted people who were "buncoing innocent investors out of hundreds of millions of dollars and embarrassing other innocent investors by unloading on them worthless stocks and bonds."

At the same time small investors were still active despite the torpid market. In May, the *Chicago Daily Tribune* began a weekly investment advice column on individual securities in answer to specific questions from readers. As the *Tribune* reported, demand for such a column was high, with a "flood of inquiries" from "financial houses welcoming an investigation of their securities," securities promoters, brokerages recommending stock they had for sale and, most of all, "from persons who have been solicited to make investments and are seeking disinterested advice." Similar columns began to appear in other newspapers and magazines that circulated among the middle class.[61]

It had been an intense winter and spring, mid-term elections were approaching, trust legislation was stalling, the economy was not moving and the market was declining. It was in this atmosphere that the president lost his cool, and it was in this atmosphere that he completed his transformation from business progressive to business defender. It was in this atmosphere that he called an end to the Progressive Era in business.

JUST BELIEVE

The end was foreshadowed on June 1 when Wilson gave a widely reported speech in which he declared that the business depression was not widespread, that other countries were in much worse shape and that the only real depression was in railroads and steel. It was then that he delivered the phrase that was to haunt him. The depression was "psychological." Like the recently created Peter Pan, the president insisted that prosperity would return if businessmen would only believe. "While admitting that he had no particular facts on which to base his assertion," he declared that the economy was sound. An outpouring of public ridicule built slowly throughout the month, tempered by the House passing the FTC and the Rayburn bills in early June.

The Wall Street Journal and the *Los Angeles Times* were especially hard on the president. The *Journal* described him as "unlearned in economics, or in business practice," and the *Los Angeles Times* suggested that "If President Wilson would only consent to psychologize into his swollen cabesa the idea that businessmen understand" the conditions for business success far better "than he ever did or ever can or ever will" there would be economic hope: "Oh, how the man in the White House needs a mind cure!"[62]

Criticism continued during the month. In mid-June, taking a page from Roosevelt's book, Wilson publicly revealed that a letter had been sent by W. P. Ahnfelt, president of The Pictorial Review Company of New York, to an undisclosed number of businesses along with a form letter to be addressed to congressmen and administration officials. Ahnfelt asked that all who agreed that Wilson's trust program should be stopped, that railroad freight rates should be increased and that business should be given a rest by the administration should send letters and telegrams along the lines of the form letter to their representatives and other officials. Wilson jumped on this as evidence of a business campaign to stop trust reform, suggesting that the wealthy and powerful were opposing the people. He continued his retaliation by publicizing supporting letters from businessmen who had written to him and meeting with the Democratic leadership to build support for pushing through the trust legislation.[63]

The president's satisfaction was short-lived. On June 25, H. B. Claflin Co., a respected dry goods wholesaler that had been in business since 1843, declared bankruptcy after surviving the Civil War, the Panics of 1873, 1893 and 1907, and several depressions. Over $30 million in notes remained unpaid, making it the largest bankruptcy in the nation's history. While its effect on the stock market was minimal, its broader impact on public opinion was far more significant. On that same day, Wilson gave a short speech in the White House to the Virginia Editorial Association. While the group was small, the newspapers were unanimous that the speech was intended to be one of the president's most important.[64]

Reading the accounts of the speech make it easy to guess at the president's emotions. He was variously described as "defiant," with snapping jaws and flashing eyes. Virtually every report commented on his "clenched fists." Perhaps the most obvious emotion that comes to mind is frustration, frustration that business failed to understand his desire to help, frustration with the pace of trust legislation, frustration with opposition members of his own party, frustration at the mockery to which he had been subjected for his psychoanalysis of the economy and frustration especially that his January prediction of a return to prosperity had fallen flat on its face. Frustration seems to have been coupled with Wilson's characteristic self-righteous anger, on display whenever his will appeared to be thwarted, the same self-righteous anger that led him to lose the graduate school battle at Princeton that led to his resignation and the same anger that would help to doom Versailles and the League of Nations.

Whatever his emotions, Wilson was indubitably ready to declare for business and almost to will a return to prosperity. Everything he said resounded with his effort to blame the depression on Roosevelt.

> There is nothing more fatal to business than to be kept guessing from month to month and from year to year whether something serious is going to happen to it or not and what in particular is going

to happen to it if anything does.... The guessing went on, the air was full of interrogation points, for ten years or more, then came an administration which for the first time had a definite programme of constructive correction.

He stated that the antitrust legislation would serve as a "new constitution of freedom" for business.

It will not be postponed, and it will not be postponed because we are the friends of business.... Because when the programme is finished, it is finished; the interrogation points are rubbed off the slate; business is given its constitution of freedom and is bidden go forward under that constitution. And just so soon as it gets that leave and freedom there will be a boom of business in this country such as we have never witnessed in the United States.

Perhaps Wilson's most astonishing statement came near the beginning of the speech. "We are in the presence of a business situation which is variously interpreted. Here in Washington ... we are perhaps in a position to judge of the actual conditions of business better than those can judge who are at any other single point in the country" and, in his judgment, a business revival was around the corner. "We know what we are doing; we purpose to do it under the advice, for we have been fortunate enough to obtain the advice of men who understand the business of the country; and we know that the effect is going to be exactly what the effect of the currency reform was, a sense of relief and security." Few presidents have ever displayed such arrogance. Few have been so fortunate as to face an impending war.[65]

Nobody was terribly impressed. Even the friendly *Times* suggested that perhaps the president had overstated the extent to which recovery was imminent. The *Los Angeles Times* headlined that *Wilson Rages Impotently*, particularly pained by the criticism he received for his psychological diagnosis of the depression. The *New York Press* asked: "Could the United States government send to the fallen house [of Claflin] 30 or 40 millions of relief in a psychological form, instead of hard cash, and lift it from its ruins? President Wilson must stop talking—and acting, too—what to ordinary business intelligence is almost criminal nonsense, or this whole country, big as it is and strong as it is, will be threatened with a Claflin collapse." B. C. Forbes, writing in the *New York American*, blamed the Claflin failure partly on the president's "perpetual attack on business," and complained that his repeated description of the depression as psychological "is worse than puerile—it is becoming exasperating to the many thousands of business men who are wrestling with heartbreaking problems to keep things going as well as to workers who have either been thrown idle or put on starvation hours." *The Wall Street Journal* also gave no ground. Wilson's optimism was, it noted, "apparently based on a plentiful absence of the right kind of information," commenting that "In Wall Street there is no such self-deception. Its aggregate information exceeds that of all the country put together, and is brought down to date." Finally, "official opinion is not only valueless but misleading. It sees what it wishes to see, when the wish is so evidently father to the thought." Wilson had called an end to economic progressivism. But the business community to whom he opened his soul responded with contempt.[66]

Business did not improve. The president's supporter, *The New York Times*, put a happy headline on a national survey of businessmen in July, but the content of their comments was no more optimistic than it had been all year. Southern and Western bankers were concerned as well, and their worry deepened as the summer progressed. Crops were predicted to be bumper, the automobile industry produced one of the economic bright spots and the trust bill was nearing passage. None of these had any discernible effect.[67]

And then the war in Europe began. The New York Stock Exchange shut down on July 31. The European sell-off of securities, many of which had been bought only that spring, had dramatically dropped stock prices over the preceding week and threatened to drain the nation's gold supply. The Exchange's closing was supported throughout the country. As the *Atlanta Constitution* put it, "the New York stock exchange would have been called upon to bear the weight of the world's financial burdens" had it not closed for business. With the NYSE closed until December and only the pending Clayton Act to finish, the administration had completed its economic reforms. A friend of business it was, and business would soon reap the benefits of the president's diplomacy. The Progressive Era in business had come to an end.[68]

PROPHET OF PROSPERITY

Wilson's June performance as an economic prophet had been rightly ridiculed. But in the event it was Wilson and not the critics who proved correct, although not for the reasons Wilson expected. The economy had indeed been suffering. Railroads in the East and related industries like steel were in genuine pain because the ICC held rates too low to permit maintenance and expansion and still allow for dividends. Railroads were in such bad shape that a group of prominent railroad presidents met with Wilson on September

9 to ask for various forms of relief, including postponement of the Rayburn bill. But the war gave the railroads what they needed. Not only was the Rayburn bill postponed for almost six years but also, on December 18, the ICC finally gave the railroads the rate relief they had been seeking, allowing an increase of 5 percent. Railroad and steel stocks reacted shortly thereafter as headlines announced that the increase would mean a "big revenue jump" of at least $30 million. By December 9, McAdoo confidently stated that prosperity already had begun to return. The absence of panic during the lengthy depression was, he said, "phenomenal" and the railroad rate increase and the easing of money that came with the operation of the new Federal Reserve banks were having good effects. Americans had started saving and had money to invest in domestic industrial expansion. "'Any war is injurious to the world, yet we have reached the point where the present war is in some ways an actual benefit.'"[69]

The benefits were not immediate. The first new order of business facing McAdoo and the bankers immediately after the declaration of war was to stave off a possible currency crisis. Gold reserves dropped by almost $160 million on a base of $1.1 billion because European creditors could not collect gold from their own debtors to pay off U.S. debt and because they dumped their American securities prior to the exchange closings. This brought McAdoo to New York immediately after July 31 to negotiate the issuance of clearinghouse certificates and increase available currency by $500 million under the Aldrich-Vreeland Act.[70]

Emergency revenue measures also placed a short-term burden on increased commerce. House Democrats backed the president's proposal for war taxes on items like beer, wine, tobacco, licenses, gasoline, bankers and brokers and a stamp tax on bonds, stock and other financial instruments, which alone was estimated to raise $35 million. Despite significant Republican opposition, the measure was supported by the NYSE as a patriotic gesture and was backed in force by Democrats, passing on October 22 as the Federal Emergency Revenue Act.[71]

American investors reflected their new optimism even before there was any discernible improvement in economic fundamentals. Despite the market closures, or perhaps because of them, there was significant pent-up investment demand. Restricted bond trading opened on the NYSE on September 20 and, on the 21st, a New York City bond issue was oversubscribed within twenty-four hours. Trading in unlisted stocks resumed on September 25 subject, like bonds, to price review by a stock exchange committee, and bond trading volume had increased significantly by the end of September.

Investor confidence continued despite dividend cuts or suspensions by railroads and industrials preparing for war finance. Plummeting foreign exchange rates, bumper wheat crops and a balance of trade increasingly in favor of the United States helped to keep confidence high. Only the South continued to suffer as the interruption in the cotton trade, especially with Britain, made the crop virtually illiquid and led to bailout plans by banks and the federal government.[72]

Signs were sufficiently good that Wilson, demonstrating perhaps that his judgment had not improved much since June but bolstered by the improving balance of trade figures, proclaimed on October 12 that business conditions were "improving rapidly," noting that "he had not made any systematic canvas, but that from reports received from here and there he is of the opinion that business is rapidly assuming normal conditions." Luckily for the president, this time he was right. The next day the New York Stock Exchange announced that it would allow restricted stock dealings to resume between members. On October 15 Wilson signed the Clayton Act and legislative reform was over.[73]

The Federal Reserve System opened for business in the middle of November, releasing $400 million into the economy. Britain took American cotton off its contraband list even as the plan to bail out cotton growers was about to be put into effect. The bond market had normalized, and indeed demand for bonds was substantial. Steel was beginning to pick up. The stock market remained sticky, but this was attributed to the fact that prices were being held where they were when the Exchange closed. In fact European investors had begun buying American securities as well rather than dumping them on the market as Wall Street had initially feared. Savings banks returned to the bond market in significant numbers by early November and as the month progressed investors' demands for stock exceeded the supply. On November 30, the NYSE reopened for bond trading, and stock trading resumed on December 12, with prices rising by month's end.[74]

The American economy was poised to take off after more than three years in the doldrums. But not just yet. Nineteen fifteen dawned with bank clearings down, business failures up and a continued "unsatisfactory state of industry and trade." No wonder Wilson had panicked in June. As one commentator noted in April 1915, "everyone seems agreed on the fact that the Wilson administration, in its first two years, has so identified itself with financial and industrial legislation that the conditions of business will have a determining effect upon the results of the next presidential campaign, unless, indeed, our foreign relations grow so acute as to sweep out of sight all the issues raised in the last ten years of agitation." Fortunately for the president, that would be precisely the case. And, as a result, the United States would engage in its first serious public war financing since the Civil War, using the same techniques that Jay Cooke had then used. The difference was that this time the securities markets had reached the threshold of their modern form and were ready for their complete integration into American culture.[75]

⊰ TEN ⊱

MANUFACTURING SECURITIES

Our branch offices throughout the United States are already working to make connections with the great new bond-buying public. Our newer offices are on the ground floor.... [We] are getting close to the public ... and are preparing to serve the public on a straightforward basis, just as it is served by the United Cigar Stores or Child's Restaurants." So "Sunshine Charley," president of the National City Company, lectured his salesmen. Mitchell, known as the greatest bond salesman of all time, was sharing his retail brokerage vision with the new recruits. And it was Charley Mitchell, perhaps more than any other American, who was the complete embodiment of the incredible transformation in American business, social and economic life that had begun more than twenty years earlier.[1]

Mitchell graduated from Amherst in 1899, four years behind his partner in prosperity, Calvin Coolidge. He started his professional life in Chicago, working as a salesman for Western Electric. After promotion to assistant manager in 1905, Mitchell moved to New York where he worked as an assistant to the president of the Trust Company of America, one of the trust companies that J. P. Morgan helped to bail out during the Panic of 1907. His education forged in this trial by fire, Mitchell formed the brokerage house of C. E. Mitchell & Co. in 1911.

In 1916, Frank Vanderlip of National City Bank called upon Mitchell to head the bank's securities affiliate, National City Company. National City, one of the new organizations used by national banks to get around the laws that prohibited them from dealing in securities, had recently absorbed N. W. Halsey, a brokerage house with an unusually developed national network. Halsey's president, Harold Stuart, left to form his own business. The resulting vacancy gave Mitchell the chance to define the modern securities market and make it a central part of American culture. National City sold bonds.

Not until 1927 would common stock form a regular part of its inventory. Regardless of the kind of securities it sold, it completed the transformation of securities from mere investments or speculative playthings into something very much like consumer products. This was Mitchell's legacy. It was the final thread that tied together the speculation economy.[2]

The National Banking Act meant to keep national banks out of the securities business. The Act limited the powers that national banks were permitted to exercise, and dealing in securities was clearly not one of them. Banks evaded this restriction by claiming it was among their incidental powers. The comptroller of the currency responded by contradicting this interpretation of the Act. Some banks still invested, and the comptroller had eased his position slightly over the years since 1902, but the stricture remained pretty clear. In response, several banks began to form separate companies known as investment affiliates to engage in underwriting, brokerage and investment activities.

Investment affiliates were separate from their banks, complying technically with the law. But they were two sides of the same coin. National City Bank declared a 40 percent dividend to encourage its shareholders to buy company stock and they did. The stock certificates for each company were printed on the opposite sides of the same sheet of paper. A stockholder could not sell one without selling the other. And the stock was held by trustees for the shareholders so they could not even vote.[3]

There were several different methods of achieving this goal of marrying a securities affiliate to a bank so that for all intents and purposes they operated as one. The First National Bank issued The First National Company's stock in the name of six trustees to be held for the benefit of its stockholders. Chase National Bank created its affiliate as a subsidiary and then spun off its shares directly to its stockholders, who in turn put the stock in trust with Bankers Trust Company. Some bolder national banks owned their trust companies directly as subsidiaries. No matter which of these or several other techniques the banks used, their shareholders remained unified so that the relationship between the bank and its affiliate was assured.

While the banks could not engage in the securities business directly, they effectively invested by providing the capital for their affiliates' activities. Needless to say, this exposed the banks' assets to precisely the kinds of risks that had brought down the trust companies in the Panic of 1907. The practice came to an end in 1933 when banks and their affiliates were torn apart by the Glass-Steagall Act. But in the days before the Crash, Sunshine Charley had built the biggest retail securities brokerage in the world, and his public cheerleading had helped to make the securities market a new national pastime.[4]

The 1920s was, of course, the explosive decade in the market and the decade when Mitchell and his company realized their promise. It was the decade in which all of the earlier sales and speculative techniques were concentrated and perfected, and new ones like investment trusts, the predecessors to today's mutual funds, were created. The vastly increasing middle class, measured by annual incomes over $5,000, expanded by two-thirds between 1922 and 1929. Consumer culture had arrived. "Rayon, cigarettes, refrigerators, telephones, chemical preparations (especially cosmetics), and electric devices of various sorts all were in growing demand.... For every $100 worth of business done in 1919, by 1927 the five-and-ten cent chains were doing $260 worth, the cigar chains $153 worth, the drug chains $224 worth, and the grocery chains $387 worth." The almost 6.8 million automobiles on the American roads in 1919 grew to 23 million by 1929. And there was yet another popular item for consumers to buy—Sunshine Charley's bonds.[5]

Mitchell's sales techniques were in the vanguard of the expanding brokerage business. But his vision was realized, and his techniques refined, during that most patriotic of capital campaigns, the Liberty Bond drives of the First World War. Americans were sold the new investments by volunteer investment banks spurred on by volunteer committees, coupling patriotism with a safe investment. The combination of advertising and salesmanship used in the Liberty Bond drives catalyzed the transformation of the American middle class into the American investing class. While a postwar slump in the market delayed things a bit, by the end of 1921 the great transformation was on its way to permanence.[6]

In its debut issue of July 30, 1919, the short-lived popular financial magazine, *The Street*, explained why it had begun publication: "Previous to the war the investing class in this country was extremely limited in numbers.... 25,000,000 Americans now own Liberty Bonds ... and are already interested as potential and actual investors in American securities." In the issue's lead article, a former assistant treasury secretary praised the brokers who volunteered their time to sell the bonds and noted that "Their reward in the future will come not in commissions from the Government for the sale of Government securities, but in a wonderfully well-educated and eager market for securities of the highest type of excellence and merit."[7]

I will conclude by tracing the critical prelude to the 1920s, the path of the American securities market as it became a consumer market. This period also included the final conceptual transformation of securities regulation from the overcapitalization concerns of antitrust and banking stability to a disclosure-based consumer protection law as the market emerged from the prewar depression and the end of Wilson's legislative program to leave America on the cusp of its "return to normalcy" and the Coolidge prosperity. For by that cold March day in 1921 when a sick, defeated and broken Woodrow Wilson rode from the inauguration of Warren Gamaliel Harding to his final home on S Street in Washington's Kalorama neighborhood, all of the ingredients of modern American corporate capitalism were in place. The ideas that would coalesce into the New Deal securities legislation had all more or less been put on the table: common stock had become accepted as an investment security suitable for the middle-class investor, and the middle class was buying; modern securities selling methods through retail brokerages and aggressive sales techniques had developed; the giant modern public corporation was a fact of life; and the business of America was finance. This is the story of those final years.

WALL STREET IN A TIME OF WAR

The New York Stock Exchange reopened for full trading on December 12, 1914, although it prohibited short sales and futures contracts and required all settlements to be in cash. The Exchange's restriction of the practices that it had defended so forcefully during the Pujo hearings made perfect sense in the new sensitive and uncertain economic environment. Europeans, desperate for money to finance the war, held $2.7 billion in American securities, suspending a Damocletian sword that could skewer the American markets in the event of a major European sell-off. The fear of a sell-off remained palpable and the balance of trade had yet to reach its extraordinary level in favor of the United States that would shore up the money markets. So it was not only reasonable of the Exchange but also perhaps its only prudent move to impose strict limits on traditional speculation. After all, part of the history of the American stock market up until that point had been concern with the destabilizing effect that speculation had on the overall economy. After almost three years of depression and an uncertain economic future, stability was crucial.

Americans had nothing to fear. Although $500 million in American securities made their way back from Europe relatively quickly, followed by another $1.5 billion by the end of July 1916, the sales were orderly and the anticipated panic never occurred. A substantial portion of the returning securities were pledged by European sovereigns who had bought them up as collateral for American loans, although the governments also liquidated many of them on the American market. Large shipments of Allied gold to the United States prevented these sales from creating massive interest rate increases. Moreover, an informal trading market had developed several weeks after the exchanges closed and prices on this market, while lower at first than before the war had begun, were reasonably stable and even returned to July levels by the time the exchanges reopened. Pundits like Roger Babson encouraged small individual investors to buy securities within two weeks after the market's close, and *The Wall Street Journal* touted investing as the way to beat the high cost of living.

Individual investors responded slowly, but surely. A bull market began to appear in March following an erratic but generally increasing market during the first quarter of 1915. The Exchange lifted all trading restrictions on April 15 and the market began to soar. According to Benjamin Graham and David Dodd, the Dow rose from 57 at about the time the exchange reopened to a peak of 110 at the end of 1916. Alexander Noyes cited a study showing a rise from 58.99 on February 15 to 101.51 in mid-November. Stock exchange historian Robert Sobel dated the beginning of the bull market to the start of the year. Regardless of the precise date, market performance was extraordinary.[8]

Return to Prosperity

There was an economic boom to match. Nineteen fifteen began with the same fear and pessimism that had come to characterize American industry despite the obvious need for war materiel in Europe. *The Wall Street Journal* was early to complain that there was not enough money around for the anticipated industrial expansion and encouraged corporations to sell securities to the public. All of the belligerents were technically insolvent, so while American industrialists understood the dramatic potential for increased demand, they remained unsure of how Europe would pay. Part of the answer lay in the shift of the world's financial capital from London to New York in the fall of 1914, with significant foreign funds left for safekeeping in New York banks. Later came massive foreign shifts of gold to New York to pay for war materiel. Foreign borrowings increased dramatically, with half a billion in Allied bonds sold in the United States during 1914 and $750 million more in 1916. The proceeds came right back to the United States to pay for U.S. exports.[9]

Noyes noted a 347 percent export expansion between 1913 and 1916, in contrast to the 112 percent increase between 1897 and 1906 that had helped to fuel the merger wave. Obviously steel and other war-related industries prospered after the first quarter of 1915. But agricultural exports, including record crops of wheat and cotton (after the near-disaster in the latter industry toward the end of 1914), and manufactured goods created record surpluses in the American balance of trade with Europe. The twelve-month value of exported wheat alone reached $333.5 million on June 15, in contrast with $88 million and $89 million during the same periods over the two preceding years. Wilson's prediction of imminent prosperity a year earlier had come to pass.[10]

Once the economy got rolling and the stock market with it, the growth in the latter was not entirely steady, although the trend for all of 1915 was up. Events like the sinking of the *Lusitania* in May 1915 caused temporary market breaks. More interesting, as Noyes reported, were the price breaks on rumors of peace. Americans had quickly become accustomed to their boom economy after years in the financial wilderness. Rumors of possible mediation in 1916 sent the market down for brief periods. The market was also soft during the lead-up to Wilson's squeak-by reelection over Charles Evans Hughes, but finished the year with some real strength.

On April 2, 1917, Wilson delivered his war message to Congress. Within two days Congress declared war. The shift from a neutral war economy to that of a belligerent had already been reflected in market prices, which had been declining since the beginning of the year. American investors might have been disillusioned under different circumstances as the market turned from its high of 110 down to 65.95 at the end of the year. But 1917 was a critically important year in the development of American corporate capitalism. That was the year that Americans of all walks of life and from every city, town and rural district of the nation began to become investors.

We have seen that the vanguard of the middle class had become avid investors in stocks and bonds by 1914. But the Liberty Bond drives were different. This time, it was war. Americans' massive, widespread participation in the Liberty Bond campaigns and the federal government's aggressive marketing techniques brought the idea of investing in securities to Americans of even the most humble circumstances and to the furthest reaches from Wall Street. Well before those bonds had a chance to mature, the new class of American investors would look to the stock market as the place to put their money.[11]

When the United States entered the war it was no longer the beneficiary of the European conflict. It now had significant financial needs of its own. The prosperity created by two years of war-financed industrial boom as a neutral meant that the nation had stored-up wealth with which to finance its effort. Taxation was always a way to tap into this wealth, but McAdoo, charged with financing the war, thought that the vast amount of money he needed would make raising it all through taxes impossible. He planned initially to raise half the money through taxes and half through bond issues. But he dramatically reduced the tax portion as the war progressed. His prewar estimate of "several billion dollars" would prove to be very much on the low side, especially in light of the fact that the United States wound up spending $2 billion a month for postwar expenses alone. The cost of war was more than taxes could handle.

McAdoo later recalled studying Civil War financing earlier in his life and it was to the financing of that war that he turned for guidance. He had little but criticism for Salmon Chase's efforts, except for his decision in the middle of the war to turn over the job of selling government bonds to Jay Cooke. McAdoo also turned to the investment bankers except, unlike Chase, he refused to pay investment banking commissions to market the bonds. He argued that "any kind of war must necessarily be a popular movement. It is a kind of crusade; and, like all crusades, it sweeps along on a powerful stream of romanticism. Chase did not attempt to capitalize the emotion of the people, yet it was there and he might have put it to work." McAdoo capitalized that emotion exceedingly well.[12]

The Liberty Loans

The president signed the first War Finance Act on April 25, 1917. It authorized the Treasury to issue debt of up to $7 billion, $5 billion of which was to be in bonds and the rest in short-term notes. McAdoo was given discretion to determine the amount and terms of each issue. Consulting with bankers and other experts, he decided to raise $2 billion in long-term debt at 3½ percent, a below-market interest rate. Paul Warburg was among the few encouraging bankers, most expressing their doubts that such an unprecedented issue could be absorbed by the people, especially at an interest rate so low. The experts were worried, McAdoo recalled, that Americans did not understand bonds. It was still a very small number who owned any. To this concern, McAdoo replied, education was the answer. They graduated from this education into modern capitalism.[13]

The problem of the low interest rate was a different matter. Money market rates in New York ranged from 4¾ to 5¼ percent. It was important to the war effort that the bonds were issued at par in order to demonstrate America's financial strength. Besides, the war effort would almost surely require additional financing, so maintaining the bonds at par was essential to ensuring public confidence in the investment. But bonds issued at rates of more than 1 percent below market would almost certainly not sell at par. Fortunately, the War Finance Act had stipulated that the bonds were to be exempt from most federal, state and local taxes. Although the bonds issued under the first act were the only ones to be fully tax exempt, the tax exemption proved to be essential in sustaining the value of the bonds.

The bankers helped McAdoo understand that public financial education was essential to the success of the bond drive. But McAdoo also knew that he had to stir up popular enthusiasm in order to get the bonds sold. His idea was to pitch the sales drive as opening a "financial front," not unlike the military front in Europe. It would give women, and men who were unable to serve overseas, the sense that they were full participants in the war effort. The bonds would also be sold on the installment plan, which made it possible for nearly every American to buy them. This method also introduced ordinary Americans firsthand to a form of margin buying.

McAdoo claimed to have been influenced by Cooke's selling methods during the Civil War, and this is surely true. But he was also influenced by the early German bond campaigns to finance their own efforts. By 1916, Germany was saturated with bond advertisements, and the "names of large subscribers were ostentatiously published in German newspapers." The German bond drive was a success, and while the British sneered, they so avidly adopted the German techniques in their own financing campaign that the Germans described the British selling effort as a distasteful circus.[14]

McAdoo's method was to sell as locally as possible. This would make it easier for volunteers to use the personal touch as a sales pitch and also would provide the chance for them to use peer pressure and public shaming as sales tactics. Each of the new Federal Reserve districts was constituted as a subcommittee of the central War Loan Organization, and in the later drives was responsible for selling its own quota, which was determined as a function of the district's wealth. The banks created Liberty Loan committees in every city in their districts. Everyone from bankers to Boy Scouts was recruited in the effort. "Widely known men and women in every walk of life immediately dropped all other business and turned their undivided attention to the loan. Bankers and business men generally accepted leading positions in the sales campaign, prominent state and national officials and other widely known orators took the platform to urge an enormous oversubscription and a veritable army of publicity men began to bombard the public with printed Liberty Loan ammunition." Bond buyers were issued buttons that proclaimed their patriotism. And the publicity drive mushroomed with the later bond issues. As Sunshine Charley would observe and adopt, "it was in the unremitting personal appeal to large audiences ... that the movement surpassed every previous demonstration of the kind."[15]

The first drive was a stunning success, as were subsequent drives. Newspapers and prominent businessmen rather hyperbolically declared the first issue to be the "best investment ever offered." But the Liberty Bond drives were nothing if not hyperbolic. Frank Vanderlip, the man who hired Charley Mitchell, called the Liberty Bonds "the highest grade investment in the world today" and encouraged wealthy investors to borrow money if they needed to in order to take up their share. Charles Clifton, president of the Pierce-Arrow Motor Car Company, was said to be investing his entire fortune in Liberty Bonds, buying on the installment plan.

It was not just the investment quality of the bonds that brought out the buyers. Newspapers and civic leaders insisted that it was the patriotic duty of all Americans to buy Liberty Bonds, aided by editorial pitches from the likes of Teddy Roosevelt and leading citizens throughout the country, not to mention the famous posters that made inducing guilt into a fine art form. The national baseball commission asked "every player, manager, business manager, and owner" of the World Series contending New York Giants and "Shoeless Joe" Jackson's Chicago White Sox to buy at least $100 of Liberty Bonds. Investing had become literally as American as baseball.[16]

According to one contemporaneous estimate, and based upon the numbers we have seen, it is likely that, at most, several million Americans were regular investors before the war. That was to change dramatically. Small investors were especially targeted during the first two Liberty Bond drives, and sales were structured so that almost everyone could afford to invest. The first drive used two thousand salesmen; the second planned to use six thousand. Bonds were sold on the installment plan with interest charges offset by interest on the bonds, creating a virtually cost-free way for small investors to buy. Banks lent bond buyers money to purchase bonds on the security of their future income and Congress expanded national bank power to lend on the security of Liberty Bonds before the fourth loan in October 1918. Vanderlip encouraged businesses to buy bonds and sell them to their own employees in monthly installments.

It worked. Every one of the four Liberty Bond issues and the final Victory Bond issue was oversubscribed, starting with the $2 billion in 3¼s receiving over $3 billion of subscriptions. Four million Americans bought bonds in the first drive, 99 percent of them in denominations of $50 to $10,000. Almost 9.5 million citizens bought bonds in the second drive, 18 million in the third, and almost 23 million in the fourth bond drive (which took place during the devastating flu epidemic of 1918). Almost 12 million bought Victory Bonds. While there was overlap, including considerable buying by banks, financial institutions and other corporations, unprecedented numbers of Americans were buying securities for the first time. And they were buying them in unprecedented amounts. By the end of the Victory

Bond drive in April 1919, conducted by McAdoo's successor, Carter Glass, the federal government had raised $21.3 billion in war debt alone, starting from a total federal debt of $1.2 billion in April 1917.[17]

Despite all the signs of war prosperity, the stock market took a substantial dive after America's declaration of war against Germany, partly because of an outflow of capital for war loans to the Allies and partly, according to Noyes, because it became clear that the combination of war taxes and the federal government's control of profiteering would limit industry's surplus war profits. But the market began a steady climb in late 1917 that did not peak until the end of 1919, when it experienced an expected postwar adjustment that lasted until the final quarter of 1921.[18]

Training Grounds for Brokers

Perhaps the most important aspect of the Liberty Bond drives for the development of the speculation economy was the participation of the new and growing national bank securities affiliates like Sunshine Charley's National City Company, as well as the national banks themselves. Few national banks had established securities affiliates by 1917, although by the time of the Glass-Steagall Act national banks had affiliates engaged in at least sixty-four different kinds of businesses legally prohibited to the national banks themselves, ranging from the securities and real estate businesses to investment trusts and insurance agencies. Some banks did not bother to establish the affiliates needed to comply formally with the law and invested in and underwrote bonds directly through their bond departments. Well before they began buying, selling and underwriting securities, these banks, with the blessing of the banking law, loaned margin money as well as longer-term money on the security of securities. This portion of the banking business grew with the stock market and was one of the factors leading national banks to develop research staffs and expertise in the securities business.[19]

The first time the banks used this expertise on a significant retail scale was during the Liberty Bond drives. "Practically all national banks became familiar with the technique of distributing securities during the War." Fifty-six percent of the total subscription to the first drive was made by national banks, both for their own accounts and for customers. National banks and 3.5 million of their customers were allotted almost half of the second drive and more than half of the total of the third and fourth drives. The same was true of the Victory Bond drive. Like the other patriotic workers ensuring the success of the loans, these banks worked without compensation. As Sunshine Charley put it: "Banking houses are not only giving up their chances of profit along ordinary lines but they are giving the salaries of their employees to the United States government, who, through the Liberty Loan committees, is now controlling such employees. The bond salesmen themselves ... are giving their services as freely as are the bankers themselves." Patriotic as this was, there would be compensation. "The only commercial reward in view ... is that which may come from the development of a large, new army of investors in this country ... who may in the future be developed into savers and bond buyers."[20]

The Liberty loan drives provided a graduate education for bankers and securities salesmen. As they learned, they developed relationships with potential investors and, as one commentator said, "won their confidence, partly because [they]... offered bonds of unquestioned soundness. Individuals, formerly prejudiced against all types of securities, became security minded and potential customers for future issues of corporate securities. The ... salesmen could argue that the corporate securities which they had for sale were as safe as government bonds and the yield far in excess." This was certainly true before the days of federal securities regulation, and the brokers took full advantage of their opportunities.[21]

Many middle-class Americans did not wait for the end of the war to become investors in corporate stock. There were reports as early as January 1917 that Western farmers were becoming significant stock buyers. And not just stock buyers, but margin buyers, anticipating that they would pay the balance of their purchase prices when their crops sold. The market was down, making it a time of bargain buying, although oddly some investors preferred to invest at higher prices. Small investors continued to show interest in the market as the war progressed and the economy boomed, even as larger investors hesitated for fear of the tax burden they would face on their expected gains. While investors were interested, they sometimes needed some persuasion to get into the market, and brokers were actively and aggressively selling. As the war went on and optimism continued, many individuals who had bought small-denomination Liberty Bonds sold them in order to invest in higher-yielding corporate securities. And investment advice columns (including the once-conservative *Wall Street Journal*) began to encourage individuals to invest, not only in bonds but also in stock.[22]

THE CAPITAL ISSUES COMMITTEE

The market was doing a remarkable job of taking care of America's war finance needs. Patriotism and peer pressure helped to raise money for the government at below-market rates. But the new habit of investing and the lure of profit began to undermine patriotism as an investment strategy. I noted earlier that the Liberty Bonds held their value reasonably well during the war, but they still dropped to 97 in 1917 and to a low of 92¼ in 1918, as buyers sold their bonds to invest in more profitable alternatives. Investment opportunities exploded as the war economy went into high gear. American industry needed large amounts of capital for production and expansion to meet the demands put on it by the war. The bull market of 1918 showed the market expanding.[23]

This situation presented a problem. At the same time that the federal government was trying to sell Liberty Bonds to raise money for the increasingly expensive war effort, private industry was working to raise money, too. Huge federal borrowings paid for huge federal orders, and American industry was scrambling to expand its production capabilities fast enough to fill them.

America was prosperous, but there was only so much cash. Vanderlip claimed that the Liberty Bonds had tapped into capital resources that did not even exist, that they would have to be bought on the strength of future income. Claiming that "all past savings are already invested," he said: "This war must be financed, not out of the past savings, but out of future savings. Future savings for the moment are not available, and some other device must, therefore, be brought into play." The devices, as we have seen, were offering Liberty Bonds on the installment plan and making bank loans available to buy the bonds. But they did not provide the funding for industry.[24]

The financial situation was serious, building toward collapse in 1920. But that was the unforeseeable future. And, foreseeable or not, the war had to be paid for. The stock market was in a steep decline. Liberty Bonds, large loans to the Allies and money used to repurchase American securities held in the belligerent nations had limited the sources of available capital for business expansion.

> The investment market was already thoroughly demoralized ... and there was practically no free money seeking investment. Savings banks held large amounts of illiquid securities at the same time that they faced the prospect of substantial withdrawals by depositors to buy Liberty Bonds, and commercial banks were saddled with heavy government loans and short-term paper, and were compelled to accept as collateral for business expansion loans securities that were unacceptable for Federal Reserve rediscounting.

As had been true of every down market since at least the Panic of 1907, illiquidity created worries about the stability of the banking system.[25]

This unprecedented financial competition between the private sector and the federal government created an extraordinary problem. Most of the money loaned to the Allies and raised during the Liberty Bond drives was being spent in government purchase orders from those very American industries that were starved by government fundraising for the expansion funds to meet those orders. War surplus taxation and the discouragement of profiteering that would be more formally (if extra-legally) enforced by Bernard Baruch and the War Finance Corporation capped corporate abilities to fund expansion with retained earnings at levels closer to those that had preceded the war. Corporations had fixed costs represented by the need to service their own debt and American investment habits at the time still demanded the regular payment of dividends on preferred stock and, typically, common stock as well. At the same time, while industrial production was critical to the war effort, not all products were created equal. Capital markets, while they might move money to profitable investments, were not the place to determine financing priorities for a nation that had temporarily reconfigured as a war machine. Somebody had to help direct the allocation of capital.

The job initially fell, as so many wartime finance jobs did, to the extraordinary treasury secretary, William McAdoo. McAdoo was helped by the banking community itself, as well as the patriotic fervor that had made the first Liberty Bonds such triumphs of finance. In November 1917, the president of the Investment Bankers' Association (IBA) repositioned bankers' traditional approaches to underwriting, putting as the first priority the question of whether a proposed financing was important to the war effort and as the last question whether the banker would profit from the deal.

As early as September 1917, members of the New York Liberty Loan Committee worked to limit money available to stock traders by raising the call money rate and rationing it by giving government and commercial borrowers priority, but this proved insufficient. Among the problems this group and other volunteers faced was that bankers and industrialists, no less than the capital markets, were ill-equipped to decide what was, and what was not, important to the war effort. Doubt often resulted in paralysis and even important financings were stalled. Bankers began to ask McAdoo for his advice and approval and he fulfilled that role. Following its annual convention in November 1917, at which the wartime conservation of capital received a great deal of attention, the IBA proposed a committee to McAdoo and the Federal Reserve Board.[26]

It is worth pausing before going on to note the unusual role played by the War Finance Corporation and, in the context of this story, the particular role played by the Capital Issues Committee (CIC). Business had called for regulation before, most prominently in the years before the FTC Act, when so many sought guidance from the Bureau of Corporations as to whether their actions would violate the Sherman Act. But the finance community—Wall Street—was, as we have seen, stubbornly resistant to the idea that any but themselves could or should have anything to do with the conduct of American capital markets. Yet even as the Bolsheviks toppled the Russian government, creating a domestic fear that would result in the Red Scare and Palmer raids of the autumn of 1919, the secretary of the treasury of the United States was telling investment bankers and industrialists whether and how much capital they could raise to run and expand their businesses. Within months this role would be assumed by a committee of members of the Federal Reserve Board, just as the federal government itself (with McAdoo at its head) would take over the operation of the nation's railroads. That committee, in its first report after its formal reconstitution by Congress in 1918, operated on "the theory of the law creating the committee that every dollar of private credit was an asset of the Government which must not be put to a nonessential use during the war." It was, perhaps, as close to a Marxian moment as the United States has ever come. And, most important for our story, it was a moment of highly intrusive, if technically noncoercive, federal intervention in the financial system that would provide a precedent for coercive, albeit far less intrusive, governmental financial regulation in another crisis just over a decade ahead. But in that later crisis Wall Street would be far less willing to cooperate.[27]

In any event, Wall Street and industry, as well as states and municipalities that had their own financing needs, cooperated so thoroughly that McAdoo was swamped. In his annual report to Congress for the year, he made it clear that he needed help. McAdoo turned to the Federal Reserve Board. He asked Paul Warburg, C. H. Hamlin and Frederick Delano to come up with a plan to review all proposed financing for consistency with the war effort. Within weeks, this small committee announced its plan, which was to create a newly constituted Capital Issues Committee consisting of those three Federal Reserve members and a staff. The CIC would examine the timing of proposed financing and its importance to the war effort. The CIC was to be aided by each of the regional Federal Reserve banks, which themselves would be helped by volunteer committees of bankers in order to enable the Committee to obtain local expertise.

This process of committee formation and procedure was, for the most part, done in a manner that could at best be described as extra-constitutional. Probably its legally saving grace was that the committee had no enforcement power and that application for approval was purely voluntary. At the same time, it was an agency organized by and within the government, and its persuasive capacities were undoubtedly for that reason greater than might have been the case with a purely voluntary organization. The New York Stock Exchange, always eager to stave off the threat of direct federal regulation, required that all issuers receive CIC approval as a condition to listing. It might therefore be exaggeration to claim, as one historian of the Committee wrote:

> Although the Capital Issues Committee of the Federal Reserve Board and its whole organization was a purely voluntary one without a legal basis and with no power of compulsion, it soon built up a system that secured the confidence of the business world and succeeded in reaching and controlling the vast majority of capital issues of sufficient size to warrant attention. This success was due to the whole-hearted and patriotic response of financial houses and organizations throughout the country.

Evidently this patriotic self-denial was insufficient, because by March McAdoo and Warburg were asking Congress for the legislative underpinning that would make the system mandatory. McAdoo wanted all corporations issuing more than $100,000 of securities outside the ordinary course of business to apply for and receive a license from the War Finance Corporation prior to selling them. Drawing upon the same military vocabulary that led him to describe the Liberty Bond efforts as a "financial front," he explained the proposal to Congress as the financial equivalent of the selective service, ensuring that slackers as well as patriotic volunteers would share the burdens of war.[28]

This time Wall Street failed to respond with enthusiasm. Patriotism, the volunteer spirit and moral suasion were one thing. Compulsion was another. The Investment Bankers Association, among others, opposed the plan, and, instead of the mandatory licensing that McAdoo wanted, the War Finance Corporation Act of 1918 created the seven-member Capital Issues Committee as a body separate from the War Finance Corporation, authorized only to determine whether a particular securities issue was "compatible with the national interest." Continuing the basic structure of the original Federal Reserve Board committee, committees on capital issues were established in each Federal Reserve district. In order to prevent the CIC from maintaining an indefinite postwar existence, it was to dissolve six months after the war ended unless the president had earlier declared its work to be unnecessary. In the event the Committee, which was created in April, disbanded in November shortly after the armistice was signed.[29]

The Committee took its role quite seriously and expanded its powers by narrowly interpreting the exceptions provided by Congress. As one historian described it, "By the end of the summer of 1918 the situation was so well in hand that it was virtually impossible to obtain large sums for capital outlay unless the project in question met with [the Committee's approval], and this applied to State and local governments, as well as to private firms." In October, the Committee's enforcement director announced that the CIC would review *every* securities issue, whether or not submitted voluntarily, and would call upon all of the resources of the government to stop the sale of those it disapproved. Economic Vigilance Committees were organized in every Federal Reserve district to investigate and report upon all unauthorized issues. McAdoo, who by then had justifiably assumed his place with Hamilton and Gallatin among America's great treasury secretaries, fully approved these new developments.[30]

By the time the Committee suspended its work on December 31, 1918, it had received 2,289 applications for new issues of securities in an aggregate amount of just over $2.5 billion. It processed an additional 1,020 applications between the armistice and December 31. According to the Committee, the simple number of applications understated its effective control over capital allocation. It noted that "numerous applications" were "voluntarily withdrawn," and that "large numbers of prospective applicants yielded to the informal suggestions made by the committee and its district committees that their enterprises or projects should be postponed until after the war." The Committee most likely did not overstate its effectiveness. In addition to the support of the NYSE, it also had the support of the Investment Bankers' Association (since the process remained voluntary), the American Bankers' Association and the United States Chamber of Commerce. Members of these associations served on the district committees and local committees that undoubtedly had influence over local businessmen and bankers whose business networks were interdependent. Moreover, the National Association of Blue Sky Commissioners, those officials who had the power to approve or forbid securities issuances in their states, also backed the Committee's work, further supporting the Committee's view of its own effectiveness.[31]

The Committee saw its work as transcending capital allocation in wartime. The same addition of 25 million, mostly new, investors in the American capital markets that had led Sunshine Charley to lick his chops also caught the attention of the regulators. In its first report to Congress the Committee wrote that if its work had continued, it would have asked for the power to protect these new investors from "unscrupulous promoters" seeking to part them from their Liberty Bonds in exchange for "worthless stocks." The Committee recommended that Congress empower a government agency to continue the "federal supervision of securities issues," stating:

> At no time has the obligation been so definitely placed upon the Government to protect its public from financial exploitations by reckless or unscrupulous promoters. The field has been greatly enlarged by the wide distribution of Liberty bonds, and the purveyor of stocks and bonds is no longer put to the necessity of seeking out a select list of prospective purchasers with money to invest. He now has the entire American public, and the transaction becomes one of persuasion to trade—to trade a Government bond bearing a low rate of interest for stocks or bonds baited with promise of high rate of return and prospect of sudden riches.

The government had taken advantage of the peoples' patriotism to use their capital. Even if securities regulation had not previously been a federal obligation, according to the Committee it was now. The Committee devoted over half of its final report of February 28, 1919, to again emphasize the need for federal action, noting that "regulation of security issues has long been an established practice among many nations which enjoy highly developed financial systems." The world had changed. The United States was the new world economic and financial leader. As the Liberty Bond market shifted to an active and more widespread stock market that for all intents and purposes became our modern stock market, Congress's perception of the need for federal securities regulation began to grow and assume its modern form.[32]

THREE WAVES OF MARKET DEVELOPMENT AND THE RISE OF MODERN SECURITIES REGULATION

The third stage of the development of the modern stock market was under way. The bull market of the merger wave of 1897 to 1903 brought middle-class Americans into the market for the first time as investors, in contrast to the random speculators and European bondholders who had long been active. While the Panic of 1903 tempered the bull market and ended the first stage of the modern securities market, it sustained a slow if steady growth in market participants up through the Panic of 1907 which, after a brief period of respite, began the second stage. The second stage, which lasted roughly until the market closings in 1914, was different from the first in that individual investors appear to have been rapidly and steadily increasing their investments in common stock. Bonds still dominated, but now high-quality industrials as well as railroads were seen as the gold standard of investment instruments, both in stocks and bonds. Speculation itself was becoming more mainstream as average investors bought common stock. The increasing availability of information in newspapers and magazines in the form of investment advice and financial reporting as well as the slowly increasing (if still rudimentary) availability of corporate information made the purchase of corporate securities somewhat less of a gamble than it might have been, although the information remained nowhere near universally reliable.

The third and final stage of the modern market began with the bull market of 1915 and did not end until the Crash of 1929. True, there were interruptions, like the bear market of 1917, the financial collapse of 1920, and the depression of 1921, but these were blips in an otherwise continuous process in which investing and, especially, investing in common stock, became not only the central ownership participation of the American middle class in American economic life but also the dominant focus of American business. Styles of investing changed, as common stock overtook bonds in the 1920s and investment trusts offered small investors the kinds of diversified portfolios that reemerged with the rise of mutual funds in the 1960s. But all of the ingredients of the modern stock market were in place by the end of World War I. Just as Sunshine Charley had predicted, "the people became educated [by the Liberty Bond drives] and accustomed to investing, owning and dealing in such bonds. It was but an easy step across to investments and dealings in industrial stocks and bonds which promised much larger returns." Thus it seems reasonable to date the start of the final stage of the speculation economy's development as the bull market of 1915.

The transformation in the American securities market was paralleled by the development of modern securities regulation, also in three stages. The first two stages ran from the dawn of the century to the enactment of the FTC and Clayton Acts in 1914. Their principal concern was antitrust. The first stage, encompassing the occasional calls for securities regulation that occurred prior to 1907, was really little more than a variant on the general issue of corporate power, the same issue that was captured by the dominant antitrust and federal incorporation movements. While investor protection was a concern, if a distant one, it was grounded in the rapid changes in the economic and financial dynamics of American life. The investment community, while growing, was still very small, and despite speculation by small investors was generally limited to the well-to-do. The issue of investor protection was thus a part of, yet deeply subordinated to, the other issues that arose in the federal attempt to control corporate power.

The second stage properly dates from the Panic of 1907 until 1914, during which we have seen a developing federal concern with securities regulation. This initial movement for federal securities regulation was also relatively unconcerned with the well-being of investors. The issue was the stability of the banking system and the national economy. The specific problems focused on were restraining overcapitalization and its monopolizing tendencies and the threat to the banking and overall economic system caused by the way that overcapitalized corporations encouraged speculation by financial institutions and individuals. Both overcapitalization and speculation increased market volatility in ways that were significantly destabilizing; securities regulation talk during this stage appropriately focused on market regulation aimed at exchanges and banks. This second stage effectively ended with the enactment of the Federal Reserve Act and the death of the Owen bill in 1914, although Untermyer and others periodically attempted to resuscitate the latter legislation. Various iterations of the Rayburn common carrier bill continued until its passage in 1920 but, as I noted in the last chapter, that bill was intended to be an antitrust measure rather than an investor protection measure.

The third stage of modern securities regulation began with the third stage of market development. As I discussed in the last chapter, its seeds lay in the Owen bill's attempt to include investor protection in what was, in essence, a measure designed to restrain speculation. But it really took its modern form, and essentially the form that the Securities Act of 1933 would take, with bills introduced in Congress in 1919, the year following the ballooning of American investors through the Liberty Bond drives.[33]

Before going on, though, it is worth taking a moment to examine the first securities bill introduced specifically for the protection of investors. Distinct from any of the other securities measures of this period, it provides a fascinating transition from the federal incorporation movement to securities regulation. Although drafted to apply only to "quasi-public" corporations, it differed from other bills in that it addressed neither stock nor exchanges but rather the individual shareholders of the corporation. This December 1915 bill, entitled "A Bill to Provide a Remedy for the Relief of Wronged and Defrauded Shareholders," gave investigatory powers to both the ICC and the attorney general to determine whether a corporation was being run in a manner that deprived the minority shareholders of their property and rights. This approach made the bill the only piece of corporate legislation introduced during a period frequently described as heavily influenced by Brandeis that truly bore the stamp of his influence and principal concerns. *Other People's Money*, Brandeis's 1915 book compiling his Pujo-inspired articles in *Harper's*, is commonly understood as focusing on securities disclosure and the dominance of the Money Trust. While this is superficially true, his undeniable goal in those essays, and in most of his corporate work, was the protection of minority shareholders from the depredations, or perceived depredations, of the control group. Although the bill went nowhere, its focus on internal corporate affairs represented perhaps the last gasp of the federal incorporation movement and, perhaps, the last attempt to ensure industrially oriented finance, before the full turn toward modern securities regulation.[34]

<h2 style="text-align:center">MODERN SECURITIES REGULATION:
THE LEGAL ACCEPTANCE OF THE SPECULATION ECONOMY</h2>

The third stage took place in two steps, embodied in two different bills that embraced two different visions of investor protective securities regulation and the federal government's role in the process. The first, introduced by Democrat John Marvin Jones of Texas, was a somewhat retrograde populist approach of the type embodied in state blue-sky laws. While more sophisticated than some, it was broker-oriented legislation that focused on disclosure of the terms of the selling effort rather than the details of the issuing corporation and, more important, on the substantive fairness of the offering to buyers.

The second bill, introduced in the House by Colorado Democrat Edward Thomas Taylor, was very close to the modern type. Drafted by Bradley Palmer, counsel to the Capital Issues Committee, and FTC member Huston Thompson, it was similar to consumer protection laws, requiring disclosure by the issuer sufficient to enable investors to make intelligent decisions in the purchase and sale of securities. Unlike the intrusive fairness inquiry to be made by the government under Jones's bill, the Taylor approach was far more in keeping with Wilsonian regulation, giving the government the power to oversee corporate self-regulation under the law rather than evaluating the quality of corporate behavior itself.[35]

Jones introduced H.R. 15399, on January 30, 1919. While aimed at investor protection, this bill was not yet in the modern form of regulation. Instead, it was a federal version of state blue-sky laws that attempted to regulate securities sales in states other than the issuer's state of incorporation. It made the payment of sales commissions to brokers the triggering factor and would have required every corporation issuing stock across state lines to file an offering plan with the FTC. The filing would describe the financing plan in detail, including promoters' compensation and brokerage agreements. The FTC would then have the authority to permit the sale following its finding that "the sale of stock will be fairly and honestly conducted both to the corporation and the public." The bill also contained an antifraud provision giving buyers a right of action against a bond required to be posted by the corporation. A similar bill would be introduced by Representative Edward Denison in 1920 and almost unanimously passed by the House.[36]

The first bill to look like modern securities regulation was introduced by Taylor on the same day, with a second version introduced two weeks later. Entitled "A Bill to Require Publicity in Prospectuses, Advertisements, and Offers for Sale of Securities," the measure specified the information that had to be required in advertisements for the sale of securities by any one person mailing or publishing more than three such ads within a given month. Specifically, it required that all such materials include information as to the commissions and expenses of the offering, as well as a notice that the issuer had filed certain mandatory information, including reasonably complete financial information, with the secretary of the treasury. That statement, which would have resembled the registration statement required under the 1933 Act, was to be signed by the issuer, its president, other chief executive officers, treasurer and a majority of the board. This bill was also the first proposed legislation providing a specific defense, a defense that ultimately would become known as the "due diligence" defense and extended to all signatories of the registration statement except the issuing corporation.[37]

The fact that securities regulation did not return to the public agenda until 1919 should come as no surprise, given the federal preoccupation with other more pressing matters. Indeed the armistice brought other problems, too, at home as well as abroad. Postwar domestic consumer prices had gone out of control. The cost of living had increased so dramatically that the president addressed the subject, and the need for legislation to control it, in a speech he delivered before a joint session of Congress in August 1919, not long after he had returned from Versailles. While a substantial portion of the speech addressed the treaty and the relationship between its ratification and economic well-being, it also represented a brief revival of Wilson's economic progressivism, couched in distinctly Wilsonian terms. Publicity was a significant remedy for the high cost of living, the president said. Goods should be "marked with the price at which they left the hands of the producer," much like the labeling required by the Pure Food and Drug Act. After all, the American consumer did not need paternalistic regulation. Instead, "the purchaser can often take care of himself if he knows the facts and influences he is dealing with and purchasers are not disinclined to do anything, either singly or collectively, that may be necessary for their self-protection."

But this was not all. Wilson, pulling a progressive regulatory thread through the preceding nineteen years, suggested that all corporations engaged in interstate commerce should be federally licensed on terms that would prevent price gouging. Finally, as an aside apparently suggested by Attorney General A. Mitchell Palmer, he said:

> May I not add that there is a bill now pending before the Congress which, if passed, would do much to stop speculation and to prevent the fraudulent methods of promotion by which our people are annually fleeced of many millions of hard-earned money. I refer to the measure proposed by the Capital Issues Committee for the control of securities issues. It is a measure formulated by men who know the actual conditions of business and its adoption would serve a great and beneficent purpose.

That bill was the Taylor bill, the clear and direct predecessor to the 1933 Act. This was classic Wilsonian economic progressivism as it had developed during his first few years in office, relatively unintrusive, disclosure-oriented regulation, designed for the needs of business to be largely self-regulatory.[38]

One can reasonably infer from the Taylor bill that the work of the Capital Issues Committee might well have made the world safe for stockholders. The bill applied to corporations issuing stock and their underwriters. It would have required highly detailed information about the issuer's finances and business, to be included in a statement signed by the same people identified in the earlier Taylor bill and filed with the secretary of the treasury before the securities could be offered to the public. Every purchaser of shares in the offering was presumed to have relied upon the information in the filed statement and could bring an action both for rescission and damages if any of the information was "false in any material respect," with strict liability imposed upon the signatories. The bill also provided criminal penalties for willful violation. The treasury secretary was given the power to make rules and regulations necessary to enforce the act, as well as the power to "prescribe forms upon which the said statements" were to be made.

Its concerns were quite different from the legislative efforts during the first two phases of securities regulation. Antitrust had gone off on its own course with the FTC Act, the Clayton Act and the Supreme Court's rule of reason. Speculation was still a concern, but the focus had shifted from the stability of the economy through the behavior of financial institutions to the well-being of the American people, who had become the new corporate financiers. Gone were the occasional attempts to tame finance in the service of industry. The new legislation accepted the speculation economy that had been embraced by the American people as the natural and correct order of things financial.

While the Investment Bankers Association had endorsed federal securities legislation at its annual convention in 1919, securities historian Michael Parrish wrote that the Taylor bill "incurred the hostility of the IBA," although IBA general counsel Robert Reed generally praised the bill while it was pending in Congress. The IBA endorsed the Denison bill. It was conceptually quite distinct from the market-oriented securities laws initiated by the Taylor bill that would ultimately flourish.[39]

Thus was the state of the market and regulation as the nation entered the presidential campaign season of 1920, the election year that would bring business back to the White House and Republican domination through the succeeding twelve years. Woodrow Wilson, embittered by the battle over the Treaty of Versailles and the League of Nations and significantly incapacitated by illness, had long since turned over economic leadership to his treasury secretary and, in any event, had lost his effectiveness in office. McAdoo had resigned to return to private life, although he would before long come back to politics, and Carter Glass had taken his place. The financially uneducated Glass had proven to be one of the most financially effective and influential congressmen in American history and would in the future return to the Senate to champion the post-Crash law that would bear his name and dismantle the securities empire that Sunshine Charley had built. But Glass's time in office was brief.

Warren Gamaliel Harding would bring to the post of treasury secretary the patrician and decidedly pro-business Andrew Mellon, whose preference for the good old days of the plutocrats would be reflected in his brief implication in the Teapot Dome scandal. The man who would replace Harding spent the fall of 1919 at the statehouse in Boston where he fulfilled his role during the days of the Red Scare by firmly suppressing a police strike. Sam Untermyer had served as an advisor to McAdoo and gone back to his law practice, from which he would be called upon in 1932 by Franklin D. Roosevelt to prepare the first, and ultimately rejected, draft of the administration's securities bill, a draft that looked very much like the Owen bill of 1914.

American investors, with their Liberty Bonds trading below par, had yet to await the outcome of a brief postwar depression, accompanied by a big enough increase in the cost of living that the term "HCL," or high cost of living, became a figure of speech. The combination of depression and HCL was brought on in part by an orgy of postwar consumer luxury spending, which Noyes contemptuously noted was a result of the workingman's failure to understand the real decline in his earnings. Instead he saw only the inflationary fact that "more money than he had ever seen before was pouring into his hands [and] his instinct was to spend it." Consumers demanded high-priced goods, and the higher the prices, the better. The inevitable downturn saw consumers' strikes, characterized by the creation of "old clothes clubs" in the spring of 1920, with retailers competing to cut prices and deflation beginning to shrink the economy. Liberty Bonds traded at new lows. But it would not be all that long before Coolidge was in the White House, prosperity returned, consumerism flourished, the stock market roared and all that money invested in Liberty Bonds began the great bull market that would end in the sickening autumn of 1929. The speculation economy in the form of the modern stock market and its regulatory correlates were in place and ready. "For the blood of the pioneers still ran in American veins; and if there was no longer something lost behind the ranges, still the habit of seeing visions persisted.... Still the American could spin his wonderful dreams—of a romantic day when he would sell his Westinghouse common at a fabulous price and live in a great house and have a fleet of shining cars and loll at ease on the sands of Palm Beach." The speculation economy had arrived.[40]

⊰ EPILOGUE ⊱

hy stop in 1919? The Roaring Twenties were only a year away. It would not be until late in that decade that Americans shifted much of their investment capital from bonds to stock and changed their investment styles from anticipating income to gambling for capital gains. It was not until the mid-1920s that the bull market really got going and collapsed into the Great Crash, one of the most spectacular and psychologically enduring events of American economic history. So one might say that my story remains incomplete.

I have two reasons for stopping where I have. The first, as I have already noted, is that finance had completed its triumph over industry and everything necessary for the modern market was in place by 1919. The second reason arises from the obvious parallels between the 1929 market crash, the stock market bubble of the late 1990s and the related corporate scandals that broke at the beginning of the twenty-first century.

One might reasonably argue that those parallels are all the more reason to extend this story through 1929 and its aftermath. But if I had given in to the temptation to do this I would have created a significant risk of distorting the history of the development of the speculation economy. I might have drawn too much attention to that manic moment in American history, a moment that was the exception, not the rule. That risk might have been exaggerated by inevitable comparisons with the more recent, and equally exceptional, events of the late 1990s. The lessons to be drawn from those episodes are important. But they are, in the main, lessons about how exceptional conditions can pervert individual and mass behavior. They do not teach the way the American economy is intrinsically speculative even under normal conditions. Manias and panics happen and speculative bubbles balloon and burst, all as episodic if unpredictable aspects of our economic life. But they are exceptional for all that.

One can, I think, draw more important and enduring lessons from the story of the formative era of American corporate capitalism, lessons all the more important precisely because they come from the stuff of everyday economic activity rather than as a sometime thing. The speculative stock market capitalism I have described seems fundamentally and inextricably embedded not only in our corporate financial structure but also in our economic and cultural consciousness and behavior. Our modern corporate economy was stock market capitalism from the moment of its conception. The stock market is in our economic genes, embedded as a mutation that formed during the great merger wave. Speculative bubbles come and go, but it is the stock market that drives American corporate capitalism. As I will shortly describe, the events of the years following 1919 continue to bear this out.

Corporate capitalism driven by the stock market produces corporate behavior fashioned by the market's demands and expectations. The market may from time to time take a long-term approach, favoring good wages and worker training, money spent for research and development, long-term strategic planning, sensible executive compensation and forthright disclosure. Or it may, as it did in the last decades of the twentieth century, demand short-term stock price increases that encourage executives to underpay workers, engage in promiscuous layoffs, cut training programs and research and development, ignore strategic planning and, in an extreme case like Enron, lie about corporate performance. In short, and as the historical development of American corporate capitalism demonstrates, the incentives created by the speculation economy make stock price the metric by which corporate performance and business behavior are measured.

There are reasonable expectations, and there are expectations that have no basis in reality. An economy characterized by widespread holdings of common stock might well be a market grounded in reality, a market that prices securities on the basis of business fundamentals such as the value of assets and past profits. Investors might hold stock for the long term, anticipating their returns as the business grows in the ordinary course, developing new markets, new efficiencies and new products. But speculation always exists in the characteristics of common stock. Speculation always exists in the capital structure of the American corporation.

John Maynard Keynes's perceptive description of the market as a psychological guessing game captures the nature of the speculation economy. Far more common than investing on the basis of fundamental values is investing on the basis of expectations that are built upon others' expectations, which themselves are floated upon the expectations of still others. Stocks trading at unsustainably high prices is a possible result. Sometimes companies, like Amazon in the late 1990s, trade at very high prices with no profits at all. Its stock, like the stock of many other companies at that time, was little different from the watered stock of the merger wave. Many other stocks regularly trade at very high multiples of earnings. But at some point expectations must give in to reality. Corporations must invest in productive assets; they must produce real cash profits. When they do and expectations are justified by performance, American corporate capitalism is at its best.[1]

But expectations built upon expectations can take on their own life, as Keynes observed, and this has often characterized the American market. During the last twenty-five years, expectations have become exaggerated. The multiples of earnings at which stock is trading are a good metric for market expectations. In his book *Irrational Exuberance*, Robert Shiller showed an almost unbroken spike in average price-to-earnings ratios beginning in the early 1980s at around ten times earnings to reach forty-five in 2000, earnings multiples that far exceeded historical averages. The more unrealistic expectations become, the more the market puts pressure on corporate managers to fulfill its sense of reality. If they fail, the market punishes them by deserting the stock, dropping its price and jeopardizing management's income and job security. The natural response is for management to do what it has to do in order to meet the market's expectations, no matter how unrealistic those expectations may be. When this occurs, the long-term health of the American corporate economy suffers.[2]

THE MANAGERIAL ERA

The effects of the speculation economy that developed during the early decades of the twentieth century receded from view during the middle of the century. The period from the late 1920s through the early 1970s is known as the managerial era, a time when directors and managers did their best to keep corporate control out of the hands of public stockholders. Its development can be detected as early as the first decade of the twentieth century. Corporate boards protected their abilities to run their businesses by creating structures that relieved them of excessive pressure from the speculation economy they created. Leading bankers sat on boards to control the combinations they helped to put together. The interlocking directorates that resulted allowed them to maintain some assurance that the businesses they financed were run profitably and responsibly, providing returns to public stockholders but preventing the market from exerting pressure on management.

Interlocking directorates were only one device. Morgan, among others, used voting trusts as one way of vesting control in boards rather than markets. In their classic 1932 study, *The Modern Corporation and Private Property*, Adolph Berle and Gardiner Means found that 21 percent of the two hundred corporations they studied were controlled by means of voting trusts, nonvoting stock, super-voting stock and pyramiding, all of which placed control in the hands of managers, directors or controlling shareholders, and held off the pressures of the market. In fact, they claimed that 44 percent of these corporations were under some form of management control. Management also quickly learned to command the proxy machinery of their companies, leading to the well-known phenomenon that stockholder voting during the whole of the twentieth century was almost entirely ineffectual.[3]

Corporate control seems to have been lodged in those with major financial interests in the corporation, whether as controlling families, banks, or executives with major assets invested in their own corporation's stock and cross-owning significant amounts of stock in other major corporations. The Temporary National Economic Committee found that 140 of the 200 largest nonfinancial corporations in 1937 had a controlling block of stock. A 1959 Conference Board study found that 27 percent of the directors of 638 industrials either were nonemployee large stockholders or represented financial institutions that had an interest in the corporation, again suggesting significant controlling shareholder influence. Robert Larner concluded that between 42.7 percent and 58.7 percent of the 300 largest public corporations among the Fortune 500 were family controlled in the mid-1960s. Robert Burch found that, as late as 1965, corporate control of almost half of American corporations lay in the stock ownership of founding families and their descendants. Other data, less carefully collected and more anecdotal, support the conclusion that a significant degree of corporate control was in the hands of small groups of large shareholders. More recent studies suggest that large stockholdings continue to characterize the ownership structures of many of the biggest American corporations.[4]

The consequence was to allow those with long-term interests in the corporation to insulate management from market pressures in making their business decisions. This was hardly perceived as an unalloyed good. On the contrary, the consensus thinking about that period is that managers worked to serve themselves at the expense of shareholders, to pay themselves high salaries and sometimes shirk their responsibilities while avoiding excessive risk taking that might produce shareholder profits if successful or jeopardize their jobs if not. There is no doubt that this was sometimes true. We cannot know what the consequences of an unrestrained speculation economy would have been had the market been given free rein, because of course it was not.

But there is evidence that despite their protection from the market, managers had strong incentives to serve the stockholders.

For one thing, stock in their companies formed a significant proportion of managers' compensation during the managerial era, making their earnings dependent on corporate profitability. One study shows that stock options alone comprised 36 percent of total executive compensation from 1955 to 1963. Still another found that 77 percent of NYSE and American Stock Exchange–listed companies had executive stock option plans by 1957. Inland Steel, for example, had set aside 11 percent of its stock for executive options, and Ford, although family controlled, allocated almost 7 percent.

In addition to managers' dependence upon their corporation's stock performance for their pay, they also invested substantial amounts of their personal wealth in their corporations. A 1939 study of executives and directors of the 97 largest manufacturing companies found that on average they together owned 7 percent of the stock of their respective companies. Another study found that the directors of the 100 largest industrials owned on average 9.9 percent of their company's stock in 1957. Several others confirmed that management stock ownership in their own corporations represented significant portions of their investment portfolios. Another study of the CEOs of 94 corporations during this period concluded that the expected annual return from managers' ownership of stock in their own corporations was equal to 41 percent of their median salary and bonuses. Recent evidence suggests that managers' ownership of their corporation's stock continued to increase throughout the century.[5]

Managers were deeply invested in their own corporations, but they were also heavily invested in stock more generally. One historian, writing of the early 1950s, identified "the managerial class [as] the largest single group in the stockholding population" with a larger proportion of that class owning stock than any other group in America. "Management is the class most interested in the highest dividends. . . . To talk of a separation between management and major stockholders in the United States is obviously quite impossible; they are virtually one and the same."[6]

Compensation and performance data support the conclusion that managers were devoted to the interests of stockholders during the managerial era. A number of careful studies showed no statistically significant correlation between board structure and executive compensation. They did find statistically significant positive correlations between corporate profitability and managers' compensation. It seems that stockholder profit was a primary determinant of executive pay during the managerial age.

The control and compensation structures of large corporations during the managerial age served the interests of stockholders even as managers were protected from the pressures of the market in running their businesses. It was also during this period, starting at the end of the 1930s, that financial institutions began to become significant investors in corporate stock in addition to the stock they held in their trusteeship roles, beginning with preferred stock and moving into common stock in the 1940s. While these institutions were decades from asserting their inchoate power, their interests were arguably aligned with those of manager-stockholders.

While the mid-century corporation continued to look after the interests of stockholders, the pressure of the speculation economy was kept in check from roughly the mid-1920s until the early 1970s by the ownership, compensation and control structures of the giant modern corporation. The twenty years between 1940 and 1960, the height of the managerial era, were, for the most part, a time when price-to-earnings ratios were maintained at one of their lowest points since the creation of American corporate capitalism.[7]

SEPARATING STOCK FROM BUSINESS

While corporate managers were concentrating on running their businesses as they saw fit during the middle of the century, theoretical developments in financial economics, theories with profound practical consequences, completed the domination of industry by finance, largely by separating stock from industrial concerns. These developments paved the way for the transformation from financial domination over industry to the full-blown triumph of the stock market over industry. The crowning glory of this line of theory was the development of the capital asset pricing model (CAPM) by William Sharpe in 1961. Sharpe's work was based on Harry Markowitz's earlier-developed portfolio theory. The common investment wisdom prior to Markowitz's work was that diversification of low-risk stocks was the safest form of investment, albeit with ordinary returns. Markowitz demonstrated that a portfolio of carefully chosen stocks, whatever their risk level, could maximize an investor's overall return as long as they moved in different directions from one another as market conditions changed.

The capital asset pricing model began with Markowitz's conclusion that the risks of investing in a specific corporation could be diversified away. Consequently, corporations did not need to compensate their stockholders for corporate-specific risks. The only nondiversifiable risk was the risk inherent in the market itself and therefore common to all securities. This was the risk for which stockholders were compensated. CAPM thus predicts a stockholder's expected return on the basis of the stock's risk with respect to market movements without any regard to the individual risks presented by a given corporation. It does so by measuring its past performance in relation to the rest of the market in a single number, the product of a regression analysis called *beta*. CAPM allows investors to build the kinds of potentially lower-risk, higher-return portfolios described by Markowitz, based solely upon a narrow range of information about the stock. The business itself matters little, if at all. All an investor needs is *beta*. No balance sheet, no profit and loss statement, no cash flow information, no management analysis of its performance and plans, no sense of corporate direction, no knowledge of what is in its research and development pipeline, no need even to know what products the corporation makes or what services it provides. Just *beta*. The stock is virtually independent of the corporation that issued it. CAPM has been adopted and is daily used by countless stock analysts and institutional money managers. Almost every American who invests in the market through mutual funds or other institutional media has invested on the basis of CAPM.[8]

Now one might object that I overstate the separation of stock from the corporation, of finance from business. There is truth in the objection, but the objection is largely hollow. That truth is that a business needs profits to survive, and to earn those profits it must grow and evolve. But stockholders in the speculation economy want their profits now, and they do not much care how they get them. Once the stock has been separated from the business, all that really matters is the movement of the stock. Modern financial derivatives take things a step further by allowing investors to profit from stock price movements without even having to take the risk of owning the stock.

THE RELEASE OF THE SPECULATION ECONOMY

Managerialism began to collapse in the 1970s, unleashing a stock market that had been restrained over the preceding four decades. A number of factors ended the managerial era. The conglomeration movement of the 1960s was rapidly reaching a crisis point and the stock market was collapsing. The new conglomerates themselves presented problems for directors, including conflicts of interest among various conglomerate boards and an overwhelming complexity of worldwide business. The Watergate investigation's revelation of illegal corporate campaign contributions followed by the SEC's questionable payments investigation discovered corporate domestic and foreign bribery that diminished confidence in corporate America and brought forth calls for reform. The impregnable Pennsylvania Railroad, once the nation's largest corporation, had gone bankrupt as the newly merged Penn Central without ever missing a dividend, and with its failure came an SEC investigation into the causes, numerous suits against directors and the development of the securities class action. A number of other bankruptcies and severe financial losses, brought on in part by recession, occurred, and with them the resignations or firings of some prominent CEOs. Chrysler was in need of its eventual federal bailout and even New York City faced bankruptcy. An activist SEC, aided by the United States Court of Appeals for the Second Circuit, had a string of successes in its attempt to make the securities laws into a body of federal corporate law with far more teeth than state law. Shareholder proposals by activist groups advocating a variety of social causes were being thrust on corporations and litigated in court.[9]

Corporate governance reform was the result and the target was the managerial board. The American Law Institute began to develop principles of corporate governance advocating a board comprised mostly of independent directors whose job would be to monitor management's performance. By definition, the independent director had no other relationship with the corporation, so the theory was that their only loyalties would be to the public stockholders. Acceptance of this model would break the barriers that had protected managers from stockholder pressure during the managerial era.

Although various business organizations initially fought the idea, the model of an independent monitoring board had become reality by the early 1980s and, by the 1990s, firmly enshrined in Delaware corporate law. Shareholder voting did not exert meaningful pressure on boards and managers, for shareholders remained largely dispersed and the rising class of institutional investors typically voted with management. But breaking the old protections in this way did provide the exposure that made stock market pressure a highly effective way of channeling managerial attention to the needs of the market.

The takeover decade of the 1980s dawned and the speculation economy that had been suppressed during the managerial era took off. As it did, a new term for American corporate capitalism came into use. Shareholder-valuism was used to describe the purpose of the corporation. Rising stock prices would be the proof that it had succeeded.[10]

The modern exaggeration of the domination of finance over industry started during the takeover decade of the 1980s, when the hostile takeover became an extreme way to satisfy stockholders' demands for short-term profit maximization by buying them out at a substantial premium over market. Stockholders began to invest in the hope of finding the next big takeover target. The looming pressure of the takeover market began to lead managers to do what they had to in order to keep their company's stock prices high and reduce the risk of hostile takeover. Corporate lawyers developed defensive devices like poison pills to keep bidders at bay, and state legislatures followed by enacting antitakeover laws to protect their corporate franchises. But stock-holders had again tasted the fruits of easy money.[11]

At the same time, institutional investors such as mutual funds, pension funds and insurance companies, whose stakes in corporate America had been swelling since the middle of the twentieth century, became major sharehold-ers in even the largest American corporations. Most observers in the late 1980s and early 1990s hoped that institutions would use their market power to demand better performance from corporate managers. They did. But better performance meant continually increasing stock prices and the institutions began to show growing impatience. As the 1990s wore on into the twenty-first century, they began to use their power to demand corporate governance reforms that reversed the effects of antitakeover devices and exposed their portfolio corporations to the market for corporate control. CEO turnover rates began to increase and boards felt threatened. Keeping their eyes on their stock prices was the key to survival, or at least to high paychecks.[12]

Institutions also reflected their short-term interests in the way they com-pensated their portfolio managers. These typically young portfolio managers, who could expect to peak in their early forties, were generally compensated on the basis of their quarterly performance. This gave them powerful incen-tives to manage their institution's portfolios to achieve the highest quarterly prices possible.

Corporate managers did not need institutions to tell them how impor-tant the stock market was. Congress amended the tax code in 1993 to encour-age corporations to compensate their executives with stock options. By the late 1990s, the average Fortune 500 executive received more than half of his or her compensation in this form. And waiting periods on exercise were few and far between. The idea was to align management's interests with those of the stockholders. But the stockholders with whose interests management was now aligned were not the controlling families and individuals whose long-term investments in their businesses had dominated during the era of managerialism. They were the impatient stockholders of the public market. It worked devastatingly well. Some companies even developed option plans like that of Computer Associates, which was triggered only when the com-pany reached and maintained a certain stock price for sixty days. Despite their best judgments as to the well-being of their corporations, managers were given irresistible incentives to maximize stock prices at almost any cost to the corporation's long-term health.[13]

The market reflected these developments, showing a dramatic increase in short-term stockholdings. Annualized turnover of all stock on the New York Stock Exchange was 118 percent in December 2006 as compared with

36 percent in 1980 and 88 percent even as recently as 2000. The average mutual fund had a 2006 turnover rate of 110 percent. There can be little question that American business is driven by finance. And the demands of finance have become short-term.[14]

As I noted in the Prologue, a 2005 survey of more than four hundred chief financial officers found that 80 percent said "they would decrease discretionary spending on such areas as research and development, advertising, maintenance, and hiring in order to meet short-term earnings targets, and more than 50 percent said they would delay new projects, even if it meant sacrifices in value creation." But the problem goes beyond business self-mutilation. As the Conference Board put it, "the pressure to meet short term numbers may induce senior managers to search for a number of business costs (i.e., the cost of a state-of-the-art pollution control system) to externalize, often to the detriment of the environment and future generations."[15]

The dominance of finance over business is, taken alone, a neutral fact. Wise and patient investors whose interests are grounded in the long-term health of the business align well with the long-term growth and sustainability of their corporations and the American economy. But we have reached a stage in the United States where our economy is characterized not simply by the triumph of finance over business, but by the domination of a stock market that has followed the logic of a widespread common stock structure to largely detach itself from business. Finance now is vested in a huge, anonymous, constantly changing market of public stockholders ranging from day traders to TIAA-CREF. When the chance to get rich quick presents itself, as it has so often in our economic history, the market takes advantage. It is only in the rare case that management can resist this pressure, usually with help like a controlling interest in the stock.[16]

—※—

Public common stock ownership is not, of course, unique to America. But the speculation economy is. Much of the rest of the industrialized world is characterized by ownership and control structures that provide some insulation for corporate management from the pressures of the market. In continental Europe and Japan, corporate ownership is characterized by concentrated stockholdings in families, investor groups or banks in a manner that centralizes control. Canada, New Zealand and Australia also have economies characterized by large blockholdings of stock. Widely dispersed stockholdings are not common in these economies, nor is frequent trading. Only Britain's corporate economy resembles that of the United States, and that economy developed historically in a very different manner.[17]

Epilogue

The history of American corporate capitalism is a story that has not ended. We continue to live in and embrace an economic order that was created at the turn of the twentieth century. The history of American corporate capitalism is living history, and the course of living history can be changed. We may choose to accept that history as we have developed it. Or we can alter it, keeping what is good and modifying or changing the aspects of our economic story that trouble us. The history of the speculation economy is a history of choice.

When corporate economies are ruled by concentrated ownership, the responsibility for success or failure is primarily on those who own the controlling interests. When a corporate economy is ruled by a stock market characterized by the dispersal of ownership throughout the society, responsibility shifts. Members of the speculation economy typically treat their participation in American corporate capitalism as a private matter with their decisions to be made on the basis of their own self-interest and without much regard for the behavior or decisions of others. But the nature and power of the speculation economy make the well-being of corporate America and, with it, the financial health of the nation, a matter of public concern. Most Americans participate in the speculation economy in one form or another. It is we who bear the responsibility for the consequences. It is we who create the demands of the market, who shape the incentives that drive corporate management. Perhaps the most important lesson of the history of the development of American corporate capitalism is that the continuing strength and health of the American corporate economy and thus American society requires market behavior that encourages management to work for the long-term economic welfare of their businesses, their people and thus of the nation. Those incentives can only be provided by the market for, in the end, the market is the master.

The speculation economy is ours. It is what we make of it.

NOTES

PROLOGUE

1. Graham, Harvey & Rajgopal, *The Economic Implications of Corporate Financial Reporting*, pp. 3–73. The study is complex and subtle, and statistics vary with respect to given behaviors. Nonetheless my generalization in the text accurately captures a principal finding in the article.

2. Tonello, Revisiting Stock Market Short Termism; CFA Centre for Financial Market Integrity/Business Roundtable Institute for Corporate Ethics, Breaking the Short-Term Cycle; Mitchell, Corporate Irresponsibility.

ONE: THE PRINCIPLE OF COOPERATION

1. Wiebe, The Search for Order, gives a wonderful portrayal of the confusion that characterized American society, including business, in the late nineteenth century. His story stands in contrast to the relatively orderly evolution of centralized, professional management that Alfred Chandler describes as beginning in the 1840s and neatly developing from that point; Chandler, The Visible Hand. But the path of industrial evolution is not part of my story. I am more interested in how the birth and growth of the giant modern corporation affected American business in the twentieth century.

2. Navin and Sears, studying the period from 1893 to 1896 "when almost no mergers were taking place" observe how the securities market and, in my view, the modern corporation with it, might have developed in the absence of the merger movement, with limited stock ownership spread from the heirs of industrialists who were looking to liquidate their positions in their family corporations; Navin & Sears, *The Rise of a Market for Industrial Securities*, p. 127.

3. Navin & Sears, *The Rise of a Market for Industrial Securities*, pp. 109–12; Dodd, Stock Watering, p. 23.

4. George Edwards, in his study of American finance capitalism, claims that what he calls "security capitalism," the system of financing business with individual savings, began in 1873 and was more or less complete by 1907; Edwards, The

EVOLUTION OF FINANCE CAPITALISM, pp. 161–62. The story I tell, using a somewhat different notion of finance capitalism, begins in 1897 and ends in 1919, both later than the period Edwards identifies.

5. The efficiency and managerial rationales form the central theses of Chandler's great work; CHANDLER, THE VISIBLE HAND; CHANDLER, SCALE AND SCOPE.

6. I rely heavily on interpretations by Kolko, Wiebe, Weinstein and especially Sklar, for the relationship between business and government and their more or less cooperative construction of corporate regulation. KOLKO, THE TRIUMPH OF CONSERVATISM; WIEBE, BUSINESSMEN AND REFORM; WIEBE, THE SEARCH FOR ORDER; WEINSTEIN, THE CORPORATE IDEAL IN THE LIBERAL STATE; SKLAR, THE CORPORATE RECONSTRUCTION OF AMERICAN CAPITALISM.

7. COWING, POPULISTS, PLUNGERS, AND PROGRESSIVES. Klein provides a revisionist account of Gould as a constructive businessman; KLEIN, THE LIFE AND LEGEND OF JAY GOULD.

8. Carnegie's statement is reported in Meade, *The Genesis of the United States Steel Corporation*, p. 542. Meade describes the Carnegie Company as "purely industrial. Financial considerations had little weight." *Id.* By contrast, finance was a driving force behind Morgan's creation of U.S. Steel.

I use Carnegie and Morgan here as ideal types. Carnegie was not a pure industrialist, and Morgan not a pure securities salesman. David Nasaw describes Carnegie's employment in the period between his career at the Pennsylvania Railroad and his creation of Carnegie Steel as consisting largely of selling bonds (including through the firm of Junius Morgan and, indirectly, his son Pierpont). While Carnegie earned his early fortune as a railroad manager, he also participated as a shareholder in a number of different enterprises, including rather unsavory railroad construction companies (explained *infra* at n. 9) and dabbled in securities speculation; NASAW, ANDREW CARNEGIE, pp. 118–36. Nonetheless, Carnegie Steel was an industrial model along the lines described by Meade and Carnegie did display later contempt for pure financiers like Morgan.

Morgan took an interest in industry, although Nasaw describes his early work in correspondence with his father as more manipulative than the financial statesmanship for which he became known; NASAW, *ibid.*, p. 136. Jean Strouse, in her magnificent biography of J. P. Morgan, places less emphasis on considerations of finance. She notes the distaste with which Morgan and his father considered the post–Civil War chaos in the railroad industry and their desire to stabilize it, albeit for the safety of the securities issued by the railroads and sold by the Morgan firms. She also credits Morgan with creating U.S. Steel convinced of the efficiency gains to be had rather than for the sake of salable watered stock; STROUSE, MORGAN, pp. 133–34, 406.

9. CLARK, HISTORY OF MANUFACTURES IN THE UNITED STATES, vol. 2, 1860–1893. Arthur Hadley's history of the railroads, while not specific, suggests that early railroads were financed by stock subscribed for by local merchants, bankers and others with free cash to invest, but bond financing predominated at least by the 1880s as the source of railroads' permanent capital. This source allowed stockholders to manipulate a railroad's wealth in order to divert profits to themselves (often in the form of what was referred to as a "construction company," which was essentially a finance

company formed to construct and control the railroad and controlled by the railroad's founders). Construction companies frequently drove the railroads into bankruptcy because the diversion of funds to the founders made it hard for the railroads either to complete construction or to meet their fixed costs if they did; HADLEY, RAILROAD TRANSPORTATION, pp. 45–55. William Ripley writes that railroad finance in the beginning was almost always in the form of stock such that, by 1855, the combined capital stock of railroads exceeded their aggregate bonded debt by 42 percent. Bonds became more common when lines moved away from Eastern money centers, and were also popular because they facilitated founders' abillities to own the railroads with other people's money by using construction companies; RIPLEY, RAILROADS: FINANCE AND ORGANIZATION, pp. 10–23. Early railroads also often received very significant state and federal financial support; HUGHES, THE VITAL FEW, pp. 363–65. Chandler provides evidence that, as early as the 1850s, railroads were financed largely with European debt, but by the 1870s, wealthy individual financiers like Vanderbilt, Gould and Forbes, among others, owned the controlling stock of railroads which remained largely financed with debt. Finally, by the 1890s, especially after an extraordinary number of railroad reorganizations, control of a number of major railroads was held by the first group of modern investment banks, including J. P. Morgan & Co.; Kuhn, Loeb & Co.; August Belmont & Co.; Lee, Higginson & Co.; and Kidder, Peabody & Co., although their control was through financial influence rather than direct investment; CHANDLER, THE VISIBLE HAND, pp. 91–172.

Railroad stock was the frequent subject of speculative activity. Chandler gives railroad speculators credit for overcoming the lassitude of permanent stockholders, whose goal simply was to maintain dividends, to force the investments necessary for the consolidation of the great railroad systems; CHANDLER, THE VISIBLE HAND, p. 148.

10. THORELLI, THE FEDERAL ANTITRUST POLICY, p. 63; CHANDLER, THE VISIBLE HAND, pp. 240–83. Thorelli shows virtually no increase in the number of factories created between 1869 and 1879 but attributes this to "the extraordinary mortality of small businesses" and instead relies upon increases in wage earners and product values to sustain his point.

11. Employment classification calculations are based on HISTORICAL STATISTICS OF THE UNITED STATES, MILLENNIAL ED., vol. 2, Table Ba 814–830. Numbers demonstrating similar trends, although slightly different, appear in UNITED STATES DEPARTMENT OF COMMERCE, HISTORICAL STATISTICS OF THE UNITED STATES, COLONIAL TIMES TO 1970, Part 1, Series D 152–166 (1976); *see also* UNITED STATES DEPARTMENT OF COMMERCE, BUREAU OF THE CENSUS, HISTORICAL STATISTICS OF THE UNITED STATES: EARLIEST TIMES TO THE PRESENT. Post-1900 data are drawn from HISTORICAL STATISTICS OF THE UNITED STATES, COLONIAL TIMES TO 1970, Part 1, Series F 6–9.

12. Throughout the book I have used dollar values as presented in the primary sources except as otherwise indicated. Thus I have adjusted for inflation neither to the present nor within the twenty-three-year period I cover.

Historians are not in complete agreement as to the dates of the merger wave. Kolko dates it from 1897 to 1901; KOLKO, THE TRIUMPH OF CONSERVATISM, p. 24. Naomi Lamoreaux considers it to have occurred from 1895 to 1904; LAMOREAUX, THE

GREAT MERGER MOVEMENT IN AMERICAN BUSINESS. Thomas McCraw agrees with Lamoreaux (relying both on his data and on Lamoreaux and several of her empirical sources); MCCRAW, PROPHETS OF REGULATION, pp. 97–98. Gardiner Means seems to have considered the most active period to have been 1898 to 1903; BONBRIGHT & MEANS, THE HOLDING COMPANY, pp. 69–70. And Arthur Dewing, writing in 1914, traces it from late 1896 until it "ceased abruptly before the depression of 1903"; DEWING, CORPORATE PROMOTIONS AND REORGANIZATIONS, p. 522.

My periodization relies both on the first post-depression jump in combination activity and the first significant effects of economic growth for the beginning of the merger wave, which were 1898 and 1897, respectively, and the break following the Rich Man's Panic of 1903 for the end. Since combination activity in 1897 was relatively modest prior to a significant increase in 1898, my starting date is somewhat arbitrary and reflects a balance of economic and combination activity. In any event, the determination of a precise date for the beginning and end of the merger wave is not critical to my argument.

The amount of new capital raised in the merger wave is unclear, and the issue is complicated by distinctions between nominal capital and the amounts of securities actually issued, and nominal value and the prices at which the securities were sold on the market, as I will discuss in Chapter Three. But the magnitude of the merger wave clearly was dramatic, and contemporary observers almost uniformly spoke in terms of nominal capital rather than actual capital so I need not resolve these distinctions for my purposes.

Conant presents the 1900 total combination capitalization as $5 billion, but this diminishes to $4.4 billion when duplications are eliminated; Luther Conant, Jr., *Industrial Consolidations in the United States*, p. 18. Thorelli is frank about the paucity of data and the consequent imperfection in the numbers; THORELLI, THE FEDERAL ANTITRUST POLICY, pp. 291–306. Navin and Sears describe the corporate landscape before 1890 as dominated by corporations with equity of less than $2 million, with a small handful having $5 to $10 million and an even smaller number exceeding $10 million. By the turn of the century there were "nearly a hundred" industrial corporations with capitalizations exceeding $10 million; Navin & Sears, *The Rise of a Market for Industrial Securities*, pp. 109–12, 134.

In emphasizing the importance of finance, I do not mean to disregard those observers who argue that there were significant efficiency gains from at least some number of these combinations. Undoubtedly there were. My point is that American corporate capitalism most likely would not have developed how it did, when it did and with the consequences it had in the absence of the alignment of financial incentives, legal possibilities and economic circumstances. It will of course require the rest of the book to sustain this assertion.

13. MOODY, THE TRUTH ABOUT THE TRUSTS, pp. 485–89; MEADE, TRUST FINANCE; NELSON, MERGER MOVEMENTS IN AMERICAN INDUSTRY, p. 37. Thorelli, based on his modification of a study by Myron Watkins, places the number of combinations at 186 between 1898 and 1901 and 163 for the period covered by Meade; THORELLI, THE FEDERAL ANTITRUST POLICY, at pp. 298–302. Both Nelson and Lamoreaux use significantly lower figures, but employ a more restricted set of crite-

ria in identifying combinations; LAMOREAUX, THE GREAT MERGER MOVEMENT IN AMERICAN BUSINESS, at p. 1, n. 1; and *see* WATKINS, INDUSTRIAL COMBINATIONS AND PUBLIC POLICY, *esp.* Appendix 2.

14. The dollar values of acquired securities are found in HISTORICAL STATISTICS OF THE UNITED STATES, MILLENNIAL ED., Table Ce42–68.

The absence of agricultural individuals from the data is not troubling, since during this period farmers tended to invest their money in land; Waring, *Life and Work of the Eastern Farmer*, ATLANTIC MONTHLY, vol. 39, no. 253 (May 1877), pp. 584–95; Mappin, *Farm Mortgages and the Small Farmer*.

Gene Smiley provides the trading volumes noted in the text; Smiley, *The Expansion of the New York Securities Market*, p. 77. NELSON, MERGER MOVEMENTS IN AMERICAN INDUSTRY, p. 90, shows an almost steady upward trend in listed securities from the Civil War until about 1895. These were, as he acknowledges, principally railroad securities. As to the 1901 trading volume, it must be remembered that 1901 was the year of the Northern Pacific battle which, for a brief but intense time, had a significant effect on trading volume. Perhaps the best general account of the fight for the Northern Pacific is provided by Strouse; STROUSE, MORGAN, pp. 418–27.

15. VEBLEN, THE THEORY OF BUSINESS ENTERPRISE, pp. 25–27, 31, 34, 89, 157, 158.

16. The intellectual and social dominance of *laissez-faire* ideology in nineteenth-century America is not inconsistent with observations that significant forms of regulation appeared during that era. *See* Novak, *Public Economy and the Well-Ordered Market*; McCRAW, PROPHETS OF REGULATION. *Laissez-faire* was an anti-regulatory philosophy and, as I discuss in this chapter and in Chapter Two, state corporate regulation was rather severe. At the same time, it was a philosophy of competition, and Supreme Court ideology of the last quarter of the nineteenth century through the New Deal, as well as significant state law, blocked cooperation in favor of competition as a business strategy.

17. For good discussions of the political and intellectual life of the era, *see* BUCK, THE GRANGER MOVEMENT; COMMAGER, THE AMERICAN MIND; CURTI, THE GROWTH OF AMERICAN THOUGHT; DORFMAN, THE ECONOMIC MIND IN AMERICAN CIVILIZATION, vol. 3, 1865–1918; GABRIEL, THE COURSE OF AMERICAN DEMOCRATIC THOUGHT, chs. 13–21; GOODWYN, THE POPULIST MOMENT; HOFSTADTER, THE AGE OF REFORM; KOLKO, THE TRIUMPH OF CONSERVATISM; MAY, THE END OF AMERICAN INNOCENCE; SKLAR, THE CORPORATE RECONSTRUCTION OF AMERICAN CAPITALISM; WIEBE, BUSINESSMEN AND REFORM; WIEBE, THE SEARCH FOR ORDER; WEINSTEIN, THE CORPORATE IDEAL IN THE LIBERAL STATE, among others.

18. THORELLI, THE FEDERAL ANTITRUST POLICY, pp. 112–17; CARNEGIE, THE GOSPEL OF WEALTH AND OTHER TIMELY ESSAYS; SUMNER, WHAT SOCIAL CLASSES OWE TO EACH OTHER; GABRIEL, THE COURSE OF AMERICAN DEMOCRATIC THOUGHT, pp. 231–35; COMMAGER, THE AMERICAN MIND, pp. 201–3; DORFMAN, THE ECONOMIC MIND IN AMERICAN CIVILIZATION, vol. 3, pp. 67–69; MAY, THE END OF AMERICAN INNOCENCE, pp. 20–21; KEYNES, THE END OF LAISSEZ-FAIRE, p. 15.

19. As Ely put it, the Industrial Revolution in America transformed an accep-

tance of laissez-faire into an understanding that it was "an anachronism"; ELY, STUD-
IES IN THE EVOLUTION OF INDUSTRIAL SOCIETY, p. 61.

For a detailed analysis of the way dominant businesses could use the railroads to
conquer smaller ones, *see* NEVINS, JOHN D. ROCKEFELLER, vol. 1, pp. 306–412 and
passim.

20. UNITED STATES DEPARTMENT OF COMMERCE, HISTORICAL STATISTICS OF
THE UNITED STATES: COLONIAL TIMES TO 1970, Part 1, Series F 287–296.

21. UNITED STATES DEPARTMENT OF COMMERCE, HISTORICAL STATISTICS OF
THE UNITED STATES, COLONIAL TIMES TO 1970, Part 2, Series Q 321–28; CHANDLER,
THE VISIBLE HAND, pp. 83, 88; RIPLEY, RAILROADS: FINANCE AND ORGANIZATION,
p. 59.

22. UNITED STATES DEPARTMENT OF COMMERCE, HISTORICAL STATISTICS OF
THE UNITED STATES, COLONIAL TIMES TO 1970, Part 2, Series Q 321–328, Series Q
284–312; CHANDLER, THE VISIBLE HAND, p. 299.

23. THORELLI, THE FEDERAL ANTITRUST POLICY, p. 237, n. 8 (reprinting table
from HISTORICAL STATISTICS OF THE UNITED STATES).

24. SELIGMAN, ESSAYS IN ECONOMICS, p. 1 (reprinting an essay published by
Seligman in 1886).

25. An excellent summary of the evolution of economic thinking during this
period, as well as a description of the principal ideas of some of the most important
economists, is found in DORFMAN, THE ECONOMIC MIND IN AMERICAN CIVILIZA-
TION, vol. 3, 1865–1918, pp. 160–213. Thorelli also gives a nice, although sometimes
narrow, picture of the economic intellectual history of this period; THORELLI, THE
FEDERAL ANTITRUST POLICY, pp. 127–32. Merle Curti provides a good description
of the difference between the capitalism of the classical economists and that of the
newer generation even as, like Clark, they modified their views over time; CURTI,
THE GROWTH OF AMERICAN THOUGHT, pp. 650–52.

26. Ely, *Report of the Organization of the American Economic Association*;
and Ely, *Constitution By-Laws and Resolutions of the American Economic Association*, p. 35.

27. Clark, *The Nature and Progress of True Socialism*; Clark, *The Limits of Competition*; CLARK, THE PHILOSOPHY OF WEALTH. As to the development of Clark's
thinking later in his career, *see* SCHUMPETER, HISTORY OF ECONOMIC ANALYSIS, pp.
867–70; THORELLI, THE FEDERAL ANTITRUST POLICY, pp. 121–23.

28. Adams, *Relation of the State to Industrial Action. See also* THORELLI, THE
FEDERAL ANTITRUST POLICY, pp. 131–32.

29. Ely, *The Nature and Significance of Monopolies and Trusts*, pp. 275–83; ELY,
STUDIES IN THE EVOLUTION OF INDUSTRIAL SOCIETY, pp. 97, 62, 89–91, 99; ELY, AN
INTRODUCTION TO POLITICAL ECONOMY, pp. 5, 14.

30. Edwin R. A. Seligman, *Railway Tariffs and the Interstate Commerce Law*,
II, pp. 372–73; HADLEY, RAILROAD TRANSPORTATION, pp. 69, 81; HADLEY, ECONOM-
ICS, *esp.* chs. 1 and 6; Gunton, *The Economic and Social Aspects of Trusts*; GUNTON,
TRUSTS AND THE PUBLIC (largely a collection of his articles defending trusts); An-
drews, *Trusts According to Official Investigation*.

31. DODD, STOCK WATERING, p. 23, notes that railroads were financed almost en-

tirely with debt, and stock sold to promoters for little or no consideration. SOBEL, THE BIG BOARD, pp. 81–82, notes that by 1869, almost 20 percent of American railroad securities were owned by foreigners. PREVITS & MERINO, A HISTORY OF ACCOUNT-ING IN AMERICA, p. 75, describe the influx of English, Dutch and German invest-ments in American railroads during the boom period of 1866 to 1873, and the way the depression of 1873, combined with the depression of 1887, led to foreign dumping of American railroad securities at significant losses, enabling Americans to purchase the securities "at greatly reduced prices, the result being that Americans had gained ownership in the railroads at a small portion of the original investment."

32. KOLKO, RAILROADS AND REGULATION, p. 7. Chandler also engages in an extensive discussion of railroad overbuilding and competition; CHANDLER, THE VISI-BLE HAND, ch. 4. For a wonderful and detailed description of the chaos in the related railroad, refining and oil producing industries in the late 1860s and early 1870s, see NEVINS, JOHN D. ROCKEFELLER, vol. 1, pp. 247 *passim.* To get a somewhat mundane but highly detailed flavor of the railroad problems, it is worth reading Robert Swaine's thorough description of the work of the law firm that became the Cravath firm from the end of the Civil War to the second decade of the twentieth century; SWAINE, THE CRAVATH FIRM, vol. 1 from p. 238 episodically through the first several hundred pages of vol. 2. *See also* CHERNOW, THE HOUSE OF MORGAN; STROUSE, MORGAN, ch. 13.

33. The U.S. Industrial Commission discussed at some length the relationship between some of the large trusts and the railroads and its effect upon public senti-ment; UNITED STATES INDUSTRIAL COMMISSION, FINAL REPORT, vol. 19, 1902, pp. 597–99, 610–11, 615–16. *See also* MOODY, THE TRUTH ABOUT THE TRUSTS, p. 112.

Attitudes toward the railroads and other big businesses tended to vary by occu-pation, region and the state of the economy. For a careful empirical study of public opinion, *see* GALAMBOS, THE PUBLIC IMAGE OF BIG BUSINESS IN AMERICA. *See also* MARCHAND, CREATING THE CORPORATE SOUL, for a study of the ways in which big corporations used public relations and the media to create public acceptance.

34. Bullock, *Trust Literature,* p. 177. UNITED STATES INDUSTRIAL COMMISSION, FINAL REPORT, vol. 19, p. 615.

35. LAMOREAUX, THE GREAT MERGER MOVEMENT IN AMERICAN BUSINESS, carefully argues that in the middle 1990s most of the truly destructive competition occurred in mass production industries with little product differentiation, high fixed costs and heavy investment made not long before the depression.

36. WIEBE, THE SEARCH FOR ORDER, pp. 7, 23; Puffert, *The Standardization of Track Gauge.*

37. CHANDLER, THE VISIBLE HAND, pp. 133–43.

38. It is perhaps more accurate to say that Ohio law was silent on the subject of corporations owning the stock of other corporations. The common law rule at the time was that silence in a statute as to a corporation's powers meant that the corpora-tion lacked those powers unless express permission had been given by the legislature in the corporation's charter.

One of the best accounts of Standard Oil's growth through predatory tactics with railroads and competitors leading to a virtual transportation shutout for almost every potential competitor is NEVINS, JOHN D. ROCKEFELLER. More critical accounts include TARBELL, THE HISTORY OF THE STANDARD OIL COMPANY and LLOYD, WEALTH AGAINST COMMONWEALTH. While Lloyd's book was published in 1894, based in part on a series of his articles beginning in 1881, I have relied upon Cochran's 1963 edition, which was prepared in response to numerous accusations of Lloyd's factual inaccuracies and distortions. Cochran's edition is an attempt to present only the verifiable facts from official sources and thus tells a more reliable (yet still gripping) story than the original publication.

39. NEVINS, JOHN D. ROCKEFELLER, vol. 1, pp. 604–17.

40. A copy of The Trust Agreement of 1882 is appended to TARBELL, THE HISTORY OF THE STANDARD OIL COMPANY, vol. 2, p. 364. It is also available as part of the House Proceedings in Relation to Trusts held in 1888. The description of Dodd is from CHERNOW, TITAN, p. 225. The story of the formation of the Standard Oil trust is carefully reported in NEVINS, JOHN D. ROCKEFELLER, vol. 1, pp. 604–17; and CHERNOW, TITAN, pp. 224–27.

41. *People v. North River Sugar Refining Company*, 121 N.Y. 582 (1890); *State v. Standard Oil Company*, 49 Ohio St. 137 (1892); MEADE, TRUST FINANCE. This was, of course, not necessarily the view of those businessmen who were destroyed in the process of combination or who believed they had sold out to the trusts too cheaply.

Exceptions to the acceptance of business combination as natural and beneficial included residents of the farm states of the Midwest, the upper Midwest and the South, who vilified the largely Eastern capitalists and businessmen and whose anger at the effect of Eastern finance on farm prices, as well as their perception that the gold standard favored by Eastern businessmen deflated the prices they could get for their products, led to the Grange and Populist movements, culminating in the presidential campaigns of William Jennings Bryan against McKinley in 1896 and 1900.

Further opposition was centered in the National Association of Manufacturers, an organization composed largely of smaller businessmen. They advocated a broad version of *laissez-faire*, within business-protective limits such as a strong tariff and good internal infrastructure, largely as a means of opposing organized labor; STEIGERWALT, THE NATIONAL ASSOCIATION OF MANUFACTURERS.

Although I will discuss the Democrats' position later in relation to the Littlefield bill of 1903, much of the story of the development of consensus on the subject is beautifully told in SKLAR, THE CORPORATE RECONSTRUCTION OF AMERICAN CAPITALISM.

42. By this time New Jersey had introduced the first of its liberalizing amendments and John D. Rockefeller and his trust reorganized safely, at least for the time being, as a corporation in New Jersey.

TWO: SANCTUARY

1. Delaware does have a state income tax, with a rather modest top marginal rate of 5.95 percent; 30 DEL. CODE ANN. sec. 1102 (a)(11)(2006).

2. UNITED STATES DEPARTMENT OF COMMERCE, BUREAU OF THE CENSUS, STATE GOVERNMENT TAX COLLECTIONS: 2005, available at http://www.census.gov/govs/statetax/0508destax.html.

3. As of 1901, the top six states in terms of corporate franchise tax receipts were

New York, New Jersey, Massachusetts, Pennsylvania, West Virginia and Maine; Calkins, *The Massachusetts Business Corporation Law*, p. 270.

4. Boyer, *Federalism and Corporation Law*, pp. 1041–42; Ballam, *The Evolution of the Government-Business Relationship*.

5. Incorporation had been outlawed in Britain since 1720, primarily because of fallout from the collapse of the South Sea Bubble; The Bubble Act, 6 GEO. 1, ch. 18 (1720).

6. *Charles River Bridge v. Warren Bridge*, 36 U.S. (11 Pet.) 420 (1837). For an extended discussion of corporate chartering and monopoly *see* Hovenkamp, *The Classical Corporation in American Legal Thought*.

7. KELLER, AFFAIRS OF STATE, pp. 184–85; CADMAN, THE CORPORATION IN NEW JERSEY, pp. 435–38.

8. CADMAN, THE CORPORATION IN NEW JERSEY, pp. 53–56.

9. Grandy discusses the Morris Canal and Banking Company, incorporated in 1824, which also enjoyed a degree of monopoly power and tax exemption and which flourished until competition with the railroads forced it into decline; GRANDY, NEW JERSEY AND THE FISCAL ORIGINS OF MODERN AMERICAN CORPORATION LAW, p. 20; RAUM, THE HISTORY OF NEW JERSEY FROM ITS EARLIEST SETTLEMENT TO THE PRESENT TIME, vol. 2, pp. 334, 340–41. Granting monopoly power to legislatively chartered corporations was not uncommon (*see* HOVENKAMP, ENTERPRISE AND AMERICAN LAW, p. 126), but New Jersey's concessions were remarkably generous.

10. ACTS INCORPORATING THE DELAWARE AND RARITAN CANAL COMPANY, THE CAMDEN AND AMBOY RAILROAD AND TRANSPORTATION COMPANY, AND THE NEW JERSEY RAILROAD AND TRANSPORTATION COMPANY, pp. 17–27, 45. The quote in the text is taken from CLEVELAND & POWELL, RAILROAD PROMOTION AND CAPITALIZATION IN THE UNITED STATES, pp. 166–67.

11. Stoke, *Economic Influences upon the Corporation Laws of New Jersey*, p. 555; Steffens, *New Jersey*; GRANDY, NEW JERSEY AND THE FISCAL ORIGINS OF MODERN AMERICAN CORPORATION LAW, p. 22; *Important Movement in New Jersey*, NILES' WEEKLY REGISTER, Mar. 19, 1836, p. 45; *Stockton's Appeal*, SATURDAY EVENING POST, Oct. 13, 1849, p. 2.

12. Stoke, *Economic Influences upon the Corporation Laws of New Jersey*, p. 567, n. 49; WATKINS, THE CAMDEN AND AMBOY RAILROAD.

13. RAUM, THE HISTORY OF NEW JERSEY FROM ITS EARLIEST SETTLEMENT TO THE PRESENT TIME, vol. 2, p. 320.

14. RAUM, THE HISTORY OF NEW JERSEY FROM ITS EARLIEST SETTLEMENT TO THE PRESENT TIME, vol. 2, p. 341. Grandy notes that heavy local property taxes were assessed to provide services for which local governments were unable to obtain adequate funding from the state. This created political resentment not only in local lawmakers, but also in local property owners who were being heavily taxed at a time when the railroads were hardly being taxed at all. The result was a fight over whether localities could tax the railroads and whether the state legislature could withdraw the railroads' tax exemptions, a fight the railroads ultimately lost; GRANDY, NEW JERSEY AND THE FISCAL ORIGINS OF MODERN AMERICAN CORPORATION LAW, pp. 23–39; AN INVESTIGATION INTO THE AFFAIRS OF THE DELAWARE & RARITAN CANAL AND

CAMDEN & AMBOY RAILROAD COMPANIES IN REFERENCE TO CERTAIN CHARGES BY "A CITIZEN OF BURLINGTON"; REPORT OF COMMISSIONERS APPOINTED TO INVESTIGATE CHARGES MADE AGAINST THE DIRECTORS OF THE DELAWARE AND RARITAN CANAL AND CAMDEN AND AMBOY RAILROAD AND TRANSPORTATION COMPANIES. This latter report is significantly more critical of the companies, especially the Canal, than the earlier investigation, but attributes financial errors to sloppiness in accounting and bookkeeping and finds nothing to suggest dishonesty or fraud on the part of the directors. *See also* STOCKTON, ADDRESS BY COMMODORE R. F. STOCKTON TO THE PEOPLE OF NEW JERSEY; WATKINS, THE CAMDEN AND AMBOY RAILROAD, p. 59.

15. *The Lease of the New Jersey Railways to the Pennsylvania Railway Company*, p. 338. The lease had been authorized by the legislature conditioned upon a two-thirds vote of the United Companies' shareholders and its payment of "fair value" for the stock of dissenting shareholders.

A number of other railroads were chartered between 1832 and 1873 but most of these were short local lines; RAUM, THE HISTORY OF NEW JERSEY FROM ITS EARLIEST SETTLEMENT TO THE PRESENT TIME, vol. 2, pp. 341–43.

16. Keasbey, *New Jersey and the Great Corporations. See also* N.J. PUB. LAWS 1846, p. 16; N.J. Laws 1849, p. 300; N.J. LAWS 1865, p. 354; N.J. LAWS 1866, p. 1034.

17. Stoke, *Economic Influences upon the Corporation Laws of New Jersey*; Dodd, *Statutory Developments in Business Corporation Law.*

18. EDWARDS, THE EVOLUTION OF FINANCE CAPITALISM, p. 158.

19. N.J. PUB. LAWS 1882, p. 76; N.J. PUB. LAWS 1884, p. 232, setting franchise tax for certain categories of companies; Stoke, *Economic Influences upon the Corporation Laws of New Jersey*, p. 570, n. 63. GRANDY, NEW JERSEY AND THE FISCAL ORIGINS OF MODERN AMERICAN CORPORATION LAW, Figure 3.4, shows the meteoric rise in New Jersey franchise tax revenues from 1884 to about 1915.

20. Upton Sinclair, *II—Justice—Bought and Paid For*, FORUM, vol. 79, no. 5 (May 1928), p. 653; *James B. Dill*, CURRENT LITERATURE, vol. 29, no. 1 (July 1900), p. 24; Earl Mayo, *The Trust Builders*, FRANK LESLIE'S POPULAR MONTHLY, vol. 52, no. 1 (May 1901), p. 8; Seligman *et al.*, *The Taxation of Quasi-Public Corporations: Discussion*; Dill, *Some Tendencies in Combinations Which May Become Dangerous*; Dill, *National Incorporation Laws for Trusts*; DILL, THE STATUTE AND CASE LAW OF THE STATE OF NEW JERSEY RELATING TO BUSINESS COMPANIES; SCHREINER, HENRY CLAY FRICK, p. 175; STEFFENS, AUTOBIOGRAPHY, pp. 192–96.

21. *James B. Dill*, CURRENT LITERATURE, vol. 29, no. 1 (July 1900), p. 24; Steffens, *New Jersey*.

22. The 1889 modifications to New Jersey's more modest 1888 holding company act were evidently drafted at least in part by lawyers from New York's Sullivan & Cromwell, counsel for the American Cotton Oil Trust; DEAN, WILLIAM NELSON CROMWELL, p. 100.

23. Steffens, *New Jersey*; Stoke, *Economic Influences upon the Corporation Laws of New Jersey*, p. 571.

24. SEAGER & GULICK, TRUST AND CORPORATION PROBLEMS, pp. 44–45. MOODY, THE TRUTH ABOUT THE TRUSTS. Arthur Dewing directly attributes the dis-

appearance of the trust form of doing business to the amendments to New Jersey law; DEWING, CORPORATE PROMOTIONS AND REORGANIZATONS, p. 520, n. 4.

25. HISTORICAL STATISTICS OF THE UNITED STATES, MILLENNIAL ED., Table Ch293–318. *See also* EVANS, BUSINESS INCORPORATIONS IN THE UNITED STATES, pp. 47–49 (noting the jump in very large corporations incorporating in New Jersey during the merger wave and the fact that many proclaimed monopolistic intent).

26. Whether or not one agrees with Chandler's argument that law had little to do with the development of big business, it is clear that the form big business took had a great deal to do with the law, a fact recognized by the Industrial Commission in 1902: "The strongest forms of combination appear to have been promoted by laws intended to prevent them"; UNITED STATES INDUSTRIAL COMMISSION, FINAL REPORT, vol. 19, p. 605; MASS. PUBLIC STATUTES 1870, ch. 224, sec. 15; MASS. PUBLIC STATUTES 1877, ch. 230, sec. 1, sec. 3; MASS. PUBLIC STATUTES 1875, ch. 177, sec. 2; Calkins, *The Massachusetts Business Corporation Law*; Dodd, *Statutory Developments in Business Corporation Law*; MASS. PUBLIC STATUTES 1903, ch. 437.

27. N.J. PUB. LAWS 1888, pp. 385–86. The 1903 sales brochure of the Corporation Trust Company of New Jersey does not even mention mergers as an attraction of New Jersey law; BUSINESS CORPORATIONS UNDER THE LAWS OF NEW JERSEY. D. E. Mowry, *The Abuse of the Corporate Charter*, ALBANY LAW JOURNAL: A WEEKLY RECORD OF THE LAW AND LAWYERS, vol. 69 (June 1907), pp. 188, 189. By 1896 almost all states provided for the interstate merger of railroad corporations upon a two-thirds vote of the stockholders. Laws permitting the interstate merger of industrial corporations were rare until late in the second decade of the twentieth century, long after the merger wave had passed.

For an interesting revision of the history of New Jersey's modern corporation law, *see* Parker-Gwin & Roy, *Corporate Law and the Organization of Property in the United States*. I believe they understate the credibility of the traditional story, much of which is consistent with my own research as presented in the text, by discounting the fact that some of the most significant changes in New Jersey law occurred during Governor Abbett's second term, which ran from 1890 to 1893; Steffens, *New Jersey*; HOGARTY, LEON ABBETT'S NEW JERSEY; HOGARTY, LEON ABBETT OF NEW JERSEY.

The fact that New Jersey was not the first state to provide legislatively for holding companies also helps to put the relative importance of the holding company act in perspective; Freedland, *History of Holding Company Legislation in New York State*. The holding company act was important and did quickly attract corporations, but it was in 1893, during Abbett's second term, that it was amended to work broadly for industrial corporations and not until 1896 that it was perfected.

28. *Elkins v. The Camden and Atlantic Railroad Company*, 36 N.J. Eq. 5 (1882); *Berry v. Yates*, 24 Barb. 199 (N.Y. 1857); *Peabody v. Chicago Gas Trust Co.*, 130 Ill. 268 (1889); *First National Bank of Concord, N.H. v. Hawkins*, 174 U.S. 364 (1899) (under national bank law); *Easun v. Buckeye Brewing Co.*, 51 F. 156 (N.D. Ohio 1892) (under Ohio law); *Buckeye Marble & Freestone Co. v. Harvey*, 20 S.W. 427 (Tenn. 1892) (apparently under Tennessee law); *Booth v. Robinson*, 55 Md. 419 (1881) (Maryland permitting intercorporate stockholdings and insisting that it was the majority

rule). *See also* ANGELL & AMES, A TREATISE ON THE LAW OF PRIVATE CORPORA-
TIONS, AGGREGATE, 7th ed., sec. 158; ANGELL & AMES, A TREATISE ON THE LAW OF
PRIVATE CORPORATIONS, AGGREGATE, 10th ed., sec. 158 (language identical to 7th
ed.); MORAWETZ, TREATISE ON THE LAW OF PRIVATE CORPORATIONS OTHER THAN
CHARITABLE, sec. 229; BOONE, A MANUAL OF THE LAW APPLICABLE TO CORPORA-
TIONS GENERALLY, sec. 107; DILL, THE STATUTORY AND CASE LAW APPLICABLE
TO PRIVATE COMPANIES, sec. 51; *Power of a Corporation to Acquire Stock of Another
Corporation. But see* Compton, *Early History of Stock Ownership by Corporations*,
detailing the extent to which corporations held stock in other corporations under
special charter provisions from at least the middle of the nineteenth century.

29. N.J. PUB. LAWS 1888, pp. 385–86; *Coler v. Tacoma Railway and Power Co.*,
64 N.J. Eq. 117 (1902); *Parsons v. Tacoma Smelting and Refining Company*, 25 Wash.
492 (1901).

30. N.J. PUB. LAWS 1893, p. 301.

31. N.J. PUB. LAWS 1896, pp. 293–94; N.J. PUB. LAWS 1896, p. 279, as amended;
N.J. PUB. LAWS 1899, p. 473 (allowing a corporation to incorporate for "any lawful
purpose or purposes"). *Dittman v. The Distilling Company of America*, 64 N.J. Eq.
537 (Ch. Ct. 1903); *Ellerman v. Chicago Junction Railways & Union Stock-Yards Co.*,
23 A. 287 (N.J. Ch. 1891); *New Jersey v. Atlantic City and Shore Railroad Company*,
69 A. 468 (N.J. S.Ct. 1907). *See* Taylor, *Evolution of Corporate Combination Law*, pp.
698–99, 749–53; SEYMOUR D. THOMPSON, COMMENTARIES ON THE LAW OF PRIVATE
CORPORATIONS, 1st ed., vol. 5, sec. 6405.

The corporate personality argument was, in part, that corporations had the same
rights as individuals to acquire property; EDDY, THE LAW OF COMBINATIONS, pp.
665–66; HORWITZ, THE TRANSFORMATION OF AMERICAN LAW, p. 87; Mark, *The Personification of the Business Corporation in American Law*.

32. As early as 1883, New Jersey permitted mergers and consolidations of specific
kinds of corporations on a majority vote of the stockholders, first those maintaining
stockyards, storehouses, piers, or docks, and, in 1888, hotels and common carriers.
The 1889 act was a significant advance in that it permitted *any* New Jersey corporation to merge or consolidate, albeit only with any other New Jersey corporation, upon
approval of the boards of directors of both companies and two-thirds of the stockholders of each company; N.J. PUB. LAWS 1883, p. 242; N.J. PUB. LAWS 1888, p. 441; N.J.
PUB. LAWS 1893, p. 121. Still, the statute authorized only horizontal mergers and consolidations. While this may seem, and was, somewhat limiting, it is important to note
that a principal reason for corporate combination at this time was to restrain and
eliminate competition and therefore most of the mergers that took place through the
early twentieth century were horizontal. LAMOREAUX, THE GREAT MERGER MOVE-
MENT IN AMERICAN BUSINESS, p. 1. So the limitation was, in practice, less significant
than it appears at first blush. A concise summary of the changes in New Jersey law
through 1896 is provided in Grandy, *New Jersey Corporate Chartermongering*.

33. I have not been able to find aggregated data detailing the technical legal
forms of combinations. Economic, business and legal historians typically use the
term "merger" to apply to any kind of corporate consolidation. Nelson, for example,
says that while "it is true that the simultaneous consolidation of a number of firms

into one company was the most common form of merger in this period, there were some important exceptions." He then contrasts this with corporations acquired one by one, suggesting that by "consolidation" he does not technically mean what we would refer to as consolidation or merger; NELSON, MERGER MOVEMENTS IN AMERICAN INDUSTRY, p. 13; LAMOREAUX, THE GREAT MERGER MOVEMENT IN AMERICAN BUSINESS; Bittlingmayer, *Did Antitrust Policy Cause the Great Merger Wave?* Thorelli argues that most of the "trusts proper" reorganized into single corporations, not holding companies. This is consistent with the idea that, at least at this early stage before the merger movement, sales of assets for stock were more common than stock-for-stock exchanges; THORELLI, THE FEDERAL ANTITRUST POLICY, p. 83. Cheffins appears to use the terms "merger" and "consolidation" interchangeably; Cheffins, *Mergers and Corporate Ownership Structure*, pp. 478–80.

Hovenkamp implies that asset transfers for stock were far more common than stock for stock transactions. HOVENKAMP, ENTERPRISE AND AMERICAN LAW, pp. 251–52. Seager and Gulick imply the same when they describe the typical initial combination proposal; "they turn over their properties and business to the new corporation to be organized in exchange for a fair proportion of the stock." In fact Seager and Gulick do not even mention mergers among the forms of combination they describe; SEAGER & GULICK, TRUST AND CORPORATION PROBLEMS, p. 65. Bonbright and Means support Thorelli's conclusion as to the early trusts. They note that during the merger wave prior to 1900, the holding company device was not frequently used. Rather, corporations engaged in "fusion." But Bonbright and Means define fusion as "merger, amalgamation, or purchase of assets," which hardly resolves the question. They do note that most fusions were "horizontal" but, as we have seen, this would have been a requirement of New Jersey law for mergers anyway. They also agree with Thorelli that most of the "trusts proper" did not use the holding company device; BONBRIGHT & MEANS, THE HOLDING COMPANY, pp. 29, 68–72. Jenks writes that the preferred form after the initial creation of the holding companies was merger, describing the transactional form as assets for stock with the dissolution of the selling corporation, which is not technically a merger but a sale of assets now characterized as a "de facto" merger. Later, holding companies became more predominant, but Jenks observed this in 1929 when holding companies had indeed become prominent and he did not set any time parameters on the evolution he describes; JENKS & CLARK, THE TRUST PROBLEM, pp. 37–38. Finally, the Industrial Commission found that although the early combinations tended to be holding companies, most of the consolidations at the height of the merger wave (that is, by 1901) were in the form of mergers or asset sales forming a single corporation; UNITED STATES INDUSTRIAL COMMISSION, FINAL REPORT, vol. 19, pp. 607–8.

It seems that the best conclusion is that combinations that did not use the holding company device used one central corporation to buy the assets of other corporations for stock rather than merge.

34. UNITED STATES INDUSTRIAL COMMISSION, FINAL REPORT, vol. 19, p. 607; BONBRIGHT & MEANS, THE HOLDING COMPANY, pp. 67–76; *People v. North River Sugar Refining Company*, 121 N.Y. 582 (1890); *United States v. Northern Securities Company*, 193 U.S. 197 (1904); *Standard Oil Co. of New Jersey v. United States*, 221

U.S. 1 (1911); *United States v. American Tobacco Co.*, 221 U.S. 106 (1911); Bittling-mayer, *Did Antitrust Policy Cause the Great Merger Wave?*.

35. REPORT OF THE COMMISSIONERS APPOINTED TO REVISE THE GENERAL ACTS OF THE STATE OF NEW JERSEY RELATING TO CORPORATIONS, p. ii. Dill, in his 1898 treatise on New Jersey corporate law, puts the language of section 49 giving directors the conclusive right to determine value in bold letters; DILL, THE STATUTORY AND CASE LAW APPLICABLE TO PRIVATE COMPANIES, sec. 49.

36. BUSINESS CORPORATIONS UNDER THE LAWS OF NEW JERSEY, p. 17. As the Industrial Commission described matters, sometimes promoters would organize a new company and pay cash to the owners of factories they wanted to buy. "More frequently," notes the Report, the plants were purchased with securities in the new corporation. When the plants were owned by corporations, the new company exchanged stock with the old, thereby acquiring ownership by stock of the constituent companies; UNITED STATES INDUSTRIAL COMMISSION, FINAL REPORT, vol. 19, pp. 607–8. It is worth noting here, although I will discuss the issue more specifically in Chapter Three, that New Jersey manufacturing corporations could not issue stock for services (N.J. PUB. LAWS 1896, pp. 286, 293, 315), although Dill suggests, despite explicit statutory limitations, that one case could be read to permit this; DILL, THE STATUTORY AND CASE LAW APPLICABLE TO PRIVATE COMPANIES, sec. 50. This limitation affected the way promoters structured deals. Typically they bought options to buy the constituent companies and sold the options to the new combination in exchange for stock.

37. Navin and Sears make the argument that there was an upper limit on the extent to which directors and promoters could overissue stock in payment for assets (Navin & Sears, *The Rise of a Market for Industrial Securities*, p. 132), but the conditions of the merger wave seem to have expanded, if not eliminated, these limits.

38. *Wetherbee v. Baker*, 35 N.J. Eq. 501 (1882); *Coit v. Gold Amalgamating Company*, 119 U.S. 343 (1886).

39. *Wood v. Dummer*, 3 Mason 308 (C.C. Me. 1824); *Wetherbee, supra* n. 38; *Boynton v. Hatch*, 47 N.Y. 225 (1872).

40. *Coit, supra* n. 38; *Van Cott v. Van Brunt*, 82 N.Y. 535 (1880).

41. *Bickley v. Schlag*, 46 N.J. Eq. 533 (1890); *Edgerton v. The Electric Improvement and Construction Company*, 50 N.J. Eq. 354 (1892) (to same effect, although decided under the New Jersey corporations statute of 1882); *Coit, supra* n. 38. One relatively contemporaneous commentator notes that the court in Bickley "ranged itself squarely on the side of the good faith rule"; Wallstein, *The Issue of Corporate Stock for Property Purchased*, p. 118.

42. BIRMINGHAM, "OUR CROWD," p. 11.

43. *Donald v. American Smelting and Refining Company*, 62 N.J. Eq. 729 (1900).

44. *American Smelting Co. Loses on Appeal*, NEW YORK TIMES, Mar. 29, 1901, p. 10; *Corporation's Safeguards*, NEW YORK TIMES, Mar. 30, 1901, p. 12; *Financial: Buying with Inflated Stock*, THE INDEPENDENT, May 2, 1901, p. 1041.

45. *American Smelting Company in Court*, NEW YORK TIMES, Feb. 17, 1901, p. 1; *Guggenheim Plant Sold*, NEW YORK TIMES, Apr. 9, 1901, p. 1; *Big Deal Closed*, BOSTON DAILY GLOBE, Apr. 9, 1901, p. 4.

46. One exception to the commentators who ignored statutory difference was Leonard Wallstein; Wallstein, *The Issue of Corporate Stock for Property Purchased.*

47. *See v. Heppenheimer*, 69 N.J. Eq. 36 (1905).

48. H. S. Richard, *Exchange of Stock for Capitalized Profits*, p. 526; H.L.W. [presumably H. L. Wilgus, a frequent legal commentator], *Creditors' Right to Hold Shareholders Liable on Corporate Stock Issued for Property Valued on the Basis of Prospective Profits*, p. 220; Wallstein, *The Issue of Corporate Stock for Property Purchased* (not discussing *See* but approving the same basic rule); *Liability for Stock Issued for Overvalued Property*, p. 366.

49. *See v. Heppenheimer, supra* n. 47 at 849.

50. Wickersham, *The Capital of a Corporation*, p. 326.

51. N.J. PUB. LAWS 1896, pp. 279, 286, 315; Dill, *National Incorporation Laws for Trusts*, pp. 280–81.

52. Testimony of Howard K. Wood before the United States Industrial Commission, Oct. 18, 1899, UNITED STATES INDUSTRIAL COMMISSION, PRELIMINARY REPORT ON TRUSTS AND INDUSTRIAL COMBINATIONS, vol. 1, p. 1089.

53. Steffens, *New Jersey*; Stoke, *Economic Influences upon the Corporation Laws of New Jersey.*

54. Pennoyer, *How to Control the Trusts*; *Remedies for Monopolistic Trusts Proposed by the St. Louis Antitrust Conference*; *Recent Trust Conferences*, NEW YORK OBSERVER AND CHRONICLE, vol. 77, no. 40, Oct. 5, 1899, p. 433; *Review of the Month*, GUNTON'S MAGAZINE, Nov. 1899, p. 337.

55. MASS. REV. LAWS 109, sec. 19; 110, sec. 44 (1903); Calkins, *The Massachusetts Business Corporation Law.*

THREE: TRANSCENDENTAL VALUE

1. Charles Conant places strong emphasis on these economic conditions in bringing about the merger wave; CONANT, WALL STREET AND THE COUNTRY.

2. ALLEN, THE GREAT PIERPONT MORGAN, p. 165. It is worth noting that Morgan had little but contempt for Gates (CAROSSO, THE MORGANS, p. 503), but he had no choice but to deal with him, especially in the U.S. Steel combination. It is also only fair to Morgan to note that he did not think of himself as a speculator like Gates, but took a serious interest in the combinations he created both for finance purposes and, relatedly, because of his desire to bring order to industry; STROUSE, MORGAN. The point in the text is not to characterize all trust promoters simply as speculators, but rather to distinguish their interest in the profits to be made from speculative securities from those of the industrialists whose profits came from industrial production in precisely the way Veblen distinguished businessmen from industrialists.

3. A significant amount of debate has taken place over the causes of the merger wave. Regardless of how they may have evaluated the business and economic consequences of the merger wave, contemporary economists almost always saw its business origins in ruinous competition; *e.g.*, MEADE, TRUST FINANCE, pp. 64, 76–78. Meade also discusses, at least theoretically, potential economies of scale from combination. *See ibid.*, pp. 67–68. *See also* MEADE, CORPORATION FINANCE, p. 27. Seager and Gulick also treat excessive competition as a major impetus for the move-

ment, although they (and Meade) acknowledge the public appetite for stock during the period with its potential for promoters' profits as a significant factor; SEAGER & GULICK, TRUST AND CORPORATION PROBLEMS, pp. 60–67. *See also* DODD, STOCK WATERING, p. 206; DEWING, CORPORATE PROMOTIONS AND REORGANIZATIONS, p. 518; and JENKS, THE TRUST PROBLEM, p. 87. Ely identifies the primary cause underlying the creation of large corporate enterprises as efficiency, which he takes pains to distinguish from monopoly; Ely, *The Nature and Significance of Monopolies and Trusts*, pp. 282–83; and ELY, STUDIES IN THE EVOLUTION OF INDUSTRIAL SOCIETY, p. 91, although Ely also explains the need for industrial cooperation in order to achieve that efficiency. *See ibid.*, pp. 89, 90. Charles Conant couples excessive competition with promoters' greed as the principal causes of the merger wave; CONANT, WALL STREET AND THE COUNTRY, p. 15. *See also* MEADE, TRUST FINANCE, pp. 56–57 (Meade argues that promoters' high profits were justifiable); NOYES, FORTY YEARS OF AMERICAN FINANCE, p. 286.

Modern historians also have debated the causes of the merger wave. Some say that it was the simple desire for monopoly, created out of the fire of competition, and the best way to achieve monopoly was to swallow your competitors. In some cases this was true. J. Fred Weston, looking at a sample of the largest mergers, as well as Moody's more comprehensive list, disputes the argument that most industries were characterized by large numbers of competing firms, and writes instead that these mergers consolidated relatively small numbers of already large plants. Most increases in corporate size, he argues, came from internal growth. But many of the corporations combined during the merger wave had themselves previously grown by consolidation. Gates's American Steel & Wire Company, for example, had acquired at least 28 different companies comprising at least 31 different plants during the few years before it was swallowed into the Steel Trust; WESTON, THE ROLE OF MERGERS IN THE GROWTH OF LARGE FIRMS, pp. 31–44.

Weston understates the number of corporations that had undergone combination prior to the merger wave. His reliance on John Moody's average of the 305 largest trusts (16) misrepresents, as do all averages, the significant competition existing in a number of industries. In addition, the 305 mergers he examines are only industrial corporations—Moody actually reports 440 "large industrial, franchise, and transportation trusts"; MOODY, THE TRUTH ABOUT THE TRUSTS, pp. xi, 485–86. Finally, Weston does not note data demonstrating significant variance in the reported number of firms that disappeared. Moody identifies 4,900 plants absorbed during the merger wave (except for the Sugar Trust which had earlier been completed).

Naomi Lamoreaux argues that too many new corporations in competitive mass production and capital intensive industries had sunk too much money into technological and marketing improvements. As a result, when the depression of 1893 brought decreased sales, these corporations were particularly "susceptible to price cutting" in order to continue operations and cover their fixed costs. This resulted in price wars that were resolved by the rationalization of industry through combination; LAMOREAUX, THE GREAT MERGER MOVEMENT IN AMERICAN BUSINESS, p. 85; O'Brien, *Factory Size*, pp. 639–49.

Alfred D. Chandler, Jr., describes the formation of the six major trusts in the

1880s as fully integrated, vertical operations that could take advantage of centralized managerial techniques, and attributes the success of the modern giant corporation to centralized and efficient management. But he also acknowledges a significant financial motivation for mergers at the end of the century; CHANDLER, THE VISIBLE HAND, pp. 331–35. The problem with Chandler's managerial argument is that while the true trusts, like Standard Oil, became vertically integrated over time, most of the mergers characterizing the merger wave were horizontal; Richard B. Du Boff and Edward S. Herman, *Mergers, Concentration, and the Erosion of Democracy*, Monthly Review, vol. 53, no. 1 (May 2001), pp. 14–29.

Yet another suggestion, supported by Ralph Nelson, is that the development of capital markets and fluctuations in securities prices at the end of the nineteenth century were a significant cause of the merger movement, as was businessmen's desire for market control; NELSON, MERGER MOVEMENTS IN AMERICAN INDUSTRY. Navin and Sears give a variety of reasons, from the desire to avoid destructive competition to plant owners' and their families' interests in liquidating their investments; Navin & Sears, *The Rise of a Market for Industrial Securities*. George Stigler, Jesse Markham and, in part, Myron Watkins conclude that it was promoters' profits from producing and selling securities that was the primary motivation; GEORGE J. STIGLER, THE ORGANIZATION OF INDUSTRY, pp. 101–3; Jesse W. Markham, *Survey on the Evidence and Findings of Mergers*, pp. 141, 162–65. WATKINS, INDUSTRIAL COMBINATIONS AND PUBLIC POLICY, p. 33; REID, MERGERS, MANAGERS AND THE ECONOMY, p. 40, found a "common thread of agreement" that the promoter was important.

Stigler notes that mergers for the purpose of monopolizing given industries would likely have been profitable long before the merger wave actually happened. Lance Davis tends to agree with Nelson, that the impetus for the merger wave was financial, but adds, through an interesting comparison with the United Kingdom, that in the latter country capital markets had been so well developed for so long that smaller enterprises had easy access to capital and did not need to combine, whereas in the traditionally poor capital markets of the United States, access to capital was available only to large enterprises. The improvement in American capital markets in the late nineteenth century led to even greater concentration as already large companies sought more capital; Lance Davis, *The Capital Markets and Industrial Concentration*. George Bittlingmayer argues that Supreme Court antitrust jurisprudence was a likely cause of the merger wave; Bittlingmayer, *Did Antitrust Policy Cause the Great Merger Wave?*.

Most economic and business historians have focused on the business consequences of the mergers in terms of productive efficiency and industrial concentration rather than on the consequences for the financial structure of the American economy.

4. *See, e.g.*, BENTLEY, THE SCIENCE OF ACCOUNTS, p. 37: "The question of value of property taken in exchange for stock is, however, left to the judgment of the directors, which frequently results in property being taken over by corporations at greatly inflated values."

5. The Drew story is found in slightly different versions in multiple sources. I have relied upon KLEIN, THE LIFE AND LEGEND OF JAY GOULD, p. 77; JOSEPHSON, THE ROBBER BARONS, p. 18; and ALLEN, LORDS OF CREATION, p. 12.

6. The description of Vanderbilt is from ALLEN, LORDS OF CREATION, p. 100. RIPLEY, RAILROADS: FINANCE AND ORGANIZATION, p. 228; RIPLEY, RAILROADS: RATES AND REGULATION, pp. 444, 448; JOHNSON, AMERICAN RAILWAY TRANSPORTA- TION, pp. 403–5. Some corporations paid these dividends in bonds. Bond dividends were more dangerous for the corporation than stock dividends because directors had legal discretion as to whether to pay dividends on the corporation's stock but they had no choice but to pay interest on the bonds. The practice burdened the railroad engaged in it with higher fixed costs but no greater capital base with which to gener- ate more profit.

7. RIPLEY, TRUSTS, POOLS, AND CORPORATIONS, pp. xxiii–xxiv, notes that over- capitalization "invites unearned profits on the part of promoters, ... stimulates ex- travagance on the part of banking syndicates, ..." in setting prices for plant owners, "facilitates internal mismanagement ... [a]nd finally, it invites speculation and stock market jobbery." At the same time, he acknowledges that it was "certainly difficult to trace a direct relation between capitalization and prices," arguing that "the evils ascribed to overcapitalization are merely concomitant rather than resultant." Ripley remained a strong opponent of overcapitalization. Even some of the most staunch defenders of overcapitalization as a legitimate means of capitalizing a corporation's future profits recognized both its possibility for abuse and the ways, both legitimate and not, that it could be used to conceal a corporation's true rate of return. *See* COO- PER, FINANCING AN ENTERPRISE, pp. 175–76, 188; GREENE, CORPORATION FINANCE, pp. 134–45.

8. I follow Marian Sears, who, in her deeply insightful article on businessmen in 1900, writes: "The goal is to discover what businessmen of that day, rather than the historian of a later day, considered important"; Sears, *The American Business- man at the Turn of the Century*, p. 383. The important thinkers in my story include politicians and other policy-makers as well as businessmen, lawyers, economists and intellectuals.

It is far from clear that the combinations resulting from the merger wave gener- ally were successful. It is not my goal in this book to examine the successes or failures of the combinations, although I discuss some of the literature in this chapter. The resolution of that issue does not affect the conclusion that combination was seen as the solution to a major business problem. As to the successes or failures of combina- tions, *compare* Shaw Livermore, *The Success of Industrial Mergers*, *with* DEWING, CORPORATE PROMOTIONS AND REORGANIZATIONS; DEWING, FINANCIAL POLICY OF CORPORATIONS; LAMOREAUX, THE GREAT MERGER MOVEMENT IN AMERICAN BUSINESS; NELSON, MERGER MOVEMENTS IN AMERICAN INDUSTRY.

Overcapitalization made a meaningful difference with respect to the railroads, frequently natural monopolies and therefore different from industrial corporations; TRANSPORTATION ACT OF 1920, 49 U.S.C. 1.

9. I am grateful to Mary O'Sullivan for reminding me that the question of value underlying the issue of overcapitalization was as much a question about corporate governance as it was about finance. Both the resolution of the issue during the early part of the century and our contemporary solutions rely on the acceptance of share- holder value maximization as the touchstone for corporate behavior. Episodically

over the century, and certainly at the turn of the twenty-first century, that premise has been called into question; MITCHELL, CORPORATE IRRESPONSIBILITY; KENNEDY, THE END OF SHAREHOLDER VALUE.

Livermore, *The Success of Industrial Mergers*, p. 84; Martin, *Overcapitalization Has Little Meaning*, pp. 407–27. Benjamin Graham and David Dodd, in their landmark work on securities valuation, note that some corporations retained earnings rather than paid dividends in order to eliminate overcapitalization, that is, to eliminate goodwill from their balance sheets, as in the case of F. W. Woolworth or, similarly, to increase the value of their equity accounts to rectify their overvaluations of their assets, as in the case of U.S. Steel, which, they write, took until 1929 fully to account for the value of its watered common stock issued in 1901. They describe managements' desires to "make good these deficiencies" as "only natural"; GRAHAM & DODD, SECURITY ANALYSIS, pp. 326, 331–32.

10. Perhaps the best valuation book from the era is COOPER, FINANCING AN ENTERPRISE, vol. 1, pp. 163–251 *passim*, which gives an extraordinarily thoughtful, thorough and grounded lesson in the various stages and components of corporate valuation. Cooper notes that economists generally were leery of capitalizing goodwill, although businessmen were not. *Ibid.*, pp. 213–14. The story I tell in this chapter bears out Cooper's observation.

"Tangible assets" was the term typically used to describe the assets covered by preferred stock. In fact preferred stock was also often used to cover some intangibles, like patents. As a matter of historical accuracy, the term tangible assets should generally be read to exclude items that ordinarily would not appear on a corporation's balance sheet or income statement, like goodwill and future profits, but the Industrial Commission observed that some combinations would value intangible assets as "the cash selling value of the properties purchased as going concerns. This, of course, includes good will in its proper sense"; UNITED STATES INDUSTRIAL COMMISSION, FINAL REPORT, vol. 19, p. 617. A combination engaging in this practice and issuing common stock as well as preferred stock was arguably double-counting goodwill. Sometimes, as I discussed in Chapter Two, courts would ignore the value of all intangibles.

11. For a good history of the Havemeyer family as well as the history of the Sugar Trust itself, *see* MULLINS, THE SUGAR TRUST.

12. Testimony of Henry O. Havemeyer, June 14, 1899, UNITED STATES INDUSTRIAL COMMISSION, PRELIMINARY REPORT ON TRUSTS AND INDUSTRIAL COMBINATIONS, vol. 1, part 2, pp. 110–11. Even thirty years after the fact, when capitalizing earnings had become broadly accepted, Jenks remained somewhat tied to physical valuation as the appropriate standard of capitalization, although one cannot help but notice his equivocation. JENKS & CLARK, THE TRUST PROBLEM, pp. 201–8.

On Havemeyer and the Sugar Trust, *see* Franklin Clarkin, *The Great Business Combination of Today*, CENTURY ILLUSTRATED MAGAZINE, vol. 65, no. 3 (Jan. 1903), p. 470; Robert N. Burnett, *Henry Osborne Havemeyer*, THE COSMOPOLITAN, vol. 34, no. 6 (Apr. 1903), p. 701; Zerbe, *The American Sugar Refining Company*; Doyle, *Capital Structure and the Financial Development of the U.S. Sugar Refining Industry*.

Navin and Sears give substantial credit to "many industrialists" for having a solidly grounded knowledge of the value of their plants; Navin & Sears, *The Rise of a Market for Industrial Securities*, p. 132; MEADE, CORPORATION FINANCE, p. 43. A very general but positive explanation of the process is provided in Fairchild, *The Financiering of Trusts*.

13. James C. Bonbright, in his preface to DODD, STOCK WATERING, p. vi, suggests that the "death knell" that had been rung for overcapitalization by corporate finance theorists proclaiming the virtues of no-par stock was premature. Dodd's book provides substantial evidence that he was right. For readers who are engaged by the techniques of watering and the problems they created, detailed examination is provided in RIPLEY, RAILROADS: FINANCE AND ORGANIZATION, at chs. 7 and 8. Some thinkers, like the members of the Hughes Committee discussed in Chapter Seven, believed that par value led unsophisticated investors to think the stock was worth its nominal, or par, value; COOPER, FINANCING AN ENTERPRISE, pp. 175–76; CLEPHANE, THE ORGANIZATION AND MANAGEMENT OF BUSINESS CORPORATIONS, 2d ed., p. 98. There were experts, like Edward Meade, who took par value seriously enough to argue that it was management's responsibility to ensure that stock traded at par; Meade, *The Genesis of the United States Steel Corporation*, p. 517.

14. Par value at $100 was most common, although "the more speculative corporations such as mining companies" typically set par at $1.00. Other common amounts of par were $10 and $50; BENTLEY, CORPORATE FINANCE AND ACCOUNTING, p. 394.

15. *Sanger v. Upton*, 91 U.S. 56, 60 (1875); COOK, A TREATISE ON THE LAW OF CORPORATIONS, vol. 1, sec. 46 (noting cases in which shareholders were held liable only for the subscription prices of their stock and not the total par value if the latter was higher).

16. Hawkins, *The Development of Modern Financial Reporting Practices*, pp. 152–53. Manning and Hanks argue that the initial purpose of par value was to ensure that each subscriber paid an equal amount for his shares and that creditor protection was an afterthought (and a poor one at that). I do not evaluate the first point because the way par value came into being does not matter to my argument, only that the law did come to treat it as creditor-protective; MANNING & HANKS, LEGAL CAPITAL, p. 24.

17. Navin & Sears, *The Rise of a Market for Industrial Securities*, trace the development of a trading market for industrial securities as it developed after the depression of the mid-1890s.

18. Navin & Sears, *The Rise of a Market for Industrial Securities*, note that there was an upper limit on the prices plant owners would demand because they knew the value of their own plants and could come up with reasonable estimates of the value of the combination. Prices that were too high meant stock that was too risky, and suspicious plant sellers would then demand cash; Navin & Sears, *The Rise of a Market for Industrial Securities*, p. 132. In contrast, MEADE, CORPORATION FINANCE, pp. 37–40, describes the difficulty promoters had negotiating with sellers on the basis of earnings alone, showing that plant owners demanded high premia in order to be induced to sell their companies. Sears also notes that prices had to be sufficiently high in order for promoters to induce plant owners to take stock instead of cash; Sears, *The American Businessman at the Turn of the Century*, p. 412.

19. By 1910, New Jersey only allowed the issuance of stock for services in quasi-

public corporations, those involved in railroads, public utilities, tunnels, wharves, canals, hotels and the like. *See* Chapter Two, note 36. But other states, like Delaware, were less restrictive; 22 DEL. LAWS, ch. 166, sec. 1 (1901); 23 DEL. LAWS, ch. 155, sec. 1 (1904). Masslich, *Financing a New Corporate Enterprise*, p. 73, discusses the ways promoters evaded the rules prohibiting bonus stock.

20. I discuss the issue of disclosure in Chapter Four.

21. UNITED STATES INDUSTRIAL COMMISSION, REPORT ON TRUSTS AND INDUSTRIAL COMBINATIONS, vol. 13, pp. 14–15; MOODY, THE TRUTH ABOUT THE TRUSTS, p. 137; ALLEN, LORDS OF CREATION, p. 34; ALLEN, THE GREAT PIERPONT MORGAN, p. 183; Meade, *The Genesis of the United States Steel Corporation*, p. 546; CONANT, WALL STREET AND THE COUNTRY, pp. 17–18. Strouse puts the syndicate fee at a more modest $50 million in stock, and notes the outraged public reaction even of such business-friendly voices as *The Wall Street Journal*; STROUSE, MORGAN, p. 408. While she is sympathetic to the problems of valuing Steel, she concedes that the common stock was water; *id.*, p. 406. It is worth noting that within two decades Steel had fully grown into its capitalization. I should also note that Steel, like a number of combinations, sold some of its new stock to raise working capital in addition to the sales made by promoters and participants in the combination.

22. DOS PASSOS, COMMERCIAL TRUSTS.

23. LUDINGTON, JOHN DOS PASSOS, pp. 2–13; CARR, DOS PASSOS, pp. 9–14.

24. Testimony of Mr. John R. Dos Passos, Dec. 12, 1899, UNITED STATES INDUSTRIAL COMMISSION, PRELIMINARY REPORT ON TRUSTS AND INDUSTRIAL COMBINATIONS, vol. 1, p. 1150; Masslich, *Financing a New Corporate Enterprise*, p. 71.

25. UNITED STATES CONGRESS, SENATE, HEARINGS BEFORE THE COMMITTEE ON BANKING AND CURRENCY ON S. 3895, pp. 35, 88.

26. SEAGER & GULICK, TRUST AND CORPORATION PROBLEMS, p. 64. *See* BENTLEY, CORPORATE FINANCE AND ACCOUNTING, p. 399.

27. Although New Jersey's statute did not reach its final form until 1896, as I noted in Chapter Two, the law already permitted the purchase of stock for assets. The merger wave did not begin until 1897, but, prior to the Panic of 1893 and the depression that followed, there had been a mini-boom in corporate combinations in the early 1890s.

28. Luther Conant, Jr., *Industrial Consolidations in the United States*. Conant only looked at combinations with capitalizations above $1 million, but it is fair to say that corporations of this size were the ones that would have a significant effect on the stock market.

Seager and Gulick note that this method of valuation aided promoters in overcapitalizing their combinations and bailing out before they had a track record of performance; Seager & Gulick, TRUST AND CORPORATION PROBLEMS, pp. 65–66.

29. Navin and Sears report that a multiple of three times earnings was relatively common, at least before the merger wave; Navin & Sears, *The Rise of a Market for Industrial Securities*, p. 108; UNITED STATES INDUSTRIAL COMMISSION, REPORT ON TRUSTS AND INDUSTRIAL COMBINATIONS, vol. 13, pp. ix–xv. On "squeezing out the water" *see* SEYMOUR THOMPSON, COMMENTARIES ON THE LAW OF PRIVATE CORPORATIONS, 2d ed., vol. 4, sec. 3674; COTTER, THE AUTHENTIC HISTORY OF THE

UNITED STATES STEEL CORPORATION, p. 31; SALIERS, PRINCIPLES OF DEPRECIA-
TION, pp. 25–26; Baker, *Regulation of Industrial Corporations*, p. 321; Dill, *Industrials
as Investments for Small Capital*, p. 110; *Jobbery in Stocks Strongly Denounced*, NEW
YORK TIMES, Apr. 21, 1900, p. 3.

30. CAROSSO, INVESTMENT BANKING IN AMERICA, pp. 82–83. WEIL, SEARS,
ROEBUCK, U.S.A.; HISTORICAL STATISTICS OF THE UNITED STATES, MILLENNIAL
ED., Table Cj1238–1242.

31. SEAGER & GULICK, TRUST AND CORPORATION PROBLEMS, p. 66.

32. CLEPHANE, THE ORGANIZATION AND MANAGEMENT OF BUSINESS CORPO-
RATIONS, 2d ed., ch. 9; LOUGH, CORPORATION FINANCE, vol. 4, p. 348; Patterson,
The Problem of the Trusts, p. 8; KOLKO, THE TRIUMPH OF CONSERVATISM; DEWING,
CORPORATE PROMOTIONS AND REORGANIZATIONS, p. 533 (table). Compared with
Dewing, who does not blame merger failure on this overcapitalization (*id.* p. 531),
Kolko (who looked at a larger number of consolidations) argues that overcapitaliza-
tion had a significant role in the failure of consolidations; KOLKO, THE TRIUMPH OF
CONSERVATISM, p. 20; UNITED STATES INDUSTRIAL COMMISSION, FINAL REPORT,
vol. 19, p. 616; DEWING, CORPORATE PROMOTIONS AND REORGANIZATIONS.

33. Luther Conant, Jr., *Industrial Consolidations in the United States*; Noyes,
The Recent Economic History of the United States, p. 192. *Common Sense in Invest-
ments*, WALL STREET JOURNAL, June 27, 1902, p. 10; BURTON, CORPORATIONS AND
THE STATE, p. 29; Dill, *Industrials as Investments for Small Capital*, pp. 109–10; SEA-
GER & GULICK, TRUST AND CORPORATION PROBLEMS, p. 224; Baker, *Regulation of
Industrial Corporations*, pp. 306–31; Beck, *The Federal Power over Trusts*; Meade, *The
Investor's Interest in the Demands of the Anthracite Miners*, pp. 36–45. I have taken
Meade's assertion at face value, but it is worth noting that the article is an argument for
giving investors priority over labor in the case of the anthracite mine railroads because
of the precarious financial position of the roads, which had led to the nonpayment
of dividends to many investors. His discussion of promoters' interests is designed to
show that both stockholders and labor should be united against the promoters. Yarros,
The Trust Problem Restudied; BURTON, CORPORATIONS AND THE STATE, p. 29. Sears
claims that it was business interest in trust formation, not promoters' interests, that
stimulated the most activity, *The American Businessman at the Turn of the Century*,
p. 388, but also notes that common stock typically was given to promoters and that
the new combinations led to "tremendous activity" on stock exchanges. *Id.*, pp. 412,
414. Dewing evaluates a handful of promotions and concludes that, on average, 10
percent of water in combination capitalization went to promoters, another 10 percent
to bankers, 20 percent to plant owners "as a gift in excess of the value of their plants,"
15 percent "to the public as bait" to persuade them to buy the stock, and 5 percent
for other work done for the combination; DEWING, CORPORATE PROMOTIONS AND
REORGANIZATIONS, pp. 541–42, 538; DODD, STOCK WATERING, p. 99.

34. COMMERCIAL & FINANCIAL CHRONICLE, vol. 67, Aug. 27, 1898, p. 427; COM-
MERCIAL & FINANCIAL CHRONICLE, vol. 67, Dec. 31, 1898, p. 1349.

35. The Company's Official Statement upon completing the initial consolidation notes that Baring Magoun & Co. and F. S. Smithers & Co. underwrote "the new
company," not the stock, suggesting perhaps that all of the stock was issued to the

sellers and promoters. Baring, Magoun was one of the two principal industrial under-writers in New York before the turn of the twentieth century and an affiliate of the respected Boston firm, Kidder, Peabody. COMMERCIAL & FINANCIAL CHRONICLE, May 6, 1899, vol. 68, p. 872; COMMERCIAL & FINANCIAL CHRONICLE, Apr. 22, 1899, vol. 68, p. 774; CAROSSO, INVESTMENT BANKING IN AMERICA, p. 44.

36. COMMERCIAL & FINANCIAL CHRONICLE, Feb. 4, 1899, p. 224; COMMERCIAL & FINANCIAL CHRONICLE, May 13, 1899, vol. 68, pp. 292, 930; COMMERCIAL & FINANCIAL CHRONICLE, Nov. 17, 1899, vol. 69, p. 1010; COMMERCIAL & FINANCIAL CHRONICLE, Dec. 30, 1899, vol. 69; *Flour Trust in Danger,* LOS ANGELES TIMES, Jan. 26, 1900, p. 12.

37. Whether shareholders relied upon nominal capital is less clear. Sears, *The American Businessman at the Turn of the Century,* p. 412 (quoting Iron Age to the effect that nobody took nominal capital seriously); CLEPHANE, THE ORGANIZATION AND MANAGEMENT OF BUSINESS CORPORATIONS, 2d ed., p. 98 (stating that the public believes nominal capital to be equal to stated capital).

38. FISHER, THE NATURE OF CAPITAL AND INCOME, p. 80. Concern for investor well-being was articulated by some reformers. Burton writes that "the investor is the one who has suffered most from … overcapitalization," yet the laws ignored him; BURTON, CORPORATIONS AND THE STATE, p. 116. The Supreme Court had sanctioned the use of goodwill in capitalization; CLEPHANE, THE ORGANIZATION AND MANAGEMENT OF BUSINESS CORPORATIONS, 2d ed., p. 100. It had also taken a sophisticated approach to the valuation of a corporation for taxation purposes by approving the assessment of the market value of its capital stock as an appropriate means of corporate valuation, clearly and expressly including the corporation's goodwill; *Adams Express Company v. Ohio State Auditor,* 165 U.S. 194 (1897); *San Francisco National Bank v. Dodge,* 197 U.S. 70 (1905). Speech of R. S. Taylor, in CHICAGO CONFERENCE ON TRUSTS, pp. 72–73 (but stressing that consumers more important); Speech of James R. Weaver, *id.,* p. 295; Speech of Edward W. Bemis, *id.,* p. 397, but investor protection was at best a tertiary theme during the period and did not attract significant federal attention.

39. U.S. Steel began a practice of retaining and reinvesting earnings shortly after its formation so that by 1929 its asset value was equal to its capitalization; COTTER, THE AUTHENTIC HISTORY OF THE UNITED STATES STEEL CORPORATION, p. 31 (claims water eliminated by 1915); Baker, *Regulation of Industrial Corporations,* p. 321; McCraw & Reinhardt, *Losing to Win,* p. 595 (noting successful distribution and long-term performance of Steel stock "despite press complaints about watering"). Other combinations reduced the outstanding amount of their securities as a means of reducing or eliminating overcapitalization; RIPLEY, TRUSTS, POOLS AND CORPORATIONS, pp. xxiv–xxv.

40. Franklin Clarkin, *The Great Business Combination of Today,* CENTURY ILLUSTRATED MAGAZINE, vol. 65, no. 3 (Jan. 1903), p. 470; Zerbe, *The American Sugar Refining Company.*

41. UNITED STATES INDUSTRIAL COMMISSION, FINAL REPORT, vol. 19, pp. 641–42. Noyes is characteristically unsympathetic, describing the public's appetite for stock during the merger wave as something of a feeding frenzy; Noyes, *The Recent*

Economic History of the United States, p. 191, *passim*. Both Cooper and Greene complained about the distorting effect of stated par value, and the securities commissions of the end of the decade, which I discuss in Chapter Seven, also recommended eliminating par as a means of reducing speculation; COOPER, FINANCING AN ENTERPRISE, vol. 1, pp. 175–76, 188; GREENE, CORPORATION FINANCE, pp. 134–35, 138–39.

42. Goodwill is, of course, an asset. But unlike tangible assets, and even intangibles like patents, it was particularly difficult to value, especially in the case of a newly formed combination.

43. Despite the unsophisticated public debate, the concept of using going-concern value by capitalizing earnings was well understood. COTTER, THE AUTHENTIC HISTORY OF THE UNITED STATES STEEL CORPORATION, p. 29; CLEPHANE, THE ORGANIZATION AND MANAGEMENT OF BUSINESS CORPORATIONS, 2d ed., pp. 99–100; ROLLINS, MONEY AND INVESTMENTS, p. 212. But its practice was heavily debated. Writing in 1928 about public utility valuation, John Sumner examines the many different ways "going value" was defined, describing it as "one of the seemingly insoluble and least understood elements encountered in the development of principles of ratemaking valuation," and "the most intangible of the intangibles"; Sumner, *Going Value*, p. 59. Railroads presented an opportunity well before the merger wave for valuation techniques to have been developed. But railroads were different. As natural monopolies, goodwill would not have been part of their valuation for ratemaking purposes. And overcapitalization of the railroads typically took the form of bonus stock where admittedly no consideration was received by the corporation. It may simply be that the obviousness of the practice required no further elaboration; RIPLEY, RAILROADS: FINANCE AND ORGANIZATION, pp. 35, 232–67. Cooper had no problem exploring the various aspects of valuing goodwill and coming up with some rather good rules for determining it; COOPER, FINANCING AN ENTERPRISE, vol. 1, ch. 20.

44. James C. Bonbright, *Preface* to DODD, STOCK WATERING, p. v (noting that judicial valuation methods vary greatly with the purpose of valuation); *id.*, p. 100 (Dodd discussing the unsuitability of other valuation methods for the purpose of valuing corporate stock), pp. 101, 102.

45. DODD, STOCK WATERING, *esp.* chs. 6 and 7 and pp. 269–70, reaches this conclusion after an exhaustive analysis of the cases.

46. As should be clear so far, practitioners like Greene, an auditor, and Conyngton, a lawyer (and Cooper, Conyngton's *nom de plume*) were far more engaged in the subject of valuation, and far more advanced in their approaches, than were the theoretical economists.

47. COMMAGER, THE AMERICAN MIND, p. 229. In 1917, William T. Lough, former professor of finance at New York University and president of the Business Training Corporation, tied the legal and economic problems together more neatly perhaps than anyone: "It may be asked why the courts do not more frequently enforce a closer adherence to the intent of the law [in valuing intangibles as well as physical assets.] . . . The intangible assets and the services which are accepted by corporations in payment for their stock are difficult to value, and for this reason it is only in exceptional cases that bad faith on the part of corporations in making their valuations can be conclusively shown"; LOUGH, BUSINESS FINANCE, p. 94.

48. COMMONS, LEGAL FOUNDATIONS OF CAPITALISM. It bears noting that the proliferation of books on corporate valuation and finance did not really begin until the mid-1920s. *E.g.*, BADGER, VALUATION OF SECURITIES (quotation from p. vii); SLOAN, EVERYMAN AND HIS COMMON STOCKS; SMITH, COMMON STOCKS AS LONG TERM INVESTMENTS; and GRAHAM & DODD, SECURITY ANALYSIS.

49. ESQUERRE, THE APPLIED THEORY OF ACCOUNTS, p. v. Thorstein Veblen, whose appreciation of the soundness of capitalizing earnings was perfectly clear, writes: "Earning-capacity is practically accepted as the effective basis of capitalization for corporate business concerns, particularly for those whose securities are quoted on the market. It is in the stock market that this effective capitalization takes place. But the law does not recognize such a basis of capitalization, nor are business men generally ready to adopt it in set form. . . ."; VEBLEN, THE THEORY OF BUSINESS ENTERPRISE, p. 70, n. 5. Irving Fisher, the first American mathematician to become an economist, was equally influenced by legal principles in discussing valuation. Although he was perhaps the first economist to introduce cash flow as a substitute for more stylized accounting concepts, like earnings, into the calculus of value, he did not venture far from the corporate balance sheet in his discussion of overcapitalization. But Fisher carefully distinguishes between corporate valuation and stock valuation in developing his theory of value; FISHER, THE NATURE OF CAPITAL AND INCOME, pp. 71–72, 77–78, 101, 103, 203, 227 *et. seq.* John R. Commons drew his entire theory of value from the history of the law; COMMONS, LEGAL FOUNDATIONS OF CAPITALISM.

During this period Clark developed a clear account of marginal theory and Veblen introduced the groundwork for institutional economics. It was also during this period that economics began to become the distinct branch of study that it is today, replacing the earlier broad discipline of political economy. DORFMAN, THE ECONOMIC MIND IN AMERICAN CIVILIZATION, pp. 369–70. *See also* LYON, CAPITALIZATION. Lyon, both a lawyer and a finance professor at Dartmouth's Amos Tuck School of Administration and Finance, as late as 1912 treated par value as the cash equivalent of asset value, and asset value as the only basis for capitalization, although he defended the practice of overcapitalization to compensate promoters. He did not even mention capitalizing earnings, although he briefly discussed separating the "speculation" from the "investment." In his extreme conservatism, Lyon strikes me as a bit of an outlier, but his book demonstrates the tenacity of legally based thinking about valuation.

50. MEADE, COPORATION FINANCE, p. 40; Meade, *The Genesis of the United States Steel Corporation*, p. 517.

51. RIPLEY, TRUSTS, POOLS, AND CORPORATIONS, pp. 121–48.

52. RIPLEY, MAIN STREET AND WALL STREET, pp. 192–93.

53. JENKS, THE TRUST PROBLEM, 1st ed., pp. 98–106.

Richard Ely wrote very little about capitalization and valuation in discussing the trust issue, but from the little he wrote he appears to have favored physical valuation. In an early discussion of corporate capitalization, he raises the subject of Wisconsin's use of physical valuation in railroad regulation, and notes that "physical valuation is one element only, but it certainly is one of very great importance." But he also claims to have modified his position in opposition to stock watering. Corporations needed capital at different rates and might legitimately keep stock payments below par for a time. This does not give us direct evidence of Ely's thoughts on valuation, but his emphasis on the legal notion of paid-in capital does reinforce the conclusion that he was committed to physical valuation. Commons, in the introduction to *Legal Foundations of Capitalism*, mentions the difficulty he and his students had encountered in determining the judicial meaning of "reasonable value"; little was to be found in the writings of economists, "except those of Professor Ely that threw light on the subject." Ely seems also to have been tied to the legal model; ELY, MONOPOLIES AND TRUSTS, p. 270; Swayze *et al.*, *Capitalization of Corporations*, pp. 424–25; COMMONS, LEGAL FOUNDATIONS OF CAPITALISM, p. vii.

54. For example, *see* MARCUS NADLER, CORPORATE CONSOLIDATIONS AND REORGANIZATIONS, p. 135 *et seq.* The particularly interesting aspect of Nadler's book is that his training was as a lawyer, yet he assumes capitalized earnings to be the only method of valuation to be used in valuing combinations. No other valuation method is even discussed. Two other relatively late contributions to the valuation debate stand out. Arthur Hadley tackles the distinction between law and finance straight on, arguing that the first and determinative question in any valuation proceeding was the purpose for which the valuation was being made. Railroad ratemaking, for example, was more in the nature of a government assessment or tax than any meaningful attempt to determine the economic value of the road; Hadley, *The Meaning of Valuation*. John R. Commons struggles to draw out of legal history an economic concept of valuation that recognizes the centrality of going-concern value and goodwill, drawing heavily (if often implicitly) on his teacher Veblen's distinction between industry and business; COMMONS, LEGAL FOUNDATIONS OF CAPITALISM, ch. 8.

55. Stockwell, *Appraisements*. Sometimes appraisers were hired by promoters. The Audit Company of New York, of which financial writer Thomas Greene was vice president, performed an appraisal for Charles Flint's Rubber Goods Manufacturing Company. Flint was the prototype of the promoter, but the underwriters of the combination were highly reputable.

56. DODD, STOCK WATERING, pp. 25–26.

57. DODD, STOCK WATERING, pp. 54, 25, 135, 98, 101, 104, 159, 118, 214 and *passim*; COMMONS, LEGAL FOUNDATIONS OF CAPITALISM, p. vii.

58. UNITED STATES INDUSTRIAL COMMISSION, FINAL REPORT, vol. 19, pp. 408–12, 415–16, 616–18.

59. UNITED STATES CONGRESS, HOUSE OF REPRESENTATIVES, REPORT NO. 3375, 57th Cong., 2d Sess., Jan. 26, 1903, pp. 20, 21; CONGRESSIONAL RECORD, 57th Cong., 2d Sess., vol. 36, pp. 1291–1915 (Feb. 5–7, 1903).

FOUR: THE NEW PROPERTY

1. MARKHAM, A FINANCIAL HISTORY OF THE UNITED STATES, vol. 1, pp. 330–33; NOYES, FORTY YEARS OF AMERICAN FINANCE; Ray Stannard Baker, *The New Prosperity*, MCCLURE'S MAGAZINE, vol. 15, no. 1 (May 1900), pp. 86–94.

2. NOYES, FORTY YEARS OF AMERICAN FINANCE, pp. 257–58; *Future of this Country*, NEW YORK TIMES, Sept. 29, 1901, p. 19 (reflecting continuing European fears of American financial dominance).

3. NOYES, FORTY YEARS OF AMERICAN FINANCE, p. 265.

4. Ray Stannard Baker, *The New Prosperity*, MCCLURE'S MAGAZINE, vol. 15, no. 1 (May 1900), pp. 86–94; NOYES, FORTY YEARS OF AMERICAN FINANCE, pp. 273–83; MEADE, TRUST FINANCE, p. 5; Henry Clews, *The Citadel of Money Power: I. Wall Street, Past, Present, and Future*, THE ARENA, vol. 18, no. 92 (July 1897), p. 1; An American, *The Degradation of Wall Street*, FRANK LESLIE'S POPULAR MONTHLY, vol. 57, no. 2 (Dec. 1903), p. 0_048 (noting 1900 as the "high water mark" of American prosperity); *Investors Inclined to Wait*, NEW YORK TIMES, Dec. 10, 1896, p. 10; *As the Brokers View It*, NEW YORK TIMES, Feb. 14, 1897, p. 17; *The Financial Situation*, NEW YORK TIMES, Jan. 10, 1897, p. 17; *Business Outlook Bright*, NEW YORK TIMES, Dec. 31, 1897, p. 8; *Early Morning Matter*, WALL STREET JOURNAL, Apr. 24, 1895, p. 2; *The Bond Market*, WALL STREET JOURNAL, Feb. 5, 1897, p. 2; *Plenty of Money to Invest*, WALL STREET JOURNAL, Nov. 19, 1897, p. 2; *A Promoter Talks*, WASHINGTON POST, July 5, 1895, p. 8; *Bond Bidders Innumerable*, WASHINGTON POST, Feb. 5, 1896, p. 6; *Why Investors Are Hesitating*, WASHINGTON POST, Jan. 6, 1897, p. 3; *The Year in Wall Street*, BROOKLYN EAGLE, Dec. 31, 1897, p. 14.

5. *How to Choose Investments*, WALL STREET JOURNAL, May 1, 1899, p. 1; *Hints on Finance for Women*, ARTHUR'S HOME MAGAZINE, vol. 46, no. 6 (June 1897), p. 382B; Mrs. Finley Anderson, *Women in Wall Street: The American Woman in Action*, FRANK LESLIE'S POPULAR MONTHLY, vol. 57, no. 5 (Mar. 1899), p. 22; *Woman as a Financier*, CHICAGO DAILY TRIBUNE, Feb. 21, 1900, p. 16; Charles H. Dow, *The Woman with a Little Money to Invest*, LADIES' HOME JOURNAL, vol. 22, no. 11 (Oct. 1903), p. 12; An American, *The Degradation of Wall Street*, FRANK LESLIE'S POPULAR MONTHLY, vol. 57, no. 2 (Dec. 1903), p. 0_048; George Morris Philips, *What to Do with Small Savings*, LADIES' HOME JOURNAL, vol. 22, no. 10 (Sept. 1905), p. 28; Alexander D. Noyes, *Finance*, FORUM, vol. 35, no. 3 (Jan. 1904), p. 353.

6. The Rev. Daniel H. Overton, *The Real Riches*, BROOKLYN EAGLE, May 13, 1901, p. 12. Some cautioned clergymen themselves to go no further than "'gilt-edged'" corporate bonds. Professor L. T. Townsend, *Christian Ministers and Money Matters IV*, CHRISTIAN ADVOCATE, May 2, 1901, p. 690; *Farmers Money in Bonds*, WALL STREET JOURNAL, Feb. 1, 1904, p. 5.

7. *Savings Versus Gambling*, NEW YORK TIMES, Apr. 18, 1900, p. 6; *The Bond Market: Investments; The Secret of Great Wealth*, WALL STREET JOURNAL, Dec. 15, 1904, p. 5; *Savings Bank Investments*, WALL STREET JOURNAL, Apr. 14, 1903, p. 8.

8. *Many Losers in Washington*, NEW YORK TIMES, May 11, 1901, p. 2; *Review and Outlook, A Remarkable Period*, WALL STREET JOURNAL, Mar. 3, 1901, p. 1; *The Mighty Power of a Few Words*, WALL STREET JOURNAL, Aug. 14, 1901, p. 8; *Studies in Value*, WALL STREET JOURNAL, Dec. 7, 1901, p. 1; *Common Sense in Investments*, WALL STREET JOURNAL, June 27, 1902, p. 1; *Sound Investments*, WASHINGTON POST, July 20, 1902, p. 4; WALL STREET JOURNAL editorial quoted in MEADE, TRUST FINANCE, pp. 150–51; *Who Own the Corporations*, NEW YORK TIMES, Oct. 4, 1908, p. 8.

9. Noyes, *The Recent Economic History of the United States*, p. 205.

10. MOODY, THE TRUTH ABOUT THE TRUSTS, pp. 479–82. Despite the fallout from the Panic of 1903, the period between 1897 and 1907 largely was characterized by a continuous bull market; SOBEL, THE BIG BOARD, pp. 153, 182. *See also* UNITED

STATES INDUSTRIAL COMMISSION, REPORT ON TRUSTS AND INDUSTRIAL COMBINA-
TIONS, vol. 13, p. ix.

11. *Investment Buying in Stocks Heavy*, NEW YORK TIMES, Nov. 16, 1907, p. 13;
A Market View, WALL STREET JOURNAL, Nov. 4, 1907, p. 7; *If A Ban Should Be Put
on Speculation*, NEW YORK TIMES, Mar. 1, 1908, p. SM1. Bargain buying evidently
"took" with the average investor; C. M. Keys, *The Buyer of Bargains*, LOS ANGELES
TIMES, Aug. 1, 1913, p. II9.

I should note that this report, while expressing the turnover rate without comment, was issued in the spring of 1908, following the fall Panic of 1907 in which
turnover could be expected to have been unusually high. Sobel describes turnover
rates of 200 percent in each of four years during the period 1900 to 1907, rates he calls
historically unprecedented as of 1965; SOBEL, THE BIG BOARD, p. 159.

12. WIEBE, THE SEARCH FOR ORDER, pp. 166, 164; HOFSTADTER, THE AGE OF
REFORM, p. 216.

13. UNITED STATES INDUSTRIAL COMMISSION, FINAL REPORT, vol. 19, pp. 804–
5. The increase in wage workers and their loss of control over their jobs had been
taking place for quite some time; MONTGOMERY, CITIZEN WORKER.

14. Romyn Hitchcock, *Corporate Regulation*, Letter to the Editor, NEW YORK
TIMES, June 2, 1900, p. 8.

15. Grosscup, *The Corporation Problem and the Lawyer's Part in Its Solution*;
Grosscup, *The Rebirth of the Corporation*, AMERICAN MAGAZINE, vol. 62, no. 2 (June
1906), p. 188; *Who Shall Own America? A Study of the Corporation Problem*, NEW
YORK TIMES, Nov. 26, 1905, p. SM6; Aldace F. Walker, *Anti-Trust Legislation*, FORUM
(May 1899), p. 257; Dill, *Some Tendencies in Combinations Which May Become Dan-
gerous*, p. 177; *The Real Danger in Trusts*, CENTURY MAGAZINE, vol. 60, no. 1 (May
1900), p. 152; Edward Godwin Johns and Duncan Macarthur, *The Concentration of
Commerce*, THE ARENA, vol. 24, no. 1 (July 1900), p. 3.

16. Editorials, *The Reign of Law and the Modern Tools of Industry*, McCLURE'S
MAGAZINE, vol. 30, no. 4 (Feb. 1908), p. 516; *Incorporating Farms*, WASHINGTON
POST, Sept. 1, 1907, p. 2.

17. *"The Tyranny of Capital,"* NEW YORK TIMES, July 6, 1899, p. 6.

18. The Vanderlip quote is found in *A Nation of Investors*, WALL STREET JOUR-
NAL, Oct. 26, 1904, p. 1. The *Journal* expressed its own opinion on the dangers of
investing as the French did only three years later; *A Timely Warning*, WALL STREET
JOURNAL, Jan. 29, 1907, p. 1.

19. *Who Own the Corporations*, NEW YORK TIMES, Oct. 4, 1908, p. 8.

20. *Workmen as Investors*, NEW YORK TIMES, May 8, 1903, p. 8.

21. *Two Million Partners Own the Corporations*, NEW YORK TIMES, Oct. 4, 1908,
p. SM1; *Steel Trust's Plan Approved*, NEW YORK TIMES, Jan. 11, 1903, p. 10; *Workmen
as Investors*, NEW YORK TIMES, May 8, 1903, p. 8; *Not Eager for Steel Stocks*, WASH-
INGTON POST, Jan. 13, 1906, p. 3; Warshow, *The Distribution of Corporate Ownership
in the United States*, p. 32. McCraw and Reinhardt provide the number of Steel workers; McCraw & Reinhardt, *Losing to Win*, p. 598.

22. *Workingmen as Capitalists*, NEW YORK TIMES, Feb. 17, 1903, p. 8.

23. *Labor's New Doctrine*, NEW YORK TIMES, Dec. 14, 1903, p. 1; *The Emancipation of Labor*, NEW YORK TIMES, Dec. 15, 1903, p. 8.

24. *Lawyers on the Trusts*, BOSTON DAILY GLOBE, Sept. 25, 1903, p. 6.

25. *Gov. Black Signs 22 Bills*, NEW YORK TIMES, Apr. 14, 1898, p. 11; *Railroad Bonds as Securities*, WALL STREET JOURNAL, Feb. 12, 1904, p. 1; *The Investing Public*, WALL STREET JOURNAL, May 5, 1904, p. 1; Davis, *The Investment Market*, p. 383. KELLER, THE LIFE INSURANCE ENTERPRISE, provides a richly detailed picture of insurance company investment practices and their move from investing primarily in real estate mortgages to corporate securities during the period he studies.

26. *Men Who Make the Market*, WALL STREET JOURNAL, Oct. 23, 1905, p. 1.

27. *Tendencies of Bank Investments*, WALL STREET JOURNAL, Nov. 4, 1905, p. 1.

28. As early as 1905, *The Wall Street Journal* noted the argument that permitting bank investments in bonds would lead to bank speculation in securities; *Tendencies of Bank Investments*, WALL STREET JOURNAL, Nov. 4, 1905, p. 1. It is fair to say that the argument was prescient. *If A Ban Should Be Put on Speculation*, NEW YORK TIMES, Mar. 1, 1908, p. SM1. NOYES, FORTY YEARS OF AMERICAN FINANCE, pp. 355–78, gives a detailed account of the Panic of 1907.

29. *The Investing Public*, WALL STREET JOURNAL, May 5, 1904, p. 1; *A Nation of Investors*, WALL STREET JOURNAL, Oct. 26, 1904, p. 1; *Two Million Partners Own the Corporations*, NEW YORK TIMES, Oct. 4, 1908, p. SM1; Hawkins, *The Development of Modern Financial Reporting Practices*, p. 145; Warshow, *The Distribution of Corporate Ownership in the United States*.

30. *Chicago News*, reprinted in THE WALL STREET JOURNAL, Sept. 21, 1907, p. 6.

31. MEADE, TRUST FINANCE, pp. 115–17.

32. MEADE, TRUST FINANCE, p. 122. The Pennsylvania listed only "capital stock," without classification, in its annual reports; COMMERCIAL & FINANCIAL CHRONICLE, vol. 82, Mar. 9, 1901, p. 489.

33. Edward Sherwood Meade, *What Chance Has a "Lamb" in the Stock Market?*, LIPPINCOTT'S MONTHLY MAGAZINE, vol. 88, no. 525 (Sept. 1911), p. 441; Meade, *Safe Methods of Speculation*, id., vol. 88, no. 526 (Oct. 1911), p. 603; Meade, *Shall I Buy Stocks or Bonds?*, id., vol. 88, no. 527 (Nov. 1911), p. 763; Meade, *Safe Investments*, id., vol. 88, no. 528 (Dec. 1911), p. 924; Meade, *The Banking House as an Aid to Investors*, id., vol. 89, no. 529 (Jan. 1912), p. 156.

34. *See generally* HAWKINS, CORPORATE FINANCIAL DISCLOSURE.

35. On the lack of disclosure and the frequency of professional manipulation *see The Financial Situation*, NEW YORK TIMES, Jan. 10, 1897, p. 17; John C. Sanborn, *The Wrong and the Remedy*, Letter to the Editor, NEW YORK TIMES, Apr. 30, 1897, p. 8; Charles A. Conant, *The Uses of Speculation*, FORUM, vol. 31, no. 6 (Aug. 1901), p. 698; Dill, *Some Tendencies in Combinations Which May Become Dangerous*, p. 177; and Edward Godwin Johns and Duncan Macarthur, *The Concentration of Commerce*, THE ARENA, vol. 24, no. 1 (July 1900), p. 3.

36. *Report of the Board of Directors of the Westinghouse Electric and Manufacturing Co. to the Stockholders*, Feb. 20, 1901, in Historic Corporate Report Collection, Baker Library, Harvard University.

37. Hawkins, *The Development of Modern Financial Reporting Practices*. Testimony of Henry O. Havemeyer, June 14, 1889, UNITED STATES INDUSTRIAL COMMISSION, PRELIMINARY REPORT ON TRUSTS AND INDUSTRIAL COMBINATIONS, vol. 1, p. 123; *Credits and Corporation Economics*, WALL STREET JOURNAL, Dec. 30, 1903, p. 1.

38. Testimony of Mr. John R. Dos Passos, Dec. 12, 1899, UNITED STATES INDUSTRIAL COMMISSION, PRELIMINARY REPORT ON TRUSTS AND INDUSTRIAL COMBINATIONS, vol. 1, pp. 1142–69.

39. For Chandler's discussion of the development of railroad accounting, *see* CHANDLER, THE VISIBLE HAND, pp. 109–20.

40. Hawkins, *The Development of Modern Financial Reporting Practices*.

41. TEWELES & BRADLEY, THE STOCK MARKET, pp. 118–19; SOBEL, THE BIG BOARD; Hawkins, *The Development of Modern Financial Reporting Practices*; *Stock Exchange Plans*, NEW YORK TIMES, Mar. 12, 1882, p. 14; *The Investing Public*, WALL STREET JOURNAL, May 5, 1904, p. 1; MCLAREN, ANNUAL REPORTS TO STOCKHOLDERS.

42. NOYES, THE MARKET PLACE, pp. 142–43.

43. PREVITS & MERINO, A HISTORY OF ACCOUNTING IN AMERICA, p. 80; SOBEL, THE BIG BOARD, p. 178. Accounting courses were taught in a handful of universities, beginning in 1883 at the Wharton School of the University of Pennsylvania.

44. *Political Economy for Beginners*, WALL STREET JOURNAL, May 19, 1904, p. 1; *Wall Street Bargains*, PORTSMOUTH (N.H.) HERALD, Nov. 24, 1900, p. 3; DES MOINES DAILY READER, Feb. 16, 1902, p. 22; CAROSSO, INVESTMENT BANKING IN AMERICA, pp. 104–6. SOBEL, THE BIG BOARD, pp. 178–80, is more critical of advertising methods than is Carosso.

45. MEADE, TRUST FINANCE, pp. 130–37; *The Incorrigible Investor*, from CHICAGO DAILY TRIBUNE, WASHINGTON POST, Feb. 18, 1903, p. 6.

46. *See, for example, General Electric Company, Sixth Annual Report—For the Year Ending January 31, 1898*, COMMERCIAL & FINANCIAL CHRONICLE, vol. 66, Apr. 30, 1898, pp. 858–60; *First Annual Report to the Stockholders of the United Fruit Company for the Fiscal Year Ended August 31, 1900; Second Annual Report to the Stockholders of the United Fruit Company for the Fiscal Year Ended August 31, 1901; Third Annual Report of the International Paper Company for Fiscal Year Ending June 30, 1900*, all available in the Historic Corporate Report Collection, Baker Library, Harvard University. MCLAREN, ANNUAL REPORTS TO STOCKHOLDERS. The change in AT&T's reports from before Morgan's involvement to after he became the corporation's main banker is dramatic; COMMERCIAL & FINANCIAL CHRONICLE, vol. 72, Mar. 30, 1901, p. 625; COMMERCIAL & FINANCIAL CHRONICLE, vol. 80, Mar. 18, 1905, p. 1110; COMMERCIAL & FINANCIAL CHRONICLE, vol. 80, Mar. 25, 1905, pp. 1180 *et seq.*; CAROSSO, THE MORGANS, p. 493; STROUSE, MORGAN, p. 563.

47. RIPLEY, MAIN STREET AND WALL STREET; Brief, *Corporate Financial Reporting at the Turn of the Century*, provides a nicely nuanced discussion of the variety of accounting practices that existed during the first decade of the century.

48. PREVITS & MERINO, A HISTORY OF ACCOUNTANCY IN THE UNITED STATES, *esp.* chs. 4 and 5; Hawkins, *The Development of Modern Financial Reporting Practices*. The British accounting profession had been developing through local societies

of accountants from the 1850s in Scotland and the 1870s in England and Wales; Mi-RANTI, ACCOUNTANCY COMES OF AGE, p. 30.

49. The sophisticated reader will note that the combination of known capitalization and dividend rate would permit interested parties to reach some conclusions as to a corporation's business performance, since rate of return could at least be calculated. But one of the problems of overcapitalization combined with nondisclosure was that the trusts could hide their true performance. This became even more complicated by the legal ability of corporations to pay dividends from accumulated surplus (and sometimes paid-in capital) and thus pay dividends even in bad years, and by the introduction and rapid acceptance of the institution of no-par stock, which I will discuss later.

FIVE: THE COMPLEX WHOLE

1. WOODWARD, ORIGINS OF THE NEW SOUTH, ch. 11.

2. *United States v. E. C. Knight Company*, 156 U.S. 1 (1895); *United States v. Trans-Missouri Freight Association*, 166 U.S. 290 (1897); *United States v. Joint Traffic Association*, 171 U.S. 505 (1898); *Addyston Pipe and Steel Company v. United States*, 175 U.S. 211 (1899).

On antitrust policy generally, including the Supreme Court's early interpretations, *see* HOVENKAMP, ENTERPRISE AND AMERICAN LAW; LETWIN, LAW AND ECONOMIC POLICY IN AMERICA; THORELLI, THE FEDERAL ANTITRUST POLICY. There is a large body of work on the Supreme Court's interpretation of the Sherman Act between 1890 and 1911. For a nice argument summarizing the claim that the Supreme Court was behaving in an economically rational manner, and summarizing the literature that supports that claim, *see* John R. Carter, *From Peckham to White*.

Interstate Commission Appeals to Congress, ATLANTA JOURNAL, Dec. 22, 1904, p. 6; Raymond, *Roosevelt Backs Garfield Plan*, CHICAGO DAILY TRIBUNE, Dec. 23, 1904, p. 1; *Federal License to Corporations*, CHICAGO DAILY TRIBUNE, Dec. 22, 1904, p. 4; KNOX, THE COMMERCE CLAUSE OF THE CONSTITUTION AND THE TRUSTS. William Jennings Bryan, speaking at the first Chicago Conference on Trusts, noted that in the preceding three years far more people who had not worried about trusts had become worried, largely because of the increase in the number of trusts and their overcapitalization; CHICAGO CONFERENCE ON TRUSTS, pp. 496–97.

The states had not been idle in the face of federal paralysis. Twenty-seven of them had passed antitrust laws by 1900 and an additional four had adopted constitutional provisions relating to trusts. State courts were active, too. In Jenks's 1900 compilation of federal and state antitrust laws for the Industrial Commission, he wrote that many states found common law principles adequate to the task and "many courts have found these principles sufficient, even when special statutes were at hand"; UNITED STATES INDUSTRIAL COMMISSION, TRUSTS AND COMBINATIONS, vol. 2, p. 3.

3. MOWRY, THE ERA OF THEODORE ROOSEVELT, pp. 8–10. While securities problems were not front and center as such, some people understood them quickly.

Some recent evidence suggests that the separation of ownership from control began considerably earlier than this period. Eric Hilt begins to identify it as early perhaps as the 1820s in New York; Hilt, *When Did Ownership Separate from Control?* While this data is interesting, and while there may well have been some early separation of ownership from control, the creation of broad public markets for widely dispersed industrial stock did not take root until the merger wave.

4. Sternstein, *Corruption in the Gilded Age Senate*, gives an excellent account of how Nelson Aldrich, as senator, became a wealthy man by legislatively protecting the Sugar Trust.

MOWRY, THE ERA OF THEODORE ROOSEVELT, pp. 115–17, gives a good overview of the power structure in the Senate. A nice brief description of the development of the Republican party as the business party is given in RUSSELL, THE PRESIDENT MAKERS. For additional discussions of the Republican leadership, *see* MERRILL & MERRILL, THE REPUBLICAN COMMAND; MORRIS, THEODORE REX, pp. 71–75; CROLY, MARCUS ALONZO HANNA.

5. While I will explore Roosevelt's takeover of regulation later, it is worth noting the comments of the *Baltimore Sun* on the Nelson Amendment: "While it is amusing to find some of the corporations protesting in the name of 'State's rights' against the proposed enlargement of Federal power, and in the same breath charging that the States usurp power in the legislation aimed at the trusts, it is clear that the tendency is to minimize the power of the States to a dangerous extent. If this tendency is to prevail it will not be long before a State will be a mere geographical expression"; *Uncle Sam's "Big Stick" For Interstate Corporations*, BALTIMORE SUN, Dec. 23, 1904, p. 4.

Taft did not shy from antitrust controversy. He brought more antitrust litigation than Roosevelt and had considerably more faith in the courts, as a number of his administration's successful antitrust prosecutions attest; WIEBE, THE SEARCH FOR ORDER, p. 203.

6. For Democratic platforms, *see* The American Presidency Project, Political Party Platforms for 1896, 1900, 1904, 1908 and 1912, available at: http://www.presidency.ucsb.edu/platforms.php.

7. TSUK MITCHELL, ARCHITECT OF JUSTICE (analyzing the role of groups and collective institutions in Progressive America).

8. LAMOREAUX, THE GREAT MERGER MOVEMENT IN AMERICAN BUSINESS; *United States v. American Tobacco Co.*, 221 U.S. 106 (1911); *Standard Oil Co. of New Jersey v. United States*, 221 U.S. 1 (1911); HOVENKAMP, ENTERPRISE AND AMERICAN LAW; Chapter Seven; GRANT, MONEY OF THE MIND, pp. 113–15; CAROSSO, INVESTMENT BANKING IN AMERICA, pp. 84–85; PEACH, THE SECURITY AFFILIATES OF NATIONAL BANKS.

9. Bullock, *Trust Literature*, p. 168. I have, except where technically necessary or when quoting, tried to avoid as much as possible the word "trust" to describe the giant corporations, because for the most part this is a legal misnomer. It is worth noting the fact that before the merger wave of the late 1890s, trusts—whether in their original legal form or in the form of holding companies or corporate consolidations—were few and far between. The only truly significant technical trusts prior to the enactment of the Sherman Act, or during the period from 1879 to 1896, to which Seager and Gulick refer as "the period of the trust proper" (SEAGER & GULICK, TRUST AND CORPORATION PROBLEMS, p. 49), were the Standard Oil Trust, the Sugar Trust,

the Cotton-Seed Oil Trust, the Linseed Oil Trust, the National Lead Trust and the Whiskey Trust. Other dominant business groups during this period, organized either as corporations or holding companies, were Diamond Match Company, American Tobacco Company, United States Rubber Company, General Electric Company and United States Leather Company. The real proliferation of giant corporations (other than, of course, the railroads), began to take place only at the end of the 1890s, and when they began to explode, they typically took the form either of consolidated corporations or holding companies.

10. STATUTES AT LARGE OF THE UNITED STATES OF AMERICA FROM MARCH, 1897 TO MARCH 1899, vol. 30, ch. 466; GOULD, THE PRESIDENCY OF WILLIAM MCKINLEY, pp. 161–64. McKinley evidently had no particular interest in the trusts while in Congress, and his first statement as president about the issue (and perhaps his only statement) was made to Congress as part of the presidential campaign of 1900. Even when he recognized the political need to address the issue of trusts he chose not to, as, for example, in his final speech on Sept. 5, 1901 in Buffalo, New York, the day before he was shot; *President M'Kinley Favors Reciprocity*, NEW YORK TIMES, Sept. 6, 1901, p. 1; LEECH, IN THE DAYS OF MCKINLEY, pp. 35, 119, 547, 575–76. RHODES, THE MCKINLEY AND ROOSEVELT ADMINISTRATIONS, only mentions trusts once in the portion of the book dealing with McKinley's administration, and that in connection with Bryan's opposition to the trusts. Only McKinley's hagiographer writes that he clearly saw the dangers posed by trusts and was working hard to develop legislation, but even this writer dates McKinley's concern to be as late as the 1899 to 1900 period; OLCOTT, THE LIFE OF WILLIAM MCKINLEY, vol. 2, pp. 298–300.

11. Salvato, *Historical Note*; KOLKO, THE TRIUMPH OF CONSERVATISM, pp. 66, 129; SKLAR, THE CORPORATE RECONSTRUCTION OF AMERICAN CAPITALISM, pp. 204 *et seq.*; WEINSTEIN, THE CORPORATE IDEAL IN THE LIBERAL STATE, pp. 8, 9; JENSEN, THE NATIONAL CIVIC FEDERATION, pp. 23, vii–viii and *passim*. The work of the NCF will be discussed more thoroughly in Chapters Seven and Eight.

12. CHICAGO CONFERENCE ON TRUSTS, pp. 5, 12–26; *Trust Conference Begun*, NEW YORK TIMES, Sept. 14, 1899, p. 1.

13. CHICAGO CONFERENCE ON TRUSTS, p. 7; the delegates are identified by affiliation and name at pp. 12–26.

14. CHICAGO CONFERENCE ON TRUSTS, Jenks at p. 27, Wooten at p. 42; *Trust Conference Begun*, NEW YORK TIMES, Sept. 14, 1899, p. 1.

15. CHICAGO CONFERENCE ON TRUSTS, Bonaparte at p. 620, Bryan at p. 496.

16. CHICAGO CONFERENCE ON TRUSTS, Howe at pp. 623–25.

17. CHICAGO CONFERENCE ON TRUSTS, p. 626.

18. Legislative data was drawn from a complete examination of the *Congressional Record* during this period as well as the bills introduced, ranging from the 47th Congress to the first year of the 56th Congress. The period from 1881 to the introduction of the Sherman Act in 1889 was not a particularly active one legislatively. Standard Oil had not taken its final form until 1882. But Congress did investigate trusts during this period and some legislation was introduced.

Another two proposed pieces of legislation beyond those mentioned in the text would have given United States district attorneys power to initiate antitrust actions without the approval of the attorney general: H.R. 8358, introduced on Feb. 12, 1900, 56th Cong., 1st Sess.; S. 5849, introduced on Feb. 2, 1901, 56th Cong., 2d Sess.; and another four were offered as amendments to the only legislatively successful antitrust bill, the Sherman Antitrust Act of 1890. The Sherman Act is codified at 15 U.S.C. 1–7.

19. *See, e.g.*, H.R. 91, introduced on Dec. 18, 1889, 51st Cong., 2d Sess.; H.R. 89, introduced on Jan. 5, 1892, 52d Cong., 1st Sess.; H.R. 11343, introduced on Sept. 3, 1888, 50th Cong., 1st Sess.; S. 1, introduced on Dec. 4, 1889 (the Sherman Act), 51st Cong., 1st Sess.; H.R. 868, introduced on Dec. 9, 1895, 54th Cong., 1st Sess. BANK, BUSINESS TAX STORIES, pp. 13–22.

20. H.R. 7505, introduced on June 20, 1894, 53d Cong., 2d Sess. A number of leading businessmen, including heads of trusts, testified before the Industrial Commission to the effect that the tariff had been important to the growth of their businesses; UNITED STATES INDUSTRIAL COMMISSION, PRELIMINARY REPORT ON TRUSTS AND INDUSTRIAL COMBINATIONS, vol. 1, pp. 23–24. For the items the Democrats wanted to put on the "free list" in 1903, *see* Henry De Lamar Clayton, *Speech on Tariffs*, CONGRESSIONAL RECORD, 57th Cong., 2d Sess., Feb. 5, 1903, p. 1757.

21. H.R. 7739, introduced on July 17, 1893, 53d Cong., 2d Sess.

22. KENKEL, PROGRESSIVES AND PROTECTION, pp. 3–7, 58.

23. H.R. 10313, introduced on Feb. 15, 1897, 54th Cong., 2d Sess.; H.R. 9509, introduced on Mar. 13, 1900, 56th Cong., 1st Sess. The importance of the change in form was nicely explained by Taft during the 1908 presidential campaign; Taft, *Mr. Bryan's Claim to the Roosevelt Policies*, Sandusky, Ohio, Sept. 8, 1908, in THE COLLECTED WORKS OF WILLIAM HOWARD TAFT, vol. 2, pp. 46–47. Davis, *Corporate Privileges for the Public Benefit*, pp. 625–28.

24. In addition to H.R. 10313, the bills for federal corporate supervision were H.R. 398, introduced on Mar. 18, 1897, 55th Cong., 1st Sess. (also introduced by Phillip Low), and H.R. 4583, introduced on Dec. 10, 1897, 55th Cong., 2d Sess. (also introduced by Low). The bills addressing overcapitalization were S. 3618, introduced on Jan. 29, 1897, 54th Cong., 2d Sess.; S. 25, introduced on Mar. 16, 1897, 55th Cong., 1st Sess.; S. 2339, introduced on Jan. 11, 1900, 56th Cong., 1st Sess.

25. North, *The Industrial Commission*, p. 708. As I noted earlier, McKinley appears to have been silent on the trust issue. He even ignored the Industrial Commission's preliminary recommendations until late in the presidential campaign of 1900 — and when he addressed the issue he was less than convincing. It appears, moreover, that the Republicans who both created and controlled the Commission varied in the strength of their real commitment to reform; LEECH, IN THE DAYS OF MCKINLEY, pp. 545–48; MERRILL & MERRILL, THE REPUBLICAN COMMAND, pp. 70–73.

26. STROUSE, MORGAN, pp. 430, 342, uses the common identification of Stetson as "Morgan's Attorney General."

27. UNITED STATES INDUSTRIAL COMMISSION, FINAL REPORT, vol. 19, pp. 642–43.

28. Supplementary Statement of Thomas W. Phillips, UNITED STATES INDUSTRIAL COMMISSION, FINAL REPORT, vol. 19, p. 669.

29. There was, not surprisingly, widespread public dispute over whether one

could distinguish "good" trusts from "bad" trusts; *Conference on Trusts*, CHICAGO DAILY TRIBUNE, Sept. 14, 1899, p. 12; *Ohio Fight Warms Up*, WASHINGTON POST, Oct. 13, 1899, p. 3; *Trust Remedy*, BOSTON DAILY GLOBE, Sept. 29, 1899, p. 4.

30. STATUTES AT LARGE OF THE UNITED STATES OF AMERICA FROM MARCH, 1913 TO MARCH, 1915, vol. 38, ch. 311. The FTC did not provide regulatory guidance until 1925; Davis, *The Transformation of the Federal Trade Commission*.

31. MORRIS, THEODORE REX, pp. 90–92; STROUSE, MORGAN, pp. 440–41.

32. UNITED STATES INDUSTRIAL COMMISSION, FINAL REPORT, p. 645.

33. Dill, *National Incorporation Laws for Trusts*, p. 274. To be fair to Dill, he did go on to explain why he believed the corporate law of New Jersey to be responsible, *id.* at 280–81, but his argument, in light of his personal history, rings rather hollow. One wonders how the contemporary listener reacted.

34. STEFFENS, AUTOBIOGRAPHY, p. 195.

35. Adams, *Federal Control of Trusts*, p. 1. Much of the work on this subject postdates the Bureau of Corporation's First Annual Report and legislative proposal and, to the extent significant, will be discussed later as I show the further development of the federal incorporation movement.

36. UNITED STATES CONGRESS, HOUSE OF REPRESENTATIVES, REPORT TO ACCOMPANY H.J. RES. NO. 138, REPORT NO. 1501, Part 1, 56th Cong., 1st Sess., May 15, 1900.

37. UNITED STATES CONGRESS, HOUSE OF REPRESENTATIVES, VIEWS OF THE MINORITY, REPORT NO. 1501, Part 2, 56th Cong., 1st Sess., May 21, 1900, p. 7.

38. Morris notes that Lodge understood Roosevelt to use the word sovereign "as a personal pronoun"; MORRIS, THEODORE REX, p. 462. Johnson, *Theodore Roosevelt and the Bureau of Corporations*. Roosevelt's insistence upon federal regulatory control increased as Taft followed a policy of Sherman Act litigation, a policy of which Roosevelt was highly critical. Theodore Roosevelt, *The Trusts, the People, and the Square Deal*.

39. TR to Hermann Henry Kohlsaat, Aug. 7, 1899; TR to Henry Cabot Lodge, Aug. 10, 1899; TR to Thomas C. Platt, Aug. 21, 1899; TR to Bellamy Storer, Sept. 11, 1899; all in THE LETTERS OF THEODORE ROOSEVELT (Morison, ed.), vol. 2, at pp. 1045, 1047, 1060, 1068.

40. TR to Lodge, Apr. 9, 1900, in THE LETTERS OF THEODORE ROOSEVELT (Morison, ed.), vol. 2, pp. 1252–54; MORRIS, THE RISE OF THEODORE ROOSEVELT, pp. 695–98, 700–702, 717–19.

41. TR to Platt, May 8, 1899; TR to Henry John Wright, Apr. 5, 1900; TR to Bishop, Apr. 11, 1900; TR to John Proctor Clark, Apr. 13, 1900; TR to Samuel Hill, May 8, 1900; all in THE LETTERS OF THEODORE ROOSEVELT (Morison, ed.), vol. 2, pp. 1004, 1247, 1256, 1259, 1292; GOSNELL, BOSS PLATT AND HIS NEW YORK MACHINE, pp. 346–47, 355–56; *Trying to Shelve Roosevelt*, WASHINGTON POST, Apr. 4, 1900, p. 6.

42. TR to Edward Oliver Wolcott, Sept. 15, 1900, in THE LETTERS OF THEODORE ROOSEVELT (Morison, ed.), vol. 2, p. 1397; Roosevelt, *Message of the President of the United States Communicated to the Two Houses of Congress at the Beginning of the Second Session of the Fifty-Seventh Congress*, ROOSEVELT, PRESIDENTIAL ADDRESSES AND STATE PAPERS, vol. 2, pp. 606, 611; TR to Lodge, Apr. 9, 1900; TR to Lodge, June

9, 1900, in ROOSEVELT, SELECTIONS FROM THE CORRESPONDENCE OF THEODORE ROOSEVELT AND HENRY CABOT LODGE, vol. 1, pp. 455, 463–64. Although Lodge was one of Roosevelt's closest friends, my reading of the Roosevelt manuscripts and published correspondence shows that Roosevelt infrequently corresponded with Lodge about the trust issue in these years. TR to Bradley Tyler Johnson, May 10, 1899; TR to Lodge, Feb. 3, 1900; TR to Henry John Wright, Apr. 5, 1900; TR to Joseph Bucklin Bishop, Apr. 11, 1900; TR to John Proctor Clarke, Apr. 13, 1900; TR to Kohlsaat, May 26, 1900; TR to Anna Roosevelt Cowles, June 25, 1900; TR to Lyman Pierson Powell, Feb. 12, 1899; TR to Henry Lincoln, Mar. 15, 1900; TR to William Tudor, Apr. 25, 1900; TR to Samuel Hill, May 8, 1900; TR to Francis Vinton Greene, June 12, 1900, all in THE LETTERS OF THEODORE ROOSEVELT (Morison, ed.), vol. 2, pp. 1009, 1166, 1247, 1256, 1259, 1313, 1339, 1181, 1225, 1271, 1292, 1332.

43. TR to Elihu Root, Dec. 7, 1899; TR to Platt, Dec. 19, 1899, in THE LETTERS OF THEODORE ROOSEVELT (Morison, ed.), vol. 2, pp. 1105, 1114.

44. Roosevelt, *Message of the Governor of New York to the Legislature, January 3, 1900*, in ROOSEVELT, PRESIDENTIAL ADDRESSES AND STATE PAPERS, part 2, pp. 770, 785–87.

45. Roosevelt, *Message of the President of the United States, Communicated to the Two Houses of Congress, at the Beginning of the First Session of the Fifty-Seventh Congress*, in ROOSEVELT, PRESIDENTIAL ADDRESSES AND STATE PAPERS, part 2, pp. 529, 541; Roosevelt, *At the Charleston Exposition, Wednesday, April 9, 1902*, in ROOSEVELT, PRESIDENTIAL ADDRESSES AND STATE PAPERS, part 1, p. 26. Roosevelt, *Just Taxation and State Regulation of Corporations, id.*, pp. 18–25.

46. Speech delivered at Cincinnati, Ohio, Sept. 20, 1902; and Speech delivered at Providence, Rhode Island, Aug. 23, 1902, both in the Theodore Roosevelt Papers, Library of Congress, Manuscript Division, Series 5A, Reel 418.

47. Kornhauser, *Corporate Regulation and the Origins of the Corporate Income Tax*, pp. 73–74; Johnson, *Theodore Roosevelt and the Bureau of Corporations*, pp. 572–73; *Fall of Mr. Littlefield*, NEW YORK TIMES, Feb. 15, 1903, p. 8; *Antitrust Bill Favored*, NEW YORK TIMES, Jan. 10, 1903, p. 8; *Trust Bill Not Ready*, WASHINGTON POST, Jan. 16, 1903, p. 4; *Bill Aimed at Trusts*, WASHINGTON POST, Jan. 23, 1903, p. 4.

Knox's speech became the touchstone of the administration's antitrust policy. The *Times* referred to it as "being accepted on all sides as a classic on the subject of trust legislation"; *Senator Hoar on Trusts*, NEW YORK TIMES, Jan. 7, 1903, p. 2.

SIX: MUCH ADO ABOUT NOTHING

1. One interesting aspect of the federal incorporation movement is that, while the bills generally were meant to supplant state regulation, none of them included provisions for dealing with the creation and structure of the corporation nor the allocation of responsibilities between directors and shareholders that traditionally are the essence of state corporate law. Perhaps the omissions are unsurprising in light of the underlying aims of federal incorporation and the predominance of federal licensing bills over federal incorporation bills, but a serious attempt at establishing federal corporations would have had to come to grips with these issues.

2. H.R. 5170, 61st Cong., 1st Sess., Mar. 26, 1909; H.R. 16360, 61st Cong., 2d Sess., Jan. 4, 1910.

3. As with the legislative census in the previous chapter, the data presented here is taken from an examination of the *Congressional Record* for this entire period, as well as a review of the Bureau of Corporation's archives. Banks and insurance companies were already subject to significant state regulation.

4. H.J. Resolution 94, 58th Cong., 2d Sess., Jan. 28, 1904 (proposing constitutional amendment to prohibit states from incorporating interstate businesses other than banks and insurance companies and giving Congress power to incorporate all corporations doing business in interstate commerce); H.R. 15792, 58th Cong., 3d Sess., Dec. 6, 1904 (prohibiting corporate activity designed to destroy competition); H.R. 473, 59th Cong., 1st Sess., Dec. 4, 1905 (requiring federal incorporation and preventing overcapitalization for businesses engaged in food and fuel supplies. Legislation on this subject was also introduced in 1906, H.R. 13095, 59th Cong., 1st Sess., Jan. 25, 1906); H.R. 9740, 59th Cong., 1st Sess., Dec. 20, 1905 (to prevent and punish overcapitalization); Senate Resolution (unnumbered) introduced by Senator Francis Newlands on Dec. 6, 1905, 59th Cong., 1st Sess. (to require ICC to propose to Congress a national incorporation act for railroads); S.R. 86, Jan. 4, 1905, 58th Cong., 3d Sess. (joint resolution to establish a fourteen-member commission for comprehensive railroad regulation, including regulation of capitalization). The archival copy of this resolution has attached to it an explanatory memo by J. W. Mitchell of the Bureau of Corporations concluding: "It is therefore fair to suspect that the real purpose of the resolution is to prevent action upon the subject-matter by the present Congress."); S. 232, 62d Cong., 1st Sess., Apr. 6, 1911. All legislation described in this section can be found in Bureau of Corporations Archives, National Archives Research Administration, Records Group 122, Stack Area 570, Row 7, Compartment 18, Shelf 2, Box 297, unless otherwise indicated in these notes.

5. The Elkins Act of 1903, Hepburn Act of 1906 and Mann-Elkins Act of 1910, while related to corporate issues, were specialized railroad legislation and oriented toward the particular problems of that industry.

6. UNITED STATES CONGRESS, HOUSE OF REPRESENTATIVES, REPORT NO. 3375, 57th Cong., 2d Sess., Jan. 26, 1903, p. 3 (quoting Philander Knox, Pittsburgh Speech), p. 2 (Roosevelt), p. 4 (Industrial Commission), pp. 5, 6 (Dill).

7. *President Not in Speaker Fight*, CHICAGO DAILY TRIBUNE, Nov. 10, 1902, p. 3; *Toasted Uncle Joe*, WASHINGTON POST, Dec. 18, 1902, p. 1. Morris suggests that Roosevelt thought Littlefield's bill was too "draconian," and while he stated he would "'go the whole distance,'" he "doubted the distance would be very long, legislatively speaking"; MORRIS, THEODORE REX, p. 196.

8. H.R. 17, 57th Cong., 1st Sess., Dec. 2, 1901.

9. H.R. 17, 57th Cong., 2d Sess., Jan. 26, 1903. Despite the Democrats' skepticism, part of the ultimately enacted legislation included an anti-rebate provision in the form of the Elkins Act.

10. *Anti-Trust Bill Favored*, NEW YORK TIMES, Jan. 10, 1903, p. 8; *Trust Bill Not Ready*, NEW YORK TIMES, Jan. 16, 1903, p. 4; *Bill Aimed at Trusts*, WASHINGTON

Post, Jan. 23, 1903, p. 4; *Agreed on a Trust Bill*, WASHINGTON POST, Jan. 24, 1903, p. 4; *Democrats' Anti-Trust View*, WASHINGTON POST, Jan. 30, 1903, p. 4; UNITED STATES CONGRESS, HOUSE OF REPRESENTATIVES, COMMITTEE ON THE JUDICIARY, REPORT TO ACCOMPANY H.R. 17: VIEWS OF THE MINORITY, HOUSE REPORT NO. 3375, Part 2, 57th Cong., 2d Sess., Jan. 29, 1903.

11. Approximately 25 percent of the members of each party did not vote on the bill, and another four Republicans and two Democrats abstained.

12. Some scholars argue as a general proposition that Americans were afraid of large aggregations of capital: ROE, STRONG MANAGERS, WEAK OWNERS. Williams quoted in CONGRESSIONAL RECORD, 57th Cong., 2d Sess., p. 1824 (Feb. 6, 1903).

13. Kitchin in *id.* at p. 1829 (emphasis added).

14. One congressman did point out that the Republican platform of 1888 had been antitrust and that the Republican Congress passed the Sherman Act. This led to an argument over the fact that the Democrats had appended a free-silver measure to the Sherman Act in an effort to derail it because the Republican platform of 1888, while antitrust, was also anti-silver. *Id.* at p. 1765.

15. *Id.* at pp. 1757, 1756.

16. UNITED STATES CONGRESS, HOUSE OF REPRESENTATIVES, COMMITTEE ON THE JUDICIARY, REPORT TO ACCOMPANY H.R. 17, REPORT NO. 3375, 57th Cong., 2d Sess., Jan. 26, 1903, pp. 19, 20.

17. *Address of President Roosevelt at Pittsburgh, July 4, 1902*, Theodore Roosevelt Papers, Library of Congress, Manuscript Division, Series 5A, Reel 424; *Mr. Roosevelt Eager for Trust Legislation*, NEW YORK TIMES, July 6, 1902, p. 1.

18. Roosevelt, Speech delivered at Providence, Rhode Island, Theodore Roosevelt Papers, Library of Congress, Manuscript Division, Series 5A, Reel 418. Roosevelt, Speech delivered at Cincinnati, Ohio, Sept. 20, 1902, Theodore Roosevelt Papers, Library of Congress, Manuscript Division, Series 5A, Reel 418 (typed, hand-revised copy); *see* same speech as finalized in ROOSEVELT, THE ROOSEVELT POLICY, vol. 1, p. 75.

19. SPROAT, THE BEST MEN; TR to Lyman Abbott, Sept. 5, 1903, in THE LETTERS OF THEODORE ROOSEVELT (Morison, ed.), vol. 3, pp. 590–92. Morris nicely develops a picture of what he refers to as Roosevelt's "autocratic tendencies"; MORRIS, THEODORE REX, p. 330.

20. The strike was, in fairness, a major episode in labor's struggle for justice. Morris provides an excellent description; MORRIS, THEODORE REX, pp. 150–61.

21. A significant conflict in assessing Roosevelt's relationship with Wall Street exists. On the one hand, as I will discuss below, there is correspondence indicating Roosevelt's belief that J. P. Morgan was a particularly strong enemy during the coal strike. On the other hand, Morgan worked closely and, in light of the pendency of the Northern Securities suit, evidently quite cordially, with Roosevelt to settle the strike; PRINGLE, THEODORE ROOSEVELT, p. 264; MORRIS, THEODORE REX, pp. 164–68; STROUSE, MORGAN, pp. 448–51. My reading of the record leads me to conclude that Roosevelt was attempting to ingratiate himself with an angry Wall Street before the midterm congressional elections of 1902, in addition to satisfying his need to be liked and his natural affinity for one who was not only a member of his class but

also had worked in several capacities with Roosevelt's father. As I have discussed, Roosevelt's editing of his trust speeches during this period shows a clear attempt to avoid inflammatory or overgeneralized condemnations of trusts, corporations and businessmen.

Lincoln was Roosevelt's hero; TR to George Otto Trevelyan, Mar. 9, 1905, in THE LETTERS OF THEODORE ROOSEVELT (Morison, ed.), vol. 4, p. 1132. His letters are replete not only with references to Lincoln but also with analogies drawn between Lincoln's struggles during the Civil War and his own fight against the trusts; TR to Lyman Abbott, Sept. 5, 1903, in THE LETTERS OF THEODORE ROOSEVELT (Morison, ed.), vol. 3, pp. 590–92.

22. Despite his cordial relationship with Morgan in the fall of 1902, Roosevelt's letters, especially in late 1903, are full of denunciations of the Wall Street interests for their attacks on him because of his role in the anthracite coal strike. *See e.g.*, TR to Richard Watson Gilder, Nov. 4, 1903; TR to Lyman Abbott, Nov. 5, 1903, both in THE LETTERS OF THEODORE ROOSEVELT (Morison, ed.), vol. 3, pp. 645, 647–48; KNIGHT, PHILANDER CHASE KNOX; TR to J. B. Bishop, Feb. 17, 1903, Theodore Roosevelt Papers, Library of Congress, Manuscript Division, Series 2, Reel 330. There is a large amount of correspondence to and from Roosevelt regarding the anthracite coal strike in this manuscript collection, Series 1, Reel 28, and Series 2, Reel 329. Indeed, most of Reel 329, going from early summer to late autumn of 1902, is taken up with Roosevelt's correspondence on the coal strike. Letters to some of his most intimate correspondents that illustrate Roosevelt's attitude toward each side and his sense of accomplishment in its resolution include: TR to Oswald Villard, Oct. 2, 1902; TR to Marcus A. Hanna, Oct. 3, 1902; TR to Grover Cleveland, Oct. 5, 1902; TR to Robert Bacon, Oct. 5, 1902; TR to Jacob Riis, Oct. 8, 1902; TR to Bacon, Oct. 7, 1902; TR to W. S. Cowles, Oct. 16, 1902; TR to Henry Cabot Lodge, Oct. 17, 1902; TR to William Allen White, Oct. 6, 1902; TR to Robert Bacon, Oct. 7, 1902, all located in Series 2, Reel 329 of the Roosevelt manuscripts. Pringle argues that Morgan, Root, Schwab and Rockefeller, among other conservatives, backed Roosevelt in the strike because of their fear that a mishandled strike could lead to Republican defeat in the 1902 midterm elections; PRINGLE, THEODORE ROOSEVELT, p. 264.

23. *Mr. Littlefield Left Off President's List*, NEW YORK TIMES, Aug. 21, 1902, p. 1; *President Starts on Trip*, NEW YORK TIMES, July 4, 1902, p. 3. The *Boston Daily Globe* suggested that Roosevelt's cancellation was a result of limited time and that his only speech in Maine would be in Bangor at the invitation of Maine's Senator Hale.

It is interesting to note that Bryan was speaking in Rockland that summer. *Know County Democrats Happy*, BOSTON DAILY GLOBE, July 18, 1902, p. 12. The incident was the cause of "much gossip." *State's Guest*, Boston, Aug. 21, 1902, p. 7.

24. Morris reports that during this first summer as president, Roosevelt remained at Sagamore Hill and engaged in as little official business as possible; MORRIS, THEODORE REX, pp. 122–29.

Given Roosevelt's view of the power of the presidency, it certainly seems as though the executive branch was preparing trust legislation; PRINGLE, THEODORE ROOSEVELT, p. 259 (noting Roosevelt's belief that the legislature should carry out the wishes of the executive); MOWRY, THE ERA OF THEODORE ROOSEVELT, p. 130

(observing that Roosevelt initiated the *Northern Securities* case and dealt with the coal strike with little or no consultation with Congress, thus antagonizing the conservatives). TR to Benjamin Barker Odell, Aug. 19, 1902, and TR to Winthrop Murray Crane, Aug. 19, 1902, both in THE LETTERS OF THEODORE ROOSEVELT (Morison, ed.), vol. 3, pp. 316–17.

25. *Senator Hoar on Trusts*, NEW YORK TIMES, Jan. 7, 1903, p. 2.

26. *A Few Whys*, WASHINGTON POST, Nov. 1, 1902, p. 6; Raymond, *Hoar Criticised [sic] for Trust Bill*, CHICAGO DAILY TRIBUNE, Jan. 4, 1903, p. 1; Jos Ohl, *G.O.P. Badly Split by Trust Problem*, ATLANTA CONSTITUTION, Jan. 4, 1903, p. 3; *President on Trusts*, WASHINGTON POST, Feb. 2, 1903, p. 3.

Morris reports that Roosevelt only finally abandoned the Littlefield bill following its passage on February 7; MORRIS, THEODORE REX, p. 206. My research suggests that he had done so, albeit without informing Littlefield, well before that date.

27. *Bitter Fight Ahead for the Speakership*, NEW YORK TIMES, Nov. 7, 1902, p. 5; *Fall of Mr. Littlefield*, NEW YORK TIMES, Feb. 15, 1903, p. 8; *Affairs in America*, CURRENT LITERATURE, vol. 34, no. 4 (Apr. 1903), p. 392; *Roosevelt Is Not Pleased*, ATLANTA CONSTITUTION, Jan. 24, 1903, p. 9. Roosevelt actually pushed the Pittsburgh Chamber of Commerce to invite Knox and to move up their meeting one month earlier (giving them one week's notice) so that Knox could attend and deliver "a speech which I regard as the most important any member of the administration is to deliver"; TR to W. H. Keach, Oct. 7, 1902, Theodore Roosevelt Papers, Library of Congress, Manuscript Division, Series 2, Reel 329.

28. Knox had signaled the administration's abandonment of the Littlefield measure no later than early January 1903; Johnson, *Theodore Roosevelt and the Bureau of Corporations*, p. 574. Nonetheless, there was wide public perception that the Littlefield bill had been moving toward passage by the House at least as late as December; *Action on Trusts*, WASHINGTON POST, Dec. 6, 1902, p. 1.

29. TR to Lawrence Fraser Abbott, Feb. 3, 1903, Theodore Roosevelt Papers, Library of Congress, Manuscript Division, Series 2, Reel 330.

30. TR to Dr. W. S. Rainsford, Dec. 27, 1902, Theodore Roosevelt Papers, Library of Congress, Manuscript Division, Series 2, Reel 330.

31. STROUSE, MORGAN, p. 440; Wm. Laffan to TR, Oct. 7, 1902; J. B. Bishop to TR, Oct. 25, 1902, both in Theodore Roosevelt Papers, Library of Congress, Manuscript Division, Series 1, Reel 30. The description of Bishop is Morris's; MORRIS, THEODORE REX, p. 526.

32. J. C. Shaffer to TR, Jan. 17, 1903; J. W. Jenks to TR, Feb. 2, 1903, both in Theodore Roosevelt Papers, Library of Congress, Manuscript Division, Series 1, Reel 32.

33. *Proceedings in Congress*, NEW YORK TIMES, Feb. 4, 1903, p. 4; *Outstrips the House*, WASHINGTON POST, Feb. 4, 1903, p. 4; *Still After Trusts*, Feb. 5, 1903, p. 4.

34. *Trust Bills in House*, WASHINGTON POST, Feb. 6, 1903, p. 4; *Friction over Trust Bills*, NEW YORK TIMES, Feb. 7, 1903, p. 3; *Agree on Bill for Department of Commerce*, NEW YORK TIMES, Feb. 8, 1903, p. 13.

35. *Turned Down by Senate*, WASHINGTON POST, Feb. 28, 1903, p. 4; *Wider in Its Scope*, WASHINGTON POST, Feb. 17, 1903, p. 4; *Anti-Rebate Bill Passed*, NEW YORK TIMES, Feb. 14, 1903, p. 8; *The Status of Anti-Monopoly Legislation*, THE WATCH-

MAN, vol. 85, no. 9 (Feb. 26, 1903), p. 5; *Not So Bad, Perhaps,* NEW YORK TIMES, Feb. 28, 1903, p. 8; *Trust and the Lottery Decision,* THE INDEPENDENT, vol. 55, no. 2831 (Mar. 5, 1903), p. 574. Some, like the avid trust-booster George Gunton, were disgusted by the Republicans and saw the Bureau of Corporations as giving the federal government unprecedented "inquisitorial power"; *The New Anti-Trust Law,* GUNTON'S MAGAZINE (Mar. 1903), p. 189.

36. In fact as late as Feb. 3, TR continued to back the anti-rebate provisions of the Littlefield bill, which he had earlier noted were similar to those drafted by Knox; TR to Lawrence Abbott, Feb. 3, 1903, Theodore Roosevelt Papers, Library of Congress, Manuscript Division, Series 2, Reel 33. Herbert Croly, Hanna's highly sympathetic biographer, underscores the importance of Hanna's role in the Department of Commerce debate and attributes it to his desire that "government might be equipped to serve the industry of the country." In light of Croly's own sympathies it is at least reasonable, if not most plausible, to understand him to be noting Hanna's support for, rather than support for regulation of, industry; CROLY, MARCUS ALONZO HANNA, pp. 373–74. Croly published THE PROMISE OF AMERICAN LIFE only three years before the Hanna biography.

37. OLAND, THE LIFE OF KNUTE NELSON, p. 272. Morris also suggests that it was this substantial executive power that led Roosevelt to abandon Littlefield for Nelson; MORRIS, THEODORE REX, p. 206.

38. *President Threatens an Extra Session,* NEW YORK TIMES, Feb. 8, 1903, p. 1.

39. *President Threatens an Extra Session,* NEW YORK TIMES, Feb. 8, 1903, p. 1; *Warned of Trusts,* WASHINGTON POST, Feb. 9, 1903, p. 1; *The President and the Standard Oil Story,* NEW YORK TIMES, Feb. 10, 1903, p. 1; *Anti-Trust Effort Strongly Resisted,* LOS ANGELES TIMES, Feb. 8, 1903, p. 1; *Treaties and Trust Laws,* THE INDEPENDENT, vol. 55, no. 2829, Feb. 19, 1903, p. 410; *The New Anti-Trust Law,* GUNTON'S MAGAZINE (Mar. 1903), p. 189; B. O. Flower, *The Corruption of Government by the Corporations,* THE ARENA, vol. 30, no. 1 (July 1903), p. 55; *The New Publicity Law,* OUTLOOK, vol. 73, no. 8, Feb. 21, 1903, p. 409. Roosevelt's story is completely discredited in BUSBEY, UNCLE JOE CANNON, pp. 221–23. Busbey identifies the senators receiving telegrams as more than the six noted by Roosevelt, and were Allison, Aldrich, Hale, Spooner, Kean, Platt, Depew, Lodge, Elkins and Nelson, few of whom would naturally have been inclined to favor trust legislation in the first place. One of Rockefeller's early biographers, John T. Flynn, notes that Roosevelt admitted he had released the information to ensure passage of the legislation. Flynn does note that "Standard Oil was in arms" over the legislation but neither affirms nor denies the existence of the telegrams. In light of the significant inaccuracies in Flynn's account of the legislation, the question is hardly resolved. FLYNN, GOD'S GOLD, p. 381. NEVINS, JOHN D. ROCKEFELLER, vol. 2, pp. 516–17. Morris does not address the issue; MORRIS, THEODORE REX, p. 206. The interesting bibliographic history of Nevins's biography and his attitude toward Rockefeller is given in COLLIER & HOROWITZ, THE ROCKEFELLERS, pp. 627–33.

40. *Fall of Mr. Littlefield,* NEW YORK TIMES, Feb. 15, 1903, p. 8; *Accept Trust Amendment,* NEW YORK TIMES, Feb. 11, 1903, p. 8; *Elkins Bill to Be Rushed,* NEW YORK TIMES, Feb. 12, 1903, p. 3; *The Interstate Penalty Not in the Trust Laws,* THE

INDEPENDENT, vol. 55, no. 2829, Feb. 19, 1903, p. 456; *Proceedings in Congress*, NEW YORK TIMES, Feb. 18, 1903, p. 8; *Trust Bill Is Passed*, WASHINGTON POST, Feb. 8, 1903, p. 5.

41. *Fall of Mr. Littlefield*, NEW YORK TIMES, Feb. 15, 1903, p. 8; *Anti-Rebate Bill Passed*, NEW YORK TIMES, Feb. 14, 1903, p. 8.

42. Hans Thorelli, in his account of the era, suggested three grounds for Roosevelt's *volte face*, although admittedly without extensive research: Roosevelt might not have actually approved of Knox's work with Littlefield; Roosevelt simply changed bills when passage of the Littlefield bill seemed improbable; and the combination of the Nelson amendment and the Elkins bill was a better, more administrable, and more "elegant" solution than the Littlefield bill.

None of this is plausible. First, the evidence is indisputable that Roosevelt was aware of Knox's work, encouraged it and described it as the administration position well after the Pittsburgh address. One study claims that Roosevelt and Knox both supported the Littlefield bill until the end of January, with Roosevelt repeating his approval after a late rumor spread that he was abandoning it. This evidently had the desired effect of creating anxiety in the Senate leadership and perhaps softening it up for the Nelson amendment, but in any event it seems clear that Roosevelt still expressed some commitment to Littlefield in the rebate provisions. Moreover, Roosevelt did not simply change horses. He shot the one he rode in on. His late animosity toward the Littlefield bill and Littlefield himself suggests that his turn had deeper causes than a simple shift in policy. Political survival panic is the most likely explanation. Finally, it is hard to argue that the Elkins and Nelson amendments were more elegant than the Littlefield bill except to the extent that their simplicity reflected a lack of substance. The Nelson amendment also gave Roosevelt virtually all the political control there was to be had over corporate America. Thorelli was correct that Roosevelt's actions were political. But they were political to a much greater purpose than the passage of antitrust legislation. They were political for the purpose of increasing Roosevelt's power. After the fact, Roosevelt would claim great pride in establishing the Bureau of Corporations, referring to it as an act of "constructive statesmanship" even as he acknowledged to his close friends that the measure was only "tentative" and a first step.

THORELLI, THE FEDERAL ANTITRUST POLICY, p. 555; Johnson, *Theodore Roosevelt and the Bureau of Corporations*; TR to J. H. Woodard, Oct. 19, 1902, in THE LETTERS OF THEODORE ROOSEVELT (Morison, ed.), vol. 3, p. 356; TR to Lawrence Fraser Abbott, Feb. 3, 1902, in THE LETTERS OF THEODORE ROOSEVELT (Morison, ed.), vol. 3, p. 416. *President McKinley's Policy*, speech delivered at the Union League, Philadelphia, Pa., Nov. 22, 1902, in THE ROOSEVELT POLICY, vol. 1, p. 107; MERRILL & MERRILL, THE REPUBLICAN COMMAND, p. 142; TR to Nicholas Murray Butler, Aug. 29, 1903, TR to Lyman Abbott, Sept. 5, 1903, TR to Lyman Abbott, Oct. 29, 1903, TR to Carl Schurz, Dec. 24, 1903, all in THE LETTERS OF THEODORE ROOSEVELT (Morison, ed.), vol. 3, pp. 579–80, 590–92, 638–39, 679–80.

43. ROOSEVELT, AUTOBIOGRAPHY, pp. 197–98. *See also* CORWIN, THE PRESIDENT, pp. 154–56 (describing Roosevelt's implementation of his "stewardship theory" during the anthracite coal strike); GOULD, THE MODERN AMERICAN PRESIDENCY, pp.

22–23 (on stewardship theory); GRAUBARD, COMMAND OF OFFICE, pp. 7–8 (noting Roosevelt's principal use of stewardship theory in foreign affairs); HARBAUGH, POWER AND RESPONSIBILITY, pp. 338–39; PRINGLE, THEODORE ROOSEVELT, pp. 254–55.

44. Garfield's appointment was almost accidental. His father's tragic political legacy allowed him unusual access in Washington, and Roosevelt had appointed him to fill TR's own old job on the Civil Service Commission for which Mrs. Roosevelt apparently suggested him; THOMPSON, JAMES R. GARFIELD, p. 73. When the Bureau was created, Roosevelt chose Garfield evidently because he "wanted an efficient administrator who would not show dangerous signs of independence," because Roosevelt intended to run the Bureau himself. *Id.*, p. 83. *See also* LEINWAND, A HISTORY OF THE UNITED STATES FEDERAL BUREAU OF CORPORATIONS, pp. 83–84.

45. *Swift and Company v. United States*, 196 U.S. 375 (1905); *Standard Oil Co. of New Jersey v. United States*, 221 U.S. 1 (1911); UNITED STATES DEPARTMENT OF COMMERCE AND LABOR, REPORT OF THE COMMISSIONER OF CORPORATIONS.

46. *Federal Franchises Is President's Plan*, NEW YORK TIMES, Dec. 22, 1904, p. 1.

47. *At the White House*, PHILADELPHIA PUBLIC LEDGER, Dec. 25, 1904, found in Bureau of Corporations Archives, National Archives Research Administration, Records Group 122, Numerical File 5451-22-2. The newspaper accounts referred to in the following discussion can, for the most part, be found in this file. Many lack page numbers as shown by citations in the following notes.

48. It is arguably difficult to generalize too much from a sampling of newspapers, especially when many of the articles appear in files kept by the Bureau of Corporations and, to that end, I have expanded the newspaper search beyond that file. The file is, however, substantial, as evidenced by the fact that even a preliminary reading of its contents took three full days, and that it covers newspapers from multiple states, large- and medium-sized cities and small towns, so it may be taken as reasonably comprehensive. In the end, all that can be generalized is that the terms of the debate described in the text were the terms engaged in by newspaper editors.

49. The *San Francisco Chronicle*'s market report blamed some degree of market gloom on the Garfield report, but hardly serious panic; *Financial News of the World*, SAN FRANCISCO CHRONICLE, Dec. 23, 1904, p. 4.

50. *Moving on the Trusts*, COLLIER'S WEEKLY, Jan. 14, 1905; *Standard Urged Control in 1899*, NEW YORK WORLD, Dec. 24, 1904. Dill's attitudes were frequently mentioned: *National Incorporations Long Urged by Magnates*, NEW YORK WORLD, Dec. 24, 1904; *Federal License Not the Remedy in Samuel Untermyer's Opinion*, NEW YORK HERALD, Dec. 22, 1904.

51. *Garfield's Plan Like Oil Trust's*, CINCINNATI COMMERCIAL TRIBUNE, Dec. 22, 1904. This comment was repeated, verbatim and without attribution, in *The New York Times* on Dec. 27 of that same year. MANSFIELD (OHIO) SHIELD, Dec. 23, 1904.

52. *First—A Corrupt-Practices Act*, NEW YORK WORLD, Dec. 26, 1904.

53. *For Federal Franchises*, WHEELING (WEST VIRGINIA) REGISTER, Dec. 23, 1904.

54. *Federal License to Corporations*, CHICAGO DAILY TRIBUNE, Dec. 22, 1904, p. 4; Raymond, *Roosevelt Backs Garfield Plan*, CHICAGO DAILY TRIBUNE, Dec. 23, 1904, p. 1; *Uncle Sam's "Big Stick" for Interstate Corporations*, BALTIMORE SUN, Dec.

23, 1904, p. 4; *Secretary Garfield's Recommendations*, RICHMOND DISPATCH, Dec. 24, 1904; *Control of Interstate Commerce*, SAN FRANCISCO CHRONICLE, Dec. 23, 1904, p. 6; *Mr. Garfield's Suggestion*, LOS ANGELES TIMES, Dec. 23. 1904, p. 4.

55. STROUSE, MORGAN, pp. 356–57; *To Abolish the States*, NEW YORK TIMES, Dec. 22, 1904; *Distinguished Rivals*, NEW YORK TIMES, Jan. 12, 1905; *A Trust Gibraltar*, NEW YORK TIMES, Dec. 28, 1904; *The New Science of Government*, NEW YORK WORLD, Dec. 28, 1904; *The Roosevelt-Garfield Scheme*, NEW YORK DAILY NEWS, Dec. 27, 1904; *Revolutionary Schemes for Regulating Corporations*, NEW YORK COMMERCIAL BULLETIN, Jan. 7, 1905.

56. *The Issue of Imperialism in a New Shape*, WALL STREET JOURNAL, Dec. 29, 1904, p. 1; *Garfield's Report*, WALL STREET JOURNAL, Dec. 22, 1904, p. 1. The *Journal* strongly supported the plan's call for increased corporate publicity and federal regulation to make it happen. Also supportive of the Garfield plan were the *New York Tribune*, *The Nation*, *Collier's Weekly* and *The Financier, New York*, among others. The need for some degree of regulation was widely acknowledged. *The Fight for Publicity*, WALL STREET JOURNAL, Dec. 24, 1904; *Mr. Havemeyer and Publicity*, WALL STREET JOURNAL, Jan. 12, 1905; *Federal Control of the Interstate Trusts?*, NEW YORK HERALD, Dec. 22, 1904; *The Fathers*, NEW YORK TRIBUNE, Dec. 27, 1904; *The Conversion of Griggs*, THE NATION, Jan. 1, 1905; *Cure and Prevention*, COLLIER'S WEEKLY, Jan. 28, 1905; *Federal Control of Corporations*, THE FINANCIER, NEW YORK, Jan. 2, 1905.

57. Federal incorporation proposals resurfaced from time to time throughout the twentieth century. All of them failed.

58. KNOX, THE COMMERCE CLAUSE OF THE CONSTITUTION AND THE TRUSTS, p. 4.

59. UNITED STATES DEPARTMENT OF COMMERCE AND LABOR, REPORT OF THE COMMISSIONER OF CORPORATIONS, pp. 16, 22, 35.

60. UNITED STATES DEPARTMENT OF COMMERCE AND LABOR, REPORT OF THE COMMISSIONER OF CORPORATIONS, pp. 35–36.

SEVEN: PANIC AND PROGRESS

1. EDWARDS, THE ROOSEVELT PANIC OF 1907; *Panic Caused by Imitators of Roosevelt*, ATLANTA CONSTITUTION, Nov. 24, 1907, p. C1; SOBEL, THE BIG BOARD, p. 188.

2. Mississippi congressman John Sharp Williams was particularly concerned with the Treasury's permission to allow national banks to accept corporate securities as security for tax revenues not yet deposited with the Treasury; Williams, *Federal Usurpations*, p. 196; *Savings Banks Conditions*, NEW YORK TIMES, Jan. 7, 1901, p. AF14; *State Trust Companies*, NEW YORK TIMES, Jan. 19, 1901, p. 14; *Trust Companies' Reports*, NEW YORK TIMES, Aug. 13, 1901, p. 9; *Statement of Trust Companies in New York*, NEW YORK TIMES, Aug. 26, 1903, p. 27; *Savings Banks Had to Meet Many Exceptional Conditions*, NEW YORK TIMES, Jan. 3, 1904, p. AFR10; *What the Year's Bond Market Tells of Past and Future*, NEW YORK TIMES, Jan. 3, 1904, p. AFR30; *Financial Markets*, NEW YORK TIMES, Aug. 4, 1907, p. C6.

3. The basic story of the Panic of 1907 is too well known to justify resorting en-

tirely to primary sources. The chronology of the story that is presented in the text that follows is principally drawn from KOLKO, THE TRIUMPH OF CONSERVATISM, pp. 153–58; GRANT, MONEY OF THE MIND, pp. 113–16; MARKHAM, A FINANCIAL HISTORY OF THE UNITED STATES, vol. 3, pp. 29–36; FRIDSON, IT WAS A VERY GOOD YEAR, ch. 1; SOBEL, THE BIG BOARD, pp. 188–92; and STROUSE, MORGAN, pp. 573–96.

4. Strouse, the exception, accepts Barney's suicide as the correct story; STROUSE, MORGAN, p. 588.

5. The Tennessee Coal & Iron deal was not a favorite of Elbert Gary, Henry Frick, or George Perkins, despite popular accounts accusing Morgan of manipulating the crisis to Steel's (and his) benefit; STROUSE, MORGAN, pp. 584–86. The Taft administration sued U.S. Steel under the Sherman Act, in part because of its acquisition of Tennessee Coal; *United States v. United States Steel Corporation*, 251 U.S. 417 (1920). Roosevelt, in an editorial in the *Outlook*, attacked the suit and Taft's approach to trust regulation, while at the same time defending his approval of the Tennessee Coal acquisition; Roosevelt, *The Trusts, the People, and the Square Deal*, OUTLOOK, vol. 99 (Nov. 18, 1911), pp. 649–56.

6. TR to Charles Joseph Bonaparte, Jan. 2, 1908, Roosevelt, *Special Message of the President of the United States to Congress*, Jan. 31, 1908, both in THE LETTERS OF THEODORE ROOSEVELT (Morison, ed.), vol. 6, pp. 883, 890, 1572, 1590.

7. The letters can be found in the Bureau of Corporations Archives, National Archives Research Administration, Records Group 122, File No. 4085.

8. PROCEEDINGS OF THE NATIONAL CONFERENCE ON TRUSTS AND COMBINATIONS UNDER THE AUSPICES OF THE NATIONAL CIVIC FEDERATION; JENSEN, THE NATIONAL CIVIC FEDERATION, pp. 273–77; SKLAR, THE CORPORATE RECONSTRUCTION OF AMERICAN CAPITALISM, p. 220.

9. Roosevelt himself told Low in Oct. 1907 that he did not see how a Sherman Act amendment would be useful in the absence of federal supervision notifying businesses whether their activities were lawful; TR to Seth Low, in THE LETTERS OF THEODORE ROOSEVELT (Morison, ed.), vol. 5, pp. 824–25. As work on the bill progressed, Roosevelt increasingly strongly asserted his desire to impose executive control over the regulation of trusts; TR to Jonathan Bourne, Jr., July 8, 1908, TR to Seth Low, Nov. 21, 1908, TR to Seth Low, Nov. 24, 1908, all in THE LETTERS OF THEODORE ROOSEVELT (Morison, ed.), vol. 6, pp. 1114–15, 1374, 1379; UNITED STATES CONGRESS, HOUSE OF REPRESENTATIVES, HEARINGS ON HOUSE BILL 19745, p. 10.

10. Low identified "the men who have been in conference more or less on the subject" in his testimony before the judiciary subcommittee holding the Hepburn hearings; UNITED STATES CONGRESS, HOUSE OF REPRESENTATIVES, HEARINGS ON HOUSE BILL 19745, p. 149 (testimony of Seth Low). To understand Jenks's view it is only necessary to read his questioning of witnesses for the U.S. Industrial Commission, his speech at the Chicago Civic Federation's National Conference on Trusts in 1899, his questioning of witnesses for the Bureau of Corporations, and his book, THE TRUST PROBLEM; UNITED STATES CONGRESS, HOUSE OF REPRESENTATIVES, HEARINGS ON HOUSE BILL 19745, p. 79 (testimony of Jeremiah W. Jenks); JENSEN, THE NATIONAL CIVIC FEDERATION, p. 279. The story of the Hepburn bill's drafting and

Teddy Roosevelt's involvement in it is well told in SKLAR, THE CORPORATE RECON-
STRUCTION OF AMERICAN CAPITALISM, pp. 228–53. *See also* KOLKO, THE TRIUMPH
OF CONSERVATISM, pp. 133–38.

11. JENSEN, THE NATIONAL CIVIC FEDERATION; SKLAR, THE CORPORATE RE-
CONSTRUCTION OF AMERICAN CAPITALISM, pp. 205–7, 228–53.

12. H.R. 19745, 60th Cong., 1st Sess., Mar. 23, 1908.

13. UNITED STATES CONGRESS, HOUSE OF REPRESENTATIVES, HEARINGS ON
HOUSE BILL 19745, pp. 13–14 (testimony of Seth Low).

14. UNITED STATES CONGRESS, HOUSE OF REPRESENTATIVES, HEARINGS ON
HOUSE BILL 19745, pp. 91–92 (testimony of Jeremiah W. Jenks).

15. UNITED STATES CONGRESS, HOUSE OF REPRESENTATIVES, HEARINGS ON
HOUSE BILL 19745, pp. 584, 606–7 (testimony of Jeremiah W. Jenks).

16. TR to Lyman Abbott, Apr. 23, 1906, in THE LETTERS OF THEODORE ROO-
SEVELT (Morison, ed.), vol. 5, pp. 217–18; TR to Charles Bonaparte, Jan. 2, 1908, TR
to George Cabot Lee, Jr., Jan. 13, 1908, Theodore Roosevelt, *Special Message of the
President of the United States to Congress*, Jan. 31, 1908, all in THE LETTERS OF THEO-
DORE ROOSEVELT (Morison, ed.), vol. 6, pp. 883, 886, 906, 1584.

17. The story I am telling is of the development of federal securities regulation.
State regulation of securities began in 1911 and, although it intersected with several
federal bills introduced after the war, followed a largely different course of development and had little to do with the increasing dominance of finance over industry. Interested readers may refer to LOSS & COWETT, BLUE SKY LAW, and HOLT, POLICING
THE MARGINS, *especially* ch. 4 (on the origins of state blue sky laws).

18. STATE OF NEW YORK, REPORT OF COMMITTEE ON SPECULATION IN SECU-
RITIES AND COMMODITIES, June 7, 1909; LOGSDON, HORACE WHITE, p. 392, n. 17;
COWING, POPULISTS, PLUNGERS, AND PROGRESSIVES, pp. 38–42. *See also* White, *The
Hughes Investigation*, pp. 528–40.

19. LOGSDON, HORACE WHITE; VILLARD, FIGHTING YEARS, pp. 125–26; WRES-
ZIN, OSWALD GARRISON VILLARD, pp. 22, 25; White, *The Stock Exchange and the
Money Market*, p. 93.

20. DICTIONARY OF AMERICAN BIOGRAPHY, vols. 9 and 10; COWING, POPULISTS,
PLUNGERS, AND PROGRESSIVES, p. 39. David Leventritt to Willard V. King, Aug. 1,
1909, Horace White Papers, New York Historical Society.

21. STATE OF NEW YORK, REPORT OF COMMITTEE ON SPECULATION IN SECURI-
TIES AND COMMODITIES, June 7, 1909, p. 5; White, *The Hughes Investigation*, p. 528.

22. Wash sales occur where a client places both buy and sell orders for the same
amount of the same security with a single broker. Matched orders occur where one
broker sells stock to another on behalf of the same client. Both types of transaction are
designed to create the appearance of market activity in a stock.

23. STATE OF NEW YORK, REPORT OF COMMITTEE ON SPECULATION IN SECU-
RITIES AND COMMODITIES, June 7, 1909, p. 9.

24. TAFT, THE COLLECTED WORKS, vol. 1, pp. 66, 70–71. Taft took a more san-
guine view of the panic, for which the Roosevelt administration received its share
of blame, than most. While he acknowledged the role of speculation and the irresponsibility of the trust companies, his principal explanation of the panic was an

exhaustion of world capital in the context of an inflexible currency system; Taft, *The Panic of 1907*, Boston, Mass., Dec. 30, 1907, in TAFT, THE COLLECTED WORKS, vol. 1, pp. 230–32.

25. Taft, *Recent Criticism of the Federal Judiciary Delivered Before the American Bar Association*, Detroit, Michigan, Aug. 28, 1895, in TAFT, THE COLLECTED WORKS, vol. 1, pp. 294, 300–301.

26. ANDERSON, WILLIAM HOWARD TAFT, pp. 51–52; Taft, *A Republican Congress and Administration, and Their Work from 1904 to 1906*, Boise City, Idaho, Nov. 3, 1906, in TAFT, THE COLLECTED WORKS, vol. 1, pp. 167, 168–69; Taft, *Mr. Bryan's Claim to the Roosevelt Policies*, Sandusky, Ohio, Sept. 8, 1908, in TAFT, THE COLLECTED WORKS, vol. 2, pp. 42, 43.

27. Taft, *The Legislative Policies of the Present Administration*, Columbus, Ohio, Aug. 19, 1907, in TAFT, THE COLLECTED WORKS, vol. 1, pp. 190, 200–201; Taft, *The Panic of 1907*, Boston, Mass., Dec. 30, 1907, in *id.*, vol. 1, p. 238; Taft, *Mr. Bryan's Claim to the Roosevelt Policies*, Sandusky, Ohio, Sept. 8, 1908, in *id.*, vol. 2, pp. 42, 50.

28. Taft's administration brought ninety antitrust lawsuits during his four-year term, in contrast to fifty-four brought by Roosevelt during his more than seven years in office; BURTON, WILLIAM HOWARD TAFT, p. 74; Taft, *Interstate Commerce and Anti-Trust Laws and Federal Incorporation*, Washington, D.C., Jan. 7, 1910, in TAFT, THE COLLECTED WORKS, vol. 3, pp. 408, 422–23; Taft, *Annual Message: Part I*, The White House, Dec. 5, 1911, in TAFT, THE COLLECTED WORKS, vol. 4, pp. 159, 170; *Taft's Bill for Federal Rule of the Trusts*, NEW YORK TIMES, Jan. 13, 1910, p. 1; H.R. 20142, 61st Cong., 2d Sess., Feb. 7, 1910.

29. Taft, *The Tariff, Income, and Corporation Taxes*, Portland, Oregon, Oct. 2, 1909, in TAFT, THE COLLECTED WORKS, vol. 3, pp. 237, 245; Taft, *Corporation and Income Taxes*, Denver, Colorado, Sept. 21, 1909, in TAFT, THE COLLECTED WORKS, vol. 3, pp. 194, 201.

30. BURTON, WILLIAM HOWARD TAFT, p. 57.

31. UNITED STATES CONGRESS, SENATE REPORT NO. 1242, *Views of Mr. Tillman*, 59th Cong., 1st Sess., Mar. 15, 1906, pp. 7–9.

32. TR to the Interstate Commerce Commission, Mar. 15, 1907, in THE LETTERS OF THEODORE ROOSEVELT (Morison, ed.), vol. 5, pp. 622–23.

33. UNITED STATES CONGRESS, HOUSE OF REPRESENTATIVES, REPORT OF THE COMMITTEE ON INTERSTATE AND FOREIGN COMMERCE TO ACCOMPANY H.R. 17536, 61st Cong., 2d Sess., REPORT NO. 923, VIEWS OF THE MINORITY, p. 160; CONGRESSIONAL RECORD, 61st Cong., 2d Sess., vol. 45, p. 4724 (Apr. 14, 1910) (remarks of Mr. Adamson).

34. CONGRESSIONAL RECORD, 61st Cong., 2d Sess., vol. 45, p. 4719 (Apr. 14, 1910) (remarks of Mr. Mann).

35. CONGRESSIONAL RECORD, 61st Cong., 2d Sess., vol. 45, p. 3384 (Mar. 18, 1910) (remarks of Mr. Cummins).

36. REPORT OF THE RAILROAD SECURITIES COMMISSION TO THE PRESIDENT, 62d Cong., 2d Sess., Dec. 11, 1911.

37. Taylor, *Hadley's "Economics,"* p. 468; MORRIS HADLEY, ARTHUR TWINING

HADLEY, pp. 79–80 (quoting Max Lerner in the *Encylopedia of Social Sciences*). Taft's move away from Roosevelt's ideal of centralized federal regulation is chronicled in SKLAR, THE CORPORATE RECONSTRUCTION OF AMERICAN CAPITALISM, pp. 285–309, 364–82.

38. MORRIS HADLEY, ARTHUR TWINING HADLEY, pp. 182–83, 60.

39. MORRIS HADLEY, ARTHUR TWINING HADLEY, p. 60; ARTHUR T. HADLEY, RAILROAD TRANSPORTATION, p. 49.

40. MORRIS HADLEY, ARTHUR TWINING HADLEY, pp. 188–91.

41. REPORT OF THE RAILROAD SECURITIES COMMISSION TO THE PRESIDENT, 62d Cong., 2d Sess., Dec. 11, 1911.

EIGHT: THE SPECULATION ECONOMY

1. SOBEL, THE BIG BOARD, p. 159.

2. NOYES, THE MARKET PLACE, pp. 194–95.

3. *Topics in Wall Street, Heavy Fall in Pressed Steel Car*, NEW YORK TIMES, Feb. 19, 1909, p. 13; *Market Movement*, NEW YORK TIMES, July 10, 1902, p. 10; *Price of Staples*, NEW YORK TIMES, Oct. 10, 1903, p. 12; *The Financial Markets*, NEW YORK TIMES, Dec. 2, 1903, p. 12; *Trading More Active*, WASHINGTON POST, Dec. 2, 1903, p. 16, all address market reactions to skipped dividends.

4. Tsuk Mitchell, *Shareholders as Proxies*, details and analyzes various attempts to reform shareholder voting and concludes that the influence of shareholders as investors through the market has been their only significant power from the rise of the giant modern corporation.

5. For an excellent account of the roots of federal securities regulation from the Panic of 1907 on, *see* Thel, *The Original Conception of Section 10(b) of the Securities Exchange Act*.

6. *Investment and Speculation*, WALL STREET JOURNAL, Jan. 30, 1906, p. 1; John Moody, *The Art of Wall Street Investing*, WASHINGTON POST, Sept. 30, 1906, p. TP3, Oct. 7, 1906, p. F2, Nov. 4, 1906, p. R4.

7. *Small Investors Careful*, reprinted from THE NATIONAL BANKER in THE WASHINGTON POST, Mar. 17, 1907, p. 14; *More Money in Sight*, WASHINGTON POST, Apr. 1, 1907, p. 10; *A Market View*, WALL STREET JOURNAL, Nov. 4, 1907, p. 7; *Investment Buying in Stocks Heavy*, NEW YORK TIMES, Nov. 16, 1907, p. 13; *If A Ban Should Be Put on Speculation*, NEW YORK TIMES, Mar. 1, 1908, p. SM1; *Two Million Partners Own the Corporations*, NEW YORK TIMES, Oct. 4, 1908, p. SM1; *The Financial Situation*, NEW YORK TIMES, Nov. 16, 1908, p. 10; *Who Own the Corporations*, NEW YORK TIMES, Oct. 4, 1908, p. 8; *Owners of Corporations*, WASHINGTON POST, Jan. 10, 1909, p. S3; *Kansas Farmers Have Lots of Money They Want to Invest*, WASHINGTON POST, Jan. 2, 1907, p. E12.

8. Alexander D. Noyes in the April *Atlantic Monthly*, quoted in *Advice for Investors*, WASHINGTON POST, Apr. 7, 1906, p. 10; Wm. E. Lewis, *When Bonds Are Good*, WASHINGTON POST, July 15, 1906, p. EA3.

9. NOYES, FORTY YEARS OF AMERICAN FINANCE, pp. 314–31; SOBEL, THE BIG BOARD, pp. 190–97.

10. *Foreign Investments of Nations*, WALL STREET JOURNAL, July 24, 1909, p. 6; *French Not Speculators*, NEW YORK TIMES, July 25, 1909, p. 6.

11. *What Is Speculation in Stocks?*, WALL STREET JOURNAL, Oct. 16, 1909, p. 6; *People with Very Large Savings*, WALL STREET JOURNAL, Oct. 23, 1909, p. 6; *Value of Legitimate Promotions*, WALL STREET JOURNAL, Dec. 18, 1909, p. 6; *Security Markets and Saving Power*, WALL STREET JOURNAL, Aug. 24, 1910, p. 1; *A View of the Bond Market*, WALL STREET JOURNAL, Oct. 4, 1909, p. 5; *The Price of Stocks*, CURRENT LITERATURE, vol. 49, no. 6 (Dec. 1910), p. 0_025; *Untitled*, THE (FAIRBANKS) ALASKA CITIZEN, May 15, 1911, p. 10; Meade, *Shall I Buy Stocks or Bonds?*, LIPPINCOTT'S MONTHLY MAGAZINE, vol. 88, no. 527 (Nov. 1911), p. 763; *Finance and Investment*, CURRENT LITERATURE, vol. 53, no. 6 (Dec. 1912), p. 34; *The Investor in Perplexity*, CURRENT OPINION, vol. 54, no. 1 (Jan. 1913), p. 84; Edward M. Reeves, *To the Investing Public*, CURRENT OPINION, vol. 55, no. 4 (Oct. 1913), p. 298.

12. NOYES, FORTY YEARS OF AMERICAN FINANCE, p. 249.

13. *A Market View*, WALL STREET JOURNAL, May 8, 1911, p. 3; *The Bond Market*, WALL STREET JOURNAL, Sept. 29, 1911, p. 5; Preston C. Adams, *"Big Business" Boom Predicts Season of General Prosperity*, INDIANAPOLIS STAR, July 30, 1911, p. 35; *Morgan on Side of Bear Market*, SYRACUSE HERALD, Aug. 20, 1911, p. 14; *The Bond Market*, WALL STREET JOURNAL, Jan. 22, 1912, p. 5; *Investment Spirit Abroad*, WALL STREET JOURNAL, Jan. 23, 1912, p. 3; *"Holland" Tells of Investments by Nation's Small Capitalists*, WASHINGTON POST, July 9, 1912, p. 10; *Holland's Letter*, WALL STREET JOURNAL, Aug. 30, 1912, p. 1; *"Holland" Discusses Puzzling Conditions in Securities Market*, WASHINGTON POST, Dec. 23, 1912, p. 9; *Attitude of Investors*, INDIANAPOLIS STAR, Mar. 29, 1913, p. 8; Richard Spillane, *Wall Street Has Fallen upon Evil Days*, SYRACUSE HERALD, Dec. 14, 1913, p. 30; *"Holland" Sees Nation's Railroads Passing into Hands of the People*, WASHINGTON POST, Mar. 12, 1913, p. 10; A STATEMENT IN REGARD TO THE AMERICAN SUGAR REFINING COMPANY, Report file no. 144, Historic Corporate Report Collection, Baker Library, Harvard University; *Steel Trust Statistics*, National Civic Federation Archives; Navin & Sears, *The Rise of a Market for Industrial Securities*.

14. *The Army of Small Investors*, LOS ANGELES TIMES, Apr. 12, 1914, p. V.18; *Public Buying*, BOSTON DAILY GLOBE, Feb. 8, 1914, p. 54; Snider, *Security Issues in the United States*.

15. Seligman was also the editor who accepted Wilson's famous article on administration, over Wilson's modest objections of inadequacy, for the *Political Science Quarterly*.

Information described as being found in the National Civic Federation Archives is contained in those archives, Reel 179, located at the main branch of the New York Public Library.

16. *Seventy-Two Roads Owned by 461,445 Shareholders*, WALL STREET JOURNAL, Feb. 28, 1913, p. 1.

17. *Million and a Quarter Owners in 327 Companies*, WALL STREET JOURNAL, Apr. 4, 1913, p. 1.

18. *Investment*, THE STREET, Sept. 3, 1919, p. 22; *Memorandum, Distribution of*

Ownership, June 14, 1915, National Civic Federation Archives. Ralph Easley (presumed) to Albert W. Atwood, June 11, 1914, provides an analysis of the decline in large shareholdings and concomitant increase in small shareholders, National Civic Federation Archives.

19. Hoffman, *Fifty Years of American Life Insurance Progress*, p. 684, notes almost 30 million policies in effect in 1910, although both the NCF's number and his number appear intuitively high for populations of 100.5 million in 1915 and 92.5 million in 1910. But when one accounts for the fact that life insurance was, at the time, one of the most important savings programs for most people, perhaps the numbers do not seem to be as extraordinary; Elmer E. Rittenhouse, *Thrift from the Life Insurance Viewpoint*, SCIENTIFIC MONTHLY, vol. 4, no. 4 (Apr. 1917), pp. 301–6. Keller notes that almost $15 billion in life insurance was in force in America in 1910, further supporting the magnitude of policyholdings. He also mentions that by 1904, insurance companies owned 10 percent of all American railroad securities; KELLER, THE LIFE INSURANCE ENTERPRISE, pp. 286, 131.

20. HEUBNER, AMRHEIN & KLINE, THE STOCK MARKET, p. 5; Baskin, *The Development of Corporate Financial Markets in Britain and the United States*, pp. 199, 230; *Memorandum* dated June 14, 1915, National Civic Federation Archives, New York Public Library; Evans Clark, *15,000,000 Americans Hold Corporation Stock*, NEW YORK TIMES, Nov. 22, 1925, p. XX5. Heubner wrote in the present tense in 1934 but the footnote to his estimate of 15 million American stockholders cites William Van Antwerp's testimony before the Senate Committee on Banking and Currency on the Owen bill, which took place in 1914; HEUBNER, AMRHEIN & KLINE, THE STOCK MARKET, p. 5, n. 3.

21. Hurdman, *Capital Stock of No Par Value*, pp. 254–55; *Smaller Municipal Bonds*, WALL STREET JOURNAL, Feb. 17, 1913; *The Birth and Rapid Growth of the Baby Bond*, CURRENT LITERATURE, vol. 53, no. 3 (Sept. 1912), p. 296; C. M. Keys, *The Buyer of Little Bonds*, SYRACUSE HERALD, July 6, 1912, p. 2; *Investments*, LIPPINCOTT'S MONTHLY MAGAZINE, vol. 89, no. 529 (Jan. 1912), p. 190; CAROSSO, INVESTMENT BANKING IN AMERICA, pp. 103–4 (on growth of installment plans).

22. Baskin, *The Development of Corporate Financial Markets in Britain and the United States*, p. 222.

23. GRAHAM & DODD, SECURITY ANALYSIS, p. 303. Graham and Dodd noted of prewar investors that their portfolios tended to be weighted heavily toward bonds and preferred stock with common stock forming small proportions. This observation is perfectly consistent with my argument that common stockholding dramatically increased in the prewar period.

24. GRAHAM & DODD, SECURITY ANALYSIS, pp. 305–6.

25. CHAMBERLAIN & HAY, INVESTMENT AND SPECULATION, pp. 3, 4.

26. CHAMBERLAIN & HAY, INVESTMENT AND SPECULATION, p. 57.

27. Robert L. Smitely, *The Economics of Speculation*, THE STREET, Aug. 13, 1919, pp. 6, 7.

NINE: THE END OF REFORM

1. Davis, *The Transformation of the Federal Trade Commission*, p. 438; STATUTES AT LARGE OF THE UNITED STATES OF AMERICA FROM MARCH, 1913 TO MARCH, 1915, vol. 38, ch. 311 (Sept. 26, 1914).

2. Perhaps the most subtle explanation of Wilson's political and business thought is Sklar's; SKLAR, THE CORPORATE RECONSTRUCTION OF AMERICAN CAPITALISM, *esp.* ch. 6. While I accept the core of Sklar's explanation, I disagree with some of his analysis as I explain in the text.

3. Abrams, *Woodrow Wilson and the Southern Congressmen*; Grantham, *Southern Congressional Leaders and the New Freedom*; Scott, *A Progressive Wind from the South.*

4. To be fair, when women's suffrage came to a vote in New Jersey during his presidency, Wilson cast his vote in favor of the measure. WHITE, AUTOBIOGRAPHY; Clements, *The Papers of Woodrow Wilson*, p. 482; *On Women Suffrage, Address to the Ladies Representing Woman Suffrage at the White House*, Oct. 3, 1918, in Wilson, WAR AND PEACE, vol. 1, p. 272; WILSON, THE STATE, p. 663; Wilson, *The New Meaning of Government*, pp. 193–95.

5. *See generally* LINK, WILSON: THE NEW FREEDOM.

6. WILSON, THE STATE, pp. 659, 661.

7. WILSON, THE STATE, pp. 650–53; Wilson, *The Study of Administration*, p. 209; Wilson, *Jackson Day Dinner Address*, Jan. 8, 1912, in WILSON, COLLEGE AND STATE, vol. 2, pp. 344, 348; Wilson, *Living Principles of Democracy*, originally published in *Harper's Weekly*, April 9, 1910, in WILSON, COLLEGE AND STATE, vol. 2, pp. 197–98; Wilson, *Speech of Acceptance*, Aug. 7, 1912, in *id.*, vol. 2, pp. 452, 464; SKLAR, THE CORPORATE RECONSTRUCTION OF AMERICAN CAPITALISM, pp. 383–430, 402.

8. WILSON, THE STATE, pp. 655, 667; Wilson, *First Inaugural Address as President of the United States*, Mar. 4, 1913, in WILSON, THE NEW DEMOCRACY, vol. 1, pp. 1, 5.

9. Wilson, *The Lawyer and the Community*, Aug. 31, 1910, in WILSON, COLLEGE AND STATE, vol. 2, pp. 254–55, 258; Wilson, *Jackson Day Dinner Address*, Jan. 8, 1912, in *id.*, vol. 2, pp. 344, 347; Wilson, *Richmond Address*, Feb. 1, 1912, in *id.*, vol. 2, pp. 367, 376; Wilson, *The Tariff and the Trusts*, Feb. 24, 1912, in *id.*, vol. 2, pp. 405, 411.

10. Wilson, *Law or Personal Power*, Apr. 13, 1908, in WILSON, COLLEGE AND STATE, vol. 2, pp. 24, 30.

11. Wilson, *The Lawyer and the Community*, Aug. 31, 1910, in WILSON, COLLEGE AND STATE, vol. 2, p. 255; Wilson, *Issues of Freedom*, May 5, 1911, in *id.*, vol. 2, pp. 283, 285; Wilson, *The Tariff and the Trusts*, Feb. 24, 1912, in *id.*, vol. 2, p. 405.

12. Wilson, *What Jefferson Would Do*, Apr. 13, 1912, in WILSON, COLLEGE AND STATE, vol. 2, pp. 424, 428.

13. WILSON, THE STATE; Wilson, *The States and the Federal Government*, in WILSON, COLLEGE AND STATE, vol. 2, pp. 32–53; Wilson, *Leaderless Government.*

14. Wilson, *Law or Personal Power*, Apr. 13, 1908, in WILSON, COLLEGE AND STATE, vol. 2, p. 29; Wilson, *The Ministry and the Individual*, Nov. 11, 1909, in *id.*, vol. 2, pp. 178, 181; Wilson, *Living Principles of Democracy*, originally published in

Harper's Weekly, April 9, 1910, in WILSON, COLLEGE AND STATE, vol. 2, p. 196; Wilson, *The Lawyer and the Community*, Aug. 31, 1910, in *id.*, vol. 2, p. 245; Wilson, *The Tariff and the Trusts*, Feb. 24, 1912, in *id.*, vol. 2, p. 413.

15. WILSON, THE NEW FREEDOM, p. 22.

16. *Money Trust Inquiry*, WASHINGTON POST, July 28, 1911, p. 4.

17. LINK, WOODROW WILSON AND THE PROGRESSIVE ERA, pp. 44–53; NOYES, THE WAR PERIOD OF AMERICAN FINANCE, p. 44.

As I have noted earlier, a number of securities bills had been introduced in Congress, but the Owen bill was the first to benefit from serious hearings and public attention.

18. CAROSSO, INVESTMENT BANKING IN AMERICA, p. 137.

19. The parallel is not perfect. Wilson retired and died after his defeat; Untermyer went on to fight many other battles.

20. Woodrow Wilson to Samuel Untermyer, Oct. 5, 1913; WW to SU, Jan. 27, 1914; WW to SU, Feb. 4, 1914; WW to SU, Aug. 15, 1914; WW to SU, Oct. 10, 1916; SU to WW, Oct. 14, 1916, all in the Woodrow Wilson Papers, Library of Congress. Wilson's initial coolness toward Untermyer appears to have been, at least in part, based on his recollection of the fraud Untermyer was found to have perpetrated in the well-publicized New Jersey *Columbia Straw Paper* case (discussed in Chapter Two), which was decided when Wilson was president of Princeton. Remarks of Simeon Fess, CONGRESSIONAL RECORD, 63d Cong., 2d sess., vol. 51, p. 9701 (June 2, 1914).

21. *Untermyer Dead in His 82d Year; Long Had Been Ill*, NEW YORK TIMES, Mar. 17, 1940, p. 1.

22. *Id.*; Editorial, *Samuel Untermyer*, NEW YORK TIMES, Mar. 18, 1940, p. 16; *Governor Attends Untermyer Rites*, NEW YORK TIMES, Mar. 23, 1940, p. 13; Coleman T. Mobley, *Firm Archives Reveal Rich History*, LEGAL TIMES, May 26, 1986, p. 26; Shannon Star, *Couple Learn History as They Rescue Home*, THE (RIVERSIDE, CALIF.) PRESS ENTERPRISE, May 11, 2002, p. B3; BROESAMLE, WILLIAM GIBBS MCADOO, pp. 104–6.

23. SU to WW, July 3, 1912; SU to WW, July 31, 1912; SU to WW, Oct. 3, 1913, all in the Woodrow Wilson Papers, Library of Congress.

24. *From the Diary of Colonel House*, Apr. 18, 1913, in WILSON, THE PAPERS OF WOODROW WILSON (Link, ed.), vol. 27, p. 334; *From the Diary of Colonel House*, May 19, 1913, in *id.*, vol. 27, p. 457; *From the Diary of Colonel House*, Nov. 29, 1913, in *id.*, vol. 28, p. 597; SU to William Gibbs McAdoo, Dec. 18, 1913, in the William Gibbs McAdoo Papers, Library of Congress; Telegram from Untermyer to McAdoo, Jan. 14, 1914, in the William Gibbs McAdoo Papers, Library of Congress. Carter Glass also suggested that a reason for Wilson's initial distaste for, and reluctance to appoint Untermyer to an official position, was his recollection of the latter's role in the Columbia Straw Paper fraud in which Untermyer was singled out by the New Jersey court as the mastermind (*See v. Heppenheimer*, discussed in Chapter Two), and there is support for this view in the fact that Untermyer continued to be publicly criticized for the deal almost twenty years later. *See* Glass's remarkable and rather vicious memo responding to Untermyer's review of Glass's book [undated, presumed 1928], found in the Woodrow Wilson Papers, Series 2, Library of Congress. I

cannot explain why a document clearly written years after Wilson's death is held in his collected papers.

25. Glass memo, *id.*

26. Robert L. Henry (RLH) to SU, Jan. 23, 1912, in the Samuel Untermyer Papers, Jacob Rader Marcus Center of the American Jewish Archives.

27. *Washington Notes,* J. POLIT. ECONOMY, vol. 20, no. 3 (Mar. 1912), pp. 276–83.

28. H.R. 405, 62d Cong., 2d Sess., Feb. 3, 1912; H.R. 429, 62d Cong., 2d Sess., Feb. 24, 1912; H.R. 504, 62d Cong., 2d Sess., Apr. 22, 1912.

29. H.R. 504, 62d Cong., 2d Sess., Apr. 22, 1912.

30. *Curbing the "Money Trust,"* NEW YORK TIMES, Dec. 28, 1911, p. 3; *Wilson Is Neutral on Exchange Bills,* NEW YORK TIMES, Jan. 24, 1914, p. 11.

31. Lawson is quoted in SCHLESINGER & BURNS, EDS., CONGRESS INVESTIGATES, vol. 3, p. 2253. RLH to SU, Apr. 9, 1912; SU to RLH, Apr. 10, 1912; SU to RLH, Mar. 15, 1912; SU to James F. Byrnes, Apr. 17, 1912; SU to A. P. Pujo (APP), Apr. 19, 1912; SU to APP, Apr. 20, 1912; RLH to SU, Apr. 25, 1912; all in the Samuel Untermyer Papers, Jacob Rader Marcus Center of the American Jewish Archives.

32. RLH to SU, Dec. 23, 1911; SU to RLH, Dec. 26, 1911; Subpoena of SU to appear before House Rules Committee from RLH, Jan. 20, 1912; RLH to SU, Jan. 26, 1912; SU to RLH, Jan. 27, 1912; RLH to SU, Jan. 30, 1912; Telegram, RLH to SU, Feb. 3, 1912; SU to RLH, Apr. 20, 1912; all in the Samuel Untermyer Papers, Jacob Rader Marcus Center of the American Jewish Archives.

33. SU to RLH, Apr. 15, 1912; SU to APP, Apr. 20, 1912. UNITED STATES CONGRESS, SENATE, HEARINGS BEFORE THE COMMITTEE ON BANKING AND CURRENCY ON S. 3895, pp. 10–12. Alfred Owen Crozier (AOC) to SU, June 10, 1912; SU to AOC, Oct. 1, 1912; AOC to SU, Oct. 16, 1912; SU to AOC, Oct 18, 1912; all Untermyer correspondence found in the Samuel Untermyer Papers, Jacob Rader Marcus Center of the American Jewish Archives.

34. SU to RLH, Apr. 30, 1912; RLH to SU, May 18, 1912; SU to RLH, May 28, 1912; SU to APP, May 30, 1912; RLH to SU, June 1, 1912; SU to RLH, June 3, 1912; APP to SU, Aug. 29, 1912; SU to RLH, Nov. 12, 1912; RLH to SU, Dec. 3, 1912; SU to William Jennings Bryan (WJB), July 18, 1912; SU to WJB, Dec. 3, 1912 and Nov. 21, 1912; WJB to SU, Nov. [illegible], 1912; all in the Samuel Untermyer Papers, Jacob Rader Marcus Center of the American Jewish Archives.

35. SU to APP, Oct. 11, 1912; SU to APP, Dec. 4, 1912; SU to George Wickersham, Dec. 16, 1912; SU to APP, Dec. 24, 1912; all in the Samuel Untermyer Papers, Jacob Rader Marcus Center of the American Jewish Archives.

36. SU to RLH, Jan. 23, 1912; SU to William G. Brown, Oct. 4, 1912; SU to the Editor of the *New York Sun,* Nov. 10, 1912; SU to WJB, Nov. 21, 1912; SU to APP, Nov. 18, 1912; SU to Andrew Freedman, Nov. 26, 1912; SU to William Randolph Hearst, Dec. 1, 1912; SU to Rollo Ogden, Dec. 17, 1912; SU to the *New York Tribune,* Feb. 11, 1913; SU to William Garver, Feb. 15, 1913; SU to APP, Feb. 17, 1913; SU to C. W. Van Ham, May 17, 1912; SU to C. W. Thompson (CWT), June 3, 1912; SU to CWT, May 31, 1912; CWT to SU, June 1, 1912; SU to CWT, June 3, 1912; all in the Samuel Untermyer Papers, Jacob Rader Marcus Center of the American Jewish Archives.

37. SU to RLH, Jan. 16, 1912; SU to RLH, June 12, 1912; SU to RLH, June 28, 1912; SU to Herman Sielcken, June 3, 1912; SU to A. H. Wiggin, Oct. 28, 1912; SU to Francis Lynde Stetson (FLS), Oct. 28, 1912; SU to FLS, Oct. 29, 1912; FLS to SU, Nov. 2, 1912; SU to FLS, Nov. 2, 1912; FLS to SU, Nov. 4, 1912; SU to FLS, Nov. 4, 1912; SU to FLS, Nov. 16, 1912; SU to FLS, Nov. 19, 1912; SU to Bernard Baruch, Oct. 28, 1912; all in the Samuel Untermyer Papers, Jacob Rader Marcus Center of the American Jewish Archives. UNITED STATES CONGRESS, SENATE, HEARINGS BEFORE THE COMMITTEE ON BANKING AND CURRENCY ON S. 3895, p. 7.

38. UNITED STATES CONGRESS, HOUSE OF REPRESENTATIVES, SUBCOMMITTEE OF THE COMMITTEE ON BANKING AND CURRENCY, MONEY TRUST INVESTIGATION, pp. 15–17.

39. It is worth noting that futures contracts and speculative activity as gambling had been a serious concern in the United States from at least the end of the eighteenth century, and persisted as a concern, particularly with respect to agricultural commodities, throughout the Progressive Era; BANNER, ANGLO-AMERICAN SECURITIES REGULATION, ch. 5; COWING, POPULISTS, PLUNGERS, AND PROGRESSIVES.

40. Responsible brokers, including those associated with the Association of Partners of Brokerage Firms, were increasingly concerned that public distrust of them was growing. They attributed part of the suspicion to public agitation stirred up by the Pujo hearings, but they also accepted responsibility themselves for misconduct within the industry. *The Brokers' Aim*, NEW YORK TIMES, Jan. 11, 1914, p. XX7. The vesting of jurisdiction in the Postmaster General was done to avoid questions over the federal government's authority to regulate the exchanges under the interstate commerce clause.

41. UNITED STATES CONGRESS, SENATE, HEARINGS BEFORE THE COMMITTEE ON BANKING AND CURRENCY ON S. 3895, pp. 26, 35, 59–63, 68, 88.

42. *Owen Stock Exchange Bill Is Charged with Dynamite*, WALL STREET JOURNAL, Jan. 20, 1914, p. 8; *Abusing the Commerce Clause*, WALL STREET JOURNAL, Jan. 24, 1914, p. 1; *Coolidge on Owen Bill*, WALL STREET JOURNAL, Jan. 28, 1914, p. 8; *The New Wall Street*, THE INDEPENDENT, Feb. 2, 1914, p. 147; *Owen Bill to Reorganize Exchanges up for Hearing*, WALL STREET JOURNAL, Feb. 5, 1914, p. 2; *Owen Says He Will Press His Bill for Passage*, WALL STREET JOURNAL, Feb. 7, 1914, p. 7; *The Owen Bill*, WASHINGTON POST, Feb. 5, 1914, p. 6; *Restricting Speculation*, WASHINGTON POST, Feb. 7, 1914, p. 6; *News Notes from Senate and House*, WASHINGTON POST, July 30, 1914, p. 5; *Mr. Untermyer Replies*, NEW YORK TIMES, Oct. 22, 1914, p. 13. CONGRESSIONAL RECORD, 63d Cong., 2d Sess., vol. 51, pp. 11075, 11116–72 (June 25 and 26, 1914). The report appears to have been destroyed. No copy exists in any of the likely locations in Washington, nor in the papers of the principals that I was able to examine.

43. CONGRESSIONAL RECORD, 64th Cong., 1st Sess., vol. 53, p. 229 (Dec. 13, 1915); UNITED STATES CONGRESS, SENATE, HEARINGS BEFORE THE COMMITTEE ON BANKING AND CURRENCY ON S. 3895, pp. 14–17, 26, 35, 39, 43, 59–68.

44. Statement of Samuel Untermyer, UNITED STATES CONGRESS, SENATE, HEARINGS BEFORE THE COMMITTEE ON BANKING AND CURRENCY ON S. 3895, pp. 45–46; Atwood *et al.*, *Speculation on the Stock Exchanges—Discussion*, remarks of

William C. Van Antwerp, p. 100. The discussion was held following Untermyer's delivery of a lengthy address on the subject. Untermyer, *Speculation on the Stock Exchanges and Public Regulation of the Exchanges.*

The history of the New York Stock Exchange bill is told in STATE OF NEW YORK, PROCEEDINGS OF THE JUDICIARY COMMITTEE OF THE SENATE IN THE MATTER OF THE INVESTIGATION DEMANDED BY SENATOR STEPHEN J. STILWELL. The Massachusetts legislature also considered and defeated a bill to require exchanges within that state to incorporate by special incorporation; THE COMMONWEALTH OF MASSACHUSETTS, AN ACT TO REQUIRE THE INCORPORATION OF STOCK EXCHANGES, House no. 71, Jan. 1, 1913.

45. Statement of Samuel Untermyer, Statement of William C. van Antwerp, Statement of Hjalmar H. Boyesen, Statement of Horace White, Statement of John G. Milburn, UNITED STATES CONGRESS, SENATE, HEARINGS BEFORE THE COMMITTEE ON BANKING AND CURRENCY ON S. 3895, pp. 60–63, 143, 150, 239–40, 278–79, 294, 347–59, 392–93, 403–4, 406.

46. In 1913 New York passed laws prohibiting wash sales, false statements in connection with the sale of securities, quotations of fictitious transactions, discrimination against non–exchange members, hypothecation of customers' securities, and brokers' trading against their customers; LAWS OF NEW YORK, 1913, chs. 253 (Apr. 10, 1913), 475 (May 9, 1913), 477 (May 9, 1913), 500 (May 14, 1913), 592 (May 17, 1913), and 593 (May 17, 1913). Article 36, sec. 390, of the Penal Law was aimed at "bucket shops" and prohibited similar fraudulent practices; LAWS OF NEW YORK, 1913, ch. 236 (Apr. 9, 1913). New York's Stock Corporation Law was similar to that of New Jersey in most relevant respects and had also been amended to permit the issuance of no-par stock. ANNOTATED CONSOLIDATED LAWS OF THE STATE OF NEW YORK, AS AMENDED TO JANUARY 1, 1910, vol. 5, ch. 59; SUPPLEMENT TO ANNOTATED CONSOLIDATED LAWS OF THE STATE OF NEW YORK, vol. 2, ch. 351.

47. UNITED STATES CONGRESS, HOUSE OF REPRESENTATIVES, SUBCOMMITTEE OF THE COMMITTEE ON BANKING AND CURRENCY, MONEY TRUST INVESTIGATION, p. 116.

48. UNITED STATES CONGRESS, HOUSE OF REPRESENTATIVES, SUBCOMMITTEE OF THE COMMITTEE ON BANKING AND CURRENCY, MONEY TRUST INVESTIGATION, p. 115; CONSTITUTION OF THE NEW YORK STOCK EXCHANGE (1918), pp. 99–100.

49. BRIEF SUBMITTED ON BEHALF OF THE NEW YORK STOCK EXCHANGE TO THE SENATE COMMITTEE ON BANKING AND CURRENCY, Mar. 5, 1914, p. 55, and REPLY BRIEF SUBMITTED ON BEHALF OF THE NEW YORK STOCK EXCHANGE TO THE SENATE COMMITTEE ON BANKING AND CURRENCY, Mar. 30, 1914; BLISS, THE NEW YORK CODE OF CIVIL PROCEDURE, vol. 3, secs. 1919, 1921, 1922; LEGG, THE LAW OF COMMERCIAL EXCHANGES, sec. 8; DOS PASSOS, A TREATISE ON THE LAW OF STOCK-BROKERS AND STOCK-EXCHANGES, vol. 1, pp. 40–46.

50. UNITED STATES CONGRESS, SENATE, HEARINGS BEFORE THE COMMITTEE ON BANKING AND CURRENCY ON S. 3895, pp. 239, 347, 357–59, 431. When the New York Stock Exchange transformed from a not-for-profit corporation to a business corporation in 2005, members did indeed exchange their seats for a combination of cash

and stock in the new entity; *Higgins v. New York Stock Exchange, Inc.*, 2005 N.Y. Misc. LEXIS 1869 (N.Y. Sup. Ct. 2005) (slip opinion), pp. 344–45.

51. Louis D. Brandeis and Samuel Gompers, *The Incorporation of Trade Unions: "No, Thank You!" Says Gompers*, GREEN BAG 2D, vol. 1 (Spring 1998), p. 308.

52. UNITED STATES CONGRESS, HOUSE OF REPRESENTATIVES, SUBCOMMITTEE OF THE COMMITTEE ON BANKING AND CURRENCY, MONEY TRUST INVESTIGATION, pp. 114–15.

53. NOYES, THE WAR PERIOD OF AMERICAN FINANCE, pp. 15–20.

54. *May Modify Legislation*, NEW YORK TIMES, Jan. 3, 1914, p. 2; *Split New Haven Without a Suit*, Jan. 11, 1914, p. 1; *Exchange Men See Flaws in Owen Bill*, NEW YORK TIMES, Jan. 30, 1914, p. 14; *Looking into the Future*, BOSTON DAILY GLOBE, Jan. 1, 1914, p. 8; *What the Brokers Think About the Stock Market*, BOSTON DAILY GLOBE, Jan. 4, 1914, p. 38; *Better Times*, BOSTON DAILY GLOBE, Feb. 1, 1914, p. 54; *Regulation of the Carriers*, CHICAGO DAILY TRIBUNE, Jan. 4, 1914.

55. *Financial Markets*, NEW YORK TIMES, Jan. 3, 1914, p. 14; *May Modify Legislation*, NEW YORK TIMES, Jan. 3, 1914, p. 2; *Morgan Firm out of Thirty Boards*, NEW YORK TIMES, Jan. 3, 1914, p. 1; *Morgan Move May Set Pace*, CHICAGO DAILY TRIBUNE, Jan. 3, 1914, p. 2; *J. P. Morgan & Co. Members Retire from Directorates*, WALL STREET JOURNAL, Jan. 3, 1914, p. 1; *Morgan Action Causes Surprise*, ATLANTA CONSTITUTION, Jan. 4, 1914, p. 3.

56. *Friendliness the Keynote*, LOS ANGELES TIMES, Jan. 21, 1914, p. 13; *Sweetens the Pill*, LOS ANGELES TIMES, Jan. 21, 1914, p. 11; *Financial Markets*, NEW YORK TIMES, Jan. 22, 1914, p. 14.

57. *Blocks Legislation on Stock Exchanges*, NEW YORK TIMES, Jan. 23, 1914, p. 3; *Wilson's Bills Made Public*, LOS ANGELES TIMES, Jan. 23, 1914, p. 13; *Wilson Will Aid Legislation on Stock Exchanges*, WISCONSIN STATE JOURNAL, Jan. 1914.

58. Quote from *Democrats in Panic Speed Legislation*, LOS ANGELES TIMES, Feb. 16, 1914, p. 11; *The Financial Situation in America and Europe*, NEW YORK TIMES, Feb. 2, 1914, p. 10.

59. *Bond Firms Object to State Control*, NEW YORK TIMES, Mar. 17, 1914, p. 14; *Taft Opposes Trust Law*, NEW YORK TIMES, Mar. 21, 1914, p. 3; *"Big Business Waiting,"* NEW YORK TIMES, Mar. 24, 1914, p. 8; *Stock Market*, BOSTON DAILY GLOBE, Mar. 16, 1914, p. 11.

60. *The General Trend of Trade*, NEW YORK TIMES, Apr. 19, 1914, p. XX12; *Delay Opposed by Wilson*, CHICAGO DAILY TRIBUNE, Apr. 14, 1914, p. 7; *Must Hurry Up "Trust" Laws*, LOS ANGELES TIMES, Apr. 14, 1914, p. 13; *What the Brokers Think About the Stock Market*, BOSTON DAILY GLOBE, Apr. 19, 1914, p. 46; *Market Oversold*, BOSTON DAILY GLOBE, Apr. 19, 1914, p. 46; *Watered Stock Is Proscribed*, LOS ANGELES TIMES, Apr. 18, 1914, p. 13; *Oppose Securities Bill*, BOSTON DAILY GLOBE, June 4, 1914, p. 15; *Senate Trust Bill Soon*, NEW YORK TIMES, Apr. 30, 1914, p. 14; *Drastic Regulation for Corporations*, ATLANTA CONSTITUTION, Apr. 30, 1914, p. 16; *Wield Club over Trusts*, LOS ANGELES TIMES, Apr. 30, 1914, p. 15.

61. *Favors Jail Clause in Railroad Bill*, NEW YORK TIMES, May 17, 1914, p. 10; *'Change Men Favor the Rayburn Bill*, NEW YORK TIMES, May 17, 1914, p. XX11;

For Federal Control of Railroad Bond Issues, ATLANTA CONSTITUTION, May 17, 1914, p. 11; *The Investor's Guide*, CHICAGO DAILY TRIBUNE, May 31, 1914, p. A5; *Remarks of Representatives McKenzie and Rayburn*, CONGRESSIONAL RECORD, 63d Cong., 2d Sess., vol. 51, p. 9687 (June 2, 1914); *Need Shown for Advice on Stocks*, CHICAGO DAILY TRIBUNE, May 31, 1914, p. A5.

62. *Some Psychological Inexactitudes*, WALL STREET JOURNAL, June 3, 1914, p. 1; *Wilson's Psychology*, LOS ANGELES TIMES, June 13, 1914, p. II4.

63. *President Insists on Trust Program*, BOSTON DAILY GLOBE, June 16, 1914, p. 1; *Wilson in Council Pushes Trust Plan*, NEW YORK TIMES, June 16, 1914, p. 1; *Wilson Explains Motive*, NEW YORK TIMES, June 19, 1914, p. 2; *Letters to Wilson Call Business Good*, NEW YORK TIMES, June 21, 1914, p. 1; *Vanderlip Urges Congress to Wait*, NEW YORK TIMES, June 23, 1914, p. 7.

64. Wilson, *The Uneasiness in Business*, June 25, 1914, in WILSON, THE NEW DEMOCRACY, vol. 2, p. 135; *Receivers Take H. B. Claflin Co.; Allies Sound*, NEW YORK TIMES, June 26, 1914, p. 1; *Claflin Firm Fails for $35,000,000*, ATLANTA CONSTITUTION, June 26, 1914, p. 3.

65. WILSON, *The Uneasiness in Business*, THE NEW DEMOCRACY, vol. 2, pp. 136, 137, 135, 137; *Stock Market*, BOSTON DAILY GLOBE, June 26, 1914, p. 14; *Big Business Boom for United States Pledged by Wilson*, ATLANTA CONSTITUTION, June 26, 1914, p. 1; *Wilson Says Boom Is Near for Business*, CHICAGO DAILY TRIBUNE, June 26, 1914, p. 1; *Wilson Predicts a Gigantic Boom*, NEW YORK TIMES, June 26, 1914, p. 1; *The Financial Situation in America and Europe*, NEW YORK TIMES, June 29, 1914, p. 12.

66. *Wilson Rages Impotently*, LOS ANGELES TIMES, June 26, 1914, p. 13; *New York Editors Want to Know If Crash Is Conspiracy or Psychology*, WASHINGTON POST, June 26, 1914, p. 3; *Developments of the Week*, WALL STREET JOURNAL, June 29, 1914, p. 1; B. C. Forbes, quoted in *Big Failure Shows the Reality of Trade Slump That Could Have Been Avoided*, WASHINGTON POST, June 27, 1914, p. 10.

67. *Business Men See Good Times Ahead*, NEW YORK TIMES, July 13, 1914, p. 1; *Views of Bankers in South and West*, NEW YORK TIMES, July 13, 1914, p. 7.

68. *Governors Close Stock Exchange*, NEW YORK TIMES, Aug. 1, 1914, p. 1; *Financial Markets*, NEW YORK TIMES, Aug. 1, 1914, p. 12; *Stock Market*, BOSTON DAILY GLOBE, Aug. 1, 1914, p. 7; *Gotham Closes Stock Exchange*, LOS ANGELES TIMES, Aug. 1, 1914, p. 18; *Many Millions Lost*, WASHINGTON POST, Aug. 1, 1914, p. 3; *Merchant's Point of View*, NEW YORK TIMES, Aug. 30, 1914, p. X12; *Security Markets of World Closed to Stop Unloading*, Aug. 1, 1914, p. 1; *War Crisis Shuts New York Stock Exchange*, BOSTON DAILY GLOBE, Aug. 1, 1914, p. 1; *Bankers Back Exchange Close*, CHICAGO DAILY TRIBUNE, Aug. 1, 1914, p. 5. The stock market closing was evidently at McAdoo's request; SILBER, WHEN WASHINGTON SHUT DOWN WALL STREET, pp. 12–13.

69. *Financial Markets*, NEW YORK TIMES, Feb. 12, 1915, p. 14; *Lines Win Fight for Higher Rates*, WASHINGTON POST, Dec. 19, 1914, p. 1; *Railways Lay Needs Before President*, NEW YORK TIMES, Sept. 10, 1914, p. 18; *President Asked to Aid Railroads*, ATLANTA CONSTITUTION, Sept. 10, 1914, p. 4; *Lines Win Fight for Higher Rates*, WASHINGTON POST, Dec. 19, 1914, p. 1; *Sees a Big Trade Boom*, WASHINGTON POST, Dec. 30, 1914, p. 9.

70. *How America Faced the European War Panic*, NEW YORK TIMES, Aug. 2, 1914, p. SM6; *Financial Ship Weathers Gale*, LOS ANGELES TIMES, Aug. 4, 1914, p. II10; *Calm in New York*, WASHINGTON POST, Aug. 4, 1914, p. 4.

71. *Agree on War Tax*, WASHINGTON POST, Sept. 16, 1914, p. 1; *Stock Exchange and War Tax*, WALL STREET JOURNAL, Sept. 2, 1914, p. 5; *Stamp Tax in Effect Tuesday*, BOSTON DAILY GLOBE, Nov. 29, 1914, p. 25.

72. *Bond Market Opens with Restrictions*, NEW YORK TIMES, Sept. 20, 1914, p. 9; *The Financial Situation in America and Europe*, NEW YORK TIMES, Sept. 21, 1914, p. 10; *Financial Markets*, NEW YORK TIMES, Sept. 26, 1914, p. 12; *Financial Markets*, NEW YORK TIMES, Sept. 29, 1914, p. 14; *Bond Demand Grows*, WASHINGTON POST, Oct. 1, 1914, p. 12; *Trade More Confident*, WASHINGTON POST, Oct. 3, 1914, p. 15; *The Financial Situation in America and Europe*, Oct. 5, 1914, p. 12; *Plan Big Cotton Loan*, WASHINGTON POST, Oct. 6, 1914, p. 11; *Confidence Gaining in the Business Channels*, WALL STREET JOURNAL, Oct. 7, 1914, p. 8; *Financial Markets*, NEW YORK TIMES, Oct. 8, 1914, p. 14.

73. *Wilson Convinced Business Is Better*, BOSTON DAILY GLOBE, Oct. 1, 1914, p. 8; *Stock Deals Revived*, WASHINGTON POST, Oct. 14, 1914, p. 12; *Favors Recess Plan*, Sept. 30, 1914, p. 5; *Wall Street Sees Lull in Radical Laws*, CHICAGO DAILY TRIBUNE, Nov. 9, 1914, p. 15.

74. *Reserve Banks Will Open Today*, NEW YORK TIMES, Nov. 16, 1914, p. 1; *Banks Open Nov. 16*, WASHINGTON POST, Oct. 26, 1914, p. 1; *England Opens Seas to Cotton*, NEW YORK TIMES, Oct. 27, 1914, p. 1; *Bond Market*, WALL STREET JOURNAL, Oct. 27, 1914, p. 5; *Steel Trade Picking Up*, NEW YORK TIMES, Nov. 1, 1914, p. XX11; *The Financial Situation in America and Europe*, NEW YORK TIMES, Nov. 2, 1914, p. 10; *Rate Increase Vital to Roads*, NEW YORK TIMES, Nov. 2, 1914, p. 11; *Stocks in Demand*, BOSTON DAILY GLOBE, Nov. 11, 1914, p. 1; *Ford Triples Despite the European War*, CHICAGO DAILY TRIBUNE, Nov. 8, 1914, p. G8; *Bond Trading Resumes on the N.Y. Stock Exchange*, WALL STREET JOURNAL, Nov. 30, 1914, p. 1; *Trading in Bonds*, WASHINGTON POST, Nov. 29, 1914, p. 11; *Financial Markets*, NEW YORK TIMES, Dec. 13, 1914, p. XX8; *Stock Trading Today*, WASHINGTON POST, Dec. 12, 1914, p. 10; *Stock Market*, BOSTON DAILY GLOBE, Dec. 29, 1914, p. 11.

75. *The Sixty-Third Congress and "The New Freedom" for American Business*, CURRENT OPINION, vol. 58, no. 4 (Apr. 1, 1915), p. 223.

TEN: MANUFACTURING SECURITIES

1. Quoted in CLEVELAND & HUERTAS, CITIBANK, p. 136.

2. Huertas & Silverman, *Charles E. Mitchell*, pp. 81–103; CAROSSO, INVESTMENT BANKING IN AMERICA, p. 274; GEISST, WALL STREET, p. 164; KLEIN, RAINBOW'S END, p. 53; CLEVELAND & HUERTAS, CITIBANK, pp. 86–87.

3. PEACH, THE SECURITY AFFILIATES OF NATIONAL BANKS, pp. 38–39.

4. PEACH, THE SECURITY AFFILIATES OF NATIONAL BANKS; CAROSSO, INVESTMENT BANKING IN AMERICA, pp. 96–98, 276–79; SELIGMAN, THE TRANSFORMATION OF WALL STREET, p. 23.

5. KLEIN, RAINBOW'S END, pp. 55–59; ALLEN, ONLY YESTERDAY, pp. 138, 136.

6. Joel Seligman quotes Ferdinand Pecora as writing that "Mitchell had astutely

foreseen as early as June 1917 that the World War I Liberty Bond drives would result in 'the development of a large, new army of investors in this country'"; JOEL SELIGMAN, THE TRANSFORMATION OF WALL STREET, p. 25.

7. *Editorial*, THE STREET, vol. 1, no. 1, July 30, 1919, p. 8; Robert B. Armstrong, *The Liberty Loans—And After, id.* at p. 1.

8. *Now Is the Time to Invest*, WASHINGTON POST, Aug. 10, 1914, p. 4; *Save and Invest*, WALL STREET JOURNAL, Oct. 7, 1914, p. 2; GRAHAM & DODD, SECURITY ANALYSIS, p. 2; NOYES, THE WAR PERIOD OF AMERICAN FINANCE, pp. 101, 135, 148; *Building Up the Financial Power of the United States*, WASHINGTON POST, Jan. 19, 1916, p. 4; SOBEL, THE BIG BOARD, pp. 213, 215.

9. NOYES, THE WAR PERIOD OF AMERICAN FINANCE, pp. 92–95, 104–5; *Federal Reserve System and Long Time Investments*, WALL STREET JOURNAL, Jan. 5, 1915, p. 8; *Safeguarding Investments*, WASHINGTON POST, Nov. 11, 1916, p. 6.

10. NOYES, THE WAR PERIOD OF AMERICAN FINANCE, pp. 98, 118, 113–14.

11. Woodrow Wilson, *An Address to a Joint Session of Congress*, April 2, 1917, in WILSON, THE PAPERS OF WOODROW WILSON (Link, ed.), vol. 41, p. 519. Noyes attributed the drop in the market to the diversion of capital to war loans as well as to the market's anticipation of governmental control of profiteering through instrumentalities like the War Industries Board; NOYES, THE WAR PERIOD OF AMERICAN FINANCE, pp. 225–26.

12. MCADOO, CROWDED YEARS, pp. 372–74. While there is no question that the Liberty Bond drives were successful in terms of the money they raised, scholars recently have questioned whether it was patriotism or market forces that made the difference; Rockoff & Kang, *Capitalizing Patriotism*.

13. MCADOO, CROWDED YEARS, pp. 382–83; NOYES, THE WAR PERIOD OF AMERICAN FINANCE, p. 175.

14. NOYES, THE WAR PERIOD OF AMERICAN FINANCE, pp. 181–83.

15. ST. CLAIR, THE STORY OF THE LIBERTY LOANS, pp. 41–42; NOYES, THE WAR PERIOD OF AMERICAN FINANCE, p. 184.

16. *Uses of National Bonds*, NEW YORK TIMES, May 18, 1917, p. 12; *Vanderlip Says War Bond Is Best Investment*, NEW YORK TIMES, May 27, 1917, p. 62; *It Is Your Duty*, NEW YORK TIMES, June 12, 1917, p. 16; *Theodore Roosevelt Writes of Duty of Every American to Invest in Liberty Bonds*, WASHINGTON POST, Oct. 20, 1917, p. 1; Sophie Irene Loeb, *Are You Preparing for the Next Liberty Loan?*, WASHINGTON POST, Aug. 19, 1918, p. 7; *Entire Savings in Liberty Bonds*, WALL STREET JOURNAL, Oct. 9, 1917, p. 8; *Suggests They Buy Bonds*, WASHINGTON POST, Oct. 17, 1917, p. S1.

17. Edward A. Bradford, *Fashions in War Bonds*, NEW YORK TIMES, Sept. 30, 1917, p. SM3; NOYES, THE WAR PERIOD OF AMERICAN FINANCE, pp. 175–90; *Must Stir Nation to Buy the Bonds*, NEW YORK TIMES, May 18, 1917, p. 1; *Liberty Loan Is Safe*, WASHINGTON POST, June 14, 1917, p. 1; *Bonds for Farmers, Slogan*, WASHINGTON POST, Aug. 5, 1917, p. 11; *Everybody Gets a Chance*, WASHINGTON POST, Oct. 3, 1917, p. 6; ST. CLAIR, THE STORY OF THE LIBERTY LOANS, p. 45. St. Clair publishes full color plates of many of the posters.

18. NOYES, THE WAR PERIOD OF AMERICAN FINANCE, pp. 225–26; GRAHAM & DODD, SECURITY ANALYSIS, p. 2; *Liberty Bonds Below Par Laid at Door of Wealthy*,

WALL STREET JOURNAL, Jan. 21, 1918, p. 8; *Selling Government Bonds*, WALL STREET JOURNAL, Apr. 15, 1918, p. 1.

19. PEACH, THE SECURITY AFFILIATES OF NATIONAL BANKS, pp. 22–31; Huertas & Silverman, *Charles E. Mitchell*, p. 85.

20. Charles E. Mitchell, "*Sound Inflation*," MAGAZINE OF WALL STREET, vol. 20, pp. 295–96; *Liberty Loan Subscriptions $3,035,226,850*, ATLANTA CONSTITUTION, June 23, 1917, p. 1; *Liberty Loan's Estimate Stands*, WASHINGTON POST, June 19, 1917, p. 2; *Loan over Top; 5 Billions*, CHICAGO DAILY TRIBUNE, Oct. 28, 1917, p. 1; *Minimum Passed by Eight Districts*, BOSTON DAILY GLOBE, Oct. 26, 1917, p. 1; *Billion in Bonds Sold, But Drive Must Go Faster*, NEW YORK TIMES, Oct. 17, 1917, p. 1; *Facts About the Third Liberty Bond Drives*, BOSTON DAILY GLOBE, Apr. 6, 1918, p. 6; *17,000,000 Buyers Set a New Record in the Bond Drive*, NEW YORK TIMES, May 6, 1918, p. 1; *Final Figures of Liberty Loan Given to Public*, CHICAGO DAILY TRIBUNE, Nov. 20, 1918, p. 10.

21. PEACH, THE SECURITY AFFILIATES OF NATIONAL BANKS, pp. 31–33; CLEVELAND & HUERTAS, CITIBANK, p. 136.

22. The financial newspaper *The Street* began publication in 1919 in order to fill a perceived demand for more investment news and advice. *Buying Is Better at Higher Prices*, WASHINGTON POST, Jan. 14, 1918, p. 9; *Hold Liberty Bonds, He Warns*, WASHINGTON POST, Jan. 21, 1918, p. 6; *Public Is Buying U.S. Steel Shares*, WASHINGTON POST, Jan. 24, 1918, p. 9; *The Financial Situation: Prices Reflecting a Return of Confidence*, NEW YORK TIMES, Jan. 7, 1918, p. 16; *100,000 Own P.R.R. Stock*, NEW YORK TIMES, Jan. 22, 1918, p. 18; *Condemns Trading of Liberty Bonds*, NEW YORK TIMES, July 9, 1918, p. 17.

23. This was hardly the low point for Liberty Bonds. They dropped to 82 in 1920, for reasons beyond the scope of my story. NOYES, THE WAR PERIOD OF AMERICAN FINANCE, pp. 202, 342.

24. *Vanderlip Says War Bond Is Best Investment*, NEW YORK TIMES, May 27, 1917, p. 62.

25. WILLOUGHBY, THE CAPITAL ISSUES COMMITTEE AND WAR FINANCE CORPORATION, pp. 9–15. *Government's Corporation Will Aid Savings Banks*, WALL STREET JOURNAL, Feb. 14, 1918, p. 5; WILLOUGHBY, *id.*, p. 10. My discussion of the basic facts surrounding the Capital Issues Committee and its work draws heavily on Willoughby.

26. WILLOUGHBY, THE CAPITAL ISSUES COMMITTEE AND WAR FINANCE CORPORATION, pp. 16–17; CAROSSO, INVESTMENT BANKING IN AMERICA, pp. 230–31; PROCEEDINGS OF THE SIXTH ANNUAL CONVENTION OF THE INVESTMENT BANKERS ASSOCIATION OF AMERICA, Nov. 12, 13 and 14, 1917, p. 152.

27. CAPITAL ISSUES COMMITTEE, [FIRST] REPORT, doc. no. 1485, 65th Cong., 3d Sess., Dec. 2, 1918, p. 3 (hereinafter, "FIRST REPORT"). An excellent description of the Red Scare of 1919 and the national turn to intolerance is provided in ALLEN, ONLY YESTERDAY, pp. 38–62.

28. WILLOUGHBY, THE CAPITAL ISSUES COMMITTEE AND WAR FINANCE CORPORATION, pp. 17–20.

29. *Ibid.*, pp. 24–33.

30. *Ibid.*, pp. 37–38. For a fascinating account of the way McAdoo protected the integrity of the United States' money supply in order to bring the nation to world monetary leadership, *see* SILBER, WHEN WASHINGTON SHUT DOWN WALL STREET.

31. CAPITAL ISSUES COMMITTEE, FIRST REPORT, p. 2; CAPITAL ISSUES COMMITTEE, [FINAL] REPORT, doc. no. 1836, 65th Cong., 3d Sess., Feb. 28, 1919, p. 1 (hereinafter "FINAL REPORT").

32. CAPITAL ISSUES COMMITTEE, FIRST REPORT, p. 3; CAPITAL ISSUES COMMITTEE, FINAL REPORT, pp. 2, 3; CAROSSO, INVESTMENT BANKING IN AMERICA, p. 233.

33. It is wrong to state, as Link does, that the Owen bill "was almost identical to the Truth-in-Securities Act of 1933"; LINK, WILSON: THE NEW FREEDOM, p. 426, n. 29. The Taylor bill of 1919, discussed below in the text, was far closer in both form and concept; 66th Cong., 1st Sess., H.R. 188, May 19, 1919. Michael Parrish places a gap between the postwar interest in federal securities regulation, which ultimately produced nothing, and the 1933 Act, PARRISH, SECURITIES REGULATION AND THE NEW DEAL, p. 20, but when the New Deal legislation was on the table it was based on the concepts and tools of the Taylor bill.

34. S. 1291, 64th Cong., 1st Sess., Dec. 10, 1915.

35. JOEL SELIGMAN, THE TRANSFORMATION OF WALL STREET, p. 41. Wall Street embraced the Taylor approach much as it would approve of the 1933 Act. Counsel to the Investment Bankers Association, Robert Reed, called the Taylor bill "perhaps the most intelligently conceived plan of enforced publicity yet proposed," except, that is, for its requirement that the underwriter sign the registration statement; Reed, *"Blue Sky" Laws*, pp. 185–86, n. 6. Reed's support is consistent with the view taken by the New York Stock Exchange in 1914, that the regulation of corporate securities was a federal matter, not an exchange matter.

36. H.R. 15399, 65th Cong., 3d Sess., Jan. 30, 1919; H.R. 15571, 65th Cong., 3d Sess., Feb. 13, 1919; SELIGMAN, THE TRANSFORMATION OF WALL STREET, pp. 49–50.

37. H.R. 15477, 65th Cong., 3d Sess., Jan. 30, 1919; H.R. 15922, 65th Cong., 3d Sess., Feb. 13, 1919. H.R. 15922 dropped the "due diligence" defense of H.R. 15477. Parrish identifies this bill as similar to one of the central models for the 1933 Act drafted at Franklin Roosevelt's request; PARRISH, SECURITIES REGULATION AND THE NEW DEAL, pp. 17–18.

38. Wilson, *An Address to a Joint Session of Congress*, Aug. 8, 1919, in WILSON, THE PAPERS OF WOODROW WILSON (Link, ed.), vol. 62, pp. 215, 214, 216; *A Memorandum by Alexander Mitchell Palmer*, c. Aug. 6, 1919, in *id.*, vol. 62, pp. 171, 180.

39. PARRISH, SECURITIES REGULATION AND THE NEW DEAL, pp. 18–19; Reed, *Blue Sky Laws*, p. 185, n. 6; SELIGMAN, THE TRANSFORMATION OF WALL STREET, pp. 49–50. In addition to the Investment Bankers Association, the bill was endorsed by the American Bankers' Association and the Mortgage Bankers' Association; CHERRINGTON, THE INVESTOR AND THE SECURITIES ACT, p. 51, n. 21.

40. NOYES, THE WAR PERIOD OF AMERICAN FINANCE, pp. 301–3; ALLEN, ONLY YESTERDAY, pp. 264–65.

EPILOGUE

1. Keynes, The General Theory of Employment, Interest, and Money, ch. 12. Lest I open myself to criticism that I am using the ideas of a British economist to explain the American market, I should note that the British stock market is the most similar to that of the United States, although based on a very different historical development and with some significant differences; Cheffins, *Putting Britain on the Roe Map*. More relevant, Keynes specifically noted the extraordinary degree of speculation in the New York market. Keynes, *id.*, pp. 158–59.

Robert Shiller shows that the period from the late 1930s through the early 1960s was a period during which price-to-earnings ratios remained at historically low levels, which tends to predict higher long-term returns; Shiller, Irrational Exuberance, p. 8. As I will later discuss, this was the age of managerialism, during which corporate managements successfully used various corporate control techniques to protect themselves from excessive stockholder pressure.

2. Shiller, Irrational Exuberance, p. 8; Mitchell, Corporate Irresponsibility, *passim*.

3. Carosso, Investment Banking in America, p. 143; Berle & Means, The Modern Corporation and Private Property; Means, *The Separation of Ownership and Control in American Industry*; Douglas, *Directors Who Do Not Direct*; Lawrence E. Mitchell, unpublished remarks delivered at Columbia University on Nov. 11, 2006 (copy on file with author).

4. Larner, Management Control and the Large Corporation; United States Temporary National Economic Committee, The Distribution of Ownership in the 200 Largest Nonfinancial Corporations; Burch, The Managerial Revolution Reassessed; Zeitlin, *Corporate Ownership and Control*; Stigler & Friedland, *The Literature of Economics*; Shleifer & Vishny, *Large Shareholders and Corporate Control*; Holderness & Sheehan, *The Role of Majority Shareholders in Publicly Held Corporations*. An excellent overview of the research done through the mid-1970s is provided in Eisenberg, The Structure of the Corporation, ch. 5.

5. Holderness, Kroszner & Sheehan, *Were the Good Old Days That Good?*

6. Lewellen, Executive Compensation in Large Industrial Corporations; Larner, Management Control and the Large Corporation, pp. 34–61; Kolko, Wealth and Power in America, pp. 67–68.

7. Based on data drawn from Shiller, Irrational Exuberance, p. 8.

8. Markowitz, *Portfolio Selection*; Sharpe, *Capital Asset Prices*; Bernstein, Capital Ideas.

9. Nader, Green and Seligman describe 1975 as a year of reckoning for a dozen major conglomerates; Nader, Green & Seligman, Taming the Giant Corporation, p. 78; Farrell & Murphy, *Comments on the Theme*. The story of this era is well told in Joel Seligman, *A Sheep in Wolf's Clothing*, pp. 325, 333–36. United States Securities and Exchange Commission, Report on Questionable and Illegal Corporate Payments and Practices. SEC *Staff Study of the Financial Collapse of the Penn Central Co. — Summary* [1972–1973 Transfer Binder], Fed. Sec.

L. REP. (CCH) PAR. 78,931 (1972). Numerous lawsuits resulted from the collapse of Penn Central: *e.g.*, *In re Penn Central Transp. Co.*, 484 F. 2d 1300 (3d Cir. 1973); *In re Penn Central Transp. Co.*, 452 F. 2d 1107 (3d Cir. 1971); *SEC v. Penn Central Co.*, Fed. Sec. L. Rep. P 94,527 (E.D. Pa. May 2, 1974). The securities class action first became a practical remedy for shareholders after 1966. Patrick, *The Securities Class Action for Damages Comes of Age*; *Escott v. BarChris Construction Corp.*, 283 F. Supp. 643 (S.D.N.Y. 1968). *See also Gould v. American-Hawaiian S.S. Co.*, 535 F. 2d 761 (3d Cir. 1976); *Securities and Exchange Commission v. Texas Gulf Sulphur*, 446 F. 2d 1301 (2d Cir. 1971), *cert. den.* 404 U.S. 1005 (1972). A history of the SEC's attempts to federalize corporate law is told in Karmel, *Realizing the Dream of William O. Douglas*. An example of shareholder activism is *Medical Committee for Human Rights v. Securities and Exchange Commission*, 432 F. 2d 659 (1970).

10. Tsuk Mitchell, *Shareholders as Proxies*; Gordon, *Independent Directors and Stock Market Prices*; Mitchell, *The Trouble with Boards*.

11. On poison pills, *see* Subramanian, *The Influence of Antitakeover Statutes on Incorporation Choice*; Kahan & Rock, *How I Learned to Stop Worrying and Love the Pill*.

12. Lucier, Kocourek & Habbel, *CEO Succession 2005*.

13. MITCHELL, CORPORATE IRRESPONSIBILITY. On executive compensation, *see* BEBCHUK & FRIED, PAY WITHOUT PERFORMANCE; CRYSTAL, IN SEARCH OF EXCESS.

14. *See* NYSE data at http://www. nysedata.com/nysedata/default.aspx?tabid=115; John Authers and Deborah Brewster, *Goldilocks Still Defies the Bears*, FINANCIAL TIMES, Jan. 9, 2007, p. 11; Philip Cogan, *Darwinian Truth Behind the Investment Struggle*, FINANCIAL TIMES, Aug. 12, 2006, p. 16; *but see Mutual Funds and Portfolio Turnover*, INVESTMENT COMPANY INSTITUTE, RESEARCH COMMENTARY, Nov. 17, 2004 (available at http://www.ici.org/stats/res/rc_v1n2.pdf) (arguing that a simple average of the turnover rate [117 percent in 2004] is misleading and a median turnover rate [76 percent in 2004] is more accurate).

15. TONELLO, REVISITING STOCK MARKET SHORT TERMISM, p. 3 (citing Graham, Harvey & Rajgopal, *The Economic Implications of Corporate Financial Reporting*); TONELLO, *id.*, p. 8.

16. The rise of private equity over the last decade has created new classes of investors who have the potential to change something of the shape of American corporate capitalism. I do not discuss this development because I believe it is too early to say anything meaningful about the phenomenon, and too complex and varied to assess in the Epilogue to a history.

17. Cheffins, *Putting Britain on the Roe Map*; La Porta, Lopez-De-Silanes & Shleifer, *Corporate Ownership Around the World*; Shleifer & Vishny, *A Survey of Corporate Governance*.

SELECT BIBLIOGRAPHY

The bibliography lists manuscript collections, governmental publications, periodicals, scholarly journals and books cited in the notes, as well as the most relevant background sources. Specific articles from the newspapers and popular magazines listed below are cited fully in the notes. Specific cases and statutes are cited in the notes, but not listed below.

NEWSPAPERS AND POPULAR PERIODICALS

THE ALBANY LAW JOURNAL: A WEEKLY RECORD OF THE LAW AND LAWYERS
THE AMERICAN MAGAZINE
THE ARENA
ARTHUR'S HOME MAGAZINE
THE ATLANTA CONSTITUTION
THE ATLANTA JOURNAL
THE ATLANTIC MONTHLY
THE BALTIMORE SUN
THE BOSTON DAILY GLOBE
THE BROOKLYN EAGLE
CENTURY ILLUSTRATED MAGAZINE
CHICAGO DAILY TRIBUNE
CINCINNATI COMMERCIAL TRIBUNE
COLLIER'S WEEKLY
COMMERCIAL & FINANCIAL CHRONICLE
THE COSMOPOLITAN
CURRENT LITERATURE
CURRENT OPINION
THE DES MOINES DAILY READER
THE FAIRBANKS (ALASKA) CITIZEN
FINANCIAL TIMES

THE FINANCIER, NEW YORK
FORUM
FRANK LESLIE'S POPULAR MONTHLY
GUNTON'S MAGAZINE
THE INDEPENDENT
INDIANAPOLIS STAR
THE LADIES' HOME JOURNAL
LEGAL TIMES
LIPPINCOTT'S MONTHLY MAGAZINE
THE LOS ANGELES TIMES
MANSFIELD (OHIO) SHIELD
MCCLURE'S MAGAZINE
THE NATION
THE NATIONAL BANKER
THE NEW YORK COMMERCIAL BULLETIN
THE NEW YORK DAILY NEWS
THE NEW YORK HERALD
NEW YORK OBSERVER AND CHRONICLE
THE NEW YORK TIMES
NEW YORK TRIBUNE
THE NEW YORK WORLD
NILES' WEEKLY REGISTER

THE OUTLOOK

THE PHILADELPHIA PUBLIC LEDGER

THE PORTSMOUTH (N.H.) HERALD

THE (RIVERSIDE, CALIF.) PRESS
ENTERPRISE

THE RICHMOND DISPATCH

SAN FRANCISCO CHRONICLE

THE SATURDAY EVENING POST

THE STREET

SYRACUSE HERALD

THE WALL STREET JOURNAL

THE WASHINGTON POST

THE WATCHMAN

WHEELING (WEST VIRGINIA) REGISTER

MANUSCRIPTS AND COLLECTIONS

Bureau of Corporations Archives, National Archives Research Administration, College Park, Md.

Carter Glass Papers, Library of Congress, Manuscript Division, Washington, D.C.

Historic Corporate Report Collection, Baker Library, Harvard University, Boston, Mass.

William Gibbs McAdoo Papers, Library of Congress, Manuscript Division, Washington, D.C.

National Civic Federation Archives, New York Public Library, New York, N.Y.

Robert Owen Papers, Library of Congress, Manuscript Division, Washington, D.C.

Theodore Roosevelt Papers, Library of Congress, Manuscript Division, Washington, D.C.

William Howard Taft Papers, Library of Congress, Manuscript Division, Washington, D.C.

Samuel Untermyer Papers, Jacob Rader Marcus Center of the American Jewish Archives, Hebrew Union College, Jewish Institute of Religion, Cincinnati, Ohio.

Horace White Papers, New York Historical Society, New York, N.Y.

Woodrow Wilson Papers, Library of Congress, Manuscript Division, Washington, D.C.

PUBLISHED LETTERS AND SPEECHES

CHICAGO CONFERENCE ON TRUSTS: SPEECHES, DEBATES, RESOLUTIONS, LIST OF THE DELEGATES, COMMITTEES, ETC. (The Civic Federation of Chicago; 1900).

HOUSE, EDWARD MANDELL. THE INTIMATE PAPERS OF COLONEL HOUSE. Charles Seymour, ed., 4 vols. (Boston; Houghton Mifflin; 1926–28).

PROCEEDINGS OF THE NATIONAL CONFERENCE ON TRUSTS AND COMBINATIONS UNDER THE AUSPICES OF THE NATIONAL CIVIC FEDERATION, OCTOBER 22–25, 1907 (New York; The McConnell Press; 1908).

ROOSEVELT, THEODORE. THE LETTERS OF THEODORE ROOSEVELT, Elting E. Morison, ed., 8 vols. (Cambridge, Mass.; Harvard Univ. Press; 1951–1954).

———. PRESIDENTIAL ADDRESSES AND STATE PAPERS OF THEODORE ROOSEVELT, 4 vols. in 2 (New York; Kraus Reprint Co.; 1970) (originally published New York; P. F. Collier & Son, 1905).

———. THE ROOSEVELT POLICY: SPEECHES, LETTERS AND STATE PAPERS, RELATING TO CORPORATE WEALTH AND CLOSELY ALLIED TOPICS, William Griffith, ed. 3

vols. (New York; Kraus Reprint Co.; 1971) (originally published New York; Current Literature; 1919).

———. THE SELECTED LETTERS OF THEODORE ROOSEVELT, H. W. Brands, ed. (New York; Cooper Square Press; 2001).

———. SELECTIONS FROM THE CORRESPONDENCE OF THEODORE ROOSEVELT AND HENRY CABOT LODGE, Henry Cabot Lodge, ed. (New York; Charles Scribner's Sons; 1925).

———. THEODORE ROOSEVELT AND HIS TIME SHOWN IN HIS OWN LETTERS, Joseph Bucklin Bishop, ed. (New York; Charles Scribner's Sons; 1920).

STOCKTON, R. F. ADDRESS BY COMMODORE R. F. STOCKTON TO THE PEOPLE OF NEW JERSEY IN RELATION TO THE EXISTING CONTRACTS BETWEEN THE STATE AND THE UNITED DELAWARE AND RARITAN CANAL AND CAMDEN AND AMBOY RAILROAD COMPANIES (Princeton, N.J.; John T. Robinson; 1849).

TAFT, WILLIAM HOWARD. THE COLLECTED WORKS OF WILLIAM HOWARD TAFT, David H. Burton, ed., 6 vols. (Athens, Ohio; Ohio Univ. Press; 2001).

WATKINS, JOHN ELFRETH. THE CAMDEN AND AMBOY RAILROAD: ORIGIN AND EARLY HISTORY, ADDRESS DELIVERED AT BORDENTOWN, NEW JERSEY (Washington, D.C.; W. F. Roberts; 1891).

WILSON, WOODROW. COLLEGE AND STATE: EDUCATIONAL, LITERARY, AND POLITICAL PAPERS (1875–1913), vol. 2. The Public Papers of Woodrow Wilson, Ray Stannard Baker and William E. Dodd, eds. (New York; Harper & Brothers; 1925–27).

———. THE COST OF LIVING: ADDRESS OF THE PRESIDENT OF THE UNITED STATES DELIVERED AT A JOINT SESSION OF THE TWO HOUSES OF CONGRESS, AUGUST 8, 1919 (Washington, D.C.; Government Printing Office; 1919).

———. THE NEW DEMOCRACY: PRESIDENTIAL MESSAGES, ADDRESSES, AND OTHER PAPERS (1913–1917), vols. 1–2. The Public Papers of Woodrow Wilson, Ray Stannard Baker and William E. Dodd, eds. (New York; Harper & Brothers; 1925–27).

———. THE PAPERS OF WOODROW WILSON, Arthur S. Link *et al.*, eds. 69 vols. (Princeton, N.J.; Princeton Univ. Press; 1966–94).

———. WAR AND PEACE: PRESIDENTIAL MESSAGES, ADDRESSES, AND PUBLIC PAPERS (1917–1924), vol. 1. The Public Papers of Woodrow Wilson, Ray Stannard Baker and William E. Dodd, eds. (New York; Harper & Brothers; 1925–27).

GOVERNMENTAL AND LEGISLATIVE MATERIAL

ACTS INCORPORATING THE DELAWARE AND RARITAN CANAL COMPANY, THE CAMDEN AND AMBOY RAILROAD AND TRANSPORTATION COMPANY, AND THE NEW JERSEY RAILROAD AND TRANSPORTATION COMPANY, WITH THE SEVERAL SUPPLEMENTS AND RESOLUTIONS RELATIVE THERETO (Trenton, N.J.; Phillips & Boswell; 1849).

ANNOTATED CONSOLIDATED LAWS OF THE STATE OF NEW YORK, AS AMENDED TO JANUARY 1, 1910 (New York; Banks Law Publishing; 1909), vol. 5.

CAPITAL ISSUES COMMITTEE. [FIRST] REPORT, doc. no. 1485, 65th Cong., 3d Sess., Dec. 2, 1918.

———. [FINAL] REPORT, doc. no. 1836, 65th Cong., 3d Sess., Feb. 28, 1919.

COMPILED STATUTES OF NEW JERSEY, vol. 2 (Newark, N.J.; Soney & Sage; 1911).

AN INVESTIGATION INTO THE AFFAIRS OF THE DELAWARE & RARITAN CANAL AND CAMDEN & AMBOY RAILROAD COMPANIES IN REFERENCE TO CERTAIN CHARGES BY "A CITIZEN OF BURLINGTON," DECEMBER, 1848 (Newark, N.J.; The Daily Advertiser; 1849).

NATIONAL BUREAU OF ECONOMIC RESEARCH, NEW YORK, BUSINESS CONCENTRATION AND PRICE POLICY: A CONFERENCE OF THE UNIVERSITIES—NATIONAL BUREAU COMMITTEE FOR ECONOMIC RESEARCH (Princeton, N.J.; Princeton Univ. Press; 1955).

REPORT OF COMMISSIONERS APPOINTED TO INVESTIGATE CHARGES MADE AGAINST THE DIRECTORS OF THE DELAWARE AND RARITAN CANAL AND CAMDEN AND AMBOY RAILROAD AND TRANSPORTATION COMPANIES, MADE TO THE LEGISLATURE, FEBRUARY 8, 1850 (Trenton, N.J.; Phillips & Boswell; 1850).

REPORT OF THE COMMISSIONERS APPOINTED TO REVISE THE GENERAL ACTS OF THE STATE OF NEW JERSEY RELATING TO CORPORATIONS (Jersey City; Jersey City Printing; 1896).

REPORT OF THE RAILROAD SECURITIES COMMISSION TO THE PRESIDENT AND LETTER OF THE PRESIDENT TRANSMITTING THE REPORT TO THE CONGRESS, HOUSE OF REPRESENTATIVES, doc. no. 256, 62d Cong., 2d Sess., Dec. 11, 1911.

SPECIAL REPORT ON TAXATION SUPPLEMENTING PREVIOUS REPORTS ON THE TAXATION OF CORPORATIONS AND COVERING THE TAX MOVEMENT THROUGHOUT THE UNITED STATES DURING 1912 (Washington, D.C.; U.S. Government Printing Office; 1914).

STAFF REPORT OF THE SUBCOMMITTEE ON DOMESTIC FINANCE COMMITTEE ON BANKING AND CURRENCY, HOUSE OF REPRESENTATIVES, FEDERAL RESERVE STRUCTURE AND THE DEVELOPMENT OF MONETARY POLICY: 1915–1935 (Washington, D.C.; U.S. Government Printing Office; 1971).

STATE OF NEW YORK. PROCEEDINGS OF THE JUDICIARY COMMITTEE OF THE SENATE IN THE MATTER OF THE INVESTIGATION DEMANDED BY SENATOR STEPHEN J. STILWELL (Albany, N.Y.; J. B. Lyon; 1913).

——. REPORT OF COMMITTEE ON SPECULATION IN SECURITIES AND COMMODITIES (1909).

STATUTES AT LARGE OF THE UNITED STATES OF AMERICA FROM MARCH, 1897 TO MARCH, 1899, vol. 30 (Washington, D.C.; Government Printing Office; 1899).

STATUTES AT LARGE OF THE UNITED STATES OF AMERICA FROM MARCH, 1913 TO MARCH, 1915, vol. 38 (Washington, D.C.; [Government Printing Office]; 1915).

STATUTES AT LARGE OF THE UNITED STATES OF AMERICA FROM MAY, 1919 TO MARCH, 1921, vol. 41 (Washington, D.C.; Government Printing Office; 1921).

SUPPLEMENT TO ANNOTATED CONSOLIDATED LAWS OF THE STATE OF NEW YORK (New York; Banks Law Publishing; 1913), vol. 2.

UNITED STATES CAPITAL ISSUES COMMITTEE. *See* CAPITAL ISSUES COMMITTEE.

UNITED STATES CONGRESS, HOUSE OF REPRESENTATIVES. HEARINGS ON HOUSE BILL 19745, BEFORE SUBCOMMITTEE NO. 3 OF THE COMMITTEE ON THE JUDICIARY, 60th Cong., 1st Sess. (Washington, D.C.; Government Printing Office; 1908).

——. REGULATION OF THE ISSUANCE OF STOCKS AND BONDS BY COMMON CARRI-

ERS, HEARINGS BEFORE THE COMMITTEE ON INTERSTATE AND FOREIGN COMMERCE, 63d Cong., 2d Sess. (Washington, D.C.; U.S. Government Printing Office; 1914).

———. REPORT NO. 3375, 57th Cong., 2d Sess., Jan. 26, 1903.

———. REPORT TO ACCOMPANY H.J. RES. NO. 138, REPORT NO. 1501, Part 1, 56th Cong., 1st Sess., May 15, 1900.

———. SUBCOMMITTEE OF THE COMMITTEE ON BANKING AND CURRENCY, MONEY TRUST INVESTIGATION: INVESTIGATION OF FINANCIAL AND MONETARY CONDITIONS IN THE UNITED STATES UNDER HOUSE RESOLUTIONS NOS. 429 AND 504 (Washington, D.C.; U.S. Government Printing Office; 1913).

UNITED STATES CONGRESS, SENATE. HEARINGS BEFORE THE COMMITTEE ON BANKING AND CURRENCY ON S. 3895, A BILL TO PREVENT THE USE OF THE MAILS AND OF THE TELEGRAPH AND TELEPHONE IN FURTHERANCE OF FRAUDULENT AND HARMFUL TRANSACTIONS ON STOCK EXCHANGES, 63d Cong., 2d Sess. (Washington, D.C.; U.S. Government Printing Office; 1914).

———. SENATE REPORT NO. 1242, *Views of Mr. Tillman*, 59th Cong., 1st Sess., March 15, 1906, pp. 1–11.

UNITED STATES DEPARTMENT OF COMMERCE. HISTORICAL STATISTICS OF THE UNITED STATES : COLONIAL TIMES TO 1970, Part 1 and Part 2 (Washington, D.C.; U.S. Government Printing Office; 1976).

———. HISTORICAL STATISTICS OF THE UNITED STATES, MILLENNIAL ED. Susan B. Carter, Scott Sigmund Gartner, Michael R. Haines, Alan L. Olmstead, Richard Sutch, and Gavin Wright, eds. (Cambridge, Eng.; Cambridge Univ. Press; 2006).

UNITED STATES DEPARTMENT OF COMMERCE, BUREAU OF THE CENSUS. STATE GOVERNMENT TAX COLLECTIONS: 2005, available at http://www.census.gov/govs/statetax/0508destax.html.

UNITED STATES DEPARTMENT OF COMMERCE AND LABOR. REPORT OF THE COMMISSIONER OF CORPORATIONS (Washington, D.C.; Government Printing Office; 1904).

———. REPORT OF THE COMMISSIONER OF CORPORATIONS ON THE STEEL INDUSTRY. PART 1: ORGANIZATION, INVESTMENT, PROFITS, AND POSITION OF UNITED STATES STEEL CORPORATION (Washington, D.C.; Government Printing Office; 1911).

UNITED STATES INDUSTRIAL COMMISSION. FINAL REPORT, vol. 19 (Westport, Conn.; Greenwood; 1970) (originally published 1900–1902).

———. PRELIMINARY REPORT ON TRUSTS AND INDUSTRIAL COMBINATIONS, TOGETHER WITH TESTIMONY, REVIEW OF EVIDENCE, CHARTS SHOWING EFFECTS OF PRICES, AND TOPICAL DIGEST, vol. 1 (Westport, Conn.; Greenwood; 1970) (originally published 1900–1902).

———. REPORT OF THE INDUSTRIAL COMMISSION ON INDUSTRIAL COMBINATIONS IN EUROPE, vol. 18 (Westport, Conn.; Greenwood; 1970) (originally published 1900–1902).

———. REPORT OF THE INDUSTRIAL COMMISSION ON THE RELATIONS AND CONDITIONS OF CAPITAL AND LABOR EMPLOYED IN MANUFACTURES AND GENERAL

Business, Including Testimony So Far As Taken November 1, 1900, and Digest of Testimony, vol. 7 (Westport, Conn.; Greenwood; 1970) (originally published 1900–1902).

———. Report of the Industrial Commission on the Relations and Condition of Capital and Labor Employed in the Mining Industry Including Testimony, Review of Evidence, and Topical Digest, vol. 12 (Westport, Conn.; Greenwood; 1970) (originally published 1900–1902).

———. Report of the Industrial Commission on Transportation, Second Volume on This Subject, Including Testimony Taken Since May 1, 1900, Review and Topical Digest of Evidence, and Special Reports on Railway Legislation and Taxation, vol. 9 (Westport, Conn.; Greenwood; 1970) (originally published 1900–1902).

———. Report on Trusts and Industrial Combinations, vol. 13 (Westport, Conn.; Greenwood; 1970) (originally published 1900–1902).

———. Trusts and Combinations: Statutes and Decisions of Federal, State, and Territorial Law, together with a Digest of Corporation Laws, vol. 2 (Westport, Conn.; Greenwood; 1970) (originally published 1900–1902).

United States Temporary National Economic Committee. The Distribution of Ownership in the 200 Largest Nonfinancial Corporations, monograph no. 29 (Washington, D.C.: U.S. Government Printing Office; 1940).

ARTICLES

Abrams, Richard M. *Woodrow Wilson and the Southern Congressmen, 1913–1916.* Journal of Southern History, vol. 22, no. 4 (Nov. 1956), pp. 417–37.

Adams, Alton D. *Federal Control of Trusts.* Polit. Sci. Quart., vol. 18, no. 1 (1903), pp. 1–16.

———. *Legal Monopoly.* Polit. Sci. Quart., vol. 19, no. 2 (June 1904), p. 173–92.

Adams, Charles Francis, Jr. *A Chapter of Erie.* North American Review, vol. 109, no. 224 (July 1869), pp. 30–106.

———. *The Granger Movement.* North American Review, vol. 120, no. 247 (Apr. 1875), p. 394.

Adams, Henry C. *Relation of the State to Industrial Action.* Publications of the American Economic Association, vol. 1, no. 6 (Jan. 1887), pp. 7–85.

American Law Review. *Legislative Control over Railway Charters.* American Law Review, vol. 1, no. 3 (Apr. 1867), pp. 451–76.

Andrews, E. Benjamin. *Trusts According to Official Investigation.* Quart. J. Econ., vol. 3, no. 2 (Jan. 1889), pp. 117–52.

Ashley, William. *Legal Foundations of Capitalism.* Econ. J., vol. 36, no. 141 (Mar. 1926), pp. 84–88.

Atwood, Albert W., *et al. Speculation on the Stock Exchanges—Discussion.* American Econ. Rev., vol. 5, no. 1 (Mar. 1915), pp. 86–111.

Baker, J. Newton. *Regulation of Industrial Corporations.* Yale L. J., vol. 22, no. 4 (Feb. 1913), pp. 306–31.

Ballam, Deborah A. *The Evolution of the Government-Business Relationship in the United States: Colonial Times to Present.* AM. BUS. L. J., vol. 31, no. 4 (Feb. 1994), pp. 553–640.

Barton, Roger Avery. *The Camden and Amboy Railroad Monopoly.* PROCEEDINGS OF THE NEW JERSEY HISTORICAL SOCIETY, n.s., vol. 12, no. 4 (Oct. 1927), pp. 405–19.

Baskin, Jonathan Barron. *The Development of Corporate Financial Markets in Britain and the United States, 1600–1914: Overcoming Asymmetric Information.* BUS HIST. REV., vol. 62, no. 2 (Summer 1988), pp. 199–237.

Bateman, Bradley W., & Ethan B. Kapstein. *Retrospectives: Between God and the Market: The Religious Roots of the American Economic Association.* J. ECON. PERSPECT., vol. 13, no. 4 (Autumn 1999), pp. 249–57.

Beck, James M. *The Federal Power over Trusts.* ANN. AMER. ACAD. POLIT. SOC. SCI., vol. 24, THE GOVERNMENT IN ITS RELATION TO INDUSTRY (July 1904), pp. 89–110.

Bittlingmayer, George. *Antitrust and Business Activity: The First Quarter Century.* BUS. HIST. REV., vol. 70, no. 3 (Autumn 1996), pp. 363–401.

——— . *Did Antitrust Policy Cause the Great Merger Wave?* J. L. & ECON., vol. 28, no. 1 (Apr. 1985), pp. 77–118.

——— . *The Stock Market and Early Antitrust Enforcement.* J. L. & ECON., vol. 36, no. 1 (Apr. 1993), pp. 1–32.

——— . *Stock Returns, Real Activity, and the Trust Question.* J. FINANCE, vol. 47, no. 5 (Dec. 1992), pp. 1701–30.

Boyer, Allen D. *Federalism and Corporation Law: Drawing the Line in State Takeover Regulation.* OHIO ST. L. J., vol. 47, no. 4 (1986), pp. 1037–76.

Brief, Richard P. *Corporate Financial Reporting at the Turn of the Century.* JOURNAL OF ACCOUNTANCY, vol. 163, no. 5 (May 1987), pp. 142–57.

Bullock, Charles J. *Trust Literature: A Survey and Criticism.* QUART. J. ECON., vol. 15, no. 2 (Feb. 1901), pp. 167–217.

Bunting, David. *The Truth About "The Truth About the Trusts."* J. ECON. HIST., vol. 31, no. 3 (Sept. 1971), pp. 664–71.

Calkins, Grosvenor. *The Massachusetts Business Corporation Law.* QUART. J. ECON., vol. 18, no. 2 (Feb. 1904), pp. 269–79.

Calomiris, Charles W. *Price Flexibility, Credit Availability, and Economic Fluctuations: Evidence from the United States, 1894–1909.* QUART. J. ECON., vol. 104, no. 3 (Aug. 1989), pp. 429–52.

Carnegie, Andrew. *The Bugaboo of Trusts.* NORTH AMERICAN REVIEW, vol. 148, no. 387 (Feb. 1889), pp. 141–51.

Carosso, Vincent P. *The Wall Street Money Trust from Pujo through Medina.* BUS. HIST. REV., vol. 47, no. 4 (Winter 1973), pp. 421–37.

Cheffins, Brian R. *Mergers and Corporate Ownership Structure: The United States and Germany at the Turn of the Century.* AM. J. COMP. L., vol. 51, no. 3 (Summer 2003), pp. 473–503.

Clark, John B. *The Limits of Competition.* POLIT. SCI. QUART., vol. 2, no. 1 (Mar. 1887), pp. 45–61.

———. *The Nature and Progress of True Socialism.* NEW ENGLANDER, vol. 38, no. 151 (July 1879), pp. 565–82.

Clements, Kendrick A. *The Papers of Woodrow Wilson and the Interpretation of the Wilson Era.* HISTORY TEACHER, vol. 27, no. 4 (Aug. 1994), pp. 475–89.

Compton, William Randall. *Early History of Stock Ownership by Corporations.* GEO. WASH. L. REV., vol. 9, no. 2 (Dec. 1940), pp. 125–32.

Conant, Luther, Jr. *Industrial Consolidations in the United States.* PUBLICATIONS OF THE AMERICAN STATISTICAL ASSOCIATION, vol. 7, no. 53 (Mar. 1901), pp. 1–20.

Cooley, Thomas, M. *Limits to State Control of Private Business.* PRINCETON REVIEW, (Jan.–June 1878), pp. 223–71.

Davis, G. Cullom. *The Transformation of the Federal Trade Commission, 1914–1929.* MISSISSIPPI VALLEY HISTORICAL REVIEW, vol. 49, no. 3, (Dec. 1962), pp. 437–55.

Davis, John P. *The Nature of Corporations.* POLIT. SCI. QUART., vol. 13, no. 2 (June 1897), pp. 273–94.

Davis, Lance E. *The Capital Markets and Industrial Concentration: The U.S. and U.K., a Comparative Study.* ECON. HIST. REV., vol. 19, no. 2 (1966), pp. 255–72.

———. *The Investment Market, 1870–1914: The Evolution of a National Market.* J. ECON. HIST., vol. 25, no. 3 (Sept. 1965), 355–399.

Davis, Theodore H., Jr. *Corporate Privileges for the Public Benefit: The Progressive Federal Incorporation Movement and the Modern Regulatory State.* VIRGINIA L. REV., vol. 77, no. 3 (Apr. 1991), pp. 603–630.

Dewing, A. S. *A Statistical Test of the Success of Consolidations.* QUART. J. ECON., vol. 36, no. 1 (Nov. 1921), pp. 84–101.

Dill, James B. *Industrials as Investments for Small Capital.* ANN. AMER. ACAD. POLIT. SOC. SCI., vol. 15, supp. 13 (May 1900), pp. 109–19.

———. *National Incorporation Laws for Trusts.* YALE. L. J., vol. 11, no. 6 (1902), pp. 273–95.

———. *Some Tendencies in Combinations Which May Become Dangerous.* PUBLICATIONS OF THE AMERICAN ECONOMIC ASSOCIATION, 3d ser., vol. 1, no. 1 (Feb. 1900), pp. 177–211.

Dodd, E. Merrick, Jr. *Statutory Developments in Business Corporation Law, 1886–1936.* HARV. L. REV., vol. 50, no. 1 (Nov. 1936), pp. 27–59.

Douglas, William O. *Directors Who Do Not Direct.* HARV. L. REV., vol. 47, no. 8 (1934), pp. 1305–34.

Doyle, William M. *Capital Structure and the Financial Development of the U.S. Sugar Refining Industry, 1875–1905.* J. ECON. HIST., vol. 60, no. 1 (Mar. 2000), pp. 190–215.

Du Boff, Richard B., & Edward S. Herman. *Mergers, Concentration, and the Erosion of Democracy.* MONTHLY REVIEW, vol. 53, no. 1 (May 2001), pp. 14–29.

Dunning, John C. *The Legal Foundations of Capitalism.* J. SOC. FORCES, vol. 2, no. 5 (Nov. 1924), pp. 759–61.

Dwight, Theodore W. *The Legality of "Trusts."* POLIT. SCI. QUART., vol. 3, no. 4 (Dec. 1888), pp. 592–632.

Ely, Richard T. *Constitution By-Laws and Resolutions of the American Economic*

Association. PUBLICATIONS OF THE AMERICAN ECONOMIC ASSOCIATION, vol. 1, no. 1 (Mar. 1886), pp. 35–46.

——. *A Decade of Economic Theory.* ANN. AMER. ACAD. POLIT. SOC. SCI., vol. 15 (Mar. 1900), pp. 92–112.

——. *Monopolies and Trusts.* CURRENT LITERATURE, vol. 28, no. 3 (June 1900), pp. 309–10.

——. *The Nature and Significance of Monopolies and Trusts.* INTERNATIONAL JOURNAL OF ETHICS, vol. 10, no. 3 (Apr. 1900), pp. 273–88.

——. *The New Economic World and the New Economics.* JOURNAL OF LAND & PUBLIC UTILITY ECONOMICS, vol. 5, no. 4 (Nov. 1929), pp. 341–53.

——. *Proceedings of the Second Annual Meeting of the American Economic Association, Boston and Cambridge. May 21–25, 1887.* PUBLICATIONS OF THE AMERICAN ECONOMIC ASSOCIATION, vol. 3, no. 3 (July 1888), pp. 43–86.

——. *Report of the Organization of the American Economic Association.* PUBLICATIONS OF THE AMERICAN ECONOMIC ASSOCIATION, vol. 1, no. 1 (Mar. 1886), pp. 5–32.

Evans, George Heberton, Jr. *Preferred Stock in the United States 1850–1878.* AMER. ECON. REV., vol. 21, no. 1 (Mar. 1931), pp. 56–62.

Fairchild, Charles S. *The Financiering of Trusts.* PUBLICATIONS OF THE AMERICAN ECONOMIC ASSOCIATION, 3d ser., vol. 1, no. 1 (Feb. 1900), pp. 149–62.

Farrell, Richard J., & Robert W. Murphy. *Comments on the Theme: Why Should Anyone Want to Be a Director?* BUS. LAW., vol. 27, special issue (1972), pp. 7–22.

Freedland, Fred. *History of Holding Company Legislation in New York State: Some Doubts as to the "New Jersey First" Tradition.* FORDHAM L. REV., vol. 24, no. 3 (Autumn 1955), pp. 369–411.

Gerstenberg, Charles W. *Legal Department; The Federal Incorporation Bill.* JOURNAL OF ACCOUNTANCY, vol. 9, no. 4 (Feb. 1910), pp. 309–11.

Gordon, Jeffrey N. *Independent Directors and Stock Market Prices: The New Corporate Governance Paradigm.* STAN. L. REV., vol. 59, no. 6 (forthcoming).

Graham, John R., Campbell R. Harvey & Shivaram Rajgopal. *The Economic Implications of Corporate Financial Reporting.* J. ACC. ECON., vol. 40 (2005), pp. 3–73.

Grandy, Christopher. *New Jersey Corporate Chartermongering, 1875–1929.* J. ECON. HIST., vol. 49, no. 3 (1989), pp. 677–92.

Grantham, Dewey W., Jr. *Southern Congressional Leaders and the New Freedom, 1913–1917.* JOURNAL OF SOUTHERN HISTORY, vol. 13, no. 4 (Nov. 1947), pp. 439–59.

Grosscup, Peter S. *The Corporation Problem and the Lawyer's Part in Its Solution.* AMERICAN LAW REVIEW, vol. 39, no. 6 (Nov/Dec 1905), pp. 835–52.

——. *Who Shall Own America?* AMERICAN ILLUSTRATED MAGAZINE, vol. 61, no. 2 (Dec. 1905), p. 146.

——. *The Rebirth of the Corporation.* AMERICAN MAGAZINE, vol. 62, no. 2 (June 1906), p. 188.

Gunton, George. *The Economic and Social Aspects of Trusts.* POLIT. SCI. QUART., vol. 3, no. 3 (Sept. 1888), pp. 358–408.

Hadley, Arthur T. *The Meaning of Valuation.* AMER. ECON. REV., vol. 18, no. 1 (Mar. 1928), pp. 173–80.

Harris, Abram L. *Veblen and the Social Phenomenon of Capitalism.* AMER. ECON. REV., vol. 41, no. 2, Papers and Proceedings of the Sixty-third Annual Meeting of the American Economic Association (May 1951), pp. 66–77.

———. *Veblen as Social Philosopher—A Reappraisal.* ETHICS, vol. 63, no. 3, Part 2: Veblen as Social Philosopher—A Reappraisal (Apr. 1953), pp. 1–32.

Hatfield, Henry Rand. *The Chicago Trust Conference.* J. POLIT. ECONOMY, vol. 8, no. 1 (Dec. 1899) pp. 1–18.

Hawkins, David F. *The Development of Modern Financial Reporting Practices Among American Manufacturing Corporations.* BUS. HIST. REV., vol. 37, no. 3 (Autumn 1963), pp. 135–68.

Herrick, Myron T. *The Panic of 1907 and Some of Its Lessons.* ANN. AMER. ACAD. POLIT. SOC. SCI., vol. 31, Lessons of the Financial Crisis (Mar. 1908), pp. 8–25.

Hilt, Eric. *When Did Ownership Separate from Control? Corporate Governance in the Early Nineteenth Century.* NBER Working Paper No. 13093 (May 2007). Available at: http://www.nber.org/papers/w13903.

Hoffman, Frederick L. *Fifty Years of American Life Insurance Progress.* PUBLICATIONS OF THE AMERICAN STATISTICAL ASSOCIATION, vol. 12, no. 95 (Sept. 1911), pp. 667–712.

Holderness, Clifford G., Randall S. Kroszner & Dennis P. Sheehan. *Were the Good Old Days That Good? Changes in Managerial Stock Ownership Since the Great Depression.* J. FINANCE, vol. 54, no. 2 (Apr. 1999), pp. 435–69.

Holderness, Clifford G., & Dennis P. Sheehan. *The Role of Majority Shareholders in Publicly Held Corporations.* J. FINANCIAL ECON., vol. 20 (1988), pp. 317–46.

Horwitz, Morton J. *Santa Clara Revisited: The Development of Corporate Theory.* W. VA. L. REV., vol. 88, no. 2 (Fall 1985), pp. 173–224.

Hovenkamp, Herbert. *The Classical Corporation in American Legal Thought.* GEO. L. J., vol. 76, no. 5 (June 1988), pp. 1593–1690.

Huertas, Thomas F., & Joan L. Silverman. *Charles E. Mitchell: Scapegoat of the Crash?* BUS. HIST. REV., vol. 60, no. 1 (Spring 1986), pp. 81–103.

Hurdman, Frederick H. *Capital Stock of No Par Value.* JOURNAL OF ACCOUNTANCY, vol. 28, no. 1 (July–Dec. 1919), pp. 246–57.

James, Clifford L. *Commons on Institutional Economics.* AMER. ECON. REV., vol. 27, no. 1 (Mar. 1937), pp. 61–75.

James, H. A. *Private Corporations and The State,* JOURNAL OF SOCIAL SCIENCE, vol. 23 (Nov. 1887), pp. 145–65.

James B. Dill. CURRENT LITERATURE, vol. 29, no. 1 (July 1900), p. 24.

Jenks, Jeremiah W. *The Principles of Government Control of Business.* AMERICAN ECONOMIC ASSOCIATION, vol. 9, no. 1 (Apr. 1908), pp. 1–20.

———. *Trusts in the United States.* ECON. J., vol. 2, no. 5 (Mar. 1892), pp. 70–99.

Johnson, Arthur M. *Antitrust Policy in Transition, 1908: Ideal and Reality.* MISSISSIPPI VALLEY HISTORICAL REVIEW, vol. 48, no. 3 (Dec. 1961), pp. 415–34.

———. *Theodore Roosevelt and the Bureau of Corporations.* MISSISSIPPI VALLEY HISTORICAL REVIEW, vol. 45, no. 4 (Mar. 1959), 571–90.

Johnson, Joseph French. *The Crisis and Panic of* 1907. POLIT. SCI. QUART., vol. 23, no. 3 (Sept. 1908), pp. 454–67.

Kahan, Marcel, & Edward B. Rock. *How I Learned to Stop Worrying and Love the Pill: Adaptive Responses to Takeover Law.* U. CHI. L. REV., vol. 69, no. 3 (Summer 2002), pp. 871–915.

Karmel, Roberta S. *Realizing the Dream of William O. Douglas: The Securities and Exchange Commission Takes Charge of Corporate Governance.* DEL. J. CORP. L., vol. 30, no. 1 (2005), pp. 79–144.

Keasbey, Edward Q. *New Jersey and the Great Corporations.* Part 1: HARV. L. REV., vol. 13, no. 3 (Nov. 1899), pp. 198–212; Part 2: HARV. L. REV., vol. 13, no. 4 (Dec. 1899), pp. 264–78.

——. *The Powers of Corporations Created by Act of Congress.* HARV. L. REV., vol. 32, no. 6 (Apr. 1919), pp. 689–708.

Kornhauser, Marjorie E. *Corporate Regulation and the Origins of the Corporate Income Tax.* INDIANA L. J., vol. 66, no. 1 (Winter 1990), pp. 53–136.

La Porta, Rafael, Florencio Lopez-De-Silanes & Andrei Shleifer. *Corporate Ownership Around the World.* J. FINANCE, vol. 54, no. 2 (Apr. 1999), pp. 471–517.

Lerner, Max. *The Supreme Court and American Capitalism.* YALE L. J., vol. 42, no. 5 (Mar. 1933), pp. 668–701.

Letwin, William L. *Congress and the Sherman Antitrust Law: 1887–1890.* U. CHI. L. REV., vol. 23, no. 2 (1955–56), pp. 221, 247–48.

Liability for Stock Issued for Overvalued Property. HARV. L. REV., vol. 19, no. 5 (Mar. 1906), pp. 366–68.

Livermore, Shaw. *The Success of Industrial Mergers.* QUART. J. ECON., vol. 50, no. 1 (Nov. 1935), pp. 68–96.

Logan, Walter S. *National Incorporation and Control of Corporations.* AMERICAN LAW REVIEW, vol. 37, no. 2 (Mar./Apr. 1903), pp. 237–54.

Lucier, Chuck, Paul Kocourek & Rolf Habbel. *CEO Succession 2005: The Crest of the Wave.* STRATEGY + BUSINESS (Summer 2006). Available at: http://www.strategy-business.com/press/article/06210?pg=0.

Mappin, W. F. *Farm Mortgages and the Small Farmer,* POLIT. SCI. QUART., vol. 4, no. 3 (Sept. 1889), pp. 3–22.

Mark, Gregory A. *The Personification of the Business Corporation in American Law.* U. CHI. L. REV., vol. 54, no. 4 (Autumn 1987), pp. 1441–83.

Markowitz, Harry. *Portfolio Selection.* J. FINANCE, vol. 7, no. 1 (1952), pp. 77–99.

Martin, T. Leroy. *Overcapitalization Has Little Meaning.* ACCOUNTING REVIEW, vol. 16, no. 4 (Dec. 1941), pp. 407–27.

Masslich, C. B. *Financing a New Corporate Enterprise.* ILLINOIS LAW REVIEW, vol. 5, no. 2 (1910), pp. 70–86.

Mayo-Smith, Richmond. *Review 1—No Title.* POLIT. SCI. QUART., vol. 15, no. 3 (Sept. 1905), p. 547.

McCraw, Thomas K., & Forest Reinhardt. *Losing to Win: U.S. Steel's Pricing, Investment Decisions, and Market Share, 1901–1938.* J. ECON. HIST., vol. 49, no. 3 (Sept. 1989), pp. 593–619.

McCurdy, Charles W. *The Knight Sugar Decision of 1895 and the Modernization of American Corporation Law, 1869–1903.* BUS. HIST. REV., vol. 53, no. 3 (Autumn 1979), pp. 304–42.

Meade, Edward Sherwood. *The Genesis of the United States Steel Corporation.* QUART. J. ECON., vol. 15, no. 4 (Aug. 1901), pp. 517–50.

——— . *The Investor's Interest in the Demands of the Anthracite Miners.* ANN. AMER. ACAD. POLIT. SOC. SCI., vol. 21, Current Labor Problems (Jan. 1903), pp. 36–45.

Means, Gardiner C. *The Growth in the Relative Importance of the Large Corporation in American Economic Life.* AMER. ECON. REV., vol. 21, no. 1 (Mar. 1931), pp. 10–42.

——— . *The Separation of Ownership and Control in American Industry.* QUART. J. ECON., vol. 46, no. 1 (Dec. 1931), pp. 68–100.

Miranti, Paul J., Jr. *Associationalism, Statism, and Professional Regulation: Public Accountants and the Reform of the Financial Markets, 1896–1940.* BUS. HIST. REV., vol. 60, no. 3 (Autumn 1986), pp. 438–68.

Mitchell, Lawrence E. *The Trouble with Boards.* In THE NEW CORPORATE FINANCE, Troy A. Paredes, ed. (forthcoming).

Mitchell, Wesley C. *Commons on the Legal Foundations of Capitalism.* AMER. ECON. REV., vol. 14, no. 2 (June 1924), pp. 240–53.

Moore Hudson, Sydney D. *Federal Incorporation.* POLIT. SCI. QUART., vol. 26, no. 1 (Mar. 1911), pp. 63–97.

The "Mother of Corporations." CURRENT LITERATURE (1888–1912), vol. 38, no. 6 (June 1905), p. 489.

Navin, Thomas R., & Marian V. Sears. *The Rise of a Market for Industrial Securities, 1887–1902.* BUS. HIST. REV., vol. 29, no. 2 (June 1955), pp. 105–38.

Neal, Larry. *Trust Companies and Financial Innovation, 1897–1914.* BUS. HIST. REV., vol. 45, no. 1 (Spring 1971), pp. 35–51.

The New Jersey Monopolies. NORTH AMERICAN REVIEW, vol. 104, no. 215 (Apr. 1867), pp. 428–76.

North, S. N. D. *The Industrial Commission.* NORTH AMERICAN REVIEW, vol. 168, no. 111 (June 1899), pp. 708–19.

Novak, William J. *Public Economy and the Well-Ordered Market: Law and Regulation in 19th-Century America.* LAW & SOC. INQUIRY, vol. 18, no. 1 (Winter 1993), pp. 1–32.

Noyes, Alexander D. *The Recent Economic History of the United States.* QUART. J. ECON., vol. 19, no. 2 (Feb. 1905), pp. 167–209.

——— . *A Year After the Panic of 1907.* QUART. J. ECON., vol. 23, no. 2 (Feb. 1909), pp. 185–212.

O'Brien, Anthony Patrick. *Factory Size, Economies of Scale, and the Great Merger Wave of 1898–1902.* J. ECON. HIST., vol. 48, no. 3 (Sept. 1988), pp. 639–49.

Parker-Gwin, Rachel, & William G. Roy. *Corporate Law and the Organization of Property in the United States: The Origin and Institutionalization of New Jersey Corporation Law, 1888–1903.* POLITICS & SOCIETY, vol. 24, no. 2 (June 1996), pp. 111–35.

Patrick, J. Vernon, Jr. *The Securities Class Action for Damages Comes of Age.* BUS. LAW., vol. 29, Special Issue (1974), pp. 159–66.

Patterson, C. Stuart. *The Problem of the Trusts.* PROCEEDINGS OF THE AMERICAN PHILOSOPHICAL SOCIETY, vol. 42, no. 172 (Jan. 1903), pp. 15–27.

Pennoyer, Sylvester. *How to Control the Trusts.* AMERICAN LAW REVIEW, vol. 33, no. 6 (Nov./Dec. 1899), pp. 876–84.

Power of a Corporation to Acquire Stock of Another Corporation. COLUMBIA L. REV., vol. 31, no. 2 (Feb. 1931), pp. 281–91.

Prentice, E. Parmalee. *Congress, and Regulation of Corporations.* HARV. L. REV., vol. 19, no. 3 (1906), pp. 168–99.

Price, Theo. H. *Speculation and the Small Investor.* ANN. AMER. ACAD. POLIT. SOC. SCI., vol. 87, The New American Thrift (Jan. 1920), pp. 155–57.

Puffert, Douglas J. *The Standardization of Track Gauge on North American Railways, 1830–1890.* J. ECON. HIST., vol. 60, no. 4 (Dec. 2000), pp. 933–60.

Rabin, Robert L. *Federal Regulation in Historical Perspective.* STAN. L. REV., vol. 38, no. 5 (May 1986), pp. 1189–1326.

Reed, Robert R. *"Blue Sky" Laws.* ANN. AMER. ACAD. POLIT. SOC. SCI., vol. 88 (Mar. 1920), 177–87.

Remedies for Monopolistic Trusts Proposed by the St. Louis Antitrust Conference. AMERICAN LAW REVIEW, vol. 33, no. 6 (Nov./Dec. 1899), pp. 905–7.

Richard, H. S. *Exchange of Stock for Capitalized Profits.* MICH. L. REV., vol. 4, no. 7 (1906), pp. 526–33.

Ripley, William Z. *Industrial Concentration as Shown by the Census.* QUART. J. ECON., vol. 21, no. 4 (Aug. 1907), pp. 651–58.

——— . *The Work of Trained Economists in the Industrial Commission.* QUART. J. ECON., vol. 16, no. 1 (Nov. 1901), pp. 121–22.

Rittenhouse, Elmer E. *Thrift from the Life Insurance Viewpoint.* SCIENTIFIC MONTHLY, vol. 4, no. 4 (Apr. 1917), pp. 301–6.

Roberts, Robert R. *The Social Gospel and the Trust-Busters.* CHURCH HISTORY, vol. 25, no. 3 (Sept. 1956), pp. 239–57.

Robinson, Maurice H. *The Federal Corporation Tax.* AMER. ECON. REV., vol. 1, no. 4 (1911), pp. 691–723.

Rockoff, Hugh, & Sung Won Kang. *Capitalizing Patriotism: The Liberty Loans of World War I.* NBER Working Paper No. W11919 (Feb. 2006). Available at: http://www.ssrn.com.

Roosevelt, Theodore. *The Trusts, the People, and the Square Deal.* OUTLOOK, vol. 99, no. 12 (Nov. 18, 1911), pp. 649–56.

Roy, William G. *The Politics of Bureaucratization and the U.S. Bureau of Corporations.* JOURNAL OF POLITICAL AND MILITARY SOCIOLOGY, vol. 10 (Fall 1982), pp. 183–99.

——— . *The Politics of Railroads in the Nineteenth-Century.* CONTEMPORARY SOCIOLOGY, vol. 23, no. 6 (Nov. 1994), pp. 819–22.

Salvato, Richard. *Historical Note.* In NATIONAL CIVIC FEDERATION RECORDS, 1894–1949, The New York Public Library, Humanities and Social Sciences Library, Manuscripts and Archives Division (Sept. 2001). Available at: http://www.nypl.org.

Sanborn, John Bell. *Federal Control of Corporations*. AMERICAN LAW REVIEW, vol. 37, no. 5 (Sept./Oct. 1903), pp. 703–12.

Scharfman, L. *Commons's Legal Foundations of Capitalism*. QUART. J. ECON., vol. 39, no. 2 (Feb. 1925), pp. 300–312.

Scott, Anne Firor. *A Progressive Wind from the South, 1906–1913*. JOURNAL OF SOUTHERN HISTORY, vol. 29, no. 1 (Feb. 1963), pp. 53–70.

Sears, Marian V. *The American Businessman at the Turn of the Century*. BUS. HIST. REV., vol. 30, no. 4 (Dec. 1956), pp. 382–443.

Seligman, Edwin R. A. *Railway Tariffs and the Interstate Commerce Law, II*. POLIT. SCI. QUART., vol. 2, no. 3 (Sept. 1887), pp. 369–413.

Seligman, Edwin R. A., et al. *The Taxation of Quasi-Public Corporations: Discussion*. PUBLICATIONS OF THE AMERICAN ECONOMIC ASSOCIATION, 3d ser., vol. 2, no. 1 (Feb. 1901), pp. 107–25.

Seligman, Joel. *A Sheep in Wolf's Clothing: The American Law Institute Principles of Corporate Governance Project*. GEO. WASH. L. REV., vol. 55, no. 2 (1987), pp. 325–82.

Seltzer, Alan. *Woodrow Wilson as "Corporate-Liberal": Toward a Reconsideration of Left Revisionist Historiography*. WESTERN POLITICAL QUARTERLY, vol. 30, no. 2 (June 1977), pp. 183–212.

Sharpe, William. *Capital Asset Prices: A Theory of Market Equilibrium Under Conditions of Risk*. J. FINANCE, vol. 19, no. 3 (Sept. 1964), pp. 425–42.

Shleifer, Andrei, & Robert W. Vishny. *Large Shareholders and Corporate Control*. J. POLIT. ECONOMY, vol. 94, no. 3, pt. 1 (June 1986), pp. 461–88.

———. *A Survey of Corporate Governance*. J. FINANCE, vol. 52, no. 2 (June 1997), pp. 737–83.

Smiley, Gene. *The Expansion of the New York Securities Market at the Turn of the Century*. BUS. HIST. REV., vol. 55, no. 1 (Spring 1981), pp. 75–85.

Snider, John L. *Security Issues in the United States, 1909–20*. REVIEW OF ECONOMICS AND STATISTICS, vol. 3, no. 5 (May 1921), pp. 98–102.

Steffens, Lincoln. *New Jersey: A Traitor State, Part 1—The Conquest*. MCCLURE'S MAGAZINE, vol. 24, no. 6 (Apr. 1905), p. 649.

———. *New Jersey: A Traitor State, Part II—How She Sold Out the United States*. MCCLURE'S MAGAZINE, vol. 25, no. 1 (May 1905), p. 41.

Sternstein, Jerome L. *Corruption in the Gilded Age Senate: Nelson W. Aldrich and the Sugar Trust*. CAPITOL STUDIES, vol. 6 (Spring 1978), pp. 13–37.

Stigler, George J., & Claire Friedland. *The Literature of Economics: The Case of Berle and Means*. J. L. & ECON., vol. 26, no. 2 (June 1983), pp. 237–68.

Stockwell, Herbert G. *Appraisements*. ANN. AMER. ACAD. POLIT. SOC. SCI., vol. 25, Business Management and Finance (Jan. 1905), pp. 21–31.

Stoke, Harold W. *Economic Influences upon the Corporation Laws of New Jersey*. J. POLIT. ECONOMY, vol. 38, no. 5 (Oct. 1930), pp. 551–79.

Subramanian, Guhan. *The Influence of Antitakeover Statutes on Incorporation Choice: Evidence of the "Race" Debate and Antitakeover Overreaching*. U. PA. L. REV., vol. 150, no. 6 (June 2002), pp. 1795–1873.

Sumner, John D. *Going Value: Its Various Interpretations and Their Validity.* JOURNAL OF LAND & PUBLIC UTILITY ECONOMICS, vol. 4, no. 1 (Feb. 1928), pp. 59–70.

Swayze, F. J., *et al. Capitalization of Corporations: Discussion.* AMERICAN ECONOMIC ASSOCIATION QUARTERLY, 3d ser., vol. 10, no. 1 (Apr. 1909), pp. 415–30.

Tawney, R. H. *Review of* LEGAL FOUNDATIONS OF CAPITALISM, BY JOHN R. COMMONS. ECONOMICA, no. 13 (Mar. 1925), pp. 104–5.

Taylor, Nelson Ferebee. *Evolution of Corporate Combination Law: Policy Issues and Constitutional Questions,* N. C. L. REV., vol. 76, no. 3 (Mar. 1998), pp. 687–1014.

Taylor, W. G. Langworthy. *Hadley's "Economics."* J. POLIT. ECONOMY, vol. 4, no. 4 (Sept. 1896), pp. 467–93.

Thel, Steven. *The Original Conception of Section 10(b) of the Securities Exchange Act.* STAN. L. REV., vol. 42, no. 2 (Jan. 1990), 385–464.

Thompson, Seymour D. *Abuses of Corporate Privileges.* AMERICAN LAW REVIEW, vol. 26, no. 2 (Mar./Apr. 1892), pp. 169–203.

Tsuk Mitchell, Dalia. *Shareholders as Proxies: The Contours of Shareholder Democracy.* WASH. & LEE L. REV., vol. 63, no. 4 (Fall 2006), pp. 1503–78.

Untermyer, Samuel. *Completing the Anti-Trust Programme.* NORTH AMERICAN REVIEW, vol. 199, no. 701 (Apr. 1914), pp. 528–31.

———. *Speculation on the Stock Exchanges and Public Regulation of the Exchanges.* AMER. ECON. REV., vol. 5, no. 1 (Mar. 1915), pp. 24–68.

Urofsky, Melvin I. *Proposed Federal Incorporation in the Progressive Era.* AM. J. LEGAL HIST., vol. 26, no. 2 (Apr. 1982), pp. 160–83.

Wallstein, Leonard M. *The Issue of Corporate Stock for Property Purchased: A New Phase.* YALE L. J., vol. 15, no. 3 (1906), pp. 111–26.

Warshow, H. T. *The Distribution of Corporate Ownership in the United States.* QUART. J. ECON., vol. 39, no. 1 (Nov. 1924), pp. 15–38.

Watkins, Myron. *Federal Incorporation: I.* MICH. L. REV., vol. 17, no. 1 (Nov. 1918), pp. 64–80.

———. *Federal Incorporation: II.* MICH. L. REV., vol. 17, no. 2 (Dec. 1918), pp. 145–64.

———. *Federal Incorporation: III.* MICH. L. REV., vol. 17, no. 3 (Jan. 1919), pp. 238–60.

———. *The Literature of the Crisis.* QUART. J. ECON., vol. 47, no. 3 (May 1933), pp. 504–32.

Whitney, Edward B. *Parasite Corporations.* JOURNAL OF SOCIAL SCIENCE, vol. 40 (Dec. 1902), pp. 110–21.

White, Horace. *The Hughes Investigation.* J. POLIT. ECONOMY, vol. 17, no. 8 (Oct. 1909), pp. 528–40.

———. *The Stock Exchange and the Money Market.* ANN. AMER. ACAD. POLIT. SOC. SCI., vol. 36, no. 3 (Nov. 1910), pp. 85–95.

Wickersham, George W. *The Capital of a Corporation.* HARV. L. REV., vol. 22, no. 5 (Mar. 1909), pp. 319–38.

H.L.W. [H. L. Wilgus]. *Creditors' Right to Hold Shareholders Liable on Corporate*

Stock Issued for Property Valued on the Basis of Prospective Profits. MICH. L. REV., vol. 4, no. 3 (Jan. 1906), pp. 220–24.

Wilgus, Horace L. *Federal License or National Incorporation.* MICH. L. REV., vol. 3, no. 4 (Feb. 1905), pp. 264–81.

——. *A National Incorporation Law.* MICH. L. REV., vol. 2, no. 7 (Apr. 1904), pp. 615–16.

——. *Need of a National Incorporation Law.* MICH. L. REV., vol. 2, no. 5 (Feb. 1904), pp. 358–95.

——. *A Proposed National Incorporation Law.* MICH. L. REV., vol. 2, no. 7 (Apr. 1904), pp. 501–96.

Williams, John Sharp. *Federal Usurpations.* ANN. AMER. ACAD. POLIT. SOC. SCI., vol. 32, Federal Regulation of Industry (July 1908), pp. 185–211.

Wilson, Woodrow. *Leaderless Government.* VIRGINIA LAW REGISTER, vol. 3, no. 5 (Sept. 1897), pp. 337–54.

——. *The New Meaning of Government.* PUBLIC ADMIN. REV., vol. 44, no. 3 (May–June 1984), pp. 193–95 (originally published 1912).

——. *The Study of Administration.* POLIT. SCI. QUART., vol. 2, no. 2 (June 1887), pp. 197–222.

Wolfe, A. B. *Institutional Reasonableness and Value.* PHILOSOPHICAL REVIEW, vol. 45, no. 2 (Mar. 1936), pp. 192–206.

Yarros, Victor S. *The Trust Problem Restudied.* AMERICAN JOURNAL OF SOCIOLOGY, vol. 8, no. 1 (July 1902), pp. 58–74.

Zeitlin, Maurice. *Corporate Ownership and Control: The Large Corporation and the Capitalist Class.* AMERICAN JOURNAL OF SOCIOLOGY, vol. 79, no. 5 (Mar. 1974), pp. 1073–1119.

Zerbe, Richard. *The American Sugar Refining Company, 1887–1914: The Story of a Monopoly.* J. L. & ECON., vol. 12, no. 2 (Oct. 1969), 339–75.

Zillmer, Raymond T. *State Laws: Survival of the Unfit.* U. PA. L. REV., vol. 62, no. 7 (1913–14), pp. 509–24.

BOOKS

ALBERT, MICHEL. CAPITALISM AGAINST CAPITALISM: HOW AMERICA'S OBSESSION WITH INDIVIDUAL ACHIEVEMENT AND SHORT-TERM PROFIT HAS LED IT TO THE BRINK OF COLLAPSE (New York; Four Walls Eight Windows; 1993).

ALLEN, FREDERICK LEWIS. THE GREAT PIERPONT MORGAN (New York; Harper & Brothers; 1949).

——. LORDS OF CREATION (Chicago; Quadrangle Paperbacks; 1966) (originally published 1935).

——. ONLY YESTERDAY: AN INFORMAL HISTORY OF THE 1920S (New York; Harper & Row; 1931).

AMERICAN NATIONAL BIOGRAPHY. John A. Garraty and Mark C. Carnes, eds. (New York; Oxford Univ. Press; 1999).

ANDERSON, DONALD F. WILLIAM HOWARD TAFT: A CONSERVATIVE'S CONCEPTION OF THE PRESIDENCY (Ithaca, N.Y.; Cornell Univ. Press; 1973).

ANGELL, JOSEPH KINNICUT, & SAMUEL AMES. A TREATISE ON THE LAW OF PRIVATE CORPORATIONS, AGGREGATE, 7th ed. (Boston; Little, Brown; 1861).

———. A TREATISE ON THE LAW OF PRIVATE CORPORATIONS, AGGREGATE, 10th ed. (Boston; Little, Brown; 1875).

BADGER, RALPH EASTMAN. VALUATION OF SECURITIES (New York; Prentice Hall; 1925).

BANK, STEVEN. BUSINESS TAX STORIES (NEW YORK; Foundation; 2005).

BANNER, STUART. ANGLO-AMERICAN SECURITIES REGULATION: CULTURAL AND PO-LITICAL ROOTS, 1690–1860 (Cambridge, Eng.; Cambridge Univ. Press; 1998).

BARRON, CLARENCE W. MORE THEY TOLD BARRON: CONVERSATIONS AND REV-ELATIONS OF AN AMERICAN PEPYS IN WALL STREET, THE NOTES OF THE LATE CLARENCE W. BARRON, ED. BY ARTHUR POUND & SAMUEL TAYLOR MOORE (New York; Harper & Brothers; 1931).

BASKIN, JONATHAN BARRON, & PAUL J. MIRANTI, JR. A HISTORY OF CORPORATE FINANCE (Cambridge, Eng.; Cambridge Univ. Press; 1997).

BAXTER, MAURICE G. THE STEAMBOAT MONOPOLY: GIBBONS V. OGDEN, 1824 (New York; Knopf; 1972).

BEBCHUK, LUCIEN, & JESSE FRIED. PAY WITHOUT PERFORMANCE: THE UNFILLED PROMISE OF EXECUTIVE COMPENSATION (Cambridge, Mass.; Harvard Univ. Press; 2004).

BELLAMY, EDWARD. LOOKING BACKWARD, 2000–1887 (Boston; Houghton Mifflin; 1887).

BENTLEY, ARTHUR F. THE PROCESS OF GOVERNMENT: A STUDY OF SOCIAL PRES-SURES (Chicago; Univ. of Chicago Press; 1908).

BENTLEY, HARRY C. CORPORATE FINANCE AND ACCOUNTING (New York; Ronald Press; 1908).

———. THE SCIENCE OF ACCOUNTS (New York; Ronald Press; 1913).

BERGLUND, ABRAHAM. THE UNITED STATES STEEL CORPORATION: A STUDY OF THE GROWTH AND INFLUENCE OF COMBINATION IN THE IRON AND STEEL INDUSTRY (New York; Columbia Univ. Press; 1907).

BERLE, ADOLF A., JR., & GARDINER C. MEANS. THE MODERN CORPORATION AND PRIVATE PROPERTY (New York; Macmillan; 1932).

BERNSTEIN, PETER L. CAPITAL IDEAS: THE IMPROBABLE ORIGINS OF MODERN WALL STREET (New York; John Wiley; 1992).

BIRMINGHAM, STEPHEN. "OUR CROWD": THE GREAT JEWISH FAMILIES OF NEW YORK (New York; Harper & Row; 1967).

BLACK, WILLIAM HARMAN. CORPORATION LAWS OF NEW YORK AND NEW JERSEY (New York; Corporations Organization; 1904).

BLAISDELL, THOMAS C., JR. THE FEDERAL TRADE COMMISSION: AN EXPERIMENT IN THE CONTROL OF BUSINESS (New York; Columbia Univ. Press; 1932).

BLISS, GEORGE. THE NEW YORK CODE OF CIVIL PROCEDURE AS IT IS JANUARY 1, 1913. 6th ed. by George A. Clement (New York; Baker, Voorhis; 1912), vol. 3.

BLUM, JOHN MORTON. JOE TUMULTY AND THE WILSON ERA (Boston; Houghton Mifflin; 1951).

————. THE REPUBLICAN ROOSEVELT, 2d ed. (Cambridge, Mass.; Harvard Univ. Press; 1977).

BONBRIGHT, JAMES C., & GARDINER C. MEANS. THE HOLDING COMPANY: ITS PUBLIC SIGNIFICANCE AND ITS REGULATION (New York; McGraw-Hill; 1932).

BOONE, CHARLES T. A MANUAL OF THE LAW APPLICABLE TO CORPORATIONS GENERALLY (San Francisco: Bancroft-Whitney; 1887).

BRANDEIS, LOUIS D. OTHER PEOPLE'S MONEY AND HOW THE BANKERS USE IT (Fairfield, N.J.; Augustus M. Kelley; 1986) (originally published 1914).

BREEN, WILLIAM J. UNCLE SAM AT HOME: CIVILIAN MOBILIZATION, WARTIME FEDERALISM, AND THE COUNCIL OF NATIONAL DEFENSE, 1917–1919 (Westport, Conn.; Greenwood Press; 1984).

BROESAMLE, JOHN J. WILLIAM GIBBS MCADOO: A PASSION FOR CHANGE, 1863–1917 (Port Washington, N.Y.; National University Publications, Kennikat Press; 1973).

BROWN, IRA V. LYMAN ABBOTT: CHRISTIAN EVOLUTIONIST: A STUDY IN RELIGIOUS LIBERALISM (Cambridge, Mass.; Harvard Univ. Press; 1953).

BRUCHEY, STUART. GROWTH OF THE MODERN AMERICAN ECONOMY (New York; Dodd, Mead; 1975).

BUCK, SOLON JUSTUS. THE GRANGER MOVEMENT: A STUDY OF AGRICULTURAL ORGANIZATION AND ITS POLITICAL, ECONOMIC AND SOCIAL MANIFESTATIONS, 1870–1880 (Cambridge, Mass.; Harvard Univ. Press; 1913).

BUNTING, DAVID. THE RISE OF LARGE AMERICAN CORPORATIONS, 1889–1919 (New York; Garland; 1986).

BURCH, PHILIP H., JR. THE MANAGERIAL REVOLUTION REASSESSED: FAMILY CONTROL IN AMERICA'S LARGEST CORPORATIONS (Lexington, Mass.; Lexington Books; 1972).

BURTON, DAVID H. WILLIAM HOWARD TAFT: IN THE PUBLIC SERVICE (Malabar, Fla.; Robert E. Kreiger; 1986).

BURTON, THEODORE E. CORPORATIONS AND THE STATE (New York; D. Appleton; 1911).

BUSBEY, L. WHITE. UNCLE JOE CANNON: THE STORY OF A PIONEER AMERICAN (New York; Henry Holt; 1927).

BUSINESS CORPORATIONS UNDER THE LAWS OF NEW JERSEY (Jersey City, N.J.; Corporation Trust Company of New Jersey; 1903).

CADMAN, JOHN W., JR. THE CORPORATION IN NEW JERSEY: BUSINESS AND POLITICS, 1791–1875 (Cambridge, Mass.; Harvard Univ. Press; 1949).

CARNEGIE, ANDREW. THE GOSPEL OF WEALTH AND OTHER TIMELY ESSAYS (New York; Century; 1901).

CAROSSO, VINCENT P. INVESTMENT BANKING IN AMERICA (Cambridge, Mass.; Harvard Univ. Press; 1970).

————. THE MORGANS: PRIVATE INTERNATIONAL BANKERS, 1854–1913 (Cambridge, Mass.; Harvard Univ. Press; 1987).

CARR, VIRGINIA SPENCER. DOS PASSOS: A LIFE (Garden City, N.Y.; Doubleday; 1984).

Carter, John R. *From Peckham to White: Economic Welfare and the Rule of Reason.* In ROBERT F. HIMMELBERG, ED., THE MONOPOLY ISSUE AND ANTITRUST 1900–1917 (New York; Garland; 1994), pp. 1–21.

CFA CENTRE FOR FINANCIAL MARKET INTEGRITY/BUSINESS ROUNDTABLE INSTITUTE FOR CORPORATE ETHICS. BREAKING THE SHORT-TERM CYCLE: DISCUSSION AND RECOMMENDATIONS ON HOW CORPORATE MANAGERS, INVESTORS, AND ANALYSTS CAN REFOCUS ON LONG-TERM VALUE (2006).

CHANDLER, ALFRED D., JR. SCALE AND SCOPE: THE DYNAMICS OF INDUSTRIAL CAPITALISM (Cambridge, Mass.; Belknap Press of Harvard Univ. Press; 1990).

——. STRATEGY AND STRUCTURE: CHAPTERS IN THE HISTORY OF THE INDUSTRIAL ENTERPRISE (Cambridge, Mass.; M.I.T. Press; 1962).

——. THE VISIBLE HAND: THE MANAGERIAL REVOLUTION IN AMERICAN BUSINESS (Cambridge, Mass.; Belknap Press of Harvard Univ. Press; 1977).

CHATFIELD, MICHAEL. A HISTORY OF ACCOUNTING THOUGHT (Huntington, N.Y.; Robert E. Krieger; 1977).

CHATFIELD, MICHAEL, ED. CONTEMPORARY STUDIES IN THE EVOLUTION OF ACCOUNTING THOUGHT (Belmont, Calif.; Dickenson; 1968).

CHAMBERLAIN, JOHN. FAREWELL TO REFORM: THE RISE, LIFE AND DECAY OF THE PROGRESSIVE MIND IN AMERICA (Chicago; Quadrangle Paperbacks; 1932).

CHAMBERLAIN, LAWRENCE. THE WORK OF THE BOND HOUSE (New York; Arno Press; 1975) (originally published New York; Moody's; 1912).

CHAMBERLAIN, LAWRENCE, & WILLIAM WREN HAY. INVESTMENT AND SPECULATION: STUDIES OF MODERN MOVEMENTS AND BASIC PRINCIPLES (New York; H. Holt; 1931).

CHEFFINS, BRIAN R. *Putting Britain on the Roe Map: The Emergence of the Berle-Means Corporation in the United Kingdom.* In CORPORATE GOVERNANCE REGIMES: CONVERGENCE AND DIVERSITY, Joseph A. McCahery, Piet Moerland, Theo Raaijmakers & Luc Renneboog, eds. (Oxford; Oxford Univ. Press; 2002).

CHERNOW, RON. THE HOUSE OF MORGAN: AN AMERICAN BANKING DYNASTY AND THE RISE OF MODERN FINANCE (New York; A Morgan Entrekin Book, Atlantic Monthly Press; 1990).

——. TITAN: THE LIFE OF JOHN D. ROCKEFELLER, SR. (New York; Random House; 1998).

——. THE WARBURGS: THE TWENTIETH-CENTURY ODYSSEY OF A REMARKABLE JEWISH FAMILY (New York; Random House; 1993).

CHERRINGTON, HOMER V. THE INVESTOR AND THE SECURITIES ACT (Washington, D.C.; American Council on Public Affairs; 1942).

CLARK, JOHN BATES. THE DISTRIBUTION OF WEALTH: A THEORY OF WAGES, INTEREST AND PROFITS (New York; Macmillan; 1899).

——. THE PHILOSOPHY OF WEALTH: ECONOMIC PRINCIPLES NEWLY FORMULATED (New York; Augustus M. Kelley; 1967) (originally published Boston; Ginn; 1886).

CLARK, JOHN BATES, & JOHN MAURICE CLARK. THE CONTROL OF TRUSTS (New York; Macmillan; 1912).

CLARK, VICTOR S. HISTORY OF MANUFACTURES IN THE UNITED STATES, Vol. 1, 1607–1860; Vol. 2, 1860–1893; Vol. 3, 1893–1928 (New York; McGraw-Hill; 1929).

CLARKSON, GROSVENOR B. INDUSTRIAL AMERICA IN THE WORLD WAR: THE STRATEGY BEHIND THE LINE, 1917–1918 (Cambridge, Mass.; Riverside Press; 1923).

CLEMENTS, KENDRICK A. HOOVER, CONSERVATION, AND CONSUMERISM: ENGINEERING THE GOOD LIFE (Lawrence; Univ. Press of Kansas; 2000).

CLEPHANE, WALTER C. THE ORGANIZATION AND MANAGEMENT OF BUSINESS CORPORATIONS (St. Paul, Minn.; West Publishing; 1905).

——. THE ORGANIZATION AND MANAGEMENT OF BUSINESS CORPORATIONS, 2d ed. (Kansas City, Mo.; Vernon Law Book Co.; 1913).

CLEVELAND, FREDERICK A., & FRED WILBUR POWELL. RAILROAD PROMOTION AND CAPITALIZATION IN THE UNITED STATES (New York; Longmans, Green; 1909).

CLEVELAND, HAROLD VAN B., & THOMAS F. HUERTAS. CITIBANK, 1812–1970 (Cambridge, Mass.; Harvard Univ. Press; 1985).

CLEWS, HENRY. FIFTY YEARS IN WALL STREET (New York; Arno Press; 1973) (originally published New York; Irving; 1908).

COCHRAN, THOMAS C., & WILLIAM MILLER. THE AGE OF ENTERPRISE: A SOCIAL HISTORY OF INDUSTRIAL AMERICA (New York; Harper & Row; 1961) (originally published 1942).

COLLIER, PETER, & DAVID HOROWITZ. THE ROCKEFELLERS: AN AMERICAN DYNASTY (New York; Holt, Rinehart and Winston; 1976).

COMMAGER, HENRY STEELE. THE AMERICAN MIND: AN INTERPRETATION OF AMERICAN THOUGHT AND CHARACTER SINCE THE 1880S (New Haven, Conn.; Yale Univ. Press; 1950).

COMMONS, JOHN R. LEGAL FOUNDATIONS OF CAPITALISM (New York; Macmillan; 1924).

——. MYSELF (Madison, Wisc.; Univ. of Wisconsin Press; 1964).

CONANT, CHARLES A. WALL STREET AND THE COUNTRY: A STUDY OF RECENT FINANCIAL TENDENCIES (New York; Greenwood Press; 1968) (originally published 1904).

CONSTITUTION OF THE NEW YORK STOCK EXCHANGE: RULES ADOPTED BY THE GOVERNING COMMITTEE PURSUANT TO THE CONSTITUTION WITH AMENDMENTS TO JANUARY 7, 1931.

CONSTITUTION OF THE NEW YORK STOCK EXCHANGE AND RESOLUTIONS ADOPTED BY THE GOVERNING COMMITTEE WITH AMENDMENTS TO JANUARY NINETEEN EIGHTEEN (New York; Searing & Moore; 1918).

CONYNGTON, THOMAS. CORPORATION PROCEDURE: LAW, FINANCE, ACCOUNTING (New York; Ronald Press; 1924).

——. THE ORGANIZATION AND MANAGEMENT OF A BUSINESS CORPORATION (New York; Ronald Press; 1900).

COOK, WILLIAM W. THE CORPORATION PROBLEM (New York; Putnam; 1969) (originally published 1891).

——. A TREATISE ON THE LAW OF CORPORATIONS HAVING A CAPITAL STOCK (Boston; Little, Brown; 1913).

COOPER, FRANCIS [pseud. for THOMAS CONYNGTON]. FINANCING AN ENTERPRISE: A MANUAL OF INFORMATION AND SUGGESTION FOR PROMOTERS, INVESTORS AND BUSINESS MEN GENERALLY, 2 vols. (New York; Ronald Press; 1907).

COOPER, JOHN MILTON, JR. THE WARRIOR AND THE PRIEST: WOODROW WILSON AND THEODORE ROOSEVELT (Cambridge, Mass.; Belknap Press of Harvard Univ. Press; 1983).

CORBIN, WILLIAM H. AN ACT CONCERNING CORPORATIONS (Newark, N.J.; Soney & Sage; 1908).

CORWIN, EDWARD S. THE PRESIDENT: OFFICE AND POWERS, 1787–1957: HISTORY AND ANALYSIS OF PRACTICE AND OPINION (New York; New York Univ. Press; 1957).

COTTER, ARUNDEL. THE AUTHENTIC HISTORY OF THE UNITED STATES STEEL CORPORATION (New York; Moody Magazine and Book Co.; 1915).

COWING, CEDRIC B. POPULISTS, PLUNGERS, AND PROGRESSIVES: A SOCIAL HISTORY OF STOCK AND COMMODITY SPECULATION, 1890–1936 (Princeton; Princeton Univ. Press; 1965).

CROLY, HERBERT. MARCUS ALONZO HANNA: HIS LIFE AND WORK (Hamden, Conn.; Archon Books; 1965) (originally published 1912).

———. THE PROMISE OF AMERICAN LIFE (Indianapolis; Bobbs-Merrill; 1965) (originally published 1909).

CROSS, GARY. AN ALL-CONSUMING CENTURY: WHY COMMERCIALISM WON IN MODERN AMERICA (New York; Columbia Univ. Press; 2000).

CRYSTAL, GRAEF S. IN SEARCH OF EXCESS: THE OVERCOMPENSATION OF AMERICAN EXECUTIVES (New York; W. W. Norton; 1991).

CURTI, MERLE. THE GROWTH OF AMERICAN THOUGHT (New York; Harper; 1943).

DAVIES, JOSEPH E. TRUST LAWS AND UNFAIR COMPETITION (Washington; Government Printing Office; 1916).

DAVIS, JOSEPH STANCLIFFE. ESSAYS IN THE EARLIER HISTORY OF AMERICAN CORPORATIONS, nos. 1–4 (New York; Russell & Russell; 1965).

DE BEDTS, RALPH F. THE NEW DEAL'S SEC: THE FORMATIVE YEARS (New York; Columbia Univ. Press; 1964).

DEAN, ARTHUR H. WILLIAM NELSON CROMWELL, 1854–1948: AN AMERICAN PIONEER IN CORPORATION, COMPARATIVE AND INTERNATIONAL LAW (New York; Ad Press; 1957).

DEWING, ARTHUR S. FINANCIAL POLICY OF CORPORATIONS (New York; Ronald Press; 1926).

———. CORPORATE PROMOTIONS AND REORGANIZATIONS (Cambridge, Mass.; Harvard Univ. Press; 1914).

DEWEY, JOHN. THE POLITICAL WRITINGS (Indianapolis; Hackett Publishing; 1993).

DICKSON, HARRIS. AN OLD-FASHIONED SENATOR: A STORY-BIOGRAPHY OF JOHN SHARP WILLIAMS (New York; Frederick A. Stokes; 1925).

DICTIONARY OF AMERICAN BIOGRAPHY (New York; Scribner; 1932 and 1933), vols. 9 and 10.

DILL, JAMES B. THE STATUTE AND CASE LAW OF THE STATE OF NEW JERSEY RELATING TO BUSINESS COMPANIES: UNDER AN ACT CONCERNING CORPORATIONS

(Revision of 1896) and the Various Acts Amendatory Thereof and Supplemental Thereto (Camden, N.J.; S. Chew & Sons; 1910).

——. The Statutory and Case Law Applicable to Private Companies Under the General Corporation Act of New Jersey (New York; Baker, Voorhis; 1898).

——. Some Aspects of New Jersey's Corporate Policy (Philadelphia; G. H. Buchanan; 1903).

Dodd, David L. Stock Watering: The Judicial Valuation of Property for Stock-Issue Purposes (New York; Columbia Univ. Press; 1930).

Dodd, Edwin Merrick. American Business Corporations Until 1860 with Special Reference to Massachusetts (Cambridge, Mass.; Harvard Univ. Press; 1954).

Dorfman, Joseph. The Economic Mind in American Civilization, Vol. 2, 1606–1865 (New York; Viking; 1946); Vol. 3, 1865–1918 (New York; Viking; 1949); Vols. 4 and 5, 1918–1933 (New York; Viking; 1959).

Dorough, C. Dwight. Mr. Sam (New York; Random House; 1962).

Dos Passos, John R. Commercial Trusts: The Growth and Rights of Aggregated Capital (New York; Putnam; 1901).

——. A Treatise on the Law of Stock-Brokers and Stock-Exchanges (New York; Banks; 1905).

Eddy, Arthur J. The Law of Combinations (Chicago; Callaghan; 1901).

Edelman, Jacob Murray. Securities Regulation in the 48 States (Chicago; Council of State Governments; 1942).

Edwards, Adolph. The Roosevelt Panic of 1907 (New York; Antirock; 1907).

Edwards, George W. The Evolution of Finance Capitalism (New York; Augustus M. Kelley; 1967).

Edwards, J. R. Studies of Company Records, 1830–1974 (New York; Garland; 1984).

Einstein, Lewis. Roosevelt: His Mind in Action (Boston; Houghton Mifflin; 1930).

Eis, Carl. The 1919–1930 Merger Movement in American Industry (New York; Arno Press; 1978).

Eisenberg, Melvin Aron. The Structure of the Corporation (Washington, D.C.; Beard Books; 2006) (originally published 1976).

Ely, Richard T. An Introduction to Political Economy (New York; Chautauqua Press; 1889).

——. Monopolies and Trusts (New York; Macmillan; 1912).

——. Studies in the Evolution of Industrial Society (New York; Chautauqua Press; 1903).

Esquerre, Paul-Joseph. The Applied Theory of Accounts (New York; Ronald Press; 1914).

Evans, George Heberton, Jr. Business Incorporations in the United States, 1800–1943 (New York; National Bureau of Economic Research; 1948).

Fisher, Irving. The Nature of Capital and Income (New York; Macmillan; 1906).

FLIGSTEIN, NEIL. THE TRANSFORMATION OF CORPORATE CONTROL (Cambridge, Mass.; Harvard Univ. Press; 1990).

FLYNN, JOHN T. GOD'S GOLD: THE STORY OF ROCKEFELLER AND HIS TIMES (Westport, Conn.; Greenwood Press; 1932).

FOLLETT, M. P. THE NEW STATE: GROUP ORGANIZATION, THE SOLUTION OF POPULAR GOVERNMENT (New York; Longmans, Green; 1923).

FOGEL, ROBERT WILLIAM. THE REINTERPRETATION OF AMERICAN ECONOMIC HISTORY (New York; Harper & Row; 1971).

FRASER, STEVE. EVERY MAN A SPECULATOR: A HISTORY OF WALL STREET IN AMERICAN LIFE (New York; HarperCollins; 2005).

FRIDSON, MARTIN S. IT WAS A VERY GOOD YEAR: EXTRAORDINARY MOMENTS IN STOCK MARKET HISTORY (New York; John Wiley; 1998).

GABRIEL, RALPH HENRY. THE COURSE OF AMERICAN DEMOCRATIC THOUGHT (New York; Greenwood Press; 1986).

GALBRAITH, JOHN KENNETH. THE GREAT CRASH, 1929 (Boston; Houghton Mifflin; 1988).

GALAMBOS, LOUIS. THE PUBLIC IMAGE OF BIG BUSINESS IN AMERICA, 1880–1940: A QUANTITATIVE STUDY IN SOCIAL CHANGE (Baltimore, Md.; Johns Hopkins Univ. Press; 1975).

GALAMBOS, LOUIS, & JOSEPH PRATT. THE RISE OF THE CORPORATE COMMONWEALTH: U.S. BUSINESS AND PUBLIC POLICY IN THE TWENTIETH CENTURY (New York; Basic Books; 1988).

GARRATY, JOHN A. RIGHT-HAND MAN: THE LIFE OF GEORGE W. PERKINS (New York; Harper & Brothers; 1957).

GEISST, CHARLES R. WALL STREET: A HISTORY (New York and Oxford; Oxford Univ. Press; 1997).

GEORGE, HENRY. PROGRESS AND POVERTY: AN INQUIRY INTO THE CAUSES OF INDUSTRIAL DEPRESSIONS AND OF INCREASE OF WANT WITH INCREASE OF WEALTH; THE REMEDY (Garden City, N.Y.; Doubleday, Page; 1915) (originally published San Francisco; W. M. Hinton; 1879).

GERSTENBERG, CHARLES W. FINANCIAL ORGANIZATION AND MANAGEMENT OF BUSINESS (New York; Prentice-Hall; 1924).

GIESKE, MILLARD L. THE POLITICS OF KNUTE NELSON, 1912–1920 (Ph.D. dissertation; Univ. of Minnesota; 1965).

GIESKE, MILLARD L., & STEVEN J. KEILLOR. NORWEIGAN YANKEE: KNUTE NELSON AND THE FAILURE OF AMERICAN POLITICS, 1860–1923 (Northfield, Minn.; Norwegian-American Historical Association; 1995).

GILPIN, ROBERT. THE CHALLENGE OF GLOBAL CAPITALISM: THE WORLD ECONOMY IN THE 21ST CENTURY (Princeton, N.J.; Princeton Univ. Press; 2000).

GOLDMAN, ERIC F. RENDEZVOUS WITH DESTINY: A HISTORY OF MODERN AMERICAN REFORM (New York; Vintage; 1958).

GOLDSCHMIDT, R. W. THE CHANGING STRUCTURE OF AMERICAN BANKING (London; George Routledge and Sons; 1933).

GOODHART, C. A. E. THE NEW YORK MONEY MARKET AND THE FINANCE OF TRADE, 1900–1919 (Cambridge, Mass.; Harvard Univ. Press; 1969).

GOODWYN, LAWRENCE. THE POPULIST MOMENT: A SHORT HISTORY OF THE AGRARIAN REVOLT IN AMERICA (Oxford; Oxford Univ. Press; 1981).

GOSNELL, HAROLD F. BOSS PLATT AND HIS NEW YORK MACHINE: A STUDY OF THE POLITICAL LEADERSHIP OF THOMAS C. PLATT, THEODORE ROOSEVELT, AND OTHERS (Chicago; Univ. of Chicago Press; 1924).

GOULD, LEWIS L. THE MODERN AMERICAN PRESIDENCY (Lawrence; Univ. Press of Kansas; 2003).

——. THE PRESIDENCY OF THEODORE ROOSEVELT (Lawrence; Univ. Press of Kansas; 1991).

——. THE PRESIDENCY OF WILLIAM MCKINLEY (Lawrence; Regents Press of Kansas; 1980).

GRAHAM, BENJAMIN, & DAVID L. DODD. SECURITY ANALYSIS (New York; Whittlesey House, McGraw-Hill; 1934).

GRANDY, CHRISTOPHER. NEW JERSEY AND THE FISCAL ORIGINS OF MODERN AMERICAN CORPORATION LAW (New York; Garland; 1993).

GRANT, JAMES. MONEY OF THE MIND: BORROWING AND LENDING IN AMERICA FROM THE CIVIL WAR TO MICHAEL MILKEN (New York; Farrar Straus Giroux; 1992).

GRAUBARD, STEPHEN. COMMAND OF OFFICE: HOW WAR, SECRECY, AND DECEPTION TRANSFORMED THE PRESIDENCY FROM THEODORE ROOSEVELT TO GEORGE W. BUSH (New York; Basic Books; 2004).

GREENE, THOMAS L. CORPORATION FINANCE (New York; Putnam; 1902).

GRIFFIN, APPLETON PRENTISS CLARK. LIBRARY OF CONGRESS LIST OF BOOKS WITH REFERENCES TO PERIODICALS RELATING TO TRUSTS (Washington, D.C.; Government Printing Office; 1907).

GUNTON, GEORGE. TRUSTS AND THE PUBLIC (New York; D. Appleton; 1899).

HADLEY, ARTHUR TWINING. ECONOMICS: AN ACCOUNT OF THE RELATIONS BETWEEN PRIVATE PROPERTY AND PUBLIC WELFARE (New York; Putnam; 1896).

——. RAILROAD TRANSPORTATION: ITS HISTORY AND ITS LAWS (New York; Putnam; 1885).

HADLEY, MORRIS. ARTHUR TWINING HADLEY (New Haven, Conn.; Yale Univ. Press; 1948).

HARBAUGH, WILLIAM HENRY. POWER AND RESPONSIBILITY: THE LIFE AND TIMES OF THEODORE ROOSEVELT (New York; Farrar, Straus and Cudahy; 1961).

HASSE, ADELAIDE R. INDEX OF ECONOMIC MATERIAL IN DOCUMENTS OF THE STATES OF THE UNITED STATES: NEW JERSEY, 1789–1904 ([Washington, D.C.]; Carnegie Institution of Washington; 1914).

HAWKINS, DAVID F. CORPORATE FINANCIAL DISCLOSURE, 1900–1933: A STUDY OF MANAGEMENT INERTIA WITHIN A RAPIDLY CHANGING ENVIRONMENT (New York; Garland; 1986).

HAYS, SAMUEL P. CONSERVATION AND THE GOSPEL OF EFFICIENCY: THE PROGRESSIVE CONSERVATION MOVEMENT, 1890–1920 (New York; Atheneum; 1969).

——. THE RESPONSE TO INDUSTRIALISM 1885–1914 (Chicago; Univ. of Chicago Press; 1995) (second edition).

HECKSCHER, AUGUST. WOODROW WILSON: A BIOGRAPHY (New York; Macmillan; 1991).

HENDRICK, BURTON J. THE AGE OF BIG BUSINESS: A CHRONICLE OF THE CAPTAINS OF INDUSTRY (New Haven, Conn.; Yale Univ. Press; 1919).

HENDRICKSON, ROBERT. HAMILTON, vol. 2, 1789–1804 (New York; Mason/Charter; 1976).

HEUBNER, S. S., G. L. AMRHEIN & C. A. KLINE. THE STOCK MARKET (New York; D. Appleton-Century; 1934).

HIBBERT, W. NEMBHARD. THE LAW RELATING TO COMPANY PROMOTERS (London; Effingham Wilson; 1898).

HIMMELBERG, ROBERT F. THE MONOPOLY ISSUE AND ANTITRUST, 1900–1917 (New York; Garland; 1994).

HIRSCHL, ANDREW J. COMBINATION, CONSOLIDATION AND SUCCESSION OF CORPORATIONS (Chicago; Callaghan; 1896).

HOFSTADTER, RICHARD. THE AGE OF REFORM: FROM BRYAN TO F.D.R. (New York; Vintage; 1955).

———. THE AMERICAN POLITICAL TRADITION AND THE MEN WHO MADE IT (New York; Vintage; 1974).

HOGARTY, RICHARD A. LEON ABBETT OF NEW JERSEY: PRECURSOR OF THE MODERN GOVERNOR (Ph.D. dissertation, Princeton Univ.; 1965).

———. LEON ABBETT'S NEW JERSEY: THE EMERGENCE OF THE MODERN GOVERNOR (Philadelphia; American Philosophical Society; 2001).

HOLT, DANIEL. POLICING THE MARGINS: THE LEGITIMACY OF AMERICAN SECURITIES MARKETS AND THE ORIGINS OF FEDERAL SECURITIES REGULATION, 1890–1938 (Ph.D. dissertation, Univ. of Virginia; in progress).

HOMER, SIDNEY, & RICHARD SYLLA. A HISTORY OF INTEREST RATES, 3d ed. (New Brunswick, N.J.; Rutgers Univ. Press; 1991).

HORWITZ, MORTON J. THE TRANSFORMATION OF AMERICAN LAW, 1870–1960 (New York; Oxford Univ. Press; 1992).

HOVENKAMP, HERBERT. ENTERPRISE AND AMERICAN LAW, 1836–1937 (Cambridge, Mass.; Harvard Univ. Press; 1991).

HUBERMAN, LEO. AMERICA, INCORPORATED: RECENT ECONOMIC HISTORY OF THE UNITED STATES (New York; Viking; 1940).

HUEBNER, S. S. THE STOCK MARKET (New York; D. Appleton-Century; 1934).

HUGHES, JONATHAN. THE VITAL FEW: THE ENTREPRENEUR AND AMERICAN ECONOMIC PROGRESS, expanded ed. (New York; Oxford Univ. Press; 1986).

INVESTMENT BANKERS ASSOCIATION OF AMERICA. PROCEEDINGS OF THE SIXTH ANNUAL CONVENTION OF THE INVESTMENT BANKERS ASSOCIATION OF AMERICA. Nov. 12, 13 and 14, 1917 (Chicago; The Association; 1917).

———. PROCEEDINGS OF THE EIGHTEENTH ANNUAL CONVENTION OF THE INVESTMENT BANKERS ASSOCIATION OF AMERICA (Chicago; Gentry Printing; 1929).

JACKSON, STANLEY. J. P. MORGAN: A BIOGRAPHY (New York; Stein and Day; 1983).

JENSEN, GORDON MAURICE. THE NATIONAL CIVIC FEDERATION: AMERICAN BUSINESS IN AN AGE OF SOCIAL CHANGE AND SOCIAL REFORM, 1900–1910 (Ph.D. dissertation; Princeton University; 1956).

JENKS, JEREMIAH WHIPPLE. THE TRUST PROBLEM (New York; McClure, Phillips; 1900).

JENKS, JEREMIAH WHIPPLE, & WALTER E. CLARK. THE TRUST PROBLEM (New York; Doubleday, Doran; 1929).

JOHNSON, EMORY R. AMERICAN RAILWAY TRANSPORTATION (New York: D. Appleton; 1904).

JONES, DWIGHT ARVEN. THE LAW AND PRACTICE UNDER THE STATUTES CONCERNING BUSINESS CORPORATIONS IN THE STATE OF NEW YORK (New York; Baker, Voorhis; 1894).

JONES, ELIOT. THE TRUST PROBLEM IN THE UNITED STATES (New York; Macmillan; 1929).

JOSEPHSON, MATTHEW. THE ROBBER BARONS: THE GREAT AMERICAN CAPITALISTS, 1861–1901 (New York; Harcourt, Brace; 1934).

KATZ, LEO. ILL-GOTTEN GAINS: EVASION, BLACKMAIL, FRAUD AND KINDRED PUZZLES OF THE LAW (Chicago; Univ. of Chicago Press; 1996).

KAYSEN, CARL. THE AMERICAN CORPORATION TODAY (New York; Oxford Univ. Press; 1996).

KELLER, MORTON. AFFAIRS OF STATE: PUBLIC LIFE IN LATE NINETEENTH CENTURY AMERICA (Cambridge, Mass.; Belknap Press of Harvard Univ. Press; 1977).

———. THE LIFE INSURANCE ENTERPRISE, 1885–1910: A STUDY IN THE LIMITS OF CORPORATE POWER (Cambridge, Mass.; Harvard Univ. Press; 1963).

———. REGULATING A NEW ECONOMY: PUBLIC POLICY AND ECONOMIC CHANGE IN AMERICA, 1900–1933 (Cambridge, Mass.; Harvard Univ. Press; 1990).

KENKEL, JOSEPH F. PROGRESSIVES AND PROTECTION: THE SEARCH FOR A TARIFF POLICY, 1866–1936 (Lanham, Md.; Univ. Press of America; 1983).

KENNEDY, ALLAN A. THE END OF SHAREHOLDER VALUE: CORPORATIONS AT THE CROSSROADS (Cambridge, Mass.; Perseus; 2000).

KEYNES, JOHN MAYNARD. THE END OF LAISSEZ-FAIRE (London; Hogarth Press; 1927).

———. THE GENERAL THEORY OF EMPLOYMENT, INTEREST, AND MONEY (San Diego; Harvest; 1964) (originally published 1936).

KILLEEN, GERALD ANDREW. THE BUREAU OF CORPORATIONS, 1903–1914 (M.A. thesis; Ohio Univ. [Athens, Ohio]; 1965).

KINDLEBERGER, CHARLES P. MANIAS, PANICS AND CRASHES (New York; John Wiley; 1978).

KIRKLAND, EDWARD C. INDUSTRY COMES OF AGE: BUSINESS, LABOR AND PUBLIC POLICY, 1860–1897, vol. 6, THE ECONOMIC HISTORY OF THE UNITED STATES (New York; Holt, Rinehart and Winston; 1961).

KLEIN, MAURY. THE LIFE AND LEGEND OF JAY GOULD (Baltimore; Johns Hopkins Univ. Press; 1986).

———. RAINBOW'S END: THE CRASH OF 1929 (Oxford; Oxford Univ. Press; 2001).

KNAUTH, OSWALD WHITMAN. STUDIES IN HISTORY, ECONOMICS AND PUBLIC LAW (New York; Columbia Univ.; 1914).

KNIGHT, MARGARET V. PHILANDER CHASE KNOX: CABINET OFFICER (M.A. thesis, Ohio State Univ.; 1934).

KNOX, PHILANDER C. THE COMMERCE CLAUSE OF THE CONSTITUTION AND THE TRUSTS (Washington, D.C.; Government Printing Office; 1902).

KOLKO, GABRIEL. RAILROADS AND REGULATION, 1877–1916 (Princeton, N.J.; Princeton Univ. Press; 1965).

——. THE TRIUMPH OF CONSERVATISM (Chicago; Quadrangle Paperbacks; 1963).

——. WEALTH AND POWER IN AMERICA: AN ANALYSIS OF SOCIAL CLASS AND INCOME DISTRIBUTION (New York; Frederick A. Praeger; 1962).

LAMOREAUX, NAOMI. THE GREAT MERGER MOVEMENT IN AMERICAN BUSINESS, 1895–1904 (Cambridge, Eng.; Cambridge Univ. Press; 1985).

LARCOM, RUSSELL CARPENTER. THE DELAWARE CORPORATION (Baltimore, Md.; The Johns Hopkins Press; 1937).

LARNER, ROBERT J. MANAGEMENT CONTROL AND THE LARGE CORPORATION (New York; Dunellen; 1970).

LARSON, HENRIETTA M. GUIDE TO BUSINESS HISTORY (Cambridge, Mass.; Harvard Univ. Press; 1948).

——. JAY COOKE: PRIVATE BANKER (New York; Greenwood; 1968) (originally published 1936).

LASSER, WILLIAM. BENJAMIN V. COHEN: THE ARCHITECT OF THE NEW DEAL (New Haven, Conn.; Yale Univ. Press; 2002).

LEECH, MARGARET. IN THE DAYS OF MCKINLEY (New York; Harper & Brothers; 1959).

LEGG, CHESTER ARTHUR. THE LAW OF COMMERCIAL EXCHANGES (New York; Baker, Voorhis; 1912).

LEINWAND, GERALD. A HISTORY OF THE UNITED STATES FEDERAL BUREAU OF CORPORATIONS, 1903–1914 (Ph.D. dissertation, New York Univ.; 1962).

LETWIN, WILLIAM. LAW AND ECONOMIC POLICY IN AMERICA: THE EVOLUTION OF THE SHERMAN ACT (Chicago; Univ. Chicago Press; 1965).

LEWIS, W. ARTHUR. GROWTH AND FLUCTUATIONS, 1870–1913 (London; George Allen & Unwin; 1978).

LINK, ARTHUR S. WILSON: THE NEW FREEDOM (Princeton, N.J.; Princeton Univ. Press; 1956).

——. WOODROW WILSON AND THE PROGRESSIVE ERA, 1910–1917 (New York; Harper & Brothers; 1954).

LIPPMANN, WALTER. DRIFT AND MASTERY: AN ATTEMPT TO DIAGNOSE THE CURRENT UNREST (New York; Mitchell Kennerley; 1914).

LEWELLEN, WILBUR G. EXECUTIVE COMPENSATION IN LARGE INDUSTRIAL CORPORATIONS (New York; National Bureau of Economic Research and Columbia Univ. Press; 1968).

LLOYD, HENRY DEMAREST. WEALTH AGAINST COMMONWEALTH, ed. Thomas C. Cochran (Englewood Cliffs, N.J.; Prentice-Hall; 1963).

LOGSDON, JOSEPH. HORACE WHITE: NINETEENTH CENTURY LIBERAL (Westport, Conn.; Greenwood; 1971).

LOSS, LOUIS, & EDWARD M. COWETT. BLUE SKY LAW (Boston; Little, Brown; 1958).

LOUGH, WILLIAM H. BUSINESS FINANCE: A PRACTICAL STUDY OF FINANCIAL MANAGEMENT IN PRIVATE BUSINESS CONCERNS (New York; Ronald Press; 1917).

——. CORPORATION FINANCE: AN EXPOSITION OF THE PRINCIPLES AND METHODS

GOVERNING THE PROMOTION, ORGANIZATION AND MANAGEMENT OF MODERN CORPORATIONS (Chicago; De Bower–Elliott; 1909).

LOWI, THEODORE J. THE END OF LIBERALISM: THE SECOND REPUBLIC OF THE UNITED STATES (New York; W. W. Norton; 1969).

LUDINGTON, TOWNSEND. JOHN DOS PASSOS: A TWENTIETH CENTURY ODYSSEY (New York; Carroll & Graf; 1980).

LUSTIG, R. JEFFRY. CORPORATE LIBERALISM: THE ORIGINS OF MODERN POLITICAL THEORY, 1890–1920 (Berkeley; Univ. of California Press; 1982).

LYON, HASTINGS. CAPITALIZATION: A BOOK ON CORPORATION FINANCE (New York; Houghton Mifflin; 1912).

——. CORPORATION FINANCE, PART I: CAPITALIZATION; PART II: DISTRIBUTING SECURITIES REORGANIZATIONS (Boston; Houghton Mifflin; 1912).

MANNING, BAYLESS, & JAMES J. HANKS, JR. LEGAL CAPITAL, 3d ed. (Westbury, N.Y.; Foundation Press; 1990).

MARCHAND, ROLAND. CREATING THE CORPORATE SOUL: THE RISE OF PUBLIC RELATIONS AND CORPORATE IMAGERY IN AMERICAN BIG BUSINESS (Berkeley; Univ. of California Press; 1998).

MARKHAM, JERRY W. A FINANCIAL HISTORY OF THE UNITED STATES, 3 vols. (Armonk, N.Y.; M. E. Sharpe; 2002).

Markham, Jesse W. *Survey of the Evidence and Findings of Mergers.* In NATIONAL BUREAU OF ECONOMIC RESEARCH, BUSINESS CONCENTRATION AND PRICE POLICY (Princeton, N.J.; Princeton Univ. Press; 1955).

MAY, HENRY F. THE END OF AMERICAN INNOCENCE: A STUDY OF THE FIRST YEARS OF OUR OWN TIME, 1912–1917 (New York; Columbia Univ. Press; 1992) (originally published 1959).

MCADOO, WILLIAM G. CROWDED YEARS: THE REMINISCENCES OF WILLIAM G. MCADOO (Port Washington, N.Y.; Kennikat Press; 1931).

MCCRAW, THOMAS K. PROPHETS OF REGULATION (Cambridge, Mass.; Belknap Press of Harvard Univ. Press; 1984).

MCCULLOUGH, DAVID. MORNINGS ON HORSEBACK (New York; Simon and Schuster; 1981).

MCLAREN, N. LOYALL. ANNUAL REPORTS TO STOCKHOLDERS: THEIR PREPARATION AND INTERPRETATION (New York; Ronald Press; 1947).

MEADE, EDWARD SHERWOOD. CORPORATION FINANCE (New York; D. Appleton; 1912).

——. CORPORATION FINANCE. 7th ed. (New York; D. Appleton; 1933).

——. TRUST FINANCE: A STUDY OF THE GENESIS, ORGANIZATION AND MANAGEMENT OF INDUSTRIAL COMBINATIONS (New York; D. Appleton; 1903).

MEANS, GARDINER C. THE CORPORATE REVOLUTION IN AMERICA (New York; Crowell-Collier; 1962).

MERRILL, HORACE SAMUEL, & MARION GALBRAITH MERRILL. THE REPUBLICAN COMMAND, 1897–1913 (Lexington; Univ. Press of Kentucky; 1971).

MIRANTI, PAUL J., JR. ACCOUNTANCY COMES OF AGE: THE DEVELOPMENT OF AN AMERICAN PROFESSION, 1886–1940 (Chapel Hill; Univ. of North Carolina Press; 1990).

MITCHELL, LAWRENCE E. CORPORATE IRRESPONSIBILITY: AMERICA'S NEWEST EXPORT (New Haven, Conn.; Yale Univ. Press; 2002).

MODLIN, GEORGE MATTHEWS, & MCISAAC ARCHIBALD MACDONALD. SOCIAL CONTROL OF INDUSTRY, vol. 3 (Boston; Little, Brown; 1938).

MONTAGUE, GILBERT HOLLAND. TRUSTS OF TO-DAY: FACTS RELATING TO THEIR PROMOTION, FINANCIAL MANAGEMENT, AND THE ATTEMPTS AT STATE CONTROL (KITCHENER, CAN.; BATOCHE BOOKS; 2003) (originally published 1904).

MONTGOMERY, DAVID. CITIZEN WORKER: THE EXPERIENCE OF WORKERS IN THE UNITED STATES WITH DEMOCRACY AND THE FREE MARKET DURING THE NINETEENTH CENTURY (Cambridge, Eng.; Cambridge Univ. Press; 1993).

MOODY, JOHN. THE TRUTH ABOUT THE TRUSTS (New York; Moody; 1904).

———. THE MASTERS OF CAPITAL: A CHRONICLE OF WALL STREET (New Haven, Conn.; Yale Univ. Press; 1919).

MORAWETZ, VICTOR. TREATISE ON THE LAW OF PRIVATE CORPORATIONS OTHER THAN CHARITABLE (Boston; Little, Brown; 1882).

MORRIS, CHARLES R. MONEY, GREED AND RISK: WHY FINANCIAL CRISES AND CRASHES HAPPEN (New York; Random House; 1999).

MORRIS, EDMUND. THE RISE OF THEODORE ROOSEVELT (New York; Coward, McCann & Geoghegan; 1979).

———. THEODORE REX (New York; Random House; 2001).

MOWRY, GEORGE E. THE ERA OF THEODORE ROOSEVELT AND THE BIRTH OF MODERN AMERICA, 1900–1912 (New York; Harper & Row; 1958).

———. THEODORE ROOSEVELT AND THE PROGRESSIVE MOVEMENT (Madison; Univ. of Wisconsin Press; 1946).

MULLINS, JACK SIMPSON. THE SUGAR TRUST: HENRY O. HAVEMEYER AND THE AMERICAN SUGAR REFINING COMPANY (Ph.D. dissertation, Univ. of South Carolina; 1964).

MYERS, GUSTAVUS. HISTORY OF THE SUPREME COURT OF THE UNITED STATES (Chicago; Charles H. Kerr; 1925).

NADER, RALPH, MARK GREEN & JOEL SELIGMAN. TAMING THE GIANT CORPORATION (New York; Norton; 1976).

NADLER, MARCUS. CORPORATE CONSOLIDATIONS AND REORGANIZATIONS (New York; Alexander Hamilton Institute; 1930).

NASAW, DAVID. ANDREW CARNEGIE (New York; Penguin; 2006).

NEILL, HUMPHREY B. THE INSIDE STORY OF THE STOCK EXCHANGE: A FASCINATING SAGA OF THE WORLD'S GREATEST MONEY MARKET PLACE (New York; B.C. Forbes; 1950).

NELSON, RALPH L. MERGER MOVEMENTS IN AMERICAN INDUSTRY, 1895–1956 (Princeton, N.J.; Princeton Univ. Press; 1959).

NEVINS, ALLAN. THE EMERGENCE OF MODERN AMERICA, 1865–1878 (New York; Macmillan; 1927).

———. JOHN D. ROCKEFELLER: THE HEROIC AGE OF AMERICAN ENTERPRISE, 2 vols. (New York; Scribner; 1940).

NEW JERSEY CORPORATION GUARANTEE & TRUST COMPANY. THE COMPANY OR-

GANIZED UNDER THE LAWS OF THE STATE OF NEW JERSEY PRINCIPAL OFFICE, CAMDEN, N.J. MINUTES OF THE MEETINGS OF STOCKHOLDERS AND DIRECTORS (Orange, N.J.; Orange Journal; 1898).

NOYES, ALEXANDER DANA. FORTY YEARS OF AMERICAN FINANCE: A SHORT FINANCIAL HISTORY OF THE GOVERNMENT AND PEOPLE OF THE UNITED STATES SINCE THE CIVIL WAR, 1865–1907 (New York; Putnam; 1909).

———. THE MARKET PLACE: REMINISCENCES OF A FINANCIAL EDITOR (Boston; Little, Brown; 1938).

———. THIRTY YEARS OF AMERICAN FINANCE (New York; Putnam; 1902).

———. THE WAR PERIOD OF AMERICAN FINANCE, 1908–1925 (New York; Putnam; 1926).

NOYES, WALTER CHADWICK. A TREATISE ON THE LAW OF INTERCORPORATE RELATIONS (Boston; Little, Brown; 1909).

OLAND, MARTIN W. THE LIFE OF KNUTE NELSON (Minneapolis; Lund Press; 1926).

OLCOTT, CHARLES S. THE LIFE OF WILLIAM MCKINLEY. 2 vols. (Boston; Houghton Mifflin; 1946) (originally published 1916).

ORTH, SAMUEL P. READINGS ON THE RELATION OF GOVERNMENT TO PROPERTY AND INDUSTRY (Boston; Ginn; 1915).

OSBORN, GEORGE COLEMAN. JOHN SHARP WILLIAMS, PLANTER: STATESMAN OF THE DEEP SOUTH (Baton Rouge; Louisiana State Univ. Press; 1943).

PARRISH, MICHAEL E. SECURITIES REGULATION AND THE NEW DEAL (New Haven, Conn.; Yale Univ. Press; 1970).

PARRINGTON, VERNON LOUIS. MAIN CURRENTS IN AMERICAN THOUGHT: THE BEGINNINGS OF CRITICAL REALISM IN AMERICA, 1860–1920 (New York; Harcourt Brace Jovanovich; 1930).

PEACH, W. NELSON. THE SECURITY AFFILIATES OF NATIONAL BANKS (Baltimore, Md.; Johns Hopkins Press; 1941).

PECORA, FERDINAND. WALL STREET UNDER OATH: THE STORY OF OUR MODERN MONEY CHANGERS (New York; Augustus M. Kelley; 1968) (originally published 1939).

PERKINS, EDWIN J. WALL STREET TO MAIN STREET: CHARLES MERRILL AND MIDDLE-CLASS INVESTORS (Cambridge, Eng.; Cambridge Univ. Press; 1999).

PESTRITTO, RONALD J. WOODROW WILSON AND THE ROOTS OF MODERN AMERICAN LIBERALISM (Lanham, Md.; Rowman & Littlefield; 2005).

PREVITS, GARY JOHN, & BARBARA DUBIS MERINO. A HISTORY OF ACCOUNTING IN AMERICA: A HISTORICAL INTERPRETATION OF THE CULTURAL SIGNIFICANCE OF ACCOUNTING (New York; John Wiley; 1979).

———. A HISTORY OF ACCOUNTANCY IN THE UNITED STATES: THE CULTURAL SIGNIFICANCE OF ACCOUNTING (Columbus; Ohio State Univ. Press; 1998).

PRINGLE, HENRY F. THEODORE ROOSEVELT: A BIOGRAPHY (New York; Harcourt, Brace; 1931).

RAUM, JOHN O. THE HISTORY OF NEW JERSEY FROM ITS EARLIEST SETTLEMENT TO THE PRESENT TIME INCLUDING AN ACCOUNT OF THE FIRST DISCOVERIES AND SETTLEMENT OF THE COUNTRY. 2 vols. (Philadelphia; J. E. Potter; 1877).

REED, ROBERT R., & LESTER H. WASHBURN. BLUE SKY LAWS: ANALYSIS AND TEXT (New York; Clark Boardman; 1921).

——. BLUE SKY LAWS (New York; Clark Boardman; 1924).

REID, SAMUEL RICHARDSON. MERGERS, MANAGERS AND THE ECONOMY (New York; McGraw-Hill; 1968).

RHODES, JAMES FORD. THE MCKINLEY AND ROOSEVELT ADMINISTRATIONS, 1897–1909 (New York; Macmillan; 1927).

RIPLEY, WILLIAM Z. MAIN STREET AND WALL STREET (Boston; Little, Brown; 1927).

——. RAILROADS: FINANCE AND ORGANIZATION (New York; Longmans, Green; 1915).

——. RAILROADS: RATES AND REGULATION (New York; Longmans, Green; 1912).

——. RAILWAY PROBLEMS (Boston; Ginn; 1907).

——. TRUSTS, POOLS AND CORPORATIONS (Boston; Ginn; 1905).

ROE, MARK J. STRONG MANAGERS, WEAK OWNERS: THE POLITICAL ROOTS OF AMERICAN CORPORATE FINANCE (Princeton, N.J.; Princeton Univ. Press; 1994).

ROLLINS, MONTGOMERY. MONEY AND INVESTMENTS. 4th ed. (Boston; Financial Publishing; 1917).

ROMASCO, ALBERT U. THE POVERTY OF ABUNDANCE: HOOVER, THE NATION, THE DEPRESSION (London; Oxford Univ. Press; 1965).

ROOSEVELT, THEODORE. THE AUTOBIOGRAPHY OF THEODORE ROOSEVELT, CONDENSED FROM THE ORIGINAL EDITION, SUPPLEMENTED BY LETTERS, SPEECHES, AND OTHER WRITINGS, EDITED BY WAYNE ANDREWS (New York; Scribner; 1958).

ROSBROOK, ALDEN IVAN. A TREATISE ON THE LAW OF CORPORATIONS IN NEW YORK: INCLUDING THE BUSINESS CORPORATIONS LAW, GENERAL CORPORATION LAW, MEMBERSHIP CORPORATIONS LAW, STOCK CORPORATION LAW OF 1923, TRANSPORTATION CORPORATIONS LAW AND MISCELLANEOUS STATUTORY PROVISIONS AS AMENDED TO JANUARY 1, 1924: WITH ANNOTATED FORMS FOR THE ORGANIZATION, MANAGEMENT AND CONTROL OF CORPORATIONS, AND PROCEDURAL FORMS. (Albany, N.Y.; M. Bender; 1923).

ROSENBERG, NATHAN, & L. E. BIRDZELL, JR. HOW THE WEST GREW RICH: THE ECONOMIC TRANSFORMATION OF THE INDUSTRIAL WORLD (New York; Basic Books; 1986).

ROY, WILLIAM G. SOCIALIZING CAPITAL: THE RISE OF THE LARGE INDUSTRIAL CORPORATION IN AMERICA (Princeton, N.J.; Princeton Univ. Press; 1997).

RUSSELL, FRANCIS. THE PRESIDENT MAKERS: FROM MARK HANNA TO JOSEPH P. KENNEDY (Boston; Little, Brown; 1976).

ST. CLAIR, LABERT. THE STORY OF THE LIBERTY LOANS, BEING A RECORD OF THE VOLUNTEER LIBERTY LOAN ARMY, ITS PERSONNEL, MOBILIZATION AND METHODS, HOW AMERICA AT HOME BACKED HER ARMIES AND ALLIES IN THE WORLD WAR (Washington, D.C.; James William Bryan Press; 1919).

SALIERS, EARL A. PRINCIPLES OF DEPRECIATION (New York: Ronald Press; 1918).

SCHLESINGER, ARTHUR M., JR. THE COMING OF THE NEW DEAL (Boston; Houghton Mifflin; 1958).

SCHLESINGER, ARTHUR M., JR., & ROGER BURNS, EDS. CONGRESS INVESTIGATES, 1792–1974 (New York; Chelsea House Publishers; 1975), vol. 3.

SCHREINER, SAMUEL A., JR. HENRY CLAY FRICK: THE GOSPEL OF GREED (New York; St. Martin's Press; 1995).

SCHUMPETER, JOSEPH A. HISTORY OF ECONOMIC ANALYSIS (Oxford; Oxford Univ. Press; 1954).

SCHWARTZ, BERNARD. THE ECONOMIC REGULATION OF BUSINESS AND INDUSTRY: LEGISLATIVE HISTORY OF U.S. REGULATORY AGENCIES, 2 vols. (New York; Chelsea House; 1973).

SEAGER, HENRY R., & CHARLES A. GULICK, JR. TRUST AND CORPORATION PROBLEMS (New York; Harper & Brothers; 1929).

SELIGMAN, EDWIN R. A. THE ECONOMIC INTERPRETATION OF HISTORY (New York; Columbia Univ. Press; 1961) (originally published 1902).

———. ESSAYS IN ECONOMICS (New York; Macmillan; 1925).

SELIGMAN, JOEL. THE TRANSFORMATION OF WALL STREET: A HISTORY OF THE SECURITIES AND EXCHANGE COMMISSION AND MODERN CORPORATE FINANCE (Boston; Houghton Mifflin; 1982).

SHILLER, ROBERT J. IRRATIONAL EXUBERANCE (Princeton, N.J.; Princeton Univ. Press; 2000).

SILBER, WILLIAM L. WHEN WASHINGTON SHUT DOWN WALL STREET: THE GREAT FINANCIAL CRISIS OF 1914 AND THE ORIGINS OF AMERICA'S MONETARY SUPREMACY (Princeton, N.J.; Princeton Univ. Press; 2007).

SKLAR, MARTIN J. THE CORPORATE RECONSTRUCTION OF AMERICAN CAPITALISM, 1890–1916 (Cambridge, Eng.; Cambridge Univ. Press; 1988).

SLOAN, LAURENCE H. EVERYMAN AND HIS COMMON STOCKS: A STUDY OF LONG-TERM INVESTMENT POLICY (New York; McGraw-Hill; 1931).

SMITH, EDGAR LAWRENCE. COMMON STOCKS AS LONG TERM INVESTMENTS (New York; Macmillan; 1934).

SOBEL, ROBERT. THE BIG BOARD: A HISTORY OF THE NEW YORK STOCK MARKET (New York; Free Press; 1965).

———. PANIC ON WALL STREET: A HISTORY OF AMERICA'S FINANCIAL DISASTERS (London; Macmillan; 1968).

SPROAT, JOHN. THE BEST MEN: LIBERAL REFORMERS IN THE GILDED AGE (New York; Oxford Univ. Press; 1968).

STEFFENS, LINCOLN. THE AUTOBIOGRAPHY OF LINCOLN STEFFENS: COMPLETE IN ONE VOLUME (New York; Chautauqua Press; 1931).

STEIGERWALT, ALBERT K. THE NATIONAL ASSOCIATION OF MANUFACTURERS: A STUDY IN BUSINESS LEADERSHIP (Grand Rapids, Mich.; Dean Hicks; 1964).

STEINBERG, ALFRED. SAM RAYBURN: A BIOGRAPHY (New York; Hawthorn Books; 1975).

STEINER, PETER O. MERGERS: MOTIVES, EFFECTS, POLICIES (Ann Arbor; Univ. of Michigan Press; 1975).

STEPHENSON, NATHANIEL WRIGHT. NELSON W. ALDRICH: A LEADER IN AMERICAN POLITICS (Port Washington, N.Y.; Kennikat Press; 1971).

STIGLER, GEORGE J. THE ORGANIZATION OF INDUSTRY (Homewood, Ill.; Richard D. Irwin; 1968).

STIGLER, STEPHEN M. THE HISTORY OF STATISTICS: THE MEASUREMENT OF UNCERTAINTY BEFORE 1900 (Cambridge, Mass.; Belknap Press of Harvard Univ. Press; 1986).

STROUSE, JEAN. MORGAN: AMERICAN FINANCIER (New York; Random House; 1999).

SUMNER, WILLIAM GRAHAM. WHAT SOCIAL CLASSES OWE TO EACH OTHER (Caldwell, Idaho; Caxton Printers; 1954) (originally published 1883).

SWAINE, ROBERT T. THE CRAVATH FIRM, 2 vols. (New York; Ad Press; 1946).

TARBELL, IDA M. THE HISTORY OF THE STANDARD OIL COMPANY. 2 vols. (New York; McClure, Phillips; 1904).

——. THE LIFE OF ELBERT H. GARY: THE STORY OF STEEL (New York; D. Appleton; 1925).

TEWELES, RICHARD J., & EDWARDS S. BRADLEY. THE STOCK MARKET. 5th ed. (New York; John Wiley; 1992).

THIMM, ALFRED L. BUSINESS IDEOLOGIES IN THE REFORM-PROGRESSIVE ERA, 1880–1914 (Univ. of Alabama Press; 1976).

THOMPSON, JACK M. JAMES R. GARFIELD: THE CAREER OF A ROOSEVELTIAN PROGRESSIVE, 1895–1916 (Ph.D. dissertation; Univ. of South Carolina; 1958).

THOMPSON, SEYMOUR D. COMMENTARIES ON THE LAW OF PRIVATE CORPORATIONS. 1st ed., 7 vols. (San Francisco; Bancroft-Whitney; 1894–99).

——. COMMENTARIES ON THE LAW OF PRIVATE CORPORATIONS. 2d ed. by Joseph W. Thompson, 7 vols. (Indianapolis; Bobbs-Merrill; 1909).

THORELLI, HANS B. THE FEDERAL ANTITRUST POLICY: ORIGINATION OF AN AMERICAN TRADITION (Baltimore, Md.; Johns Hopkins Press; 1955).

TONELLO, MATTEO. REVISITING STOCK MARKET SHORT TERMISM (New York; Conference Board; 2006).

TRESCOTT, PAUL B. FINANCING AMERICAN ENTERPRISE: THE STORY OF COMMERCIAL BANKING (New York; Harper & Row; 1963).

TSUK MITCHELL, DALIA. ARCHITECT OF JUSTICE: FELIX S. COHEN AND THE FOUNDING OF AMERICAN LEGAL PLURALISM (Ithaca, N.Y.; Cornell Univ. Press; 2007).

VAN ANTWERP, W. C. THE STOCK EXCHANGE FROM WITHIN (New York; Doubleday; 1913).

VAN HISE, CHARLES R. CONCENTRATION AND CONTROL: A SOLUTION OF THE TRUST PROBLEM IN THE UNITED STATES (New York; Macmillan; 1912).

VANGERMEERSCH, RICHARD. FINANCIAL REPORTING TECHNIQUES IN 20 INDUSTRIAL COMPANIES SINCE 1861 (Gainesville; Univ. of Florida Press; 1979).

VEBLEN, THORSTEIN. THE THEORY OF BUSINESS ENTERPRISE (New York; New American Library of World Literature; 1958) (originally published 1904).

VILLARD, OSWALD GARRISON. FIGHTING YEARS: MEMOIRS OF A LIBERAL EDITOR (New York; Harcourt, Brace; 1939).

WATKINS, MYRON C. INDUSTRIAL COMBINATIONS AND PUBLIC POLICY: A STUDY OF COMBINATION COMPETITION AND THE COMMON WELFARE (Boston; Houghton Mifflin; 1927).

WEIL, GORDON L. SEARS, ROEBUCK, U.S.A.: THE GREAT AMERICAN CATALOG STORE AND HOW IT GREW (New York; Stein and Day; 1977).

WEINSTEIN, JAMES. THE CORPORATE IDEAL IN THE LIBERAL STATE: 1900–1918 (Boston; Beacon Press; 1968).

WEISSMAN, RUDOLPH L. THE NEW WALL STREET (New York; Harper & Brothers; 1939).

WESTBROOK, ROBERT B. JOHN DEWEY AND AMERICAN DEMOCRACY (Ithaca, N.Y.; Cornell Univ. Press; 1991).

WESTON, J. FRED. THE ROLE OF MERGERS IN THE GROWTH OF LARGE FIRMS (Berkeley; Univ. of California Press; 1953).

WHITE, WILLIAM ALLEN. THE AUTOBIOGRAPHY OF WILLIAM ALLEN WHITE (New York; Macmillan; 1946).

WIEBE, ROBERT H. BUSINESSMEN AND REFORM: A STUDY OF THE PROGRESSIVE MOVEMENT (Cambridge, Mass.; Harvard Univ. Press; 1962).

——. THE SEARCH FOR ORDER, 1877–1920 (New York; Hill and Wang; 1977).

WILLIAMS, NATHAN B. LAWS ON TRUSTS AND MONOPOLIES: DOMESTIC AND FOREIGN WITH AUTHORITIES (Washington, D.C.; Government Printing Office; 1914).

WILLOUGHBY, WOODBURY. THE CAPITAL ISSUES COMMITTEE AND WAR FINANCE CORPORATION (Baltimore, Md.; Johns Hopkins Press; 1934).

WILSON, WOODROW. CONGRESSIONAL GOVERNMENT: A STUDY IN AMERICAN POLITICS (Gloucester, Mass.; World Publishing; 1973) (originally published 1885).

——. THE NEW FREEDOM: A CALL FOR THE EMANCIPATION OF THE GENEROUS ENERGIES OF A PEOPLE (New York and Garden City; Doubleday, Page & Company; 1913).

——. THE STATE: ELEMENTS OF HISTORICAL AND PRACTICAL POLITICS (Boston; D. C. Heath & Co., Publishers; 1889).

WOODWARD, C. VANN, ORIGINS OF THE NEW SOUTH, 1877–1913 (Louisiana; Louisiana State Univ. Press; 1951).

WRESZIN, MICHAEL. OSWALD GARRISON VILLARD: PACIFIST AT WAR (Bloomington, Ind.; Indiana Univ. Press; 1965).

WRIGHT, HERBERT F. PHILANDER CHASE KNOX: SECRETARY OF STATE, MARCH 15, 1909 TO MARCH 4, 1913 (New York; Alfred A. Knopf, Inc.; 1929).

WRIGHT, ROBERT E. THE HISTORY OF CORPORATE FINANCE (London; Pickering & Chatto; 2003).

INDEX

Abbett, Leon, 40, 41, 291n.27
Abbott, Lawrence, 152
Abbott, Lyman, 20, 152
accounting, 108–10, 111–12, 310n.43.
  See also disclosure
Adams, Alton, 128
Adams, Henry Carter, 20, 21, 87–88
Adamson, William, 186, 238
Addams, Jane, 118
advertising securities, 110, 180. *See also*
  brokers and brokerage firms; invest-
  ment
AEA. *See* American Economic Associa-
  tion
Ahnfelt, W. P., 238
Aldrich, Nelson, 114, 155, 172, 218;
  and Rockefeller family, 156–57
Aldrich-Vreeland Act of 1908, 168
Allison, William B., 114
Amalgamated Association of Iron,
  Steel, and Tin Workers, 100
American Bankers' Association, 260
American Bar Association, 101
American Chicle Company, 72
American corporate capitalism. *See*
  corporate capitalism
American Economic Association (AEA),
  39, 213; Saratoga Springs platform,
  20–21
American Law Institute, 276

American Law Review, 97
American Smelting and Refining
  Company, 50, 51
American Sugar Refining Company,
  200. *See also* Havemeyer & Elder;
  Sugar Trust
American Telephone and Telegraph,
  annual reports, 111
American Tobacco case, 45
Andrews, Benjamin, 21
anthracite coal miners' strike of 1902,
  148–49
anticipated earnings. *See* prospective
  profit
antitrust concerns, 43, 76–77, 97–98, 114
antitrust reform, 115, 121–24, 176–77,
  311n.2. *See also* Chicago Conference
  on Trusts; federal incorporation;
  Hepburn bill of 1908; Littlefield
  bill of 1903; railroads, regulation of;
  Sherman Antitrust Act of 1890
Archbold, John, 156, 160
asset-for-stock transfers, 293n.33,
  294n.36. *See also* mergers
Audit and Appraisement Company
  of America, 84

Babson, Roger, 249
"baby bonds," 204
Bacon, Robert, 148

ABOUT THE AUTHOR

Lawrence E. Mitchell is Theodore Rinehart Professor of Business Law at The George Washington University Law School. After practicing corporate law for several years in New York, he entered academia and has been a leading corporate and business law scholar for twenty years. One of the founders of the progressive corporate law movement, named after his 1995 edited collection, *Progressive Corporate Law*, Mitchell has written extensively on a variety of topics ranging from corporate governance and the stock market to the history of anti-Semitism in the New York bar. His books include *Stacked Deck: A Story of Selfishness in America* and *Corporate Irresponsibility: America's Newest Export*, as well as casebooks on corporate law and corporate finance. At George Washington, Mitchell created the Sloan Program for the Study of Business in Society to support multidisciplinary research in corporate law, and the Institute for International Corporate Governance and Accountability to explore a range of issues arising from globalizing capitalism. He is a sought-after speaker in academic and nonacademic settings, and a frequent commentator in the news media. Mitchell holds a B.A. from Williams College and a J.D. from Columbia Law School.